Floating Charges in Comparative Perspective

Floating Charges in Comparative Perspective

Edited by

Alisdair MacPherson

Senior Lecturer in Commercial Law, University of Aberdeen, UK

Caroline Sophie Rapatz

Professor of Civil Law, European and International Private and Procedural Law and Comparative Law, Christian Albrechts University of Kiel, Germany

EE Edward Elgar PUBLISHING

Cheltenham, UK • Northampton, MA, USA

Published by
Edward Elgar Publishing Limited
The Lypiatts
15 Lansdown Road
Cheltenham
Glos GL50 2JA
UK

Edward Elgar Publishing, Inc.
William Pratt House
9 Dewey Court
Northampton
Massachusetts 01060
USA

Authorised representative in the EU for GPSR queries only: Easy Access System Europe – Mustamäe tee 50, 10621 Tallinn, Estonia, gpsr.requests@easproject.com

A catalogue record for this book
is available from the British Library

Library of Congress Control Number: 2025931104

This book is available electronically in the **Elgar**online
Law subject collection
https://doi.org/10.4337/9781035317141

MIX
Paper | Supporting responsible forestry
FSC® C014540

ISBN 978 1 0353 1713 4 (cased)
ISBN 978 1 0353 1714 1 (eBook)

Printed in the UK by Short Run Press Ltd, Exeter EX2 7LW

Contents

Contributors

Reghard Brits, Extraordinary Professor, University of the Western Cape and Research Fellow, Stellenbosch University, South Africa.

Alexandra Dal Molin-Kränzlin, Dr. iur., MLaw, Attorney at Law, Legal Counsel at Accenture and University Lecturer, Zurich, Switzerland.

Chike Emedosi, Lecturer in Banking and Finance Law, University of Aberdeen, Scotland, UK.

Vincent van Hoof, Associate Professor, Department of Legal History, Radboud University Nijmegen, the Netherlands.

Teemu Juutilainen, Professor, Faculty of Law, University of Turku, Finland.

Patrik Lindskoug, Docent, Associate Professor, Department of Law, Lund University, Sweden.

Bjørn Løtveit, PhD, Senior Associate, Kvale Law Firm, Norway.

Alisdair MacPherson, Senior Lecturer in Commercial Law, University of Aberdeen, Scotland, UK.

Astrid Millung-Christoffersen, Associate Professor, Department of Law, Aarhus University, Denmark.

Christopher K. Odinet, Professor of Law and Mosbacher Research Fellow, Texas A&M University, USA.

Caroline Sophie Rapatz, MPhil (Cantab), Professor, Faculty of Law, Christian Albrechts University of Kiel, Germany.

Muriel Renaudin, LLM, Lic. en droit, Maître en droit, Senior Lecturer in Law, School of Law and Politics, Cardiff University, Wales, UK.

Radu Rizoiu, Professor, Faculty of Law, University of Bucharest, Romania.

Tibor Tajti, Professor, Legal Studies Department, Central European University – Private University, Vienna, Austria.

Andreas Televantos, MSt (Oxon), Associate Professor, Lincoln College, University of Oxford, England, UK.

Catherine Walsh, BA, LLB, BCL, Full Professor, McGill University, Québec, Canada.

Zhicheng Wu, LLB, MJur, MPhil (Oxon), Associate Professor, School of Law, Renmin University of China, China.

Hao Zhang, Associate, Zhong Lun Law Firm, China.

Acknowledgements

As with any extensive book project, there are many people to thank in relation to the present volume, only some of whom can be mentioned here. Firstly, and most importantly, we would like to thank the experts who provided responses to the questionnaire which formed the core of our comparative overview chapter, and the authors who contributed individual chapters to this volume. The book would simply not have been possible without them and we are (figuratively) indebted to them. We are grateful to the Young Property Lawyers Forum, the Institute of European and Comparative Law at the University of Oxford and the Gesellschaft für Rechtsvergleichung e.V. for facilitating our project meetings and for hosting presentations by one or both of us, and to attendees who provided comments on, and support for, our ongoing project. Furthermore, it would be remiss not to acknowledge the support we have gratefully received over the years from our own institutions, the University of Aberdeen, the Julius-Maximilians-Universität Würzburg and the Christian-Albrechts-Universität zu Kiel, as well as from our excellent colleagues. We also especially wish to thank Professor Andrew Steven of the University of Edinburgh for his kindness and encouragement.

We very much appreciate the initial funding provided by the Gesellschaft für Rechtsvergleichung e.V. through the Ernst Rabel Preis that we devoted to this project, and the financial assistance provided by the CB Davidson Fund, which enabled some of the research in this book to be undertaken.

We would also like to thank Edward Elgar Publishing, and especially Stephanie Tytherleigh and Caroline Cornish, for offering us the opportunity to publish the book and helping us bring it to fruition. Its final version benefited significantly from the editorial assistance by 'Team Rapatz', led by Fynn Baas, at the Christian-Albrechts-Universität zu Kiel.

Finally, we must acknowledge the forbearance of our friends and families, and the distractions they provided, which kept us afloat during this project's long journey. We owe you a lot (metaphorically speaking, and without providing security).

Alisdair MacPherson and Caroline Sophie Rapatz
Aberdeen and Kiel, January 2025

Introduction to *Floating Charges in Comparative Perspective*

Alisdair MacPherson and Caroline Sophie Rapatz

"FLOATING" SECURITY: A WIDESPREAD PHENOMENON

Security rights are an important feature of legal systems. They are generally recognised as being advantageous to both creditors and debtors and support economic activity more broadly.[1] A creditor benefits by receiving protection for the repayment of debt (by being able to enforce against particular assets) and obtaining priority over other creditors, while a debtor is able to access finance more readily and at lower rates of interest.[2] Secured lending, therefore, underpins modern economic systems. This is especially applicable in relation to corporate finance. Security rights over specific assets have existed for millennia; however, in the modern age, the need for a security covering a collection of assets, including as those assets change, has become more pronounced. Consequently, many legal systems seek to address this by providing a flexible form of security that can cover a number of different assets, particularly in the context of enterprises.

The most prominent example of this type of security is the English floating charge. It emerged in the mid-nineteenth century and is closely connected to the rise of modern companies.[3] The English floating charge has been described

---

[1] See e.g. UNCITRAL, *Legislative Guide on Secured Transactions* (2010) 1–3. Similar views are held by various other international organisations. However, there is ongoing debate regarding the extent to which secured credit is economically advantageous or disadvantageous for various parties and more generally – for a summary of the issues and relevant sources, see L Gullifer and J Payne, *Corporate Finance Law: Principles and Policy* (3rd edn, Hart 2020) 348–358.

[2] The notion that security provides benefits for both parties was also acknowledged historically, including under Roman law: Justinian, *Institutes* III, XIV, 4.

[3] See *Re Panama, New Zealand and Australia Royal Mail Co* (1870) 5 Ch App 318; RR Pennington, "The Genesis of the Floating Charge" (1960) 23 MLR 630; and Chapter 2 (A Televantos), and the sources cited there.

as both one of equity's "most brilliant" and "most subtle" creations.[4] Despite various changes to the law of floating charges and ongoing uncertainty regarding the security's conceptual status, it continues to endure. Its appeal for creditors and debtors derives from its key operational features. The floating charge is a non-possessory security[5] that can cover a class of assets (both present and future) up to all of the grantor's property at any given time, and importantly, allows for the grantor to deal with their assets in the ordinary course of business, including by way of disposal, without needing to obtain the permission of the security holder regarding specific dealings.[6] It is understandably counterposed against fixed security, for which there is less liberty for a grantor to dispose of security property free from the security and a greater necessity of control by the creditor, including with respect to dealings with such property. Yet the higher-ranking priority of fixed security in comparison with floating charges means that creditors will often seek to have security characterised as fixed, while trying to obtain the flexibility that comes with floating security.[7]

It seems undeniable that floating charges are most associated with English law, and the English floating charge bears features of its origins in equity. However, it would be a mistake to think that other systems, both past and present, do not have security rights with features that may be considered those of a "floating" security. Of course, the English floating charge has been particularly influential in systems deriving from English law. Many of those jurisdictions have retained such security (albeit with variations). Yet its influence has also extended to jurisdictions beyond the Common Law world, sometimes with conscious adoption of security with its characteristics.[8] In addition, even

---

[4] R Goode, "The Case for the Abolition of the Floating Charge" in J Getzler and J Payne (eds), *Company Charges: Spectrum and Beyond* (OUP 2006) 11; R Goode and L Gullifer, *Goode and Gullifer on Legal Problems of Credit and Security* (7th edn, Sweet & Maxwell 2023) para 4-01.

[5] In other words, the creditor does not need to take possession of the collateral.

[6] See *Re Yorkshire Woolcombers Association Ltd* [1903] 2 Ch 284 per Romer LJ at 295; and *Re Spectrum Plus Ltd* [2005] UKHL 41, [2005] 2 AC 680 per Lord Scott of Foscote at paras 106–107.

[7] See e.g. *Re Spectrum Plus Ltd* [2005] UKHL 41, [2005] 2 AC 680, and, more recently, *Re Avanti Communications Ltd* [2023] EWHC 940 (Ch) and *Re UKCloud Ltd* [2024] EWHC 1259 (Ch).

[8] This and various related matters are discussed in many of the chapters of this book. The transposition of rules or institutions of law from one jurisdiction to another is often known as a "legal transplant"; however, the suitability of the term and concept can be contested – see e.g. A Watson, *Legal Transplants: An Approach to Comparative Law* (2nd edn, University of Georgia Press 1993); P Legrand, "The Impossibility of Legal Transplants" (1997) 4 MJECL 111; E Örücü, "Law as Transposition" [2002] 51 ICLQ 205.

where there is a lack of evidence about the direct influence of the English floating charge, there is security that can be considered "floating" at least in a broad sense. In fact, one can trace such security back at least as far as Roman law, thus long before the emergence of English law and equity. Different jurisdictions have therefore also developed solutions to respond to the practical need for a flexible security right over multiple assets. Consequently, functional equivalents to floating charges exist in many legal systems, but there is significant divergence across jurisdictions, in terms of both the features of the security rights in practice and their doctrinal foundations. It is therefore a worthwhile and interesting endeavour to identify the functional characteristics of floating security and to compare the English floating charge with equivalent security elsewhere, and in turn to compare different security rights elsewhere with one another – including not only Common Law jurisdictions, but also Civil Law and "mixed" legal systems.[9]

EMBARKING ON A LARGE-SCALE RESEARCH PROJECT

The project that led to this book began in 2018 as a joint post-doctoral research idea. We share a strong interest in security rights generally and floating charges specifically,[10] and we were particularly interested to discover the extent to which experts in other jurisdictions considered that their legal systems also had floating security, and what similarities and differences the large-scale comparison of such security might show. This proved to be an unexplored area. Although there is significant scholarly interest in floating security, academic works from recent decades either deal with wider aspects of security rights in comparative perspective,[11] but include floating security only to a limited extent, or provide

[9] "Mixed" in this context is often considered to be a combination of elements of the Common Law and Civil Law traditions (see e.g. VV Palmer, "Mixed Jurisdictions" in JM Smits (ed.), *Elgar Encyclopedia of Comparative Law* (2nd edn, Edward Elgar Publishing 2012) 590–599); however, if a wider understanding is adopted, the mixture may be a combination of elements of one or more other legal traditions too.

[10] See e.g. ADJ MacPherson, *The Floating Charge* (ELET 2020); J Hardman and ADJ MacPherson (eds), *Floating Charges in Scotland: New Perspectives and Current Issues* (EUP 2022); CS Rupp, *Grundpfandrechte zwischen Flexibilität und Schutz* (Mohr Siebeck 2015); CS Rupp, §§ 1204–1296 BGB, in G Dannemann and R Schulze (eds), *German Civil Code/Bürgerliches Gesetzbuch (BGB). A Commentary to the German Civil Code* (CH Beck 2020).

[11] See e.g. E-M Kieninger (ed.), *Security Rights in Movable Property in European Private Law* (CUP 2004); J de Lacy (ed.), *The Reform of UK Personal Property Security Law* (Routledge-Cavendish 2009); L Gullifer and O Akseli, *Secured Transactions Law Reform: Principles, Policies and Practice* (Hart

in-depth studies on floating security but with a limited comparative scope of two or, at most, three jurisdictions.[12] Given the growth of comparative law in recent times and the academic and practical significance of security rights, including floating charges, throughout the world, it is surprising that many aspects of floating security have never been extensively studied before from a comparative perspective and that no in-depth studies specifically focussing on floating charges on a larger comparative scale have previously been undertaken.[13] The academic importance of the relevant law makes it an exciting area for scholars to explore in more detail, while in practice, there is a growing need for in-depth knowledge of the different types, features and possibilities of the practically useful and widely utilised form of "floating" security, particularly in commercial cross-border transactions. Examining the intersection of scholarly and practical aspects of law has always been of particular interest with regard to security rights.

Building a network of contacts, we have endeavoured to collectively produce the largest specific study of floating charges and their functional equivalents yet undertaken. We decided that the first stage should be to collect information regarding floating security rights from a number of jurisdictions. To ensure comparability, we formulated a questionnaire with questions covering key aspects of this type of security right, ranging from their historical and doctrinal roots via their operational components to enforcement issues. Open questions

---

2016); G McCormack and R Bork, *Security Rights and the European Insolvency Regulation* (Intersentia 2017); M Dubovec and L Gullifer, *Secured Transactions Law Reform in Africa* (Hart 2019); L Gullifer and D Neo (eds), *Secured Transactions Law in Asia: Principles, Perspectives and Reform* (Hart 2021).

[12] See, e.g. relevant German publications of recent years: F Kleweta, *Die Sicherungsfunktion der Floating Charge in Deutschland* (Mohr Siebeck 2018); T Grädler, *Die Möglichkeiten der globalen Belastung von Unternehmen im deutschen Recht* (Mohr Siebeck 2012); J Ungerer, "Die floating charge – wie man Kredite mittels einer Wolke sichert" (2015) Zeitschrift für Europarecht, Int Privatrecht und Rechtsvergleichung 31–46; S Enchelmaier, "Die englische floating charge: Aufstieg und Fall eines Sicherungsrechts" (2013) 112 Zeitschrift für Vergleichende Rechtswissenschaft 403–437. The private international law angle is also typically explored with a focus on England, e.g. A Schall, "Die neue englische floating charge im Internationalen Privat- und Verfahrensrecht (2009) Praxis des Internationalen Privat- und Verfahrensrechts 209–217; M Wenckstern, "Die englische Floating Charge im deutschen Internationalen Privatrecht" (1992) 56 Rabels Zeitschrift für ausländisches und internationales Privatrecht 624–695.

[13] One of the present authors contributed a chapter, "Floating Charges" in S van Erp and K Zimmermann (eds), *Research Handbook on European Property Law* (Edward Elgar Publishing 2024), that covers various jurisdictions; however, the contribution is a short one and some jurisdictions are dealt with only briefly.

were used to allow contributors to expand upon the different approaches in their respective jurisdictions as needed, and to introduce aspects of importance to their legal systems not addressed by the core questions. Experts, including both academics and practitioners, were identified from a selection of jurisdictions aimed at covering a representative sample with regard to geography and legal traditions. Although almost inevitably some regions are represented more than others, we were successful in gathering responses from contributors for countries in Africa, the Americas, Asia, Australasia and Europe. The project currently encompasses over 40 jurisdictions from across the world, albeit in different and sometimes relatively limited ways.

In terms of the project's progression, we encountered an unexpected obstacle in the form of the COVID-19 pandemic. By the spring of 2020, we had successfully completed the initial phase of the project – gathering information from a first group of contributors, evaluating it at a meeting in Edinburgh, discussing our preliminary findings with colleagues at the 2019 Young Property Lawyers Forum in Glasgow, and proceeding to systematically add information for further jurisdictions. As we were poised to commence the next phase of the project with a presentation in New Orleans at the Association for Law, Property and Society's 2020 Annual Meeting, the worldwide pandemic brought our plans to a halt. Owing to the pressing needs these extraordinary times brought for many of our contributors, we decided to put the project on hiatus until the pandemic was over (not knowing that it would take almost two years). As we returned to our work after this gestational period, we decided to concentrate on the publication of a comparative book as the first tangible output of our project. From the collation and analysis of the questionnaire responses, we produced an extensive comparative overview chapter. From the issues stressed by the contributors regarding the forms of floating security in their respective systems, we also identified particular issues in different jurisdictions (and often across jurisdictions) that merited in-depth study. Selected contributors were therefore invited to write individual chapters on topics exemplified by their jurisdictions that provide especially interesting case studies highlighting or explaining particular issues in relation to floating security rights.

The resulting present volume is the first work to specifically cover floating charges in comparative perspective in such a depth and range. It provides information about floating security rights in various jurisdictions, also inviting and enabling future comparison. The comparative overview chapter outlines and explores a range of common threads and points of disparity. The other chapters examine discrete aspects of floating charges and their equivalents in selected jurisdictions, considering matters of particular scholarly and/or practical value, such as historical developments, the creation of "floating" security rights, their interaction with property law rules and their enforcement.[14] Inevitably, however, even in a book of this length, it is not possible to cover everything relating to floating security and some issues are only dealt with briefly.

The principal aim of this volume is to provide the first wide-ranging exploratory overview and analysis of floating security rights in a global perspective. As it evidences their significant practical, economic and academic interest, it strives to offer information and inspiration to practitioners, law reformers and scholars alike. We are hopeful that the comparative law knowledge that will be provided by this book will assist parties in navigating the complexity of such work and minimising risks and costs. From an academic perspective, this volume may provide a starting point and template for further exploration, discussion and exchange in this area. There is certainly scope for such work, whether comparatively focussing on particular issues in more detail or examining additional jurisdictions.

Furthermore, in the wider context of comparative law, this project is an opportunity to consider the extent to which there are convergences and divergences among "legal families"[15] and the ways in which jurisdictions have influenced one another in the formulation of their laws. Consequently, the project can serve as a case study that considers wider comparative issues such as legal transplants. Methodologically, it is based on a functional approach to comparison, through identifying functional equivalence between security rights examined and comparing and contrasting accordingly.[16] While to some extent this is adopted in each chapter, no single methodology is adopted across the chapters. The different particular approaches, details of which are provided in each chapter, as well as the questionnaire method used for the comparative overview chapter, provide insights into the varying approaches to comparative law currently in use. The insights contained in this volume may provide a starting point for the utilisation of alternative and supplementary methodologies, including through the use of scenario-oriented questionnaires, additional questions that can be more easily coded or leximetric techniques.[17]

---

[14] Further details regarding these chapters are provided in the next section.

[15] For legal families, see e.g. K Zweigert and H Kötz, *Introduction to Comparative Law* (T Weir tr, 3rd edn, OUP 1998) ch 5 onwards; J Husa, "Legal Families" in JM Smits (ed.), *Elgar Encyclopedia of Comparative Law* (2nd edn, Edward Elgar Publishing 2012) 491–504.

[16] For functional approaches in comparative law more generally, see e.g. R Michaels, "The Functional Method of Comparative Law" in M Reimann and R Zimmermann (eds), *The Oxford Handbook of Comparative Law* (2nd edn, OUP 2006); Zweigert and Kötz, ibid, ch. 3.

[17] For examples of such approaches, see e.g. M Siems and D Cabrelli, *Comparative Company Law: A Case-Based Approach* (2nd edn, Hart 2018); PP

STRUCTURE AND CONTENT

The present book has 13 chapters, excluding this introduction. It contains a comparative overview chapter, followed by 12 chapters examining floating security in a particular jurisdiction or group of jurisdictions. Related to the initial exploratory scope of the project, significant latitude has been given to authors to showcase the analytical, structural and stylistic characteristics of their jurisdictions instead of requiring them to conform to a predetermined strict format. While there is of course a level of standardisation and consistency across the volume, we have endeavoured to respect differences in legal thinking, reasoning and writing styles, which hopefully enrich the book by reflecting the multifaceted approaches to floating security rights in a global context.

As already noted, the comparative overview (Chapter 1) is the product of questionnaire responses from contributors in 40 jurisdictions. The chapter has been structured around the relevant questions and responses. These focus on whether the chosen jurisdictions have a floating charge or functional equivalent, the history and development of such security (including the influence(s) of other legal systems), its scope, rules regarding its creation (such as registration requirements) and how property leaves its ambit, its integration into the wider legal system (including property law), how it is enforced and how it ranks in competition with other rights. The content in the chapter is divided into four substantive parts on: (i) approaches to floating security; (ii) history and development; (iii) property matters; and (iv) enforcement and ranking. This exploratory study provides a foundation for future work, including the possibility of testing the preliminary conclusions outlined.

Given that the English floating charge is often considered as the template for floating security, the first chapter examining a particular legal system in detail (Chapter 2) focusses on England and Wales. Andreas Televantos considers the floating charge in English law from historical, theoretical and practical perspectives, with reference to its emergence and evolution in the nineteenth century, the rights held by a chargeholder and practical issues with floating charges in the present day. The chapter assesses the extent to which the nature of a chargeholder's rights is consistent with aspects of property in an equitable sense. It also discusses whether the separate treatment of fixed and floating charges in the context of insolvency procedures is justified. This chapter, therefore, picks up on key issues concerning floating charges in English law, but which are likely to be of interest to those dealing with security in other

Lele and M Siems, "Shareholder Protection: A Leximetric Approach" (2007) 7 JCLS 17.

systems modelled on the English floating charge or at least which share some of its features.

In Chapter 3, attention turns to African legal systems that have inherited the floating charge of English law but modified it in some respects. Chike Emedosi analyses the history and evolution of the law of floating charges in Ghana, Kenya and Nigeria, and presents a compelling study of these jurisdictions. He shows that while floating charges were received in each of them in the colonial era, the reception of later developments depended upon local circumstances and law-making. Since independence for the selected countries was obtained, there have been some divergences from both English law and from one another. While English law is still a key reference point for all jurisdictions, the changes adopted have led to inconsistencies and problems in the operation of floating charges. Consequently, the chapter highlights that new issues can emerge as the law is reformed in ways that represent a departure from English law.

The following chapter (Chapter 4) switches focus to the counter-model(s) offered by the Civilian tradition. Vincent van Hoof considers the recognition of non-possessory security rights in Continental Europe following the revival of interest in Roman law in the late medieval and early modern periods. It is pointed out that aspects of Germanic law remained, leading to a fusion of rules. He moves on to discuss the rejection of non-possessory security over movables in the wake of the emergence of national civil codes from the late eighteenth century, and then the return of non-possessory security rights in various countries in the twentieth century. The pledging of business assets was often permitted, along with the allowance of transfers in the ordinary course of business. The chapter provides an important platform for other contributions examining jurisdictions in the Civilian tradition.

South Africa has a mixed legal system but with Civilian elements prevalent in property law. Reghard Brits notes in Chapter 5 that the general hypothecation of movable property in South Africa, using a general notarial bond, has its historical roots in Roman and Roman-Dutch law. It is contended that this form of security is a broad equivalent of the English floating charge. However, there are also notable differences, particularly in terms of the steps necessary to obtain third-party effect. There is insightful discussion as to how the general notarial bond compares with other forms of security and its relationships with them. The chapter identifies the value of general notarial bonds as a security device while also noting weaknesses that could be usefully addressed.

Chapter 6 explores the "floating lien" of the USA as a further alternative floating security, which has proved to be influential in other jurisdictions. Christopher K. Odinet examines the history and development of this form of security, providing background and context to its emergence, including the motivations for such a mechanism (in political and financial terms). There is a detailed discussion of the Uniform Commercial Code, Article 9, which allows for security interests in present and future assets that can amount in some instances to a floating security. The chapter offers an absorbing story of the involvement of legal professionals and legislators in developing floating security in order to meet commercial needs and also reflects upon the use of the security in the context of digital assets in the modern day, a matter with which many systems are currently wrestling.

In Chapter 7, we move to China, a system that is outside the Common Law world but has been influenced by jurisdictions in that tradition in terms of its own floating security. Zhicheng Wu and Hao Zhang discuss the arrival of such security by legislation in 2007 to support the financing of small and medium-sized enterprises and also reflect upon whether and to what extent English law has been more influential than US law in relation to this security. They also discuss more recent changes to the law, which were made to increase the attractiveness of the security in wider economic terms, and doctrinal matters relating to the security grantor, security property and "crystallisation" events. Given the rise of China as a superpower, it is important to understand its legal mechanisms and the extent to which these may have been influenced by Western models, while recognising that its own version may prove influential for other systems in the future.

While France does not have a precise equivalent of the English floating charge, Muriel Renaudin shows in Chapter 8 that security in that country does have features that are recognisably "floating", and this has become more apparent with legal reforms. There appear to be trends in the direction of allowing for a more expansive "global" security, and it is contended that many advantages would be provided by such a floating security, not least greater opportunities for raising finance. In the chapter, the English floating charge is used by way of a comparator in identifying French functional equivalents. The laws of Mexico and Québec, systems with closer similarities to France, are also referred to in order to identify whether their forms of security could provide some inspiration or conceptualisation of a broader French floating security.

Québec itself offers an interesting case study, as a mixed legal system combining elements of English law and French law, and surrounded by other Canadian provinces and territories with functionalist systems of secured transactions. Chapter 9, by Catherine Walsh, focusses on Québec, explaining various rules applicable to the creation, ranking and enforcement of hypothecs on the universality of an enterprise debtor's present and future movable property. She demonstrates how this model of floating security has been accommodated in Québec and considers that such a model could be successfully transplanted elsewhere, but with some caveats identified. On a related note, the chapter also shows the significance that constitutional arrangements can have in the operation of floating security, specifically in terms of the interrelationship between the law in Québec and Canadian federal law.

Other jurisdictions also have a form of floating security comparable with the Quebec hypothec over a universality. Chapter 10 by Radu Rizoiu concerns the hypothec over *universitas facti* in Romanian law. The chapter explains the arrival of this security in the context of the transition of Romania towards becoming a market economy in the 1990s. It is clear that the introduction of floating security was viewed as helping the legal system to move towards facilitating finance. However, the chapter shows that the security has not been used to its full potential by participants and there are problems with its operation, including its treatment in insolvency, that ought to be resolved in order to enhance its use.

Like Romania, other countries such as Hungary embraced floating security as they emerged as market economies following the collapse of the socialist (or communist) states of the Eastern Bloc. Tibor Tajti in Chapter 11 discusses the influence of other systems and the role of the European Bank for Reconstruction and Development in the introduction of floating security in Hungary. However, unusually, the closest functional equivalent to the English floating charge was abolished in Hungary within two decades of its arrival owing in part to enforcement issues in insolvency (albeit that alternative security with some floating characteristics remains). The chapter provides details regarding its demise and the cautionary lessons that can be learnt by other systems in terms of reforming their laws in this area.

Remaining in Europe, the Nordic legal systems have atypical features in matters of property law, owing to their functional systems, and there is considerable value in exploring their approach(es) to floating security. Chapter 12 examines such security in Denmark, Norway, Sweden and Finland, and has been written by a team of scholars: Bjørn Løtveit, Astrid Millung-Christoffersen, Patrik Lindskoug and Teemu Juutilainen. From their chapter, it is apparent that there is less fragmentation in security rights than in property law generally, and all of the systems have some form of floating security. While discussing the rules applicable to such security, the influences and similarities of aspects of the systems become apparent, albeit that some of the systems are more closely aligned with one another than others.

Finally, Chapter 13 offers a special case regarding floating security only being permitted over a narrow type of asset. Alexandra Dal Molin-Kränzlin discusses the law of Switzerland, which has generally rejected non-possessory security rights such as floating charges. However, perhaps unsurprisingly given Switzerland's focus on financial activity, legal changes earlier this century have allowed for intermediated securities to be encumbered with a form of security with floating features. The chapter compares this security with the English floating charge. The Swiss example may provide a blueprint for countries that are generally resistant to non-possessory security but see economic value in the creation of floating security over a limited class of assets.

We have avoided simply grouping the chapters using geographical location or by using firm divisions based on "legal families". Rather, we have opted for their arrangement along an identifiable thread connecting each chapter with preceding and following chapters. Nevertheless, alternative narratives may emerge from reading the chapters in a different order, as various other connections between the chapters and the jurisdictions examined are apparent and have been explained above. Whichever approach a reader may choose, collectively, they provide valuable insights regarding the law of floating charges and functional equivalents in various jurisdictions and with respect to the features and merits of floating security in comparative terms.

As already noted, much more could be written about the topic of floating security from a comparative perspective, whether in relation to the chosen jurisdictions on matters like the treatment of such security in insolvency law (which is only covered in detail in a few chapters) or with reference to other jurisdictions. However, for now, and whatever the future of floating charges, we and the other contributors hope that this work will advance academic and practical understanding of floating security and will be a useful contribution to scholarship on the law of secured transactions.

A NOTE ON TERMINOLOGY

The term "charge" is a technical one in English law (particularly English equity) and therefore may not be considered appropriate for use in relation to other systems. Given the greater neutrality of the term "security", the use of "floating security" can be considered more technically appropriate elsewhere. In addition, this book is more focused on the floating aspect than charges in a narrow sense. Yet it needs to be acknowledged that "floating charge" is a more common and better understood term in many places, reflecting the prevalence of English law and concepts, and the fact that the English floating charge is often used as the measuring stick for comparable security. As it also provided the point of origin for our project, we have chosen to title the book *Floating Charges in Comparative Perspective*, even though we ourselves often refer to floating security. However, it should also be noted that we have not been prescriptive in terms of how contributors refer to relevant security in examined jurisdictions in the various chapters of this book. This avoids the impression that the systems have a homogeneous security without variation and allows an appreciation of the linguistic differences in terms of how contributors in different jurisdictions refer to the "floating" form(s) of security in those places.

1. A comparative overview of floating charges and functional equivalents

Alisdair MacPherson and Caroline Sophie Rapatz

INTRODUCTION

The present study is ambitiously intended as a first exploration of floating security rights on a broad comparative basis, undertaking to provide an overview of the different approaches to this phenomenon in jurisdictions across the world. Its goal is to take stock of the current situation, identify key questions and the answers and solutions provided for them, and develop an integral understanding of floating security. It strives to include major legal issues currently surrounding floating security and to encompass a wide range of legal systems with a view to systematising their approaches.

The present chapter provides a comparative overview of the law of floating charges and their functional equivalents in 40 jurisdictions around the world, spanning countries in Africa, the Americas, Asia, Australasia and Europe. Jurisdictions were chosen for various reasons – among others, their status as "major" commercial jurisdictions, the existence of unusual features in their laws concerning security rights (including floating security), their interconnections with other legal systems, and their experience of recent law reform. The overall aim was to cover a representative sample with regard to geography and legal traditions, albeit that some areas (particularly in Europe) are more heavily represented than others.

As no large-scale comparative work specifically on floating charges has to date been undertaken, gathering and collating information for so many legal systems was the first challenge encountered in this study. The availability and (linguistic) accessibility of primary and secondary literature for different jurisdictions varies greatly; in addition, more theoretical or conceptual works do not always reflect the entirety of the problems and possibilities of security rights in their current application. Therefore, the decision was made to approach experts from the selected jurisdictions with the request to provide information and insights regarding their domestic legal system on the basis of a questionnaire. The expert contributors comprise both academics and legal practitioners; they were chosen on the basis of their experience in the field of security rights.[1] A complete list of the jurisdictions covered and the expert contributors is contained in Appendix 1.

For the questionnaire, a semi-structured method with essay-style questions covering a range of matters was chosen. This approach upholds a significant degree of consistency across responses, thus supporting their comparability; also, it ensures that all key issues could be addressed for each jurisdiction. At the same time, questions had to be formulated in an open manner – on the one hand, in order to grant contributors the freedom to expand upon the different approaches in their respective jurisdictions as required and to provide necessary explanations, and on the other hand, in order to approach answers on a blank slate and analyse them without predetermination in this initial study. Furthermore, the formulation of more specific questions (with potentially "quantifiable" answer possibilities) would have been contingent on comparative insights on the different approaches, which were the aim and not the starting point for this study, and might have falsified input. The questionnaire, along with the explanatory note provided to contributors, is provided in full in Appendix 2.

Questionnaire responses were then collated and subsequently analysed – the results of this analysis are presented in this chapter.[2] It follows the order of the questionnaire by considering, in turn: a first comparative approach to the existence and understanding of floating charges and their functional equivalents; the history and development of floating security; the property law aspects of such security (from their scope and creation to coherence with property law principles and mechanisms for encumbrance and unencumbrance); and finally how they are dealt with in the context of enforcement and ranking. The result is a comparative overview of the fundamental issues of floating security. Owing to the constraints of its broad scope and holistic approach, it remains restricted to a general character. Its focus lies on charting the heretofore unknown territory of floating security by classifying responses, grouping approaches and identifying general models; it does not aim to draw a detailed map of specific jurisdictions or solutions through in-depth micro-comparison of individual answers. Hence, the present study concentrates on the broad strokes and outlines which form common threads between different legal systems. It needs to generalise and cannot reflect nor do justice to the richness of details provided

---

[1] Many contacts were facilitated by colleagues from the Young Property Lawyers Forum network, to whom we are deeply grateful.

[2] Unless otherwise indicated, all information in this chapter is drawn from the questionnaire answers provided by the contributors.

in the questionnaire responses. This is in keeping with the exploratory character of this initial study: it is intended to provide an overview of the possibilities and potential of floating security and comparative research into them, and to inspire further in-depth study. One of its main results is the identification of questions and aspects that merit further analysis – hopefully, it will serve as a springboard for future research.

It should be noted that the open format of the questionnaire made the comparative evaluation of responses fascinating yet challenging. The differences between responses in style, depth and approach offer insights into the variants of general understanding and working techniques in diverse legal traditions and backgrounds, which have greatly enriched this study and allowed for some comparative deductions of their own. At the same time, divergences in interpretation, approach and treatment have sometimes hampered the comparability of responses. The questionnaire does not match the solutions of all jurisdictions exactly, so that sometimes issues are examined in a different context or not addressed at all. While wary of comparing apples and oranges, for the purposes of this overview study, such lacunae were filled, if possible, by recourse to the response as a whole and inference from the information provided in other parts of the questionnaire; when no clear indication was provided for a jurisdiction with regard to a specific issue, it was not included in the evaluation of this aspect.

We would like to express our heartfelt gratitude to our contributors for their expertise and diligence in responding to our questionnaire, for their enthusiasm in participating in this study and for their unwavering support over a long period of time. It goes without saying that any errors of reproduction and interpretation are our own.

APPROACHES TO FLOATING SECURITY (QUESTION 1)

1. Does (or did) your system have a floating charge or does (or did) it have a functional equivalent?

The initial question was deliberately formulated in a general manner, asking for the past or present existence of floating charges or functional equivalents in each jurisdiction. The aim behind this was twofold. Firstly, the question was intended to provide confirmation of whether floating security exists in different jurisdictions. Secondly, its open formulation left room for interpretation by respondents, allowing for different understandings and approaches to what may be considered a "floating" security. Together, these aspects permit an initial classification of security rights and legal systems, as well as a first indication of potential points of interest, in order to establish a basis for the following, more specific questions.

The Responses in Overview: First Impressions

In keeping with the introductory and general nature of the question, responses were mostly brief. Apart from an indication of the existence of a floating charge-style security, they frequently provided basic information about its provenance and type.

With regard to the existence of a floating charge or functional equivalent, the answers were surprisingly homogeneous – for the vast majority of jurisdictions covered, the existence of a floating security was indicated. The current existence of a "floating charge" was confirmed for China, England and Wales, Hong Kong, India, Ireland, Israel, Nigeria, Scotland and Singapore, with respondents for Australia, Canada (excluding Quebec) and New Zealand indicating that it technically still exists but is no longer used in practice.[3] A functional equivalent was identified for Australia, Belgium, Bosnia and Herzegovina, Canada, Chile, Croatia, Czechia, Denmark, Finland, France, Italy, Japan, Jordan, Lithuania, Mexico, the Netherlands, Norway, Poland, Quebec, Romania, Russia, Serbia, South Africa, Turkey and the USA. Only for three jurisdictions (Austria, Germany and Switzerland) was the question answered in the negative, and in one jurisdiction (Hungary) it was stated that a functional equivalent has been both introduced and abolished in the past. However, the answers for all of these jurisdictions pointed out the existence of security featuring partial similarities to floating charges – the negative answers constitute a "qualified no" rather than a complete rejection.

Some first conclusions may already be drawn from this initial self-assessment of jurisdictions. There must be a very strong practical need for security featuring all or some characteristics of the floating charge – if this was not the case, their popularity would not be as high across different legal systems. Apparently, a modern jurisdiction has to cater to this need at least in some measure, regardless of its geographical location, historical developments or legal family's traditions. At the same time, the spectrum of what may be considered a "floating charge" or functional equivalent is broad. Although there is an apparent consensus that such security covers a pool of assets, the individual components of which may change over time, responses indicate that the meaning of these terms may be understood and interpreted in different ways, depending to a great extent, but not exclusively, on the jurisdictional

[3] These jurisdictions have not given up the floating charge entirely, but largely replaced it by a functional equivalent.

background. "Floating charge" may be interpreted, *inter alia*, as a security over a company or business, a security over general assets, or a security over a fluctuating asset pool. A fundamental challenge for further comparative work in this area will lie in arriving at a universally valid definition of what constitutes a floating security, as well as establishing a common terminology as a basis for dialogue.[4]

In some jurisdictions, several security rights with floating charge characteristics exist. Various reasons for such coexistence can be discerned. It may be due to the parallel availability of old and new security rights (for example, there are "new" functional equivalents in Australia, Canada and New Zealand, but the old floating charge remains technically available in narrow circumstances). Some legal systems supplement their general security rights with additional security available only to businesses (for example, the business security of Lithuanian and Mexican law) or by special security for certain situations (for example, the sector-specific security of Norwegian law). Some jurisdictions (for example, France) offer different security rights for tangibles and intangibles, with the possibility of approximating an all-encompassing security by a combination of security rights (as indicated, for example, for Germany and the Netherlands). For some jurisdictions, additional security rights were mentioned in passing but not explored in depth, as they were not considered full functional equivalents of the floating charge (for example, the general mortgage in Japan and the factory mortgage in South Korea). Notably, however, none of the jurisdictions currently using a floating charge indicated the existence of a functional equivalent as a competing alternative.

As the relevance of the different security rights varies, and answers were not provided throughout for all of them, their inclusion in the analysis proved challenging. For the purposes of this study, the "main" floating security of each jurisdiction (as indicated by the responses) was taken as the point of reference throughout,[5] while selectively adding information on other security rights if pertinent. The focus of this initial exploration lies on security over tangible movables – immovables[6] and intangibles (e.g. receivables, intellectual property rights or shares) are only considered within the context of encompassing security, but not with regard to security devoted exclusively to them.

---

[4] This should include, for example, definitions for the meaning of terms like "business" or "universality of assets".

[5] If no other indication is given, references to jurisdictions relate to this security right.

[6] As well as security rights on registered movables (e.g. motor vehicles, ships, aircraft) which typically follow similar rules as immovables.

Initial Classification: Legal Traditions and Basic Models

A first insight into the different lines of development towards the current state of floating-style security can be deduced from the responses to the first question. The close links between the legal systems at the respective ends of the spectrum are remarkable. The majority of the jurisdictions affirming the current existence and use of a "floating charge" belong to the Common Law legal tradition and have historically very close ties to English law; a strong influence of English law is also manifested in the existence of a "floating charge" in the hybrid legal systems of Israel and Scotland. It is somewhat more surprising to find a "floating charge" affirmed for China, a jurisdiction usually considered principally part of the Civil Law tradition. On the other hand, the jurisdictions which are sceptical vis-à-vis floating charge-style security all belong to the Germanic legal tradition, traditionally limiting the development of security by adherence to strict principles of property law.[7] In the middle of the spectrum, an openness towards functional equivalents can be noted especially for jurisdictions which have – more or less recently – reformed their law of security and/or adopted a functionalist approach.

Similarly, the indications provided in the responses allow for a preliminary classification of the fundamental conceptualisations underlying floating security. Security rights directly following in the tradition of English law typically adhere to the floating charge model. Functional equivalents to the floating charge usually follow one of three conceptions:

- *Functionalist model:* the possibility of security fulfilling the same purpose as the floating charge is integrated into the "functionalist" approach to security. The most prominent representative of this model, the USA's security interest under Art 9 of the Uniform Commercial Code, has strongly influenced other jurisdictions. In Australia, Canada and New Zealand, the model has been realised as the "Personal Property Security Scheme" (PPSS), enacted in various "Personal Property (and) Security Acts" (PPSAs). Furthermore, Art 9 UCC also served as the inspiration for the security rights of Bosnia and Herzegovina, Croatia and – together with the United Nations Commission on International Trade Law (UNCITRAL) model secured transactions law – Jordan.
- *Non-possessory pledge model:* the majority of jurisdictions utilise a non-possessory security in the tradition of the Civil Law pledge to

[7] The historically strong influence of the German legal tradition may have been a contributing factor in the ultimate reticence of Hungarian law towards a floating security.

create a functional equivalent to the floating charge (depending on terminological preferences, called a [movables] hypothec, a lien or a [non-possessory] pledge). This model forms the dogmatic basis in Belgium, Chile, Czechia, Denmark, Finland, France, Italy, Lithuania, Mexico, the Netherlands, Norway, Poland, Quebec, Romania, Russia, Serbia, South Africa, Switzerland and Turkey. The broad range of variations of this model includes its most notable subgroups – "general" security, security over a plurality of assets, and security specific to businesses or enterprises. Different forms of security may coexist.

- *Fiduciary model:* in a few jurisdictions, security rights with floating characteristics take the form of a transfer of ownership for security purposes. Following the concept established by German law, this type of security can also be encountered in Austria, Japan and South Korea.

HISTORY AND DEVELOPMENT OF FLOATING SECURITY (QUESTIONS 2–4)

2. When, how and why was such a security introduced?
3. Was the law in any other legal systems especially influential when the security was introduced? If so, how did this influence manifest itself?
4. If your system formerly had a floating charge or functional equivalent, when, how and why was such a security abolished? And what (if anything) was it replaced with?

Introduction of Floating Security

Floating charges are, of course, most closely associated with the Common Law tradition generally and English law in particular. However, security with "floating" characteristics can also exist in and be considered compatible with other systems. In Roman law, which forms the foundation of the Civilian tradition, there was a general hypothec that could cover changing property, and later commentators have referred to this as a floating charge.[8] Yet Civil Law systems departed from the liberal Roman law position on security for a considerable period, and only later was there a revival of non-possessory security over movable property in Civilian jurisdictions.[9]

[8] See especially D.20.1.34.pr (Scaevola). And see e.g. HLE Verhagen, *Security and Credit in Roman Law: The Historical Evolution of Pignus and Hypotheca* (OUP 2022) ch 9.

[9] See WJ Zwalve, "A Labyrinth of Creditors: A Short Introduction to the History of Security Interests in Goods" in E-M Kieninger (ed.), *Security Rights*

The Common Law floating charge, in its modern form, was first accepted in England in the mid-nineteenth century. Registered companies began to follow the practice of companies established by a private Act,[10] in granting security over their "undertaking".[11] In *Re Panama, New Zealand and Australian Royal Mail Co*[12] it was held that such a purported security would create an equitable security over all of the grantor company's present and future property.[13] Later cases also upheld floating charges and identified their features, and there has been legislation relating to floating charges too.[14] English law's reach (especially owing to the British Empire), and the perceived advantages of floating charges for business and trade, owing to their wide-ranging scope, flexibility and the continuing ability of the chargor to deal with assets, meant that floating charges were recognised in Common Law jurisdictions, including Australia,[15] Canada, Hong Kong, India,[16] Ireland, New Zealand,[17] Nigeria and Singapore, as well as the mixed legal system of Israel. In some jurisdictions, such as Ireland, the floating charge was apparently recognised around

in Movable Property in European Private Law (CUP 2004) 38; and Chapter 4 (V van Hoof).

[10] As, for example, many railway companies were.

[11] See e.g. RR Pennington, "The Genesis of the Floating Charge" MLR 23 (1960) 630; and Chapter 2 (A Televantos).

[12] (1870) 5 Ch App 318.

[13] See e.g. E McKendrick, *Goode and McKendrick on Commercial Law* (Penguin 2020) para. 25.03. *Holroyd v Marshall* (1862) 10 HL Cas 191 is also an important case in the emergence of floating charges. The term "floating charge" seems to first appear in a reported case in *Re Colonial Trusts Corporation* (1879) 15 Ch D 465.

[14] See e.g. *Re Florence Land and Public Works Co* (1878) 10 Ch D 530; *Government Stock and Other Securities Investment Co Ltd v Manila Railway Co Ltd* [1897] AC 81 at 86 per Lord Macnaghten; *Illingworth v Houldsworth* [1904] AC 355. For relevant legislation, see e.g. formerly Companies Act 1900, Companies (Consolidation) Act 1908, Companies Act 1948, Companies Act 1985 (which still remains in force for the creation of floating charges in Scotland), and now the Insolvency Act 1986 and the Companies Act 2006.

[15] See e.g. *Purcell v Queensland Public Curator* (1922) 31 CLR 220.

[16] See e.g. *Nallaperumal Pillai v Krishna Aiyangar* (1915) 30 Ind Cas 286; AIR (1916) Mad 7.

[17] We understand that the first reported reference is in *Geoghegan v Greymouth Point Elizabeth Railway and Coal Company (Limited)* (1898) 16 NZLR 749 (NZ CA).

the same time as in England and, as there, seems to have been connected with the rise of industrialisation, as well as the arrival of railways.[18]

The questionnaire responses reveal that in a number of countries (including beyond the Common Law world), floating security was introduced by legislation, usually in order to meet a perceived business or economic need.[19] Floating security has variously been introduced to address strained economic circumstances in the event of war[20] or political change,[21] and/or merely (growing) dissatisfaction regarding the existing legal position and its insufficient support for economic growth (sometimes in comparison to a neighbouring jurisdiction).[22] The last of these is true for Scotland, which is part of the UK but a mixed legal system. The courts in Scotland rejected floating charges[23] but a statutory floating charge was introduced by legislation in 1961 to meet perceived commercial needs.[24] There was demand from various businesses and commercial organisations to make it easier to raise finance, and Scottish businesses were disadvantaged compared with their English counterparts. Greater uniformity with English law was considered desirable in this area. South Africa, like Scotland, is ordinarily considered to be a mixed system, and did not accept the English floating charge. Instead, the functional equivalent of a floating charge in South Africa, the general notarial bond, was the product of inheritance from Roman-Dutch law.[25]

The USA was historically an outlier in the Common Law world (excluding mixed systems), as a standard floating security was rejected by the US Supreme Court in a 1925 case,[26] which required that a creditor needed to have a certain

---

18 See *Re Bagnalstown and Wexford Railway Co Ltd* (1867) 1 Ir Eq Rep 278, with the term "floating charge" being used in *Re Old Bushmills Distillery Company Ltd* [1896] 1 IR 301.

19 E.g. Belgium's Law of 25 October 1919, allowing for security over assets of a business, replaced by the Law of 11 July 2013 (effective 1 January 2018) modifying the Civil Code regarding security over movables.

20 E.g. Belgium in the wake of the First World War.

21 Such as in many former Eastern Bloc countries, and those who have otherwise gained independence from another state. In addition, sometimes conflict and political change accompany one another and can lead to change in the law of secured transactions, e.g. in Bosnia and Herzegovina.

22 Sometimes it can also lead to a reform to amend the law so that a more evidently functional equivalent to a floating charge is introduced, e.g. in Chile in 2007.

23 *Carse v Coppen* 1951 SC 233.

24 Companies (Floating Charges) (Scotland) Act 1961. Subsequent legislation has retained the floating charge.

25 See Chapter 5 (R Brits).

26 *Benedict v Ratner*, 268 US 353 (1925). See further Chapter 6 (C Odinet).

degree of control over security property in order to hold a security interest. It was, however, possible to use a combination of security devices to approximate floating security, but this was complicated and cumbersome. The obstacles can be viewed as the product of an environment that was sceptical of the notion of supporting certain forms of lending. The arrival of the Uniform Commercial Code (UCC) Art 9 brought with it a single security interest, which could be of a floating nature over changing assets (and if so is referred to as a "floating lien"), with the debtor in control of the assets. There was clearly a desire to make it easier to use this type of security as part of an economy supported by secured credit, albeit that its introduction was not free from criticism. The initial rejection of a streamlined floating security by the courts, followed a relatively short time later by legislative intervention introducing floating security, is comparable with how the law developed in Scotland.

In some jurisdictions, floating security first appeared in a limited context, such as to support agricultural businesses in the raising of finance, before being expanded or joined by a more general floating security.[27] The floating features of security have sometimes become more apparent or enhanced over time, constituting incremental development of a truer form of floating security.[28] Such developments can be a response to growing financial demands in specific contexts or industries or more widely. In Norway, a general floating security was introduced by legislation in 1980, but there were pre-existing limited floating security rights in specific industries, including for mining companies (in limited form initially, but later expanded), and subsequently railway and bus companies, communications companies, agricultural enterprises and fishing businesses.[29] Finland introduced an enterprise mortgage (*yrityskiinnitys/företagsinteckning)* covering most types of movable property in 1986, but this followed on from a more limited form of security over certain types of enterprises, including agricultural enterprises, that had existed since 1923.[30] The main aim of the relevant legislation was to support the raising of finance by businesses, particularly small and medium-sized enterprises (SMEs).

Similar developments are perceptible elsewhere. The expansion of floating security has been apparent in Mexico, where the industrial mortgage (*hipoteca industrial*) was introduced in 1941 for the purpose of encouraging

---

27 E.g. in Chile (as early as 1926) and in Scotland (from 1929): ADJ MacPherson, "The Pre-History of Floating Charges in Scots Law" in J Hardman and ADJ MacPherson (eds), *Floating Charges in Scotland: New Perspectives and Current Issues* (EUP 2022) 48–53.

28 E.g. in Chile, with legislation in 1982 and 2007.

29 Albeit with some differences depending on the type of business, and in particular instances being limited to loans from specific state banks.

30 Following legislation in 1984.

the development of particular industries that would benefit the country's economy, while the non-possessory pledge (*prenda sin transmisión de posesión*) and the security trust were introduced by legislation in 2000, in order to support the re-emergence of the credit market (which had been badly impacted by an economic crisis in 1994) by easing SMEs' access to credit. In Quebec, legislation from the early twentieth century allowed certain corporate entities to create non-possessory security over various types of movable property. This was expanded to corporate entities generally in 1914, but with the exclusion of some property types. The law was developed further with the arrival of agricultural pledges (1942) and commercial pledges (1962). The Civil Code of Québec of 1991, in force since 1994, allows for trustees, corporations and other legal persons carrying on an enterprise (and others in limited circumstances) to create a hypothec on a universality of present and future property of the security provider (*hypothèque qui grève une universalité de biens*).[31] The reform was intended to streamline and modernise the law with a view to supporting business financing.

Relatively recent reforms in France have also been intended to support economic efficiency and finance, while also protecting debtors. Although the security over business components (*nantissement du fonds de commerce*) was introduced in 1898, other security rights with floating elements were the product of more recent reforms, especially in 2006 with the introduction of the general non-possessory pledge (*gage*), and with some modifications in 2021.[32] Of course, if a party takes a combination of such security, a wide range of movable collateral will be encumbered, akin to a floating charge. The French security over business components was influential in Romania in the early twentieth century, leading to the recognition of a similar security. However, it became inapplicable owing to the absence of private businesses in the socialist era. After the end of that period in 1989/1990, there seems to have been some recognition of the pledge of an enterprise. In 1999, legislation expressly recognised the ability to create security in a *universitas facti* (a collection of assets treated as a whole), with the security attaching to every item in the collection.[33]

More generally, from the 1990s onwards, countries from Central and Eastern Europe have moved away from their socialist (or communist) pasts and have sought to develop economically, identifying access to credit as an important contributor. Floating security has clearly been viewed as offering a useful function in this context. In some jurisdictions, the Model Law on Secured Transactions (1994) produced by the European Bank for Reconstruction and

---

[31] See Chapter 9 (C Walsh) for further details.

[32] See Chapter 8 (M Renaudin).

[33] See Chapter 10 (R Rizoiu).

Development (EBRD) has been influential.[34] In Hungary, a floating security called the property encumbering charge (*vagyont terhelő zálogjog*) was introduced in 1996, upon the initiative of the EBRD, as the country transitioned to a post-socialist economy.[35] Floating security also arrived in Poland via legislation in 1996 and came into force in 1998. The previous law was considered inimical to business and the developing economy, as debtors wanted to be able to retain and use their assets.[36] Lithuania first introduced a form of security with floating characteristics under the new Civil Code, which came into force in 2001. This was followed by the reform of security rights in 2012, introducing a company hypothec. Meanwhile, legislation introduced the pledge of (part of) an enterprise in Czechia (2001, *zástava [části] závodu*) and floating security in Croatia (2006, *lebdeće založno pravo*).

Effective lobbying by, and support from, relevant stakeholders seems to often be important in the introduction of floating security by legislation. As well as being the case for a number of countries already mentioned, this also applies to China, where representatives of small enterprises and banks pressed for such security to be made available, and the perceived economic desirability of introducing floating security overrode concerns as to how it would fit with wider (principally Civilian) property law principles.[37] China was not the first country in East Asia to develop floating security. For example, Japan introduced a form of floating security (enterprise security) in 1958, in order to address difficulties encountered by companies wishing to create security over business assets generally when raising finance. Separately, the Japanese courts recognised ownership transfers for security purposes for different property types, including inventory of businesses. South Korea was influenced by both Germany and Japan and may be considered not to have a true functional equivalent to the floating charge. However, (functional) security over a changing pool of movable assets, identifiable by their location, kind and quantum, was recognised under the Civil Code (*YangDoTamBo* and *JipHamMulYangDoTamBo*), and Korean legislation from 2010, in force from 2012, provides for the registration of non-possessory security.

The past decade or so has also witnessed the arrival or expansion of floating security in certain jurisdictions with few obvious connections to one another in this area. In Russia, the total assets pledge was introduced by legislation in 2013, coming into force in 2015, and can be granted by a business, whether

[34] E.g. Czechia.

[35] However, see below regarding the abolition of this security.

[36] There was a pre-existing form of pledge of an enterprise, but it was little used.

[37] See Chapter 7 (Z Wu and H Zhang).

a company or sole trader.[38] This security and the pre-existing goods in circulation pledge indicate a belief that supporting such security is conducive to facilitating business. The law of security rights in Belgium has also undergone reform, with legislation of 2013 allowing for security over a class of goods such as a business or patrimony coming into force in 2018.[39] This followed a different form of business security that had existed since 1919. For Italy, 2016 witnessed the introduction of a non-possessory pledge (*pegno non possessorio*) over various categories of movable property, but this did not become fully effective until the arrival of an electronic registry system in 2023.

Meanwhile, in the Middle East, Jordan introduced floating security in 2018, with a newly established register becoming operational in 2019. The reform was intended to modernise the law in Jordan, introducing a more functionalist approach to secured transactions and expanding the scope of assets that could be used as collateral. Another Middle Eastern country that has reformed its secured transactions laws in the last 10 years is Turkey. In contrast with Jordan, however, Turkey already had a non-possessory pledge over a commercial undertaking (*ticari işletme rehni*) with floating characteristics since 1971, introduced to support economic growth and access to finance. Yet legislation from 2016, which entered into force the following year, expanded the debtors who could create the security and allowed for security to be established over particular items and groups of assets, rather than just all movables. The ability for SMEs to use the security to raise finance is regarded as important.

As already noted, some jurisdictions, particularly the Germanic jurisdictions in our study, have been more resistant to the recognition of floating charges or functional equivalents in a strict sense. In doctrinal terms, this has often been due to a desire to uphold long-standing publicity requirements for security over movable property, focused on the giving of possession,[40] and the failure to introduce a suitable registration system as an alternative means of publicity. In Germany, there is no exact functional equivalent to a floating charge. However, the transfer of ownership (and assignment of receivables) for security purposes (*Sicherungsübereignung*), which as a "package" of various security can resemble floating security for movables, has existed since the late nineteenth century and also been recognised since the introduction of the BGB.[41] As in Germany, the Netherlands accepted security

[38] Introduced by way of amendment to the Russian Civil Code.

[39] The Belgian Pledge Act of 11 July 2013.

[40] *Faustpfandprinzip.*

[41] See the cases cited by M Brinkmann, "The Peculiar Approach of German Law in the Field of Secured Transactions and Why It Has Worked (So Far)" in L Gullifer and O Akseli (eds), *Secured Transactions Law Reform: Principles, Policies and Practice* (Hart 2016) 339, 341.

transfers of movables (and claims) from 1929 onwards, and these could cover present and future movables. Yet Dutch law has now somewhat departed from German law by introducing non-possessory pledges (*pandrecht*) via the Civil Code of 1992. Switzerland presents an example of a system that has generally eschewed floating security but has permitted such security in the limited context of the encumbrance of intermediated securities since 2010.[42] It is perhaps not surprising that Switzerland has sought to adopt this innovation in the area of finance, given the country's emphasis on such activity. Austria seems to be the staunchest opponent of floating security among the Germanic jurisdictions and has not specifically introduced such security, albeit it may be recognised in very limited circumstances.

Influence of Other Systems

English law has been particularly influential in the emergence of floating charges in various jurisdictions. This has, in large part, been due to the reach of the British Empire and the UK's historical role as a colonial power. In jurisdictions such as Australia, Canada, Hong Kong, India, Ireland, Israel, New Zealand, Nigeria and Singapore, English law was adopted, and this included the acceptance of floating charges. Even after independence, many jurisdictions in the Common Law world continued to be heavily influenced by the English law of security rights and did not drastically depart from it.[43] In those jurisdictions which still recognise floating charges on the English model, English authorities continue to be frequently drawn upon in relation to such security.

Within the UK itself, the legislation that brought floating charges into Scots law was inspired by English law's floating charge, albeit with adaptations.[44] Given the commercial, economic, social and political ties between Scotland and England and Wales, this is not surprising, and various interested parties pressed for greater alignment with English law. It was also suggested, however, in a report preceding the introduction of the security that a non-possessory security (potentially with floating characteristics) would not be inconsistent with the Civilian tradition.[45] South Africa is another mixed legal system but, as noted above, the general notarial bond in South African law arose from the

42 See Chapter 13 (A Dal Molin-Kränzlin).

43 See e.g. Chapter 3 (C Emedosi).

44 The term "floating charge" itself was taken from English law.

45 Law Reform Committee for Scotland, *Eighth Report of the Law Reform Committee for Scotland: The Constitution of Security over Moveable Property; and Floating Charges* (Cmnd 1017: 1960), Appendix I – "Historical Note" by TB Smith.

country's Roman-Dutch legal heritage, rather than English law. Yet it was supplemented by procedural and registration systems that were established during the period of English colonial rule.

Where Common Law jurisdictions have reformed their secured transactions laws in recent decades, functionalist systems emphasising the substance or function of security transactions rather than their form,[46] emanating from the approach taken by the USA's UCC Article 9, have often been adopted, including in Australia, Canada and New Zealand. In the USA, there was no particular model for the floating lien (as a form of the security interest) under UCC Article 9, yet some components of the security that already existed in US law were originally derived from English legal concepts. The influence of UCC Art 9 has not just been limited to Common Law jurisdictions, with countries including Belgium and Bosnia and Herzegovina introducing some aspects of such a system when reforming their laws.[47]

There are, however, also examples of Civil Law systems, or at least non-Common Law systems, being influenced by the English floating charge. For instance, English law seems to have been particularly influential for floating security introduced in Japan[48] and China.[49] It also appears to have been somewhat (indirectly) influential in the emergence of the Hungarian floating security, principally through the mechanism of the EBRD's Model Law.[50] The influence of the English floating charge and the EBRD is also apparent in Lithuania, while in Poland, there was some inspiration taken from comparative studies in relation to both Common Law and Civilian systems.[51] International instruments have also played a role in relevant reforms outside Europe. In Jordan, both the UNCITRAL Legislative Guide on Secured Transactions (2007) and the UNCITRAL Model Law on Secured Transactions (2016) were highly

[46] So that e.g. using ownership/title for security purposes can be recharacterised as the creditor holding merely a security interest with the debtor owning the collateral.

[47] However, note the continued conceptualisation of the Belgian security as a pledge identified above.

[48] The enterprise security was modelled after the English floating charge. The ownership transfer for security purposes is primarily of domestic origin but possibly with some German influence.

[49] Albeit that legal provisions in other systems also seem to have had an impact, including Japan.

[50] See Chapter 11 (T Tajti).

[51] However, it did not go as far as introducing a single security interest as in e.g. UCC Art 9.

influential.[52] EBRD and UNCITRAL publications have also been reference points for Turkey, as discussed further below.

It is commonplace that when a country introduces floating security, the law in multiple other jurisdictions is referred to or utilised in certain respects. The Danish company charge (*virksomhedspant*) was influenced by the law on floating security and security rights more generally in England, Finland, Norway and Sweden.[53] And while Finland was heavily influenced by Swedish law, in Norway, the preparatory works for the general floating security apparently referred to various systems, including the other Nordic systems, England, France, the Netherlands, Switzerland, Germany and the USA.[54]

For some jurisdictions, no other system has had a notable influence on the introduction of floating security, or it is at least not obvious or clear whether another system has played such a role.[55] In Russia, while it is sometimes suggested that the Common Law was a source for relevant provisions, it cannot be said that English law or indeed any other legal system had a direct influence on the Russian floating security. In Switzerland, the introduction of floating security in a limited context appears to have been driven by practical concerns and seems to not have taken place in imitation of another jurisdiction. For France, no other jurisdiction appears to have been particularly influential, but in recent times there has been scholarly consideration of other approaches, including under English law and US law.[56]

French law itself has been impactful elsewhere, with the non-possessory pledge and industrial mortgage of Mexican law having been inspired to some extent by French law (as well as Spanish law).[57] French law unsurprisingly influenced the previous Belgian law in terms of the possibility of security being granted over certain assets of a business, albeit that there has since been some divergence of the two systems.[58] The original floating security in Romanian law partly derived from French law in the early twentieth century. Yet since the 1990s, and the move towards a market economy, there has been growing

[52] The laws of other Middle East jurisdictions, such as Palestine and the UAE, apparently utilised drafts that were originally prepared for Jordan.

[53] The Danish floating security may be considered most similar to the Norwegian version, but it is not obvious to what extent this was intentional.

[54] See Chapter 12 (B Løtveit, A Millung-Christoffersen, P Lindskoug and T Juutilainen).

[55] E.g. in Chile.

[56] See Chapter 8 (M Renaudin).

[57] The security trust of Mexican law, in contrast, seems to have been an attempt to emulate the trust of Anglo-American law.

[58] The Belgian law of 1919 was partly influenced by an earlier French law regarding security over businesses.

American and Canadian influence in this area, with Quebec generally having an impact in private law, because of its mixture of Civilian and Common Law elements. However, the provisions on floating security may be more influenced by UCC Art 9 and the Canadian PPSAs, with the floating charge of English law having had a more limited impact.[59]

In relation to Quebec, the 1991 Code reflects the Civilian tradition, especially as embodied in French law, but the relevant rules for floating security involve a notable degree of alignment with the PPSAs of the Canadian (Common Law) provinces, and thus less directly the USA's UCC Article 9 from which they ultimately derive. The changing focal points of influence away from France are also evident in the case of Turkey. There were apparently significant references to French law, including security over a commercial fund, when floating security was introduced in 1971. However, the current form of floating security introduced in 2016/2017 has taken some inspiration from more international sources, namely the UNCITRAL Model Law on Secured Transactions 2010 and the EBRD Model Law on Secured Transactions.

There does not seem to have been a particularly influential system for Germany in its refusal to recognise a true functional equivalent to floating charges. And there has only been limited debate about floating charges, principally with reference to English law.[60] Germany is of course itself an influential jurisdiction in private law both historically and in the present day, but few countries in our sample continue to adopt the same course in relation to floating security. The law in the Netherlands was historically shaped by German law in the early twentieth century in accepting security transfers of movables. The non-possessory pledge over present and future assets that now exists in the Netherlands has no equivalent in German law and does not seem to have been specifically influenced by the law in any other country.[61] In South Korea, the German and Japanese legal systems were important reference points when the general modern law of security rights was developed, in the form of the Korean Civil Code. The country has not followed Japan in the introduction of enterprise security but has created a non-possessory security register for movables, in a departure from the German position.

---

59 See Chapter 10 (R Rizoiu).

60 See e.g. F Kleweta, *Die Sicherungsfunktion der Floating Charge in Deutschland* (Mohr Siebeck 2018); T Grädler, *Die Möglichkeiten der globalen Belastung von Unternehmen im deutschen Recht* (Mohr Siebeck 2012).

61 But note the historical influence of Roman law, which meant that expansive security over various types of assets was available until the nineteenth century: see Chapter 4 (V van Hoof).

Abolition and Replacement

As noted above, some systems in their modern form have not admitted floating security, except sometimes in very limited contexts. However, these systems, or their predecessor(s), may have inherited the expansive hypothec of Roman law, at least over movables, but departed from that position historically or abolished the security. Yet it is often unknown when precisely and how this occurred.[62] Of course, other systems that did have the general hypothec, or at least wide-ranging security with floating characteristics, and subsequently abolished it, later replaced it with a modern functional equivalent and now have floating security in a general sense.[63]

With reference to recent centuries, once floating security has been introduced, it is unusual for it to be abolished entirely without replacement. Of course, one could point to formerly socialist countries (as noted above), where any flexible security that did exist was rendered unavailable by the nature of the regimes. However, post-socialist jurisdictions have generally (re-)introduced such security. Hungary, though, presents an interesting example, as the floating security ("property encumbering charge") introduced in the post-socialist era was subsequently abolished by the 2013 Civil Code. The reasons for this are not entirely clear, but enforcement issues appear to have been prominent.[64] There does, however, seem to remain a form of security with some floating characteristics.

Various Common Law jurisdictions, including Canada, New Zealand and Australia, have turned away from the English model of floating charges in the past half-century and have embraced the American UCC Art 9-style functionalist model instead. Such reforms have meant that floating charges, in a narrow sense, and other formal types of security have been replaced by a broader security interest that can also encompass future property. Nevertheless, in some of these jurisdictions, floating charges in the narrow English law sense have not technically been abolished, and it may still be possible for them to be created (at least over property not covered by the PPSAs), albeit they seem to be falling into obsolescence.[65] Other Common Law countries which admitted floating charges based on the English model continue to allow them, yet there has been divergence from English law in certain ways.[66] There have also sometimes been unsuccessful attempts or arguments made to abolish floating charges, or at least to place greater limitations on them, including as early as the late

---

[62] E.g. in Austria.

[63] See e.g. Chapter 4 (V van Hoof).

[64] This is discussed in more detail in Chapter 11 (T Tajti).

[65] E.g. in Australia and New Zealand.

[66] See e.g. Chapter 3 (C Emedosi).

nineteenth century in Ireland, and also more recently in relation to English law itself.[67] This has often been due to the perceived unfairness of floating charges in terms of the priorities conferred in comparison with ordinary unsecured creditors.

Some systems have experimented with different forms of floating security.[68] There are jurisdictions in which an existing version of floating security has been replaced by a different version, which may be more expansive.[69] In others, multiple types of floating security have been introduced, and this has sometimes led to one or more of them being used far less commonly. Poland's enterprise security was little used anyway, but has largely been usurped by the more general registered pledge, and, although still technically available, has fallen even further into obsolescence owing to the existence of the competing floating security. The enterprise security in Japan has become uncommon owing to the availability of an alternative form of security that can serve an equivalent purpose but with a higher-ranking priority.[70] In Quebec, a type of floating security more akin to the Common Law floating charge, the floating hypothec, is very rarely used in practice, with the common ordinary hypothec, which also has floating characteristics as it covers a class of property, far more common.[71]

There would be merit in further exploring the particular reasons why one form of security succeeds another in terms of usage and desirability. Additional work could also examine the extent to which there is pressure from different quarters to reform, abolish or replace floating security in the focus jurisdictions. In relation to jurisdictions where such abolition, replacement or reform has taken place, the grounds for these steps would be of particular interest. Archival research might shed significant light in this regard, as it could in relation to other historical aspects of floating security discussed above.

FLOATING SECURITY IN TERMS OF PROPERTY LAW (QUESTIONS 5–8)

5. What assets does the floating charge (or equivalent) extend to in your system? In what situations/by whom can it be created?

---

67 See e.g. RJ Mokal, *Corporate Insolvency Law: Theory and Application* (OUP 2005) ch 6.

68 See e.g. Chapter 12 (B Løtveit, A Millung-Christoffersen, P Lindskoug and T Juutilainen).

69 E.g. Belgium, discussed above.

70 Such as the transfer of ownership package covering inventory and receivables in Japanese law.

71 See Chapter 9 (C Walsh) for further details.

6. How is (or was) the security created over property in your system? (Particular reference is to be made to publicity/registration.)
7. How does (or did) the security function in the broader legal system, including with respect to coherence with property law?
8. How do (or did) specific assets become encumbered by the security and how do (or did) specific assets become unencumbered?

Scope

Question 5 is aimed at assessing the scope of security with floating characteristics. At the heart of this issue lies the question of which assets such a security may, or must, cover. In addition, the personal and situational availability of such security is of interest – are they generally available, or is their use restricted to specific creditors, security providers or situations? Potentially, an interrelation between the configuration of these factors may be observed.

Scope: assets

By necessity, a security cannot be "floating" if it covers only single, specific items – by its nature, it has to be established over a group of (changeable and changing) assets. This central criterion of a "blanket" security over a multiplicity of items can be realised in different ways. From the questionnaire answers, three major approaches can be identified: security covering all the property of a company; security covering a universality of present and future movable assets; and security covering only specific (collections of) assets. These different approaches lead to rather marked differences in the extent of the security, which may in turn influence their availability.

The most extensive approach is that of establishing security over an enterprise as such. Frequently, its object is called the "undertaking of a company" or the "business itself as a going concern" – it includes all present and future property of the debtor company (especially all immovables and movables, including receivables [choses in action] and other intangibles).

For the floating charge established under English law, this is the traditional scope, although it may be limited to a subset of assets.[72] A broad scope also forms the basis in the jurisdictions which closely follow the English floating charge model. Similar conceptions have been affirmed in the questionnaires for Scotland,[73] Ireland,[74] Nigeria,[75] Singapore and the now-abolished

[72] See Chapter 2 (A Televantos).

[73] Companies Act 1985 s 462(1).

[74] The inclusion of registered immovables leads to practical difficulties regarding the accommodation of the floating charge in land registration systems.

[75] See Chapter 3 (C Emedosi) for more details.

Hungarian property encumbering charge; while not explicitly stated, a similar scope is indicated for Hong Kong, India and Israel. The same goes for the traditional English-type floating charge in Australia and New Zealand, and the unpopular enterprise security as well as the general mortgage available only to specified public companies in Japan.

A comparable extent of security is achieved by "enterprise pledges" or "company mortgages" such as the Mexican industrial mortgage and the company security rights introduced in Czechia, Lithuania and Poland. However, the responses indicated a certain amount of unease with the general "all property" scope: in Lithuania, an inventory of the assets needs to be included; in Czechia, their clear description by the parties is highly recommended; and in Poland, the enterprise pledge enjoys very limited popularity. The traditional French approach of the security right over business components (*nantissement du fonds de commerce*) is somewhat more limited: The security always covers incorporeal assets such as the trading name and sign, the clientele or the business goodwill, with the option for the parties to add to its scope commercial movables, materials, business equipment or tools, or intellectual property (IP) rights – not, however, immovables, trade stocks or book debts. Notably, it has fallen out of favour in practice, while its Belgian equivalent, the *gage du fonds de commerce*, has been abolished and the Turkish pledge over the commercial undertaking has been similarly replaced.

The second approach to "blanket" security rights allows for a universal scope but limited to a homogeneous class of assets – movables, frequently including not only tangibles but also receivables and (at least certain specified) intangibles, and sometimes limited to those used by a business.[76] Such a security over a "(factual) universality" of assets may either cover the security provider's entire personal property or be limited to a certain group or class of goods as specified by the parties, typically equipment, inventory, raw materials or similar collections of goods. In either case, it typically extends not only to present property but also to future assets (acquired after the creation of the security right).

This approach is at the core of the functionalist security rights. In the USA, Art 9 UCC permits the use of a type of movables including future movables (e.g. inventory) as collateral. Similar results are achieved under the PPSA/PPSS model in Australia, Canada and New Zealand, albeit with some differences in

76 This is the case e.g. in Italy and Romania.

scope.[77] The floating security interests of Bosnia and Herzegovina and Croatia are other examples of the functionalist approach.[78]

Similar results can be achieved by the more traditional pledge/movables hypothec model if it is extended to allow for the pledge of asset "universalities", comprising either types or groups of movables or "all property". This is the case, e.g., for the non-possessory pledges in Chile, Italy and the Netherlands as well as for the movables hypothec model followed in Quebec and Romania; similar results are achieved in Belgium, Lithuania and South Africa. Some jurisdictions allow for general "all (movable) property" security rights, e.g. Quebec, the Netherlands and South Africa, while others demand a more detailed indication, e.g. Chile. In a few cases, the current state clearly reflects earlier stages of development: Belgian law allows the pledge of a business or agricultural exploitation as a factual universality in the tradition of the former *gage du fonds de commerce*, while the Lithuanian security interest over property complexes (of movable assets) originated in a security interest over goods in circulation, which was subsequently expanded to include other types of property.

A notable subgroup of "blanket" security rights are those specially provided for but also limited to businesses. Finland's enterprise mortgage constitutes a security covering (with a few exceptions) the entire movable property of tangible and intangible fixed assets, changing assets (raw materials, supplies, finished products and goods) and financial assets. Russian law permits a "universal" or "total" all-assets pledge, which, however, does not constitute a special security right but rather allows for the broad scope and general description of the pledged assets via "all assets" clauses in B2B scenarios. Similarly, Turkish law has introduced the option of a security over all present and future movable assets allotted to a commercial undertaking, effectively re-introducing a version of the commercial undertaking pledge. On the other hand, the French *gage sur stock*, available to businesses as a pledge over inventory and fungible goods, was integrated into the general non-possessory pledge in 2021.

The narrowest scope for an encompassing security is achieved by the approach limiting it – in availability or applicability – to specific assets or asset groups. Security rights of this type typically cover various assets, both present and future, but impose stricter limits on the criteria defining the group

---

77 For Canada, inventory and accounts were indicated, while in New Zealand, the possibility to extend the security typically leads to "all present and after-acquired personal property" clauses. In Australia, Sec. 8 PPSA (Australia) contains a wide range of exclusions, mostly regarding other security interests.

78 While in Bosnia and Herzegovina, the security interest can potentially extend to all the debtor's movable assets, in Croatia, it may cover a collection of goods or a specific group of goods situated in a specific space.

or collection of assets. While details vary greatly, under this approach three major types of security can be identified.

The first type is that of security rights available only to businesses and limited to specific types of business assets. The Chinese law floating charge covers manufacturing facilities, raw materials, semi-manufactured goods and products owned by the chargor, with an option to limit its extent to one or more specific groups. Similarly, the Danish company charge covers specific asset groups (e.g. inventories, operating fixtures and equipment, or IP rights), while Norwegian law provides for general floating security rights over operating assets, inventory or trade receivables, the scope of which cannot be adapted by the parties.[79] The inventory pledge of Serbian law and the Japanese special security devices under the "mortgage on foundation" (e.g. factory mortgage) also fall within this category.

The second type is that following the pledge model and allowing for the pledging of assets specified by their belonging to a certain group or category. Examples of this are the French and Mexican non-possessory pledges and the Jordanian security interest which can be established over present and future tangible and intangible movables.[80] Some jurisdictions are more restrictive regarding the pledgeable asset groups. In Poland, a set of (changing) movables may be pledged as such if it constitutes an "economic unit"; notably, this option is typically used in commercial transactions to allow for a pledge over the debtor's entire enterprise with the possible exception of certain elements, effectively coming close to a universal pledge. In Russia, a pledge over "goods in turnover" can be constituted over the pledgor's items intended for circulation or sale (e.g. raw materials, goods in a warehouse) and located at a specified site, making this security right available to professional merchants and manufacturers.

The third type is the security rights, which are not per se of a floating type but show partial similarities, especially those based on a fiduciary transfer of ownership for security purposes. In Austria, such a security can cover all goods (including future goods) stored in a warehouse or comparable room, or all receivables; German law is more flexible and also allows for security ownership of any group of (future) assets as long as they are clearly described and can be individualised. Japanese and South Korean law arrive at similar

---

[79] Assets for which Norwegian law provides special (floating) security rights are excluded from its general floating security. For further details, see Chapter 12 (B Løtveit, A Millung-Christoffersen, P Lindskoug and T Juutilainen).

[80] In France, there is a distinction between the *gage* (for corporeal movables which may be fungible) and the *nantissement* (for incorporeal assets, especially book debts); historically, specific pledge rights were developed for particular types of assets, a number of which still exist.

results. Notably, this technique of security right has largely been shaped by commercial practice and case law, and the combination of various security rights allows for establishing revolving security over fluctuating aggregate entities with a scope rather similar to the English floating charge, albeit ordinarily limited to movables. In addition, security with floating characteristics but covering only specific assets falls within this group. This is the case for the Swiss security right over intermediated securities, which may cover all intermediated securities credited to a securities account or a proportion of them up to a specific value. Less obviously, a hypothec or land charge under German law extends not only to the mortgaged plot of land, but also to its separated products, other components and accessories owned by the land owner;[81] a security right over premises will thus include the objects forming an economic unit with the land, allowing for a fluctuation in their scope.

There is a consensus regarding the requirement for security covering a multiplicity of items – especially with regard to asset totalities typically fluctuating in their composition as specific items are constantly replaced by similar new ones owing to trade or processing. "Fixed" security, invariably covering the items originally individualised, would be highly impractical in this context. Rather, the notion at the core of this type of security is that of "revolving" or "circulating" assets: it is established over a pool of assets, the single components of which may be exchanged or replaced. This presupposes, on the one hand, a certain fungibility of the components in the sense that the security right does not depend on individual items but rather on a collection of items (of a certain value). On the other hand, the security provider must be permitted to use the original items and replace them, with the security covering the "current" composition of the asset pool (sometimes described as present "from time to time"). As a result, the security extends to present property (assets at the time of its creation) as well as future property (assets acquired afterward). The details regarding the encumbrance and unencumbrance of specific items were explored in a separate question (see the analysis of question 8 below).

Three different approaches to establishing such "collective" security can be discerned. For the purposes of the evaluation of the questionnaire responses, the distinction was drawn along theoretical lines. Security rights are considered "over an enterprise" if they cover all property belonging to a business, sometimes also including immovables, and/or if their scope explicitly covers an enterprise as such. They are considered to extend to a "(factual) universality" if they potentially cover all movables, allowing for limitation by the parties. They are considered security rights over "specific assets or asset groups" if they can cover only assets of a certain type, determined either by law or by

81 Extended mortgage liability (*Haftungsverband*), §§ 1120 et seq. BGB.

the parties. However, the delineation of boundaries between the approaches and the classification of security rights under them may prove challenging. An "enterprise" may be considered to be the "universality of all its assets"; for example, while the Czech pledge of (part of) an enterprise is classified as an enterprise security according to the criteria established, the Czechian response noted that an enterprise is understood as a "*universalitas rerum*", indicating a dogmatic relationship to the universal pledge model rather than the business security model. Similarly, the line between universal and asset type-specific security is blurred, with some security rights potentially covering all assets but in practice typically employed only for specific asset groups.

For further research, the potential of a security right to cover "mixed" asset groups (not only assets of a homogeneous type) as a determining factor appears worth exploring. Generally, there appears to be a tendency towards preferring security over asset groups or universalities with a more or less clear description of the assets covered to security over business entities as such. The extent to which this is a result of general developments with respect to security rights, especially regarding the modern possibilities for registration, remains to be studied. With regard to the types of assets, detailed scrutiny needs to be imparted to intangibles, especially receivables. Most responses focused on tangible movables, and the fragmentary information provided regarding intangibles typically concentrated on rights (such as IP rights); however, some also indicated the (potential) inclusion of receivables in the scope of floating security rights.

The relationship between encompassing floating security rights and security rights over specific individual assets merits further in-depth research. Notably, in many jurisdictions,[82] "registered property" (typically immovables and registered movables such as motor vehicles, ships and aircraft) is explicitly excluded from the scope of floating security rights, granting precedence to the specific security rights designed for these assets. However, several jurisdictions[83] explicitly refer to the practice of combining different asset (type)-specific security rights (e.g. security rights over specified tangible movables and/or receivables and/or immovables) into a "security package" in order to obtain results similar to an encompassing all-assets security. This solution, encountered especially in jurisdictions with a restrictive approach to the scope of security rights, invites further study as a functional equivalent.

82 For example, Jordan, Poland, South Korea and Turkey.

83 For example, Germany, Japan, the Netherlands and Poland.

Scope: situational and personal restrictions

With regard to the situational and personal scope of application of floating security, the questionnaires either provided rather straightforward answers or did not even explicitly address the issue; the answer is closely linked to or may be inferred from the extent of asset coverage.

Interestingly, a restriction of the situations in which the security is available was indicated for only two, rather marginal, scenarios: the use of the remnants of the traditional floating charge in Canada as a specific form of security right over immovables[84] and the Japanese general mortgage for public enterprises. This result is in keeping with the general tendency of security rights moving away from situation-, sector- or asset-specific security rights (e.g. the traditional *warrants* of French law) towards universally applicable security rights (culminating in the functionalist model gaining ever more popularity).

With regard to the personal scope of application, on the debtor side, a restriction to businesses (companies, enterprises) or business owners (entrepreneurs) is common. It necessarily follows for security rights over businesses "as such"[85] or over business assets.[86] There is, however, some variation in detail. While some jurisdictions allow natural persons to act as security providers (e.g. China), others restrict the availability of encompassing floating security to companies and comparable entities (e.g. Scotland, Ireland). In addition, security rights over specific types of assets may only be available to apposite businesses.

On the other hand, non-business-specific security rights are usually available to all debtors, in keeping with their more general nature. This is most notably the case for security rights following the functionalist model, for which no personal restrictions were indicated.[87] Similarly, availability to all kinds of security providers was indicated for the security rights over specific assets or

---

[84] The floating charge still finds application in scenarios of transaction financing involving mineral interests and other land interests with a high asset turnover, as it offers a more practical solution compared to fixed registration under a land titles system.

[85] This is the case for the relevant security rights in England and Wales, Scotland, Ireland, Nigeria, Singapore, Hong Kong, India, Israel, Mexico, Czechia, Lithuania, Poland, Japan and France as well as the (previous) floating charges of Australia, New Zealand and Hungary and the former Belgian *gage du fonds de commerce*.

[86] Either with a broad scope, e.g. in Finland, Russia and Turkey, or limited to certain asset groups, e.g. in China, Denmark, Norway, Serbia and Japan.

[87] USA, Australia, Canada, New Zealand, Bosnia and Herzegovina and Croatia.

asset groups.[88] While this is also the starting point for universal pledge-type security,[89] in jurisdictions that allow for a far-reaching "general pledge", its restriction to the use of business security providers may be observed. Both Quebec and Romania restrict the "universal" movables hypothec in this way; a similar limit can be encountered for the Lithuanian security interest over property complexes and the Italian non-possessory pledge (again, the definition of "enterprise" may vary from a broad understanding [e.g. Quebec] to a stricter one [e.g. Italy]). Notably, for some jurisdictions, a *de facto* restriction was mentioned, with a security right theoretically available universally being used in practice only in commercial transactions (Poland, Russia and South Africa). In addition, some responses addressed the issue of consumer protection, pointing out exceptions and special provisions in this regard (e.g. Jordan, New Zealand, Quebec and the USA).

Limitations of the personal scope on the creditor side were indicated only rarely, with financial institutions or banks as the sole takers of collateral. In Turkey, the scope of security providers is limited if the secured creditor is not a credit institution. A restriction to banks can also be observed for some security rights over businesses, such as the French *nantissement du fonds de commerce*, the Mexican industrial mortgage and the abolished Belgian *gage du fonds de commerce*. It was also a requirement for the abolished French *gage sur stock*; *de facto*, financial credit institutions still enjoy a monopoly as creditors of the French non-possessory pledge.

From the answers provided, the following tendency can be deduced: The broader the scope of a security right is, the more likely it is that access to the use of this security right will be restricted. The common restriction to "professional" security providers reflects the widespread scepticism towards both non-possessory and general security rights over movables, which are frequently perceived as potentially perilous and detrimental to the security provider. The correlation between scope and availability merits in-depth study, exploring further the reasons behind the limitations of the use of floating security and the techniques employed for their implementation. Additional insights may be gained from a comprehensive scrutiny of the possibilities and risks of this type of security in the context of consumer credit.

---

[88] France, Jordan, Mexico, Poland, Russia, Germany, Austria, Japan, South Korea and Switzerland.

[89] Chile, the Netherlands, Belgium and South Africa.

Creation

The goal of question 6 is to explore the mechanisms for the creation of different types of floating security. With regard to the steps necessary to establish the security right, aside from formal requirements, the nature and extent of publicity play a central role. While registration typically forms the means of publicity, strong differences can be observed both on the substantive level concerning its effects and on the implementation level concerning the type of register chosen for the publication of floating security. A systematisation of the solutions encountered allows for the discernment of approaches, which may be interdependent with the varying scopes of security right.

Formal requirements: security agreement

At the basis of the constitution of a voluntary security right, there is always a security agreement – containing the parties' concordant declarations to create the security. The designation for this may vary (e.g. "security agreement", "pledge contract"), as well as the prominence accorded to it. A broad range can also be observed with regard to the level of formality required to validly conclude such an agreement; the formal conditions can be grouped into three categories.

The highest level of form that may be required for a security agreement is that of a public instrument. Under this heading, different state-authorised documents are grouped, the most prominent among which are notarial deeds, private documents with a signature authorised by a notary and documents registered with a public body. Their common denominator is the involvement of a public authority, typically a notary, tasked with the authentication of the agreement. While allowing for legal certainty and strong evidence value as well as protection of the parties (through raising their awareness of the significance of their transaction), this approach has the downside of comparatively high effort and costs. The requirement of a form of public instrument was indicated for Chile, Croatia, Czechia, Japan (enterprise security), Lithuania (both company mortgage and security interest over property complexes), the Netherlands, South Africa and Turkey; a deed was also the formal requirement for the now-abolished Belgian *gage du fonds de commerce*. Some jurisdictions offer alternative forms: in the Netherlands, a written deed needs to be either executed before a notary or registered with the tax authority; in Lithuania, while a non-possessory security right requires a notarised and registered agreement, the simple written form is sufficient if the creditor obtains possession of the collateral. Turkish law provides for an electronic conclusion of the agreement using an official electronic signature as an alternative to the traditional paper agreement with notarised signatures concluded before the registry's clerk. An indirect form requirement results for the assets falling within the scope of a hypothec or land charge under German law: as security rights over immovables necessitate notarial involvement, this constitutes a prerequisite also for their extension to land-related movables.

A middle road is taken by the jurisdictions demanding a security agreement be concluded in written form, signed either by both parties or only by the security provider, but without the involvement of official bodies. Writing is required in China, Denmark, Finland, France (both *nantissement du fonds de commerce* and non-possessory pledge), Italy, Mexico (both industrial mortgage and non-possessory pledge), New Zealand, Poland, Quebec and Romania; it was also the form required for the abolished French *gage sur stock*. Again, some variations can be observed. For example, under Danish law, traditional writing has been replaced by a digital document with a digital signature, which is then submitted electronically for registration. The Finnish enterprise mortgage requires the inclusion of a standardised negotiable promissory note.[90] Under the law of New Zealand, the form requirement does not affect the validity of the security right but its effect against third parties: while it is possible to conclude the security agreement orally, for its enforcement against third parties, the debtor's assent in writing is required.

In a fairly large number of jurisdictions, there are no specific form requirements for the creation of the security right by party agreement. The conclusion of the security agreement free of any form is possible in Belgium, England and Wales, Germany, Hong Kong, Ireland, Japan (transfer of ownership), Jordan, Nigeria, Scotland, Singapore and South Korea. In addition, no form requirements were indicated in the questionnaires for Australia, Austria, Canada (floating charge), Hungary, India, Israel, Norway, Russia, Switzerland and the USA. It is notable, however, that despite the freedom of form, for practical and evidence reasons, transactions are usually executed or documented in writing, especially when a security right for a large value and/or a long term is envisaged. For example, the response for Ireland indicated that in practice, floating charges are granted by deed (in writing and executed in accordance with the requirements of company law and the constitution of the relevant companies with regard to the company seal), while in South Korea, the standard practice is a written (including electronic) security agreement signed by the parties, and in Belgium, the demand for a deed may result from evidence law. In addition, form requirements for the security agreement may result indirectly from those established for publicity mechanisms – such is the case, e.g. in Australia, where a written security agreement is required when publicity is effected through the creditor's control of the collateral, and in Hong Kong, where the subsequent

90 For details, see Chapter 12 (B Løtveit, A Millung-Christoffersen, P Lindskoug and T Juutilainen).

registration of a floating charge requires a certified copy of the charge instrument, effectively necessitating its conclusion in writing, which is comparable to the position in various other jurisdictions (see below).[91]

Generally, a fairly strong interrelation between the security right's type and scope and the formal requirements for its constitution can be observed. Freedom of form is typically encountered for asset-specific security rights – but also for floating charges in the English tradition. The high threshold of a public instrument, on the other hand, is usually required for universal and enterprise pledges, with the compromise of "simple" writing as the standard under the functionalist model and also frequently encountered in a business-specific context.

The formal requirements for the security agreement are also influenced by registration – the type of register and the level of formality required for registration may have repercussions on the formalities at the level of the underlying agreement. If registration is conditional upon the submission of a written, or even formalised, document, an (at least indirect) form requirement for the creation of the security right between the parties results. This correlation merits further study within the larger context of registration.

Publicity: requirement and effect

The efficiency of security rights depends to a large extent on their effectiveness towards third parties – in property law terms, on their effects *in rem* or *erga omnes*. Typically, this is connected to publicity requirements. Today, registration is the most common mode of publicity for floating security, frequently introduced as an alternative to the traditional, highly impractical approach of possession as a means of publicity. This development can be observed both in jurisdictions basing their floating security right on a non-possessory pledge[92] and in jurisdictions following the functionalist approach.[93] Frequently, registration is superimposed on the older publicity model, offering the parties a choice between delivery of the collateral to the creditor and registration.[94] The availability of electronic registration systems with low expense and effort has greatly contributed to the growing popularity of publicity by registration in the

[91] Similarly, while no form requirement was mentioned in the questionnaire for Russia, written form can be presumed to be a prerequisite for (voluntary) pledge registration with a notary.

[92] E.g. France.

[93] E.g. under the PPSAs in Australia, Canada and New Zealand.

[94] This can be observed e.g. under the functionalist approach in Australia, New Zealand and Jordan, with the pledge model in Belgium, France and Quebec, and for the transfer of ownership in Japan and South Korea.

past decades. The majority of questionnaire responses indicated a requirement for the publication of floating security by registration.

A dichotomy can be observed, however, with regard to the effects of publicity. While some legal systems demand registration as a constitutive element for the existence of the security right ("creation"), others require it only for it to produce its full effects ("perfection"). This distinction is not peculiar to floating security, however; rather, the extent of the effects of publicity is a characteristic of security rights models in general (depending, among other factors, on the legal tradition,[95] and with the distinction between *inter partes* and *erga omnes* effects through publicity featuring prominently, especially under the functionalist approach). With regard to their floating security, some jurisdictions follow the traditional idea that publicity is a constitutive requirement for *in rem* rights to come into existence and demand registration for the security to be validly created – without publicity, it is not (yet) existent and has no effect. Such a strong need for publicity can be encountered in Bosnia and Herzegovina, Chile, Czechia, Finland, Lithuania (both company mortgage and security interest over property complexes), Poland, South Africa, South Korea and Turkey; under German and Russian law, publicity is constitutive as far as the security right involves immovables. A more differentiated approach to publicity is taken by a large number of jurisdictions under which the agreement of the parties concerned is sufficient for the security right's existence between them, but publicity (by registration) is required for it to take full effect against third parties – especially for the determination of the secured creditor's priority and position in enforcement and insolvency proceedings (see question 10 below). This is the position in Australia (both floating charge and PPSA), Belgium, Canada (both floating charge and PPSA), China, Croatia, England and Wales, France (both *nantissement du fonds de commerce* and non-possessory pledge), Hong Kong, India, Ireland,[96] Israel, Japan (transfer of ownership), Jordan, Mexico (both industrial mortgage and non-possessory pledge), New Zealand, Nigeria, Norway, Quebec, Scotland, Singapore[97] and the USA. The answers regarding the effects of registration under Danish, Italian and Serbian law cannot be clearly classified into one of the two groups. For the Finnish enterprise mortgage, registration is needed; however, third-party effects result from it only once a security agreement has been concluded and the promissory

[95] For example, while German law traditionally accords constitutive value to publicity requirements for *in rem* rights, French law has established a clear distinction between the right's existence and its enforceability towards third parties.

[96] Irish law recognises some exceptions for non-registrable assets.

[97] Registration is required for company charges over assets contained in a specified list; however, the majority of assets fall within this group.

note (with the registration entered on it by the competent authority) has been delivered to the creditor.[98]

For several jurisdictions, time limits for registration were indicated. On the one hand, registration may have to be applied for within a certain time period after the creation of the security right between the parties – this is the case, for example, in England and Wales and Scotland,[99] Ireland,[100] Hong Kong[101] and Nigeria.[102] On the other hand, the register entry may not be effective indefinitely, but may expire after a certain duration – for example, in Belgium, Denmark, France and Quebec.

Only a small number of responses described a publicity regime deviating from a registration mechanism. On one side of the spectrum, Austria is the only legal system to still adhere to the very strict, traditional publicity rules initially established for the possessory pledge and applied also to the transfer of ownership for security purposes. The only alternative to the creditor's full physical control over the assets consists in affixing a "sign" advertising the security right and transferring exclusive control over the assets to a "trusted third party". Owing to a narrow interpretation, these requirements have proved incompatible with the operation of an ongoing business (especially the creation of security over goods stored in a warehouse or similar place), which has led to security rights over tangible movable groups not being used in practice.[103] On the other side of the spectrum, some jurisdictions allow for floating security without publicity. No true publicity mechanism is required for the German transfer of ownership for security purposes or the Dutch non-possessory pledge over movables;[104] for the Swiss encumbrance of intermediated securities, publication is not even envisaged as possible. An interesting middle road is taken by Russian law, which does not demand publicity for the pledge

---

98 For an in-depth discussion, see Chapter 12 (B Løtveit, A Millung-Christoffersen, P Lindskoug and T Juutilainen).

99 Twenty-one days after creation.

100 Twenty-one days after creation, but allowing for advance registration.

101 One month after creation.

102 Ninety days after creation.

103 The practice of a (global) pledge of receivables or their assignment for security purposes is, however, quite common under Austrian law, as its publicity requirements of either a notification to the third-party debtor or an entry of the security into the security provider's bookkeeping system can be fulfilled fairly easily, especially by banks.

104 Creation requires a written deed, either executed before a notary or registered with the tax authority; this registration, however, does not constitute a publicity mechanism, but only serves as a means of officially dating a private deed.

over movables, but offers and indirectly encourages its voluntary enrolment with a notary.[105]

The ensemble view shows a certain interrelation between the type of security right and the registration model. Constitutive publicity appears limited to the Civil Law tradition (especially in jurisdictions with a certain influence of German law), whereas a third-party effect can be encountered under the floating charge model, the functionalist approach and the pledge model (especially in the French tradition) and alternative publicity requirements remain reserved for asset-specific security. A complete lack of publicity requirements is rare; notably, when practice creates publicity-free security rights (e.g. the transfer of ownership for security purposes in Germany), their implementation by legislation usually includes publicity requirements (e.g. the transfer of ownership in Japan and South Korea).

The details of registration provide a worthwhile topic of exploration, with regard to both the requirements for and the effects of registration. For example, encompassing information should be gathered and compared regarding the time limits for the effectuation and the expiration of register entries (including phenomena like "temporary perfection" rules or "grace periods"). Such a study will require contextualisation within the general regime of security rights, as the conceptions and technical aspects of publicity are often not specific to floating security but rather contingent on the general model and functioning of security. This may also serve to deepen knowledge on how far floating security is integrated into the security rights system and to what extent it remains separate, possibly even foreign.

Registration: type of register

The majority of jurisdictions have established a registration requirement for their floating security. This entails the question of what kind of register forms the basis of publicity in this context. The most frequent types of register are company or enterprise registers and security interest or pledge registers, with some jurisdictions taking (additional) recourse to land registers. The choice of register type depends strongly on which assets are covered by the security. Additionally, a certain correlation between the type of register and the effects of registration can be observed.

Registration in a companies or enterprise register is, with one exception, encountered exclusively in jurisdictions that use security over enterprises as such, modelled on the English floating charge. In England and Wales, the

[105] Enrolment entails constructive notice of third parties as the notary's pertinent data are open to the public, effectively prohibiting the loss of the pledge through *bona fide* acquisition of the pledged assets.

registration of floating charges is effected at Companies House. Following this approach of registering the security over the enterprise with the authority in charge of enterprise registration, the floating charges of Hong Kong, India, Ireland, Israel, Nigeria, Singapore and Scotland require registration with the corresponding authority.[106] Similarly, the former floating charges of Australian and Canadian law had to be registered in registers for security over companies.[107] Notably, the traditional floating charge registration in the companies register does not constitute a creation requirement, but only leads to the security right's effectiveness vis-à-vis (at least some) third parties. The only other jurisdiction indicating an enterprise-specific registration is Japan: the creation of an enterprise security depends on its entry in the Corporate Registration system. The main advantages of the company registration model are the recourse to an already existing register, simply adding the security right to the company's established register entry, and the resulting apparentness at one glance whether a given enterprise is encumbered for all interested parties. However, as this type of registration is available exclusively to (registered) companies and similar entities, its scope is necessarily limited.

A more general scope, in terms of both registrable security and security providers' registration, is available through security registers (frequently called security interest or pledge registers), conceived either as general registers for all types of security rights or as special registers for specific types of security rights. A general, unified approach to security registration lies at the core of the functionalist approach – hence, the floating securities of Australia, New Zealand and the USA are registered in the security registers.[108] For non-possessory pledges (and movables hypothecs), registration is typically effected in a pledge register – this is the case, for example, in Chile, France, Italy, Jordan, Mexico, Poland, Quebec and Romania.[109] Registration in a security register is also required or available for the security rights based on a transfer of ownership in South Korea and Japan. Security over business assets that do not follow the floating charge model is also typically registered in a register for security rights rather than for companies – this can be observed for security over enterprises as such (the Czech pledge of [part of] an enterprise, the

[106] For example, the Company Registration Office in Ireland or the Companies Registrar in Hong Kong and Israel.

[107] As Australian law has abandoned the floating charge in favour of the functional approach, the Australian Register of Company Charges has consequently been discontinued.

[108] E.g. in the applicable UCC registry in the USA; see Chapter 6 (C Odinet) for details.

[109] For example, the French centralised online pledge register established in 2023; for details, see Chapter 8 (M Renaudin).

Mexican industrial mortgage and the abolished Hungarian property encumbering charge), for "blanket" security over business assets (the Finnish enterprise mortgage and the Turkish security over all present and future movable assets allotted to a commercial undertaking) and for security over specific business assets (the Chinese floating charge, the Danish company charge and the Norwegian security rights over operating assets, inventory or trade receivables).[110] As the characteristics of security registers vary greatly, so do their effects: within this group, both constitutive registration requirements ("creation") and registration requirements for third-party effect ("perfection") can be encountered.

For both registration models, some responses indicated a need for coordination with other registration systems for certain types of assets. For assets for which registration in a specialised register is required (typically, registrable mobile equipment such as motor vehicles, ships and aircraft, or IP rights), intricate practical problems may arise with regard to the registration of a floating charge in the company register.[111] Similarly, assets subject to specialised registration need to be accommodated by exceptions from registration in a general security register.[112] Even more difficulties may arise when the floating security also covers immovables and the requirements of land registration need to be fulfilled. Different solutions are available, but all of them detract from a straightforward registration of the floating security. An additional registration in the land register for floating charges covering registered land is required in Hong Kong, Ireland, India and Nigeria.[113] In Mexico, in such cases, the registration of an industrial mortgage is "split", with registration in the movables securities register for movable assets and the land register for immovables. In Russia and Romania, if land is included in a "total" all-assets

---

[110] Register types, names and authorities may vary greatly – for example, in China the uniform register for charges/pledges is maintained by the Market Regulation Bureau while in Finland the Register of Enterprise Mortgages falls within the domain of the Patent and Registration office.

[111] This is the case, for example, for a variety of assets in Ireland (with priority with regard to these assets governed by the specialised registration) as well as Nigeria and Singapore.

[112] Typically, registrable mobile equipment (motor vehicles, ships and aircraft) – for example, in New Zealand and South Korea.

[113] Notably, under Hong Kong law, the registration of a floating charge on interests in land with the Land Registry is required, but can only be effected once the floating charge has crystallised and become a fixed charge. Similarly, Nigerian law does not require registration of the creation of a floating charge in the land registry as it does not constitute a transfer of interest, but requires it for enforcement purposes or upon occurrence of a crystallising event.

pledge or universal hypothec, the security over the immovable property has to be registered according to the rules applicable to real estate;[114] similarly, in Japan, a transfer of ownership of real property only becomes effective against third parties after the apposite registration. As already noted, many jurisdictions avoid such coordination difficulties by excluding immovables and other registered assets from their floating security right.[115] The price to be paid for this simplification, however, is a substantial limitation of the scope of the floating security.

Alternatively, coordination issues may be avoided by attaching the registration of floating security rights entirely to the land registration system. A few legal systems have chosen this approach of extending land registration also to movables. This is the case in South Africa, where the general hypothec requires the registration of the general notarial bond with the Deeds Office, mainly tasked with the registration of rights in immovables.[116] In Lithuania, registration of the company mortgage is effected with the land register (Hypothec Register), treating the company as real estate. A similar approach is used for the Japanese "mortgage on foundation", with the assets treated collectively and registered according to real property rules. Under German law, a security right over immovables (hypothec or land charge) requires its constitutive registration in the land register; its floating extension to the movables connected with the land follows as an automatic consequence, without additional registration.

On the whole, a marked tendency to integrate the registration of floating security in existing register systems can be observed, with the issues of interest for the general development of register law (e.g. formalities, proceedings and digitalisation) reflected throughout. A point of interest is, again, the localisation of floating security within the general context of security rights – their registration in an encompassing security register indicates a stronger integration in the security rights model, whereas their registration in a different register points to their position as a special instrument. Further attention should also be devoted to the complicated and frequently competitive relationship with land registration encountered in several jurisdictions. Exploring these issues may also contribute to the understanding of registration systems, in the security rights context and beyond.

114 In Romania, the effect of registration in the land registry varies: in the regions where the general cadaster is finalised, registration is a creation requirement, while in the remaining regions, it still only entails perfection.

115 See e.g. Turkish law.

116 For details, see Chapter 5 (R Brits).

Floating Security and Property Law Rules

Question 7 aims at identifying the potential problems that may be raised by the integration of floating security within the context of general property law. While the English floating charge has its roots in the notoriously flexible equity, and the approach to its regulation stems largely from the fairly adaptable company law, the security rights of the Civil Law legal tradition are typically based on property law with its more rigid rules and principles. It is thus of interest to explore which challenges the integration of floating characteristics poses for such legal systems – how far are they compatible with the principles of property law, and are conflicts resolved by limitations to the floating security or by loosening the rules of property law?

It is important to note that responses to this question varied greatly, with regard to length and depth as well as the aspects addressed. There was a wide variety of interpretations, ranging from the observance of core principles of property law to issues of coherence with other security rights, depending on the different jurisdictions' backgrounds and context. Generally, responses remained brief, with some contributors indicating that this type of reasoning was foreign to their legal system – possibly, the question was formulated too strongly from the angle of Civil Law dogmatics. As not all aspects were addressed by all contributors, the following evaluation cannot claim to provide a definitive picture. It does permit, at this stage, the identification of potentially problematic facets, in preparation for further study with a more nuanced and detailed approach.

Coherence with property law: general observations

As they grant the creditor (limited) rights over the debtor's assets, floating security rights are closely connected to property law – in many legal systems, they are construed as (limited) real rights. However, their floating character may conflict with the demands of property law, which typically requires clarity and definition. This is potentially problematic, especially when a floating security is introduced owing to practical and economic needs, taking inspiration from a foreign model and challenging the limits of traditional domestic property doctrine.

Interestingly, many jurisdictions for which responses indicated good general functioning of floating security within the framework of property law, with only occasional problems with regard to specific situations, are part of the Common Law legal tradition. This is the case for the floating charges in Australia, India, Ireland and Nigeria, as well as for the functionalist security rights in Australia, New Zealand and the USA.[117] In several legal systems from the Civil Law or hybrid legal traditions, the integration of floating security rights is generally not considered problematic from a dogmatic point of view – this was stated for Belgium, Finland, Hungary, Jordan, Lithuania, the Netherlands, Norway and South Africa.[118]

However, for a significant number of legal systems, it was indicated that floating security gives rise to a need for reconciliation with the principles and doctrines of property law. This is the case for all Civil Law legal systems from the German legal family (Austria, Germany and Switzerland) as well as for the transfer of ownership for security purposes in Japanese law, which is strongly inspired by the German model.[119] Various other Civil Law jurisdictions also noted issues regarding the compatibility of floating security and general property law rules – among them, Bosnia and Herzegovina, China, France and Russia.[120] However, an at least somewhat problematic relationship with the general property law rules was also indicated for the hybrid legal system of Scotland, where the integration of the floating charge into a mainly Civilian property law system proves challenging, especially with regard to its conceptualisation and publicity aspects. Most notably, some controversy regarding the reconciliation of the equitable floating charge with the property law models of the nature and priority of security rights was attested even for English law.

As information regarding coherence with property law dogmatics remains rather rudimentary and strongly divergent, further in-depth research on specific aspects will be necessary. While the floating, flexible nature of the security may raise problems in all legal traditions, it appears especially difficult to reconcile with Civil Law legal systems, with their perception of security rights as real rights adhering to the principles of property law. At the same time, it

---

[117] In New Zealand, some difficulties arise from the parallel existence of security interests in personal property under the Property Law Act 2007, particularly at the level of enforcement. In Nigeria, problems have been created by the partial adoption of a functionalist approach to security owing to its lack of coordination with the traditional approach to floating charges (based on English law).

[118] The Hungarian response stressed that the difficulties leading to the eventual abolition of the property encumbering charge were related to its enforcement as well as its coordination with mortgages over immovables, but not rooted in a fundamental dogmatic incompatibility.

[119] While this was not indicated for South Korea, owing to the structural similarities, comparable issues can be presumed for the South Korean transfer of ownership for security purposes.

[120] For example, the clear distinctions of French property law between movable and immovable, corporeal and incorporeal, and fungible and non-fungible property pose a conceptual obstacle to the "global" security rights.

can be deduced that the practical and economic need for floating security leads to their increasingly generous accommodation in spite of theoretical reservations. There appear to be two driving factors: the development of mechanisms reconciling floating characteristics with traditional property law dogmatics and a pragmatic disregard for academic worries about theoretical coherence. These tendencies and their interrelationship merit further exploration from both academic and practical perspectives.

Coherence with property law: the principles of speciality and publicity

Detailed responses about the potential conflict between floating security and general property law principles were provided only for jurisdictions from the Civil Law legal tradition. The aspect addressed most frequently as potentially problematic is the principle of speciality (or specificity), demanding the clear determination and identification of all objects of real rights. The resulting need to individualise all assets encumbered by a security right is problematic for collections of assets, especially for the revolving groups of assets forming the basis of floating security. The responses for several jurisdictions explicitly stressed the need for an accommodating exception from the (strict) speciality principle – among them Finland,[121] Italy and Switzerland.[122]

Concerns with regard to compliance with the principle of speciality were indicated from a broad range of Civil Law legal systems: Austria, Belgium, Bosnia and Herzegovina, Chile, China, Denmark, Finland, France, Germany, Italy, Jordan, the Netherlands, Quebec, Russia, Serbia, South Africa and Switzerland. Additionally, similar reservations were not explicitly mentioned but can be inferred for Japan, Mexico, Romania, South Korea and Turkey. However, the solution to this dogmatic issue is as widespread as the issue itself: the speciality principle is interpreted generously, especially with regard to future assets, allowing for greater flexibility in their individualisation.

The most common approach to accommodate security over (revolving) collective assets under the principle of speciality is to let the individualisability and determinability of the assets suffice instead of the individual identification and determination of each encumbered object. For practical reasons, when security covers groups of assets, legal systems do not require a description of every single asset, but allow for a general description of the collectivity – while

---

[121] The Finnish response noted that for the enterprise mortgage, a different standard is used for speciality (and publicity) than for traditional security rights, owing to its different use, with the greater leniency for the enterprise mortgage counterbalanced by its weaker priority in insolvency.

[122] On the relationship of the Swiss security right over intermediated securities with the principle of speciality, see Chapter 13 (A Dal Molin-Kränzlin).

some jurisdictions permit this explicitly,[123] in others this solution has evolved in practice by a loosened interpretation of the speciality principle.[124] Typically, this approach considers the specificity requirement fulfilled by a description of the asset group – either specified by the designation of the type and location of the assets,[125] or, even more generously, by a generic and potentially broad formula.[126] The speciality principle is considered fulfilled as long as the identification of the group of assets enables the determination of whether a specific object falls within the encumbered class. This mechanism also allows for the encumbrance of revolving asset groups, especially the inclusion of future assets (see the analysis of question 8 below). Difficulties were indicated, however, with regard to the individualisation of future receivables.[127]

In some jurisdictions, the focus lies not on the encumbered assets as such, but (additionally) on their value. Chilean law requires an indication of their global monetary value (alternatively, further details about them must be provided). Similarly, Italian law allows for the determination of the encumbered assets by reference to either categories or to an overall value, conceptualising the non-possessory pledge as a "pledge of value" with their economic value rather than the goods themselves forming the object of security.

A different route towards safeguarding the speciality requirement for encumbered assets is taken by South African law. Drawing inspiration from the English floating charge rather than the Civil Law tradition, it distinguishes the phases before and after the attachment of specific assets. Once the security right is "fixed" as an *in rem* right in this manner, speciality is fulfilled with regard to the specific assets it has attached to. During the "floating" phase before this, the creditor is accorded only a special preference in insolvency, not necessitating adherence to the speciality principle required for *in rem* security rights.[128]

The other property law principle of fundamental relevance for security rights, the principle of publicity, was explicitly addressed by only a small number of respondents (Austria, Chile, Japan, Norway and South Africa). No

---

123 E.g. Bosnia and Herzegovina.

124 E.g. Germany.

125 For example, under German law, a general collective designation (e.g. "inventory" or "raw materials") has to be combined with a clear marking of the individual assets or their localisation in a clearly defined room (e.g. a warehouse). Japanese law typically requires the specification of the encumbered assets by type, volume and location.

126 For example, general descriptions like "all of the debtor's present and future movable property" are sufficient in the Netherlands or Quebec.

127 E.g. in the responses from France and the Netherlands.

128 See Chapter 5 (R Brits).

difficulties are noted in this regard – as seen previously (see the discussion of question 6 above), the traditional strict requirement for the creditor's physical control of the assets (delivery, *traditio*) is broadly replaced by registration as a publicity mechanism. This alternative approach to publicity guarantees compliance with this principle of property law, also with regard to future assets, the encumbrance of which can be publicised in advance by registration. It can be assumed that in the other jurisdictions, especially of the Civil Law tradition, the principle of publicity is similarly considered to be adhered to.

An in-depth analysis of the relationship of floating security with the individual principles of property law appears promising, also as an example of the development and interpretation of general property law dogmatics. Regarding speciality, the techniques for accommodating revolving and future assets under a more flexible understanding of this principle are of interest; regarding publicity, the relationship with registration merits further scrutiny. Additionally, the issue of the *numerus clausus* of real rights – not addressed by any of the responses – merits examination. The design of such a study should explore, on the one hand, the interdependence of the dogmatic solutions with the different models of floating security and their scope,[129] and on the other hand, the parallels and differences between floating and non-floating security. For the long-term development and practical functioning of floating security, especially in Civil Law jurisdictions, the possibilities for their seamless dogmatic integration into the context and system of property law are of considerable importance.

Encumbrance and Unencumbrance of Specific Items

The floating character of the security lies at the core of question 8. Its goal is to identify the mechanisms allowing for the encumbrance and unencumbrance of specific objects falling within the scope of the security right as established upon its creation: How do individual items become part of the pool of assets covered, and how can they be removed from it? Which techniques can be used to achieve its "revolving" character? Aside from the security's scope with regard to the assets potentially covered (question 5), this issue presents a close link to the speciality principle (question 7).

---

[129] For Civil Law jurisdictions, comparing the approaches to the accommodation of legal transplants and the development of Civilian functional equivalents appears especially interesting.

Encumbering specific assets

With regard to the fundamental concept behind the encumbering of assets by floating security, a widespread, if not even universal, consensus can be observed. "Global" or "revolving" security rights are designed to cover not only the debtor's present property when the security right is created, but also future assets, frequently designated "after-acquired property". The future assets covered by the scope of the security right typically "enter" it automatically once they become the security provider's property. This position lies at the basis of the English floating charge model (as was explicitly noted for Australia, England and Wales, Hungary, Ireland and Scotland and can be inferred for Hong Kong, India, Israel, Nigeria and Singapore) as well as its functional equivalents under the functionalist model (Australia, New Zealand, the USA and presumably Canada) and other approaches, notably the pledge model (stated expressly for Austria, Czechia, Denmark, Finland, Germany, Japan, Lithuania, Mexico, the Netherlands, Norway, Poland, Quebec, Romania, Russia, Serbia, South Africa and Turkey and presumably similar in Belgium, France, South Korea and Switzerland).

Some differences in detail can be observed with regard to the requirements for considering an asset as having become a part of the encumbered "universality", "group" or "class" of assets. While under some laws (e.g. Danish law) acquisition by the security provider is sufficient, others may require possession or physical control (e.g. Turkish law) or physical transfer into a certain space (e.g. Austrian, German and Russian law) in addition to the security provider's ownership.[130] Exceptions may be made for specific assets governed by special legal regimes, for example in the law of New Zealand for consumer goods or serially numbered assets. Some jurisdictions may pose limits for the encumbrance of new assets: In the Netherlands, once the security provider is formally insolvent, the assets they newly acquire will not become encumbered.

In addition, within the consensus noted above, very distinctive concepts of the encumbrance of specific assets can be discerned. For the floating charge, the key aspect is the moment of crystallisation – the event transforming the "floating" charge into a "fixed" charge. While today, the floating charge in the tradition of English law constitutes more than the mere promise to create a fixed security at a later date, before crystallisation it does not unfold *in rem* effects towards specific assets but rather constitutes a potential encumbrance.[131] Upon crystallisation, the charge "attaches" to the specific assets present at this time, activating their encumbrance, and Scots law also only

130 This is a necessary corollary of defining the security right's scope by reference to assets located at a specific site or in a certain space.

131 For detailed discussion, see Chapter 2 (A Televantos) as well as Chapter 3 (C Emedosi).

recognises the creation of a proprietary interest in specific assets at this point. Crystallisation typically is triggered automatically once the conditions agreed by the parties or specified by law (e.g. debtor's insolvency) are met.[132] Some legal systems (e.g. England and Wales, Ireland, Nigeria) allow for its effects to be reversed (i.e. for the fixed charge to become floating again, "detaching" from the specific assets) through so-called de-crystallisation. Furthermore, crystallisation does not necessarily stop newly acquired assets from entering the scope of the floating charge.[133]

For security rights not modelled on the English floating charge, there typically is no crystallisation. For a few jurisdictions, similarities can be deduced – most notably, the "perfection" of the South African general hypothec. An understanding that specific assets become encumbered only upon enforcement measures taken by the creditor was indicated also for the Italian non-possessory pledge, interpreted as a "pledge of value".[134] Constructively, however, with security rights designed as traditional property rights (especially following the pledge model), there can be no distinction between "floating" and "fixed" stages owing to the demands of property law for clarity and certainty, embodied especially in the requirements for speciality and publicity (see the analysis of question 7 above). It follows that the *in rem* encumbrance of single assets has to occur immediately once they enter the scope of the security. Consequently, under this conception, mechanisms for the unencumbrance of specific items are of central importance. Additionally, the unconditional encumbrance of all assets falling within the category covered by the security raises the issue of over-collateralisation. For jurisdictions following the functionalist model, these aspects appear to be less problematic; the responses did not provide details on the dogmatic construction of specific asset encumbrance.

Conceptually, there appears to be a spectrum for the possible encumbrance mechanisms of floating security: at one extreme, a mere promise to create a fixed security in the future; at the other, a real right or proprietary interest over particular items from the moment of creation onwards; and existing but not yet item-specific proprietary interests as the middle ground. Localisation on this spectrum generally corresponds with the general model and scope of the security – follow-up research will need to be tailored to this and explore, e.g.,

---

[132] See Chapter 2 (A Televantos), also for a critical discussion of automatic crystallisation clauses. Under Scots law, such clauses are ineffective and only legislatively specified events give rise to crystallisation.

[133] This was indicated e.g. for the floating charge under Australian law. It is also true to some extent in England and Wales and Scotland.

[134] It can also be argued that with a German land charge or mortgage, regarding the movables covered, the seizing of the land has some effects similar to crystallisation.

distinctions between enterprise and movables pledges. It should focus on specific mechanisms like "attachment" and "crystallisation" and their interplay with general property law rules as well as on the details of requirements for items to enter and leave the asset pool covered by the security, time limits and exceptions. The issue of over-collateralisation also merits further attention as a potential obstacle for floating security, at least in some jurisdictions.

Unencumbering specific assets

In two situations, the unencumbrance of assets follows as a necessary consequence. Once the secured debt has been discharged, the security has served its purpose and will either cease to exist automatically or be terminated by the parties;[135] this entails a release of the encumbered assets. Similarly, enforcement procedures will lead to the assets enforced against becoming free of the relevant security. As these mechanisms are not specific to floating security, they were only mentioned in passing for a few jurisdictions and will not be explored further.[136]

The floating character of security depends, however, on the possibility of unencumbering specific assets while the security as such remains intact. Its "revolving" nature results from continually adding new assets while extracting other items from its coverage. Thus, a central aspect lies in the power of the security provider to dispose of specific items, and of third parties to acquire them, free of encumbrance. Irrespective of the dogmatic construction of the floating security, a consensus between jurisdictions can be observed in this regard. The vast majority of responses explicitly addressed the possibility to unencumber specific assets by their disposal to third parties (Australia, Austria, Belgium, Bosnia and Herzegovina, Chile, China, Croatia, Denmark, England and Wales, Finland, France, Germany, Hungary, Ireland, Israel, Italy, Lithuania, Mexico, the Netherlands, New Zealand, Nigeria, Norway, Poland, Quebec, Russia, Scotland, Serbia, South Africa, Turkey and the USA), with such an option inferable for several other jurisdictions (Czechia, Hong Kong, India, Japan, Romania, Singapore and Switzerland).

Differences can be observed with regard to the conditions for unencumbrance. In some jurisdictions, especially those following the floating charge and functionalist models, the security provider is always free to dispose of

135 Depending on the security right, action by the secured creditor may be required (e.g. the release of a charge or a re-transfer of ownership). There may also be a need for the deletion of the register entry.

136 This issue was briefly addressed in, e.g., the responses from France, Israel, Jordan, Mexico and Singapore.

specific assets (until crystallisation occurs).[137] Contrarily, in Civil Law jurisdictions with security rights based on the pledge model, the power to dispose is frequently contingent on an agreement by the parties – either an explicit agreement is required[138] or power is considered granted unless there is an agreement to the contrary.[139] Some legal systems provide differentiated rules. Under French law, while the power to dispose under a movables pledge requires authorisation by the creditor, this prerequisite was abolished with regard to a pledge of fungible goods, which the security provider may dispose of subject to an obligation to replace them.[140] On the other hand, with a *nantissement du fonds de commerce*, the security provider's ability to dispose of charged assets is limited, with certain modifications requiring authorisation by the creditor.[141] Similarly, under Norwegian law, details are nuanced according to the type of security. German law provides an intricate regime for the unencumbrance of movables falling within the scope of a mortgage or land charge, contingent on the temporal sequence of disposal, removal and seizing.

Furthermore, unencumbrance may occur upon acquisition (of ownership) by the third party, or may additionally be dependent upon physical delivery of the assets to them or their removal from the space specified for the security. While the disposal of the assets by the security provider typically takes the form of a sale to third parties, it may also be understood more broadly to include other uses. Most prominently, this comprises the processing or transformation of raw materials, which may entail (*ex lege*) their loss and the generating and legal allocation of new assets. This issue was addressed in passing for a number of Civil Law jurisdictions, with conditions and consequences comparable to those of a third-party sale indicated.[142]

Typically, the security provider's power to dispose of assets, removing them from the security's coverage, is limited to transactions in the ordinary course of business. Such a requirement can be observed either expressly or tacitly in all jurisdictions, with different designations, such as "lawful sale

---

[137] This was also stated, for example, for the Chinese floating charge; to some extent, it applies as well to the Swiss encumbrance of intermediated securities.

[138] E.g. in Austria, Germany and the Netherlands.

[139] For example, in Chile, Italy, Poland (in the form of a negative pledge clause) and South Africa.

[140] For details, see Chapter 8 (M Renaudin).

[141] Art 143-1 Code de Commerce.

[142] For a transfer of ownership for security purposes over goods to be processed under German law, for example, this is frequently addressed by a "processing clause" (*Verarbeitungsklausel*), allowing the security provider to dispose of the assets by processing or transformation.

to third parties"[143] or "within the limits of what is required under proper management",[144] or as the consequence of the power to dispose ending once business is not transacted regularly.[145] Similar results may be achieved by negative pledge clauses that contractually prohibit the security provider from selling or otherwise encumbering the collateral.[146] Closer scrutiny reveals, however, that this requirement is based on pragmatic rather than dogmatic needs: while economically, limiting the security provider's power to dispose to regular transactions is necessary to avoid a (fraudulent) "depletion" of the security, such a limitation is not required for the legal-technical construction of a revolving security right (but rather, restricts its function). The question of whether disposals free from the floating charge need to be in the "ordinary course of business" is reflected, for example, in the uncertainty in Scots law on this point.[147]

However, outside of the security provider's power to dispose (i.e. outside the ordinary course of business), an acquisition of assets free of encumbrance may be subject to further conditions. For a broad range of jurisdictions, it was indicated that assets may be unencumbered if third parties acquire ownership of them *bona fide*, not being aware that they are subject to a security – explicit reference to this possibility was made for Belgium, Czechia, England and Wales, Finland, France, Germany, Japan, Nigeria, Norway, Poland, Russia, South Korea and Turkey, and it can be assumed that acquisition free of encumbrance is possible according to general *bona fide* rules in other jurisdictions as well.[148] The threshold for good faith is, however, frequently rather high, especially for registered security rights. While some jurisdictions impose an obligation on acquirers to check the register (for example, Belgium with regard to professionals), others consider registration to convey constructive notice, destroying good faith per se (for example, Czechia;[149] in Russia, this effect is one of the main advantages of voluntary pledge enrolment). The exact scopes

[143] E.g. under Mexican law.

[144] See, for example, § 1122(1) BGB with regard to the German extension of mortgage liability to products and components.

[145] In the Netherlands, the creditor's permission to dispose is ended by specific events, such as defaulting on the secured credit or the opening of insolvency proceedings, which are symptomatic of regular business ceasing to be conducted.

[146] E.g. in Nigeria and Poland.

[147] See e.g. ADJ MacPherson, *The Floating Charge* (ELET 2020) para 2–03.

[148] The questionnaire responses from India, Ireland and Italy, for example, suggest this.

[149] For Poland, it was noted that the legal presumptions following from the register's existence make it exceedingly difficult to prove that the assets were acquired in good faith.

of good faith and registration effects frequently form the subject of debate, as was indicated for Nigeria, South Korea and Turkey. In the same vein, the extent to which registration leads to constructive notice of negative pledge clauses was mentioned. In sum, the requirements and limitations for unencumbrance by good faith acquisition are strict and becoming stricter.

For a number of jurisdictions, reference was made to specific mechanisms for the substitution of assets unencumbered through disposal by the assets replacing them in the disposing security provider's property. Most importantly, this is the case for the proceeds realised in the sale of the assets; again, the rules may also encompass the resulting products in scenarios of processing. Under the functionalist model, such a mechanism is widespread. For example, under the New Zealand PPSA, the creditor's security interest and priority are extended to comprise both the proceeds and the products resulting from the original collateral; likewise, a security interest under Art 9 UCC *ex lege* includes the original assets' proceeds (understood broadly[150]). With the pledge model, jurisdictions from the French legal family frequently rely on a mechanism of real subrogation, automatically transferring the pledge to assets replacing the originally pledged items – apart from France, such a mechanism was described for Chile, Italy, Mexico and Quebec. German law does not provide a comparable mechanism for the transfer of ownership for security purposes, but similar results are arrived at by party agreement.[151] Notably, some jurisdictions formulate an obligation for the debtor to replace or substitute assets used or sold – such a "depletion control" mechanism exists, for example, under Croatian[152] and French[153] law.

In conclusion, the unencumbrance of specific assets appears closely linked to the *in rem* character of the security right. For security rights following the English floating charge model, in the "floating" phase the security has not yet attached to specific items – as there are no encumbrances *in rem*, the removal of individual items from the security's coverage is unproblematic and typically envisaged as an automatic consequence of dispositions. Contrarily, freeing

---

150 UCC Art 9-102(a).

151 Usually, the parties will anticipatorily assign the resulting receivables for security purposes when assets are intended for sale, and stipulate a "processing clause" ensuring the creditor's ownership for security purposes of the resulting new goods when assets are intended for processing.

152 The obligation does not require the security provider to substitute item by item, but to cover the so-called "recoverability margin" in terms of the assets' value; it can be excluded by party agreement.

153 With a pledge over fungible assets, the security provider's right to use assets is subject to a replacement obligation (Art 2341 Code Civil). The now-abolished *gage sur stock* also protected the creditor against asset depletion.

items from *in rem* encumbrances, especially under the pledge model, poses a greater challenge – a successful unencumbrance usually depends on the security provider being granted power to dispose (with authorisation playing an especially important role with ownership transfer models) and is frequently accompanied by a substitution mechanism. Additional information is needed on the details of the conceptualisation under the functionalist model. For further research, the necessity and interpretation of the requirement of dispositions "in the ordinary course of business" will be a central issue, especially in their interrelation with the possibilities for *bona fide* acquisition free of encumbrance and other reasons for unencumbrance. A comparison between *bona fide* acquisition rules relating to floating security and fixed security respectively may also produce interesting insights regarding the boundaries of different types of security.

ENFORCEMENT AND RANKING OF FLOATING SECURITY (QUESTIONS 9–10)

9. How is (or was) the security enforced?
10. How is (or was) the security dealt with in competition with other rights, e.g. in a ranking context?

Enforcement

The following discussion is focused on what is usually known as "enforcement" of security, which principally means the mechanism(s) by which the security holder can utilise it for the purposes of satisfying the secured debt that is due to them.[154] As will be seen, a variety of approaches are adopted in relation to enforcement of floating security. The extent to which there are special enforcement rules for floating security seems to be partially determined by the extent to which it is viewed as clearly distinct and separate from other forms of security available.

In English law, some remedies applicable to other security rights can be utilised for floating charges too, but there are also special rules for floating charges in relation to e.g. administration and receivership. Given the wide-ranging nature of floating charges, insolvency procedures such as administration and liquidation, as well as the enforcement procedure of receivership, are often viewed as important, as control is taken over the debtor's assets (or

[154] Given the widespread use of the term "enforcement" it has been adopted here, rather than equivalents such as "exercise" of security, which may be more technically accurate in certain contexts.

at least a large proportion of them), enabling expansive realisation. In addition, such processes often give rise to the crystallisation of floating charges. Regarding the particulars of enforcement itself, various remedies are often specified in the instrument (debenture) creating the floating charge.[155] These include the power to take possession of assets and to sell them, to appoint an administrator,[156] and in limited cases, to appoint a receiver (despite the general prohibition on administrative receivership).[157] The ability to appoint an administrator and, where still available, a receiver, can happen out of court, but a court application is also possible. A qualifying floating charge holder is the only creditor able to appoint an administrator out of court.[158] The position in Scotland is broadly aligned with England and Wales, with many of the same statutory provisions, including for administration, applying to both jurisdictions or doing so with only minor variations. The general replacement of (administrative) receivership with administration as the main enforcement mechanism for floating charges in English law and Scots law was largely driven by a desire to try and rescue businesses and to give control to an insolvency practitioner acting in the interests of all creditors, rather than just in the interests of the floating charge holder.

The enforcement of floating charges in other Common Law jurisdictions such as Hong Kong and Singapore bears similarities to the approach in English law; however, in those jurisdictions, receivership has not been usurped by administration as an enforcement mechanism for floating charges and it remains a principal mechanism of enforcement. Likewise, in Ireland, enforcement by appointing a receiver has remained the standard approach, yet such an appointment can be overridden by a court order if the debtor company later enters the insolvency process of examinership.[159] For Nigeria, the chargeholder may appoint a receiver or manager, or the court may do so on the chargeholder's application. Other remedies are available too, including taking possession and the sale of the property.[160] Israeli law also allows for a petition to court to appoint a receiver, who can then conduct a public sale of security assets. As such, receivership has been widely retained where English-style

---

155 Reliance on contractual provisions regarding enforcement was also reported in other Common Law jurisdictions with an English-style floating charge, such as India.

156 Whose primary objective is the rescue of the company as a going concern: see Insolvency Act 1986, Sch B1, para 3.

157 See Insolvency Act 1986 ss 72A–72GA for the prohibition and exceptions.

158 Insolvency Act 1986 Sch B1, para 14.

159 Companies Act 2014 s 522.

160 See Chapter 3 (C Emedosi).

floating charges are available, despite it having been pushed to the margins in England and Wales.

In those jurisdictions where floating charges on the English model have been displaced by security interests in a functionalist security regime, the approaches to enforcement previously aligned with English law. For example, in Australia, a floating charge holder was generally able to appoint a receiver (which would crystallise the charge), and where crystallisation had occurred, remedies such as an order for sale or possession were available.[161] Under the personal property security regime, legislation provides the rules for personal property security interests, and the seizure, disposal and retention of security property are provided for. Similar points can be made in relation to Canada and New Zealand.[162] Sometimes though there are special rules, such as for consumer goods in relation to repossession, which are intended to give protection to consumer borrowers.[163]

For some systems, the enforcement mechanisms depend on the type of property in question, and there is no general mechanism applicable to all property. One such example is the USA, where if inventory or other tangible movable property is covered, the creditor can obtain possession judicially or extra-judicially (which can support the exercise of other remedies), whereas for accounts receivable (claims), the creditor can give notice to account debtors to pay the creditor instead.[164] More broadly, however, there is also the ability to sell, lease, licence or otherwise dispose of collateral after default. In other jurisdictions where enforcement of floating security is not distinguished from alternative security rights, the methods of enforcement may also depend on the property in question.[165] This is true of various Civilian countries, such as Austria,[166] Germany,[167] France[168] and Norway, which represent a spectrum in terms of the availability of true floating security.

---

161 See WJ Gough, *Company Charges*, 2nd edn (1996) 129–130 and 159–160.

162 In New Zealand, there is also a separate Receiverships Act 1993, where a security holder uses a receiver for enforcement purposes.

163 See Credit Contracts and Consumer Finance Act 2003 in New Zealand.

164 See UCC Art 9-601 *et seq*. See also other jurisdictions such as Quebec.

165 Of course, if security collateral is incorporeal, possessory remedies are not available.

166 In Austria, enforcement regarding security for warehouses and receivables is by a court sale or extra-judicial enforcement, and for receivables by seeking payment from the claim debtor: §§ 466a–466e ABGB.

167 For the transfer of ownership for security purposes, realisation rules are ordinarily identified in the security agreement, including sale by private agreement and forfeiture to the creditor.

168 See further below and Chapter 8 (M Renaudin).

More generally outside the Common Law world, various different approaches are adopted regarding the enforcement of floating security. In some jurisdictions, the ordinary rules for enforcement of security over property apply, allowing seizure, sale and/or appropriation of assets depending upon the precise rules of the jurisdiction in question.[169] Many countries, such as China, Jordan and Russia, allow for enforcement by sale with the agreement of the security provider; otherwise, authorisation by a court is necessary.[170] In the Netherlands, a pledgee has a right to sell security property without approval from the court, but they must do so via public sale. However, a pledgee can request court permission to sell property privately, or the parties can agree, but only if the debtor is in default. Similarly, in Czechia, the parties can agree on how the security should be enforced, which could be a direct sale, and if there is no agreement, then a sale by public auction or judicial sale is used. In Italy, no judicial decision is required for enforcement of a non-possessory pledge, but there are notification requirements to the debtor (and any pre-existing security holder).[171] The position under French law is more complicated and depends on the type of security in question. For the *nantissement du fonds de commerce*, the business can be sold and the creditor has a preferential right to payment from the proceeds.

As already indicated, the method of enforcement in certain jurisdictions can be significantly determined by whether or not there is a contractual agreement. That is also true for the following countries, which adopted different approaches and have no obvious legal connection to one another. In Turkey, the creditor can demand transfer of ownership from the debtor (at least in some circumstances where such *pactum commissorium* is provided for), assign the secured claim to asset management companies or use rental and licence rights over movable assets. Under Mexican law, extra-judicial procedures can be utilised for non-possessory pledges and security trusts, with an expert giving an appraisal of the assets; such an expert can be agreed upon by the parties, either at the time of the security agreement or later. If there is disagreement between the parties, then judicial procedures are to be used. Judicial procedures are

---

169 E.g. Chile; see also Bosnia and Herzegovina and Croatia, where enforcement is in accordance with generally applicable laws on enforcement and insolvency. In the limited context in which floating security exists in Swiss law, secured creditors can realise the assets themselves via sale or appropriation.

170 For Jordan, enforcement would involve summary procedures. In Russia, if the parties agree, enforcement can be e.g. by auction, sale by a commissioner, transfer of assets to the pledgee, or through a notary (without court approval), if the pledge agreement has been certified by the notary.

171 Thereafter, the creditor can sell the property, transfer the secured claim, lease the property or obtain possession.

also required for the industrial mortgage, unless the parties have agreed that extra-judicial enforcement can be utilised. In Korea, enforcement of a non-possessory pledge can be by a court-authorised public auction, or in certain contexts by extra-judicial sale, while in some instances an application can be made to acquire security property, and there is also scope under legislation to agree on another method of enforcement.[172]

For the mixed jurisdictions of Quebec and South Africa, there is also (unsurprisingly) no uniformity in approach. For Quebec, enforcement is relatively liberal and wide-ranging, as any type of hypothec, irrespective of the property type, enables the secured creditor to obtain surrender of the security property, to take possession for administration purposes, to acquire the property in payment, and to sell the property privately or by public auction or with judicial authority (and the sale can be of items separately or collectively).[173] South African law is more unusual in certain respects. Enforcement necessitates "perfection" of the bond and attachment of the goods, such perfection requires that the agreement provided for the creditor to obtain possession and to identify the circumstances in which perfection can occur.[174] The sale of the assets ordinarily requires a judgment debt, and the sale can be by auction. Court authorisation is the default position but the agreement can provide for extra-judicial sale.

There are non-Common Law jurisdictions that allow for enforcement processes with similarities to receivership. This is the case in Poland, where options for extra-judicial enforcement include, if agreed, lease of a pledged enterprise or administration of that enterprise. This is a form of private receivership where a party becomes the administrator of the enterprise to utilise income generated to seek to satisfy the debt. In Lithuania, while enforcement takes place as for other security, crystallisation causes security interests to attach to relevant assets. For a company hypothec, all of the property is covered, and an administrator must be appointed, which can then involve running the company for the purposes of generating funds to pay the debt or seeking to auction the business or particular assets. Under Japanese law, enforcement of enterprise security is by a court-appointed receiver, who seizes the assets and disposes of them by way of public sale (either individually or collectively). While in the Canadian Common Law provinces, receivership is available as an enforcement method (which assists with dealing with the business as a going concern), in Quebec the ability to appoint an administrator provides a similar

172 Extra-judicial enforcement is apparently also possible in relation to commercial claims if the parties agree.

173 However, as an alternative to the sale for receivables, the creditor can choose to receive payment instead.

174 See Chapter 5 (R Brits) for further details.

mechanism. Yet the role is more burdensome than a receiver, and so creditors have frequently applied to the courts for the appointment of a receiver under the federal insolvency legislation.[175] In Romanian law, the creditor can have a judicial officer (bailiff equivalent) undertake the full enforcement process or just part of it. If the creditor enforces extra-judicially, after the officer's involvement with notification, the creditor can use any reasonable method specified in the agreement, such as selling the assets, managing the security property as an enterprise, or becoming the owner of the property to discharge the debt.

For security that can be created by consumers, this sometimes gives rise to more onerous enforcement requirements than in relation to non-consumer debtors. This is true in e.g. Belgium where judicial authorisation for appropriation or sale (whether publicly or privately) is necessary for enforcement against consumer debtors but not against others. In South Africa, it is broadly accepted that court authorisation is necessary in relation to enforcement in the consumer context. Sometimes the relative protections in a jurisdiction are more modest, such as the greater time period between notice of default and exercise of a security right for security connected to a consumer contract, as in Quebec.

In many jurisdictions across different legal traditions, floating security is heavily connected to insolvency and restructuring law. This is certainly true for English law itself, where the law of corporate insolvency has been significantly influenced and shaped by floating charges. Floating charges on the English model often "crystallise" and become effective against particular items of property in the context of insolvency law,[176] and enforcement ordinarily takes place through an insolvency procedure (such as administration and liquidation) or a process that is at least comparable in some ways to such procedures (e.g. [administrative] receivership). It is logical that a wide-ranging security is connected with insolvency procedures and may be dependent upon enforcement by a third party in that context.[177] In English law and Scots law, it has been concluded that the power of a floating security holder should not override the purposes of the insolvency procedure (including potentially the saving of the debtor's business), and regard should be had to the interests of other creditors. This is more difficult to achieve in the Common Law jurisdictions with an English-style floating charge, which have retained receivership (or an equivalent) that is principally focused on returns to the floating charge

---

175 See Chapter 9 (C Walsh) for further details.

176 See L Gullifer, *Goode and Gullifer on Legal Problems of Credit and Security*, 7th edn (Sweet & Maxwell 2023) paras 4–32 et seq, for the situations in which floating charges in English law crystallise. Such an effect is not, however, only limited to the Common Law, as the response for Turkey revealed.

177 It is interesting to note the issues that have existed in Hungary in these areas: see Chapter 11 (T Tajti).

holder. The USA, in contrast, is often considered to be a less creditor-friendly jurisdiction and operates a general stay on the enforcement of security in insolvency procedures, but permission can be obtained to have the stay lifted and the security enforced despite the procedure.

Jurisdictions in the study ordinarily accept the effectiveness of security (including floating security) in insolvency procedures, and this is often the context in which a floating charge holder receives payment.[178] Yet there are matters for which there is divergence. For example, the effect of insolvency procedures on future acquired property that would otherwise fall under floating security gives rise to differing results, ranging from such property being ordinarily covered if this is provided for in the instrument creating the security (e.g. England and Wales) to the result depending on the type of insolvency procedure and with a degree of uncertainty as to the law (e.g. Scotland), to after-acquired property being generally excluded on the basis that the commencement of insolvency requires protection of the interests of the creditors as a whole (e.g. Denmark).

Competition and Ranking

It is often the case that the assets of a debtor are insufficient to pay all creditors in full. As such, the law needs to determine who has priority, and this is done by ranking different claims in order of priority, with secured creditors usually receiving a high degree of priority. The wide-ranging scope of floating security and its non-possessory nature (allowing for multiple security rights over the same property) mean that ranking competitions involving such security are commonplace. It also leads to a significant degree of complexity in many jurisdictions as to how the floating security ranks against other interests. A floating security holder can be in competition with the holder of other floating security, with other secured creditors or with preferential or ordinary unsecured creditors.

In English law (and Scots law), the perceived power of a floating charge, owing to its scope and the rights it confers, and the consequent perceived unfairness that it would otherwise give rise to, mean that various parties have been given priority over floating charges: the expenses of liquidation and administration (in general), preferential creditors (such as unpaid employees to a limited extent and the state for some unpaid taxes) and a ring-fenced percentage of the assets subject to the charge for unsecured creditors.[179] In addition,

---

178 This was noted in the responses for e.g. Finland and France, and can be inferred for other jurisdictions.

179 Insolvency Act 1986 ss 175(2)(b), 176ZA, 176A, 386 and Sch 6 para 8 onwards.

the limited effects of a floating charge in property terms mean that the default position is that it will rank behind fixed security,[180] whether created before or after the charge's creation, but before its crystallisation. However, in practice, many floating charges contain negative pledges, which will mean the floating charge will have priority over later fixed (as well as floating) securities, if those security holders have notice of the earlier charge and the negative pledge.[181] In Scotland, the position is similar, but negative pledges have effect from creation without the necessity of such notice.[182]

Equivalent rules to England and Wales in relation to the ranking relationship between floating charges and fixed security, including the effects of negative pledges, also largely apply in other jurisdictions with English-style floating charges, such as Hong Kong, Nigeria and Singapore.[183] In Nigeria, there is some uncertainty as to whether a purchaser would be deemed to have notice where there is registration, but this is perhaps only true for those reasonably expected to check the register, which appears aligned with the position in English law regarding those bound by a negative pledge. In Common Law jurisdictions with floating charges, it is commonplace for such security to rank behind preferential creditors such as the state for certain unpaid taxes and unpaid employees to varying degrees.[184] There is also sometimes express provision, such as in Nigeria, that insolvency expenses, especially liquidation expenses, rank ahead of a chargeholder too. In Israel, the standard position is that a floating charge ranks lower than a fixed security, and preferred creditors such as unpaid employees and the tax authorities ordinarily also rank ahead.[185]

In countries like England and Wales and Nigeria, an execution creditor (i.e. a previously unsecured creditor who is enforcing) will only have priority and take free of the security if they complete execution before crystallisation so that they acquire the property in question. However, in Scotland, despite some contrary earlier authority, a bare execution (diligence) will take priority over a floating charge, even if not completed prior to crystallisation (in the sense that

---

180 Under English law, this fixed security may be equitable (e.g. a fixed charge) or legal (e.g. a legal mortgage), with the latter ordinarily having priority over equitable security.

181 Notice may be actual or constructive owing to the registration of the security and the negative pledge in the companies register following its creation.

182 Companies Act 1985 s 464(1)(a) and (1A).

183 See e.g. Chapter 3 (C Emedosi).

184 E.g. in Ireland and Nigeria.

185 However, the precise ranking may depend on whether the floating charge materialises (crystallises) before or after the commencement of liquidation proceedings.

the creditor has not acquired the asset[s] by that point).[186] This is the product of a conscious attempt in legislation to give such otherwise unsecured creditors a priority over chargeholders and may be considered to reflect the property status accorded to such execution rights in Scots law. In Scots law, it is also expressly stated that fixed security arising by operation of law (another category of involuntary security) has priority over a floating charge.[187]

Most responses did not specifically address the ranking positions of execution creditors or those with security arising by law, and so it is difficult to draw wider conclusions. However, for Quebec, it was noted that various claims have prior status ahead of hypothecs, including the claim of an unpaid seller for the price of a movable sold to a natural person not operating an enterprise; claims of persons having the right to retain movables (lien rights); state claims under fiscal laws; and claims of municipalities and school boards for property taxes. For competing hypothecs, they usually rank according to their publication (e.g. by registration). Conventional and legal hypothecs, including judgment creditors' claims, rank according to the same rules. In the responses for a few other jurisdictions, such as Finland and Norway, it was stated that (certain) rights of retention (lien rights) have priority over floating security.

For Australia, the position was historically broadly comparable to English law. This law has now been largely overtaken by the functionalist regime. Under the current law, a perfected security interest has priority over an unperfected one, while if there are multiple perfected security interests, priority depends on the timing of perfection (whether by e.g. registration or taking and retaining possession or control), and the priority of unperfected interests is determined by the order of attachment. Again, similar points can be made about other functionalist jurisdictions such as Canada and New Zealand. Secured transactions laws enacted in recent times ordinarily have relatively clear ranking rules, which are intended to be close to comprehensive. While these often depend upon the date of creation or becoming enforceable (by perfection), purchase money security interests are frequently given a super priority.[188] In the USA, the position is usually that priority is by the date of filing of a financing statement (where a security is later made effective between debtor and creditor [referred to as attachment]) or perfection.[189] Yet there are exceptions, e.g. priority is given to a purchase money security interest holder (i.e. where credit

186 See e.g. Companies Act 1985 s 463(1)(a); *MacMillan v T Leith Developments Ltd* [2017] CSIH 23.

187 Companies Act 1985 s 464(2).

188 E.g. Jordan and New Zealand.

189 UCC Art 9-322(a).

is advanced to a debtor for the purpose of acquiring particular property) ahead of a party with a normal security interest (whether floating or not).[190]

Ranking priority is, to some extent, dependent upon whether there is a property interest following the security's creation and, if so, what type of property right it is. In many systems in the Civilian tradition in particular, the usual rules of ranking of security also apply to floating security, particularly where such security is not recognised as being entirely distinct from other security types (e.g. where it is viewed as an expansive type of pledge). The most significant rule is that security rights rank according to when they are created by registration or some other publicity step.[191] This is known by the Latin brocard "*prior tempore potior jure*" but also by terms such as timing priority, anteriority principle and *Altersprioritüt*. However, as is the case for the Common Law functionalist systems noted above, in at least a few other jurisdictions, there is a priority in particular situations for a purchase money security interest, even if it is registered after a competing security.[192] Interestingly, in France, the creation and ranking position of a *nantissement du fonds de commerce* do not entirely correspond with all registration requirements being fulfilled. It appears to be less normal outside the Common Law for fixed security to be given automatic priority over floating security. However, Japan is apparently a system in which the enterprise security is generally subordinated to security over specific assets. In the Netherlands, those with a possessory security can have priority over those with a non-possessory security, if the party with the possessory pledge is unaware of, or not expected to have been aware of, the earlier non-possessory pledge.

In some jurisdictions, the applicability of ranking depends on the particular type of security involved, and some security defeats the possibility of ranking contests. For Austria, in relation to security for warehouses and receivables, priority of security for limited proprietary rights is determined by the time of creation, whereas for the transfer of ownership as security, there is no ranking as no additional security can be created.[193] A similar position arises in German law, where the transfer of ownership as security stops the security provider from creating further security over the same property, even though it

---

190 UCC Art 9-324; but this depends upon timely perfection.

191 E.g. in Belgium, Bosnia and Herzegovina, Chile, Croatia, Denmark, Finland (where it is possession of the promissory note containing the register authority's security entry), France, Italy, Korea, Lithuania, Mexico, the Netherlands, Norway, Poland, Romania, Serbia, Switzerland and Turkey (but see below). There may, of course, be some variations in certain cases.

192 E.g. Bosnia and Herzegovina and Denmark.

193 Albeit it may be possible that pre-existing security still affects the property.

may still be encumbered by earlier created security.[194] Of course, there may be a dispute between competing transferees, and under Japanese law, the perfection of transfers determines priority if there is a dispute, and this is presumably largely true elsewhere. In jurisdictions such as Croatia, property subject to the transfer of ownership by way of security or retention of title can be separated from the insolvency estate and thereby receive priority over a floating security. In France, a party with a retention of title clause can also ordinarily recover their property.

As with the Common Law systems noted above, other jurisdictions give certain creditors preferences (sometimes in the form of security),[195] so that they rank ahead of floating security (and potentially also fixed security). Our responses indicate that some countries make such provision for employee claims for unpaid wages,[196] tax claims,[197] insolvency expenses[198] and some other expenses for the benefit of creditors generally.[199] There are also examples of more unusual claims being given priority, such as for individuals' claims for damages relating to personal injury.[200]

In general, there is an absence of an equivalent to the "prescribed part" that exists in the jurisdictions of the UK, which ringfences a proportion of assets for unsecured creditors. However, Finland has an equivalent. As well as claims secured by pledge rights or rights of retention having priority over enterprise security, in insolvency proceedings, the enterprise security holder only has priority in respect of 50% of the assets covered, and this is intended to benefit the unsecured creditors. South Africa also represents an interesting example, as an unperfected floating security (general notarial bond) gives rise to a ranking status similar to that of a preferential creditor, as priority lies between the secured creditors and unsecured creditors, in spite of the absence of security in the strict sense.[201]

There can be a degree of uncertainty regarding ranking relationships and outcomes involving floating security. The likelihood of such issues increases with the complexity and multiplicity of ranking rules. In China, the floating security has an inchoate effect against later registered rights but will not

---

194 The law of over-collateralisation (*Übersicherung*) may also be relevant.

195 E.g. by statutory lien over the general assets in Japan.

196 E.g. France, Japan, Korea, Mexico, Russia.

197 E.g. Korea and Mexico.

198 E.g. France.

199 E.g. Japan.

200 E.g. Russia.

201 In some respects, this may be viewed as the equivalent of a non-registered charge in English law; however, the latter would also be ineffective against a liquidator or administrator.

bind purchasers of movables in the ordinary course of business (even if they have knowledge of the floating charge). It does not appear to be entirely clear whether the same rule can be interpreted to apply to later charges or pledges.[202] The responses also identified uncertain ranking issues elsewhere, e.g. in Denmark in relation to trade receivables, and in Italy as regards conflicts between non-possessory and possessory pledges, and between the former and those with special privileges or purchasers. There is also some complexity in Korea regarding buyers of security property acting in good faith, e.g. whether they are expected to have checked the registry.[203] In Hungary, there was uncertainty after the introduction of the property encumbering charge as to whether it ranked from the date of its registration or the equivalent of crystallisation, with the former ultimately prevailing. English law is also affected by ranking problems, and this includes the phenomenon of circles of priority, where there is no clear discernible hierarchy of priority.[204] There are ways to resolve such problems when they arise, whether in English law or in the laws of other systems such as Canada, the USA and Scotland, but the most appropriate approach to doing so can also be a matter of contention.[205]

The discussion above principally represents the default rules of ranking. There is, however, the possibility of ranking agreements between parties, where a multitude of different arrangements are possible. The precise rules for these, as well as their effects and the extent to which they can affect third parties without their agreement, are not identified here, but there is no doubt a notable degree of variation.[206] Sometimes there is statutory provision for the effects of ranking agreements, such as in Scotland. An interesting approach is adopted in Turkey, where a default ranking system based on the date of creation operates in parallel with a system in which the debtor can specify the ranking of secured creditors in an agreement. Registration of an agreement under the latter approach ought to be registered to be fully effective against

---

[202] Once the floating security crystallises, it will rank equivalent to a fixed security against later security rights.

[203] South Korea adopts this approach rather than the ordinary course of business approach.

[204] E.g. security A ranks ahead of B, and B ranks ahead of C, but C ranks ahead of A.

[205] See e.g. J Hardman and ADJ MacPherson, "The Ranking of Floating Charges" in J Hardman and ADJ MacPherson (eds), *Floating Charges in Scotland: New Perspectives and Current Issues* (EUP 2022) 386–394 and the sources cited there.

[206] Even within the UK, there are differences between English law and Scots law.

third parties, but the competing systems operating at the same time can cause ranking complexity and disputes.[207]

It must be noted that the above discussion does not (and could not) fully take into account all of the details and complexities that exist in each jurisdiction in the study. There are various aspects of ranking that would repay further study, including the effects of ranking agreements, the priority status of preferential claims and involuntary security against floating security, and how ranking is dealt with more generally in insolvency.

CONCLUSIONS AND REFLECTIONS

Floating security is a widespread phenomenon, appearing in many different shapes and sizes in jurisdictions of all continents and legal traditions. This initial analysis from a wide comparative angle has yielded a number of preliminary results, as well as providing impulses for further exploration.

A Working Definition of "Floating Security"

Our first conclusion relates to definitional matters. Within the course of this study, a central aspect emerged again and again: the understanding of what may constitute a floating charge or functional equivalent to it varies greatly, depending, among other things, on legal tradition and system, dogmatic background and individual interpretation. A key challenge is, therefore, to arrive at a working definition of floating security for the purposes of comparative study. Only on the basis of a common understanding and terminology can different security rights be classified definitively as floating, compared with regard to their characteristics, advantages and shortcomings, and the dogmatic background and practical application of floating security be explored and understood in a conclusive and comprehensive manner. Such a definition must necessarily depart from the notion of the "floating charge" in the sense of the traditional instrument of English law. Rather, it must approach the issue functionally and with a broader horizon, taking into account the various interpretations, notions and approaches from different jurisdictions emerging from the responses. As has been shown decisively, the phenomenon of floating security may comprise far more than the traditional approach under English law. To illustrate this terminologically (and to avoid confusion with the specific security right under English law), "floating security" would seem to be preferable to "floating charge(s)".

---

[207] Thus adopting one such approach may be preferable in any given case.

Collating the self-assessments provided for the different jurisdictions with regard to their respective security rights, it becomes clear that there is no one single type of floating security. Nevertheless, as the comparative analysis has shown, certain elements are recurring as common threads for groups of jurisdictions or even all of them. There appears to be a spectrum of what can be understood as a floating security, with graduations of the intensity of the "floating" nature depending on various factors. A definition must be flexible enough to accommodate and reflect this, while allowing for the localisation of individual security rights on the spectrum according to their adherence to certain criteria.

The evaluation of the responses and their comparative analysis show that the key factor, evidenced by the floating security of all jurisdictions, is that the security covers an asset pool of multiple present and future assets, the composition of which may change over time, with individual assets moving "in and out" of the security's ambit. Typically, the security provider is granted the power to dispose of individual assets, while newly acquired assets automatically become covered by the security. Consequently, the main criterion is that of a "revolving" security, in the sense of a security right covering a revolving pool of assets in its current composition. Such an understanding allows for terminological clarity: "revolving" refers to the asset pool covered, over the changing constituents of which the security "floats".

In addition to this central element, further characteristics can be distilled from the comparative overview. In a significant number of jurisdictions, a revolving security can comprise not only one type of asset, but be granted over assets belonging to different classes, and frequently also over the totality of the security provider's (movable) assets (and sometimes also including immovable assets), subject perhaps to only minor exceptions. While such a "global" nature does not appear as a *conditio sine qua non* for floating security, it is nevertheless one of its typical features. Similarly, access to floating security is frequently limited to companies or businesses as security providers, either through providing specific security rights over enterprises or through restricting the availability of security rights to businesses, including natural persons acting in a business capacity. Although not discernible in all floating security, the character as an "enterprise security" is an important feature for many of them. Finally, within the context of enterprise security, a special enforcement mechanism can be encountered in a significant number of jurisdictions, allowing for comprehensive enforcement against all assets by replacing the security provider's control of the enterprise. While not a necessary condition for the floating nature of a security, and not even for its character as an enterprise security, this feature can nevertheless be considered a distinguishing characteristic within the spectrum of floating security.

On the other hand, several characteristics can be observed that, although they may be of importance for the security rights of specific jurisdictions, do not have major significance for defining floating security from a comparative perspective. This is the case for the method of creation – from the overview of jurisdictions, no uniform criteria emerge in this regard. Similarly, the ranking relationships of floating security against other (security) rights do not follow a generally discernible pattern. A central characteristic of the English law floating charge, its changing nature dependent on an event of "crystallisation", is likewise not a prominent feature of floating security rights stemming from other legal traditions and concepts. A transformation of the security right from one type to another can thus not play a role in a comprehensive comparative law definition.

Based on these insights, a definition of floating security should include both necessary and optional criteria. A broad definition, based on necessary elements, enables a clear delimitation of "common" floating security rights vis-à-vis non-floating security rights. Narrowing this definition through the application of optional elements permits grouping and differentiating between varying types of "special" floating security rights, further discerning their spectrum. The following working definition of "floating security" is proposed:

- The core element for affirming the floating character of a security right is that it is of a revolving nature, allowing for the coverage of an asset pool consisting of multiple present and future assets and permitting individual items to be brought in and removed from under its coverage over the course of time. Under a broad definition, all security of such revolving character can be considered floating security, while security not permitting this type of coverage cannot be classified as such.[208] Security rights do not need to be originally conceptualised and expressly tailored as "floating" to be classified as such; rather, this wide understanding comprises all security with basic floating characteristics. Under this broad definition, at least one security right in all jurisdictions covered in this study can be understood as "floating", evidencing the practical and economic need for such security.
- Requiring compliance with this core characteristic, a narrow definition may further refine the understanding of what constitutes a floating security right by means of the following criteria:
  - Floating security, allowing for the constitution of security covering various classes of assets and potentially the universality of the

[208] Under this broad definition, pledges (e.g. France, Netherlands) and transfers of ownership for security purposes (e.g. Germany, Japan) are considered "floating security" if they can be of a revolving nature.

security provider's (movable) assets, can be defined as "global floating security".[209]

- Floating security available only to businesses or companies and specifically tailored to them can be defined as "enterprise floating security".[210]
- Floating security, which provide for comprehensive enforcement by a special mechanism designed to transfer the security provider's control over the encumbered enterprise, can be defined as "special enforcement floating security".[211]

Individual security rights may fulfil one or more of the criteria under the narrow definition. This allows for their gradation on a scale of intensity, depending on the number of elements displayed. Notably, while the "global" and "enterprise" criteria may exist in combination but also independently of each other,[212] comprehensive enforcement necessarily requires the existence of an enterprise security right, and in practice is encountered only for security rights fulfilling both the global and enterprise criteria. The criteria of this more narrow definition are fulfilled only by security consciously intended and conceptualised to be "floating".[213]

Findings of the Comparative Analysis

From the comparative analysis conducted in this study, some initial findings regarding floating security may be deduced. They do not constitute certified facts, but rather preliminary conclusions drawn from the responses to the exploratory questionnaire. Their main purpose is to provide an overview of the most pertinent issues in this context and to serve as a basis for further in-depth study.

It is clear that floating security rights arrived in jurisdictions at different points and for a variety of reasons, albeit that the desire to improve access

---

[209] This is a typical feature of the functionalist model (e.g. Australia, USA), but it can also be achieved under the pledge model (e.g. Belgium, Mexico, South Africa).

[210] Examples are the Chinese floating charge and the French *nantissement du fonds de commerce.*

[211] This very specific feature is most notably typical of the traditional English floating charge model (e.g. England and Wales, Hong Kong, Nigeria, Scotland), but may also be introduced in other jurisdictions (e.g. Lithuania, Romania).

[212] In fact, the majority of enterprise security seems to also be global; "global enterprise security" can be found e.g. in Czechia, Finland, Italy, Quebec and Turkey.

[213] Including, of course, the English model of floating charge.

to finance has been a core consideration. In the Common Law world, floating charges ordinarily appeared as a result of colonial inheritance from the latter part of the nineteenth century onwards. The sample also identifies outliers, such as South Africa, where floating security emerged from a non-English colonial inheritance (Roman-Dutch law) and the USA, which generally rejected floating security despite its inheritance of English law more broadly. The USA later developed a floating lien as part of its functionalist model, which has proved to be influential. Although a number of countries introduced floating security at various points in the twentieth century, there seems to have been a wave of floating security appearing from the 1990s into the early twenty-first century, with a relatively large number of countries in Central and Eastern Europe adopting floating security as they emerged from socialist regimes. This development somewhat slowed down, but in the past 10 years or so, there have been examples of jurisdictions in different geographical areas where floating security has been (further) embraced.

It is not surprising that the English floating charge has been inherited by a number of Common Law jurisdictions, often because of colonial heritage and the ongoing significance of English law for such jurisdictions. It has, however, also served as a model for other jurisdictions, including those outside the Common Law, when the introduction of a floating security was desired. Yet often it has not simply been a case of a straightforward transplant, which may be expected given the different systems involved. Frequently, a number of jurisdictions and sources from elsewhere, including neighbouring countries, have been influential, albeit that these may themselves have been influenced by English law. Of course, various Common Law systems in recent times have turned away from English law in this area and towards the functionalist model presented by the USA's UCC Art 9, and subsequently adopted in various PPSAs. French law, which has been influential in many Civilian jurisdictions historically, has also somewhat diminished as a model for security against the rise of the functionalist model(s), as well as the development of international instruments produced by organisations such as the EBRD and UNCITRAL. The approach adopted by Germany, which is also a leading Civilian system but remains relatively hostile to floating security, has become unusual. Yet even where floating security has been adopted, the external sources of influence, if any, are not always discernible.

In broad terms, once a floating security has been introduced, it is unusual for it to be abolished without being replaced by some form of functional equivalent. It can be speculated that this is in part due to the interests that lenders have in retaining a powerful security and the benefits for the debtor in being able to deal with their assets in the (ordinary) course of their business. Various jurisdictions of different traditions have supplemented or replaced certain forms of floating security with other versions of such security. However, some types of floating security have fallen into obsolescence. Where there are various forms of security with floating characteristics, the likely usage of a particular floating security is ordinarily dependent upon its advantages in terms of matters such as ranking and the extent to which alternative, higher-ranking security offers what the creditor is seeking. If a more attractive alternative is available, how much the security rights respectively correspond to e.g. the English floating charge is likely to be immaterial.

The scope of floating security rights, in terms of the assets covered, is the key feature for their classification as such. As reflected in the working definition established in the preceding section, all floating security covers a collection of revolving assets. While some jurisdictions limit the possibilities for security over specific assets or asset groups of a certain type, others permit universal security potentially extending to all (movable) assets or even the entire patrimony of a business (resulting in "global floating security"). A character as an "enterprise floating security" may result from a business as such forming the object of the security, or from the availability of certain security rights only to businesses as security providers.

A wide range of approaches can be observed with regard to the creation of floating security. In respect to the requirements for the valid creation and enforceability of a security right, as well as of the formal standards to be adhered to, groups of jurisdictions can be discerned, but no common denominator stands out as typical of floating security. Rather, the approaches largely conform to the general rules for the establishment of security rights under different conceptions, especially regarding the conditions and effects of publicity. Registration emerges as the publicity mechanism of choice; however, the type of register differs depending, among other factors, on the scope of the security.

The integration of floating security within the general dogmatics of property law merits further scrutiny. Apart from publicity, the most pressing issue appears to be the principle of speciality central to the Civil Law legal tradition, which raises problems with regard to revolving asset collections. Typically, the need for floating security is met by a more generous interpretation of the requirements of asset description, allowing for generalised descriptions of the asset group covered, which enable the exact determination of the individual items at a later date.

Different dogmatic conceptions are also reflected in the approach to the encumbrance and unencumbrance of specific assets. In the tradition of the floating charge of English law, the security initially "hovers" over the pool of assets but encumbers individualised items only after a specific event triggering "crystallisation". Before this point in time, items may unproblematically enter and leave the security provider's property and thus the (potential) encumbrance. In legal systems constructing floating security rights as *in rem* rights and requiring adherence to the principle of speciality, however, the encumbrance of each individual asset has to be unconditional and determined precisely at any time. Items falling within the description of covered assets will automatically become encumbered upon their acquisition by the security provider, and items can be freed from encumbrance through acquisition by a third party (and will often be substituted by the assets replacing them). Under both models, however, importance is accorded to the circumstances under which the security provider is permitted to dispose of (potentially) encumbered assets (typically, in the "ordinary course of business") and the requirements for overcoming this condition (typically, by good faith acquisition).

There is a mixed picture regarding the enforcement of floating charges. A number of jurisdictions recognise the value of third-party involvement in enforcement. However, in English law (and Scots law), there has generally been a departure from utilising receivership in favour of procedures that depend upon regard being paid to the interests of all creditors, whereas in other Common Law jurisdictions with floating charges deriving from English law, the value of receivership has largely been recognised and it has been retained as a principal enforcement method for such security. An equivalent of receivership is also adopted in some countries outside the Common Law. Elsewhere, there is a wide variety in terms of the enforcement mechanisms and the extent to which enforcement of floating security differs from other security. Some jurisdictions are more liberal than others in terms of remedies and give more credence to what the parties contractually agree. In the absence of such an agreement, a court order is often required for enforcement, which is ordinarily by sale but sometimes appropriation or other forms of enforcement are available. There are special protections in certain jurisdictions where the security can be granted by consumers, but these vary and the extent to which consumer protections exist in various other jurisdictions is not wholly clear based on the responses we received. While the relationship between floating security and insolvency is undeniably important and leads to diverging results across jurisdictions, this study necessarily only touches the surface of the interrelationship between enforcement of floating security and insolvency.

As regards ranking, it is apparent that many jurisdictions, particularly those with English-style floating charges, give a lower ranking priority to such security compared with fixed security, and various other claims are frequently elevated over floating charges, as a response to their power and scope. Elsewhere, floating security often ranks in accordance with the normal rules based upon the time of creation, usually through registration or its equivalent, but there are exceptions and departures from this for policy or doctrinal reasons. It is commonplace for parties such as unpaid employees and fiscal claims to have priority over floating security, and sometimes other security too. Ranking problems are identifiable in various jurisdictions, particularly as the complexity of ranking rules increases. In practice, such issues and default ranking rules can be circumvented in some countries by the use of ranking agreements; however, there is insufficient information to draw conclusions and the outcomes seem to vary.

The Way Forward

The results of the present study invite further research in a variety of respects. First of all, the conclusions resulting from this initial overview should be tested and refined by further study. The ideal endurance test for the working definition of "floating security" established on the security rights analysed will be the subsumption of additional instruments under its categories. Naturally, a "control group" should include (potentially) floating security from other jurisdictions. In addition, it would be beneficial to apply this definition to all security rights available in the jurisdictions covered in this study, as it is possible that security rights or mechanisms that fall within the broad understanding this study has arrived at were not initially envisaged as "floating" by contributors. For example, concepts and institutions such as trust and proprietary estoppel may result as "floating" at least in the broad sense. In return, the application to security rights beyond the basis of its conception will show the strengths and shortcomings of the current definition and allow for its further refinement.

Comparative research could and should then be undertaken on a variety of aspects and phenomena connected to floating security. In the course of this study, with regard to each question, several specific issues meriting further scrutiny were identified. Some of them stand out as especially pressing and promising. Taking into account its importance in the classification of floating security, the scope of assets covered needs to be explored in more detail – comprehensively considering its potential coverage of immovables and intangibles. With regard to publicity, a cross-cutting study should explore the connections between the technical aspects of registration and the various effects publicity unfolds with regard e.g. to the creation of floating security rights, their priority, or the possibilities of unencumbrance through good faith acquisition. Specific issues resulting from certain approaches, like the mechanism of crystallisation or the problem of over-collateralisation, merit further study, as well as the details of ranking and enforcement inside and outside the context of insolvency.

Taking a more general view, some overarching issues stand out as especially promising for additional comparative research. On the basis of the initial findings of this study, the dogmatic foundations of floating security and the different models used to achieve such constructions merit a fundamental comparative study of their own – contrasting the features considered formative for the floating charge of English law with the mechanisms of the functionalist model, the pledge tradition, and other approaches including the combination of several security rights. Closely connected to this is the history and development within different legal traditions, including aspects like the influence of specific jurisdictions or models, the impact of economic and legal transformations, and the differences between developments driven by legislators and practitioners respectively. Archival research would no doubt bear fruit on this front. Ongoing reforms and tendencies also provide further material for continuing study. Additional insight into the practical application of floating security may be gathered from statistics on their present-day popularity as well as an inquiry into the motivations behind their introduction to legal systems and their use (especially their perceived commercial advantages and disadvantages). In cross-border scenarios, the private international law dimension, especially the extent of the acceptance of floating security rights created under foreign law, is of additional importance.

All further comparative research will need a sound basis of information on national jurisdictions. It would be worthwhile to continue the cooperation established with the expert contributors to this study by developing their questionnaire responses into an information platform on floating security, and subsequently expanding it to include further jurisdictions, especially from the global south. Such a platform could ideally be established as an online database containing structured data sets for all jurisdictions as well as bibliographies to initiate further research – allowing its use both for informational and comparative purposes. The availability of detailed information in an accessible and comparable format could be of immense benefit to practitioners, especially in cross-border cases, as well as academics; using English as a *lingua franca*, it would also serve to establish a common terminology. The Herculean task of its preparation will depend not only on the willingness of a reliable number of long-term participants, but also on the acquisition of funding for such an ambitious, large-scale project.

The further comparative study of floating security offers a plethora of options also from a methodological angle. Additional theoretical work may integrate interdisciplinary approaches, which appear promising especially with regard to including economics and history. For in-depth comparative work on specific aspects, scenario-based approaches as well as empirical and quantitative methods (e.g. leximetrics), especially when allowing for a visualisation of results, are attractive – the initial findings presented in this study may serve as a point of departure for the preparation of the refined and nuanced questions needed for such approaches.

The demands of credit security continue to drive the creation and development of floating security – covering a wide range from the traditional floating charge of English law to more recent and less obvious functional equivalents. Varying in technique, popularity and intensity, a recurring theme with these security rights is their flexible and pragmatic character, continually adjusting to real-life needs through solutions oriented towards and frequently shaped by practice. The need for a coherent and contemporary regulatory framework becomes more and more pressing, as evidenced for many jurisdictions by the responses provided for this study. Legislative introductions and reforms of floating security rights are a worthwhile pursuit, whether at the national level or with a view to regional or global harmonisation. Hopefully, the present study may contribute as an inspiration and starting point for such endeavours.

APPENDIX 1: JURISDICTIONS AND CONTRIBUTORS

Table 1A.1 Compilation of jurisdictions and their corresponding contributors

Jurisdiction	Questionnaire Contributor(s)
Australia	Professor Murray Raff Emeritus Professor, Canberra Law School, University of Canberra, Australia Dr Jenny Fu Senior Lecturer, Canberra Law School, University of Canberra, Australia Dr Geoffrey Nicoll Senior Lecturer, Canberra Law School, University of Canberra, Australia Professor Benedict Sheehy Professor of Law, Canberra Law School, University of Canberra, Australia
Austria	Professor Dr Wolfgang Faber Professor, Faculty of Law, University of Salzburg, Austria
Belgium	Johan Van de Voorde PhD, Senior Researcher at the University of Antwerp, Research Group Personal and Property Rights, Belgium Dr Inge Van de Plas University of Antwerp, Belgium
Bosnia and Herzegovina	Dr Patricia Živković Senior Lecturer, University of Aberdeen, Scotland, UK
Canada (excluding Quebec)	Professor Ron Cuming Emeritus Professor, College of Law, University of Saskatchewan, Canada
Chile	Professor María Paz Gatica Rodríguez Facultad de Ciencias Jurídicas y Sociales, Universidad Austral de Chile – Sede Puerto Montt, Chile
China	Professor Dr Zhicheng Wu, MJur, MPhil (Oxon.) Associate Professor, School of Law, Renmin University of China, China
Croatia	Dr Patricia Živković Senior Lecturer, University of Aberdeen, Scotland, UK
Czechia (Czech Republic)	Dr iur. Magda Schwandt LLM, MA (LIS) Law Librarian, European Legal Studies Institute, Osnabrück University Library, Germany
Denmark	Professor Dr Astrid Millung-Christoffersen Associate Professor, Department of Law, Aarhus University, Denmark

Jurisdiction	Questionnaire Contributor(s)
England and Wales	Professor Andreas Televantos Lincoln College, University of Oxford, England, UK
Finland	Prof. Dr Teemu Juutilainen Professor, Faculty of Law, University of Turku, Finland
France	Dr Muriel Renaudin, LLM, Lic. en droit, Maître en droit Senior Lecturer in Law, School of Law and Politics, Cardiff University, Wales, UK
Germany	Professor Dr Caroline Sophie Rapatz, MPhil (Cantab.) Professor, Faculty of Law, Christian Albrechts University of Kiel, Germany
Hong Kong	Eva Tam Principal Lecturer, Faculty of Law, The University of Hong Kong
Hungary	Professor Dr Tibor Tajti (Thaythy), SJD, LLM Professor, Legal Studies Department, Central European University – Private University, Vienna, Austria
India	Dr Anil R. Nair Associate Professor, National University of Advanced Legal Studies, Kochi, India
Ireland	Dr Noel McGrath Lecturer in Law, University College Dublin, Ireland
Israel	Ehud (Udi) Schaffer LLB, LLM Managing Partner, E. Schaffer & Co. Shiri Ish-Shalom LLB Partner, Arnon, Tadmor-Levy, Tel Aviv, Israel
Italy	Dr Gabriele Conni Senior Business Development Officer, e-Pol SRL, Milan, Italy Dr Vittorio Pozzi Partner, Legance – Avvocati Associati, Milan, Italy
Japan	Professor Noriyuki Aoki Professor of Law, Waseda University, Japan Professor Dr Souichirou Kozuka Professor of Law, Gakushuin University, Japan
Jordan	Lana Salameh JC Law, Jordan
Lithuania	Dr Lina Aleknaitė-van der Molen Counsel, Sorainen, Vilnius, Lithuania

Jurisdiction	Questionnaire Contributor(s)
Mexico	Professor Rafael Ibarra Garza Dean of Faculty of the School of Law, Universidad de Monterrey, Mexico Roberto Helio Colyer Ayala Research Fellow, Universidad de Monterrey, Mexico Cynthia Alejandra Sánchez Torres Research Fellow, Universidad de Monterrey, Mexico
Netherlands	Professor Dr Vincent van Hoof Associate Professor, Department of Legal History, Radboud University Nijmegen, Netherlands
New Zealand	Barry Allan Associate Professor – Law, University of Otago, New Zealand
Nigeria	Dr Chike Emedosi Lecturer in Banking and Finance Law, University of Aberdeen, Scotland, UK
Norway	Professor Dr Bjørn Løtveit Professor, Faculty of Law, The Arctic University of Norway Tromsø, Norway
Poland	Krzysztof Kaźmierczyk Counsel, Dentons, Warsaw, Poland
Quebec	Professor Dr Catherine Walsh, BA, LLB, BCL Full Professor, McGill University, Quebec
Romania	Professor Dr Radu-Alexandru Rizoiu Professor, Faculty of Law, University of Bucharest, Romania
Russia	Professor Alexander A Vishnevskiy Professor, Department of Private Law, Higher School of Economics (Moscow), Russia
Scotland	Dr Alisdair MacPherson Senior Lecturer, University of Aberdeen School of Law, Scotland, UK
Serbia	Dr Patricia Živković Senior Lecturer, University of Aberdeen, Scotland, UK
Singapore	Professor Dora Neo Associate Professor, Faculty of Law, National University of Singapore, Singapore
South Africa	Professor Dr Reghard Brits Extraordinary Professor, University of the Western Cape; Research Fellow, Stellenbosch University, South Africa
South Korea	Professor Dr WooJung Jon Assistant Professor, Korea Advanced Institute of Science and Technology, South Korea

Jurisdiction	Questionnaire Contributor(s)
Switzerland	Dr Alexandra Dal Molin-Kränzlin, MLaw, Attorney at Law Legal Counsel at Accenture and University Lecturer, Zurich, Switzerland
Turkey	Dr Yaman Gürsel, LLM, LLB International Arbitration Lawyer, Washington DC, USA
USA	Professor Christopher K Odinet Professor of Law and Mosbacher Research Fellow, Texas A&M University, USA

APPENDIX 2: THE QUESTIONNAIRE

Floating Charges in Comparative Perspective

This project aims at a comparative analysis of the law of security rights in a range of jurisdictions. In particular, it will focus on floating charges and their functional equivalents. A floating charge is a type of non-possessory security interest that emerged in English equity in the mid-to-late nineteenth century. As a mechanism for obtaining security over present and future assets of a debtor, it enables the grantor to continue to trade with the "charged" property, including being able to dispose of the property in the ordinary course of business. The grantor's freedom to deal remains until particular later events take place and cause the charge to take on the characteristics of a fixed security over the property then subject to the charge ("crystallization").

The floating charge has been introduced into other jurisdictions, especially those in the Common Law world. However, in some of those systems the floating charge has since been replaced and in others (including England and Wales) the abolition of the floating charge has been proposed. On the other hand, a general interest in floating charges among scholars and practitioners in Civilian systems can be noted. In recent years, some jurisdictions have even introduced security interests that lawyers refer to as floating charges, despite the absence of equity in those systems. In other jurisdictions, distinct forms of security interest serve some of the purposes of a floating charge.

This project is likely to be the most extensive specific study of floating charges on a comparative basis. It will allow for a greater understanding of the nature of floating charges, as well as their historical and present-day value and significance. The project will also enable us to consider a number of comparative law issues. For example, the floating charge provides an interesting case study of a legal transplant across different types of system. In addition, the wide-ranging nature of the project will also allow for conclusions regarding the extent to which there has been convergence or divergence of the law in this area. It may provide starting points for future legislative projects or even harmonization in this area of law.

As a starting point, we propose to ask participants to briefly answer some questions. We would be grateful if you could respond to the following:

1. Does (or did) your system have a floating charge or does (or did) it have a functional equivalent?
2. When, how and why was such a security introduced?
3. Was the law in any other legal systems especially influential when the security was introduced? If so, how did this influence manifest itself?
4. If your system formerly had a floating charge or functional equivalent, when, how and why was such a security abolished? And what (if anything) was it replaced with?
5. What assets does the floating charge (or equivalent) extend to in your system? In what situations/by whom can it be created?
6. How is (or was) the security created over property in your system? (Particular reference is to be made to publicity/registration.)
7. How does (or did) the security function in the broader legal system, including with respect to coherence with property law?
8. How do (or did) specific assets become encumbered by the security and how do (or did) specific assets become unencumbered?
9. How is (or was) the security enforced?
10. How is (or was) the security dealt with in competition with other rights, e.g. in a ranking context?

2. Floating charges in England

Andreas Televantos

INTRODUCTION

A floating charge in English law is a security interest over present and future property, under which a corporate[1] debtor is nevertheless able to use the assets subject to the security in its ordinary course of business until it either ceases to trade or the secured creditor intervenes.[2] At that stage the charge 'crystallises', and the debtor is no longer free to use the charged assets. Significantly, because of statute,[3] security held by a floating charge creditor today grants only a qualified priority upon the insolvency of the debtor – further differentiating it from other security interests. Charges of this kind have been used for over 150 years in England, and from England such charges spread to other areas of the Commonwealth and inspired various other jurisdictions. However, the modern English law on floating charges is seen by many as problematic.[4] Other common law jurisdictions have swept away the common law rules on floating charges, subsuming them within personal property securities acts or other statutory codes governing security. Further, these common law rules, still applicable in England, are perceived as needlessly complex and the legislature

[1] There is an exception for farmers (see the Agricultural Credits Act 1928), but beyond that it is usually taken for granted that unincorporated persons and partnerships cannot grant floating charges, e.g. see *Aquachem Ltd v Delphis Bank Ltd* [2008] UKPC 7 at [6] (Lord Hoffmann); L Gullifer, *Goode & Gullifer on Legal Problems of Credit and Security* (7th edn, Sweet & Maxwell 2023) at [4–01]. For a counterargument that such charges are conceptually possible, but simply impractical, see M Raczynska, 'The Species and Structure(s) of the Floating Charge: The English Law Perspective on the Scottish Floating Charge', in J Hardman and A MacPherson (eds), *Floating Charges in Scotland* (Edinburgh University Press (EUP), 2022), 316–317.

[2] For the classic definition, see *Re Yorkshire Woolcombers Association Limited* [1903] 2 Ch 284, 295 (Romer LJ).

[3] Discussed below.

[4] See discussion below.

has heightened the problem by attaching drastically different consequences to floating charges as compared with other kinds of security interests, particularly in the twenty-first century.

This chapter looks at the doctrinal theory and history behind floating charges on the one hand, and the practical problems surrounding them on the other. It is divided into three parts. The first examines the legal concepts that shape the modern concept of a floating charge. It will be shown why floating charges are often thought to be difficult to explain at the level of legal doctrine. The difficulties stem in part from uncertainties concerning the nature of equitable charges more broadly, and in part from the apparent contradiction inherent in a debtor's right to trade with assets that are charged in equity. It will be suggested that such inconsistencies might be explained by reference to historic concerns about the general incorporation of joint stock companies with limited liability. The introduction of the general incorporation of limited liability companies was itself controversial, and judges were willing to sanction attempts by creditors to take more extensive security over the business of such debtors than was possible when dealing with natural persons. The second part looks more specifically at the debate surrounding the nature of the rights of a creditor with an uncrystallised floating charge, and how such charges should be legally characterised. The third part looks at some modern issues surrounding floating charges, in particular automatic crystallisation clauses, the impact of twenty-first-century legislation on the position of the floating charge creditor, the characterisation of charges as fixed and floating and potential avenues of reform for the floating charge.

THE BASICS OF THE ENGLISH FLOATING CHARGE

Although the floating charge in English law is well established, and such charges remain popular forms of security, their doctrinal building blocks are not always well understood. Understanding these basic elements is crucial for comprehending why the floating charge looks, at least at first blush, difficult to justify as a matter of legal doctrine.

First, a floating charge is a kind of equitable interest held by a creditor. Although the nature of equitable interests is much debated,[5] an equitable interest is a right which relates to other (primary) rights, which binds some classes

---

[5] E.g. F Maitland, Equity (eds Chaytor and Whittaker), (1929); R Nolan, 'Equitable Property' (2004) 122 Law Quarterly Review 232; B McFarlane and R Stevens, 'The Nature of Equitable Property' (2010) 4 Journal of Equity 1; H Dagan and I Samet, 'The Beneficiary's Ownership Rights in the Trust Res in A Liberal Property Regime' (2022) <https://papers.ssrn.com/sol3/papers.cfm?abstract_id=4050514> accessed 22 September 2022.

of third parties in a way that resembles a common law property right. In particular, an equitable interest confers a priority[6] claim to the relevant assets upon the insolvency of the primary right holder and can bind certain kinds of purchasers of the assets subject to the interest.[7] Further, equitable interests can be held outright or by way of security only. The archetypical example of the holder of an equitable interest outright is the beneficiary of a trust. A creditor with a charge also has an equitable interest but holds it as security only – that is to say, the creditor retains it only so long as the secured obligation remains unperformed.

Secondly, a floating charge governs at least a class of present *and future* assets of the debtor. English law has long recognised that where A promises to grant B an equitable interest in an asset that A does not yet own, once B has performed her part of the bargain, B will acquire an equitable interest in the asset automatically and immediately upon A's receipt of it.[8] The principle applies as much to promises to grant interests by way of security as it does to promises to hold on trust or convey absolutely.[9] Floating charges make use of this mechanism: the debtor grants the creditor security over a present asset and a class of future assets.[10] In other words, the promise to grant an interest over the future property is self-executing.

Thirdly, where a debtor grants a floating charge, the debtor can nevertheless use and dispose of the charged assets in the ordinary course of business until it ceases to trade or the secured creditor intervenes as permitted by the terms of the charge. Ordinary course of business is understood broadly in this context and can in principle include transactions that are unusual or might amount to fraudulent preferences or breach of fiduciary duty by directors.[11] This free-

---

6 Throughout this paper, charges and other equitable interests are described as giving 'priority' in the sense that assets subject to an equitable interest do not generally form part of the debtor or trustee's estate available for distribution to general creditors, and so are made available to the beneficiary or secured creditor 'in priority' to unsecured creditors. This is simply a shorthand common in commercial law literature, and the language is not intended to deny that equitable interests generally prevent the encumbered assets vesting in an insolvent estate; see W Swadling, 'Policy Arguments for Proprietary Restitution' (2008) 28(4) Legal Studies, 506–523.

7 See Nolan (n 5).

8 See J Getzler, 'Assignment of Future Property and Preferences' in J Glister and P Ridge (eds), '*Fault Lines in Equity*' (Hart 2012), 73–106.

9 E.g. *Holroyd v Marshall* (1862) 10 HL Cas 191 (security); *Pullan v Koe* [1913] 1 Ch 9 (beneficial interest).

10 *Re Yorkshire* (n 2).

11 *Ashborder BV v Green Gas Power Ltd* [2004] BCC 634 at [227] (Sir Terrence Etherton MR).

dom to deal with and dispose of the assets in the ordinary course of business differentiates a floating charge from a fixed charge over a class of present and future property.

It is this third and final feature of the floating charge that presents the greatest difficulty for doctrinal lawyers. Chancery first justified the insolvency priority of equitable interests on the basis that, just as the insolvent could not have freely used the assets to pay its unsecured creditors before insolvency, those claiming through the insolvent in a bankruptcy or liquidation should not be able to do so either.[12] This principle came to be an integral part of the law governing when fixed charges and trusts arise. A fixed charge only arises where the assets in question are unconditionally appropriated as security for the obligation, and the debtor comes under duties to the creditor not to use them for other purposes until the obligation is performed.[13] Likewise, a trust only arises if the settlor intends the assets held on trust not to be at the free use of the trustee, but only according to the trust's terms.[14] In other words, a fundamental premise of private law is that equitable interests only arise where a person holds rights that they cannot freely use for their own benefit.[15] If restrictions on use are a basic feature of trusts and equitable charges, yet a floating charge does not restrict the debtor's free use of the assets, then why does equity recognise a charge as arising at all? After all, a purported 'declaration of trust' which gave the trustee extensive powers to trade the trust assets for its *own* benefit would probably[16] be found by a court to be illusory: the

[12] See A Televantos, *Capitalism Before Corporations* (OUP 2020) 128–132.

[13] E.g. see *National Provincial and Union Bank of England v Charnley* [1924] KB 431, 449–450 (Atkin LJ); *Re TXU Group Europe Group Plc* [2003] EWHC 1305; *Swiss Bank Corporation v Lloyds Bank* [1989] AC 584.

[14] E.g see *Paragon Finance v Thakerar* (1999) 1 All ER 400, 451–456 (Lord Millett); *Lehman Brothers Finance SA* [2010] EWHC 2914 (Ch) [250]–[252] (Briggs J); *Angove's Pty Ltd v Bailey* [2016] UKSC 47 at [29].

[15] J Getzler, 'Securities Lending, the Right to Use, and Financial Trusts: Lessons (Imperfectly Learned) from the Lehman Insolvency' (forthcoming).

[16] Courts have been more willing to find trusts in such cases in the commercial context, even though this is very difficult to reconcile with orthodox trusts law principles – see *Re Lehman Brothers International Europe* [2009] EWHC 2545 [1]–[97]; *Re Lehman* (n 14); R Stevens, 'Floating Trusts' in P Davies and J Penner (eds), *Equity Trusts and Commerce* (Hart 2017); R Salter, 'Securities Lending: Does a "Right of Use" Prevent the Existence of a Trust?' (2020) Journal of International Banking & Financial Law 3. See too *Barclays Bank v Quistclose Investments Ltd* [1970] AC 567 and *Twinsectra v Yardley* [2002] 2 AC 164 (Lord Millett and Lord Hoffmann).

trustee's extensive powers would be inconsistent with a finding that there was an intention to declare a trust in favour of another.[17]

The case law gives little explanation. It remains unclear how and why English law came to recognise equitable charges at all. It has been said that eighteenth- and nineteenth-century English law did not, outside of maritime law, recognise security in the form of 'hypothecation', at least of personalty.[18] Hypothecation means a security interest arising without a change in ownership (at law or in equity), or change in possession, from the debtor to the creditor.[19] For centuries, the doctrine of reputed ownership provided that personalty in the possession of a bankrupt with the consent of its 'true owner' would vest in the possessor's bankrupt estate, rendering non-possessory security interests over personalty prima facie unenforceable upon bankruptcy.[20] At first sight, both rules would seem to suggest that English law did not recognise charges of personal property. Nevertheless, from the mid-nineteenth century it was taken for granted that reputed ownership did not apply to corporate insolvency,[21] and that equity's willingness specifically to enforce agreements to give security would give rise to equitable charges of real and personal property.[22] Specific performance remains the dominant explanation for the law's recognition of equitable charges,[23] but there has been little discussion of the content of the promise that is being specifically enforced to give rise to a charge, nor why specific performance is available in the first place. Buckley LJ's explanation in *Swiss Bank Corporation v Lloyds Bank*[24] that no priority could be given without specific enforcement, and so the promise would be rendered void, is circular. Surely if the agreement is simply to grant priority on insolvency, the

---

17 E.g. see *Webb v Webb* [2020] UKPC 22; *JSC Mezhdunarodniy Promyshlenniy Bank v Pugachev* [2017] EWHC 2426 (Ch).

18 E.g. see *Howes v Ball* (1827) 7 B & C 481, 484; 108 ER 802, 804; cf *Stainbank v Shepard* (1853) 13 CB 418; 138 ER 1262, 1270. Civilian readers should note that 'personalty' and 'personal property' in English law encompass tangible movables, but also *in personam* rights such as debt claims.

19 C Sweet, *A Dictionary of English Law* (1882) 412–413.

20 21 Jac I c 19 (1623–24), s 10, eventually abolished in the Insolvency Act 1986. See F Stolker, 'The Rise and Fall of the Reputed Ownership Clause' (MSt thesis, University of Oxford 2016).

21 *In Re Crumlin Viaduct Works Company* (1879) 11 Ch D 755.

22 *Tailby v Official Receiver* (1888) 13 App Cas 523.

23 E.g. see *In the Matter of Lehman Brothers International Europe* [2012] EWHC 2997 (Ch) at [43] (Briggs J); *Equity Trust (Jersey) Ltd v Halabi* [2022] UKPC 36 at [110]–[111] (Lord Richards and Patten LJ).

24 [1989] AC 584 at 595.

promise should be rendered unenforceable as a fraud on the insolvency statutes, and not specifically enforced?[25]

The process by which courts came to recognise that corporate debtors could grant floating equitable charges is more difficult still. As Nolan[26] and Stebbings[27] have recognised, before incorporation by registration, companies created by statute ('statutory companies') were sometimes specifically empowered to grant mortgages over 'their undertaking' as a means of raising finance. This was typically to carry out some public infrastructure project: examples include canal navigation companies, turnpike companies, and later, railway companies. It is generally thought that lawyers created the floating charge by imitating the drafting of such mortgages following the introduction of general incorporation and limited liability, and courts gave effect to such arrangements.[28] However, the statutory antecedents of the floating charge are of limited help in understanding how to characterise the floating equitable charge outside of that context. First, statutory companies were empowered to mortgage their undertakings directly by statute. In contrast, the power of modern companies to grant floating charges is not rooted in any statutory provision, but the exercise of the powers they have under the general law.[29] Second, as Raczynska has convincingly shown,[30] the authorisation of statutory companies to grant charges over their undertaking was seen as only authorising the company to charge its profits – not the underlying capital assets, a point that makes sense given that such companies owned public infrastructure. Nevertheless, in *Re Panama*,[31] Giffard LJ rejected counsel's argument that a charge on an undertaking of a company incorporated under the Companies Act 1862 only covered profits but not capital assets.

This change was significant, and we need to look beyond legal doctrine for an explanation. It may be that this lies in early attitudes towards limited liability corporations. As Taylor argues, when limited liability incorporation was first introduced, it was controversial and was generally opposed by the

[25] See *Belmont Park Investments Pty Ltd v BNY Corporate Trustee Services Ltd* [2011] UKSC 38, [2012] 1 AC 383 at [1]–[15] (Lord Collins).

[26] R Nolan 'Property in a Fund' (2004) LQR 108, 117–131.

[27] C Stebbings, 'Statutory Railway Mortgage Debentures and the Courts in the Nineteenth Century' (1987) 8 JLH 36.

[28] Nolan, 'Property in a Fund' (n 26).

[29] See *Re Anchor Line Ltd* [1937] Ch 483 at 487–488 (Luxmoore J).

[30] Raczynska (n 1). Note, though, that courts did, in other contexts, treat debentures granted by turnpike companies as interests in their underlying real property, e.g. see *Robinson v Robinson* (1851) 1 De GM & G 247, 262; 42 ER 547, 553.

[31] *In re Panama, New Zealand, and Australian Royal Mail Company* (1869–1970) LR 5 Ch App 318.

business community.[32] In turn, this explains why suspicion of the corporate form lingered throughout the nineteenth century,[33] and uptake of incorporation was slow and happened sector by sector.[34] At the same time, much of the motivation in Parliament for the introduction of limited liability was as a means of stabilising the economy. Earlier companies without limited liability had destabilised the economy: creditors had been willing recklessly to extend credit to such entities,[35] relying on claims against prominent shareholders in the event of default.[36] In the minds of some legislators at least, creditors of limited liability companies, lacking such redress, would lend on more responsible terms.[37] Against this backdrop, the judicial recognition of the floating charge makes sense: creditors bargaining for such charges were seen as extending credit prudently. Although the courts would not have recognised partnerships or natural persons as capable of granting a charge over circulating stock, they were willing to recognise limited liability corporations as having such power. It was legitimate for creditors dealing with debtors *of that type* to seek so-called 'floating' security because they did not have the protection of a claim against the natural persons that owned the business. In turn, as Getzler argues, the floating charge ultimately became a standard requirement of the risk-averse British banking sector, which increasingly would only make loans to businesses in return for a floating charge, thereby ultimately encouraging use of the corporate form.[38]

---

[32] See J Taylor, *Creating Capitalism: Joint Stock Enterprise in British Politics and Culture, 1800–1870* (Boydell Press, 2006) 170–171.

[33] Ibid 172–175. For a vivid illustration, see A Trollope, *The Way We Live Now* (Chapman and Hall 1875).

[34] M Daunton, *Wealth and Welfare: An Economic and Social History of Britain 1851–1951* (OUP 2007) 105; P Johnson, *Making the Market: The Victorian Origins of Corporate Capitalism* (CUP 2010) 122–124.

[35] Taylor (n 32) 161. See too Televantos (n 12) at 172–176.

[36] M Lobban, 'Joint Stock Companies' in W Cornish, A Anderson, R Cocks, M Lobban, P Polden and K Smith, *The Oxford History of the Laws of England, Volume XII, 1820–1914: Private Law* (OUP 2010) 613, 624.

[37] Taylor (n 32) 161.

[38] J Getzler, 'The Role of Security over Future and Circulating Capital: Evidence from the British Economy *circa* 1850–1920' in J Getzler and J Payne (eds), *Company Charges, Spectrum and Beyond* (OUP, 2006).

THE NATURE OF UNCRYSTALLISED FLOATING CHARGES

Even if we can posit plausible historical explanations of *why* the floating charge was recognised, these tell us nothing about the legal form of the rights involved. This ambiguity subsists in modern discussions about the nature of uncrystallised floating charges as a matter of legal doctrine. What is the nature of the rights of a creditor with an uncrystallised floating charge? Does such a creditor have an equitable proprietary security in a class of assets held by the debtor? Can such a right be in any sense 'proprietary' if the assets in the class are constantly changing – as when they are being traded? And how can the creditor have an equitable property right given that, subject to a promise not to make dispositions of particular types (a 'negative pledge clause'), the debtor can freely use the assets for business purposes?

One response to the apparent problem is to deny that the floating charge creditor pre-crystallisation has a proprietary right at all[39] – and instead to treat his rights as personal before this time,[40] conferring a degree of insolvency priority simply because of statute.[41] Such models, however, do not fit well with judicial articulations of the rights of a floating charge creditor in English law, nor are they consistent with the existing legal rules. Courts have always recognised the floating charge creditor as having a *present* security right, rather than a future security right, even before crystallisation.[42] Further, this right is treated as an equitable interest capable of binding a purchaser. For example, imagine a case where a debtor disposes of an asset subject to a floating charge, despite a negative pledge clause in the terms of the charge prohibiting such a disposition. Later, the charge crystallises. In such a case, the floating charge creditor would have a priority over the disponee by virtue of having an equitable interest which had arisen before the purchase. Accordingly, the purchaser would be bound unless the disponee could make out a defence sufficient to bar a prior equitable interest.[43] This reasoning is inconsistent with any model that characterises the creditor's rights before crystallisation as personal only.

---

[39] E.g. see *Equity Trust (Jersey Ltd) v Halabi* (n 23) at [248] (Lord Briggs).

[40] W Gough, *Company Charges* (2nd edn, Butterworths 1996).

[41] For an argument along these lines in relation to Scots law, where the legal position differs from English law and the floating charge is a statutory creation, see A D J MacPherson, *The Floating Charge* (Edinburgh Legal Education Trust 2020).

[42] E.g. see *Evans v Rival Granite Quarries Ltd* [1910] 2 KB 979, 999–1000.

[43] *English & Scottish Mercantile Investment Co Ltd v Brunton* [1892] 2 QB 700 at 707 (Lord Esher MR); *Wilson v Kelland* [1910] 2 Ch 306 (Ch D).

Another response is exemplified by Buckley LJ's dicta in *Evans v Rival Granite Quarries Limited*,[44] and developed by Roy Goode and Louise Gullifer.[45] On this model, the creditor with an uncrystallised floating charge does have an equitable property right, but this interest is not 'attached' to any specific asset – it is a right to a 'fund' only,[46] and in this sense, it 'floats'.[47] Upon crystallisation, however, the charge 'attaches' to specific assets. This model also has difficulties. Property rights both at law and in equity require certain subject matter.[48] This is because a common law property right is a right to possess a particular tangible thing,[49] while an equitable property right is a right which relates to a specific right of another.[50] If this is accepted, how can the creditor have a property right which does not relate to any specific rights until the moment of attachment? On these definitions, a creditor's floating charge could not be a 'property right' either at law or in equity, lacking a certain subject matter at the time at which it ostensibly comes into being. The model has been described as a 'metaphor': it describes how the floating charge works at a high level of abstraction, but it provides no rationalisation or modelling of the entitlements of the creditor in orthodox private law terms.[51]

The most persuasive view is instead that a creditor with an uncrystallised floating charge does have an equitable interest in the charged assets.[52]

---

44 [1910] 2 KB 979.

45 L Gullifer, *Goode and Gullifer on Legal Problems of Credit and Security* (7th edn, Sweet & Maxwell 2022) [4-02] to [4-06].

46 Note that there are different theories as to the nature of 'funds' in English law, and Goode and Gullifer's is distinct because it claims that such a right does not involve a right to the underlying assets in the fund, ibid. Similar views are taken elsewhere by Roy Goode, see e.g. R Goode, 'The Right to Trace and its Impact in Commercial Transactions – I' (1976) 92 LQR 360, 384. For rather different conceptions, see Nolan, 'Property in a Fund' (n 26) 111–115; S Elliott (ed.), *Snell's Equity* (35th edn, Sweet & Maxwell 2025) at [2-010]–[2-011]; J Getzler, 'Plural Ownership, Funds, and the Aggregation of Wills' (2009) 10(1) Theoretical Inquiries in Law 241, 243; 249–250.

47 *Goode and Gullifer, i*bid [4-03].

48 E.g. see *Re Goldcorp* [1994] 2 All ER 806.

49 See L Rostill, *Possession, Relative Title, and Ownership in English Law* (OUP 2021).

50 B McFarlane & R Stevens, 'The Nature of Equitable Property' (n 5).

51 J Getzler (n 8) 82; R Calnan, R Oliver & M Raczynska, *Calnan on Taking Security, Law and Practice* (5th edn, Butterworths 2024) at [5.26]–[5.31].

52 Nolan, 'Property in a Fund' (n 26); Calnan ibid, Chapter 5; S Worthington, *Proprietary Interests in Commercial Transactions* (OUP 1996), 79–86; Raczynska (n 1); B McFarlane, *The Structure of Property Law* (Hart 2008) 599–604; R Stevens, 'Contractual Aspects of Debt Financing' in D Prentice and A Reisberg

Although this theory has variants,[53] the most comprehensive exposition is given by Nolan, drawing analogies with the working of trusts.[54] Imagine a case where T holds business assets on fixed trust for B, yet has powers under the terms of the trust to trade the assets. In such a case, B would have an existing equitable interest in the original assets but, upon T trading one asset for another, B's interest in the original asset would be destroyed or 'overreached'[55] and B would acquire an equitable interest in the substitute. Nolan's theory is that the floating charge is much the same: the debtor's rights to specific assets are encumbered by the creditor's equitable interest, yet the debtor has powers[56] to use those assets in its ordinary course of business. The exercise of those powers overreaches the equitable interest of the creditor in the asset disposed of but gives the creditor an immediate charge over any new assets received of the class specified in the charge. As explained by Esher MR in *Driver v Broad*:[57]

> It seems to me perfectly clear that these debentures [i.e. the debt instrument] constitute a charge on the company's land and buildings, ... It was argued that that was not so, because the charge was expressed to be a 'floating security'. The meaning of that expression appears to be that, notwithstanding the charge, the company is to have power to sell the property charged under certain circumstances, and so the charge may be defeated; but there is none the less a charge on the land, subject to

(eds), *Corporate Finance Law in the UK and the EU* (OUP 2011) 220; *Snell's Equity* (n 46) [40-007]–[40-009]. The approach seems to be implicitly recognised in the nineteenth-century cases treating a floating charge simply as a present charge over the assets of the debtor, e.g. see *Governments Stock and Other Securities Investment Co v Manila Railway Co* [1897] AC 81 at 86.

53 In outline, on some versions the debtor's power to deal with the assets comes from a licence or agency mandate (Worthington ibid; Raczynska (n 1) *pace* Buckley LJ's rejection of the idea in *Evans* (n 42)), while on others it comes from powers that form part and parcel of the charge more analogous to the powers of a trustee (Nolan n 16, Calnan n 51). A third variant treats the creditor as having a power to acquire an equitable interest, akin to a mere equity or claim by proprietary estoppel, until crystallisation (McFarlane ibid; Stevens ibid) – a novel claim in analogising inchoate equities that arise by operation of law to expressly created interests.

54 Nolan, 'Property in a Fund' (n 26).

55 D Fox, 'Overreaching' in P Birks and A Pretto (eds), *Breach of Trust* (Oxford, Hart 2002) 95–101.

56 These equitable powers are, in fact authority for the debtor to make use of the rights it has charged, rather than powers in a Hohfeldian sense. See J Hudson, 'Justifying Equity's Control of Power: Fiduciary Status and Beyond' in P Miller and J Oberdiek (eds), *Oxford Studies in Private Law Theory Volume II* (Hart 2023).

57 See *Driver v Broad* [1893] 1 QB 744, 747 (Esher MR).

the power given to the company to dispose of the property in the ordinary course of its business.

Where the charge contains a negative pledge clause prohibiting a particular type of disposition, the debtor has no power to make a disposition of that kind, and if it does so, this will not overreach the interests of the creditor in the asset – explaining the creditor's prima facie priority over any such disponee. Finally, on this view, upon crystallisation of the charge the debtor's power to deal with the assets simply comes to an end. The creditor retains the same charge that it had all along. The major advantage of this model is that it goes further than any of the others: it not only describes the working of the relevant rules but explains them in doctrinal terms which can stand alongside both the outcome and the reasoning in cases.

MODERN CONTROVERSIES

The debate concerning the nature of rights under a floating charge is sometimes criticised as purely academic. However, practically significant controversies surrounding the nature of floating charges and their reform turn on the view one takes about the nature of a floating charge creditor's rights. This section will consider a number of those controversies.

Automatic Crystallisation Clauses and Decrystallisation

One controversy relates to so-called automatic crystallisation clauses. The term refers to clauses which provide that, upon the happening of specified events, a floating charge will automatically crystallise. In the 1970s, such clauses played a useful function, in that a charge which crystallised before insolvency was treated as a fixed charge for insolvency purposes, and so gave complete priority rather than the qualified priority floating charges give.[58] By specifying crystallisation events that are likely to pre-date insolvency, an automatic crystallisation clause could be used by a floating creditor to evade the statutory restrictions placed on floating charges in insolvency proceedings. However, the Insolvency Act 1986 provides that any charge created as floating is to be treated as such for insolvency purposes.[59] While automatic crystallisation clauses might be useful in specific cases, for instance where monitoring the debtor's business might be impractical, this does not explain their continued widespread use in floating charges.

---

[58] See *Goode & Gullifer* (n 45) at [4-53], [4-56].

[59] Insolvency Act 1986 ss 40(1) and 251; Companies Act 2006, s 754(1).

In fact, such clauses have the potential to frustrate the intentions of both creditor and debtor. Unless carefully drafted, a crystallisation clause can be triggered by something very minor, yet its effects will be drastic: crystallisation revokes the debtor's authority to use the assets in its business. This can paralyse the business and in turn can imperil the value of the encumbered assets. For instance, suppose a charge provides that it is to crystallise upon the debtor breaching any of the covenants in the debenture, that is to say the terms of the loan. The typical scope of covenants is such that a minor breach could trigger crystallisation – e.g. a delay in providing information or documents required by the terms of the charge to be shown to the creditor on a particular date.[60] As Hoffman J put it in *Re Brightlife Ltd*,[61] 'the commercial inconvenience' means that courts will be slow to infer that automatic crystallisation was intended by the parties, although this is of no help where the clause is unambiguous.

In practice, most commercial parties ignore technical breaches – in essence allowing the charge to 'de-crystallise', to 're-float' – yet this comes with its own dangers. The nature of a 're-floated' charge would be controversial. There is certainly an argument that such a charge is a brand new floating charge, and this leads some practitioners to register the re-floated charge as a brand new charge to ensure its enforceability. This not only comes with additional costs, but the priority of such a charge might be dated to the time of de-crystallisation, rather than when the original charge was given.[62] At the level of doctrine, the question is whether a charge can 're-float' in such circumstances. Goode and Gullifer see the answer to this question as turning on the view one takes of the nature of an uncrystallised floating charge.[63] On the view that the creditor's pre-crystallisation rights are personal or an 'unattached' property right, they suggest that de-crystallisation must involve the creation of a new floating charge, which therefore would have to be registered.[64] This is because, on these approaches, upon creation of the charge the creditor has no right to specific assets, which are only acquired upon crystallisation, and then are lost upon de-crystallisation.[65] More appealing – both practically and theoretically – is the view that a floating charge creditor has the same charge before

---

[60] *Goode & Gullifer* (n 45) at [4-56].

[61] [1987] Ch 200.

[62] *Goode & Gullifer* (n 45) at [4-60].

[63] Ibid.

[64] Ibid.

[65] Note, though, that Goode and Gullifer do not consider the argument that it might be possible to construe the floating charge, even after de-crystallisation, as a single charge for the purpose of the registration provisions in the Companies Act 2006, ss 859A-859Q. I am grateful to Mitchell Cleaver for this suggestion.

and after crystallisation, subject to the effects of overreaching. On this view, upon crystallisation the debtor's authority to deal with the assets is revoked, and upon de-crystallisation the debtor once again acquires such authority. The creditor's charge remains the same throughout, and there is no need to regard the creditor as acquiring a new charge upon de-crystallisation, with all the disadvantages that involves.

The Distinction Between Fixed and Floating Charges

The next set of controversies concerns the distinction between the fixed and floating charge. Under modern law, the holders of fixed and floating charges are subject to drastically different treatment upon insolvency. This differing treatment is premised on a supposed doctrinal distinction between them. Can this distinction bear the weight placed upon it?

Different treatment

The Insolvency Act 1986, as modified by the Enterprise Act 2002, the Finance Act 2020, and the Corporate Insolvency and Governance Act 2020, makes specific provision for the treatment of floating charges upon insolvency. These twenty-first-century changes essentially erode the value of the floating charge as a device for ensuring priority upon insolvency.

First, a floating charge does not give unqualified priority on insolvency in the way most security interests do.[66] The Enterprise Act 2002 provided that a 'prescribed part' (a calculated proportion) of the assets subject to a floating charge be made available to unsecured creditors.[67] Originally the prescribed part was capped at £600,000,[68] but this has been raised to £800,000 for charges created since 6 April 2020.[69] This measure originally replaced His Majesty's Revenue and Customs' (HMRC's) claim to charged assets, which had priority over the floating charge. However, priority claims in respect of certain tax debts such as VAT have been reintroduced by the Finance Act 2020.[70] This is particularly difficult for creditors: before the 2020 Act, a floating charge creditor could at least estimate the maximum value of the prescribed part when deciding the terms on which to lend. However, as a debtor's possible tax liabilities in the

---

[66] Insolvency Act 1986, Schedule 6.

[67] Insolvency Act 1986, s 176A; Insolvency Act 1986 (Prescribed Part) Order 2003; Insolvency Act 1986 (Prescribed Part Amendment Order) 2020.

[68] Insolvency Act 1986 (Prescribed Part) Order 2003 (affected floating charges created on or after 15 September 2003).

[69] Insolvency Act 1986 (Prescribed Part Amendment Order) 2020.

[70] Finance Act 2020, s 98, modifying Insolvency Act 1986, s 386(1) and (1B), and Schedule 6 Paragraph 15C.

event of insolvency are less certain, rationally pricing borrowing *ex ante* will become more difficult.[71]

Second, the historical control that floating charge creditors were given over a debtor company has also been eroded. This has been done in a way that further dents the value of a floating charge as security. Before 2003, a floating charge creditor could appoint an administrative receiver[72] to manage the debtor company in the circumstances specified by the terms of the charge.[73] Although still possible in specified contexts,[74] that general power was removed by the Enterprise Act 2002,[75] which instead allows a qualifying floating charge creditor[76] – namely a creditor with charges over the whole or substantially the whole of the debtor company's property, at least one of which is a floating charge – to put a company into 'administration'. Further, if permitted by the terms of the debenture, this can be done without showing that the debtor is insolvent.[77] This procedure was designed to facilitate corporate rescue and operate for the benefit of creditors generally, not only the floating charge creditor.[78] For that reason, unlike administrative receivership, administration is not simply a remedy for a floating charge creditor following default by the borrower – indeed there are various routes by which a company can be put into administration,[79] and in practice company directors do appoint

---

[71] See S Davies and K Gunaratna, 'Crown Preference, Corona and the Continued Assault on Floating Charge Lending' [2020] *Journal of International Banking and Financial Law* 306.

[72] See Insolvency Act 1986, s 29(2).

[73] The grounds for appointment turn on the scope of the power in the debenture, not general law rules. See K van Zwieten, *Goode on Principles of Corporate Insolvency Law* (5th edn, 2018) at [10–26].

[74] Insolvency Act 1986, ss 72A to 72G. The power can still matter in the context of project finance (s 72E); see L Gullifer and J Payne, *Corporate Finance Law: Principles and Policy* (3rd edn, Hart 2020) 319.

[75] See the Insolvency Act 1986, s 72A.

[76] Insolvency Act 1986, sch B1, para 14.

[77] The administrator can be appointed if the floating charge has, according to its terms, become enforceable, ibid. See discussion in K van Zweiten, *Goode on Principles of Corporate Insolvency Law* (n 73) at [11-09].

[78] Insolvency Act 1986, para 3.

[79] E.g. See Insolvency Act 1986, sch B1, paras 10 and 22.

administrators.[80] Further, administrators[81] and liquidators[82] can claim their expenses from floating charge assets, and administrators can even dispose of floating charge assets in the course of administration as if the assets were not charged.[83] Nevertheless, following the Enterprise Act 2002, a qualifying floating charge holder typically had control of the identity of any administrator, and in that way could de facto retain control over the debtor's insolvency.[84] Typically, the creditor could pre-agree an administration deal with a 'friendly' insolvency official and present this as a 'pre-pack' administration to a debtor running into difficulties.[85] In this way, floating charge assets would be protected, in that the 'friendly' administrator would not freely resort to them to fund the administration.[86]

However, the 'control' given to a qualifying floating charge holder has been affected by the Corporate Insolvency and Governance Act 2020. The Act creates a new free-standing moratorium procedure,[87] although so far it has not been much used in practice.[88] This allows directors of a distressed company to apply to court for a payment holiday from its non-financial obligations,[89] which also restricts the ability of both secured and unsecured creditors of the company to take enforcement action against its assets.[90] The purpose of the procedure is to protect the company from creditors while it pursues a rescue

---

80 S Frisby, 'Not Quite Warp Factor 2 Yet? The Enterprise Act and Corporate Insolvency (Pt 1)' (2007) 22 Journal of International Banking and Finance Law 327; K van Zweiten, *Goode on Principles of Corporate Insolvency Law* (n 73) at [11–46].

81 Insolvency Act 1986, sch B1, paras 70 and 99.

82 Insolvency Act 1986, s 176ZA, reversing the position taken in *Re Leyland DAF Ltd* [2004] 1 AC 298.

83 Insolvency Act 1986, sch B1, para 70.

84 See Insolvency Act 1986, sch B1, para 36.

85 See *Corporate Finance* (n 74) at 319–320.

86 E.g. see *Graham Review into Pre-Pack Administration* (June 2014) para 7.36.

87 Inserting the new Part A1 into the Insolvency Act 1986.

88 Between 26 June 2020 and 31 January 2025 in England and Wales, 50 Moratoria were obtained only; see *Commentary – Monthly Insolvency Statistics January 2025*, <https://www.gov.uk/government/statistics/company-insolvencies-january-2025/commentary-company-insolvency-statistics-january-2025> accessed March 2025.

89 Insolvency Act 1986, s A18.

90 Insolvency Act 1986, s A20 (restrictions on insolvency proceedings); s A21 (restrictions on enforcement and legal proceedings); s A22 (restrictions on floating charge creditors crystallising the charge during the moratorium); s A23 (restrictions on creditors given security during the moratorium).

plan. Crucially, a company can invoke this procedure without any input from a floating charge holder. Further, creditor interests are protected during the procedure by the appointment of a 'monitor', an insolvency practitioner appointed to oversee the running of the company during the moratorium and monitor the chances of it being rescued as a going concern.[91] Moreover, the 'monitor' can dispose of floating charge assets during the moratorium other than for the purpose of discharging the secured debt, where it has permission to do so from a court that takes the view that the disposition will support the rescue of the company as a going concern.[92] In addition, the monitor can be chosen without any input from the floating charge creditor. This combination is potentially problematic for floating charge creditors, who thereby lose the oversight over a struggling business that they might otherwise have had through administration. In particular, monitors appointed without consultation with the floating charge holder might be more willing to use floating charge assets than a friendly administrator might have been.[93] Although floating charge holders can nevertheless claim substitute assets as part of the floating charge,[94] this will be of little comfort where floating charge assets are sold, for instance, to pay debts or to buy consumables. Lenders might respond to this danger by seeking contractual commitments to consult and provide additional information prior to the appointment of a monitor,[95] but this is only a partial solution. The net result is that floating charge holders are left with weaker priority and weaker control than they have ever had.

In sum, then, floating charges do not provide clear insolvency priority of the same kind as other security. The combination of the priority claims of HMRC and the 'prescribed part' scheme, combined with an administrator's and, in particular, a monitor's powers to use floating charge assets, means that a floating charge creditor cannot *ex ante* be sure what assets it will receive on insolvency. This makes lending against circulating stock riskier than secured lending of other kinds, potentially increasing the cost of credit for debtors with few fixed assets but valuable circulating stock like high street retail chains.[96]

---

91 Insolvency Act 1986, s A35.

92 Insolvency Act 1986, s A31.

93 Insolvency Act 1986, sch B1 para 70.

94 Insolvency Act 1986, s A31.

95 G Quenby, 'The Impact of the Corporate Insolvency and Governance Act 2020 and the Finance Act 2020 on Drafting Loan Documentation and Practice: Update' [2022] Journal of International Banking and Finance Law 269, 270–271.

96 See Davies and Gunaratna (n 71).

Characterising charges as fixed or floating

The statutory restrictions on the rights of floating charge holders have necessarily put further stress on the doctrinal distinction between the fixed and the floating charge. As Quenby argues, the recent reforms have created two new classes of persons incentivised to challenge whether charges drafted as fixed are actually floating: HMRC with its re-introduced preference, and monitors of moratoria, who can dispose of assets subject to a floating charge for reasons other than paying off the secured debt, but cannot do so with assets subject to fixed security.[97] Accordingly, the doctrinal boundary between fixed and floating charges is likely to matter more than ever.

How, then, does English law distinguish fixed from floating charges? As set out by Lord Millett in *Agnew v Commissioner of Inland Revenue*,[98] courts characterise charges by first looking at the rights and duties created by the purported charge, and then identifying the legal relationship created based on those rights and duties. Crucially, the mere fact a debtor and creditor have labelled their arrangement as a 'fixed' charge in a debenture is not conclusive: freedom of contract allows parties to determine their rights and duties, but not to legally categorise the relationship they have created. Accordingly, the court will characterise the charge based on the actual content of the rights and duties created. As outlined above, the process of characterising a charge as fixed or floating depends on the degree of restrictions, if any, placed on the debtor's ability to use the charged asset. To summarise, if the asset is *immediately* and unconditionally appropriated as security for performance of the obligation, the charge is fixed. However, if the charge's terms do not restrict the debtor's freedom to use the asset to this degree, it will be construed as floating. While Lord Millett's reasoning in *Agnew* was not binding on English courts, being a Privy Council case only, it was affirmed as representing English law by the House of Lords in *Re Spectrum Plus*.[99]

The distinction between fixed and floating charges has been a significant focus of academic commentary on floating charges, especially since the decisions in *Agnew* and *Re Spectrum*, and a range of criticisms have been made. Some issues relate to the scope of the decisions. *Re Spectrum* and *Agnew* both made it clear that it is not possible for a debtor company to grant a floating charge over rights to payment it has against customers if the terms of the charge allow it to draw upon the proceeds of those rights. However, uncertainties

---

97 Insolvency Act 1986, s A31. See too G Quenby, 'The Impact of the Corporate Insolvency and Governance Act 2020 and the Finance Act 2020 on Drafting Loan Documentation and Practice: Update' (n 95).

98 *Agnew v Commissioner for Inland Revenue* [2001] UKPC 28, [2001] 2 AC 710.

99 *Re Spectrum Plus Ltd* [2005] UKHL 41, [2005] 2 AC 680.

remain. For instance, what kinds of assets can be charged separately from their proceeds?[100] When a court is deciding whether a charge is fixed or floating, of what relevance is conduct outside of the terms of the debenture?[101] And how stringent does control of the debtor's use of the assets have to be for the charge to be fixed rather than floating?[102]

Reform: is the difference justified?

The fundamental issue in this area is, given their doctrinal differences, does anything justify the different treatment of fixed and floating charges upon insolvency? Why should the debtor's right of use affect how the floating charge creditor is treated upon insolvency?

An historical justification related specifically to debtors in the manufacturing industry, where charged assets included raw materials and manufactured products. Upon insolvency, it was thought that the employees of the firm – whose labour had improved the value of the raw materials – should have a claim for wages protected against floating charge creditors.[103] That reasoning today, though, is obviously of more limited application, given that it applies only to particular industries, and there are other protections given to employees in the insolvency setting.[104] More general arguments can be made, though. First, it can be argued that the law's recognition of floating charges, if left unchecked, would allow a single creditor to take all the assets of a debtor firm upon insolvency.[105] This might be seen to justify qualifying the priority of a floating charge holder. Secondly, floating charges allow the debtor to carry on trading with charged assets and so contract more unsecured debts with

---

[100] See *Goode & Gullifer* (n 45) at [4-11]–[4-20]; N Frome and K Gibbons, 'Spectrum – an End to the Conflict or the Signal for a New Campaign?' in J Getzler and J Payne (eds), *Company Charges:* Spectrum *and Beyond* (OUP 2006).

[101] E.g. *Re Beamtube Products* [2006] EWHC 486; *Re UKCloud Ltd (in liquidation)* [2024] EWHC 1259 (Ch), [56]-[72].

[102] E.g. *Re Avanti Communications Ltd* [2023] EWHC 940 (Ch). See also S Atherton and R Mokal, 'Charges over chattels: issues in the fixed/floating jurisprudence' (2005) 26 Company Lawyer 10; *Goode & Gullifer* (n 45) at [4-11]–[4-20]; N Frome and K Gibbons, 'Spectrum – an End to the Conflict or the Signal for a New Campaign?' in J Getzler and J Payne (eds), *Company Charges: Spectrum and Beyond* (OUP 2006).

[103] See R Goode, 'The Case for the Abolition of the Floating Charge', in J Getzler & J Payne (eds), *Company Charges: Spectrum and Beyond* (OUP 2006) 12–13; *Corporate Finance Law* (n 74) 314.

[104] See *Corporate Finance Law* (n 74) at 355.

[105] *Agnew* (n 98) at [8]–[9]. See too *Salomon v Salomon* [1897] AC 22, 53.

creditors who might be left with nothing on insolvency: this could be seen as justifying giving unsecured creditors a priority claim.[106]

A final possible explanation relates to the nature of equitable interests. As seen above, historically equitable interests were given priority upon insolvency because the insolvent had herself been limited in her use of the asset.[107] Just as she could not use assets subject to a trust or charge to pay her general debtors, nor could those debtors claim the asset upon insolvency. In this way, the restriction on free use requirement acted as a check on when equity would recognise priority claims that disrupted insolvency distribution. The principle thus protected unsecured creditors. The floating charge appears anomalous because equity treats the floating charge holder as having an equitable interest, despite the debtor retaining free use of the assets.[108] While Victorian judges pragmatically tempered basic doctrines of equity to facilitate creditors lending responsibly to limited liability corporations, this came at a cost.[109] Unsecured creditors of corporations were the casualty of this adaptation of the rules of equitable property, in being unable upon insolvency to claim assets that the debtor company could have used to pay unsecured debts. In other words, judges broke the normal rules of equity by recognising floating charges in a way that harmed the unsecured creditors of companies, forcing the legislature to step in to protect those creditors by other means.

On this reasoning, we can see the statutory qualifications to the priority that the floating charge confers as the price the legal system demands for breaking its own rules: rules that otherwise protect unsecured creditors.

The problem with the above views is that each of them essentially focusses on why a floating charge creditor should not have unqualified priority against unsecured creditors, or a subset of them. None explains why assets subject to floating charges, but not other types of security, should be subject to a priority claim by HMRC, or be available to an administrator or monitor to fund an administration or moratorium, or to claims for liquidation expenses, or subject to different anti-preference rules compared with security interests of other kinds.[110]

It is perhaps unsurprising then that academic criticism of the current position has been trenchant, with many advocating for the abolition of the floating charge as a distinct category. The point is put best by Richard Calnan.[111]

---

106 *Agnew* (n 98) at [10]. See, too, *Corporate Finance Law* (n 74) 314.

107 See text above from (n 10) to (n 17).

108 See text above from (n 15) to (n 25).

109 See text above from (n 25) to (n 38).

110 See Insolvency Act 1986, s 245.

111 R Calnan, 'Floating Charges: A Proposal for Reform' (2004) 19 Journal of International Banking and Financial Law 341.

Calnan views a floating charge in much the same terms as Nolan, essentially as a modified fixed charge, differentiated only by the debtor's power to trade with the assets.[112] Unsurprisingly then, Calnan argues that floating charges should be treated like fixed charges on insolvency, because he sees them as doctrinally similar. While he acknowledges that there might be good reason to give certain classes of claimant priority claims over secured creditors,[113] he argues that it is hard to see why those reasons justify priority claims over floating charge holders but not fixed charge holders. A similar conclusion was reached by the Financial Law Committee for Secured Transaction Reform,[114] while Roy Goode, Louise Gullifer and Jennifer Payne all argue in much the same terms,[115] the latter arguing that in the UK non-adjusting unsecured creditors are already sufficiently protected.[116] It is along these lines that Canada has reformed the law, abolishing the distinction between fixed and floating charges and providing priority claims for unpaid wages (up to a defined sum) over all security interests, and tax claims over all security interests other than mortgages of land.[117]

The argument perhaps seems all the more appealing given that the law already gives creditors so many other means of obtaining insolvency protection. Even if one were to accept that the legal system should prevent a single creditor from obtaining security over the whole of a debtor's assets, or that there are good reasons for treating floating charges differently, it is questionable whether the legal system as a whole gives effect to such policy concerns. Of course, creditors seeking security will take *fixed* charges over as many of a debtor's assets as possible, which can in practice give significant priority where the debtor has a substantial amount of fixed assets. As regards assets over which fixed charges cannot be taken, there are other potential workarounds, although these can increase transaction costs.

One such example is cash pooling arrangements. Take a case where a creditor takes a fixed charge over book debts, insisting that the proceeds are paid into a particular blocked bank account but, at the same time, the creditor wants to make another line of credit available to the debtor as the proceeds of the

---

112 See text above from (n 51) to the end of that section.

113 LA Bebchuk and JM Fried, 'The Uneasy Case for Secured Credit' (1996) 105 Yale Law Journal 857.

114 CLLS Financial Law Committee Secured Transactions Reform Discussion Paper 2: Fixed and Floating Charges on Insolvency (24/02/2014).

115 Goode (n 103); *Corporate Finance Law* (n 74) 318, 358–369.

116 Ibid 352–358.

117 For a summary, see L Gullifer and J Payne, 'The Characterisation of Fixed and Floating Charges' in Getzler and Payne (eds) *Company Charges: Spectrum and Beyond* (OUP 2006) 90–95.

book debts are paid into the blocked account. Obviously, if that credit were made available by allowing the debtor to draw on the very same account into which the book debts were paid, following *Spectrum* a court might well characterise the charge on the book debts as floating rather than fixed. However, if the creditor instead were to provide the credit through a separate bank account, with another bank, there would be no such risk. In *Re Keenan*,[118] the High Court of Ireland recognised that in such a case the creditor could take a fixed charge over the book debts, and *Re Keenan* itself was approved of in *Agnew* and *Spectrum*. Accordingly, by using two bank accounts, a creditor might safely take a fixed charge over receivables, while at the same time advancing further credit to the debtor. Such an arrangement would be economically equivalent to the arrangement in *Spectrum*, but would allow the creditor to take a fixed charge.

A second workaround for financiers seeking to avoid the effect of the decisions in *Agnew* and *Spectrum* involves outright assignment. Since those decisions, financiers who in the past would have lent against the security of a charge over book debts instead extend finance simply by 'buying' outright assignments of book debts. Such arrangements do not involve the creation of a charge and so do not need to be registered.

Indeed, there is some suggestion that following the reforms of 2020 such workarounds will become more and more common. Quenby has suggested that creditors might increasingly wish to structure their secured lending outside of traditional debentures using chattel mortgages and pledges, as well as assignments in order to protect against recharacterisation risks.[119] The argument is that courts are willing, within a single debenture, to recharacterise charges labelled as 'fixed' as 'floating' but are less willing to do so for security interests created separately. That creates an incentive for creditors to make greater use of security devices outside of traditional debentures.

However, it should be emphasised that the existence of these workarounds does not make the question of reform of the floating charge academic only. Some kinds of borrowers will struggle to offer security to a creditor through the devices discussed above – especially borrowers with large circulating tangible inventory and few fixed assets. In effect, then, the restrictions placed by statute on floating charge creditors target the ability of those classes of borrowers to raise finance. Viewed in that light, it is hard to see what sensible policy the restrictions achieve.

---

[118] [1986] BCLC 242.

[119] G Quenby, 'Back to the Future – Old Legal Techniques for Modern Transactions' in Recovery Magazine (Autumn 2021) 16–18.

CONCLUSION

The floating charge in English law is filled with apparent contradictions. As a matter of doctrine, it is a kind of security, yet one which gives much more limited insolvency protection than security of other kinds. It is an equitable property right, yet one which does not prevent the holder of the charged assets from trading with them for its own benefit. Nevertheless, while creditors are increasingly likely to look to other ways of ensuring insolvency priority, the device will probably remain popular. The floating charge is valuable for lenders seeking to meet regulatory capital adequacy requirements – in that lending against such charges is treated as 'asset backed'.[120] Further, while creditors will seek fixed charges wherever possible, the floating charge remains the best device for ensuring a priority claim over circulating tangible stock – and the power to appoint an administrator remains useful too.[121]

The final point to be emphasised is that the continued clampdown on the floating charge looks strange. English law has for centuries treated equitable property rights as effectively conferring priority upon insolvency but has protected unsecured creditors through restrictive requirements on when such rights arise.[122] In a rightly celebrated article, Roy Goode suggested that equity, in effect, undermined insolvency regimes by conflating property and obligation – by giving what should have been unsecured creditors' priority claims.[123] However, there is a deeper point here that is often missed. Equity's willingness to recognise 'property rights' in any given asset has always depended on that asset not being at the free use of its owner – this is a policy limit on the law's recognition of equitable interests designed to protect third parties such as unsecured creditors. It is this which prevents the effects of equity on insolvency distribution from being arbitrary and might be seen as justifying some limitation on a floating charge holder's priority. What makes any qualification seem anomalous is the simultaneous increasing willingness of English law to allow the creation of insolvency priority without limiting the debtor's use of any particular asset, as in cases involving rights of use and commercial trusts[124] and netting arrangements,[125] especially where financial collateral is

---

120 See J Benjamin, *Financial Law* (OUP 2007) at [17.41].

121 See *Corporate Finance Law* (n 74) 319–320.

122 See text above from (n 11) to (n 17) and (n 107) to the end of paragraph.

123 R Goode, 'Ownership and Obligation in Commercial Transactions' (1987) 103 LQR 433.

124 See n 16.

125 E.g. See *Lomas v JFB Firth Rixson Inc* [2012] EWCA Civ 419; P Peach, 'The Value of Financial Market Insolvency Safe Harbours' [2016] OJLS 1.

involved.[126] Whether these developments are desirable or not – at least outside of certain contexts[127] – is an open question,[128] but these wider developments make the qualifications imposed on floating charges look difficult to explain.

ACKNOWLEDGEMENT

I am grateful to Mitchell Cleaver and the editors for their very helpful comments and suggestions.

---

126 Financial Collateral Arrangements (No 2) Regulations 2003 (SI 2003/3226, amended by SI 2009/2462 and SI 2010/2993).

127 For an overview of the issues specifically concerning Financial Collateral, see *Goode and Gullifer* (n 45) Chapter 6.

128 For a view that insolvency priority is generally only justified where security restricts the debtor's use of the secured assets, see R Mokal, *Corporate Insolvency Law: Theory and Practice* (OUP 2005) 179–186. For counterarguments, see Peach (n 125) and Benjamin (n 120).

3. The evolution of floating charges in Ghana, Kenya and Nigeria

· **Chike Emedosi**

INTRODUCTION

This chapter traces, for the first time, the history and evolution of the law of floating charges in a selection of common law jurisdictions in Africa, using Ghana, Kenya and Nigeria as focus jurisdictions.[1] Much of the existing literature tends to conflate the law in these jurisdictions with English law. It assumes that they automatically received the floating charge from England owing to colonisation and that their laws on floating charges have followed English law ever since. As a result, the literature has mostly been written in the shadow of English law.[2] This approach misses the opportunity to examine the local circumstances and jurisprudence in the focus jurisdictions in order to (i) determine the extent to which the English rules on floating charges were received in the focus jurisdictions and (ii) ascertain how the laws in the jurisdictions have evolved in terms of their similarity to, and divergence from, English law.

The chapter seeks to remedy this by examining the law in light of the local jurisprudence in the focus jurisdictions. It makes two main findings through this approach. First, it finds that the principles of the floating charge as laid

---

1 These jurisdictions are arguably the most prominent common law systems in Africa; hence the focus on them.

2 See e.g. Gregory Esangbedo, "Conceptual or Pragmatic? Differentiating Floating Charges from Unitary Security Interests under Nigerian Law" (2022) 66(3) JAL 491 (particularly on the discussion of the nature of the floating charge and priority rules); Emuobo Emudainohwo, "A Critical Analysis of the Nature and Effectiveness of a Floating Charge as a Security in Nigerian Law" (2021) 12 Beijing Law Review 191. It is not intended to make light of the quality of the cited papers. On the contrary, the papers are insightful, and their findings have helped inform arguments in the present chapter. The intention, however, is to shine a light on an aspect of the analysis in the literature that seems to have been ignored.

down in *Re Panama, New Zealand and Australian Royal Mail Co*[3] and subsequent cases were received in the focus jurisdictions despite the limitations in the colonial statutes. Furthermore, although the subsequent developments made by English case law to the floating charge were received in the focus jurisdictions, the reception of statutory reforms was restricted by local circumstances. Part one of this chapter, which focusses on the pre-independence era evolution of the floating charge, discusses this finding.

Part two focusses on the post-independence era and discusses the second finding. It demonstrates that while the focus jurisdictions' recent partial adoption of functional approaches to security rights has incorporated notable deviations from English law, the lack of coordination between these regimes and the English fragmented regime that was received in the jurisdictions creates problems in the operation of floating charges in the focus jurisdictions.

PRE-INDEPENDENCE ERA

English law has undoubtedly played a significant role in the development of law in the focus jurisdictions. This is especially true in relation to the law of floating charges, the history of which dates back to the jurisdictions' colonial roots. The focus jurisdictions were former UK colonies, and as was the practice at the time, Western powers that colonised Africa came with their laws.[4] In the case of the focus jurisdictions, English law was introduced in two ways.

First, English law was introduced directly by legislation in the UK. This method of introduction required the relevant legislation to have an express provision (or provisions) intending that the legislation be extended to a colony.[5] An example was the Copyright Act of 1911, which was extended to British colonies, including the focus jurisdictions, by virtue of Order in Council No. 12 of June 1912. This mode of introduction was rare[6] and is of little relevance to this study, as none of the extending statutes directly related to the floating charge.

The second method by which English laws were introduced was through the received laws. Under this method, the common law, the doctrines of equity and the statutes of general application that were in force in England at the date a colony was constituted were introduced in the colony by local legislation. This differs from the first method because it arises from local legislation (i.e.

3 *Re Panama, New Zealand and Australian Royal Mail Co* (1870) 5 Ch.App. 318.

4 William Blackstone, *Commentaries on the Laws of England* (9th edn, 1783) Vol 1, 107–08.

5 UK Colonial Laws Validity Act 1865, s 1.

6 Kenneth Roberts-Wray, "Adaptation of Imported Law in Africa" (1960) 4(2) JAL 66, 69.

the reception statute). The reception statutes for the focus jurisdictions were the Gold Coast Supreme Court Ordinance of 1876 (Ghana), the Kenya Colony Order in Council 1921[7] and the Nigeria Supreme Court Ordinance 1914.[8] This method of introduction is more relevant to this study and will therefore be examined in the following discussion.

Section 14 of Ghana's 1876 Ordinance provided that:

> the common law, the doctrines of equity, and the statutes of general application which were in force in England … on 24 July, 1874, shall be in force within the jurisdiction of the Court.

There were very similar reception provisions for Kenya and Nigeria, although different cut-off dates applied. Kenya's cut-off date was 12 August 1897,[9] reflecting the date the East Africa Colony was constituted.[10] The cut-off date

---

[7] Kenya's reception statute dated back to 1897, when the East Africa Order in Council 1897 was introduced to apply to the East Africa Protectorate, an area that later became the Colony and Protectorate of Kenya in 1920. The 1921 Order superseded the 1897 Order. See generally Eugene Cotran, "The Development and Reform of the Law in Kenya" (1983) 27 JAL 42.

[8] The history of reception statutes in Nigeria is long and complex. It dates back to 1863 when Ordinance 3 of that year introduced English law into what was then the Lagos Settlement, a jurisdiction located in the southern part of present-day Nigeria. In 1874, the British constituted a unified colonial administration, comprising Lagos and the Gold Coast, under the name the "Gold Coast Colony". The Gold Coast Supreme Court Ordinance of 1876 was subsequently enacted to introduce English law to the unified "Gold Coast Colony". In other words, the 1876 Ordinance superseded the former Lagos Ordinance of 1863. This appears to explain why the 1876 Ordinance has been referred to as "Nigeria and the Gold Coast Supreme Court Ordinance" in some literature. See e.g. Julius Lewin, "The Recognition of Native Law and Custom in British Africa" (1938) 20 Journal of Comparative Legislation and International Law 16, at notes 1 and 4. Such reference is technically not correct for the following reasons. The British dissolved the union in 1886 and incorporated Lagos into a new Protectorate of Southern Nigeria in February 1906. Following the amalgamation of Southern and Northern Nigeria on 1 January 1914, the 1914 Supreme Court Ordinance was introduced to make the received English law applicable in the whole of Nigeria. See generally TO Elias, *The Nigerian Legal System* (2nd edn, Routledge & Kegan Paul Limited 1963) 17f; RB Bening, "Integration and Disintegration in British Colonial West Africa: The Case of the Gold Coast and Lagos 1874–1886" (2009) 1 Ghana Journal of Geography 1, 2ff.

[9] Kenya Colony Order in Council 1921, s 4(2).

[10] See discussion in note 7 above.

in Nigeria was 1 January 1900,[11] reflecting the date the Southern Nigeria and Northern Nigeria colonies were constituted before their amalgamation in 1914.[12]

While the meanings of the terms "common law" and "doctrines of equity" were relatively straightforward, the interpretation of the phrase "statutes of general application which were in force in England" attracted much judicial attention. Owing to limited space, a detailed analysis in this chapter will not be possible.[13] However, in Nigeria, the two criteria suggested by Osborne CJ in *Attorney General v John Holt & Co Ltd*[14] gained popularity in the literature.[15] Osborne CJ observed on page 21 that there is a "strong likelihood" that a statute applicable (a) by all civil or criminal courts in England and (b) to all classes of the community in England as of the cut-off date would be held as a statute of general application.[16] This approach has been considered "faulty", and subsequent cases have held statutes applied only by certain courts as statutes of general application in England.[17] Unfortunately, the issue has remained unsettled, and the judicial approach to the interpretation has been inconsistent.[18] The effect of this uncertainty on the present study is minimal since, as will be

---

[11] Nigeria Supreme Court Ordinance 1914, s 14.

[12] See discussion in note 8 above.

[13] For discussion from Nigeria's perspective, see AEW Park, *The Sources of Nigerian Law* (African University Press/Sweet & Maxwell 1963) 24ff; AO Obilade, *The Nigerian Legal System* (Sweet & Maxwell 1979) 72ff.

[14] (1910) 2 NLR 1.

[15] The principles were cited with approval in TO Elias, *The Nigerian Legal System* (2nd edn, Routledge & Kegan Paul Limited 1963) 19 and followed by later case law. See e.g. *Braithwaite v Folarin* (1938) 4 WACA 76; *Lawal v Younan* [1961] 1 ANLR 245.

[16] A leading case on this subject in Kenya, *I v I* [1971] EA 278, supported the second part of the test: that a statute would be of general application if it was applicable to all subjects of the Crown as of the cut-off date.

[17] See Obilade (n 13) 72f, and the cases discussed in the text.

[18] For instance, it was held in *Re Estate of James Sholu* (1932) 11 NLR 37 that the Land Transfer Act of 1897 was not of general application because it applied only in England and not in the rest of the United Kingdom (i.e Ireland and Scotland). This decision was rejected by the West Africa Court of Appeal in *Young v Abina* (1940) 6 WACA 180, where the court held that "[t]he words 'of general application' are used with reference to the matter of the statutes and not only geographically" and suggested that "England is the test of geographical generality". Seven years later, the same court in *Okpaku v Okpaku* [1947] WACA 2491 adopted the view it had rejected in *Young*. The view of the court in *Okpaku* was later considered *per incuriam* by the Nigerian Federal Supreme Court in *Lawal v Younan* [1961] 1 ANLR 245, 256.

seen below, the relevant law concerning the floating charge that was caught by the reception statutes was mainly case law based on the doctrines of equity.[19]

In light of the reception provisions, it would appear at first sight that the floating charge was recognised in the focus jurisdictions early in their colonisation. The charge was a creation of English equity and was formally accepted in 1870 following the Chancery decision in *Re Panama, New Zealand and Australian Royal Mail Co* (1870) 5 Ch App.[20] This was an Appeal Court case involving a steamship company that issued mortgage debentures, charging all its "undertaking" and "all sums of money arising therefrom". Giffard LJ held that the term "undertaking" meant all the property of the company, both present and future. He went on to establish the three fundamental features of the floating charge: (a) that the charge enabled the company to freely deal with its property in the ordinary course of business; (b) that such freedom would cease and the charge would attach to all the company's property on the occurrence of a crystallisation event, i.e. the company's winding up or the enforcement of the charge; and (c) that the occurrence of a crystallisation event entitled the charge holder to realise the security over the company's property in priority to general creditors.[21]

However, the application of the received laws was limited in two ways. The first limitation could be gleaned from the provisions themselves: their application was subject to a cut-off date, and it appeared that only the laws in force as of the relevant cut-off date were received under the statutes.[22] The second limitation concerned the interaction between the received laws and

---

[19] The single exception to this is the Preferential Payments in Bankruptcy Amendment Act 1897, which was a statute introduced to reform the floating charge but did not extend to Scotland (see s 5 of the Act). The Act was caught by the reception statutes of Kenya and Nigeria in that it predates their cut-off dates. See discussion below.

[20] Some writers have associated the floating charge with the Roman general hypothec. See e.g. WW Buckland, *A Text-book of Roman Law from Augustus to Justinian* (3rd edn, rev by P Stein (1963) 475; HLE Verhagen, "*Ius Honorarium*, Equity and Real Security: Parallel Lines of Legal Development" in E Koops and WJ Zwalve (eds), *Law and Equity: Approaches in Roman Law and Common Law* (2014) at 135ff. However, while there are some similarities, there are notable differences too – see e.g. ADJ MacPherson, "The 'Pre-History' of Floating Charges in Scots Law" in J Hardman and ADJ MacPherson (eds), *Floating Charges in Scotland: New Perspectives and Current Issues* (EUP, 2022) 21ff.

[21] *Re Panama* (n 3).

[22] Some qualification is necessary here. The wording of the reception statutes was not entirely clear as to whether the cut-off dates applied only to "the statutes of general application" and not to all three laws (i.e. including "the common law" and "the doctrines of equity"). See below for a discussion of this issue.

local circumstances. The English recognised that not all English laws were transplantable into the colonies. The local circumstances of a colony may have made the reception of the laws difficult or impossible, in which case the colonial courts were empowered to modify or exclude the application of such laws as appropriate (see discussion below). As such, it was common to make the received laws applicable only so far as local circumstances permitted.

Further scrutiny of these limitations is required to determine (a) whether the new security (i.e. the floating charge) as introduced in *Re Panama* was received in the focus jurisdictions when the case was decided and (b) the extent to which subsequent judicial advancements and statutory reforms made in England to the floating charge were received.

The Reception of Floating Charges in the Focus Jurisdictions

Re Panama was decided before the three cut-off dates (i.e. 24 July 1874 for Ghana, 12 August 1897 for Kenya and 1 January 1900 for Nigeria). As such, the limitation by date did not apply to prevent the reception of it, and thus the floating charge, in the colonies.[23] The following discussion therefore focusses on the limitation by local circumstances.

Kenya's reception provision had a proviso that stated that "the said common law [sic] doctrines of equity and the statutes of general application shall be in force in the Colony … subject to such qualifications as local circumstances render necessary".[24] In contrast, the reception statute for Ghana provided that "[a]ll Imperial laws declared to extend or apply to the jurisdiction of the Courts shall be in force only as the limits of the … local circumstances permit".[25] The effect of these limiting provisions manifested in several cases, two of which are highlighted below.

In *Nyali Bridge Ltd v Attorney-General* (Kenya), the Court of Appeal found the common law rule requiring the grant of a royal franchise of tolls to be made by matter of record (such as charter or letters patent) to be unnecessary in the Kenya Protectorate.[26] The court reasoned that the English Crown was not sovereign in the Protectorate, and as such the formality would not be

23 Even if *Re Panama* was decided after the cut-off dates, it is not clear if the limitation by date would have still applied given the ambiguity in the wording of the reception statutes as pointed out earlier. See below for more discussion on this.

24 Kenya Colony Order in Council 1921, s 4(2).

25 Gold Coast Supreme Court Ordinance of 1876, s 17. See s 17 of Nigeria Supreme Court Ordinance 1914 for a similar provision.

26 *Nyali Bridge Ltd v Attorney-General* [1956] 1 QB 1.

applicable.[27] In *Halliday v Alapatira*[28] (Nigeria), Smith J stated that the UK Bankruptcy Act 1869 was not in force in the Colony of Lagos. While he did not give any reason for the statement, it has been observed that applying the Act in the colony would have been impracticable since the "special administrative" condition and "judicial machinery" required for its operation were not available in the colony.[29]

The relevant question, therefore, is whether the focus jurisdictions had the necessary conditions in place, at the time of the ruling in *Re Panama*, for the effective operation of the floating charge. To answer that, it is necessary to consider whether the colonies had a legal framework that enabled the incorporation of limited liability companies. That is because the circumstances and principles on which the decision in *Re Panama* was based suggested that, on a narrow view, the floating charge was available only to companies, or that in practical terms it would be most relevant for companies and therefore having such a framework was arguably a precondition to the operation of the charge at the time.[30] Another necessary condition was whether the administrative structures for registering limited liability companies were present in the colonies. The existence of the legal framework needed to be complemented by the presence of an administrative system that oversaw company registrations and management.

Both conditions appear to have been in place at the time the colonies were constituted. First, the UK Companies Act of 1862, which provided a legal framework for the registration and administration of companies, was received in the colonies as a statute of general application.[31] Secondly, while most of the companies that operated when the colonies were constituted were foreign companies,[32] the possibility of statutory incorporation indicates that the local

---

[27] Ibid, 16–17.

[28] *Halliday v Alapatira* (1881) 1 NLR 1.

[29] Park (n 13) 32; Obilade (n 13) 78.

[30] The principles of floating charges as laid down in *Re Panama*, as well as the conditions for their application, were premised on a company acting as the grantor. For instance, the concept of "borrowing on the undertaking" was introduced by the Companies Clauses Consolidation Act 1845, see s 38, for use by companies incorporated under specific Acts.

[31] See e.g. Ike Oraegbunam and CJ Ubanyionwu, "Examining Some Gains and Pitfalls of Nigeria's Companies and Allied Matters Act: Urgent Need for Review" (2019) 1(2) IRLJ 48, 49.

[32] These were mainly companies chartered by the English government. See e.g. the British United Africa Company, formed in 1879, and the Imperial British East Africa Company, formed in 1888.

legislatures were able to pass special Acts incorporating local companies with borrowing powers.[33]

The conclusion that can be drawn from the foregoing is that local circumstances would not have made the operation of the floating charge in the colonies impossible. Moreover, trade and commerce were prevalent in the colonies at the time the colonies were constituted, and there was evidence that forms of security with familiar features existed in the colonies in the pre-colonial era.[34]

Therefore, neither the cut-off dates nor the local circumstances limitations applied to prevent the reception of the decision in *Re Panama*, and thus the floating charge, in the focus jurisdictions.

The Reception of Subsequent Floating Charge Developments

This subsection is concerned with the reception of subsequent refinements and reforms made to floating charges under English law. As noted earlier, the application of the received law was subject to a cut-off date in the reception statutes. The reception provision for Ghana (i.e. s 14 of the 1876 Ordinance) has been cited above and was identical to Nigeria's provision (i.e. s 14 of the 1914 Ordinance).[35] Kenya's reception provision had a similar effect to Ghana's and Nigeria's. However, it was worded differently, providing that the jurisdiction of the Supreme Court and subordinate courts was to be exercised in accordance with "the substance of the Common law, the doctrines of equity and the statutes of general application in force in England on 12 August 1897".[36] This suggests that any judicial development or reforms made to a received law after a cut-off date did not apply in the colonies unless such development or reform was effected through another piece of local legislation or extended through English legislation.

The wording of the reception provisions attracted much debate as to whether the cut-off date applied only to the "statutes of general application" or whether it also extended to the common law and doctrines of equity. If it applied to all three laws, it meant that developments involving the floating charge in

---

[33] The company statutes that were received by the colonies allowed the formation of limited liability companies through special Acts of Parliament.

[34] The literature makes references to pledges and mortgages as existing even before the jurisdictions' colonisation. See e.g. RJH Pogucki, *Gold Coast Land Tenure* (Accra 1955) Vol 2, at 38 and 90; NA Ollennu, *Principles of Customary Land Law in Ghana* (Sweet & Maxwell London 1962) 94–107, 122–123; SNC Obi, *The Ibo Law of Property* (Butterworths London 1963) 120ff, 145–146.

[35] Nigeria's reception provision is identical to Ghana's. See Nigeria's 1914 Ordinance, s 14.

[36] Kenya Colony Order in Council 1921, s 4(2).

England (either by case law or statute) which post-dated the cut-off date had no automatic effect in the former colonies. For instance, the cut-off date of 24 July 1874 in Ghana would mean that the improvements introduced in *Moor v Anglo-Italian Bank* (1878)[37] and *Re Hamilton's Windsor Ironworks Co* (1879)[38] regarding the ranking of the floating charge with a fixed security were not received in the former colony. Both cases established that a fixed security taken with notice of a prior floating charge ranked ahead of the floating charge. Conversely, the law as determined in these cases would be received in colonial Kenya and Nigeria since the cases were decided before their cut-off dates (i.e. 12 August 1897 for Kenya and 1 January 1900 for Nigeria).

Despite its significance, the question of whether the cut-off date applied to the common law and the doctrines of equity was never resolved. Professor Seidman provided an interesting analysis of this subject in an article published in 1969, suggesting that the cut-off date was intended to apply to all the received laws.[39] His conclusion revolves around the information he gathered from correspondence between relevant colonial officials before the Gold Coast Supreme Court Ordinance 1876 was formulated. However, the correspondence Seidman cites in support of his argument does not offer a definitive statement that an expansive application was intended, and some material appears to lend credence to the contrary. For example, Seidman cites the following on page 48:

> Imperial Law in force in the colony should be limited to the Common Law and Statute law of general application in force at the date of the Charter. It is necessary to draw the line there or the greatest confusion will arise, as to what *statutes* are repealed or altered in England, and at what time new *English statutes* should operate in the colony. The Law of England at the date of the Charter is quite sufficient and if necessary the colony can improve upon it by local legislation following any *new Imperial acts*. [Italics have been added for emphasis]

The various references to statutes after the first statement, in justifying a cut-off date, suggest that the cut-off might have been intended for statutes only. It is significant that no such reference was made to the common law. The reference to "Imperial acts" further strengthens this view. "Imperial acts" was a term more commonly associated with English Acts of Parliament than with the common law and principles of equity.[40] Interestingly, most notable African

---

[37] *Moor v Anglo-Italian Bank* (10) Ch D 681.

[38] *Re Hamilton's Windsor Ironworks Co* (12) Ch D 707.

[39] RB Seidman, "A Note on the Construction of the Gold Coast Reception Statute" (1967) 13(1) JAL 45. See also AN Allott, *New Essays in African Law* (Butterworths 1970) 63ff.

[40] Park (n 13) 37 (suggesting that the word "Imperial" was mostly a reference to the Imperial Parliament at the time the reception provisions were first drafted

authors have argued that the cut-off date applied to the statutes only.[41] Some noted, in respect of the Gold Coast Supreme Court Ordinance, that the language and punctuation suggested that the cut-off date applied only to the statutes.[42]

The wording of the reception provisions that were subsequently enacted for regional High Courts in Nigeria suggests that the intention was for the cut-off date to apply to the statutes only.[43] The various High Court Laws of the regions contained reception provisions that had clearer wording on the subject. The High Court Law of Northern States listed each of the received laws in separate paragraphs, and the cut-off date was applied to the statutes only.[44] The High Court Law of Western States received only the English common law and the principles of equity. As a result, it had no cut-off date.[45] In relation to the Federal Territory of Lagos, s 2(1) of the provision was worded as follows: "the common law of England and the doctrines of equity, together with the statutes of general application that were in force in England on 1 January, 1900".[46] The use of a comma and the conjunction "together with" (rather than "and" as used in the 1914 Supreme Court Ordinance) implies that the received laws were not

---

and noting that "certainly the phrases 'Imperial common law' and 'Imperial equity' have never existed"). See also Obilade (n 13) 80. Statutes have also used the term "Imperial Acts" in reference to enactments. See e.g. the New South Wales Imperial Acts Application Act 1969; the Australia Imperial Acts Application Act 1980.

41 See e.g. WCE Daniels, *The Common Law in West Africa* (Butterworths London 1964) 122–124; Elias (n 15) 21; Obilade (n 13) 70f. In an earlier article, Elias suggested that post-cut-off English court decisions were received automatically in the colonies, including those that extended the scope of pre-cut-off decisions, but only to the extent that the post-cut-off decision was not based on a post-cut-off statute or enactment. See TO Elias, "Colonial Courts and the Doctrine of Judicial Precedent" (1955) 18(4) MLR 356, 369f.

42 Editors, *Gold Coast Assize* (1884) Vol 2, No 5, at page 3. See also WB Harvey, "The Evolution of Ghana Law Since Independence" (1962) 27(4) Law and Contemporary Problems 581, 588.

43 Nigeria became a fully federal state under the Lyttleton Constitution of 1954, comprising three regions (i.e. Eastern, Northern and Western regions) and the Federal Territory of Lagos. The constitution shared legislative powers between the regional and central governments. It established a Supreme Court at the federal level and a high court for each of the regions and Lagos. The high courts exercised jurisdiction as vested under their respective regional legislatures. See Elias (n 15) 171.

44 High Court Law (No 8 of 1955), s 28.

45 Law of England Application Law (WRN Laws 1959, Cap 4), s 3.

46 Law (Miscellaneous Provisions) Law (Lagos Laws 1973, Cap 65), s 2(1).

referred to as a group, and the cut-off date applied to the statutes alone.[47] The conclusion that can be drawn from the foregoing analysis is that the cut-off date might have been intended to apply to the statutes only, and post-cut-off English court decisions in relation to the floating charge were received.

Yet even if the cut-off date applied only to the statutes, that mode of application was problematic. It implied that the colonies would be stuck with the statutes as they were at the cut-off date. Any legislative reforms made in England after the cut-off date had no effect unless the reform was expressly (or by necessary implication) extended to the colony by English legislation or received through local legislation.[48] This was particularly problematic with the floating charge as reforms introduced to address the excesses of the charge[49] were mostly statutory, and they generally came into force after the cut-off dates.

The first such reform was the Preferential Payments in Bankruptcy Amendment Act 1897. Sections 2 and 3 of that Act gave certain claims, which had been granted preferential status under the Preferential Payments in Bankruptcy Act 1888, priority over the claims of a floating charge holder during liquidation or receivership.[50] The 1897 Act was a direct response to the perceived injustice attributed to the Chancery decision in *Richards v Overseer of Kidderminster*.[51] It was held in that case that the preference granted to employees and the Crown under the 1888 Act did not extend to floating charges – meaning that the floating chargee had priority over unsecured creditors (preferential or not) in insolvency.[52] The reform did not apply in Ghana since the 1897 Act was enacted on 15 July 1897, after Ghana's 24 July 1874 cut-off date. However, it seemed to apply in Kenya and Nigeria.[53] The last statement

---

47 The wording is retained under s 32 of the Interpretation Act 1964 (Nigeria), a federal law that is still in force today. It should be noted, however, that the High Court Law of Eastern States adopted wording that is identical to the controversial wording used under the Supreme Court Ordinance. See High Court Law (EN Laws 1963, Cap 61), s 15. See generally Park (n 13) 20ff.

48 Allot (n 39) 63.

49 These problems related to the concerns that the floating charge holder was too powerful – a floating charge could encompass all the assets of the company upon enforcement, leaving nothing for general creditors. See e.g. the opinion of Lord Macnaghten in *Salomon v Salomon & Co Ltd* [1897] AC 22, 53.

50 These claims included accrued employees' wages, pension contributions, holiday pay and certain taxes accruing to the Crown. For a discussion of the current position on this subject in the focus jurisdictions and England see below.

51 *Richards v Overseer of Kidderminster* [I896] 2 Ch 2 12.

52 See generally Kayode Akintola, *Creditor Treatment in Corporate Insolvency Law* (Edward Elgar Publishing 2020) paras 4.15–4.18.

53 The Act pre-dated the cut-off dates for Kenya (i.e. 12 August 1897) and Nigeria (i.e. 1 January 1900).

is debatable because it is unclear if the 1897 Act can be regarded as a "statute of general application" as contemplated under the reception provisions, given that the Act does not extend to Scotland.[54]

Two other key statutory reforms introduced later are noteworthy. The first was the Companies Act 1900, in which s 14 introduced a requirement for floating charges (and certain other charges) granted by a company to be registered within 21 days after the date of their creation.[55] The second was the Companies Act 1907, in which s 13 introduced a rule that allowed liquidators to set aside floating charges granted within three months before the commencement of winding-up proceedings, except where a new advance was given.[56] Given their cut-off dates, these two reforms were not automatically received in Ghana, Kenya and Nigeria.[57]

The three statutory reforms were subsequently re-enacted in the Companies (Consolidation) Act 1908, then the Companies Act 1929 and later the Companies Act 1948. It was not until the enactment of the Companies Ordinance 1912 in Nigeria (the first locally enacted company statute in Nigeria), which was generally a transplant of the English Companies (Consolidation) Act 1908,[58] that the reforms were introduced to the country.[59] The same is true for Kenya.[60] Ghana was, however, not as responsive. Its first Companies Ordinance of 1906 was based on the UK Companies Act 1862 and remained unchanged until 1963, five years after its independence.[61] The 1963 amendment was mostly based on the UK Companies Act 1948.[62] As such, the statutory reforms were not adopted in Ghana until 1963.

This part has made two main findings in relation to the pre-independence evolution of the floating charge in the focus jurisdictions. First, it has shown that the floating charge as laid down in *Re Panama* was received in the former

---

[54] See s 5 of the 1897 Act. See also above for a discussion of the issues related to the definition of the phrase "statutes of general application".

[55] For a discussion of the current position of the law on this subject in the focus jurisdictions and England see below.

[56] See now Insolvency Act 1986, s 245(3), which has extended the relevant period from 3 to 12 months.

[57] In respect to Nigeria, the 1900 Act was enacted on 8 August 1900 and therefore post-dated Nigeria's cut-off date of 1 January 1900.

[58] LCB Gower, *Final Report of the Commission of Enquiry into the Working and Administration of the Present Company Law of Ghana* (Accra, 1961) para 15.

[59] The 1912 Ordinance only applied to Lagos. It was extended to the rest of Nigeria by the Companies Amendment and Extension Act 1917 following the amalgamation of Southern and Northern Nigeria in 1914.

[60] See the Companies Ordinance 1921 (Kenya).

[61] Gower's Report (n 58) para 15.

[62] Ibid.

colonies despite the limitations of the reception provisions. The second finding reveals that though the subsequent developments made by case law to the floating charge were received in the former colonies, the reception of statutory reforms was delayed until the reforms were adopted by local legislation. The next part of the chapter focusses on the post-independence evolution of the floating charge.

POST-INDEPENDENCE ERA

The focus jurisdictions attained independence from colonial rule on 6 March 1957 (Ghana), 12 December 1963 (Kenya) and 1 October 1960 (Nigeria). This, however, did not necessarily result in a legal revolution, as their pre-independence body of laws was largely unchanged. For instance, the reception clauses were retained by post-independence statutes.[63] This means that the independent systems inherited the English laws on floating charges received before independence.[64] Also, the jurisdictions retained the English legal system of divided property ownership, which recognises two property rights: equitable and legal. This makes it conceptually possible for the courts to refer to and adopt English judicial decisions.[65] Hence, the floating charge in the focus jurisdictions remains equitable.[66]

However, a major change initiated by independence is to be found in the hierarchy of the new legal order in the systems, in which local enactments

---

[63] See Ghana Courts Act 1960, s 154(4) – the Act repealed the Court Ordinance 1935 (the reception statute that succeeded the Supreme Court Ordinance of 1876) but provided in s 154(4) that the repeal shall not affect the continued application of the statutes of general application which were in force in England on 24 July, 1874; Ghana Republican Constitution 1960, art 40 and the Interpretation Act 1960, s 17(1) – both were to the effect that the English common law and doctrines of equity continued to be part of the law of Ghana. For Nigeria, see the Interpretation Act 1964, s 32 – preserving the reception provision; for Kenya, see Eugene Cotran, "The Development and Reform of the Law in Kenya" (1983) 27(1) JAL 42, 47. The various Independence Acts of the systems, however, abolished the direct extension of English statutes passed on or after the independence date of each system. See Ghana Independence Act 1957, s 1(a); Kenya Independence Act 1963, s 1(2); Nigeria Independence Act 1960, s 1(2).

[64] See discussion in the part above.

[65] In Nigeria, for example, it has been suggested that English decisions were highly regarded and were at a time "slavishly" followed by local courts. See BO Nwabueze, *A Machinery of Justice in Nigeria* (Butterworths 1963) 37.

[66] See discussion below.

became the principal sources of law.[67] English laws, and other foreign laws, were made subordinate to local enactments and only operated in areas not dealt with by local enactments. This is relevant for the present study because, as will be seen, the legal framework underpinning the floating charge in the focus jurisdictions is primarily statutory, unlike English law which is based mainly on case law.[68] The other significant change is that the courts became independent and were no longer considered to be bound by English precedents.[69] These changes were significant, as they allowed the local parliament and courts to formulate policies and laws that suited the needs of the relevant society.

The various company law enactments in the focus jurisdictions are the primary sources of law for floating charges after their independence. These laws have been amended on different occasions, with the latest enactments being the Companies Act 2019 (Ghana), Companies Act 2015 (Kenya) and Companies and Allied Matters Act 2020 (Nigeria) – hereafter jointly referred to as the CAs and individually as CA or CAMA for Nigeria. Various other statutes that affect the operation of the floating charge in these systems have been enacted, including secured transactions laws (hereafter, the STLs).[70] The

---

67 Ghana Republican Constitution 1960, art 40; Kenya Judicature Act 1967, s 3(1); Nigeria Interpretation Act 1964, s 32.

68 The codification approach in the focus jurisdiction was inspired by the influential Gower's Report (n 58) – this is at least the case for Ghana and Nigeria. That Report, in a bid to make Ghana's company law simple and accessible, recommended for Ghana the codification of not just the English Companies Act 1948 but also the background body of common law and equity surrounding the Act (see paras 16ff of the Report). The annotated Companies Code Bill accompanying the Report was later enacted into the Ghana Companies Act 1963. Other African countries, such as Nigeria, subsequently adopted the codification model. For an interesting review of the Report, see Otto Kahn-Freund "Final Report of the Commission of Inquiry into the Working and Administration of the Present Company Law of Ghana" (1962) 25(1) MLR 78.

69 Ghana Republican Constitution 1960, art 42(4); Judicature Act 1967 (Kenya), s 3(1); *Alli v Okulaja* [1970] I UILR 72, 77 (per Beckley J – stating the following about the binding effect of an English precedent on a Nigerian High Court: "I do not think that this Court can be held bound by that decision of the Court of Appeal of England, this country now being an independent sovereign state"). Although it has been argued that the courts were still following English precedents "slavishly" despite the independence. For Nigeria, see e.g. BO Nwabueze, *A Machinery of Justice in Nigeria* (Butterworths 1963) 37. See also Jill Cottrell, "An End to Slavishness? A Note on *Alli v Okulaja*" [1973] 17(2) JAL 247.

70 The relevant STLs include Ghana's Borrowers and Lenders Act 2020, Kenya's Movable Property Security Rights Act 2017 and Nigeria's Secured Transactions in Movable Assets Act 2017.

floating charge laws of the respective systems have also been further developed through indigenous case decisions. These enactments and case law arose based on the freedom attained pursuant to independence. Therefore, it is inevitable that the post-independence body of laws will diverge in some measures from the English model and from one another.

The following sections discuss the extent of the divergences. Owing to space limitations, the analysis is focused on three key aspects of the charge: (i) the nature of the charge; (ii) registration; and (iii) priority ranking. These three areas have been selected in part because they raise important issues regarding the floating charge's creation and operation, and in part because these are areas where the floating charge created under the CAs fundamentally differs from a floating security right created under the STLs, and therefore many issues arise in these areas in terms of law reform.[71]

Nature of the Floating Charge

There are two main stages to consider when examining the nature of the interest created by a floating charge: (i) the pre-crystallisation stage; and (ii) the post-crystallisation stage. In England and the focus jurisdictions, the position of the law concerning the latter stage is uncontroversial: upon crystallisation, the charge becomes a fixed charge and creates a proprietary interest in specific assets of the company that are subject to the charge.[72] What remains unclear is the interest the charge creates in the pre-crystallisation stage. The main debate on this subject has been whether or not the charge creates a property right. Where it is agreed that a property right is created, there is another debate about the nature of the property right since a core element of the charge is that the grantor is free to dispose of the charged assets without the chargee's specific concurrence – an element that seems to contradict the general rules of property rights. The literature analysis in this area has largely turned on the nature and composition of the property covered by the charge.

The dominant view in English law is that the charge creates a property right from inception.[73] Several theories have been advanced to explain the character

---

[71] See discussion below. Other aspects of the charge worth considering for future research are crystallisation and enforcement, both of which raise issues at later stages of the charge.

[72] *Re Spectrum Plus Ltd (in liquidation)* [2005] UKHL 41; [2005] 2 AC 680, [138–139] (England); Companies Act 2019 (Ghana), s 90(3); *JK Kahagi v Kencity Clothing Ltd* [1977] eKLR 3 (Kenya); Companies and Allied Matters Act 2020 (Nigeria), s 203(2).

[73] *Evans v Rival Granite Quarries Ltd* [1910] 2 KB 979, per Buckley LJ at 999. Compare WJ Gough, *Company Charges* (2nd edn, Butterworths 1996) 79ff

of the property right, with one particularly prominent view being that the property right is attached to a circulating fund of assets rather than the specific assets the fund comprises.[74] The specific assets can change from time to time, but the proprietary interest attached to the fund remains the same. Upon crystallisation, the charge attaches to these specific assets and becomes fixed.

The position in the focus jurisdictions is mostly similar to English law, albeit that the CAs in Ghana and Nigeria attempt to describe the pre-crystallisation nature of the charge. Ghana's CA describes the charge as "an equitable charge over the whole or a specified part of the undertaking and assets of the company both present and future".[75] It goes on to note that the charge "does not preclude the company from dealing" with its assets until the occurrence of some specified events.[76] However, where any of the events occur, the Act provides that "the charge crystallises and becomes a fixed equitable charge on those of the

---

and 347ff, arguing at 347 that "[p]rior to crystallisation, the rights of the chargee remain contractual. The proprietary rights conferred on the chargee … are suspended or deferred until crystallisation".

[74] See e.g. Ewan McKendrick (ed), *Goode and McKendrick on Commercial Law* (6th edn, Penguin 2020) para 25.06; Louise Gullifer (ed), *Goode and Gullifer on Legal Problems of Credit and* Security (7th edn, Sweet & Maxwell 2022) para 4-03f. This view also appears to have judicial support – see e.g. *Re Spectrum Plus Ltd* (n 72) [139]. Compare S Worthington, *Proprietary Interests in Commercial Transactions* (1996) 81ff; RC Nolan, "Property in a Fund" (2004) 120 LQR 108 at 126 – where it is suggested that the charge holder has a property interest in the specific assets, but such interest is defeasible or over-reachable where the chargor engages in permitted dealings with the assets. The problem with this view is that it considers the floating charge as equivalent to a fixed charge, an idea that has been rejected by the court on different occasions – see e.g. *Evans v Rival Granite Quarries Ltd* (n 73) 999. For a recent analysis of the theories, see Michael Bridge and others, *The Law of Personal Property* (3rd edn, Sweet and Maxwell 2021) para 16-089f; Louise Gullifer and Jennifer Payne, *Corporate Finance Law: Principles and Policy* (3rd edn, Hart 2020) 301ff; Duncan Sheehan, *The Principles of Personal Property Law* (2nd edn, Hart 2017) 420.

[75] Companies Act 2019, s 90(1).

[76] Companies Act 2019, s 90(2). The specified events, as provided in s 90(2)(a)–(c), include where: (a) the charge becomes enforceable, and the chargee takes possession or appoints a receiver or a manager pursuant to the charge instrument; (b) the Court appoints a receiver or manager of the charged assets on the application of the chargee; (c) the company goes into liquidation. It should be observed that the stated events in (a) and (b) do not include the appointment of an administrator. However, it is arguable that it is contemplated under the Corporate Insolvency and Restructuring Act 2020 that the appointment of an administrator either by the chargee (in accordance with the charge instrument) or the court would be a crystallisation event. See e.g. s 3(5) CIRA.

assets of the company that are subject to the charge".[77] Nigeria's CAMA adopts a similar wording, although its description of the assets to which the charge can apply expressly includes "cash and uncalled capital of the company".[78]

The foregoing description of the charge as an "equitable charge over the undertaking or assets" of the grantor suggests that it creates an immediate security interest that relates to property. The Nigerian Supreme Court has judicially acknowledged this interpretation.[79] It is also apparent from the subsequent wording of the provision that the charge is not attached to specific assets of the grantor until crystallisation occurs. In *Olalomi Industries v NIDB Ltd*, the Supreme Court held that the floating charge does not create a charge over specific assets but relates only to "floating assets".[80] That seems to be in line with the concept of a "circulating fund of assets" in English law.

There is no similar description of the charge in Kenya's Companies Act 2015. However, it has been established in a number of cases that the floating charge creates an immediate proprietary interest.[81] In *Sokhi International (K) Ltd*, the Kenyan High Court attempted to shed some light on the proprietary nature of the charge, describing the property as "circulating assets which are not definitely identified" and "a floating charge remains dormant and inoperative as regards any particular assets until it is converted into a [fixed] charge by the intervention of the debenture holder".[82] The reference to "circulating assets" and the description that follows appear to make the position similar to that of English law.

---

[77] Companies Act 2019, s 90(3).

[78] Companies and Allied Matters Act 2020 (CAMA), s 203(1)&(2). The specified crystallisation events are also very similar to those of Ghana, with the appointment of an administrator by a chargee or the court also contemplated. See s 452(4) CAMA.

[79] See *Olalomi Industries v NIDB Ltd* (2009) LPELR-2564, at 30 – in respect of a predecessor provision that had identical wording, i.e. s 178(1) CAMA 1990. See also *JIA Enterprises (Electrical) Ltd v British Commonwealth Insurance Co Ltd* (1962) LPELR-25052, at p 9 – another Nigerian Supreme Court case in respect of a predecessor provision, Companies Act 1954, s 101(1).

[80] (2009) LPELR-2564, at p. 30. See also *George Cohen (W.A.) Ltd v Comet Construction Co. Ltd and another* [1966] GLR 777 (Ghana).

[81] *JK Kahagi v Kencity Clothing Ltd* [1977] eKLR 3 (per M.G Muli holding at p. 3 that the floating charge "confers upon the debenture holder … equitable interest over the assets"). See also *Lochab Brothers v Kenya Furfural Co Ltd* [1983] eKLR; *Sokhi International (K) Ltd v Giro Commercial Bank Limited* [2006] eKLR.

[82] *Sokhi International (K) Ltd v Giro Commercial Bank Limited* [2006] eKLR 2.

Moreover, English jurisprudence has greatly influenced the judicial analysis of the pre-attachment nature of the floating charge in the focus jurisdictions.[83] This is also true of the statutory descriptions of the charge under the CAs in Ghana and Nigeria, the foundations of which are based on a Report and a Draft Bill that largely adopted English judicial principles.[84] This continuing influence of English jurisprudence reinforces the argument that the position in the focus jurisdictions as to the nature of the floating charge is highly similar to that of England.

Registration

This section examines the role of registration in relation to the creation and third-party effectiveness of the charge. It will be seen that there are major differences between the registration rules in England and the focus jurisdictions on these subjects. This is in part because the CAs of some of the focus jurisdictions (particularly Kenya and Nigeria) still retain elements of the UK registration regime that operated before the 2013 reforms (see discussion below). Another reason for the difference is the reforms introduced by the various STLs.

In English law, the registration of floating charges is governed by the Companies Act 2006. Registration is not a constitutive requirement for creating a floating charge under this regime, as floating charges are created by mere agreement between the security parties.[85] Registration is also not compulsory to make the charge enforceable against third parties: an unregistered charge is only void against those parties contemplated under the Companies Act, i.e. the chargor's secured creditors,[86] liquidator and administrator.[87] An unregistered charge remains valid against other third parties not contemplated, such as an outright purchaser of the charged assets and unsecured creditors of

---

[83] This is apparent in the cases cited in notes 79–81 above.

[84] See discussion in note 68 above.

[85] For more discussion on the creation of the floating charge, see Goode and McKendrick (n 74) paras 23.03 and 25.10.

[86] The actual term used in the Act is "creditors". However, that term has been held to mean creditors who have acquired rights in the charged property. Such creditors include a subsequent chargee, an execution creditor, and an unsecured creditor where, and only where, the company has gone into liquidation before the charge is registered. See *Re Ashpurton Estates Ltd* [1983] Ch 110, per Lord Brightman at 123. See also *Goode and McKendrick* (n 74) para 24.51.

[87] Companies Act 2006, s 859H(3).

the non-insolvent chargor.[88] Lastly, registration under the Companies Act is not a priority point in that priority is determined by reference to the date the charge is created rather than the order of registration (see below for discussion of priority issues).[89] Instead, the purpose of registration is to give the charge maximum third-party effect by making it valid against the above-mentioned third parties (i.e. the grantor's insolvency officers and secured creditors).[90] Registration is therefore not mandatory but is only a matter of commercial decision.[91]

In respect of the focus jurisdictions, registration is subject to two regimes, i.e. the CAs and the STLs.[92] The STLs introduce reforms aimed at simplifying security taking in the jurisdictions.[93] Unfortunately, the reform processes were not coordinated with existing registration rules under the CAs, and the STLs leave the registration system under the CAs generally untouched. This implies that security interests created by companies and registrable under both regimes may have to be registered twice, making secured transactions in the jurisdictions more burdensome. A related difficulty is that registration serves different purposes under both regimes, thereby making the relationship between the two regimes complicated. These matters are discussed below. Before that, it is necessary to note a couple of points.

---

88 *Goode and McKendrick* (n 74) para 24.50. However, where the outright purchaser acquires the legal title for value and without notice of any restrictive term of the charge as regards the ability of the chargor to sell, the purchaser will take the title free of the charge. *Goode and McKendrick*, para 24.52.

89 *Goode and Gullifer* (n 74) para 5.16.

90 Although non-registration has priority consequences in some instances. See discussion below.

91 Department for Business, Energy & Industrial Strategy, *Revised Scheme for Registration of Charges created by Companies and Limited Liability Partnerships: proposed revision of Pt 25, Companies Act 2006* (August 2011), comments to s 860.

92 This also means that each of the STLs establishes a collateral register distinct from the CA's register. See s 18 Borrowers and Lenders Act 2020 (Ghana) – hereafter BLA; s 19 Movable Property Security Rights Act 2017 (Kenya) – MPSRA; s 10 Secured Transactions in Movable Assets Act 2017 (Nigeria) – STMAA.

93 In terms of the scope of their application, the BLA applies to security interests in movable and immovable assets, whether tangible or intangible (see s 1 BLA and the exceptions mentioned there). The MPSRA and STMAA apply only to security interests created over movable assets, tangible or intangible (see s 4 MPSRA and s 2 STMAA, and the exceptions mentioned in them).

The first is that the various STLs adopt a functional approach (i.e. they treat all applicable security interests unitarily),[94] and each law has features that enable floating security. That means it is possible for a borrower to create a security interest over present and future assets, and the assets only need to be identified generically.[95] Therefore, to create a floating security under the laws, parties only need to include in the security agreement terms that give the borrower freedom to deal with the assets in the ordinary course of business, subject to the occurrence of certain events of default.[96] Parties may also qualify the freedom by including terms that restrict the debtor's powers to dispose of the security assets, such as a negative pledge clause. The functional approach adopted under the secured transactions laws would imply that the need to distinguish between a floating and fixed charge is no longer relevant for the purposes of the laws, since all security rights are treated as one and governed by the same rules. However, this has not been the case (at least in Nigeria and Kenya) for reasons discussed below. The other point is that since the STLs adopt a functional approach and the term "security interest" (or "security right" in the case of Kenya) is used rather than "charge", the phrase "floating security interest" will hereafter be used to refer to floating charges created under the STLs, while the phrase "floating charge" will be used to refer to those created under the CAs. This distinction is made only to aid the understanding of the discussions hereof and not necessarily to indicate that the security rights are two entirely separate types of security.

In Ghana, registration is compulsory under its CA for a floating charge to be effective, even against security parties.[97] Section 110(1) of the CA is to the effect that a floating charge is "void" unless certain prescribed particulars and the charge document are delivered to the registrar for registration within 45 days after the date of the charge's creation.[98] Conversely, under the Borrowers and Lenders Act 2020 (hereafter the BLA), registration is not compulsory for

[94] The definitions of the term "security interest" (or "security right") under the STLs include all devices intended to provide security for a payment obligation. See Ghana's BLA, s 85; Kenya's MPSRA, ss 3 and 4(1)(a); and Nigeria's STMAA, s 63(1).

[95] See ss 6(3) and 8 BLA; ss 6(2) and 8 MPSRA; and ss 3(2) and 6(1)(b) STMAA.

[96] The nature of this type of floating security right is different from that of the floating charge in that it is considered as a fixed security from inception.

[97] Ghana's CA, s 110(1).

[98] Section 118 of the CA provides for judicial leave to register out of time in certain circumstances, in which case the charge will be subject to any interest acquired before the date of actual registration unless the court orders otherwise. See *Ghana Timber Board v Ashanti Curl & Lumber Products* [1968] GLR 931.

the validity of a floating security interest against the security parties.[99] Instead, s 14 BLA makes registration compulsory for the validity of the security interest against third parties.

The BLA does not expressly repeal or amend the registration rules under the CA. This raises difficulties regarding the relationship between the two registration regimes. It has been suggested that the conflicting provisions should be resolved in favour of the BLA so that an unregistered floating charge would remain effective (not void) against the security parties.[100] This view appears correct, given that s 86 BLA provides that the Act will prevail where it conflicts with any other enactment as regards creation, third-party effectiveness, and priority of security interests.

Yet the law is not entirely free from uncertainty. The most straightforward way to address the relationship between the two pieces of legislation would have been to expressly repeal the provisions of the CA in the BLA. However, that has not been the case.[101] Section 17(2) instead provides that registration under the Act "does not discard with registration under other Acts",[102] which implies that the Act does not intend to repeal the registration requirement under the CA. Section 17(2) would be meaningless if the provisions of the BLA on registration truly superseded those of the CA because there would be no point in registering under other registries if the BLA superseded them. It is therefore difficult not to think that the CA registration rules still apply and companies need to register twice, i.e. in the BLA and CA registries, for the floating charge to be effective in terms of the CA and achieve third-party effectiveness in terms of the BLA. Moreover, given the stated uncertainty, it is unlikely that the borrowing company and the lender will be willing to risk not registering with the CA registry considering the consequences.[103] In relation to the borrowing company, s 114(3) of the Act provides that the company and its officers will be liable to pay an administrative penalty, and s 110(4) provides

---

[99] See s 6(1) BLA. However, non-registration attracts certain sanctions, including disentitlement to extrajudicial enforcement on the part of the lender (s 61(1)(b)) and an administrative penalty where the lender is under the supervision of the Bank of Ghana (s 22(2)).

[100] Jonathan Amable, "Key Issues to Note from the Enactment of the Borrowers And Lenders Act, 2020 (Act 1052)" (Mondaq, 2022) <https://www.mondaq.com/financial-services/1257482/key-issues-to-note-from-the-enactment-of-the-borrowers-and-lenders-act-2020-act-1052> accessed 24 July 2023 – noting that the BLA "impliedly amended" the Companies Act regarding rules on registration of charges.

[101] BLA, s 88.

[102] BLA, s 17(2).

[103] See e.g. Ghana's CA, ss 110(1), 114(3) and 114(4).

that the loan will immediately become payable. Regarding the lender, s 110(1) provides that the charge will be void. All these provisions remain effective, as the BLA did not repeal them. The double registration outcome is unfortunate, given that the BLA was introduced to simplify (and not complicate) secured transactions in Ghana.[104]

In Kenya, the relationship between the Movable Property Security Rights Act 2017 (hereafter the MPSRA) and its CA with regards registration presents a similar difficulty. As noted earlier, the MPSRA only applies to security interests in movable property, including floating charges.[105] Hence, a distinction between a floating and fixed charge remains relevant for securities outside its scope (e.g. security rights over immovables). One of the purposes of the MPSRA was to replace the CA registration rules for in-scope security rights with MPSRA rules so that e.g. dual registration is avoided.[106] However, this has not been achieved. As a result, it is argued below that a distinction between a floating and fixed charge is also relevant for securities within the MPSRA scope.

Under the MPSRA, registration serves a similar function as that of the BLA, i.e., registration is only required to make a security interest enforceable against third parties. It is not a constitutive requirement. Therefore, registration is not mandatory and is only a matter of commercial decisions.[107] This contrasts with the Kenya CA, where registration is mandatory. The consequences of a failure to register within time (i.e. 30 days)[108] under the CA mirror the position in the UK before the 2013 reforms, in that: (i) it is a criminal offence on the part of the chargor and its officers, which is punishable by fine,[109] and (ii) it makes the charge void against the chargor's liquidator, administrator and (secured) creditors.[110] Therefore registration is not compulsory for the creation

---

104 For an interesting analysis of these issues in a wider security context as regards an earlier draft of the Bill that introduced the BLA 2020, see Marek Dubovec and Louise Gullifer, *Secured Transactions Law Reform in Africa* (Hart, 2019) 78ff.

105 MPSRA, s 4(1).

106 See s 94 MPSRA, which provides for various consequential amendments and repeals to the CA intended to achieve this purpose.

107 It should be noted that registration has priority effects in some circumstances. See the discussion below.

108 The CA, s 885(1)(a). The deadline is extendable by the court in certain circumstances – s 888(1) and (2) CA.

109 The CA, s 878(8)&(10).

110 The CA, s 889(1). While the CA only mentions the chargor's creditors (not "secured" creditors), it appears that the position is similar to English law, where secured creditors are contemplated, given the lack of authority in Kenya to the contrary. See note 86 above.

and third-party effectiveness of the charge. However, the provision for criminal sanction makes registration mandatory in reality.

In a bid to harmonise the provisions of the CA with the MPSRA and make registration under the MPSRA supersede the CA rules, the MPSRA amended (ii) above to the effect that a registered security right under the MPSRA will not be void against parties mentioned there even if the charge is unregistered under the CA.[111] This implies that the MPSRA intended to avoid double registration for security rights subject to it. However, the scope of the amendment is limited, as it does not extend to the criminal sanction consequence. That sanction still applies to floating charges,[112] meaning that registration under the CA remains mandatory, and dual registration is still required. This is unfortunate since the MPSRA was introduced "to facilitate the registration of security rights in movable assets".[113] The MPSRA should have also expressly amended s 878(4) CA[114] to exclude charges within its scope from the CA registration scheme.[115] That would have removed the criminal sanction and truly facilitated a single registration.

In Nigeria, the relationship between the CAMA and the Secured Transactions in Movable Assets Act 2017 (STMAA) is equally problematic. The STMAA was introduced to facilitate the creation and perfection of security interests in movable assets. Yet its ability to achieve this objective is limited, given that it left the registration system under the CAMA entirely untouched. This raises several legal issues regarding third-party effectiveness and the priority of floating charges.

Under the CAMA, a floating charge must be delivered to the companies registry for registration within 90 days of its creation.[116] A failure to deliver the charge within time renders it void against "the liquidator and any creditor of the company".[117] This means that registration is not a constitutive requirement under the CAMA since an unregistered charge is valid against the security parties and is void only against the parties mentioned above.[118] It should be observed that the chargor's administrator is not mentioned, unlike in Kenya and

---

111 The s 94 MPSRA; s 889(1)(c) CA.

112 See the combined effect of ss 878(4)(g) and 878(8).

113 MPSRA, s 3(c).

114 This section lists charges to which the CA registration scheme applies.

115 See also Dubovec and Gullifer (n 104) 102 f.

116 CAMA, s 222(1).

117 CAMA, s 222(1). The 90-day deadline is extendable by courts on grounds similar to those of Kenya – see s 230 CAMA.

118 See e.g. the Appeal Court case of *African International Bank Ltd v Lee and Tee Ind Ltd and Another* [2003] 7 NWLR (Part 819) 366. While the word "creditor" is used, it appears that the position is similar to English law, where

England. This is interesting, given that one of the major reforms the recently revised CAMA introduced was the inclusion and prioritisation of business rescue processes (such as administration) to Nigeria's corporate insolvency system.[119] It would have been expected that the unregistered charge should also be made void against the administrator. The non-inclusion suggests that an unregistered charge is binding on an administrator, and the administrator cannot disregard an unregistered charge in its dealings with the charged property, especially in realising property, in order to make a distribution to creditors.[120]

In addition to being void against the stated parties, a failure to register the charge within time is a criminal offence on the part of the company granting it and its officers.[121] This indicates that registration is mandatory.

Under the STMAA, registration is not necessary to create a security interest. There is, however, no explicit provision as to whether registration is compulsory to make a security interest enforceable against third parties.[122] The STMAA merely provides in s 8(1) that "a security interest is perfected when a financing statement in respect of that security interest has been registered". But that does not necessarily mean that registration is a prerequisite for third-party effectiveness. Perfection is not always a precondition for third-party effectiveness. In England, for example, while registration is a perfection event, it is not a prerequisite for third-party effectiveness.[123] The STMAA provides a comprehensive list of what perfection means for security holders, all of which are stated in terms of priority effects.[124] For example, the Act provides that the order of registration determines priority between two perfected security rights[125] and that an outright buyer who takes title for value has priority over an unperfected security interest.[126] No provision is made as to whether an

secured creditors are contemplated (see note 86 above), given the lack of authority in Nigeria to the contrary.

[119] Hon Justice Nnamdi Dimgba, "Changes to Nigeria's Insolvency System by the Companies and Allied Matters Act, 2020: A Judicial Perspective" (Commercial Law Research Network Nigeria, March 2021) <https://www.clrnn.net/2021/03/05/changes-to-nigerias-insolvency-system-by-the-companies-and-allied-matter-act-2020-a-judicial-perspective/> accessed 23 January 2023.

[120] On the objectives of the administration procedure, see s 444(1) CAMA.

[121] CAMA, s 224(3).

[122] What the STMAA provides is that registration is a priority point (see s 23 STMAA).

[123] Goode and Gullifer (n 74) para 2.23.

[124] See Part V of the STMAA.

[125] Section 23 STMAA.

[126] Section 32 STMAA.

unperfected security interest is effective against unsecured creditors (or creditors with a later unperfected security interest in the same collateral).

To the author's knowledge, existing literature has not taken notice of this omission, and some have assumed that the Act requires registration for third-party effectiveness in all cases.[127] Such an assumption does not entirely reflect the law for the preceding reasons. It is, in fact, arguable that registration under the STMAA only serves as a priority point. The express subordination of an unperfected security interest in certain circumstances, such as when a buyer takes title for value, suggests that an unperfected security right may be enforceable in other circumstances, e.g. when the third party takes title without value or when a later unperfected security is created over the same asset. An express provision stating the drafter's intention would have avoided this uncertainty.

The relationship between the registration rules under the STMAA and CAMA is also problematic. Section 2(3) STMAA provides that "nothing in this Act shall prevent the creation of security interest [sic] in the form of charges by companies registered under the Companies and Allied Matters Act". While this provision confirms that the Act intends to retain the charges and registration rules under the CAMA, its exact meaning is unclear. Dubovec and Gullifer note that the provision is capable of two different interpretations, depending on whether the term "registered under the Companies and Allied Matters Act" refers to the word "charges" or the word "companies".[128] Suppose the term referred to "companies". In that case, the provision could be seen to mean that charges created under the CAMA would be recognised as a security interest under the STMAA and therefore registrable under that Act. However, if the term referred to "charges", the provision could be read as creating a dual system where companies can choose between creating a floating security interest under the STMAA or a floating charge under the CAMA.[129]

Each of these interpretations raises difficulties. The problem with the first interpretation is that a floating charge would have to be registered twice, under both registries, for it to attain maximum third-party effectiveness. (In contrast, the second interpretation would require a single registration under the chosen regime.) Also, either interpretation would result in conflicts of priority outcomes since the priority rules under the Acts are entirely different – while

[127] See e.g. Williams Iheme, "The Defects of Nigeria's Secured Transactions in Movable Assets Act 2017 and Their Potential Repercussions on Access to Credit: A Comparative Analysis and Lessons from the Anglo-American Law" (2021) 27 Comparative Law Review 9, 32.

[128] Dubovec and Gullifer (n 104) 152.

[129] This interpretation appears to be preferred in the literature. See e.g. Iheme (n 127) 21ff.

registration is a priority point under the STMAA, it is not under the CAMA (see discussion below).

In addition, the failure to repeal the CAMA rules on charges means that the concept of the floating charge remains relevant in Nigeria, despite the STMAA's functional approach. Hence, a distinction between a floating and fixed charge will continue to be required in order to determine the priority rules applicable to the charge.[130] This is unfortunate, as the failure to repeal the CAMA and the difficulties associated with s 2(3) of the STMAA considerably limit the scope of the STMAA in realising its objectives of facilitating secured transactions in Nigeria.[131] Based on the author's experience in practice, lenders generally prefer to create charges under the more familiar rules of CAMA, despite the benefits available under the STMAA, including the exclusion of stamp duties costs and the possibility of securing priority by registering a financing statement in advance of a security interest.[132] This practice unwittingly adopts the second interpretation above, where registration is only done under the CAMA.

Priority

This section considers the priority rules that apply to a floating charge in the focus jurisdictions pre- and post-crystallisation and how the rules compare with English law. Also, given that the STLs create a dual system to some extent and that the laws enable a floating security right (see discussion above), the discussion below considers the priority rules applicable under the STLs and the consequent tensions arising from their relationships with the various CAs.

Pre-crystallisation priority rules under company laws

A discussion under this subsection requires consideration of three categories of subsequent interests arising prior to crystallisation. These include the interest of a buyer, a secured creditor and an execution creditor. Given the focus jurisdictions' closeness to English law on the nature of the floating charge at the pre-crystallisation stage (discussed above), some similarities are to be expected. For example, since it is the essence of a floating charge in the jurisdictions to allow the chargor to freely dispose of the charged assets in the course of business, the charge does not affect third parties who subsequently acquire an interest in the course of the chargor's business. Hence, an outright purchaser of the charged assets or a lender who has been granted fixed

---

[130] For a discussion of the effects of the dual system in the broader secured transactions law, see Dubovec and Gullifer (n 104) 152ff.

[131] See s 1 STMAA.

[132] See respectively ss 54 and 12(1) STMAA.

security[133] over the charged assets in the course of business takes title free of the charge (subject to the doctrine of notice as discussed below).[134] Also, since the charge does not attach to specific assets until it crystallises, an execution creditor who has completed the execution[135] before crystallisation takes free of the charge in the jurisdictions.[136]

The regimes are also generally similar in their priority treatment of disposals made in breach of the security agreement, where the buyer or fixed security holder takes title with actual notice of the breach.[137] Hence, if a security holder or a purchaser takes title with actual notice of a negative pledge clause,[138] the floating charge will have priority on crystallisation. Furthermore, registration within the relevant periods allowed is not a priority point in all jurisdictions.[139]

---

133 The term "fixed security" is a convenient term used here to refer to mortgages, pledges, contractual liens, fixed charges and security rights created under the secured transactions laws. It does not include a floating charge because competing floating charges are subject to a different priority rule, as will be seen below.

134 See e.g. CA, s 90(2)&(5) (Ghana); *Noor Abdikadir Abdalla v Grofin East Africa Fund LLC and another* [2009] Civil Case 316 (Kenya); CAMA, ss 203 and 204; *Goode and Gullifer* (n 74) para 5.40.

135 There is also a broad similarity between the regimes as to what counts as completion of execution, in that execution against goods is completed by seizure and sale, an attachment of debt requires the execution creditor's receipt of the debt, and execution against land requires seizure or the appointment of a receiver. See Insolvency Act 1986 (England), s 183(3); Insolvency Act 2015 (Kenya), s 481(3); CAMA 2020 (Nigeria), s 666(2). There are no similar provisions in Ghana's companies and insolvency laws. However, it seems to be accepted that the position is equally similar in Ghana. See e.g. JEA Mills, "Priority between a Debenture Holder Secured by a Floating Charge and an Execution Creditor" (1986–1990) 17 U Ghana LJ 27, 52f.

136 *Re Opera Ltd* [1891] 3 CH 260 (English); *George Cohen (W.A.) Ltd. v Comet Construction Co. Ltd and another* [1966] GLR 777 (Ghana); *Lochab Brothers v Kenya Furfural Co Ltd* [1983] eKLR (Kenya); Emudainohwo (n 2) 199 (Nigeria).

137 *English & Scottish Mercantile Investment Co Ltd v Brunton* [1892] 2 QB 700, 707; CA (Ghana), s 90(5); CAMA, s 204. It appears there is an absence of authority in Kenya on this point; however, it is expected that the law will be similar to the preceding rules.

138 A negative pledge clause is a term that restricts the chargor's ability to create any subsequent security right ranking in priority to or pari passu with the floating charge or to sell any of the charged assets outside the ordinary course of business. *Goode and Gullifer* (n 74) para 2.28.

139 However, failure to register has priority consequences in some circumstances. This is the case, for example, where a floating charge with a negative pledge clause is registered. A subsequent fixed security holder may be considered

Instead, priority is determined by reference to the date the charge is created.[140] This means that the "invisibility period" problem (i.e. the period between creation and registration when the registries will not disclose the existence of the security) applies in all jurisdictions, but it is profound in the focus jurisdictions given the longer period applicable under their CAs.[141] Furthermore, where there are competing floating charge holders, the first in time to be created will have priority.[142] Given the broad similarities between the jurisdictions, discussing these points in detail will not be productive.

One area of difference that is worth noting is the question as to whether registration of the charge constitutes constructive notice of its contents. This point is significant for determining the effect of a registered charge that has a negative pledge clause. If registration constitutes notice, subsequent fixed security holders and purchasers of the charged assets may be deemed to have actual notice of the restriction and therefore will take title subject to the charge. Two questions need to be considered in order to address this issue. The first is whether registration constitutes notice of the existence of a negative pledge clause. Secondly, who is considered to have such notice? The following paragraphs discuss how the laws in the jurisdictions answer these questions. It will be seen that the law in Ghana and Nigeria is clearer compared with Kenya and England.

Ghana's CA provides that registration constitutes actual notice of the particulars required for registration, but not the content of the charge instrument,

---

to have constructive notice of the negative pledge by reason of the registration, and that can have priority effects. See below for discussion.

140 Although unlike in English law, where registration is only a perfection requirement, registration is compulsory in the focus jurisdictions given the criminal sanctions applicable in Nigeria's and Kenya's CAs, and the fact that an unregistered charge under Ghana's CA is void. See, respectively, CA (England), s 859H; CA (Ghana), s 110(1); CA (Kenya), ss 878(8) and 889(1); CAMA, ss 224(3) and 22(1).

141 That is 45 days in Ghana (s 110(1) A), 30 days in Kenya (S 885(1)(A) CA), and 90 days in Nigeria (S 222(1) CAMA), compared with 21 days in England (s 859A(4) CA).

142 *Re Benjamin Cope & Sons Ltd* [1914] 1 Ch 800. It appears there is no direct authority in the focus jurisdictions on this point, but the insolvency laws in Kenya and Nigeria, regarding the definition of a prior floating charge in an administration proceeding, suggest the same position. See e.g. Insolvency Act (Kenya), ss 535 and 612; CAMA, ss 453 and 534. A case authority in England suggests that a later floating charge will rank ahead of an earlier one where the later charge covers part of the assets comprised in the earlier charge. See *Re Automatic Bottle Makers Ltd* [1926] Ch 412.

"to all persons and for all purposes as from the date of registration".[143] Nigeria's CAMA has a similar provision, although without the quoted phrase.[144] In both Acts, the particulars required to be filed include a statement indicating the existence of a negative pledge clause.[145]

The combined effect of the provisions in Ghana is that registration amounts to notice of the existence of a negative pledge clause. It is also clear from the quoted words above that such notice applies to the whole world. Therefore, any subsequent title, whether legal or equitable, taken either by a purchaser or a fixed security holder in breach of the negative pledge will be subject to the charge, and the charge will have priority upon crystallisation. The same applies to Nigeria regarding the first question – i.e. registration amounts to notice. However, given the absence of the quoted words or anything to that effect under Nigerian laws, notice cannot be said to apply to the whole world. The better view is that notice may only apply to those third parties that are reasonably expected to search the register. Such parties would include commercial financiers and lenders such as banks, but not purchasers who take title in the ordinary course of business.[146]

The position in Kenya and England is not as clear-cut. In both jurisdictions, it is stated that the particulars required to be filed include a statement indicating the existence of a negative pledge clause.[147] However, their CAs do not answer the two questions above. Case law in both jurisdictions has also not been very helpful. The closest case authority is an *obiter* opinion in an English case, where it is suggested that registration gives notice of the existence of the charge but not of any negative pledge provisions in the charge.[148] This vacuum has been filled by English academic literature, in which it is generally accepted that registration constitutes notice of the particulars required for filing as regards third parties that would reasonably be expected to search the register.[149] If this view is applied to the questions under consideration, it would mean that registration constitutes notice of the existence of negative pledge

143 CA, s 121.

144 CAMA, ss 204 and 222(1).

145 CA, s 110(6)(f); CAMA, s 223(1)(v).

146 The wording of the proviso to s 204 CAMA appears to support this view by suggesting that registration only amounts to notice to fixed security holders.

147 CA (England), s 859D(2)(c); Companies (General) Regulations 2015 (Kenya), regs 58 and 59.

148 *Wilson v Kelland* [1910] 2 Ch 306. For a discussion see J de Lacy, "Constructive Notice and Company Charge Registration" (2001) 65 The Conveyancer 122, 127ff.

149 See e.g. *Goode and Gullifer* (n 74) para 2.28; *Goode and McKendrick* (n 74) paras 24.46ff.

clauses (since the clause is one of the prescribed particulars to be filed), and that notice will be imputed to commercial lenders and security holders such as banks.

However, it is necessary to examine the principles on which that view is based and consider whether they remain applicable. It appears that the view was originally predicated on the common law doctrine of constructive notice of public registers[150] and the fact that registration was compulsory under the pre-2013 CA, as non-registration was a criminal offence.[151] As such, a searcher can reasonably expect the company charges register to be definitive where applicable.[152] In addition, Goode and McKendrick have alluded to the relative simplicity of the register and the clarity with which the particulars filed in it are set out as justifying such a view.[153] However, since the abolition of the criminal sanction in the post-2013 CA means that registration is no longer compulsory, the validity of the stated view has become questionable.[154]

The position in Kenya is even more uncertain owing to the paucity of case authority and academic literature on the questions. However, if the above approach adopted in the English literature were applied to Kenyan law, the resulting view would be more persuasive since registration remains mandatory under Kenya CA.[155]

It can be seen from the foregoing discussion that the position of the floating chargee is strengthened under Ghanaian law, as registration imputes notice of the existence of a negative pledge on all third parties. However, this advantage is somewhat academic, as parties in the jurisdictions will most often seek to govern priorities through agreements such as an inter-creditor agreement.[156] This probably (partly) explains why there has been a paucity of case authority on these questions since these agreements provide clarity on the priorities of charges. However, it is essential that the background law on which practice is based is clear on these issues.

Priority competitions with security interests under secured transactions laws

As noted above, the focus jurisdictions have each enacted STLs that run parallel with their CAs. Under the STLs, a distinction between a floating and a fixed charge is irrelevant since the laws treat all applicable security interests

---

150 *Wilson v Kelland* [1910] 2 Ch 306, 313.
151 The relevant provisions were the Companies Act 2006, s 860(4)–(6).
152 *Goode and Gullifer* (n 74) paras 2.27ff.
153 *Goode and McKendrick* (n 74) paras 24.47f.
154 See e.g. *Goode and Gullifer* (n 74) para 2.29.
155 Non-registration is a criminal offence under s 878(8) and (10) CA (Kenya).
156 See e.g. *Goode and Gullifer* (n 74) para 5.41.

unitarily and apply the same rules (including priority rules).[157] Thus, for example, if a CA-registered floating charge is also registered under an STL, the distinction that exists between the floating and fixed security as regards priority disappears under the STL. Given this unitary approach of the STLs, discussing the priority rules as they relate to floating and fixed security interests will not be productive for the purposes of this chapter. It is, however, necessary to examine how the priority rules under the STLs interact with those under the CAs and consider possible issues that may arise from such interaction. These issues are discussed below in light of where a CA-registered floating charge competes with an STL-registered floating security interest.

A major element as regards priority is that the rules under the STLs are completely different from those under the CAs. Priority under the STLs is determined by the date of registration.[158] In other words, the first party to register takes priority.[159] Under the CAs, priority is determined by reference to the date the charge is created (see discussion above). This difference in approach makes it necessary that the relevant laws clarify which priority rule takes precedence in the event of a conflict.

In Ghana, such clarity is found in s 33 of the BLA, where it is stated that a "security interest registered under [the BLA] shall, irrespective of the time of registration, have priority over any other security interest registered under any other enactment".[160] Hence, if a company's asset is subject to a floating charge duly registered under Ghana's CA and the company subsequently grants another security interest over the same asset and registers it under the BLA, the later security interest will have priority.

The position is less clear in Kenya for two reasons. First, neither the MPSRA nor Kenya's CA has a provision that is equivalent to Ghana's s 33 BLA – i.e. neither Act provides a priority rule to resolve the conflict. Secondly, the MPSRA does not make a wholesale repeal of the relevant rules applicable under the CA. Instead, it makes specific changes to various CA provisions to

---

157 This is a major departure from the fragmented system that exists under the CAs, where a floating charge is subject to unique priority rules and therefore needs to be distinguished from a fixed charge for that purpose.

158 BLA, s 34; MPSRA, 38; STMAA, s 23.

159 Certain exceptions apply to the "first to register" rule, particularly as regards an acquisition security interest, a transferee of negotiable instruments and securities, a buyer or lessee in the ordinary course of business, and a holder of a non-consensual possessory lien in respect of movable property. See respectively BLA, ss 38, 43, 44(2) and 48; MPSRA, ss 45(4)–(8), 46(3), 47, 52 and 55; STMAA, ss 27, 30, 31, 32(2).

160 See also s 86 BLA.

replace the CA's relevant rules with those under the MPSRA.[161] The problem with this approach is that the priority rules applicable under the CA are contained in case law (see the relevant cases in footnotes 134 and 136 above) and not in the CA. Hence, the amendments made under s 94 of the MPSRA do not expressly affect the rules.[162] It may be argued that a purposive interpretation of s 94 MPSRA would resolve the conflict in favour of the MPSRA since the overarching aim of the provision is to replace the CA rules with those of the MPSRA. This argument is strengthened by the fact that s 94 of the MPSRA expressly amends relevant provisions of the Insolvency Act (i.e. ss 535(2) and 612(4)) to make the MPSRA determinative of the priority of floating charges for the purposes of appointing and replacing an administrator. Section 535 requires the holder of a qualifying floating charge who intends to appoint an administrator to give notice to the holder of a prior floating charge, and s 612 empowers a prior floating charge holder to apply to the court to replace an administrator.

Furthermore, a Kenyan High Court has suggested in a recent case that the MPSRA is "a statute of general application" and the Act applies to "all transactions" creating security rights in movable property.[163] While that implies that the MPSRA has an overriding effect as regards movable security rights within its scope, the relevance of the statement to the present inquiry should not be overstated, given that the opinion is an *obiter* and the case is concerned with the priority of floating charges for the purposes of ss 535 of the Insolvency Act, an area on which the MPSRA is undoubtedly determinative. The law would have been clearer if there had been a wholesale repeal of the relevant CA rules or a s 33 BLA-like provision in the MPSRA.

A similar difficulty is found in Nigeria, in that neither the STMAA nor the CAMA provides a wholesale repeal of the relevant rules under the CAMA or has a s 33 BLA-like provision. The difficulty is even more profound in Nigeria, as the STMAA makes no attempt to replace or amend relevant provisions of the CAMA. Instead, s 2(3) STMAA confirms that the STMAA retains the charges system under the CAMA. The interpretational difficulty associated with s 2(3) STMAA has been discussed above, where it is noted that the provision is capable of two interpretations. The first interpretation is said to result in all charges being registrable under the CAMA and the STMAA. The second interpretation is said to result in a dual system where companies can choose to register under either Act. Each of these interpretations creates a priority conflict for which neither of the Acts provides a resolution.

---

161 See s 94 MPSRA.

162 The difficulty arising from this approach in relation to registration is discussed above.

163 *I & M Bank Ltd v ABC Bank Ltd and another* [2021] eKLR [48].

Take the first interpretation, for example. Suppose a floating charge over movable assets is registered under the CAMA on day one and under the STMAA on day three, and one or more of the same assets is used as collateral in another security that is registered under the STMAA on day two and under the CAMA on day four. The priority result in this scenario is unclear. Unfortunately, there is an absence of judicial consideration of these issues. This is perhaps unsurprising, given that in practice parties usually regulate priorities through inter-creditor agreements. It is, however, essential that the law is clear on these issues since it is the framework on which practice is based.

It has been suggested that the priority conflict should be resolved in favour of the CAMA so that the first to create the floating charge would prevail.[164] That view revolves around a common law principle of statutory interpretation that states that where two laws apply to the same subject matter, the more specific law should have priority.[165] Therefore the view considers the CAMA as the more specific law on floating security rights. The problem with this approach is that it assumes that the security will always relate to the floating charge as contemplated under the CAMA. What if the security parties intend to create a *floating security right* as contemplated under the STMAA?[166] In that case, the STMAA (not the CAMA) would be considered the more specific law. Also, given that the STMAA is security-specific legislation (unlike the CAMA, which is company-specific) and focusses particularly on movable assets security rights, it is arguable that the STMAA should generally be seen as the specific law and should therefore prevail.

An alternative approach, which achieves the same outcome (i.e. the STMAA having priority), is to resort to a basic common law rule that prioritises a legal interest over an equitable interest. This rule is most clearly expressed by the Nigeria Court of Appeal in *Ajayi v. Osunuku and Others*: "the basic rule of temporal order of priority [is] modified by the maxims in stating that where equities are equal, the first in time ought to prevail; where however there [exist] both legal and equitable interests, ... the former would supersede".[167] Hence, since registration under the STMAA creates a legal interest (as against the

164 Iheme (n 127) 25f.

165 See e.g. Anja Lindroos, "Addressing Norm Conflicts in a Fragmented Legal System: The Doctrine of Lex Specialis" (2005) 74(1) Nordic Journal of International Law 27.

166 As noted above, the STMAA has features that enable the creation of a floating security right, and one advantage this type of security has over the floating charge is that it is considered as a fixed security from inception.

167 (2008) LPELR-8332, at 36, per Ogunbiyi JCA.

equitable floating charge created under the CA), the rule under the STMAA should prevail so that the first party to register under the STMAA gets priority.[168]

The application of the alternative approach faces difficulty when used to determine a prior floating charge in an insolvency proceeding under ss 453 and 534 CAMA. These sections are similar to ss 535 and 612 of Kenya's Insolvency Act (see above), except that they make the CAMA determinative of the priority of floating charges.[169] The fact that the STMAA does not amend these sections of the CAMA means that a floating security interest that has priority under the STMAA (i.e. because it is registered first under that Act) may lose priority for the purposes of ss 453 and 534 CAMA. This is another undesirable consequence of the lack of coordination between the STMAA and the CAMA. Unfortunately, the lawmakers missed the opportunity to resolve these issues during the revision of the CAMA in 2020.

Post-crystallisation priority rules

Once a floating charge crystallises, it becomes a fixed charge in the focus jurisdictions and will have priority over subsequent interests.[170] Earlier in this chapter, attention was drawn to the excesses of the floating charge and the reform introduced under English law to protect certain unsecured debts from the excesses. The reform allowed certain preferential debt claims to rank ahead of the floating charge, even where the claims arise after the charge crystallises.

---

[168] See also Esangbedo (n 2) 102f.

[169] There is an apparent confusion on how the sections define a prior floating charge. While s 453(2)(a) defines it as the charge that "was first created", s 534 defines it as that which "was first registered [at the Companies Registry] or, in default of registration, it was first created". This confusion is unfortunate, as it can lead to an outcome that is contrary to the purpose of s 534, which is to give a prior chargee an opportunity to replace an administrator appointed by a subsequent chargee. In other words, the conflicting definitions can cause a situation where the notice under s 453 is owed to one party, and another party (who could well be the party who gave the notice under s 453) gets the power to replace an administrator under s 534. For example, suppose Floating Charge A is created on day 1 and registered on day 4, and Floating Charge B is created on day 2 and registered on day 3. If Floating Charge B wishes to appoint an administrator, it will need to notify Floating Charge A. However, the same Floating Charge B will have the power to replace going by the definition under s 534.

[170] *Goode and Gullifer* (n 74) observe that in accordance with the principle of apparent authority, a subsequent purchaser or chargee who concludes a transaction after crystallisation but without notice of the crystallisation may take title free of the crystallised charge (see para 5.52). This view, however, appears to be lacking in case authority in England and the focused jurisdictions.

This area of law has evolved over time, and the classes of preferred creditors have been widened. Table 3.1 provides relatively detailed information on the current position of the law in England and the focus jurisdictions.

Much could be written about how the jurisdictions compare, but owing to limitations of space, the following analysis is selective, and the reader is encouraged to consult Table 3.1 for a broader comparative view. The table shows that Kenya is the closest to English law, followed by Nigeria. The hierarchy of interests to which the floating charge is subject is similar in the three jurisdictions, albeit there is no provision for the prescribed part in Nigeria.

The approach in Ghana is fascinating for at least three reasons.[171] Firstly, liquidation expenses and certain preferential debts have priority over both fixed and floating charges.[172] The actual wording used in the Corporate Insolvency and Restructuring Act 2020 (CIRA) does not differentiate between floating and fixed charges.[173] Instead, CIRA provides that "a secured debt" that "shall be secured by *a fixed charge* against an asset of the company" (italics added) is a Class C debt, i.e. it ranks after Class A and Class B debts.[174] It is unclear what is meant by "a fixed charge," and the wording of the provision is capable of at least three interpretations: (i) that the security can only be a fixed charge; (ii) that the security includes other fixed securities such as a mortgage;[175] and (iii) that the fixed charge includes other fixed securities and floating charges.

Sadly, the CIRA neither defines the term "fixed charge" nor the word "charge".[176] In fact, various references are made to floating charges and mortgages in other parts of the Act, suggesting that these types of security are distinct from a fixed charge.[177] Yet adopting the first interpretation would lead to an absurd result that would make a mortgage holder subordinated to ordinary shareholders' claims (i.e. Class H debts). The same argument can be made in

---

171 For a recent analysis of Ghana's insolvency legal framework, see KNO Ghartey, "Local Public Entities in Distress: A Critical Analysis of the Ghanaian Approach" in L Coordes, Y Marique and E Vaccari (eds), *When Liquidation is Not an Option: A Global Study of Local Public Entities in Distress* (INSOL International, November 2022) 202ff. For an interesting historical analysis of the framework, see SB Adarkwah, "The Development of Insolvency Law in Ghana" (2016) 42(4) Commonwealth Law Bulletin 485.

172 CIRA, ss 107, 129 and 130.

173 See s 107(3)(c) CIRA.

174 Ibid. Class A debts are debts qualifying as Post-Commencement Financing, and Class B debts include preferential debts (see Table 3.1).

175 In Ghana CA, a charge is defined to include "a security on property or a mortgage" – see s 383, First Schedule.

176 There has also been an absence of attention on this point, both in case law and in the literature.

177 See e.g. ss 36(1)(b)(iii) and 117(3)(b) CIRA.

respect of the floating charge if the second interpretation is adopted. As such, the better view will be to adopt the third interpretation, which considers the term "a fixed charge" as including a mortgage (and other fixed securities) and a floating charge. This view suggests that there is no difference between a floating and fixed charge for priority purposes in insolvency, and hence both charges rank equally. It also redefines the policy underlying the protection afforded to preferential debtors, which traditionally has been to address the excessive nature of the floating charge. Including fixed security is an unusual approach, and it is not clear what the rationale is, especially given that the prior law, which the CIRA repealed, restricted the priority of preferential debtors to competitions against the floating charge.[178]

The foregoing discussion and earlier discussion of ss 33 and 86 BLA imply that a distinction between a fixed and floating charge is no longer necessary in Ghana, at least for security interests within the scope of the BLA.[179] The combined effect of ss 33 and 86 BLA is that the priority rules under the BLA, which do not distinguish between fixed and floating securities, supersede those under the CA where such a distinction exists. Also, since the same priority ranking applies to both fixed and floating charges during insolvency (see discussion above), the distinction becomes irrelevant.[180] This entails that both before and during insolvency, competing security interests will rank in the order of their registration and not whether they are fixed or floating.[181] This outcome contrasts with the position in Kenya and Nigeria. In Nigeria, the combined effect of s 2(3) STMAA (which retains the priority rules under the CA – see discussion above) and ss 657(4)(b) and 657(6)(a) CAMA (which differentiate between fixed and floating charges for priority purposes in insolvency – see Table 3.1) is that a distinction continues to be relevant, even for security interests within the scope of the STMAA. In Kenya, the distinction appears to be relevant (including for securities within the scope of the MPSRA) because of the limited effect of s 94 MPSRA, in that it does not expressly affect the priority rules applicable under the CA, and the absence of a wholesale repeal of the relevant rules in the CA (see the discussion above). The distinction is

---

178 The Bodies Corporate (Official Liquidations) Act, 1963, s 41(3).

179 As noted above, the BLA has a wider scope (than the MPRSA and STMAA) in that it applies to both movable and immovable assets. Section 1(3) BLA, however, provides for a few securities that are outside the scope of the Act, which include security interests in a ship or an aircraft.

180 Perhaps, the need to avoid the distinction may have informed the approach adopted in the CIRA of not differentiating between floating and fixed charges for priority purposes during insolvency. However, if that was the case, the wording of s 107(3)(c) CIRA should have been clearer on the inclusion of the floating charge.

181 See ss 33, 34 and 86 BLA.

also relevant under Kenya's insolvency laws since both charges are subject to different priority rules in insolvency (see Table 3.1).[182]

The second interesting feature of Ghana's approach is the inclusion of post-commencement financing debts as a first-priority preferential debt. The CIRA distinctly provides that such debts "shall be paid in full".[183] Post-commencement financing is defined as including "any financing obtained by the company … during the administration or restructuring proceedings of the company".[184]

The third feature relates to the nature of a crystallised floating charge in Ghana and how that affects the charge's priority ranking during the distribution of assets in administration or liquidation. It was noted earlier in this chapter that the floating charge becomes a fixed charge upon crystallisation.[185] The consequence of this is, barring any statutory (or case law) intervention, the subordination of the floating charge to preferential debts and the prescribed part can be avoided if the charge crystallises before the commencement of a winding-up or administration. That is because the crystallised charge would have converted to a fixed charge by the time of distribution. This position was confirmed in the English case of *Re Griffin Hotel Co Ltd*[186] in respect of s 264 of the Companies Act 1929, a predecessor provision on preferential debts. It was held in that case that preferential debts incurred after the crystallisation of a floating charge were subordinate to the charge on the ground that the charge "was no longer a floating charge" at the time the debts were incurred.[187]

This issue has been addressed in England, Kenya and Nigeria by the introduction of statutory provisions that expand the definition of the floating charge to refer to "a charge that is a floating charge on its creation".[188] Hence, a charge remains a floating charge even after crystallisation for the purposes of insolvency processes such as the distribution of assets. However, such statutory provision has not been introduced in Ghana,[189] and there is sadly a lack of

---

182 See ss 471, 473 and 474 of the Insolvency Act 2015.

183 CIRA, s 107(3)(a).

184 CIRA, s 169.

185 CA (Ghana), s 90(3); CAMA, s 203(1) and (2). No similar statutory provision exists in Kenya, but case law establishes the same position. See cases cited in notes 81 and 82 above.

186 [1941] Ch 129.

187 Ibid.

188 Insolvency Act 2015 (Kenya), s 474(8); CAMA (Nigeria), s 549(1). For England, see Insolvency Act 1986, ss 40(1) and 251; Companies Act 2006, s 754.

189 Section 383 of Ghana's CA adopts the definition provided under s 90 CA for all purposes under the Act, including for insolvency processes. The s 90 definition in turn is to the effect that the floating charge converts to a fixed charge upon

Table 3.1 *Priority ranking of floating charges on distribution of assets by the administrator or liquidator*

England	Ghana	Kenya	Nigeria
Fixed security holders[a]	*Liquidation expenses* (CIRA ss 63(2), 129 and 130)	*Fixed security holders* (Insolvency Act 2015 (IA), s 471)	*Fixed security holders* (CAMA, s 657(6)(a))
Liquidation expenses (Insolvency Act 1986 (IA), s 175(1)(b), Sch B1 para 99(3), s 176ZA)	*Preferential creditors* Class A (1st priority) – Post-Commencement Financing (CIRA ss 107(3)(a) and 130(2)) Class B (2nd priority) – Four months employee remunerations; taxes due within the year preceding the commencement of liquidation (CIRA s 107(3)(b))	*Liquidation expenses* (IA s 471, Sch 2(para 2))	*Liquidation expenses* (CAMA, s 657(4)(a) and (5))

England	Ghana	Kenya	Nigeria
Preferential creditors Ordinary preferential debts (1st priority) – pension contributions; four months' employee remunerations (with a monetary limit), coal and steel production levy; Financial Services Compensation Scheme debts and deposits.Secondary preferential debts (2nd priority) – VAT, PAYE, National Insurance and Construction Industry Scheme deductions (IA s 175(1A)–(1B), s 385, Sch 6)	*Charge holders* (including *floating charge holders, both crystallised and uncrystallised – see discussion above*) (CIRA s 107(3)(c))	*Preferential creditors* 1st priority – Four months' employee remunerations; employee holiday and compensation for redundancy; deductions from wages to satisfy 3rd party obligations (e.g. pensions). All not exceeding 200,000 shillings. 2nd priority – Tax deductions made under PAYE rules and withholding tax rules of the Income Tax Act; duty payable under the Customs and Excise Act (IA s 471, Sch 2 (paras 3 and 4))	*Preferential creditors* All local rates, charges, assessed property or income taxes, PAYE tax deductions due within the year preceding liquidation; deductions from wages pursuant to the Pension Reform Act; contributions payable under the Employees' Compensation Act; wages and accrued holiday pay for clerks, servants and workmen (CAMA, s 657(1))
Prescribed part 50% of the first £10,000 of net assets, 20% of the excess, with £800,000 maximum (IA, s 176A; Insolvency Act 1986 (Prescribed Part) Order 2003 as amended)	–	*Prescribed part* 20% of the net assets worth at least 500,000 shillings (IA ss 474(2)(a) and 474(3)(a); Insolvency Regulations 2016, r 96)	*Floating charge holders* (CAMA, s 657(4)(b))
Floating charge holders (IA, s 175(2))	–	*Floating charge holders* (IA ss 471, 473 and 474)	–

Notes: The distribution of assets by a receiver also follows the same ranking in England, Ghana and Nigeria. See respectively Insolvency Act 1986, ss 40 and 176A; CA, s 92 (referring to the CIRA's predecessor legislation); CAMA, s 207. [a] *LB Holdings Intermediate 2 Ltd (In Administration)* [2020] EWHC 1681.

judicial treatment of the issue. It, therefore, appears that the problem persists in Ghana, albeit its impact on the floating charge ranking during liquidation or administration is minimal since the CIRA uses the term "fixed charge" (and not necessarily "floating charge") – see discussion above.

It may be that the term "fixed charge" is used in the CIRA in order to resolve the foregoing issue, as that seems to make all floating charges (crystallised or not) subordinate to preferential debts. However, that is doubtful, as it does not explain why charges originally created as fixed charges are equally made subject to preferential debts. If the intention was to avoid situations where a crystallised floating charge avoids subordination to preferential debts, the law should have targeted only floating charges.

CONCLUSION

This chapter has sought to investigate the history and evolution of floating charges in the focus jurisdictions by paying attention to their local circumstances and jurisprudence. Through this approach, the chapter makes a number of important findings on the pre- and post-independence evolution of the charge. Regarding the pre-independence evolution, it is shown that while the principles of the floating charge as laid down in *Re Panama* and subsequent developments made by English case law to the floating charge were received in the focus jurisdictions by virtue of their reception statutes, the reception of statutory reforms was restricted by local circumstances. The significance of this is that while the floating charge was in operation in the colonial jurisdictions, the statutory reforms that were introduced to address its excesses were not automatically received by the reception statutes. The reforms needed to be enacted through other local legislation.

On the post-independence evolution, it has been demonstrated that the body of laws related to the floating charge continued to be largely based on English law until the enactment of the STLs (i.e. the secured transactions laws), which introduced functional approaches to security rights in the jurisdictions and made their floating charge laws diverge in many respects from the more formalist and fragmented English approach. Their divergence from English law follows a similar path, albeit there are sub-divergences in their approaches. A recurring proposition in this part of the chapter is that despite the STLs' objectives to facilitate secured transactions, they have made the creation and operation of floating charges in the jurisdictions problematic and burdensome. They made floating charges subject to two regimes (i.e. the various CAs and STLs),

---

crystallisation. The CIRA makes no attempt to define the floating charge; hence, the s 90 CA definition also applies.

whose rules on key aspects of the charge (such as its nature, registration, priority ranking and enforcement) are starkly different and poorly harmonised. The chapter demonstrates the difficulties in the areas of registration and priority ranking.

On registration, it shows that a floating charge created over assets covered under the STLs will need to be registered twice under the STL and CA registries. That is because the various STLs in the jurisdictions failed to repeal or appropriately amend relevant provisions of the CAs. This contrasts with English law, where a single regime applies. A similar difficulty arises regarding priority ranking, where the difference in approach creates priority conflict for competing floating security interests, for which neither Act provides an adequate resolution in Kenya and Nigeria. In Ghana, the conflict is resolved under s 33 BLA, where the STL is given priority. While an attempt is made in Kenya's MPRSA to replace the CA rules with those of the MPSRA through changes made to specific provisions of the CA, it is argued that the changes are limited in scope and do not extend to case law that is the source of CA priority rules. The difficulty is profound in Nigeria, as no attempt is made to resolve the conflict.

It is further argued that despite the functional approach adopted in the STLs, a distinction between a floating and fixed charge continues to be relevant in Kenya and Nigeria for security rights within the scope of the STLs. This distinction is necessary to address the unique priority rules applicable to floating charges under the CAs, as the CA rules have not been expressly superseded by the relevant STL. The chapter also shows that the distinction is required to address the unique priority rules applicable to floating charges under the insolvency laws of both countries, as these too were not changed by the STL. The chapter demonstrates that the distinction is not relevant in Ghana for security rights covered by the STL, both before and during insolvency.

All these point to the need for reform of relevant laws in the focus jurisdictions. Rather than the piecemeal changes (or none in the case of Nigeria), this chapter recommends a wholesale repeal of the relevant CA rules to better harmonise them with the STLs. It is conceivable that the existing laws impede the success of the STLs in their bids to facilitate secured transactions. Indeed, as noted earlier, lenders in Nigeria generally prefer to create charges under the CAMA, despite the benefits available under the STMAA, which include the exclusion of stamp duties costs and the possibility of securing priority by registering a financing statement in advance of a security interest.

ACKNOWLEDGEMENTS

I am greatly indebted to the editors for their insightful comments on previous drafts of this paper. I am also thankful to Professor Marek Dubovec, Mr Kenneth Ghartey and Dr Samuel Adarkwah for providing valuable comments on aspects of the paper. I benefitted from resources accessed during my stay at the Max Planck Institute for Comparative and International Private Law in Hamburg, for which I am grateful to the Institute. Any errors remain my own.

4. The decisive influence of publicity on the historical development of continental European floating security rights

Vincent van Hoof

INTRODUCTION

Nowadays, many countries on the European continent allow for the creation of "floating" security rights. As stated in the introduction to this volume,[1] a floating security right in a broad sense has two core characteristics: (1) it is a security right over multiple present and future assets; and (2) the security grantor ordinarily has the power to dispose of property "covered" by the security right without the explicit consent of the security right holder. The security grantor may often transfer assets free of any encumbrance in his ordinary course of business prior to an event of default.

Some countries, such as Germany and the Netherlands, have known non-possessory security rights (over multiple present and future movables and claims) since the beginning of the twentieth century. Other countries, such as France, Italy and Belgium, have only recently introduced all-encompassing security rights in movable assets.

A common characteristic of the recent modernisation efforts in many European countries is the required registration of security rights in a public register. This underlines the international trend towards the publicity of security rights. Soft law instruments such as UNCITRAL's model law on secured transactions highlight the importance of public registration.[2] The

[1] A MacPherson and C Rapatz, "Introduction to *Floating Charges in Comparative Perspective*" in A MacPherson and C Rapatz (eds), *Floating Charges in Comparative Perspective* (Edward Elgar Publishing 2025).

[2] Art. 18 (Primary methods for achieving third-party effectiveness) of UNCITRAL Model Law on Secured Transactions (2016).

World Bank's Doing Business report (2016) calls publicity one of the "pillars of a modern secured transactions system".[3] Some countries, such as Italy, have expressed willingness to align their new pledge provisions with the standards set by UNCITRAL and the World Bank.[4] Other countries, such as Germany and the Netherlands, contrast sharply with these modernisation efforts because of their lack of public registration of non-possessory security rights or any inclination to introduce such a requirement. From a comparative point of view, it seems that public registration is the next logical step in the evolution of security rights for all European countries and that jurisdictions without publicity are just lagging behind. However, a legal historical perspective will show that we certainly must not jump to that conclusion.

In this chapter, I will use a legal historical perspective to explain modern differences between European countries regarding the recognition of non-possessory security rights and the role of public registration. By investigating the historical development of non-possessory security rights in movables (and the principle of publicity), I will provide an overview of a recurring reluctance to accept non-possessory security rights and the various concepts that shaped modern security rights. The appreciation and understanding of differences between legal systems will contribute to the debate on modernisation and harmonisation of security rights at a national as well as an international level.

Modern security rights in movables are – despite all national differences – essentially an amalgamation of two different approaches to security rights in movables. The first approach is that of Germanic law, the customary law of the Germanic peoples who lived across Europe in the medieval period. Germanic law rejected non-possessory security rights in movables and only recognised possessory rights of pledge. Control (or a lack thereof) entailed some kind of publicity. In the next section, I will elaborate on this Germanic approach. The second approach is that of Roman law. Roman jurists and emperors developed the concept of all-encompassing (non-possessory) security rights in the second and third centuries CE. In Roman law, secured creditors had priority over other creditors regarding the proceeds of the encumbered assets and could even recover encumbered assets from third parties. Publicity was lacking. In the third section, I will investigate the scope and legal effects of these so-called general rights of pledge or hypothec.[5] The revival in the study and application

---

3 World Bank Group, Doing Business 2016, 109, available at <https://www.doingbusiness.org/content/dam/doingBusiness/media/Annual-Reports/English/DB16-Full-Report.pdf> accessed 1 January 2024.

4 Fascicolo Iter DDL S. 2362 (Senato della Repubblica, 19 March 2018).

5 In this chapter, the term "pledge" will be used as the generic term for a possessory or non-possessory security right, that is, a limited property right, not an ownership right, in the debtor's assets. The grantor of a right of pledge to secure

of Roman law in the late medieval and early modern period led to an amalgamation of the Germanic approach and the Roman approach towards security rights in many regions across Europe. The extent to which Roman law was adopted varied throughout Europe. In the fourth section, I will discuss the recognition of non-possessory security rights in four different European regions to illustrate the various degrees to which Roman law superseded Germanic law. Consequently, I will explain why non-possessory rights of pledge were lacking in the civil codes of the nineteenth and twentieth centuries (fifth section). From the introduction of the national civil codes onwards, the gradual return of all-encompassing (and non-possessory) security rights in movables has been a matter of national law. As I will illustrate in the final section, a clear distinction arose between countries in the twentieth century which is still reflected in modern provisions on security rights: security rights with and security rights without public registration.

GERMANIC APPROACHES TO LIABILITY AND SECURITY

Liability for Debts in Medieval Europe

During and after the decline of the Western Roman Empire, Germanic peoples, such as the Visigoths, Ostrogoths and Franks, migrated across Europe. They eventually settled, and their kingdoms filled the power vacuum left by the fall of the Western Roman Empire. These peoples had their own customary private law, often called Germanic law. This term does not refer to a single law system, but to a family of legal systems.[6] Roman law was still applied in many parts of the former empire. Germanic kings authorised the use and application of Roman law in their kingdoms. The indigenous Roman people continued to live under Roman law. The surviving sources of Roman law were used by the Germanic kings to compile codifications of Roman law, the so-called *leges Romanorum*.[7] In the more Romanised parts of Europe, such as Italy, Spain and southern France, Roman law remained a relevant source of law throughout the Middle Ages. In less Romanised parts of Europe, such as the north of France and the greater part of northern Europe, Germanic law gradually became more

---

his own obligation will mostly be referred to as "debtor". It will be stated expressly if the grantor created a right of pledge to secure the obligation of another person. The party whose claim is secured by a right of pledge will mostly be referred to as the "(secured) creditor".

[6] R Lesaffer, *European Legal History* (CUP 2009) §129, 159.

[7] F Wieacker and R Zimmermann, *A History of Private Law in Europe* (Clarendon 2003) 78; Lesaffer (n 6) §132, 163.

important and pushed Roman law further into the background. Roman law was also applied by the courts of the Roman Catholic Church to settle private law disputes between (the Church and) clergymen.[8]

Unlike in Roman law, a debtor was not liable for his debts by default. Germanic law distinguished between obligation (*Schuld*) and liability (*Haftung*).[9] This meant that a debtor was not automatically liable when a creditor had a claim against him. A creditor could only enforce his claim if the debtor had made one of his assets liable for the claim. Movable assets were often the primary type of collateral, since immovable assets regularly belonged to a feudal lord or were regarded as inalienable family property.[10]

Mobilia non habent sequelam

Initially, a debtor could only create possessory pledges in movables and had to hand over the asset(s) to the creditor.[11] A lack of non-possessory pledges followed from the Germanic approach to the protection of interests in movables in general. Unlike Roman law and many modern continental approaches to property law, Germanic law made no real distinction between ownership and possession.[12]

In Roman law, the most comprehensive right in a movable thing was ownership (*dominium*). Ownership was protected by an action, the so-called *reivindicatio*. The owner could bring this action against any possessor to recover the thing. A possessor was someone who had control over the thing (*corpus*) and had the intention to retain the thing for himself (*animus possidendi*). A possessor was distinguished from a detentor, someone who had factual control over the thing on behalf of someone else (the possessor) and thus lacked the intention to retain the thing for himself.

Pursuant to Germanic law, a person who had actual control over an asset had *Gewere* or *seisin*. The *Gewere* was protected against any interference. From a Roman law perspective, even a *detentor* had *Gewere*. If someone who

---

[8] Lesaffer (n 6) §154, 184; Wieacker and Zimmermann (n 7) 84ff.

[9] O von Gierke, *Schuld und Haftung* (Marcus 1910) 1ff; R Hübner, *Grundzüge des deutschen Privatrechts* (Deichert 1930) 493ff. See with references: R. Zimmermann, *The Law of Obligations* (Clarendon 1996) 5.

[10] A Egger, *Vermögenshaftung und Hypothek nach fränkischem Recht* (Marcus 1903) 102–103; Hübner (n 9) 505ff; J Bart, *Histoire du droit privé de la chute de l'Empire romain au XIXe siècle* (LGDJ 2009) 379; D Deroussin, *Histoire du droit privé (XVIe–XXIe siècle)* (Ellipses 2010), nr 418.

[11] Egger (n 10) 98–99; Von Gierke (n 9) 123; Hübner (n 9) 470; Bart (n 10) 382.

[12] Possession was protected by legal remedies (interdicta), but a possessor would generally have to hand over the thing to the owner of the thing.

had *Gewere* voluntarily handed over the asset to someone else, *Gewere* was transferred to that person, even if that person was supposed to give it back at one point. If this "holder" transferred *Gewere* to a third party, the original possessor only had an action against his counterparty (the "holder") for breach of contract. He could not bring an action against the third party. This effect is sometimes described by the legal maxim *Hand wahre Hand* or "let hand indemnify hand".[13] After the reception of Roman law, the legal maxim *mobilia non habent sequelam* ("movables cannot be followed") was used to describe this Germanic lack of third-party effects as opposed to Roman law. In Germanic law, only someone who lost *Gewere* involuntarily (i.e. by means of theft) could bring an action against any third party who had acquired *Gewere* of the thing. The third party was acting unlawfully by not giving back the asset and was liable for damages. The Germanic approach to movables influenced the way in which security rights functioned in the early modern period. For a long time, it was required to provide the *Gewere* to a creditor in order to create a right of pledge in movables.[14] The requirement of control over movables led to transparency or publicity of rights of pledge. As long as movables remained in the hands of a debtor, his creditors were certain that the assets were not encumbered by a non-possessory right of pledge.

Contractual Liability by Means of *obligationes*

From the thirteenth century onwards, debtors could go before a (local) court and make specific *immovable* assets liable by means of a so-called *obligatio* without having to hand over the asset to the creditor.[15] This practice is often referred to by the term *jüngere Satzung* in modern literature.[16] An *obligatio specialis* gave a creditor priority over other creditors. The chronological order of the *obligationes* determined the priority between competing creditors whose claims were enforceable against the same encumbered asset by means of an *obligatio specialis*.[17] A secured creditor could enforce his security right over the charged asset even if the debtor had transferred ownership of the asset to a third-party.[18]

---

[13] Hübner (n 9) 433ff; Deroussin (n 10) nr 418.

[14] Hübner (n 9) 470.

[15] Von Gierke (n 9) 333ff; Hübner (n 9) 505ff; Ph. Godding, *Le droit privé dans les Pays-Bas méridionaux* (Palais des Académies 1987) nr 367; Bart (n 10) 379.

[16] Egger (n 10) 136; Von Gierke (n 9) 31; Hübner (n 9) 407; Bart (n 10) 383.

[17] Egger (fn 10) 138–139; Von Gierke (n 9) 33; Godding (n 15) nr 365; Bart (n 10) 383.

[18] Von Gierke (n 9) 31–32; Hübner (n 9) 410; Godding (n 15) nr 367; Bart (n 10) 383.

Apart from the *obligatio (specialis)* that made specific immovable assets liable, a general *obligatio (generalis)* regarding all of a debtor's assets was recognised.[19] The *obligatio* was evidenced by a sealed deed and passed before a local court. According to the thirteenth-century jurist Philippe de Rémi, sire de Beaumanoir (c. 1247–1296), the debtor would sometimes write: "I have bound myself and my heirs, and all that is mine now and in the future, movables and immovables".[20] The *obligatio generalis* did not encumber the assets with a right in rem, since the debtor was able to transfer any of his assets free of any encumbrance.[21] The *obligatio* enabled the creditor to take recourse against all of the debtor's assets at the moment the debtor was in default. Only then did the creditor have the right to take possession of the assets, have them sold and use the proceeds to satisfy his claim against the debtor. The creditor was, however, protected against gratuitous transfers by the debtor to third parties prior to the seizure of the obligated assets.[22] The creditor could recover donated assets from third parties despite the fact that they no longer belonged to the debtor. An *obligatio generalis* gave no priority to a creditor over other creditors whose claims were also enforceable by means of an *obligatio generalis*, even when their claim or *obligatio* was from a later date.[23] A special *obligatio*, however, had priority over a general *obligatio*.[24]

These medieval *obligationes* paved the way for the reception of Roman security rights in the late medieval period and early modern period. As I will now discuss, Roman law also distinguished between general and special security rights. These security rights did not, however, completely replace the medieval concepts of the *obligationes* and the Germanic approach to movables.

THE REDISCOVERY OF ROMAN LAW AND ITS (GENERAL) SECURITY RIGHTS

In the sixth century, the Eastern Roman emperor Justinian wanted to restore the Roman empire to its former glory *armis legibusque*, with weapons and laws. He re-conquered parts of the former Western Roman Empire such as

19 Von Gierke (n 9) 333; Hübner (n 9) 411; Godding (n 15) nr 365; Bart (n 10) 383.

20 P de Beaumanoir, *Les coutumes du Beauvoisis* (Renouard 1842) II, XXXV, 49: "J'ai obligié moi et mes oirs, et tout le mien present et a venir, meubles et eritages".

21 Egger (n 10) 138; Von Gierke (n 9) 77; Hübner (n 9) 411; Godding (n 15) nr 366; Bart (n 10) 383.

22 Egger (n 10) 148–149, and 164; Bart (n 10) 383.

23 Godding (n 15) nr 366.

24 Egger (n 10) 140 and 152; Godding (n 15) nr 366.

Italy, and he codified Roman law. A few copies of his codification reached Italy but failed to make a lasting impact in western Europe in that period. Lesaffer remarks that the Byzantine dominion was "too brief and the text too extensive and complex for widespread distribution in the West. After the Byzantines had been driven out of northern and middle Italy, the Justinian codification fell into oblivion."[25] At the end of the eleventh century, a copy of the Digest of Justinian's codification was discovered in Florence. Scholars like Irnerius lectured on the Digest in Bologna. In the following centuries, Roman law was studied and taught at universities across Europe. The church and secular jurisdictions in Europe increasingly adopted particular concepts and rules of material law (from Justinian's codification), a process often referred to as the reception of Roman law. In the more Romanised southern parts of Europe such as Spain, Italy and southern France, the reception started as early as the thirteenth century.[26] In the north of Europe, the reception took place from the fourteenth, fifteenth and sixteenth centuries.[27] I will first discuss the non-possessory security rights of Roman law and the debtor's ability to deal with his assets in the ordinary course of business. In the fourth section, I will analyse how some of these concepts were adopted in medieval Europe.

The *generalis hypotheca*

In Roman law, a right of non-possessory pledge (*hypotheca* or *pignus*) in movable and immovable assets was created by a pledge agreement, provided that the asset(s) belonged to the debtor (*in bonis*). According to Ulpian, a pledge agreement was concluded as soon as the parties reached *nuda conventio*.[28] For this, they needed to agree on the encumbered asset(s) and the secured obligation. Parties often put the pledge agreement in writing, although this was not required.[29] Gaius pointed out that a written agreement obviously made it easier for the parties to prove what they agreed on.[30] In Post-Classical Roman law, a written agreement had another advantage compared with an oral agreement. In 472 CE, Emperor Leo I gave pledges that were created by means of public

---

[25] Lesaffer (n 6) §152, 183.

[26] Lesaffer (n 6) §232, 272.

[27] Lesaffer (n 6) §232, 272.

[28] Cf. D.13,7,1 pr. (Ulp. 40 ad Sab.): pignus contrahitur … etiam nuda conventione.

[29] Cf. HLE Verhagen, "Secured Transactions in Classical Roman Law" in G. Dari-Mattiacci/D.P. Kehoe, *Roman Law and Economics*, II (OUP 2020) 141.

[30] D.20,1,4 (Gaius *formula hypothecaria*).

deeds priority over pledges that were created by other means.[31] Public deeds were prepared by a notary (*tabellio*) and sealed in the presence of witnesses. A written agreement that was signed by three respectable witnesses was put on par with public deeds. True publicity in the sense that outsiders could establish whether or not assets were encumbered, was lacking.

If the asset belonged to the debtor or was encumbered with permission from the owner, a limited real right in the asset was created.[32] This meant that the right of pledge was effective against third parties. For example, the secured creditor could recover the encumbered asset(s) from a third party with the *actio Serviana*.

The parties could either describe the pledged assets specifically in the pledge agreement or describe the assets in an all-encompassing manner. A debtor could, for example, pledge all of his present and future assets at once. Future assets would then automatically be encumbered when the debtor acquired the assets. According to Gaius, it was standard contractual practice for Roman debtors to describe some assets specifically and state that the rest of the debtor's present and future assets (*cetera bona*) were pledged "as if specifically pledged".[33]

This so-called general pledge or hypothec (*generalis hypotheca*) was distinguished from a *specialis hypotheca*. A debtor created a right of pledge *specialiter*[34] if he specified the encumbered asset in the agreement (non-possessory pledge) or handed over the asset to the creditor (possessory pledge). Jurists often noted that a general pledge covered future assets, whereas a special pledge could only encumber assets that belonged to the debtor at the time the

---

31 C.8,17,11,1. Cf. Nov. 73,1 (Imp. Just.); P Frezza, *Le Garanzie delle Obligazioni*, II (Milani 1963) 266–267; M Kaser, *Das römische Privatrecht*, II (Beck 1975) 318; WJ Zwalve, "A Labyrinth of Creditors" in E Kieninger (ed.), *Security Rights in Movable Property in European Private Law* (CUP 2004) 42; Verhagen (n 29) 146–147.

32 D.20,1,4 (Gaius 1 de form. hyp.); D.20,1,1 pr (Pap. 11 resp.); C.8,15(16),1 (Imp. Sev. and Car., a. 194). Cf. Kaser, RP I, § 110, 464–465.

33 D.20,1,15,1 (Gaius form. hyp.). Cf. M Kaser (n 31) 466.

34 D.20,1,6 (Ulp. 73 ad ed.); D.20,1,15,1 (Gaius form. hyp.); D.20,2,6 (Ulp. 73 ad ed.); D.20,4,7,1 (Ulp. 3 disp.); D.20,4,8 (Ulp. 7 disp.); D.20,4,11,2 (Gaius form. hyp.); D.20,6,4,2 (Ulp. 8 disp.); D.20,6,8,7 (Marc. ad form. hyp.); C.4,10,6 (Imp. Diocl. and Max.); C.8,16(17),9 pr and 1 (Imp. Just.).

contract of pledge was concluded.[35] This difference ensued from the *formula* of the *actio Serviana*, as Marcianus pointed out.[36]

The way in which parties described the encumbered assets in the pledge agreement had several other legal effects. I have argued that by opting for a general pledge, the parties intended to give the debtor the right to dispose of his generally pledged assets free of the right of pledge.[37] The *generalis hypotheca* was a floating security right in the sense that it was a security right over multiple present and future assets, and the security grantor ordinarily had the power to dispose of property "covered" by the security right without the explicit consent of the security right holder. I will elaborate on this interpretation of the pledge agreement in the next section.

Another difference between special and general pledges was that a debtor needed the secured creditor's permission to sell specifically encumbered assets. If he sold specifically encumbered assets without permission, he committed embezzlement (*furtum*).[38] Paul implied that permission was not required for the sale of generally encumbered assets.[39] He only considered the sale of assets as an act of *furtum* if they had been encumbered by a possessory pledge or a non-possessory special pledge (*sive eam tradiderat creditori sive speciali pactione tantum obligaverat*). The previous point was demonstrated in Roman law in relation to enslaved persons. Slaves could be objects of property and could therefore be pledged to a creditor. The owner of a slave could free the slave so that the freed person was no longer property, and if the slave was pledged, was no longer encumbered by the security right. However, a debtor could no longer free the slaves he had encumbered with a special right of pledge, whereas he could set free his slaves if he had created a general right of pledge.[40] A debtor who had encumbered his assets with a general pledge could still free

---

35 D.20,1,1,pr. (Papinianus 11 responsorum); D.20,1,6 (Ulpianus 73 ad edictum); D.20,4,21,pr. (Scaevola 27 digestorum); D.22,3,23 (Marcianus 4 regularum); C.8,16(17),9,1 (Imp. Justinianus in 528).

36 D.22,3,23 (Marcianus *ad formulam hypothecariam*); Also: D. 20,4,9,3 (Africanus 8 quaestionum); C. 8,15(16),5 and 6 (Imp. Diocletianus and Maximianus in 286 and 293); C. 8,16(17),6 (Imp. Diocletianus and Maximianus in 293).

37 VJM van Hoof, "The 'generalis hypotheca' and the sale of pledged assets in Roman law" *TR* 85 (2017) 490; cf. D Schanbacher, review of VJM van Hoof – Generale zekerheidsrechten in rechtshistorisch perspectief, *TR* 85 (2017) 617.

38 D.47,2,19,6 (Ulp. 40 ad Sab.); D.47,2,67(66) pr (Paul. 7 ad Plaut.); C.7,26,6 (Imp. Philippus).

39 D.47,2,67(66) pr (Paulus 7 ad Plaut.).

40 C.7,8,3 (Imp. Sept. Sev. and Car., a. 209); see also D.40,9,5,2 (Jul. 64 dig.).

his encumbered slaves unless he was insolvent and the liberation was harmful to his creditor.[41]

The way in which parties described the encumbered assets in the pledge agreement did not necessarily affect the secured creditor's priority. Roman jurists recognised the rule that the chronological order of the creation of rights of pledge determined the priority between competing rights of pledge with regard to the same encumbered asset(s). This rule was expressed in the famous legal maxim *prior tempore, potior iure*, earlier in time, stronger in right (hereafter: the *prior tempore* rule).[42] This meant that the first secured creditor could use the proceeds from a sale of the encumbered assets to satisfy the secured obligation before lower-ranking secured creditors. Exceptions to the *prior tempore* rule were made in favour of specific categories of secured creditors, such as a creditor who provided finance to the debtor for the acquisition of assets and obtained a hypothec (non-possessory pledge) over these assets. His right of pledge was privileged, in the sense that he had priority over secured creditors with earlier non-privileged pledges.[43] Papinian made it clear that the *prior tempore* rule applied to special and general pledges alike.[44]

Express and implied terms of the pledge agreement affected the enforcement of the right of pledge in case the debtor failed to pay or otherwise satisfy a secured obligation (for example, by providing a guarantee). The enforcement of rights of pledge developed throughout the first centuries of the common era.[45] In the presumed first stage of this development, the secured creditor would become the owner of the encumbered assets after the debtor's default.[46] If the value of the asset(s) exceeded the secured obligation, the secured creditor would benefit. However, the parties sometimes expressly agreed on the (re) payment of the surplus.[47] In the second stage, the obligation to pay the surplus

41 Fragmentum quod vulgo Dositheanum dicitur; D.40,9,29 (Gaius 1 de manum.); Inst. Gaius I,37; C.7,8,3 (Imp. Sept. Sev. and Car., a. 209).

42 Derived from C. 8,17,3 (Imp. Car., a. 213): (…) *sicut prior es tempore, ita potior iure.*

43 D.20,4,7 pr (Ulp. 3 disp.); C. 8,17(18),7 (Diocl. et Maxim.) and Nov. 97,3. Cf. VJM van Hoof, "The priority of acquisition secured creditors in classical Roman law" SZ, Rom.abt. 139 (2022) 192–213.

44 D.20,4,2 (Papinianus *3 responsorum*). Cf. C.8,17(18),6 (Imp. Val. and Gall.).

45 See M Kaser, *Studien zum römischen Pfandrecht* (Jovene 1982) 75–78; HLE Verhagen, The evolution of pignus in classical Roman law, Ius honorarium and "ius novum" *TR* 81 (2013) 69.

46 The term "default" will be used to describe the failure of a debtor to pay or otherwise perform a secured obligation and any other event that constitutes default under the terms of an agreement between the debtor and the secured creditor.

47 Cf. Verhagen (n 45) 69.

to the debtor may have been implied. The encumbered assets needed to be valued. In the third and final stage, unless the parties agreed otherwise, the creditor had to sell the encumbered assets and pay the surplus proceeds to the debtor.[48] A conditional sale of the encumbered asset by the debtor to the creditor for its market value, triggered by an event of default, was valid.[49] The use of a forfeiture clause, the so-called *lex commissoria*, was eventually prohibited by Emperor Constantine in the first half of the fourth century (C. 8,34,3, a. 326 CE). This meant that parties could not effectively agree that an event of default resulted in the acquisition of ownership of the encumbered assets by the creditor without paying the surplus to the debtor.

Pledging a Group of Things as a Whole

A debtor could not only pledge *all* of his assets but also a specific class or group of assets, such as a herd (*grex*) or the contents of a shop (*taberna*). By doing so, the parties intended to pledge the group as a whole and not the individual assets. According to the jurist Pomponius, there were three types of things (*corpora*):

> One is that suffused by a single spirit, which the Greeks call unitary, a slave, for instance, a beam of wood, a stone, and the like; another is that compounded of cohering individual elements, which is described as constructed, a house, say, a ship, or a cupboard; the third is that which is composed of individual entities, subsumed under one designation, such as a nation, a legion, or a flock.[50]

Pomponius referred to the third category as a *corpus ex distantibus*.[51] The identity of this type of *corpus* remained the same despite the changing of its assets. In medieval literature, this category was also called a *universitas rerum*.[52] If a debtor pledged his herd to a creditor, animals which were born afterward were also encumbered. Marcianus pointed out that the herd itself remained encumbered, even if all the animals which had formed the herd at

---

48 C.8,34,1 (Imp. Alex. Sev.); see for exceptions to this rule (conditional sales of the pledged object by the debtor to the creditor): Verhagen (n 45) 73–78.

49 D.20,1,16,9 (Marc. ad form. hyp.); cf. HLE Verhagen, "'Verfallpfand in early classical Roman Law: real security in the archive of the Sulpicii" *TR* 79 (2011) 18.

50 D.41,3,30pr (Pomponius 30 ad Sabinum). For the translation of Digest texts, I have used A Watson (ed.), *The Digest of Justinian* (University of Pennsylvania Press 1998) (unless stated otherwise), and I have exchanged the word mortgage for hypothec (or pledge) as the translation of *hypotheca* and *pignus*.

51 Also Justinian in Inst. 2,20,18.

52 Bartolus ad D.20,1,13 (ed. Polara, G. (ed.), *Bartolus Commentaria* II, Rome: Il Cigno Galileo Galilei, 1996, fo. 134va.

the time of the pledge agreement had died in the meantime.[53] Roman jurists did not regard every random group of animals as a *grex*. A group of animals needed to be big enough to reproduce and recover from the loss of some animals.[54] Moreover, the animals had to be accustomed to each other to live in relative harmony.[55]

In a case discussed by the jurist Scaevola, a debtor had pledged his shop (taberna) to his creditor:

> When a debtor pledged a stall (*taberna*) to the creditor, the question was put whether this was invalid or whether by "stall" the merchandise in the stall was to be taken as pledged. And if he sold goods from time to time, bought others, brought them into the stall, and then died, could the creditor in the action on pledge sue for all that was then on the premises, in view of the turnover of stock? Scaevola replied: What was in the stall at the debtor's death was subject to the pledge.[56]

Scaevola stated that a pledge of a *taberna* resulted in a pledge of all assets on the debtor's premises at the time of his death.[57] Several different interpretations of this text exist in modern literature. Some authors believe that the Roman jurists regarded the pledge of a *taberna* as a special right of pledge in one particular asset, the *taberna*. In this view, the *taberna* itself was an ever-changing group of things which were treated as a whole (*universitas*) or a *corpus ex distantibus* like a herd (*grex*).[58] According to Mentxaka, a debtor who

---

[53] D.20,1,13pr (Marcianus ad formulam hypothecariam).

[54] J Hammerstein, *Die Herde im römischen Recht: Grex als rechtliche Sachgesamtheit und Wirtschaftseinheit* (Musterschmidt 1975) 41 and 127.

[55] In 7.6.5 of his *res rustica*, Columella remarked that a purchase of separate animals ran the risk that the animals would not get along with each other. Cf. Hammerstein (n 54) 42.

[56] D.20,1,34pr (Scaevola *27 digestorum*): Cum tabernam debitor creditori pignori dederit, quaesitum est, utrum eo facto nihil egerit an *tabernae* appellatione merces, quae in ea erant, obligasse videatur? Et si eas merces per tempora distraxerit et alias comparaverit easque in eam tabernam intulerit et decesserit, an omnia quae ibi deprehenduntur creditor hypothecaria actione petere possit, cum et mercium species mutatae sint et res aliae illatae? Respondit: ea, quae mortis tempore debitoris in taberna inventa sunt, pignori obligata esse videntur.

[57] Cf. H Wagner, "Zur wirtschaftlichen und rechtlichen Bedeutung der Tabernen" in: *Studi in onore di Arnaldo Biscardi* 3 (Istituto Editoriale Cisalpino-La Goliardica 1982) 412; F Sturm, "Exegese von Scaevola" D.20,1,34pr., JuS 1962, 427ff in H Schlosser, F Sturm and H Weber, *Die rechtsgeschichtliche Exegese* (Beck 1993) 412; EA Daubermann, *Die Sachgesamtheit als Gegenstand des klassischen römischen Rechts* (Lang 1993) 117.

[58] Cf. D.7,1,70,3 (Ulpianus 17 ad Sabinum); D.41,3,30,pr (Pomponius 30 ad Sabinum) and D.20,1,13,pr (Marcianus ad formulam hypothecariam).

pledged a *taberna* could transfer individual assets free of any encumbrance, because the *taberna* was pledged as a whole and not the individual assets.[59] Roman jurists did not, however, label the *taberna* as a *corpus ex distantibus* or *universitas*. Göppert has argued that a *corpus ex distantibus* required a common soul (ψυχή) and that a *taberna* had no such soul.[60] Baron pointed out that there was some kind of connection between the assets of *universitates rerum* that was acknowledged throughout time and by different peoples: "The *universitates rerum* form by themselves, by virtue of a natural necessity, by virtue of needs of life and transactions".[61]

It is more likely that by pledging the *taberna* the debtor created a general right of pledge. This meant that all present and future assets in the shop were pledged as if they were specifically pledged. If the debtor defaulted, the secured creditor could not only take recourse against the assets in the shop but, in theory, also follow (or trace) encumbered assets in the hands of third parties. As a general rule, pledged assets remained encumbered by a right of pledge if the pledgor transferred the assets without the permission of the pledgee.[62] A pledgee's silence was not enough to constitute permission. A pledgee who remains silent when he is aware that a pledgor intends to transfer a pledged asset does not lose his right of pledge.[63] A creditor and his debtor could agree that assets were no longer encumbered.[64] If the parties opted for a general description of the encumbered assets, such as *taberna*, *bona debitoris*, or *cetera bona*, the interpretation could lead to the conclusion that the pledgor was free to transfer generally pledged assets in his ordinary course of business, prior to an event of default. In the case discussed by Scaevola, the security grantor apparently had the right to transfer the assets in the shop prior to his death.

---

59 R Mentxaka, *La pignoracion de colectividades en el derecho romano clasico* (Universidad del Paĭs Vasco 1986) 227. Cf. CF von Mühlenbruch, "Ueber die s.g. *juris* und *facti universitates*" in *Archiv für die civilistische Praxis*, Band 17, Heft 3 (1834) 378.

60 HR Göppert, *Über einheitliche, zusammengesetzte und Gesammt-Sachen nach römischem Recht* (Verlag der Buchhandlung des Waisenhauses 1871) 49.

61 Sie bilden sich von selbst, vermöge Naturnotwendigkeit, vermöge der Bedürfnisse des Lebens und Verkehrs; J Baron, *Die Gesamtrechtsverhältnisse im römischen Recht* (Elwert 1864) 62.

62 C.8,25(26),10 (imp. Diocletianus en Maximianus in 293).

63 D.20,6,8,15 (Marcianus ad formulam hypothecariam). See E Koops, *Uitleg van afstand van zekerheidsrechten*, *AA* 2013, with references, 704.

64 D.20,6,8,1 (Marcianus ad formulam hypothecariam).

THE RECEPTION OF ROMAN GENERAL SECURITY RIGHTS IN MOVABLES AND *MOBILIA NON HABENT SEQUELAM*

The medieval *obligationes,* which were already present across the continent, provided a basis for the above-mentioned reception of Roman security rights. The legal effects of the special *obligatio* were relatively similar to those of the Roman hypothec, and the distinction between general and special hypothecs showed a certain similarity to the distinction between general and special *obligationes.* Roman security rights did not, however, completely replace the medieval concepts of the *obligationes.* Moreover, the medieval appreciation of publicity was not diminished. I will provide a rough outline of the law of secured credit in a variety of regions: Italy, the Dutch Republic, the German-speaking countries, France and Belgium. I have selected these European regions because they illustrate the various degrees to which Roman law superseded Germanic law in early modern Europe and the principle of publicity was applied.

Italy

Perhaps the most comprehensive reception of the Roman security rights took place in Italian cities and regions. The distinction between general and special security rights of pledge (*ipoteca generale* and *speciale*) was recognised.[65] A general right of pledge encumbered all of a debtor's assets, such as immovables, movables, claims, money, etc.[66] These security rights were true rights in rem, and a secured creditor could recover pledged assets from third parties. However, pledgor and pledgee could agree that the pledgor could dispose of pledged assets in his ordinary course of business. When a debtor pledged his shop (*taberna* or *bottega*), the interpretation of the pledge agreement was that the debtor could continue to deal with the pledged assets in his ordinary course of business.[67] Publicity of the security rights was not required.

---

65 *Pratica civile composta dall'avvocato Domenico Moro,* tomo III (Pauria 1763), cap. XXXV, §1, 5.

66 *Selectarum Rotae Florentinae decisionum thesaurus ex bibliotheca Johannis Pauli Ombrosi,* tomus III (Bonducciana 1770), dec. 27 (30 July 1694) 191.

67 Selectarum Rotae (n 66) dec. 67, 506.

The Dutch Republic

In the seventeenth century, the Dutch Republic's private law was an amalgamation of Roman law and (indigenous) customary law. From the fifteenth century onwards, the revival in the study and application of Roman law (*ius commune*) across Europe strongly influenced Dutch private law. Because of this mixed character, the law of Holland is often referred to as Roman-Dutch law (*Rooms-Hollands recht*).[68] In the Dutch Republic, the right of pledge (*pand*) was recognised as a creditor's limited property right in the debtor's assets (*ius in re aliena*) to secure the performance of an obligation.[69] Roman-Dutch law distinguished between special and general rights of pledge based on the description of the encumbered assets, as Roman law did.[70] For example, a debtor created a general right of pledge by referring to "all of his property, movable and immovable, claims and credits, present and future, without any excluded".[71] As this example illustrates, the general right of pledge affected, among other things, movable property, claims and immovable property. The general right of pledge was known by different names, such as *generaal pandrecht* or *generale hypotheek, algemene onderzetting* or *algemeen verband*.[72] It was common practice to combine a special right of pledge with a general right of pledge by specifying one or more assets and indicating the rest of the

---

[68] S van Leeuwen, *Het Rooms-Hollands-Regt* (Hackens 1664); See also RW Lee, *An Introduction to Roman-Dutch Law* (Clarendon 1953) 2–7; R Zimmermann, *Das römisch-holländische Recht in Südafrika* (Wissenschaftliche Buchgesellschaft Darmstadt 1983).

[69] Hugo de Groot, *Inleiding tot de Hollandsche Rechts-geleertheyd* (Van Wou 1631), 2.48.1, 136 recto; S. Groenewegen van der Made, *Tractatus de legibus abrogatis et inusitatis in Hollandia vicinisque regionibus* (Waesberge 1669) ad D.20,1,1; Voet, *Commentarius ad Pandectas* (De Hondt 1726) I, ad D.20,1,1, 849; Van Leeuwen (n 68) 4.13.24, 325; DG van der Keessel, *Voorlesinge oor die hedendaagse reg na aanleiding van De Groot se "Inleiding tot de Hollandse rechtsgeleerdheyd"* (translation of: Praelectiones juris hodierni ad Hugonis Grotii introductionem ad jurisprudentiam Hollandicam) (Balkema 1964) III, ad. Gr.2.48, 407; VJM van Hoof, "Grotius's Contribution to the Law of Secured Credit" *Grotiana* 44 (2023) 247–275.

[70] Van Hoof (n 37) 476–478.

[71] "alle zijn goederen roerende en onroerende Actien en Crediten tegenwoordige en toekomende geen dien uitgezondert" in J. Naeranus, *Consultatien, advisen en advertissementen, gegeven en geschreven bi verscheiden treffelike rechtsgeleerden in Holland en elders* (Naeranus 1689) V 49, 181.

[72] See for an elaborate analysis of the development of the general right of pledge in the Netherlands: VJM van Hoof, *Generale zekerheidsrechten in rechtshistorisch perspectief* (Wolters Kluwer 2015).

debtor's assets as also pledged.[73] A right of pledge had to be created before the local aldermen (*schepenen*) court or a notary to create a non-possessory pledge over movables. The deeds of pledge were recorded in the local court's registers, which were publicly accessible. Registration was required within eight days after the deed was passed under penalty of nullity of the right of pledge.[74] Registration was not required if the encumbered assets were handed over to the secured creditor (possessory security right).[75] The recordation of the pledge deeds aimed to prevent back-dating of a transfer or encumbrance.[76] Interested parties could make use of the services offered by the city's secretary to look up any encumbrances.[77]

Despite the comprehensive reception of Roman law in general, Roman-Dutch legal practitioners and scholars were reluctant to adopt all legal effects that ensued from a Roman right of pledge. In particular, the secured creditor's right to follow (or trace) encumbered movable assets in the hands of third parties was not recognised (in its entirety). In Roman-Dutch law, pledged movables could not be traced into the hands of third parties if there was a transfer of ownership. This rule was often referred to by the legal maxim *mobilia non habent sequelam* or *roerend goed heeft geen gevolg van hypotheek* and was strongly influenced by the aforementioned customary law of Germanic origin.[78]

---

[73] Van Leeuwen (n 68) 4.12,4, 313; Voet (n 69) I, ad D.20,1,10, 854; Van der Keessel (n 69) III, ad. Gr.2.48.32, 455; O Gelderblom, M Hup and J Jonker, "Public Functions, Private Markets: Credit Registration by Aldermen and Notaries in the Low Countries, 1500–1800" in M. Lorenzini et al. (eds), *Financing in Europe* (Palgrave Macmillan 2018) 174.

[74] Art. 2 in: *Handvesten, privilegien, octroyen, costumen en willekeuren der stad Amstelredam* (Amsterdam: Joost en Otto Smient 1662/3) 3.1.11 (Vande Desolate Boedels) 4, 259.

[75] Art. 4 in: *Handvesten, privilegien, octroyen, costumen en willekeuren der stad Amstelredam* (Amsterdam: Joost en Otto Smient 1662/3), 3.1.11 (Vande Desolate Boedels) 4, 259–260.

[76] Cf. O Gelderblom, M Hup and J Jonker, "Public Functions, Private Markets: Credit Registration by Aldermen and Notaries in the Low Countries, 1500–1800" in M Lorenzini et al. (eds), *Financing in Europe* (Palgrave Macmillan 2018) 188.

[77] *Amsterdamsche secretary, bestaande in formulieren van scheepenen- kennissen, quytscheldingen, schatbrieven en ander die gewoonlyk daar gebruikt worden* (Amsterdam: Bos 1737) 316; C van Bochove, H Deweneth and J Zuijderduijn, "Real estate and mortgage finance in England and the Low Countries, 1300–1800", *Continuity and Change* 30 (2015) 15.

[78] Cf. Zwalve (n 31) 44ff; WJ Zwalve and AJB Sirks, *Grundzüge der europäischen Privatrechtsgeschichte* (Böhlau 2012) 427.

As a general rule, the application of the rule *mobilia non habent sequelam* in the Dutch Republic did not require that the pledged assets were sold in the pledgor's ordinary course of business. According to Van Leeuwen, a "sufficient title" (*behoorlijke tijtel*), in other words, any legal basis for the transfer of ownership, was sufficient.[79] Voet expressly mentioned that it was irrelevant whether the movables were transferred for consideration or gratuitously.[80] Van der Keessel concurred and added that a secured creditor could only recover pledged assets if the transferee had knowledge of prejudice to creditors.[81] Grotius remarked that a right of pledge ended after a transfer pursuant to a legal basis (*wettige titule*),[82] but in one of his opinions this rule was limited to transfers for consideration.[83] Grotius gave his opinion in an Amsterdam case of 1632, where 20 lawyers confirmed the rule that a right of pledge was extinguished when a movable was transferred "to a third party pursuant to any legal basis for consideration" ("*aan een derde bij eenig tijtel onereux*"). In a different opinion, Van Assendelft explained that the rule "*roerend goed heeft geen gevolg*" aimed to protect commerce.[84] Perhaps the city of Amsterdam deviated from the law of secured credit in the rest of Holland in this matter. Nevertheless, the (Roman-Dutch) notion that a transferee only acquired unencumbered movables for consideration was adopted in South Africa.[85]

German-speaking Countries

The concept of *mobilia non habent sequelam* was also applied to security rights in the German-speaking countries of the early modern period. German law initially only recognised possessory pledges of movables. From the 1400s, however, non-possessory rights of pledge were also recognised in some

---

[79] Van Leeuwen (n 68) IV, XIII, 353.

[80] Voet (n 69) I, D.20,6 nr 6, part III (1787) 355 (632); cf. AG Pos, *Hypotheek op roerend goed (bezitloos pandrecht)* (Kluwer 1970) 153.

[81] Van der Keessel (n 69) III, 441 and 449.

[82] De Groot (n 69) II, 48, 29.

[83] J Naeranus, *Consultatien, Advysen en Advertissementen gegeven ende geschreven by verscheijden Treffelijke Rechtsgeleerden in Hollant en elders* (Naeranus 1662), III 174, 466–470 (26 February 1632).

[84] Van Assendelft in J Naeranus, *Consultatien, Advysen en Advertissementen gegeven ende geschreven by verscheijden Treffelijke Rechtsgeleerden in Hollant en elders* (Naeranus 1660) IV 319, 578 (6-7-1656).

[85] *Francis v Savage and Hill* (1881–1884) 1 SAR TS 33; *Hare v Trustee of Heath* (1884–1885) 3 SC 32; *Cooper NO en andere v Die Meester en 'n ander* [1992] 2 All SA 20 (A).

German-speaking regions, such as Lübeck and later Frankfurt.[86] The creation of such rights of pledge required formal registration in the town register. Registration prevented back-dating, since the chronological order of the rights of pledge determined the priority between competing creditors whose claims were enforceable against the same encumbered asset. If the debtor lost or transferred possession of the pledged assets to someone else, the secured creditor could not recover the assets from the third party. Hübner remarked that this ensued from the rule *Hand wahre Hand*.[87] The reception of Roman security rights changed the security rights in the German countries. Secured creditors could recover pledged assets from a third party, unless the third party was a *bona fide* possessor.[88] Hübner added to that: "Though a general hypothec in chattels was, as such, recognized, this did not restrict the debtor in his power of disposing of individual chattels. Furthermore, a subsequent possessory pledgee had priority over an earlier secured creditor whose claim was secured by a non-possessory pledge."[89]

France and Belgium

Some regions in France and Belgium recognised non-possessory and general security rights in movables (*l'hypothèque mobilière*) and applied the rule *mobilia non habent sequelam*. These general rights of pledge were created by means of notarial deeds, and some regions required the public registration of those deeds.[90] In 1653, King Philippe IV of Spain harmonised the formal requirements for the creation of non-possessory security rights in movables in the Spanish Netherlands. All transfers or encumbrances of movables where no control had been handed over were deemed null and void, unless a deed was passed before the aldermen of the city where the transferor or debtor lived.[91] The king noted that "collusion, abuse, fraud, and simulation" occurred on a

---

86 Hübner (n 9) 476–477; W Hromadka, *Die Entwicklung des Faustpfandprinzips im 18. und 19. Jahrhundert* (Böhlau 1971) 30.

87 Hübner (n 9) 477.

88 Hübner (n 9) 477ff; P Altorfer, *Die Mobiliarhypothek* (Schulthess 1981) 12.

89 Hübner (n 9) 478.

90 For example, art. 177 and 178 of the Coutume of Bretagne. See: Sauvageau, *Coutumes de Bretagne* I (Vatar 1737) 42.

91 Placcaet's Konincx, rakende de solemniteyten gherequireert tot het vertransporteren ende oppignoreren van Catheylen, Vruchten ende andere mobiliare Goederen, vanden 29. Julij 1643, in: *Derden placcaet-boeck van Vlaenderen* (Ghendt 1685) 428–430.

daily basis owing to transfers and encumbrances without control being handed over.[92]

The *prior tempore* rule determined the priority between secured creditors.[93] Secured creditors were unable to recover pledged assets from third parties because of the application of the rule *mobilia non habent sequelam*.[94] As a general rule, the application of the rule *mobilia non habent sequelam* in these French regions did not require that the pledged assets were sold in the pledgor's ordinary course of business. A secured creditor could only recover pledged assets if the transferee had knowledge of prejudice to creditors.[95] The main argument against the right to trace was "the public interest and the freedom of commerce."[96]

In a large part of France, including Paris and its surrounding regions, the rule *mobilia non habent sequelam* was applied in a stricter manner. The rule was said to impede non-possessory security rights altogether.[97] According to Loyseau, the essence of non-possessory Roman security rights was that they enabled secured creditors to recover the encumbered assets from third parties. Since the French common law was unwilling to accept a secured creditor's right to trace movables, such a hypothec was not recognised.[98] Exceptions were

---

92 "Vande collusien, abuysen, frauden, ende simulatien die daghelijckx by den schuldenaeren worden ghecommitteert inde verkoopinghen, transporten, cessien, alienatien, oppignoratien, ofte verpandinghen, ende engagementen van huys-catheylenn, beesten, granen, vruchten te velde staende, ende alle andere meubelen, sonder daer van overleveringhe te doen aen hunne gepretendeerde Crediteuren, in prejudicie van hunne rechte ende waerachtighe Schuldenaeren, ende dickwils vande Rent-meesters, Collecteurs vande Beden ende Subsidien aen ons gheaccordeert."

93 J Brissaud, *Le créancier, "premier saisissant'" dans l'ancien droit français* (Presses universitaires de France 1972) 42–46; J Yver, "Note sur l'hypothèque mobilière dans quatre coutumes de l'Ouest de la France" in *Dix ans de conférences d'agrégation, Etudes de droit commercial offertes à Joseph Hamel* (Dalloz 1961) 488.

94 TJA Cottereau, *Le droit général de la France, et le droit particulier à la Touraine et au Lodunois* (Vauquer-Lambert 1778) I, nr 5058–5070, 423–424; BJ Bretonnier, *Recueil par ordre alphabétique des principales questions de droit* (Onfroy 1783) 195–196.

95 For Lille: F Patou, *Commentaire sur les coutumes de la ville de Lille et de sa châtellenie, et conférences de ces coutumes avec celles voisines et le droit commun* (Dumortier 1788) 8,2,1,V, 191. For Metz: Egger (n 6) 164.

96 Patou (n 95) 8, 2, 1, VI, 191.

97 For example: art. 170 of the Coutume de Paris. Cf. Zwalve and Sirks (n 78) 433; J-L Halpérin, *Histoire du droit des biens* (Economica 2008) 104–105.

98 C Loyseau, *Cinq livres du droit des offices* (Angelier 1614) 325.

recognized for, *inter alia* unpaid sellers, creditors who were prejudiced by a transfer to a transferee who knew of the transferor's insolvency, creditors who had attached the goods prior to the transfer, and lessors with regard to the lessee's movables.[99] Guyot added that non-possessory security rights in movables were too precarious for secured creditors because movables were easily lost, commingled with another person's assets, transferred by the debtor, and so on.[100] Pothier remarked that non-possessory pledges were rejected "to secure and facilitate commerce."[101] Only possessory pledges of movables were recognised. The possessory pledge was called *nantissement* and required continuous control over the pledged asset by the pledgee. In many cities, unsecured creditors could attach movables and attachment created priority. The priority between attaching creditors was determined by the *prior tempore* rule.[102]

THE TRIUMPH OF INDIGENOUS (GERMANIC) PRINCIPLES (*FAUSTPFANDPRINZIP*) OVER ROMAN LAW

The recognition of non-possessory security rights in movables was met with suspicion by eighteenth- and nineteenth-century lawmakers, particularly in the German-speaking countries and France. The Prussian hypothec and bankruptcy ordinance of 1722 rejected non-possessory security rights in movables.[103] The *Allgemeines Landrecht für die Preußischen Staaten* of 1794 only recognised the possessory pledge of movables.[104] Other German-speaking regions, such as Hessen, Bavaria and Saxony also followed this approach.[105]

In the German-speaking countries, several different arguments were put forward to justify the rejection of non-possessory security rights.[106] The requirement of control over movables led to transparency or publicity of rights of pledge.[107] As long as movables remained in the hands of a debtor, his creditors were certain that the assets were not encumbered by a non-possessory

---

[99] Cottereau (n 94) I, nr 5066–5070, 423–424.

[100] PJJG Guyot, *Répertoire universel et raisonné de jurisprudence civile, criminelle, canonique et bénéficiale* (Panckoucke en Depuis 1784) VIII, 621.

[101] RJ Pothier, Traité de l'hypothèque (1767) in *Oeuvres de Pothier* IX (Plon, Cosse et Marchal 1861) nr 36, 434.

[102] Cf. Brissaud (n 93) 31ff.

[103] Hübner (n 9) 478; Hromadka (n 86) 51ff. Some exceptions were made, for example, for non-possessory pledge of ships.

[104] ALR I 20 §§ 6–10. Hromadka (n 86) 54; Zwalve and Sirks (n 78) 473.

[105] Hromadka (n 86) 86, 97 and 113.

[106] See with references: Hromadka (n 86) 41ff.

[107] Hromadka (n 86) 37; Altorfer (n 88) 75ff; T. Quantz, *Besitz und Publizität im Recht der beweglichen Sachen* (Duncker & Humblot 2005) 81ff.

right of pledge.[108] Control was said to prevent a false appearance of a debtor's creditworthiness. Third parties who wanted to acquire ownership or a right of pledge in a movable asset did not have to fear the existence of a prior non-possessory right of pledge, since only possessory pledges were recognised. Moreover, possessory pledges were automatically in accordance with the principle of speciality (specificity), the requirement that pledged assets were specified in the pledge agreement.[109] Only those assets which were handed over to the creditor were encumbered. This prevented the overcollateralization of secured creditors, since the debtor could still pledge the movables he still controlled. The prevention of over-indebtedness was another aim of the rejection of non-possessory security rights.[110] Many debtors could not afford to lose control over their assets and could thus not provide these assets as collateral for credit. Control over the pledged assets also prevented a debtor from prejudicing the position of the secured creditor by disposing of the pledged assets.[111] There was also a more systematic argument for the requirement of (handing over of) control over the movable. Modern codifications often provided that limited real rights were created in the same manner as the encumbered assets were transferred in ownership. For movables, this meant that control was required to create a right of pledge, since delivery was required for a transfer of ownership.[112]

Non-possessory pledges were rejected for similar reasons in France.[113] After Napoleon Bonaparte came to power in 1799, a draft civil code was made for the whole of France. In accordance with the law of many French regions, including the law of Paris, non-possessory pledges in movables were not recognised in the draft. The draft contained the provision that "les meubles n'ont pas de suite par hypothèque" (*mobilia non habent sequelam*).[114] Only possessory pledges were accepted. Despite the fact that many French regions still recognised non-possessory pledges at that time, there was very little debate about the new provisions.[115] Article 2119 of the civil code of 1804 rejected non-possessory pledges. The possessory pledge was called *gage*.[116] The pledgor could hand

---

108 Hromadka (n 86) 36; Altorfer (n 88) 18 and 76; Zwalve and Sirks (n 78) 486.

109 Hromadka (n 86) 43; Altorfer (n 88) 82.

110 Altorfer (n 88) 85.

111 Hromadka (n 86) 31ff; Altorfer (n 88) 83.

112 Altorfer (n 88) 19; Zwalve and Sirks (n 78) 469.

113 Hromadka (n 86) 70ff.

114 Book III, title VI, art. 8 jo. art. 16, in: PA Fenet, *Recueil complet des travaux préparatoires du Code civil* (Videcoq 1836) II, 211–215.

115 Fenet (n 114) III, 150.

116 Art. 2071 Cc. Cf. Zwalve and Sirks (n 78) 439ff.

over control to either the creditor or to a third party (*entiercement*). A pledge deed had to be drawn up and registered.[117] A notarised pledge deed was not required for tradesmen, however.[118] If the debtor defaulted, the creditor could have the movable asset sold and use the proceeds to satisfy his claim. The use of a forfeiture clause, the so-called *pacte commissoire*, was prohibited.

The new French legislation had a knock-on effect throughout Europe because of Napoleon's geopolitical conquests. This eventually led to the rejection of non-possessory rights of pledge in regions that previously recognised such rights.[119] In 1810, the French emperor Napoleon Bonaparte annexed the Dutch territories and decreed that the French civil code of 1804 should take effect in the Dutch territories in 1811. The French civil code only recognised possessory pledges, and so the Dutch non-possessory pledges were abolished.[120] After the (United) Kingdom of the Netherlands regained its independence in 1815, the non-possessory pledges did not return. One of the parliamentary committees favoured the principle of speciality, the requirement that pledged assets were specified in the pledge agreement. This principle was aimed at preventing overcollateralization. The committee expressly commended the application of speciality in the Prussian Allgemeines Landrecht, which only recognised possessory pledges.[121] The Dutch civil code of 1838 provided that a right of pledge in a movable could not exist as long as the movable remained in the hands of the pledgor.[122]

Napoleon came to power in Italy in 1800, after the Battle of Marengo.[123] In 1804, he introduced the French civil code in Italy. Non-possessory pledges were rejected as a result of that.[124] After the fall of Napoleon and the Congress of Vienna in 1815, Italy disintegrated into city states.[125] The French civil code was no longer applied, but new civil codes were introduced. These new codes, however, progressed from the French civil code. After the unification of Italy in 1861, the new *Codice Civile del Regno d'Italia,* or *Codice Pisanelli,* was introduced in 1865. This new civil code relied heavily on the French civil code

---

117 Art. 2076 jo, 2074 Cc. Cf. Zwalve and Sirks (n 78) 445.

118 Art. 91 in 109 Code de Commerce.

119 See §4.1 and §4.2.

120 The general hypothec survived the change from the Dutch Republic into the Batavian Republic in 1795, the Batavian Commonwealth in 1801 and subsequently the Kingdom of Holland in 1806. See: Van Hoof (n 72), §7.2.1, §7.2.2 and §7.2.3.

121 Pos (n 80) 61ff.

122 Art. 1196 jo. 1213 jo. 1198 Burgerlijk Wetboek (1838).

123 Lesaffer (n 6) §360, 413.

124 Art. 2071 Code civil.

125 Lesaffer (n 6) §363, 416.

of 1804. The Italian civil code of 1865 only recognised possessory pledges, as does the present Italian civil code (1942).[126]

The rejection of non-possessory security rights in movables was widespread in the nineteenth century, as the Austrian empire followed the approach taken by France and Prussia. Separate states that emerged from the Austrian empire after its dissolution, such as Hungary and Czechoslovakia, adopted a similar approach.[127] The German civil code of 1900 also applied the Faustpfandprinzip.

A SLOW RETURN TO NON-POSSESSORY SECURITY RIGHTS

The Recognition of Security Transfers of Ownership

The rejection of non-possessory security rights meant that a pledgor could not encumber his movable assets with a security right and still use his movables in the ordinary course of business. He had to give control over the assets to someone else. For business debtors who needed to have control over their movable assets to conduct a feasible business, possessory pledges were problematic. At the beginning of the nineteenth century, tradesmen often relied on capital provided by (one of their) partners in a partnership or by banks whose claims were secured by personal security rights.[128] Tradesmen who were not able to get capital in that way and who only had movables were not considered to be creditworthy.[129] The industrial revolution, however, changed the way of thinking about creditworthiness.

Some debtors resorted to the security transfer of ownership to circumvent the restrictions of possessory pledges. This meant that a debtor transferred ownership of movable assets to the creditor to secure the payment of an obligation.[130] Possession was granted by means of constructive delivery or *constitutum possessorium*, as the debtor kept control over the thing. If the debtor satisfied the secured obligation, the creditor had to transfer ownership back to the debtor. If the debtor defaulted on the secured obligation, the creditor remained the owner of the thing and could recover it from the debtor. The creditor was sometimes under the obligation to repay the debtor if the value of the asset exceeded the sum of the secured claim. Before and after the introduction of the German

---

126 Art. 2784–2807 Codice civile (1942). Cf. Altorfer (n 88) 173ff.

127 K Andová, *Das Mobiliarpfandrecht in Österreich, Ungarn, Tschechien und der Slowakei* (Manz 2004) 13, 56, and 140.

128 Zwalve (n 31) 48; Zwalve and Sirks (n 78) 450ff.

129 Zwalve and Sirks (n 78) 451.

130 A similar development took place regarding the security assignment of claims.

civil code in 1900, the German *Reichsgericht* held that a security transfer of ownership (*Sicherungsübereignung*) of a movable was a valid way of creating security.[131] In 1929, the Dutch Supreme Court (*Hoge Raad*) followed suit and recognised the security transfer of ownership (*zekerheidsoverdracht*).[132] The Austrian Supreme Court (*Oberster Gerichtshof*) recognised the security transfer but ruled that actual delivery to the secured creditor was required.[133] This meant that a security transfer did not enable the debtor to keep using the transferred assets to conduct his business.

The recognition of the security transfer in Germany and the Netherlands at the beginning of the twentieth century was the starting point of a development that eventually led to debtors transferring all of their present and future movables (in advance) to their secured creditors.[134] Secured creditors were the legal owners of the assets and could, in theory, recover these assets from third parties. In business transactions, however, it became standard practice to allow the debtor to freely transfer the assets to third parties in the ordinary course of business. German and Dutch law protected third parties in good faith if no such permission was granted by the secured creditor. Publicity has not been required in the Netherlands and Germany ever since the recognition of security transfers in the first half of the twentieth century.[135]

Security transfers of ownership were rejected in various other countries. The French supreme court (*Cour de cassation*) held that the effects of such a transfer conflicted with the statutory prohibition of the forfeiture clause, the *pacte commissoire*, since the creditor could keep the (total value of the) asset if the debtor defaulted on the secured claim.[136] The Italian supreme court (*Corte di Cassazione*) rejected the security transfer for similar reasons.[137] Although the Austrian supreme court recognised security transfers, the movable had to be handed over to the creditor and the rules regarding the enforcement of rights of pledge were applied.[138] The rejection of (unrestricted) security transfers meant that debtors could not create security in their essential business

---

131 Reichsgericht 9. Oktober 1880, RGZ 2, 170–171; Reichsgericht 8. November 1904, RGZ 59, 146ff; cf. Zwalve (n 31) 51; Zwalve and Sirks (n 78) 479ff.

132 HR 25 januari 1929, *NJ* 1929, 616 and HR 21 juni 1929, *NJ* 1929, 1096.

133 OGH 09.03.1955 7 Ob 12/55, ECLI:AT:OGH0002:1955:RS0010391. Cf. Altorfer (n 88) 206; Andová (n 127) 49.

134 See for the Netherlands: Van Hoof (n 37) §8.3.6.

135 Cf. Quantz (n 107) 95ff.

136 Req. 24 Mai 1933, D. P. 1933, 378. Cf. Altorfer (n 88) 153; Zwalve and Sirks (n 78) 444 and 452.

137 *Corte di Cassazione*, 3 June 1983, n. 3800, in *Il Foro Italiano* 1984 I, 212, annotated by Macario.

138 Andová (n 127) 49.

assets, stock-in-trade, and future assets. Alternatives had to be used or developed to meet the needs of the market.

Public Registration of Non-possessory Pledges

In France, the abovementioned *entiercement* was used to create rights of pledge in movables without handing the movables over to the pledgee. Instead, the pledgor handed over control to a third party as agreed upon by the parties. Movables were often placed in third-party-owned warehouses as a way of *entiercement*. The warehouse gave the pledgor a receipt (*récépissé*) and another document, a so-called *warrant*. A pledgor could create a right of pledge in the movables by handing over (*endosser*) the *warrant*.[139] The legislator eventually allowed for the use of warrants in agricultural credit, even without *entiercement*. A farmer could pledge his crops, cattle and equipment by handing over a warrant to his creditor. This warrant had to describe the encumbered assets and had to be registered in a public register.[140] The handing over of the movables for the creation of a right of pledge was effectively replaced by public registration of the warrant. Similar warrants were created for industrial products and oil stocks. Furthermore, specific creditors were awarded legal preferences.

At the beginning of the twentieth century, the French legislator responded to the (credit) needs of tradesmen with relatively small businesses by introducing a non-possessory pledge over business assets.[141] This right of pledge in a so-called *fonds de commerce* is publicly registered and encumbers assets such as patents, clientele, inventory and trade name.[142] After-acquired assets are also encumbered if they replace previously encumbered assets.[143] Initially, movables such as stock-in-trade were not part of the *fonds de commerce* and were thus not encumbered.

The creation of particular security rights for specific economic sectors was also the approach taken by the Italian legislator, who introduced a customised publicly registered non-possessory right of pledge over dry-cured ham (1985)

---

139 Altorfer (n 88) 152; Zwalve and Sirks (n 78) 449. Even before the introduction of the French civil code, tradesmen could pledge assets that were stored elsewhere by pledging the bills of lading.

140 Altorfer (n 88) 154; Zwalve and Sirks (n 78) 454.

141 G Kunzler, Das Nantissement du Fonds de Commerce (Metzner 1960) 34ff; Altorfer (n 88) 168ff; Zwalve and Sirks (n 78) 456. This approach was followed by the Belgian legislator in 1919 (Wet van 25 Oktober 1919 betreffende het beroepskrediet ten bate van de kleine burgerij in handel en nijverheid).

142 Article L142-2 Code de Commerce. Cf. Kunzler (n 141) 46ff.

143 Kunzler (n 141) 51.

and cheese (2001).[144] Moreover, the Italian legislator created all kinds of privileges regarding movables to meet the financing requirements of businesses.[145]

In France and Italy, the legislator repeatedly stepped in to create particular security rights for specific economic sectors. The public registration of non-possessory rights of pledge replaced the requirement of granting control for the creation of possessory rights of pledge. Unlike Germany and the Netherlands, the role of judges in creating new forms of security was limited.[146] The recent modernisation of security rights continues along the same lines, and some examples will now be mentioned. In 2006, the French legislator introduced a non-possessory registered right of pledge (*gage sans dépossession*).[147] A debtor can pledge his present and future movables. The pledgor can dispose of pledged assets free of any encumbrance unless the parties agreed otherwise.[148] The commercial code also allows a publicly registered non-possessory right of pledge in a debtor's (present and future) stock-in-trade.[149] The pledgor can dispose of these assets in his ordinary course of business.[150] From 2016 onwards, the Italian legislator has been preparing the introduction of a general non-possessory registered pledge (*pegno non possessorio*) for business debtors.[151] On the first of January 2018, the new Belgian Pledge Act came into force and introduced a publicly registered non-possessory right of pledge in movables. Parties can also still opt for possessory pledges. Article 21 of the Pledge Act provides that a debtor may dispose of encumbered assets free of rights of pledge in their ordinary course of business unless the parties agreed otherwise.[152] The creditor's security right will automatically extend to the receivable that replaces the asset if it has been sold (*zakelijke subrogatie*).[153] Similar developments have been taking place in Hungary, the Czech Republic and Slovakia.[154]

---

144 Altorfer (n 88) 178ff; M Natale, "Sul pegno non possessorio e rotativo d'impresa: principi in divenire, ricadute effettuali di margine?" *Comparazione e diritto civile* (2020) 532 n 4 with references.

145 A Veneziano, *Le garanzie mobiliari non possessorie. Profili di diritto comparato e di diritto del commercio internazionale* (Giuffrè 2000) 20.

146 Zwalve and Sirks (n 78) 457.

147 Art. 2336 Cc.

148 Art. 2343 Cc.

149 Art. L. 527-1 CdC.

150 Art. L. 527-5 CdC.

151 D.l. 59/2016 converted into l. n. 119/2016. Cf. Natale (n 144) 534ff.

152 J Baeck, *Voorrechten en hypotheken OVH, Commentaar bij Art 21 Pandwet*, 56 (23 September 2015) 39.

153 Art 9 Pandwet.

154 Andová (n 127) 249ff.

CONCLUDING REMARKS

Throughout history, continental Europe has known a variety of security rights over a group or class of assets, which allowed for the debtor to use and dispose of the encumbered assets in his ordinary course of business. The best-known example of such a security right is the Roman general hypothec or right of pledge. A pledgor could pledge all of his present and future assets or a group of assets, and the parties were free to agree on whether the pledgor could dispose of his encumbered assets in his ordinary course of business. For example, a pledgor who pledged his shop could probably trade with the assets in the shop until there was an event of default. The legal effects of a general right of pledge bear a strong resemblance to the modern floating charge, because both rights concern a security right over a group of present and future assets, with that group changing from time to time and where the chargor can carry on its business in the ordinary way until the charge crystallises and attaches to assets.[155]

The reception of Roman law in Europe in the early modern period did not supersede private law principles of Germanic origin with regard to movable assets and security rights therein. Some regions, such as Paris and its surrounding areas, did not adopt non-possessory pledges and only recognised possessory pledges. Roman rights of non-possessory pledge were adopted in various parts of Europe, but these were hardly *rights in rem*. The rule *mobilia non habent sequelam* often prevented secured creditors from recovering encumbered assets from third parties. Exceptions were mainly limited to cases where assets were gifted or the transfer caused prejudice to the secured creditor. In other words, the pledgor was free to dispose of his assets until there was an event of default. Non-possessory security rights were practically quite similar to the modern floating charge, given the fact that the security rights allowed for the chargor to deal with the charged assets and withdraw them from the security without the consent of chargee.[156] These early modern non-possessory rights of pledge were often publicly registered. Registration was aimed at preventing the backdating of pledge agreements and at safeguarding

---

[155] See also: WW Buckland, *Text-book of Roman Law from Augustus to Justinian* (CUP 1921) 475; RR Pennington, "The Genesis of the Floating Charge" (1960) 23 MLR 646; RJ Goebel, "Reconstructing the Roman Law of Real Security" (1961) 36 TulLRev 47; HLE Verhagen, "Ius honorarium, Equity and Real Security: Parallel Lines of Legal Development" in E Koops and WJ Zwalve (eds), *Law & Equity, Approaches in Roman Law and Common Law* (Nijhoff 2014) 141–142; HLE Verhagen, "Secured Transactions in Classical Roman Law" in G Dari-Mattiacci and D Kehoe, *Roman Law and Economics*, Vol II (OUP 2020) 125.

[156] HG Beale et al (eds), *The Law of Security and Title-Based Financing*, 3rd edn (OUP 2018) para 6.101.

the application of the *prior tempore* rule to determine priority between secured creditors.

From the end of the eighteenth century onwards, non-possessory pledges were rejected in more and more regions. All the national civil codes of the nineteenth and twentieth centuries required that a pledgor had to hand over control of the assets to create a security right in movables. Several different reasons for this were mentioned. The requirement of control led to some kind of publicity and was aimed at preventing overcollateralization, over-indebtedness, and, among other things, a false appearance of creditworthiness.

From the beginning of the twentieth century, the approaches to non-possessory security in movables diverged. One approach, taken by *inter alia* Germany and the Netherlands, is the recognition of security transfers of ownership to secure a debt. These transfers quickly became all-encompassing since a debtor could transfer all of his present and future assets to his creditor. No (public) registration was required. The parties often agreed that the debtor could transfer the assets in his ordinary course of business. The second approach, taken by *inter alia* France, Italy and Hungary, was the rejection of security transfers and the piecemeal creation of specific rights of pledge for specific economic activities. The main characteristic of these pledges was that handing over control over a movable was replaced by the public registration of the pledge. Pledgors could often dispose of pledged assets free of any encumbrance in the ordinary course of business.

The recent modernisation of non-possessory rights of pledge in movables in countries such as France (2006), Italy (2016) and Belgium (2018) has led to a convergence of security rights in the sense that (business) debtors across Europe can encumber all of their present and future assets in a relatively easy manner. The (lack of) publicity of these security rights, however, clearly echoes the different approaches to security rights from the beginning of the twentieth century. Publicity has not been required in the Netherlands and Germany ever since the recognition of security transfers in the first half of the twentieth century. The Dutch civil code of 1992 introduced non-possessory pledges and requires the registration of pledge deeds to prevent backdating, but the register is not publicly accessible. Countries such as France and Italy required public registration when they introduced particular rights of pledge in the twentieth century and kept that requirement when they enhanced the scope of rights of pledge in the twenty-first century. The debtor's ability to transfer encumbered assets in his ordinary course of business follows these same lines. In Germany and the Netherlands, the parties often agree that the debtor can do so until there is an event of default. In Belgium, France and Italy, statutory provisions automatically enable the debtor to do so.

Many countries on the European continent allow for the creation of non-possessory security rights in a debtor's present and future movable assets and claims. The debtor may often transfer assets free of any encumbrance in his ordinary course of business prior to an event of default. However, the ways in which different jurisdictions achieve these equivalents to the English floating charge differ greatly. The modern differences evolved out of a country's (un)willingness to accept the creation of security rights without any form of publicity as an alternative to the possessory right of pledge. Jurisdictions that require no publicity are not lagging behind in the evolution of security rights but have willingly accepted non-possessory security rights without any form of publicity. Publicity, however, has momentum and could be the next step in the European development of security rights. Should the European legislator ever consider harmonising public registration of security rights, it must first try to appreciate and understand the differences between legal systems and how they came to be, since there is not one pan-European approach to non-possessory security rights evolving, but several.

5. The general hypothecation of movable property in South African law

Reghard Brits

INTRODUCTION

Movable property can be used as collateral in South Africa by creating either a special security right (hypothec, pledge or mortgage)[1] over a specific asset (or specific assets) or a general security right over all of the debtor's movable assets. There are no formality requirements for the conclusion of an agreement in this regard, as long as there is consensus between the parties regarding (i) their intention to create a security right, (ii) the property to be hypothecated and (iii) the debt to be secured. However, an agreement alone does not create a right *in rem* in the creditor's favour and the hypothec will have no third-party effect unless a further step is taken to 'perfect' the security. The security can be perfected in two ways: either by the creditor receiving possession of the movable property (voluntarily or through judicial attachment), or by registering the security agreement in a public registry. In both cases, the purpose is to create publicity of the security right so as to justify it becoming enforceable against third parties. However, in the case of registration, the legal consequences will differ depending, for instance, on how the property is described, whether the security is special or general, whether the debtor is insolvent and whether the creditor has also taken possession of the property.

The registration of an agreement hypothecating movable property in South Africa is done through the registration of a so-called 'notarial bond'.[2] The

[1] For purposes of this chapter, the terms 'pledge', 'hypothec' and 'mortgage' all generally convey the same meaning, namely a security right. In practice, different terms are often used in different contexts – such as pledge for movable property and mortgage for immovable property, or pledge if possession is transferred to the creditor and hypothec or mortgage if the security is non-possessory, but nothing turns on the particular word used.

[2] For general discussions of notarial bonds, see e.g. Gustav Muller, Reghard Brits, Juanita M Pienaar and Zsa-Zsa Boggenpoel, *Silberberg and Schoeman's*

bond is 'notarial' in the sense that, before it is registered, the parties must execute (sign) the deed (the written security agreement) before a notary public, who must also sign it as a witness. If the bond purports to create a general hypothec over all of the debtor's movable property, it is called a 'general notarial bond', while the term 'special notarial bond' is used when a specific asset is (or specific assets are) hypothecated. As shown in this chapter, the registration of a general notarial bond over all the movable property of a debtor creates a security right that is roughly comparable with a floating charge as understood in the English legal tradition. However, the general bond in South Africa has its roots in the general hypothecation of property in Roman and especially Roman-Dutch law.[3] Roman-Dutch law was transplanted into South Africa in the seventeenth century when a part of the country was a Dutch colony and is still a primary source of many areas of South African private law, although it has been developed and adapted throughout the years by the courts and the legislature.

The registration of a general bond creates a 'floating' security right in the sense that registration alone does not vest the creditor with a 'fixed' right *in rem* that is enforceable against third parties. Instead, the security must be 'perfected' (or 'fixed') for it to have third-party effect. Before the security is perfected, the creditor has a mere personal right against the debtor – not a right in the property – and is not regarded as a secured creditor. However, the holder of an unperfected bond will at least have a preference over concurrent[4] (unsecured) creditors upon the debtor's insolvency. The holder of an unperfected bond also cannot prevent the debtor from disposing of the property and thus will lose its security once the property is transferred to a third party, although the security will also cover any new property acquired by the debtor. On the other hand, if the bond is perfected by taking possession of the property, the

The Law of Property (6th edn, LexisNexis 2019) 462–668; Reghard Brits, *Real Security Law* (Juta 2016) 193–72.

[3] For a historical discussion of general security rights in Roman and Roman-Dutch law, see Vincentius Johannes Maria van Hoof, *Generale Zekerheidsrechten in Rechtshistorisch Perspectief* (Wolters Kluwer 2015) 13–70 and 85–140.

[4] In South African insolvency law, the term 'concurrent creditors' refers to unsecured creditors with no preferent claim whatsoever. This is distinguished from certain unsecured creditors (called 'statutory preferent creditors') who, although they do not hold any security rights, are afforded a statutory preference above other unsecured creditors (the concurrent creditors). As explained below, the holder of an unperfected general notarial bond, although unsecured, is such a statutory preferent creditor with a claim preferred over other (concurrent) unsecured creditors.

creditor will be a fully secured creditor who can prevent the disposal thereof to third parties.

The purpose of this chapter is to discuss these matters pertaining to general hypothecation in South Africa in closer detail. I will first set the scene by explaining the broader context of both special and general hypothecation through the registration of notarial bonds, including a summary of the registration process (second section). Secondly, the nature of an unperfected general bond is discussed with reference to the rights of a creditor who holds such a bond (third section). Thereafter, the perfection of a general bond as well as the consequences of such perfection are explored (fourth section). Although the general notarial bond is a very useful and relatively popular security device in South Africa, it has its limitations, and thus it might be necessary to reform this area of law.[5]

GENERAL AND SPECIAL NOTARIAL BONDS

If movable property is pledged by giving possession of the property to the creditor, nothing further is necessary to vest the creditor with a real (*in rem*) security right enforceable against third parties, also upon the debtor's insolvency.[6] In other words, delivery of the property to the creditor has the effect of perfecting the creditor's security right. This applies to the pledging of specific movables, a collection of movables or all of the debtor's movables in general. However, if the parties enter into a security contract in which the debtor agrees to pledge his movable property to the creditor, but this agreement is not followed by delivery of the property to the creditor, the contract will only create personal rights enforceable between the parties and will have no effect upon the debtor's insolvency.[7]

The only alternative way to create a real security right with third-party effect, other than by transferring possession to the creditor, is to register the deed embodying the security agreement in a public registry. In South Africa, this can only be achieved through the registration of a notarial bond in one

[5] Since the entire system of security rights in movable assets is outdated, a wider reform initiative might even be called for. See e.g. Michel Marlize Koekemoer, *A Framework for Reforming the South African Law of Security Rights in Movable Property* (LLD thesis, University of Pretoria 2020). However, despite calls for reform, it is not on the government's agenda at the moment.

[6] On the requirement to transfer possession to the creditor, see e.g. *Vasco Dry Cleaners v Twycross* 1979 (1) SA 603 (A) 611; *Oertel NO v Brink* 1972 (3) SA 669 (W) 674–675; *Smith v Farrelly's Trustee* 1904 TS 949, 954–955.

[7] See e.g. *Ward v Barrett NO and Another NO* 1963 (2) SA 546 (A) 552; *Vasco* (n 6) 611.

(or more than one) deeds registry in terms of the Deeds Registries Act.[8] If, in terms of the security agreement, the debtor committed himself to having the agreement registered in the form of a notarial bond, the creditor may claim specific performance of this duty and therefore can approach a court to compel the debtor to register the bond.[9]

There are a number of deeds registries (deeds offices) across the country, each managed by a Registrar of Deeds with jurisdiction over a certain geographical area. The primary function of the deeds registries is to serve as the public registers for the transfer and creation of rights in immovable property, but they also serve certain other functions, one of which is the registration of notarial bonds with respect to movable goods. The Deeds Registries Act defines a notarial bond as 'a bond attested by a notary public hypothecating movable property generally or specially'.[10] The phrase 'attested by a notary public' means that the parties must execute the bond (that is, sign it) in the presence of a notary public, who must affix his signature to the bond as a witness to their agreement. However, notarial attestation of the bond is not enough. The Act stipulates that the bond must also be registered in a deeds registry within three months after it has been executed before a notary public, but an application can be brought to court to request a longer time if necessary.[11] The moment of registration is when the Registrar of Deeds affixes his signature to the bond.[12] As explained further below, in some instances, the moment of registration will be the point at which the security right is perfected and thus becomes effective against third parties. However, in other cases, registration alone will not be enough but must be followed by the transfer of possession of the relevant property to the creditor, either voluntarily or through judicial attachment.

Regarding the parties to notarial bonds, there are no rules restricting these bonds only to certain categories of debtors or creditors. For example, any natural or juristic person debtor can register a notarial bond over his or its movable property in favour of any natural or juristic person creditor, as long as they have the contractual capacity to do so. Consumers can, therefore, also make use of notarial bonds, but they are more common in the commercial sphere. If the debtor is a consumer, the rules set out in consumer credit legislation[13] must be complied with when concluding and enforcing the credit transaction. Also,

---

[8] Deeds Registries Act 47 of 1937, ss 61–62.
[9] See e.g. *Pattinson and Another v Fell and Another* 1963 (3) SA 277 (D).
[10] Deeds Registries Act 47 of 1937, s 102 (def of 'notarial bond').
[11] ibid, s 61(1).
[12] ibid, s 13(1).
[13] National Credit Act 34 of 2005.

as pointed out below, the registration process is somewhat less cumbersome for debtors who are companies.

Regarding the nature of the debt secured by the bond, it can essentially entail any debt agreed to by the parties. It can be an existing debt or a future debt. It is also common for such bonds to secure the payment of a fluctuating current and future debt, in which case it is referred to as a 'covering bond'.[14] The creditor's security is accessory to the existence of a valid debt and, therefore, the security will be extinguished automatically once the debt is discharged or is invalidated for some reason.[15] The aforementioned covering bond is an exception to the latter principle since the bond will continue in existence even though there are times during which the fluctuating debt is zero.

Since notarial bonds deal with movable assets that can be situated or moved anywhere in the country, the exact deeds registry (or registries) in which the bond must be registered can be a complex matter. The place of registration is not based on the area in which the movables are situated (since they can be moved or spread across the country) but based on the area in which the debtor resides and/or carries on business at the time of registration. If he resides and carries on business in the same area, the bond should be registered in the deeds registry of that area only, in which case the registration will be effective across the entire country.[16] If the debtor resides and carries on business in different areas (or more than one area), the bond must be registered in the deeds registry of each area in which he resides and carries on business.[17] If this is done, the bond will be effective across the entire country.[18] However, if the bond is registered in only one of the relevant deeds registries (that is, despite the debtor residing and/or doing business in other areas as well), the registration will only be effective in the area where it is registered, not across the entire country.[19] In cases where the bond must be registered in more than one deeds registry, the second registration must take place within one month after the first, the third within one month after the second, and so forth.[20] If the debtor is a company, the matter is simpler in that, for effectiveness across the entire country,

---

14 Deeds Registries Act 47 of 1937, s 50(2).

15 See, e.g. *Land and Agricultural Development Bank of South Africa v Phato Farms (Pty) Ltd and Others* 2015 (3) SA 100 (GP) [96]; *Coloured Development Corporation Ltd v Sahabodien* 1981 (1) SA 868 (C) 870. Although the security lapses once the debt is extinguished, a formal process must still be followed to remove the notarial bond from the deeds registry.

16 Deeds Registries Act 47 of 1937, s 62(1)–(2).

17 ibid, s 62(1).

18 ibid, s 62(2).

19 ibid, s 62(3).

20 ibid, s 61(5).

the bond only has to be registered in the deeds registry of the area where the company's registered office is situated, not also in each area where it conducts business.[21] If the bond was registered in the correct registry (or registries) at the outset, the effectiveness of the bond will not change should the debtor subsequently move its residence, business activities or registered office to a different area. In other words, the legal consequences of the bond at registration will subsist for as long as it remains registered and the debt remains owing, regardless of any subsequent geographical movements by the debtor.

Although movable property can be hypothecated specially or generally through the registration of a notarial bond, immovable property can only be hypothecated specially through the registration of a mortgage bond. It is similarly not possible to create a general hypothec that covers all of the debtor's movable and immovable property.[22] Effectively, therefore, movable and immovable property must be bonded separately.

As illustrated in the above summary of the attestation and registration process, the system is relatively archaic and not in line with the global tendency towards modern electronic registries dedicated to security rights in movable property.[23] Instead, the current system in South Africa is paper-based, time-consuming and cumbersome, especially when registration must occur in more than one registry. Information in the deeds registries is also not as easily accessible to the public as would be the case with a single electronic registry.

As seen in the definition quoted above, a notarial bond can be used to hypothecate movable property either 'generally or specially'.[24] The Deeds Registries Act does not say anything more about what this distinction means, nor does it provide for the legal consequences of the registration of a notarial bond or the differences in this regard between general and special hypothecs. For these answers, one must consult provisions in other statutes, case law and/or the Roman-Dutch common law.

---

[21] ibid, s 62(4).

[22] See the Deeds Registries Act 47 of 1937, s 53(1) read with the Insolvency Act 24 of 1936, s 86.

[23] See especially the United Nations Commission on International Trade Law (UNCITRAL), *Legislative Guide on Secured Transactions* (UN 2010); UNCITRAL, *Model Law on Secured Transactions* (UN 2019).

[24] Deeds Registries Act 47 of 1937, s 102 (def of 'notarial bond'). It is also possible to create a special and general security right in the same bond. Such a bond would, for example, specify a particular movable object and then add a general clause covering the rest of the debtor's movable assets. See *Reeskens v Registrar of Deeds* 1964 (4) SA 369 (N) 372.

If a bond complies with the requirements of the Security by Means of Movable Property Act,[25] which came into force in 1993,[26] the hypothec is regarded as having the same effect as a pledge created through the delivery of the movables to the creditor, despite no such delivery actually having taken place.[27] In other words, the registration of the bond in compliance with the statutory requirements creates a true non-possessory pledge with the same legal status as a possessory pledge,[28] also upon the debtor's insolvency (where it is classified as a 'special mortgage').[29] With such bonds, therefore, the moment of registration is the moment when the security is perfected and becomes effective against third parties – provided that the requirements of the Act are fulfilled. Importantly though, the Act only applies to tangible movables.

The main requirement of the Act is that the bond must specify and describe the movable property in a manner that renders it readily recognisable.[30] This requirement is interpreted strictly and basically means that the exact movable object must be identifiable with reference to the information in the bond alone,

---

25 Act 57 of 1993.

26 Prior to 1993, the system was fragmented. In the Natal Province (now known as KwaZulu–Natal), the Notarial Bonds (Natal) Act 18 of 1932 provided for the registration of a special notarial bond which, if it complied with the asset-description requirements in the latter Act, made the bondholder a secured creditor in the same position as a special mortgage upon the debtor's insolvency, without the need to transfer possession to the creditor. However, in the rest of the country, the common law applied, since there was no special statute like the one in Natal. Therefore, in the rest of the country, the registration of a special notarial bond did not make the bondholder a secured creditor unless the creditor also took possession of the property. As explained later in the chapter, such special bonds were regarded (apparently by mistake) as placing the creditor in the same position as a general bondholder, namely that the creditor at least had a preference over concurrent creditors upon the debtor's insolvency. The Security by Means of Movable Property Act 57 of 1993 replaced the Natal Act in 1993 when it became apparent that the fragmented approach was no longer sustainable, especially in light of the weak position of special notarial bonds outside of Natal. For a more detailed historical overview of these statutes, see Brits (n 2) 231–238.

27 Security by Means of Movable Property Act 57 of 1993, s 1(1).

28 See, e.g. *Ikea Trading und Design AG v BOE Bank Ltd* 2005 (2) SA 7 (SCA) [22]; *Bokomo v Standard Bank van SA Bpk* 1996 (4) SA 450 (C) 457. See further Reghard Brits, 'Two Decades of Special Notarial Bonds in terms of the Security by Means of Movable Property Act' (2015) 27 South African Mercantile Law Journal 246, 253–261.

29 Security by Means of Movable Property Act 57 of 1993, s 4 read with the definitions of 'security' and 'special mortgage' in the Insolvency Act 24 of 1936, s 2.

30 Security by Means of Movable Property Act 57 of 1993, s 1(1).

without reference to any external evidence.[31] If the description of the property does not comply with this standard, the bond will not have the desired effect of making the creditor a secured creditor. Instead, the security will have to be perfected through the transfer of possession. One of the problems with the current system is that compliance with the description requirement in the Act is not formally checked (or at least, required to be checked) by the notary or any official of the deeds registry before or at registration of the bond. In other words, there is no guarantee that a registered special bond complies with the Act and thus that the security has been perfected. Compliance will be a factual question and, therefore, disputes might have to be resolved via litigation.

The above statutory measure relates to a special hypothec (or pledge) of movable property via registration, and thus it is usually called a 'special notarial bond'. However, the Act does not exclude other ways of hypothecating movable property via notarial bonds. The Deeds Registries Act does not restrict the registration of notarial bonds to those that fall under the Security by Means of Movable Property Act, since the latter only deals with the legal consequences of bonds that comply with its requirements. Bonds that do not comply with these requirements (particularly the strict way in which the property must be described), such as bonds that hypothecate movables (including intangibles) in more general terms, are governed by common law principles. The Insolvency Act[32] also has an impact on the priority ranking of certain notarial bonds.[33]

Accordingly, movable property can be hypothecated through the registration of a notarial bond in three ways: (1) through a special notarial bond in terms of which specific tangible movable property is described in compliance with the Security by Means of Movable Property Act; (2) through a general notarial bond that covers all of the debtor's movables, nothing excluded, and including intangibles and future property; and (3) something in between, that is, a bond that is not special enough to comply with the Security by Means of Movable Property Act, but also not general enough to cover all of the debtor's movables – for example, where a category of goods is hypothecated. The first option is not a general (or 'floating') hypothecation, since registration alone is enough to perfect (or 'fix') the security. Therefore, most of what is explained in the rest of the chapter applies to both the second and third options, since both qualify as 'floating' security devices. Importantly, though, as will become clear in the next section, South African law draws a somewhat archaic distinction between the second and third options in cases where the bond was not perfected prior to the debtor's insolvency.

---

[31] *Ikea* (n 28) [18]–[24]; *Scheltema Beleggings CC v Commercial Truck and Trailer Sales CC* (35420/08) [2010] ZAGPPHC 28 (1 April 2010) [8]–[11].

[32] Act 24 of 1936.

[33] See Section 3, "Effect of an unperfected bond", below.

EFFECT OF AN UNPERFECTED BOND

An agreement generally hypothecating movable property that has not yet been registered or that has been registered but not yet perfected through attachment[34] provides the creditor with very limited rights. If the agreement is neither registered nor perfected through attachment, it merely creates a personal right against the other party – not a right in the property. It only binds the parties to the agreement and will provide no protection against third parties (unless they have actual knowledge of the terms of the agreement) and no preferential rights upon the debtor's insolvency. The contractual relationship alone also cannot prevent the debtor from disposing of the assets, unless a contractual clause expressly prohibits disposal. However, a disposal in contravention of the contract will merely amount to a breach of contract that could render the debtor liable for damages towards the creditor, but will not invalidate the disposal or otherwise bind third parties (again, unless the third party has actual knowledge of the clause prohibiting disposal). Therefore, once the debtor disposes of the property, the effect of the bond over such movables will end and the bondholder will have no recourse against such assets.[35] Nevertheless, since the bond creates a floating security, any new assets acquired by the debtor will automatically also be covered by the bond. Another consequence of a bond that has not yet been perfected is that the bondholder cannot prevent other creditors from judicially attaching the property to enforce their claims against the debtor.[36] This also means that the holder of an *unperfected* security cannot prevent another creditor from perfecting its security over the relevant property.

The only added benefit of registering the security agreement in the form of a general notarial bond is that it will give the creditor some protection upon the debtor's insolvency. Registration will not afford any other rights, such as a stronger ability to prevent the disposal of the property. When the debtor enters insolvency proceedings (sequestration in the case of individuals or liquidation (winding-up) in the case of companies),[37] the hypothec will not automatically change from a 'floating' to a 'fixed' security right, and thus it will still not be

[34] See Section 4, "Perfection of the security", below on perfection through attachment.

[35] Brits (n 2) 203–5; CG van der Merwe, *Sakereg* (2nd edn, Butterworths 1989) 669–70. cf. also Philip Sacks, 'Notarial Bonds in South African Law' (1982) 99 South African Law Journal 605, 616, 619–20.

[36] *Phato* (n 15) [4]; *Standard Bank v Wentzel & Lombard* 1904 TS 828, 835.

[37] The sequestration of individual debtors is regulated by the Insolvency Act 24 of 1936, while the liquidation of companies is regulated by the Companies Act 61 of 1973. Although the latter statute has been repealed by the Companies Act 71 of 2008, the provisions regarding liquidation in the 1973 Act are still in force.

binding on all third parties. In this sense, there is not much difference between a registered and unregistered general hypothec. However, upon the registration of a general notarial bond, the hypothec will become binding on other unsecured (concurrent) creditors in the event of the debtor's insolvency. When the free residue of the debtor's insolvent estate (that is, the surplus funds after secured creditors have been paid) is distributed, the Insolvency Act sets out a list and sequence in which certain unsecured creditors with special preferential rights (known as 'statutory preferent creditors') must be paid.[38] The last item on this list of statutory preferent creditors is the holders of unperfected general notarial bonds. In other words, a creditor holding a registered yet unperfected general bond will be paid as the last creditor in the list of statutory preferent creditors but in preference to those unsecured creditors (concurrent creditors) who enjoy no statutory preference.[39] To summarise, a creditor with an *unperfected* general notarial bond does not have a real security right in the bonded property. Instead, such a creditor only has a personal right against the debtor as well as a special statutory preference over other (the lowest-ranking) unsecured creditors in the case where the debtor has been declared insolvent. Outside of insolvency law, the holder of an *unperfected* general bond has no security right enforceable against third parties whatsoever, except against third parties with actual knowledge of the bond.

The 'second to last' position of an unperfected general bond in the ranking of creditors in insolvency law might not provide great comfort in all cases. Nevertheless, provided that there are sufficient funds available, the general bondholder should be able to receive payment of most of its claim – or at least significantly more than would have been the case if it had it been a mere concurrent creditor. It is also possible for more than one general bond to be registered over the movables of a debtor, and if both are unperfected (thus 'floating'), they will rank according to the time sequence in which they were registered.[40] Importantly, the general bondholder's preference will not extend to property burdened with something like a possessory pledge (including where a general bond had been perfected via attachment) or a special notarial bond that complies with the Security by Means of Movable Property Act, since these are 'fixed' security rights that are always preferred over 'floating' ones. If there are funds available after the secured creditors' claims have been settled from the proceeds of their collateral, the surplus will be available for lower-ranking creditors, including the holders of unperfected general bonds who will be paid before concurrent creditors.

---

[38] Insolvency Act 24 of 1936, ss 96–102.

[39] ibid, s 102.

[40] Van der Merwe (n 35) 669 n 553.

In the case of an unperfected bond, the general bondholder's statutory preference under the Insolvency Act will not extend to the proceeds of immovable property but only to those of movable (including intangible) property. This may appear obvious, since the bond only hypothecates the debtor's movable property, but there used to be some uncertainty in this regard. For instance, some assumed that the general bondholder's preference extended to all funds available after the secured and other preferent creditors had been paid, regardless of the origin of the funds.[41] However, the Supreme Court of Appeal has clarified this matter by confirming that the general bondholder's preference over concurrent creditors only applies to proceeds deriving from movable assets.[42]

When providing for this preference, the Insolvency Act uses the term 'general mortgage bond',[43] which is just another word for 'general notarial bond' in this context. An important implication of the word 'general' in this section is that the special statutory preference accorded to this bond only applies to bonds that hypothecate the debtor's movables generally in the literal sense. If any movable assets are excluded or if only a category of movables is indicated in the bond, it will not qualify as a 'general' bond for purposes of the Insolvency Act and, consequently, the creditor holding such a bond will not enjoy a statutory preference upon the debtor's insolvency. Instead, such a non-general bond will effectively amount to a 'special' bond – albeit one that probably does not comply with the Security by Means of Movable Property Act and thus will not be 'special' enough to grant the creditor a fixed security right enforceable against third parties or with any meaningful status in insolvency. Such a creditor will be entirely unsecured. Prior to 1993, a contrary assumption was held in practice, namely, that special notarial bonds that did not create a real security right due to non-compliance with the statutory requirements[44] at least granted such a creditor the same preference over concurrent creditors

---

41 See, e.g., Konrad M Kritzinger, *Principles of the Law of Mortgage, Pledge & Lien* (Juta 1999) 56–57; Van der Merwe (n 35) 671; Sacks (n 35) 611.

42 *Firstrand Bank Ltd v Land and Agricultural Development Bank of South Africa* 2015 (1) SA 38 (SCA). See also *Contract Forwarding (Pty) Ltd v Chesterfin (Pty) Ltd and Others* 2003 (2) SA 253 (SCA) [3]; *Cooper NO en Andere v Die Meester en 'n Ander* 1992 (3) SA 60 (A) 82.

43 Insolvency Act 24 of 1936, s 102.

44 As explained in n 26 above, the applicable statute prior to 1993 was the Notarial Bonds (Natal) Act 18 of 1932, but in terms of this Act, only special notarial bonds registered in the Natal Province could make the creditor a secured creditor, provided that the property was described correctly in accordance with the statutory requirements.

as that of a general bondholder.[45] Although there seems to be no reason, in principle, why a general bondholder should enjoy this preference but a special bondholder should not, the Appellate Division (as the Supreme Court of Appeal was known then) overturned this widely held assumption. The court found that the preference in insolvency only applies to bonds that are literally 'general' in nature, as per the wording of section 102 of the Insolvency Act.[46] As a result of this judgment, special notarial bonds that do not fall under the pre-1993 statutory regime have practically no value whatsoever.

The legislature stepped in soon after to partially overturn the negative effects of this judgment for such special bondholders and thus restored their status as enjoying the same preference over concurrent creditors as general bondholders.[47] However, this only applies to special notarial bonds registered prior to 1993. Any special notarial bond registered after 1993 but that does not comply with the Security by Means of Movable Property Act, therefore, does not afford a perfected security right or a preference over concurrent creditors. Effectively, such a bond is not 'special' enough to grant a right *in rem* but also not 'general' enough to bind concurrent creditors upon the debtor's insolvency. In other words, there currently exists a 'missing middle' in the law concerning the hypothecation of movables through the registration of notarial bonds in South Africa. A creditor who wants to enjoy a form of security via a notarial bond must get the debtor to follow one of two routes: either (1) register a (special) notarial bond that complies with the Security by Means of Movable Property Act or (2) register a (general) notarial bond that covers all present and future movable property without exception. Any bond that is somewhere in between these two options, such as a bond covering a category of movables (like stock-in-trade), will have no effect beyond the contractual rights enforceable between the parties. The only way for the creditor to enjoy meaningful security in such cases is to perfect the bond by having the movables attached.[48] Currently, if a creditor wants to receive an effective form of security over a category of movable objects, like stock-in-trade or a flock of livestock, the solution is simply to include all of the debtor's movables in the bond; otherwise, the creditor will enjoy no preference over unsecured creditors upon the debtor's

---

45 See, e.g. *Vrede Koöp Landboumaatskappy Bpk v Uys* 1964 (2) SA 283 (O) 285–286. See also TJ Scott and Susan Scott, *Wille's Law of Mortgage and Pledge in South Africa* (3rd edn, Juta 1987) 68; B Wunch, 'What Rights of Preference are Enjoyed by a Special Notarial Bond?' (1960) 23 Journal for Contemporary Roman-Dutch Law 112; Sacks (n 35) 611–613.

46 *Cooper* (n 42).

47 Security by Means of Movable Property Act 57 of 1993, s 1(3).

48 See Section 4, "Perfection of the security", below.

insolvency.[49] Reforming the law in this regard could also be a good idea, since there is no reason, in principle, why a hypothec over a category of movable objects should not, similar to an all-asset general hypothec, grant the creditor a preference over concurrent creditors – especially if that hypothec is registered.

PERFECTION OF THE SECURITY

As explained thus far, unregistered security agreements not accompanied by the transfer of possession to the creditor, as well as registered security agreements that do not comply with the Security by Means of Movable Property Act, are all of a 'floating' nature. If the agreement is unregistered, it merely creates rights enforceable between the parties, while in the case of a registered agreement that qualifies as a 'general' bond, the creditor's rights are preferred over those of concurrent creditors upon the debtor's insolvency. Except for the latter preference, such a creditor's security right is not of much value in competition with other creditors. And even if the hypothec is registered, the creditor cannot prevent the disposal of the property or otherwise control the debtor's use of the property, except for what they might have agreed to in the security agreement. Nevertheless, as mentioned earlier, it is possible for the creditor to perfect its security by having the relevant property judicially attached and placed under its control.

The form of control (possession) necessary to perfect the security will depend on the nature of the property and the broader context of the transaction. In addition to the classic example of the movables being removed by the sheriff and placed in the creditor's custody, it is also possible for the creditor to receive possession by taking control of the debtor's premises, especially if the intention is for the creditor to temporarily take over the debtor's business.[50] For instance, it might be sufficient for the sheriff to remove the keys to the premises from the debtor and hand them to the creditor.[51] It could also be enough to place a security guard, who is in the employ of the creditor, at the premises

---

[49] It is common practice for parties to describe a specific property in the notarial bond but then also to include a so-called 'general clause' whereby, in addition to the specified property, the bond also covers all of the debtor's movable property in general. This practice caters for the risk that the description of the specific property does not comply with the statutory requirements, thus at least ensuring that the creditor will enjoy the statutory preference over concurrent creditors in the event that the debtor is declared insolvent.

[50] See e.g. *Juglal NO and Another v Shoprite Checkers (Pty) Ltd t/a OK Franchise Division* 2004 (5) SA 248 (SCA).

[51] See e.g. *Firstrand Bank Ltd t/a RMB Private Bank v Miko NO 166 (Pty) Ltd, Miko NO 166 (Pty) Ltd v Firstrand Bank Ltd t/a RMB Private Bank, Firstrand*

to prevent the debtor from gaining access and removing any assets.[52] In other instances, sufficient possession might require controlling the keys, placing a security guard outside the premises and, if necessary, placing a representative of the creditor in charge of the debtor's business.[53] The ultimate question is whether the creditor has been placed in effective legal control of the debtor's assets.[54]

Although the debtor can voluntarily hand the property to the creditor,[55] it is more typical for the creditor to apply for a court order in terms of which the sheriff is instructed to attach the property and place it in the creditor's custody.[56] In fact, if the debtor does not cooperate by voluntarily handing over the property, the creditor may not take the law into its own hands by taking possession without a court order. A contractual clause authorising self-help will also not be effectual. If the creditor does take possession without the debtor's permission or without a court order, this will amount to spoliation (the unlawful disturbance of peaceful possession) and, consequently, the debtor will be entitled to institute a spoliation remedy (the *mandament van spolie*) for the return of his property.[57] Thus, unless the debtor voluntarily hands over the property, a court order will be required to facilitate the perfection of the creditor's security. The nature of this perfection remedy is nothing other than a claim for specific performance of the terms of the security agreement,[58] whether registered or not. Because the agreement basically entails a promise on the part of the debtor to pledge his movables to the creditor, the performance of this

---

Bank Ltd t/a RMB Private Bank v Ezard and Others (16183/2012, 17089/2012, 19033/12) [2012] ZAWCHC 346 (7 November 2012) [24].

52 See e.g. *Huma t/a Spar Supermarket v North-West Development Corporation Limited* (679/96) [1998] ZANWHC 2 (3 September 1998).

53 See e.g. *Contract Forwarding* (n 42).

54 CFC van der Walt, 'Aspekte van die Reg insake Notariële Verbande' (1983) 46 Journal for Contemporary Roman-Dutch Law 332, 334.

55 In this case, no court order is necessary. See *SAPDC (Trading) Ltd v Immelman* 1989 (3) SA 506 (W) 508–509.

56 The earliest reported cases in which perfection orders were granted are *Paruk v Glendale Estate Co* (1924) 45 NPD 1 and *Pietersburg Cold Storage Ltd v Cacaburas* 1925 TPD 295, but such orders might have been granted earlier than that already. See Johan Roos, 'The Perfecting of Securities held under a General Notarial Bond' (1995) 112 South African Law Journal 169, 169.

57 See e.g. *Miko* (n 51) [26].

58 *Boland Bank Ltd v Vermeulen* 1993 (2) SA 241 (E) 243; *Barclays National Bank Ltd and Another v Natal Fire Extinguishers Manufacturing Co (Pty) Ltd and Others* 1982 (4) SA 650 (D) 654–655; *International Shipping Co (Pty) Ltd v Affinity (Pty) Ltd and Another* 1983 (1) SA 79 (C) 84.

duty through the transfer of possession will have the effect of perfecting the creditor's security.

It is important that the security agreement (also when it is registered in the form of a notarial bond) should contain an express clause entitling the creditor to receive possession of the property – a so-called 'perfection clause'.[59] The clause must also set out the circumstances under which the creditor may demand possession of the property.[60] The most common circumstance entitling the creditor to demand possession is when the debtor defaults on his payment obligations, but it could include other circumstances as well, such as when the debtor's business starts running into financial difficulties. The onus is on the creditor to prove that it is entitled to a perfection order,[61] that is, that one of the conditions for possession set out in the bond has been triggered. Although there has been some uncertainty whether it is truly necessary to make express provision for the creditor's right to take possession via a perfection clause, the courts have confirmed that it is indeed necessary to do so expressly, since the creditor has no implied or automatic right in this regard.[62] Therefore, in the absence of a perfection clause, the creditor will be unable to perfect its security, and the bondholder's only right will be its preference over concurrent creditors upon the debtor's insolvency.[63]

In cases where a party to a contract requests a court to compel the other party to perform under their contract, the court always has discretion whether or not to grant the order. However, since a perfection order is practically the only remedy available to the holder of a general bond, the courts are not eager to exercise their discretion against the granting of a perfection order, provided that the creditor has a clear right to receive possession.[64] Nevertheless, the debtor may try to argue that the terms of the perfection clause in question

---

59 In general, see Brits (n 2) 212–27; Roos (n 56). See also Marlize Jansen, 'More Legal Security Regarding Security by Means of General Notarial Bonds' (2003) 15 South African Mercantile Law Journal 486; Susan Scott, 'Notarial Bonds and Insolvency' (1995) 58 Journal for Contemporary Roman-Dutch Law 672, 675–677; Sacks (n 35) 619–620.

60 Roos (n 56) 171–173.

61 *Pick 'n Pay Retailers (Pty) Ltd v Pine Valley Supermarket (Pty) Ltd* (8209/2014) [2015] ZAKZDHC 27 (20 March 2015) [6].

62 *Eerste Nasionale Bank van SA Bpk v Schulenburg* 1992 (2) SA 827 (T); *Boland Bank Bpk v Spies en 'n Ander* 1993 (1) SA 402 (T) 403–404; *Vermeulen* (n 58) 243–244; *Atmore NO v Tobacco Sales Warehouse (Pvt) Ltd* 1978 (3) SA 215 (R).

63 *Spies* (n 62) 403; *Atmore* (n 62) 216.

64 *Contract Forwarding* (n 42) [10]; *International Shipping* (n 58) 84. See also Jansen (n 59) 495.

should not be enforced due to the unjust results that will follow under the circumstances of the case.[65]

Depending on the nature of the property and the general context of the transaction, the parties can also cover other matters in the agreement, such as the scope of the creditor's rights and duties with reference to the debtor's property while in possession thereof. It can also contain provisions on using the attached property to enforce the secured debt. For instance, the contract could provide for the creditor's right to sell the property without court authorisation (*parate executie*)[66] or to take over the property at a fair value (a *quasi*-conditional sale).[67] However, a clause authorising the creditor to appropriate the property regardless of the value of the property or the size of the debt (a *pactum commissorium*) is invalid.[68] Moreover, despite the ability to include a provision permitting a private sale, the position is more restrictive in the consumer law context, where court authorisation is always necessary to enforce the security.[69]

In the commercial context, it is relatively common for the agreement to permit the creditor to take over the temporary management of the debtor's business.[70] The purpose of this step is usually to enable the creditor to sell the

---

[65] Such arguments were made but were unsuccessful in, e.g. *Juglal* (n 50); *Pick 'n Pay Retailers* (n 61).

[66] Clauses authorising *parate executie* are valid in pledge agreements pertaining to movable property. See, e.g. *Bock and Others v Duburoro Investments (Pty) Ltd* 2004 (2) SA 242 (SCA) [7], [13]; *Juglal* (n 50) [11]; *SA Bank of Athens Ltd v Van Zyl* 2005 (5) SA 93 (SCA) [10]–[16]; *Osry v Hirsch, Loubser & Co Ltd* 1922 CPD 531. However, such a clause is not valid in the case of a mortgage of immovable property. See *Iscor Housing Utility Co and Another v Chief Registrar of Deeds and Another* 1971 (1) SA 613 (T).

[67] *Mapenduka v Ashington* 1919 AD 343, 352–353. See also *Graf v Buechel* 2003 (4) SA 378 (SCA).

[68] See e.g. *Bock* (n 66) [8]; *Graf* (n 67) [9]–[11]; *Vasco* (n 6) 611.

[69] In *ABSA Bank Ltd v Prochaska t/a Bianca Cara Interiors* 2009 (2) SA 512 (D) [60], it was held that a loan agreement and a general notarial bond registered as security for such a loan together qualify as a 'secured loan' for purposes of the National Credit Act 34 of 2005. To the extent that the Act applies to such transactions, the enforcement of notarial bonds must therefore comply with the consumer protection measures in the Act. See Reghard Brits, 'Pledge of Movables under the National Credit Act: Secured Loans, Pawn Transactions and Summary Execution Clauses' (2013) 25 South African Mercantile Law Journal 555 for an explanation of how certain provisions in the Act have the effect of prohibiting *parate executie* clauses – thus rendering extra-judicial enforcement unlawful.

[70] Roos (n 56) 173–175.

business as a whole or to sell the individual assets to recover the debt.[71] Taking over the management of the business could also be aimed at the creditor attempting to save the business, thus bringing it back to a place of profitability before handing it back to the debtor. Either way, in cases where the parties intend for the creditor to have the right to take over the debtor's business temporarily, the security agreement should specifically set out the creditor's rights and powers in this regard.[72] A general bondholder who is in possession of their debtor's property has a duty of care towards the debtor with reference to such property and must account to the debtor for how the property is managed.[73] If the creditor is given the power to sell the debtor's property, this must be done in a way that does not prejudice the debtor's rights; otherwise, the latter can approach the court to protect his interests.[74]

The result of perfecting a general bond is that such a creditor, who is now in possession of the debtor's assets, will be a fully secured creditor for all intents and purposes.[75] The security has changed from being 'floating' to 'fixed'. The creditor will no longer only have the statutory preference over the concurrent creditors upon the debtor's insolvency but will be a secured creditor by virtue of holding a 'pledge' in such assets.[76] However, the statutory preference will continue to exist with regard to any movables that were not attached under the perfection order, since such assets are still covered by the general bond should any portion of the debt remain outstanding.

Interestingly, the power to perfect the security can be exercised right up until the moment before the debtor enters into insolvency proceedings. In the case of an individual, this will be when the provisional sequestration order is granted,[77] while in the case of a company, it will be when the application for the liquidation order is filed.[78] The insolvency practitioner (trustee in the case

---

[71] See e.g. *Spar Group Limited v Sea Spirit Trading 162 CC t/a Paledi and Others* (JA47/2017) [2018] ZALAC 15 (7 June 2018). See also *Juglal* (n 50).

[72] Such a clause would effectively be in the nature of a *pactum antichreseos* (an agreement to use the pledged property). See Brits (n 2) 217.

[73] See e.g. *Simon NO and Others v Mitsui and Co Ltd and Others* 1997 (2) SA 475 (W); *Federal Supply and Cold Storage Company of South Africa Limited v Schultze and Fly* (1906) 27 NLR 82. On a possessory secured creditor's duty of care in general, see also e.g. *Lourens v Du Toit* (1879) 8 Buch 182; *Vassen v Garett* 1911 EDL 188; *National Bank v Tayob & Co* 1919 TPD 133; *Retmil Financial Services (Pty) Ltd v Sanlam Life Insurance Company Ltd and Others* [2013] 3 All SA 337 (WCC).

[74] *Osry* (n 66) 547.

[75] Scott (n 59) 676–77.

[76] Insolvency Act 24 of 1936, s 2 (def of 'security').

[77] ibid, s 2 (def of 'sequestration order').

[78] Companies Act 61 of 1973, s 348.

of an individual and liquidator in the case of a company) will not be able to have the perfection of the creditor's security set aside if the creditor had taken possession on the basis of a court order and if such attachment took place before the commencement of the insolvency proceeding. This is true even if the perfection court order was merely provisional at that point but made final after the insolvency proceeding commenced, as long as attachment took place before the insolvency proceeding commenced.[79] Although there are other instances where a trustee or liquidator can have certain pre-insolvency transactions set aside, for instance if one creditor was given an undue preference shortly before the debtor entered an insolvency proceeding,[80] this power does not apply to the perfection of a general bond prior to insolvency. The main reason for this is that the perfection was authorised by a court order and it would not have been appropriate for the trustee or liquidator to have the power to set aside an action that was authorised by a court.[81] However, if the bond was perfected via a voluntary handing over of the property to the creditor shortly before insolvency (hence without a court order), it may be possible for the trustee or liquidator to have it set aside as an undue preference, provided that the relevant requirements in the Insolvency Act are complied with.[82]

Therefore, although the commencement of insolvency itself does not have the effect of perfecting the bondholder's security, the creditor can perfect its security by keeping an eye on the debtor's affairs and ensuring that it obtains an attachment order and takes possession of the relevant property before the debtor enters into insolvency – even immediately before this moment. One might question whether it is a good thing, from an insolvency law perspective, to allow the perfection of a general bond so soon before insolvency without the ability of the trustee or liquidator to overturn such perfection if it prejudices the other creditors.[83] However, the power to perfect the security is one of the few advantages of holding a general bond, and provided that the perfection is authorised by a court, there appears to be no reason to change the current state of affairs in this respect.

---

79 *Development Bank of Southern Africa Ltd v Van Rensburg and Others NNO* 2002 (5) SA 425 (SCA) [17]–[24]; *Contract Forwarding* (n 42) [8]–[12]. See also Jansen (n 59) 491–497.

80 Insolvency Act 24 of 1936, s 30.

81 *Contract Forwarding* (n 42) [7].

82 See the Insolvency Act 24 of 1936, s 30, for the specific requirements for having an undue preference set aside.

83 See, e.g. *Chesterfin (Pty) Ltd v Contract Forwarding (Pty) Ltd and Others* 2002 (1) SA 155 (T) 169.

CONCLUSION

The registration of a general notarial bond is a useful, albeit imperfect, credit security device in South Africa. The cumbersome and outdated nature of the registration process seems to be outweighed by the other benefits of holding a notarial bond over all the movable assets of one's debtor, and thus this form of general hypothecation is still relatively popular in commercial practice. The registration of a general notarial bond creates the rough equivalent of a 'floating charge' over all of the tangible and intangible movable property of the debtor.[84] Although the term 'floating charge' is not often used in South Africa, the operation of a general bond is broadly comparable with that of a floating charge. Registration alone does not make the creditor a secured creditor with a 'fixed' real security right enforceable against third parties. The closest it gets to impacting third parties is that the bond gives the creditor a preference over concurrent creditors upon the debtor's insolvency. Other than that, the creditor's rights are very limited. For instance, it cannot prevent the debtor from disposing of the bonded movables and, as a result, the security will not persist over any objects that leave the debtor's ownership, although it will cover new property acquired in the place of the disposed property. The general bondholder's rights will also be subservient to the rights of other creditors with fixed security rights, even if such rights were created after the registration of the bond.

The bondholder's floating security can be transformed into a fixed security by obtaining a perfection order and taking possession of the property in accordance with the terms of a clause entitling the creditor to receive possession under certain stipulated circumstances, such as when the debtor defaults or when the debtor's business starts experiencing financial difficulties. Perfection of the bond can entail attaching the debtor's movables and placing them in the creditor's custody, or the creditor taking over the debtor's premises and, for example, taking over his business with the aim of selling the assets or even restoring the business to profitability before handing it back to the debtor. Perfection can take place up until the moment before the debtor enters into an insolvency proceeding, as long as the creditor receives possession before the debtor enters a formal state of insolvency. Upon perfection, the creditor will be in the same position as a creditor with a possessory pledge or special

[84] For a comparison between the general bond and the floating charge, see Natania Locke, 'Security Granted by a Company over its Movable Property: The Floating Charge and the General Notarial Bond Compared' (2008) 41 Comparative and International Law Journal of Southern Africa 136.

mortgage, meaning that the bondholder will be a secured creditor with reference to the attached property for all intents and purposes.

One of the interesting consequences of the way in which general notarial bonds work is that the creditors under such bonds are effectively compelled to keep a close eye on the affairs of their debtors. Unlike fully secured creditors, a general bondholder cannot stand by passively, expecting full protection in the event that its debtor runs into financial problems. It must keep an eye on the debtor's affairs, and the agreement can even entitle the creditor to inspect the debtor's business and have access to its financial records, which the creditor will need in order to establish whether it is necessary to perfect its security to strengthen its position. If such due diligence is not exercised, the bondholder's only guarantee will be its statutory preference over concurrent creditors, which in many cases will not be a bad position to be in either.

In conclusion, therefore, the South African system has proven that it is possible to take a historical concept like the general hypothecation of movable property, with its roots in Roman and Roman-Dutch law, and make it relatively useful and thus popular in a modern commercial context. The principles surrounding general bonds are largely clear and settled, and they operate reasonably well in practice. A more general reform of South African secured transactions law might be necessary, especially to improve the efficiency of special security rights over movable property, but in the meantime, the general hypothecation of movables can go a long way towards fulfilling the demands of commercial practice.

ACKNOWLEDGEMENTS

Thank you to Michel Koekemoer for reading and providing very helpful comments on this chapter. All errors are my own.

6. The floating lien in American law: from historical accounts to digital assets

Christopher K. Odinet

INTRODUCTION

The desire for a so-called *floating lien* in American law, akin in ways to the English *floating charge*,[1] has a long and bumpy history in the United States.[2] That story, as outlined in this chapter, has much to do with political motivations driven by limited sources of funding for small businesses alongside the slow progression of overcoming theoretical legal obstacles when it came to granting a security interest in property that one does not yet own: specifically, *accounts receivable* and *inventory*, both of which are at the "immediate core of a commercial debtor's enterprise"[3] but that "are like water flowing through

[1] For a discussion of the origins of the floating charge in English law, see George L Gretton, "Reception Without Integration? Floating Charges and Mixed Systems" (2003) 78 Tul L Rev 307. In the United States, the term lien is used broadly to include a variety of security interests, including those created voluntarily and involuntarily by the debtor. See *Bates v. Chicago Lumber Co. of Omaha*, [2016] 375 P.3d 732, 738 (Wyo) ("a lien is a right to encumber property until a debt is paid"). In this chapter, the term lien refers to the voluntary creation of a security interest under Article 9 of the Uniform Commercial Code and its various predecessor laws.

[2] Notably, Article 9 only allows a floating charge for certain types of property capable under the law of being encumbered with a nonpossessory security interest; the English floating charge is more all-encompassing in terms of debtor assets. See Jeanette L Goldsberry, "Perfection of Nonpossessory Security Interests Under Revised Article 9: Consequences of the Practical and Conceptual Incompatibility of US and English Secured Transactions Law" (2002) 3 Chi J Int'l L 241, 243–44.

[3] *Commercial Asset-Based Financing* (Callaghan, 2023 edn), Part III, s 18:1.

a river bed".[4] The combination of these factors led to the eventual drafting of Article 9 of the Uniform Commercial Code and its provisions that allow for a lien over the property of a debtor.

Yet, the road to Article 9 was paved with an assortment of security devices that attempted to achieve the idea of a floating lien but never quite hit the mark.[5] By a floating lien, I mean a consensual lien securing a revolving line of credit that could encumber present and future acquired property maintained in the possession of the debtor and which could be sold or otherwise disposed of in the ordinary course of business,[6] but also where the lien allowed the debtor to make use of the proceeds arising out of the collateral in a variety of ways apart from immediately paying down the debt.[7]

Even after courts slowly became comfortable with the idea of allowing debtors to grant security interests in property they had not yet acquired (i.e. after-acquired property), it could only be for assets that were fixed in the possession of the debtor.[8] A prime example was equipment.[9] But as for things that would turn over in the everyday course of business, like inventory and accounts receivable, courts resisted.[10] Legal issues relative to giving notice to third persons, encumbering property *en masse*, and the chance of misleading unsecured creditors as to their avenues of recourse when faced with nonpayment caused courts to resist allowing after-acquired property clauses in security contracts to apply to "shifting stock" collateral.[11]

Judicial resistance could, however, only last for so long.[12] As explained in this chapter, lawyers and legislatures eventually came to draft and legislate a variety of different security devices that would circumvent or override judicial roadblocks in creating a floating lien—or at least come as close as possible to

---

[4] Eldon H Reiley, *Security Interests in Personal Property* (West Group, 2022 edn) para 34:35.

[5] See Robert W Weeks, "'Floating Liens' in Inventory Financing" (1956) 1956 U Ill LF 557, 559–75.

[6] For a discussion of the nature of transactions involving inventory and third persons, see *Commercial Asset-Based Financing* (2023 edn), Part III, para 18:2.

[7] Eldon H Reiley, *Security Interests in Personal Property* (West Group, 2022 edn) para 34:33; see also Richard L Barnes, "Tracing Commingled Proceeds: The Metamorphosis of Equity Principles into UCC Doctrine" (1990) 51 U Pitt L Rev 281, 287.

[8] D Benjamin Beard, "The Purchase Money Security Interest in Inventory: If It Does Not Float, It Must Be Dead" (1990) 57 Tenn L Rev 437, 463.

[9] ibid.

[10] ibid 463–464.

[11] ibid.

[12] D Benjamin Beard, "The Purchase Money Security Interest in Inventory: If It Does Not Float, It Must Be Dead" (1990) 57 Tenn L Rev 437, 465.

creating one.[13] Yet, as Benjamin Beard explained, one would need to spend a great deal of time and money in order to use one of these devices to the fullest.[14] Grant Gilmore,[15] a giant of American commercial law, described the process of creating a floating lien on inventory as, although doable, both complicated and difficult.[16]

Finally came Article 9 of the Uniform Commercial Code (UCC). Its general aim was "to encourage the extension of commercial credit by reducing transaction costs and economic legal risks, especially in long-term commercial relationships".[17] To do so, it essentially blessed the notion of a floating lien through various provisions that individually validated components of what was previously unachievable.[18] This chapter aims to tell the story of the floating lien in the United States—from pre-UCC Article 9 to the eventual passage of this most important commercial law—as well as raise some issues about the future of the floating lien in the digital age.[19]

---

13 ibid.

14 ibid.

15 Professor Grant Gilmore was an American scholar of commercial law and one of the principal drafters of the Uniform Commercial Code. See generally Anthony J Waters, "For Grant Gilmore" (1983) 42 Md L Rev 865. One of his most famous works is titled *The Death of Contract*. See Grant Gilmore, *The Death of Contract* (Ohio St UP 1974).

16 D Benjamin Beard, "The Purchase Money Security Interest in Inventory: If It Does Not Float, It Must Be Dead" (1990) 57 Tenn L Rev 437, 465.

17 Bruce A Campbell, "Contracts Jurisprudence and Article Nine of the Uniform Commercial Code: The Allowable Scope of Future Advance and All Obligations Clauses in Commercial Security Agreements" (1986) 37 Hastings LJ 1007, 1041.

18 Those individual provisions of Article 9 are Sections 9-204(1), (3) (validating after-acquired property clauses and future advances of credit), 9-205 (making clear that a debtor need to account to the creditor relative to proceeds received from the disposition of collateral), 9-203(3), 306 (providing that a security interest attaches automatically to the proceeds of collateral), 9-307(1) (allows a buyer in the ordinary course to receive collateral unencumbered by a pre-existing security interest), 9-110 (allows for broad descriptions of collateral to be used in security agreements and otherwise), 9-201 (allows for new forms of security agreements) and 9-108 (defines more broadly the notion of a pre-existing debt). See Eldon H. Reiley, *Security Interests in Personal Property* (West Group, 2022 edn) §34:33.

19 For a discussion of commercial law's doctrinal workings and points of private law risk with regard to property—particularly digital assets, see Kara J Bruce, Christopher K Odinet, and Andrea Tosato, "The Private Law of Stablecoins" (2022) 54 Ariz St LJ 1073; Juliet Moringiello and Christopher K Odinet, "Blockchain Real Estate and NFTs" (2023) 64 William & Mary L Rev

FLOATING LIEN BEFORE THE UCC

The Problem of Small Business Financing

The issue of the floating lien has long been important in American law, largely because of its connection to small business financing.[20] In the United States, as Homer Kripke explains, the ability to attract capital to finance small business operations has always been a major challenge.[21] Small businesses are "chronically undercapitalized" but have few options in terms of obtaining funding.[22] Specifically, equity investors are generally not interested in or able to provide capital in this regard because of the extensive underwriting and monitoring costs of doing so.[23] As such, the public market for the buying and selling of securities is generally not hospitable to small businesses.[24] For the few equity investment opportunities that do exist, they are highly selective, thereby leaving out a great deal of the small business financing demand.[25]

In terms of credit, rather than equity, institutional lenders have historically also been very hesitant to lend to small businesses.[26] As Bruce Campbell notes, the "cost, complexities, and risks" involved in small business lending resulted in only a few lenders—specifically, commercial finance companies and only the very largest banks—actually engaging with this market.[27] Indeed, "[m]any banks simply did not engage in asset-based financing at all'.[28]

1131; Juliet Moringiello and Christopher K Odinet, "The Property Law of Tokens" (2022) 74 Fla L Rev 607.

[20] Homer Kripke, "Current Asset Financing as a Source of Long-Term Capital" (1952) 36 Minn L Rev 506, 506–09.

[21] ibid.

[22] ibid 511.

[23] ibid 508.

[24] Homer Kripke, "Current Asset Financing as a Source of Long-Term Capital" (1952) 36 Minn L Rev 506, 506–09.

[25] ibid 509–13.

[26] Bruce A Campbell, "Contracts Jurisprudence and Article Nine of the Uniform Commercial Code: The Allowable Scope of Future Advance and All Obligations Clauses in Commercial Security Agreements" (1986) 37 Hastings LJ 1007, 1013.

[27] ibid.

[28] ibid.

The Inadequacies of the Chattel Mortgage

The lack of lending to small businesses was due in large part to the fact that the primary form of collateral available for securing such financing was the small business's inventory and accounts receivable.[29] That is not to say that it was impossible to obtain a security interest in such assets.[30] The laws of almost every state allowed for such a thing.[31] These included specific laws permitting the creation of chattel mortgages, trust receipt transactions, assignments of accounts receivable and other contracts, and factor's lien agreements.[32] Of these, the oldest was the *chattel mortgage*,[33] which provided a method of granting a security interest over personal property of a debtor.[34] Yet, as Allison Dunham recounts, this device was meant to collateralize "goods at rest".[35] In other words, the chattel mortgage was only meant to cover personal property of a debtor-business that was not intended to be sold or transferred in the ordinary course and scope of the business.[36] If a debtor business was authorized to sell personal property subject to a security interest (such as in the case of inventory), then courts would view this as "no security at all".[37]

Interestingly, Dunham notes that a fear among judges was that between two owners of a business (the example he gives is a grocery store), one would grant a security interest to the other over all of the business's stock of inventory.[38] In doing so, this would create a first priority lien in favor of one of the owners

---

29 ibid.

30 Bruce A Campbell, "Contracts Jurisprudence and Article Nine of the Uniform Commercial Code: The Allowable Scope of Future Advance and All Obligations Clauses in Commercial Security Agreements" (1986) 37 Hastings LJ 1007, 1018.

31 ibid.

32 "Article IX of the Uniform Commercial Code: The 'Floating' Lien" (1963) 37 St. John's L Rev 392, 394 [hereinafter Article IX].

33 See Grant Gilmore and Allen Axelrod, "Chattel Security: I" (1948) 57 Yale LJ 517, 529–30 (explaining the history of the chattel mortgage).

34 Allison Dunham, "Inventory and Accounts Receivable Financing" (1949) 62 Harv L Rev 588, 590. For a discussion of the history of the chattel mortgage, see John H Wigmore, "The Pledge-Idea: A Study in Comparative Legal Ideas" (1896) 10 Harv L Rev 321; Garrard Glenn, "The Chattel Mortgage as Statutory Security" (1939) 25 Va L Rev 316.

35 Allison Dunham, "Inventory and Accounts Receivable Financing" (1949) 62 Harv L Rev 588, 590.

36 ibid.

37 ibid.

38 Allison Dunham, "Inventory and Accounts Receivable Financing" (1949) 62 Harv L Rev 588, 590.

that would defeat (or, rather, be given priority over) the claims of the business's other, true creditors.[39] The idea was that this confected security interest would be faux security in that it was designed solely with the notion of undermining the suppliers and other creditors of the grocery store.[40]

Over time, courts and legislatures attempted to accommodate a chattel mortgage that would float over, as Gilmore described them, "goods in motion"[41] in various ways (like inventory and accounts), but never with great effectiveness.[42] For example, some courts allowed the chattel mortgages to cover goods in motion if the funds from their sale had to be furnished to the secured lender immediately.[43] Additionally, sometimes the ability to engage in this kind of secured transaction was limited by statute to just a certain kind of merchant.[44] The scope of what lenders and borrowers could agree to, however, was inherently limited. Gilmore notes that "a chattel mortgage with mortgagor in possession with power of sale clause plus after acquired property clause was about the largest camel which could be swallowed".[45] Even this, however, did not truly account for a floating lien because the proceeds from the sale of the collateral still had to be given to the lender upon sale and could not be used, even in part, to invest in new inventory or otherwise cover other business expenses.[46] Attempts to do anything like this were met with "judicial condemnation".[47]

Conditional Sales as Substitutes

Finding the above-noted situation unsatisfactory, suppliers began to facilitate the acquisition of goods by their merchant-buyers through something called *conditional sales*.[48] In these instances, the goods would not be sold from the supplier to the merchant under a financing arrangement, but rather the goods

39 ibid.

40 ibid.

41 Grant Gilmore and Allen Axelrod, "Chattel Security: I" (1948) 57 Yale LJ 517, 533.

42 Allison Dunham, "Inventory and Accounts Receivable Financing" (1949) 62 Harv L Rev 588, 594–97.

43 ibid 595.

44 ibid 592.

45 Grant Gilmore and Allen Axelrod, "Chattel Security: I" (1948) 57 Yale LJ 517, 534.

46 ibid 534–35.

47 ibid 535.

48 Allison Dunham, "Inventory and Accounts Receivable Financing" (1949) 62 Harv L Rev 588, 591.

would be conveyed to the merchant on the condition that the merchant pay the supplier for them—even if doing so would occur at a later date and with interest.[49] The transfer of title, however, would not occur until the price was actually paid. In other words, the sale was conditional on payment of the price.

In this way, the merchant had possession of the goods, but only on behalf of the supplier who retained ownership.[50] By maintaining title with the supplier-seller, no security device was used, and thus the limitations of the chattel mortgage were avoided although, to be sure, the supplier-seller was acting in the position of a lender and the substance of the transaction was very much one of security.[51] However, as Gilmore observed, the conditional sale was limited in that it always required a sale.[52] There had to be a seller and a buyer of goods, thereby cutting out possible participation by third party lenders.[53]

Trust Receipts as Substitutes

Soon enough, lenders wanted to become involved in the conditional sale market.[54] To do so, they either purchased the conditional sale contract rights from the supplier-seller or else they engaged in a new kind of transaction involving so-called *trust receipts*.[55] These latter arrangements originated at least prior to 1850 but became popular by the end of the nineteenth century.[56]

In the case of trust receipts, the supplier-seller would sell goods to the lender.[57] The lender, now the owner of the goods, would entrust the goods to a merchant-buyer, who would in turn issue a trust receipt evidencing that the merchant-buyer's possession of the goods was one of limited authority.[58] Yet, the lender would authorize the merchant-buyer to sell the goods, provided the proceeds from the sale would be handed over to the lender.[59] Thus, as Dunham explains, "a new breed of security resulted" and financing attorneys argued,

---

49 ibid.

50 ibid.

51 ibid.

52 Grant Gilmore and Allen Axelrod, "Chattel Security: I" (1948) 57 Yale LJ 517, 541.

53 ibid 542.

54 Allison Dunham, "Inventory and Accounts Receivable Financing" (1949) 62 Harv L Rev 588, 592.

55 ibid 591.

56 Grant Gilmore, "Chattel Security: II" (1948) 57 Yale LJ 761, 761.

57 Allison Dunham, "Inventory and Accounts Receivable Financing" (1949) 62 Harv L Rev 588, 591.

58 ibid.

59 ibid.

with some success, that despite its clear nature, this was neither a conditional sale nor was it a secured transaction using a chattel mortgage.[60]

From a historical perspective, as Gilmore explains, the trust receipt was initially used as a method to finance imports of raw materials from foreign locales.[61] However, in the late 1930s, courts began to uphold these as devices that could be used to finance domestic transactions.[62] The explosive advent of the automobile served as the impetus for such domestic use, and it soon became the preferred method of dealer financing.[63]

Factor's Liens as Substitutes

Yet another security-like device devised by commercial finance lawyers was the *factor's lien*.[64] This device emerged from the textile manufacturing industry and the practice of factoring.[65]

A factor was a person who took possession of goods on behalf of a seller and attempted to sell them on consignment.[66] While in possession of the goods, the factor had a long-recognized lien on the property, which extended to the proceeds of the sale of the property, both of which served as security for the obligation of the seller to compensate the factor for their services.[67]

Eventually, however, factors wanted to engage in lending, and those buying from the factor wanted possession of the goods prior to having to pay for them.[68] To accommodate this demand, the New York legislature passed a law that extended the factor's lien to the goods after they were sold to buyers, provided that the buyer posted a sign on its door indicating the existence of the lien and a document was filed into the public record that similarly accounted for the factor's security rights.[69] Other states eventually followed suit, and the factor's lien became common in the retailer market.[70]

---

[60] ibid.

[61] Grant Gilmore, "Chattel Security: II" (1948) 57 Yale LJ 761, 764.

[62] ibid 764–65.

[63] ibid 765.

[64] Allison Dunham, "Inventory and Accounts Receivable Financing" (1949) 62 Harv L Rev 588, 592.

[65] ibid.

[66] ibid.

[67] ibid.

[68] Allison Dunham, "Inventory and Accounts Receivable Financing" (1949) 62 Harv L Rev 588, 592.

[69] ibid.

[70] ibid.

Analysis and Summation

In order to accommodate the demand for the lien as a method of financing and in the face of these attempts by clever lawyers to confect varying kinds of floating charge substitutes, as described above, a number of uniform acts were created by the Uniform Law Commission and passed by the various state legislatures.[71] These included the Uniform Conditional Sales Act, the Uniform Trust Receipts Act, the Factors Lien Acts, and the amendments that were made to Section 60a of the Bankruptcy Act in 1951.[72]

Yet, these devices varied depending on the form of collateral at issue and each was laden with technical pitfalls.[73] The validity of a given security interest in a particular piece or class of the debtor's property depended on various components, such as "form, timing, recording, and other circumstances" such that while a creditor might enjoy priority over one rival lender, it could very easily be subordinated to another.[74] Moreover, neither the trust receipt transaction nor the conditional sale arrangement actually achieved a true floating lien in that they could only collateralize property acquired prior to when the credit was advanced.[75] In other words, they could not cover so-called after-acquired property, and as Dunham remarks, neither device could probably be used to secure pre-existing debts from prior transactions, which made them unavailable to secure revolving lines of capital loans.[76] And then there was also a complication that existed for quite some time—until 1980—under the Bankruptcy Act that allowed a trustee to claim non-perfection for property acquired by the debtor during the bankruptcy despite pre-existing collateralization under an after-acquired property clause.[77]

---

71 Allison Dunham, "Inventory and Accounts Receivable Financing" (1949) 62 Harv L Rev 588, 591; Homer Kripke, "Current Asset Financing as a Source of Long-Term Capital" (1952) 36 Minn L Rev 506, 514.

72 Homer Kripke, "Current Asset Financing as a Source of Long-Term Capital" (1952) 36 Minn L Rev 506, 514.

73 Bruce A Campbell, "Contracts Jurisprudence and Article Nine of the Uniform Commercial Code: The Allowable Scope of Future Advance and All Obligations Clauses in Commercial Security Agreements" (1986) 37 Hastings LJ 1007, 1012–16.

74 ibid 1021.

75 Allison Dunham, "Inventory and Accounts Receivable Financing" (1949) Harv L Rev 588, 592.

76 ibid 592.

77 Eldon H Reiley, *Security Interests in Personal Property* (West Group, 2022 edn) para 34:35.

In sum, to quote one observer: "only the most expert lawyers [could] hope to avoid the many hidden pitfalls" involved in such secured lending.[78]

Much of the resistance to creating an all-purpose and easy-to-use security device that would encumber and float over all the debtor's major assets in motion stemmed from "the ancient policy of preserving a cushion of free assets" to satisfy the debts owed to various unsecured creditors.[79] Despite these various uniform acts, state legislatures and courts had not quite moved away from this policy point of view, nor had they been ready to grant carte blanche in terms of debtor-creditor freedom of contract[80] when it came to commercial financing transactions.[81] Grant Gilmore describes this as "the early 19th century bias in favor of the unsecured creditor", which resulted in devices like the chattel mortgage being "uneasily tolerated" by courts.[82]

It is also worth noting that attempts to create a floating *lien* in the United States should not be confused with attempts to create a floating *charge* in the United States. While there are some similarities, the English floating charge and the American floating lien have major differences. I will not attempt to describe fully the English floating charge in these pages, as that will be accomplished by other contributions within the larger work of which this chapter is only a part. I will only note, as Dunham explains, that there was never a floating charge in the United States akin to what exists in England.[83]

Recall from above that in the United States, many of the various methods of collateralizing inventory and accounts receivable required what is described

---

[78] Bruce A Campbell, "Contracts Jurisprudence and Article Nine of the Uniform Commercial Code: The Allowable Scope of Future Advance and All Obligations Clauses in Commercial Security Agreements" (1986) 37 Hastings LJ 1007, 1013.

[79] ibid 1018.

[80] Richard L Barnes, "Tracing Commingled Proceeds: The Metamorphosis of Equity Principles into UCC Doctrine" (1990) 51 U Pitt L Rev 281, 320–21.

[81] Bruce A Campbell, "Contracts Jurisprudence and Article Nine of the Uniform Commercial Code: The Allowable Scope of Future Advance and All Obligations Clauses in Commercial Security Agreements" (1986) 37 Hastings LJ 1007, 1018.

[82] Grant Gilmore and Allan Axelrod, "Chattel Security: I" (1948) 57 Yale LJ 517, 533.

[83] Allison Dunham, "Inventory and Accounts Receivable Financing" (1949) Harv L Rev 588, 595. Jeanette Goldsberry, "Perfection of Nonpossessory Security Interests under Revised Article 9: Consequences of the Practical and Conceptual Incompatibility of US and English Secured Transactions Law" (2002) 3 Chi J Int'l L 241.

as *self-liquidation*.[84] This meant that as goods were sold or accounts were collected upon, the funds had to go straight to the lender.[85] The borrower could not keep them, lest the security interest be compromised.[86] This was considered to be a significant flaw in American secured lending law, because it deprived the debtor of the useful deployment of income from the business.[87]

Lastly, the benefit of automatically obtained security in after-acquired property was not often achievable.[88] For example, while the trust receipt transaction had many benefits, the entruster's lien could only attach to the goods described in the trust receipt.[89] This meant that each time goods were handed over to a merchant, a new trust receipt had to be issued.[90] The factor's lien had a similar constraint in that the lien would only attach to the goods that were designated in writing by the borrower: hardly a rule that would allow for the kind of general security interest that the floating lien contemplates.[91]

FLOATING LIEN AFTER THE UCC

Enactment Concerns, Drafting, and Commentary

As noted above, early case law in the United States "stunted free development of financing arrangements" and therefore led to "a movement to reconceptualize security arrangements" as well as to "provide a total legal framework to address credit and security".[92] In essence, the result was the creation of the Uniform Commercial Code's Article 9 and related provisions, which allowed for the creation of a floating lien[93] over a wide variety of personal property that would meet the needs of commercial parties and those seeking to finance their activities using working capital credit facilities.[94]

---

84 Allison Dunham, "Inventory and Accounts Receivable Financing" (1949) Harv L Rev 588, 597.

85 ibid.

86 ibid.

87 ibid 598.

88 See generally Grant Gilmore, "Chattel Security: II" (1948) 57 Yale LJ 761.

89 ibid 768.

90 ibid.

91 ibid 770.

92 Iris H-Y Chiu, "The Legal Fabrication of Security Interests in the United Kingdom" (2005) 31 N.C.J. Int'l L & Com Reg 703, 727.

93 See D Benjamin Beard, "The Purchase Money Security Interest in Inventory: If It Does Not Float, It Must Be Dead" (1990) 57 Tenn L Rev 437, 438.

94 John F Dolan, "Changing Commercial Practices and the Uniform Commercial Code" (1993) 26 Loy L A L Rev 579, 592.

The enactment of Article 9's provisions relative to the floating lien was not, however, without its controversy.[95] Indeed, when the legislation was introduced in the California legislature in the early part of the 1960s, unsecured lenders and their trade representatives warned that the new law would give far too much power to creditors with a broad, first priority lien.[96] And, in turn, this outsized power over the most important property of the debtor would hurt all the various parties who provide important forms of unsecured credit to businesses, such as suppliers of materials and laborers.[97]

Yet, eventually, these concerns were defeated and Article 9 was enacted across all jurisdictions in the United States,[98] thereby bringing a true floating lien to the American commercial market.[99] As Dana McAlister explained, Article 9 broadly gave validation to the floating lien.[100] The drafters of Article 9 decided that "rather than insist on a series of complex transactions that ultimately had the same effect as a floating lien" (which is to say, the pre-UCC law), it was better to outright bless the use of the device in a "more efficient and more certain" manner.[101]

The only limitation placed on the floating lien—and one that had been developed by judges in the nineteenth century—was that dealing with *purchase money security interests*.[102] These were security interests in which the

---

95 Bruce A Campbell, "Contracts Jurisprudence and Article Nine of the Uniform Commercial Code: The Allowable Scope of Future Advance and All Obligations Clauses in Commercial Security Agreements" (1986) 37 Hastings L J 1007, 1013.

96 ibid.

97 ibid.

98 The final jurisdiction to enact UCC Article 9 was the USA's sole mixed jurisdiction, Louisiana, which did not enact the legislation until 1988, taking effect in 1990. See 1988 La. Acts No. 528; 1989 La Acts No. 135. See also Christian Paul Callens, "Louisiana Civil Law and the Uniform Commercial Code: Interpreting the New Louisiana UCC-Inspired Sales Articles on Price" (1995) 69 Tul L Rev 1649; James A. Stuckey, "Louisiana's Non-Uniform Variations in UCC Chapter 9" (2002) 62 La L Rev 793.

99 Robert H Skilton, "Tradition and Change: The Law of Mortgages on Merchandise" (1963) Wis L Rev 359, 422.

100 Dana L McAlister, "Purchase Money Security Interests and Their Continuing Priority as to Proceeds: MBank Almo National Association v Raytheon Co." (1993) 34 B C L Rev 655, 666.

101 ibid 667.

102 ibid; see also D Benjamin Beard, "The Purchase Money Security Interest in Inventory: If It Does Not Float, It Must Be Dead" (1990) 57 Tenn L Rev 437, 438.

secured debt was related to the acquisition of the collateral itself.[103] In order to address the concern that a debtor might pledge all of its assets to a single creditor, thereby "leaving nothing for later creditors", the UCC drafters chose to give priority to purchase money secured creditors over those holding an otherwise first priority floating lien.[104]

UCC Article 9 also eliminated prior distinctions between fixed collateral and collateral in motion by validating the use of after-acquired property clauses in security agreements for many types of collateral.[105] Parties were given free rein to collateralize an assortment of property types and to do so with regard to then owned and later acquired assets of a debtor.[106] And of course, the ability to have the floating lien secure obligations that would arise in the future, such as with revolving lines of credit, was also authorized.[107]

To make matters explicit, the UCC drafters included a comment to Section 204 of Article 9. Section 9-204 provides the specific authorization for after-acquired property and the ability for a security interest to secure future advances of credit.[108] Importantly for the purposes of this chapter, Comment 2 provides:

> [This section] makes clear that a security interest arising by virtue of an after-acquired property clause is no less valid than a security interest in collateral in which the debtor has rights at the time value is given. A security interest in after-acquired property is not merely an "equitable" interest; no further action by the secured party—such as a supplemental agreement covering the new collateral—is required. This section adopts the principle of a "continuing general lien" or "floating lien." It validates a security interest in the debtor's existing and (upon acquisition) future assets, even though the debtor has liberty to use or dispose of collateral without being required to account for proceeds or substitute new collateral.[109]

By moving away from a property-based approach, which struggled with the notion that one could grant a security interest in a thing that one did not yet

---

[103] Dana L McAlister, "Purchase Money Security Interests and Their Continuing Priority as to Proceeds: MBank Almo National Association v. Raytheon Co." (1993) 34 B C L Rev 655, 667.

[104] ibid 673; see also D Benjamin Beard, "The Purchase Money Security Interest in Inventory: If It Does Not Float, It Must Be Dead" (1990) 57 Tenn L Rev 437.

[105] Dana L McAlister, "Purchase Money Security Interests and Their Continuing Priority as to Proceeds: MBank Almo National Association v. Raytheon Co." (1993) 34 B C L Rev 655, 664.

[106] ibid 665.

[107] ibid.

[108] UCC § 9-204.

[109] UCC § 9-204, comment 2.

own, and moving to a contract-based approach, the UCC drafters created the conditions whereby "a bargain concluded today can include a commitment which will bind you as an encumbrance on property you acquire in the future".[110] And moreover, the new law allowed the debtor to maintain control of the collateral,[111] including by commingling it with other property as well as by selling or otherwise disposing of it.[112]

As Bruce Campbell noted, Article 9 "was, and was intended to be, revolutionary".[113] And, in terms of achieving a broad and easy-to-use floating lien in American commercial financing, it was indeed that.

Doctrinal Summary

The final section in this part sets forth the mechanism by which a floating lien under UCC Article 9 over inventory and accounts receivable can be created and maintained. It also points out places where there are exceptions to the normal rules of priority.

Attachment

There are three requirements that must be met for a security interest to *attach* to the collateral. Attachment is the process by which a security interest comes into existence between the debtor and the creditor—it establishes the necessary privity. There are three elements to attachment.[114] First, value must be given by the secured party to the debtor in exchange for receiving the security

---

110 Bruce A Campbell, "Contracts Jurisprudence and Article Nine of the Uniform Commercial Code: The Allowable Scope of Future Advance and All Obligations Clauses in Commercial Security Agreements" (1986) 37 Hastings L J 1007, 1022.

111 Eldon H Reiley, *Security Interests in Personal Property* (West Group, 2022 edn) para 34:35.

112 See Article IX at 395 and Richard L Barnes, "Tracing Commingled Proceeds: The Metamorphosis of Equity Principles into UCC Doctrine" (1990) 51 U Pitt L Rev 281, 320 (both discussing the case of *Benedict v. Ratner* and its overturning by the UCC Article 9 drafters). The Supreme Court in that case invalidated an assignment of accounts receivable on the ground that, because the debtor was allowed to maintain control over the accounts and their collection—rather than handing such management over to the creditor—this was a fraudulent conveyance. See *Benedict v. Ratner* [1925] 268 US 353, 364–65.

113 Bruce A Campbell, "Contracts Jurisprudence and Article Nine of the Uniform Commercial Code: The Allowable Scope of Future Advance and All Obligations Clauses in Commercial Security Agreements" (1986) 37 Hastings L J 1007, 1018.

114 UCC § 9-203.

interest. However, value is defined very broadly[115] to include not only value given at the time the security interest is granted but also value that was given in the past (such as for a pre-existing loan) or, importantly, value given in the future (such as a line of credit that will only be drawn on in the future).

Second, the debtor must have the necessary rights in the collateral that would allow them to grant a security interest. This idea comes back to fundamental property law—one cannot grant a right that one does not have. If one lacks a property right in something, then one cannot thereby give a property right in that thing to someone else. However, it is important to note that Article 9 allows one to grant a security interest prospectively. In other words, one can grant a security interest in property that the debtor will come to own in the future.[116] This is the after-acquired property concept.

The third and final element for the attachment of a floating lien over accounts and inventory under Article 9 is that the debtor must authenticate a security agreement. The term authenticate is broad and means a signature or some other form of authorization, such as when consent is given electronically.[117] The security agreement is simply a written contract that contains words evidencing a desire by the debtor to grant a security interest in collateral. This, of course means that the security agreement must actually describe the collateral. Although this description can be quite broad,[118] super-generic descriptions such as "all assets" or "all personal property" of the debtor are expressly prohibited.[119] Rather, the standard is that the description must *reasonably identify* the property to be collateralized,[120] and the statute provides a series of examples, including using a series of set definitions that are provided in the law itself.[121] Two such definitions are *inventory*[122] and *accounts*.[123]

Lastly, the security interest created hereby can secure, as noted above, value of a future kind. Therefore, the parties can agree—and this will typically be in the security agreement, although it is not one of the formal requirements under UCC Article 9—that the security interest secures future advances of funds from the creditor to the debtor.

Therefore, one can simply include in the security agreement a statement that the debtor is granting a security interest in all of its now owned and thereafter

115 UCC § 1-204.
116 UCC § 9-204.
117 UCC § 9-102(a)(7).
118 UCC § 9-108.
119 UCC § 9-108(c).
120 UCC § 9-108(a).
121 UCC § 9-108(e).
122 UCC § 9-102(a)(48).
123 UCC § 9-102(a)(2).

acquired accounts and inventory to secure any and all advances—past, present or future—made by the creditor to the debtor. This simple formulation is all that is required in order to then attach a long-desired floating lien to goods in motion.

Perfection

Once the lien has become effective between the debtor and the creditor, it is necessary to cause it to become effective against third persons, including other creditors of the debtor and buyers of the debtor. This process is known as *perfection*. For the purposes of perfecting a floating lien in inventory and accounts, one must file a financing statement in the proper public recording office. Notably, perfection cannot occur until attachment has been accomplished.[124]

The document that must be filed is called a *financing statement*, which is a brief document that contains three essential pieces of information.[125] These consist of the name of the debtor, the name of the secured party, and a description of the collateral. Since we are discussing a floating lien, we will assume the debtor is a business entity.[126] In such a case, the name that should be included on the financing statement is the legal name of the debtor as shown on its charter if the business is registered (like a corporation). For unregistered businesses, such as partnerships, the name should be either the name by which the partnership is known or the individual names of each of the partners. The method of determining the name of the secured party is the same.

In terms of describing the collateral, one can simply recite the same description contained in the security agreement, or one can use a broad, omnibus description.[127] For example, one can simply state "all assets" of the debtor or "all personal property" of the debtor.[128] Notably, this formulation can be used even if the security agreement contains a much narrower class of collateral. The reason for this has to do with the filing system itself. It is not a system that is meant to convey facts to third parties. Rather, it is meant to convey the potential for facts. One who searches the public filings will find the financing statement and see that potentially all of the debtor's assets have been encumbered. It is then incumbent upon the searcher to seek more information from

---

[124] UCC § 9-308.

[125] UCC § 9-502.

[126] UCC § 9-503. This assumption is made by virtue of the fact that the floating lien is a device used to finance business operations, which means that the debtor will almost always take the form of a business entity.

[127] UCC § 9-504.

[128] Notably, the prohibition on super-generic descriptions in the security agreement does not have a corollary when it comes to the financing statement. UCC § 9-504.

the debtor as to whether this is true. To do so, one must look to the security agreement, which contains the true agreement between the parties. It is important to observe, however, that one may not use such an omnibus description of collateral in the security agreement, although one could achieve essentially the same substantive result by simply listing all the UCC Article 9 collateral categories individually.

These three simple elements are all that are needed for the financing statement to be effective. The fact of after-acquired property or future advances need not be included in the financing statement. In terms of where to file,[129] if one is dealing with a business entity as a debtor, then one simply files in the applicable public office of the jurisdiction where the business is registered.[130] If the business is not registered, then one files in the public office of the jurisdiction where it has its place of business, if it has only one, or where it has its principal place of business, if it has more than one.[131] Once one determines the applicable jurisdiction for filing (and by jurisdiction, this typically means which state among the various states that comprise the United States), one files in whatever public office is designated for such filings. In many jurisdictions, this is the Office of the Secretary of State.

Once the filing is made, the security interest has now attached and is perfected. The effect of perfection will last for five years from the date of the filing—this is known as the lapse date.[132] To cause perfection to continue for a longer period, the creditor must file another document in the same filing office—this document is known as a continuation statement.[133] If filed no sooner than six months before the date of lapse but not after the date of lapse, this will cause the effects of perfection to continue for another five years from the date of making this additional filing.[134]

General ranking rules

Once perfection is achieved, as the debtor acquires inventory, those assets are immediately encumbered with a security interest. The same is true when accounts receivable are generated. Moreover, the date for the existence of this security interest will be retroactive to the date when perfection was achieved.[135] For example, Debtor grants a security interest in its inventory

---

[129] UCC § 9-301.

[130] UCC § 9-307. For a definition of a registered organization, see UCC § 9-102(a)(71).

[131] UCC § 9-307.

[132] UCC § 9-515.

[133] UCC § 9-515.

[134] UCC § 9-515.

[135] UCC § 9-322.

and after-acquired inventory to Creditor 1, which is perfected on January 1. Debtor then grants another security interest in its inventory and after-acquired inventory to Creditor 2, which is perfected on February 1. Then, on March 1, Debtor acquires a stock of inventory, followed a week later by Debtor defaulting on both of the secured obligations. As between the two of them, Creditor 1 prevails because its security was perfected first. This is true even though at the time of perfection, Debtor had not yet acquired the inventory. The reasoning behind the ordering of the creditors' rights is reflected in UCC Article 9's general rule of *first in time, first in right*. Whichever creditor perfects first prevails over those that perfect later.

Special rules: buyers in the ordinary course

In general, once perfected, a security interest in inventory will continue even after the inventory has been conveyed to third persons—unless one of Article 9's specific "take-free" rules apply.[136] And indeed, one of the most important of Article 9's take-free rules when it comes to inventory lending is that of the *buyer in the ordinary course*.[137] If a purchaser qualifies as a buyer in the ordinary course, then that person acquires the property free and clear of any security interest under Article 9 created by the seller, even if that security interest has otherwise been and remains perfected. However, the definition of a buyer in the ordinary course is limited. First, the seller of the good must be in the business of selling these sorts of items. Thus, buying a book from a bookstore would be sufficient, but purchasing kitchenware from a bookstore would not.

Second, the buyer must act in good faith. For example, if the buyer has actual knowledge of the fact that the seller is not permitted under its agreement with its lender to sell certain goods, but the buyer purchases the goods anyway, then the buyer would not be in good faith. However, the buyer's mere knowledge of the existence of a security interest in the goods is not alone sufficient to constitute bad faith. Third and lastly, the buyer must actually take possession of the goods (rather than purchasing them but leaving them in the possession of the seller), and the buyer must actually pay for the goods with new value (one cannot claim payment by forgiving a prior debt).

The reason for the buyer-in-the-ordinary-course rule makes a great deal of sense in the retailer-consumer setting. Sellers obtain financing from lenders and thereby grant floating liens under Article 9 in their inventory. However, buyers who purchase that inventory do not want security interests of third-party lenders with whom they have no relationship to continue to encumber the property once it is taken home by the buyer. The provisions of Article 9 resolve

136 UCC § 9-315.
137 UCC § 9-320.

this issue by making what is otherwise within the expectations of the parties explicit in the law itself.

Special rules: purchase money security in inventory

The final matter worthy of mention here relates to an item described above—the exception to the floating lien when it comes to purchase money security interests. One might imagine a situation whereby Debtor has granted and perfected a security interest in all of its inventory and after-acquired inventory to Secured Lender on January 1. Later, Debtor purchases inventory on credit from Supplier, thereby granting and perfecting a security interest in the recently acquired inventory in favor of Supplier. Now there is a conflict between Secured Lender and Supplier, both of whom have perfected security interests in this newly acquired inventory. However, under the general rule of first in time, first in right, Secured Lender would prevail in a ranking competition due to its prior perfected, floating lien.

The Article 9 drafters thought that this result was unfair, since it was only through the accommodation of Supplier that this new inventory was acquired by Debtor at all. It would seem unjust, then, to give priority to Secured Lender when Supplier had yet to be paid. To ameliorate the injustice, Article 9 provides that a purchase money security interest (which is the security interest in favor of Supplier) will prevail over a prior perfected security interest in the same inventory (which is the security interest in favor of Secured Lender) if the purchase money security interest is perfected before the debtor receives possession of the goods and the holder of the purchase money security interest furnishes notice to the pre-existing secured creditor stating the fact of the subordination of security.[138] Thus, to apply it to the example above, Supplier would rank ahead of Secured Lender if Supplier perfected (in this case, by filing a financing statement) before Debtor took delivery of the goods sold to it and Supplier also sent notice to Secured Lender alerting it to the fact that its pre-existing security interest would be subordinated to the security interest in favor of Supplier.

In sum, the floating lien long sought by American commercial finance lawyers and their clients can now be achieved under UCC Article 9. Through a combination of targeted provisions in Article 9, each of the obstacles previously thrown up by courts has been overcome, although not without some continued controversy. Indeed, as the detractors warned, it does allow a creditor to largely take a broad and all-encompassing lien over a debtor's major property, thereby giving it outsized control over the business in a way that some might find objectionable.

---

[138] UCC § 9-324.

FLOATING LIEN IN THE DIGITAL AGE

Moving beyond traditional forms of collateral subject to the floating lien, i.e. tangible personal property in the form of inventory and intangible rights such as accounts receivable—the remainder of this chapter considers the collateralization of digital assets using a floating lien.

NFTs as Inventory

To help envision the applicable scenario in terms that are realistic (at least as of the time of this writing), consider a company that is in the business of minting so-called non-fungible tokens (NFTs). As written elsewhere, the central concept around NFTs relates to the concept of crypto *tokenization*.[139] This generally refers to the process whereby the owner of tangible or intangible property creates a digital asset (in actuality, an entry in a distributed ledger), and that digital item is intended to represent or be associated with another asset or service.[140] The digital asset is called a non-fungible token because it is uniquely identifiable and one of a kind within the distributed ledger network in which it exists—and it is the tangible or intangible asset or service that is now ostensibly tokenized.[141] According to their issuers, ownership of these NFTs also conveys ownership or other stipulated rights in the underlying asset to which it is supposedly tethered.[142]

There are presently two primary models for tokenizations.[143] The first is largely *intermediated*, and it is prevalent in the high-volume, low-value NFT market.[144] An individual creates and then sells an NFT through an online

---

[139] Juliet Moringiello and Christopher K Odinet, "The Property Law of Tokens" (2022) 74 Fla L Rev 607, 609.

[140] ibid; see also Christopher K Odinet and Andrea Tosato, "The Intersection of NFTs and Structured Finance" (2023) 103 BU L Rev 1005 <https://papers.ssrn.com/sol3/papers.cfm?abstract_id=4357533>.

[141] Juliet Moringiello and Christopher K Odinet, "The Property Law of Tokens" (2022) 74 Fla L Rev 607, 609; Christopher K Odinet and Andrea Tosato (n 140). Whether the external thing—being the asset—is actually not linked or tethered to the NFT is subject to other law. See Juliet Moringiello and Christopher K Odinet, "The Property Law of Tokens" (2022) 74 Fla L Rev 607, 609.

[142] Juliet Moringiello and Christopher K Odinet (n 140).

[143] Juliet Moringiello and Christopher K Odinet, "The Property Law of Tokens" (2022) 74 Fla L Rev 607, 628; Christopher K Odinet and Andrea Tosato (n 140).

[144] Christopher K Odinet and Andrea Tosato (n 140).

"minting" platform.[145] This is done initially by creating an account with a minting platform and linking it to a crypto digital wallet, through which the creator will send and receive funds in relation to the minting and disposing of NFTs.[146] Relying on the platform provided by the minting company, the NFT creator then uploads a digital image, text, music file, or other digital file they desire to be linked to their soon to be created NFT.[147] Thereafter, the creator selects the manner in which they want to monetize their NFT; typically, this will be through a sale.[148]

At this juncture, the minting platform both mints the NFT[149] and produces a webpage devoted to the NFT, typically featuring the uploaded image, text, or sound file, as well as related metadata.[150] This webpage and its contents are managed by the minting platform and are typically hosted by a web services provider, such as Amazon, Microsoft or Google. The NFT is created using a "smart contract" that is coded by the minting platform and executed through a distributed ledger technology system of its choice, such as Ethereum, Solana, or Avalanche.[151] Once all these operations have been carried out, the NFT is offered to the public.[152] Generally, both the minting platform and the person who created the NFT strive to attract prospective purchasers by advertising through social media and other channels.[153] When a buyer wishes to acquire the NFT, the minting company acts as an intermediary, handling both the processing of the payment and the transfer of the NFT.[154] Once the transfer is complete, depending on how the minting platform holds the NFT itself,

---

145 "Top Minting Platforms in 2023" (*Coinbound*) <https://coinbound.io/top-nft-minting-platforms/> accessed 28 February 2023; Christopher K Odinet and Andrea Tosato (n 140).

146 Juliet Moringiello and Christopher K Odinet, "The Property Law of Tokens" (2022) 74 Fla L Rev 607, 628–29; Christopher K Odinet and Andrea Tosato (n 140).

147 Mitchell Clark, "NFTs, Explained" (*The Verge*, 6 June 2022) <https://www.theverge.com/22310188/nft-explainer-what-is-blockchain-crypto-art-faq> accessed 28 February 2023.

148 Juliet Moringiello and Christopher K Odinet, "The Property Law of Tokens" (2022) 74 Fla L Rev 607, 628–29; Christopher K. Odinet and Andrea Tosato (n 140).

149 ibid.

150 ibid.

151 ibid.

152 Juliet Moringiello and Christopher K Odinet, "The Property Law of Tokens" (2022) 74 Fla L Rev 607, 628–29; Christopher K Odinet and Andrea (n 140).

153 ibid.

154 ibid.

the minting platform's public cryptographic information will be replaced with the buyer's public cryptographic information on the relevant blockchain, thus making the transfer complete.[155]

The second tokenization model is *disintermediated*, and it has been used in most large price tag NFT transactions, such as with corporate issuers and major artists.[156] The process works as follows. Relying on either a major public DLT network (such as Ethereum) or one under their control (such as Dapper Labs' FLOW Blockchain), the issuer mints one or more NFTs and then allies them with a creative work, such as a digital image, video, or sound file.[157] This allying typically involves the storing of the relevant images, videos or sound on servers connected to the internet and then linking each NFT to a specific creative work through a hyperlink or a functionally similar mechanism.[158]

Thereafter, the NFTs are offered to the public either by the issuers directly or via specific agents, such as firms like Christie's and Sotheby's.[159] Along with the NFT, the issuer may also offer services or other items.[160]

With that background in mind, consider the second NFT business model—that which involves corporate issuers. Here, the issuer mints hundreds of NFTs and then sells them to the public, either through direct sale or via auction. The NFTs sell at significant prices and represent one of the principal means by which the issuing company obtains its income. In this case, the NFTs are inventory, in a layman's sense, to the seller. The next section explores how one might go about obtaining a floating lien over this novel *crypto inventory*.

---

[155] ibid. It is possible, however, that the minting platform holds all of the NFTs that it mints through a single public cryptographic key (like an omnibus account). Then, all transfers of the NFT are actually confined to the books and records of the minting platform, just as a bank keeps track of the accounts of its various customers through an internal accounting system, but where all of the deposited funds are pooled together. See Christopher K Odinet and Andrea Tosato (n 140).

[156] Christopher K Odinet and Andrea Tosato (n 140); "Yuga Labs" <https://www.yuga.com> accessed 6 February 2023; "Dapper Labs" <https://www.dapperlabs.com> accessed 6 February 2023; "Merge by Pak" <https://www.niftygateway.com/collections/pakmerge> accessed 6 February 2023; "Beeple" <https://www.beeple-crap.com> accessed 6 February 2023.

[157] Christopher K Odinet and Andrea Tosato (n 140).

[158] Joshua AT Fairfield, "Tokenized: The Law of Non-Fungible Tokens and Unique Digital Property" (2022) 97 Ind LJ 1261, 1296; Christopher K Odinet and Andrea Tosato (n 140).

[159] "NFT Art Auction Department" (*Sotheby's*) <https://www.sothebys.com/en/departments/nft> accessed 6 February 2023; "Christie's NFT" <https://nft.christies.com> accessed 6 February 2023; Christopher K Odinet and Andrea Tosato (n 140).

[160] Christopher K Odinet and Andrea Tosato (n 140).

NFT Inventory Financing

Assume that the corporate issuer of NFTs wishes to use them as collateral. In a colloquial sense, the NFTs being held out for sale are in fact inventory to the corporate issuer, although they are not considered inventory within the meaning of UCC Article 9, which confines such items to tangible personal property held out by a business for sale, lease, or furnished under a service arrangement.[161] In this case, the items held out for sale consist of intangible personal property. Nevertheless, UCC Article 9 has a category for them: *general intangibles*.[162] This final part of the chapter explores how the UCC's most recent 2022 revisions—specifically, the introduction of Article 12 and its accompanying provisions—can provide for a floating lien over crypto inventory. This part also considers how such collateralization might be accomplished in those jurisdictions that will be influenced by the Principles on Digital Assets and Private Law, created by the International Institute for the Unification of Private Law (UNIDROIT).[163]

Under UCC Articles 9 and 12

The sponsoring entities of the UCC, the Uniform Law Commission (ULC) and the American Law Institute (ALI), recognized the growing use of crypto assets in commercial transactions, as well as the desire in various states of the US for crypto-supportive law.[164] As such, the ULC and the ALI drafted revisions to the UCC that are aimed at facilitating and clarifying the rules regarding transactions involving cryptoassets.[165] These UCC amendments, issued in 2022, create a new collateral subcategory under the UCC's definition of general intangibles: the *controllable electronic record*.[166]

A controllable electronic record is defined as "information that is stored in an electronic or other medium and is retrievable in perceivable form" and that

---

161 UCC § 9-102(a)(48).

162 UCC § 9-102(a)(42).

163 "Principles on Digital Assets and Private Law" (*UNIDROIT*, January 2023) <https://www.unidroit.org/wp-content/uploads/2023/01/Draft-Principles-and-Commentary-Public-Consultation.pdf> accessed 28 February 2023.

164 See "2022 Amendments to the Uniform Commercial Code" (*Uniform Law Commission*, 2022) <https://www.uniformlaws.org/committees/community-home?CommunityKey=1457c422-ddb7-40b0-8c76-39a1991651ac> accessed 28 February 2023.

165 See ibid.

166 ibid; UCC § 12-102(a)(1).

is susceptible to control.[167] The drafters intended that this category include assets such as NFTs.[168] Notably, the definition of a controllable electronic record is predicated on the ability to take *control* of the record.[169] The new rules set up a three-prong test for control: the person claiming control must have the power to enjoy "substantially all the benefit" of the controllable electronic record, must be able to prevent others from enjoying "substantially all the benefit", and must have the power to transfer control to someone else.[170] And importantly, the person claiming such control must have the ability to identify to a third party that all three components are satisfied.[171]

As described in the NFT minting summary earlier in this chapter, an NFT will typically meet the definition of a controllable electronic record.[172] The reason for this is because, aside from consisting of an electronic record, one whose public cryptographic key is identified with the NFT on that NFT's particular blockchain will meet the necessary control prerequisites. That individual can claim substantially all of the benefits of the NFT (whatever those might be) to the exclusion of others, since no other person can lay claim to the asset on the relevant blockchain. Additionally, typically through the use of a digital wallet and through a crypto exchange company, the individual can transfer the NFT to someone else. Lastly, the ability to identify oneself as having such control can be achieved by sharing the public cryptographic key or other relevant crypto-based identifying information. Thus, the NFT will almost always qualify as a controllable electronic record.

In terms of granting security rights in the NFT to another person, the new rules provide for perfection[173] and take-free acquisition.[174] Specifically, the attachment process would not materially change, since the NFT is still considered to be a type of general intangible (which remains the umbrella category

---

[167] Certain kinds of electronic records, particularly electronic chattel paper, electronic documents, electronic money, investment property and transferable records. See "2022 Amendments to the Uniform Commercial Code" (n 164); UCC §12-102(a)(1).

[168] "2022 Amendments to the Uniform Commercial Code" (n 164); Edwin E Smith and Steven O Weise, "The Proposed 2022 Amendments to the Uniform Commercial Code: Digital Assets" (*Business Law Today*, 25 March 2022) <https://businesslawtoday.org/2022/03/proposed-2022-amendments-uniform-commercial-code-digital-assets/> accessed 28 February 2023.

[169] UCC § 12-105(a).

[170] UCC § 12-105(a)(1)(A), (B).

[171] UCC § 12-105(a)(2).

[172] ibid.

[173] UCC § 9-306B, 310(b)(8), 312(a), 314(a).

[174] UCC § 12-317(h).

for this asset).[175] Thus, the collateral description in the security agreement could describe the specifics of the NFT (such as its metadata or other identifying information) or could merely list all the debtor's general intangibles.

But what do the new rules do differently than what existed before? They modify the process for perfection of the security interest. It should be noted that a creditor could still simply file a financing statement and perfect the security interest in the NFT, just as they could before the new rules became effective.[176] However, the new rules also create a preferable alternative: perfection can also occur by taking control of the NFT.[177] This goes back to the definition of what constitutes *control* of a controllable electronic record (the multi-pronged test described above).[178] So, for example, a secured creditor could perfect a security interest in an NFT by having the debtor transfer the NFT to the creditor. This would be accomplished by having the NFT associated with the creditor's cryptographic key on the relevant blockchain, rather than the debtor's. Additionally, the secured creditor could use other methods, such as using specific NFT metadata configurations or smart contracts which require the creditor to sign off (provide a digital signature of sorts through the use of an additional private cryptographic key) before the NFT can be transferred by the debtor. This is, in essence, the value of the broad standards-based framework for control—it allows parties to harness whatever technology might be available to achieve the satisfaction test for control. The drafters aimed to be technologically neutral.

Lenders involved in these kinds of crypto financings will probably want to achieve perfection by control for yet another reason—the so-called *take-free* rules.[179] The idea of taking free comes up in two main contexts—taking free as a buyer and taking free (or, better said, taking priority) as a secured creditor. As for buyers, one who purchases a controllable electronic record for value, in good faith, and without notice of a pre-existing claim to the controllable electronic record may do so and thereafter disregard any competing property claims to the digital asset.[180] For secured parties, a creditor who perfects a security interest in a controllable electronic record using control—as well as for value, in good faith, and without notice of a pre-existing interest in the digital asset—takes priority over that pre-existing interest. The name the new

---

175 UCC § 9-102(a)(42).

176 UCC § 9-312(a).

177 UCC § 9-314(a).

178 UCC §§ 9-314(a), 107A(a); UCC § 12-105 (providing for the definition of control of a controllable electronic record).

179 UCC § 9-317(h).

180 UCC §§ 9-317(h), 12-102(a)(2), 12-104(e).

rules give to such individuals is that of a *qualifying purchaser.*[181] In essence, this makes the controllable electronic record have the same kind of attributes as a negotiable instrument.[182] It allows a second-in-time secured creditor with an interest in the controllable electronic record who perfects by taking control to take priority over a first-in-time secured creditor with an interest in that same controllable electronic record who perfects through merely filing a financing statement.

Now consider how a lender would take a blanket lien over all of the debtor's NFTs. As to attachment, our crypto financier has two options when using controllable electronic records as collateral. First, as these crypto assets are a subcategory of the broader "general intangibles" category, a creditor and debtor can create a security interest with a "signed" agreement that adequately describes the collateral. Specifically for NFTs, a contract clause stating that the collateral consists of "all debtor's present and future general intangibles" or "all debtor's present and future controllable electronic records" would be effective. But there would also be no issue with using a narrower description that more precisely focuses on the crypto assets in question, such as "all NFTs minted by the debtor" and, possibly, also specifying the relevant blockchain network, smart contract and cryptographic identifying information.

The second option to create a security interest in crypto inventory takes advantage of the concept of control. Dispensing with the requirement of a signed security agreement, the 2022 UCC Amendments provide that a security agreement can be created if "the collateral is ... controllable electronic records... and the secured party has control under Section ... [12–105] ... pursuant to the debtor's security agreement". By extending to controllable electronic records the rules previously available for deposit accounts, electronic chattel paper, investment property, or letter-of-credit rights, the 2022 UCC Amendments recognize that taking control of controllable electronic records adequately evidences what collateral the parties objectively intended to encumber.

The 2022 UCC Amendments also introduce a new set of rules for the perfection of security interests in controllable electronic records that further highlight the central role of control. As with many types of collateral,[183] a creditor can perfect a security interest in crypto inventory (which is to say, general intangibles) by filing a financing statement in the relevant registry, just as it could before the new rules came into effect.[184] However, the 2022 UCC

---

[181] UCC § 12-102(a)(2).

[182] Edwin E Smith and Steven O Weise (n 168).

[183] Note the exception of a security interest in money, which can only be perfected by possession. *See* UCC § 9-313(a).

[184] UCC § 9-312(a).

Amendments also provide that a creditor can perfect a security interest in controllable electronic records by taking control of these items.[185] A creditor can also obtain control through a third party who acknowledges that it has or will obtain control on the creditor's behalf.[186] Control can be accomplished by having all newly minted NFTs automatically transferred to the creditor's digital wallet rather than that of the debtor. In the alternative, all NFTs could be held through an escrow-like smart contract that would be jointly governed by the debtor and the creditor through a multi-signature agreement.[187]

Crypto inventory lenders will likely want to achieve perfection by control for two more reasons. First, under Article 9, the general rule for ranking competing interests over the same collateral is that the party first to file a financing or to otherwise perfect has priority over others.[188] The 2022 UCC Amendments introduce a special priority rule to rank competing security interests over controllable electronic records.[189] A secured creditor who perfects by control "has priority over conflicting security interests held by a secured party that does not have control".[190] Copying the same approach historically adopted by the UCC for the priority regime regarding deposit accounts and investment property, the 2022 UCC Amendments recognize a preference for secured creditors that have direct dominion over the digital asset.

The second reason why crypto financiers will want to take control of controllable electronic records comes from the *take-free* regime introduced by the 2022 UCC Amendments for the commercial circulation of these items.[191] Under these new rules, a person who acquires a controllable electronic record for value, in good faith, and without notice of any conflicting property claims is deemed a "qualifying purchaser" and, as such, takes the controllable electronic record free from any pre-existing property claims.[192] Drawing heavily from the UCC Article 3 regime for negotiable instruments, these provisions confer attributes of negotiability on controllable electronic records.[193] Thus, if a secured creditor obtained a security interest in crypto inventory and only perfected by filing, they would be at risk of the debtor disposing of the collateral

[185] UCC § 9-314(a).

[186] UCC § 9-307.

[187] See Kevin Werbach and Nicolas Cornell, "Contracts Ex Machina" (2017) 67 Duke LJ 313, 344-46. See also UCC § 12-105 and accompanying comment.

[188] UCC § 9-322(a)(1).

[189] UCC § 9-322.

[190] UCC § 9-326A.

[191] UCC § 9-317(h).

[192] UCC §§ 9-317(h), 12-102(a)(2), 12-104(e).

[193] Edwin E Smith and Steven O Weise (n 168).

and transferring control to a qualifying purchaser that would take it free from any competing claim.

Under UNIDROIT Principles on Digital Assets and Private Law

Lastly, I turn to the UNIDROIT Principles.[194] UNIDROIT's program of work for 2020–2022 (called the Triennial Work Programme) created a working group, the goal of which was "to develop a future legal instrument containing principles and legislative guidance in the area of private law and digital assets".[195] As of May 2023, a public draft of the Principles was presented to the Governing Council of UNIDROIT, and that document forms the basis of the discussion that follows.[196]

In terms of the impact of the Principles, it is hoped (and dare I say, likely) that in jurisdictions that have not yet developed their law governing security interests (including floating liens) in digital assets, lawyers, legislators and courts will look to these Principles in guiding the way they structure, legislate and judicially resolve digital asset collateralizations.

Turning to the substantive provisions, the definition of digital asset is familiar: "an electronic record which is capable of being subject to control".[197] Although not specifically set forth in the body of the text, the commentary to the definitions makes clear that the drafters had cryptoassets in mind.[198]

For purposes of the Principles, the notion of transferring a digital asset includes not only what would normally be considered a sale but also the granting of a security interest in the asset.[199] In terms of how one actually goes about validly creating a security interest in a digital asset, the Principles explicitly leave that to "other law"—meaning, the law of security rights in

---

194 UNIDROIT, "Principles on Digital Assets and Private Law" (n 163).

195 UNIDROIT, "Study LXXXII: Digital Assets and Private Law Project" <https://www.unidroit.org/work-in-progress/digital-assets-and-private-law/> accessed 28 February 2023.

196 UNIDROIT, "Principles on Digital Assets and Private Law" (n 163).

197 UNIDROIT, "Principles on Digital Assets and Private Law" § I.2.2.

198 UNIDROIT, "Principles on Digital Assets and Private Law" § I.2, comments 4, 9, 10 (describing cryptographic information associated with a digital asset, as well as distributed ledger technology).

199 UNIDROIT, "Principles on Digital Assets and Private Law" § I.2.5(d); UNIDROIT, "Principles on Digital Assets and Private Law" § I.2, comment 22 ("In these Principles, the term 'transfer' is also used to denote the grant of a security right in favor of a secured creditor, and a 'transferee' includes a secured creditor".).

a given jurisdiction.[200] This includes making a security interest effective as against third persons (perfection, in UCC terms).[201]

Much as the UCC's 2022 amendments devote specific provisions to how one takes control of a controllable electronic record, the UNIDROIT drafters elaborate in Principle 6 how one takes control of a digital asset.[202] An individual has control if they possess "the exclusive ability to prevent others from obtaining substantially all of the benefit from the digital asset", if they have "the ability to obtain substantially all the benefit from the digital asset", and if they and only they have the ability to transfer the two aforementioned rights (those being the right to exclude and the right to enjoy) to another person.[203] Lastly, the person possessing all three abilities must be able to evidence this fact because "the digital asset, or the relevant protocols or system, allows" for such a demonstration of control to be made.[204] Importantly, for purposes of considering security rights, the comments to these provisions make clear that control does not necessarily mean a transfer—one may have control for purposes of security but not for ownership.[205]

One can easily see that the definition of *control* in the UNIDROIT Principles is quite similar to the *control* definition in UCC Article 12. This is due, I suspect, to some overlapping membership in these two groups. Indeed, Professor Charles Mooney and Professor Carla Reyes are both members of the UNIDROIT working group. Professor Mooney was the reporter for the UCC 2022 amendments and Professor Reyes was heavily involved in the technical research and drafting process.[206] In fact, the comments to Principle 6 on

---

200 UNIDROIT, "Principles on Digital Assets and Private Law" § I.3.3(c); UNIDROIT, "Principles on Digital Assets and Private Law" § I.3. comment 10 ("[These Principles] make explicit that the relationships between … a grantor of a security right and the relevant secured creditor … continue to be a matter of other law and are not, as a matter of principle, dealt with by these Principles".).

201 UNIDROIT, "Principles on Digital Assets and Private Law" § I.3. comment 11 ("Pursuant to these Principles … whether a transfer and a security right, respectively, can be asserted against third parties, continue to be, as a matter of principle, a matter of other law".).

202 UNIDROIT, "Principles on Digital Assets and Private Law" § III.6; see also comment 1 (comparing control of digital assets to possession of movables).

203 UNIDROIT, "Principles on Digital Assets and Private Law" § III.6(a).

204 ibid.

205 UNIDROIT, "Principles on Digital Assets and Private Law" § III.6, comment 4.

206 See UNIDROIT, "The Digital Assets and Private Law Working Group" (January 2023) <www.unidroit.org/work-in-progress/digital-assets-and-private-law/#1622753957479-e442fd67-036d> accessed 23 February 2023; ULC, "Final Act, With Comments: Uniform Commercial Code Amendments" (2022)

control explicate how taking control of an NFT, as described under the UCC above, would mirror how control would be achieved under the UNIDROIT Principles. For example, comment 14 provides an illustration of how one effectuates a change in control. The example given is very crypto-centric:

> A Beta is a digital asset, as it satisfies all the requirements of Principles 2 [definition of digital assets] and 6 [definition of control]. Person A changes control of a Beta to Person B by disassociating the Beta from a public key for which only Person A knows the private key, and associating it with a public key for which only Person B knows the private key.

Principle 7 further explains that identifying oneself as a person with control can be accomplished by, among other things, "an identifying number, a cryptographic key, an office, or an account number, even if the identification does not indicate the name or identity of the person to be identified".[207] This would be a classic case of a person who holds a crypto asset on a particular blockchain, but where the asset is associated only with a public cryptographic key that in no way actually identifies the natural person or entity behind it.

Like the UCC concept of a qualifying purchase, the UNIDROIT Principles have a concept called an innocent acquirer. Just as with the UCC corollary, the UNIDROIT drafters desired to provide "attributes similar to those of negotiability".[208] This is meant to recognize that digital assets are "often traded on a distributed ledger system or other electronic networks that permit near instantaneous transactions".[209] Combined with "the fact that many transferors are pseudonymous and often based in different jurisdictions", this in turn makes discerning whether there are "conflicting proprietary rights" in a given digital asset "highly impractical".[210] The power of negotiability—through the concept of an innocent acquirer, as with a qualifying purchaser—facilitates digital asset "transactions and contribute[s] to legal certainty".[211] The requirements to be an innocent acquirer are virtually the same as those required to be

---

<https://higherlogicdownload.s3-external-1.amazonaws.com/UNIFORMLAWS/2e456b4d-7e6a-18b7-116c-7971f84a8393_file.pdf?AWSAccessKeyId=AKIAVRDO7IEREB57R7MT&Expires=1677621075&Signature=KZtHaxDq7K%2BFecKDAImgOyJzVrY%3D> accessed 28 February 2023 (listing the drafting committee membership and roles).

207 UNIDROIT, "Principles on Digital Assets and Private Law" § III.7.

208 UNIDROIT, "Principles on Digital Assets and Private Law" § III.7, comment 1.

209 UNIDROIT, "Principles on Digital Assets and Private Law" § III.7, comment 2.

210 ibid.

211 ibid.

a qualifying purchaser,[212] although jurisdictions are given the option of developing their own requirements.[213] In addition, just as with the qualifying purchaser under the UCC, an innocent acquirer also includes a secured creditor.[214]

Lastly, Section V of the Principles states precisely that "[d]igital assets can be the subject of security rights".[215] The UNIDROIT drafters state that this provision "reflects the general principle that secured transactions regimes should enable the use of any type of movable asset as collateral".[216] It should be noted, however, that the Principles do not create a security interest regime for digital assets, in the way the UCC 2022 amendments do, which provide more precise rules for digital asset collateralization. The UNIDROIT drafters provide that their Principles "are not intended to interfere with domestic conception of security right or domestic security law".[217] Instead, "[t]he Principles presuppose the existence of some rules" on the granting of a security interest in what would be considered a digital asset.[218] Thus, the actual ability to grant a security interest over a digital asset and make that interest effective as against third persons all comes back to "other applicable law" of the jurisdiction, which the UNIDROIT Principles do not attempt to create or define.[219]

The drafters do admit, however, that "[i]n adopting these Principles, a State may need to amend existing secured transactions legislation by including special rules for digital assets".[220] This is because, in addition to whatever law already exists for secured transactions involving digital assets, the Principles aim to expand the rules. For instance, much like UCC Article 12, the Principles state that a security interest in a digital asset may be made effective through control by the creditor or a custodian acting on their behalf.[221] But here again, the comments to the applicable section encourage a given jurisdiction to

[212] UNIDROIT, "Principles on Digital Assets and Private Law" § III.8.6.

[213] UNIDROIT, "Principles on Digital Assets and Private Law" § III.8.1.b.

[214] UNIDROIT, "Principles on Digital Assets and Private Law" § III.8, comment 2 (discussing collateral value and the benefits of the take-free rule for those holding a security interest in the digital asset).

[215] UNIDROIT, "Principles on Digital Assets and Private Law" § V.14.a.

[216] UNIDROIT, "Principles on Digital Assets and Private Law" § V.14, comment 1.

[217] UNIDROIT, "Principles on Digital Assets and Private Law" § V.14, comment 2.

[218] ibid.

[219] UNIDROIT, "Principles on Digital Assets and Private Law" § V.14, comment 3.

[220] UNIDROIT, "Principles on Digital Assets and Private Law" § V.14, comment 4.

[221] UNIDROIT, "Principles on Digital Assets and Private Law" § V.15 and comment 1.

"incorporate 'control' as defined in [the Principles] in its secured transactions law".[222] And similar to UCC Article 12, the UNIDROIT drafters desire for perfection by control to prevail "over a security right in the digital asset that is made effective against third parties only by a method other than control".[223]

In summary, the similarities between the two regimes are striking. The Principles adopt many of the themes and components that proved popular among the ALI and ULC drafters of the 2022 UCC amendments. Critically, much is left to the gap-filling of a given jurisdiction's secured transactions and underlying property law. Yet the UNIDROIT Principles strike a balance between yielding to the reasoned policy decisions of a given locale while, at the same time, gently and appropriately pushing the jurisdiction toward a set of rules that will support and encourage a robust yet principled commercial market for digital assets.

CONCLUSION

The floating lien in American law has come a long way since its early days when the US commercial market was still in a decidedly developing stage. The variability of devices evidences a tension between achieving a commercial transaction that facilitates the flow of credit on the one hand and providing necessary guardrails for warding off creditor overreaching and maintaining coherence with the law of property on the other.

The story of the American floating lien is one of savvy lawyers, cautious courts, innovative reformers and careful legislators. The twenty-first century and the advent of the digital age have seen yet another wave of commercial law reforms, this time dealing not with tangible goods and their money claim offspring (those being inventory and accounts) but rather with the complex and ever-growing world of cryptoassets. As explained in these pages, the US and international experience with creating a floating lien over such novel things as digital assets is happening at the very moment this chapter is being written. Indeed, we should expect to see more reforms as the chronicle of secured transactions law—and the story of the floating lien in particular—continues to unfold.

---

222 UNIDROIT, "Principles on Digital Assets and Private Law" § V.15 and comment 5.

223 UNIDROIT, "Principles on Digital Assets and Private Law" § V.16.

ACKNOWLEDGMENTS

This chapter is partly derived from Christopher K Odinet and Andrea Tosato, "Floating Liens Over Crypto-in-Commerce" (2023) 99 Indiana LJ 367 <https://papers.ssrn.com/sol3/papers.cfm?abstract_id=4424022>. I thank the Office of International Programs at the University of Iowa for the generous funding support that allowed me to spend time as a visiting researcher at the *Institut International pour l'Unification du Droit Privé* [The International Institute for the Unification of Private Law] (UNIDROIT) in February 2023. I also thank Professor Ignacio Tirado, Hamza Hameed, Bettina Maxion, Laura Tikanvaara and the entire staff at UNIDROIT for their friendship, engagement, workspace and access to library resources during my time at the Villa Aldobrandini. Finally, I thank Jordan Jenquin and Lucas Wetsch (Iowa Law Class of 2024) for their invaluable research support and editing.

7. The floating charge in Chinese law: following the English model?

Zhicheng Wu and Hao Zhang

INTRODUCTION

This chapter aims to give an analysis of the rules regarding the floating charge (浮动抵押, *fudong diya*) in Chinese law. It starts with an overview of the relevant legislation from 2007 and 2020 in the next section. The third section illustrates the constituent elements of the creation of a floating charge. The fourth section depicts the crystallisation events in Chinese law, followed by a comparison with its English counterpart. The effects as between the chargee and the chargor and effects as between the chargee and third-party right-holders are analysed in the fifth and sixth sections, respectively, each followed by a comparison with English law. The final section concludes.

LEGISLATION: AN OVERVIEW

The Introduction of the Floating Charge

If one confines the timeline to post-1949 mainland China, then the floating charge did not become a concept formally recognised in a primary source of law until 2007, when Property Law 2007 (中华人民共和国物权法, *zhonghua renmin gongheguo wuquanfa*) was promulgated in March and took effect in October of that year. There were three provisions directly relevant to the floating charge in that statute. Article 181 was a general provision on floating charges.[1] Article 189 dealt with the effect of a floating charge on third parties.[2] Article 196 concerned the crystallisation of floating charges.[3] Property Law 2007 was replaced in its entirety in 2021 by the Chinese Civil Code (promulgated in May 2020 and taking effect in January 2021). The codification continues to allow for floating charges but in a modified way. Regardless of the modifications depicted immediately below, the nature of the floating charge as a non-possessory security interest over movables remains unchanged.[4]

The Current Rules

The Chinese Civil Code has made merely minor changes to the three rules on the floating charge in Property Law 2007. At first blush, article 396 of the Chinese Civil Code[5] implies that the formality requirement (i.e. that the

---

1 Article 181 provides: 'An enterprise, industrial and commercial household, or agricultural manufacturer or trader may, by way of agreement in writing, create a charge over existing and future manufacturing equipment, raw materials, semi-finished products, and products, so that the creditor is entitled to have the debt repaid with priority to the extent of the value of the aforementioned movables at the moment of materialisation, in cases of the debtor's non-performance of the due debt, or other circumstances of enforcing the charge as agreed by the parties.'

2 Article 189 has two paragraphs. Para 1 provides: 'Where an enterprise, industrial and commercial household, or agricultural manufacturer or trader creates a charge over movables in accordance with article 181 of this Law, registration shall be done in the administration department for industry and commerce at the domicile of the chargor. The charge is created when the underlying contract of charge takes effect, though the charge does not bind bona fide third-parties without registration.' Para 2 provides: 'Where the subject-matter of a charge is movable property, the right of charge cannot be alleged against the purchaser of such movable property who has paid a reasonable price in the ordinary course of business.'

3 Article 196 provides: 'Where a charge is created in accordance with article 181 of this Law, the subject-matter of the charge is crystallized under any of the following circumstances:

(1) the personal right is not yet realized when the debt becomes due;

(2) the chargor is declared insolvent or is abolished;

(3) in other circumstances of enforcing the charge as agreed by the parties; or

(4) in other circumstances which severely affect the realization of the personal right.'

4 Chinese Civil Code, art 1260.

5 Article 396 provides: 'An enterprise, industrial and commercial household, or agricultural manufacturer or trader may create a charge over existing and future manufacturing equipment, raw materials, semi-finished products, and products, so that the creditor is entitled to have the debt repaid with priority to the extent of the value of the aforementioned movables at the moment of crystallization, in cases of

underlying contract of charge must be in writing) is no longer applicable to the creation of a floating charge, as this provision deletes the phrase 'by way of agreement in writing' contained in article 181 of Property Law 2007. However, such a formality requirement is nevertheless still there. This is because the legislator considers that the general rule in article 400 of the Chinese Civil Code, stating that the underlying contract to create every type of charge must be made in writing, also covers the floating charge. It would thus be redundant for a special provision on floating charges to say that again, as a matter of codification technicality.[6] Articles 403 and 404 of the Chinese Civil Code have made two changes to article 189 of Property Law 2007.

Compared to article 189, paragraph 1 of Property Law 2007, article 403 of the Chinese Civil Code[7] no longer provides for a specific body in charge of floating charge registration. The reason for this is that, most probably owing to the government's acceptance of the World Bank's promotion of a uniform collateral registry in its Ease of Doing Business methodology,[8] the Chinese Civil Code legislator has decided to pave the way to establishing a uniform registration system for movables and rights (i.e. 'incorporeal things'; 'choses in action') by deleting the rules on sectoral registration in Property Law 2007. Implementing this, the Measures for the Unified Registration of Security Interests Over Movable Properties and Rights 2021 were later issued by the central bank, namely the People's Bank of China, in which an institution the called Credit Reference Center is in charge of many types of security

the debtor's non-performance of the due debt, or other circumstances of enforcing the charge as agreed by the parties.'

6 Huang Wei, *Interpretation of the Chinese Civil Code: Book on Property Rights [中华人民共和国民法典解读]* (China Legal Publishing House 2020) 599.

7 Article 403 provides: 'Where the subject-matter of a charge is movable property, the right of charge is created when the underlying contract of charge becomes effective. Such right of charge cannot be alleged against a bona fide third party without prior registration.'

8 World Bank, 'Getting Credit Methodology', at <https://archive.doingbusiness.org/en/methodology/getting-credit> accessed 26 February 2024.

registration including floating charges.[9] Article 404 of the Chinese Civil Code[10] makes the rule allowing the chargor to deal with assets in the ordinary course of business not only applicable to the case of the floating charge (as article 189, paragraph 2 of Property Law 2007 already provided), but extends it to other types of charges over movables, namely, the fixed charge[11] and the maximum amount charge.[12] Article 411 of the Chinese Civil Code[13] simply modifies article 196 of Property Law 2007 by a single word in item 2 with no substantial change as to the crystallisation events.

---

9 People's Bank of China, Measures for the Unified Registration of Security Interests Over Movable Properties and Rights [动产和权利担保统一登记办法] (promulgated on 28 December 2021), arts 2, 4. Notably, apart from the floating charge, this system does not cover all types of fixed charge over movables and rights. It covers charges over receivables, certificates of deposit, warehouse bills and bills of lading. It also covers financial leases, factoring and retention of title. However, it does not cover fixed charges over motor vehicles, vessels, aircraft, bonds, mutual fund units, company shares and intellectual property rights.

10 Article 404 provides: 'Where the subject-matter of a charge is movable property, the right of charge cannot be alleged against the purchaser of such movable property who has paid a reasonable price in the ordinary course of business.'

11 Chinese Civil Code, art 394. A fixed charge is a type of non-possessory security interest over specific corporeal things but not a class of things (as in the case of a floating charge), where the secured creditor is entitled to have the debt repaid with priority to the extent of the value of such subject matter, in the event of the debtor's non-performance of the due debt or in other circumstances of enforcing the charge as agreed by the parties.

12 Chinese Civil Code, art 420. A maximum amount charge is a type of non-possessory security interest over specific corporeal things but not a class of things (as in the case of a floating charge) to secure the repayment of debts up to a maximum amount within a certain period of time in the future, according to which the chargee is entitled to have the debts up to such maximum amount repaid with priority to the extent of the value of the charged subject matter in cases of the debtor's non-performance of the due debt or other circumstances of enforcing the charge as agreed by the parties.

13 Article 411 provides: 'Where a charge is created in accordance with Article 396 of this Code, the subject-matter of the charge is crystallized under any of the following circumstances:

(1) the personal right is not yet realized when the debt becomes due;

(2) the chargor is declared insolvent or is dissolved;

(3) in other circumstances of enforcing the charge as agreed by the parties; or

(4) in other circumstances which severely affect the realization of the personal right.'

Why the Floating Charge Was Introduced

Given that the Chinese Civil Code does not make major changes to the floating charge, the reason why Chinese law has adopted this type of security interest should be traced back to the time of the drafting of the Property Law 2007. Antagonists contended that the domestic credit system was not well developed, so introducing a floating charge would increase financial risk. Nonetheless, for the purpose of increasing the efficiency of using the full value of assets,[14] and facilitating trade and liquidity,[15] the legislator decided to embrace the floating charge concept in 2007. Notably, apart from the 'yes or no' question, there were debates as to its scope, such as whether the subject matter was to be limited to movables, whether it should be possible to include future assets, and whether the ability to grant a floating charge should be limited to enterprises and thereby exclude individuals.[16] However, the legislator ultimately decided to largely retain the rules as they had been drafted during the codification stage.

Outside Influence

Scholars in China have not reached a consensus as to the external origins of the Chinese version of the floating charge. The majority contend that China adopted it from US law, while the minority consider that it is based on the English law floating charge,[17] causing the Chinese Supreme Court's pro-US reaffirmation in 2020.[18] Strangely, this notion seems to be based on a prevailing misunderstanding that the English floating charge before crystallisation

---

[14] Wand Shengming (ed.), *Understanding Property Law 2007 [中华人民共和国物权法解读]* (China Legal Publishing House 2007) 387.

[15] Civil Law Branch of the Law Affairs Commission of the National People's Congress Standing Committee, *Collection of Thoughts and Background regarding Legislating the Property Law 2007 [物权法立法背景与观点全集]* (Law Press 2007) 65–66.

[16] Ibid, 176–177.

[17] Wand Hongliang, 'Analysing the Independence of the Effect of Registration of Charges over Movables [动产抵押登记效力规则的独立性解析]' [2009] 11 Law Science [法学] 88, 97; LI Min, 'Systemically Improving the Regime of Floating Charge in Chinese Law [论我国浮动担保制度的系统性完善]' [2020] 1 Law Science [法学] 60, 75; Sun Xianzhong and Zhu Guangxin (eds), *Commentaries of the Civil Code [民法典评注:物权编]* (China Legal Publishing House 2020) 89; JI Hailong, 'Law of Secured Transactions in the Civil Code of China from a Systematic Perspective' [2021] 1 The Jurist [法学家] 40, 45–46.

[18] Enforcement of Civil Code Group of the Supreme People's Court (ed.), *Understanding and Applying the Book on Property Rights of the Chinese Civil*

has no third-party binding effect at all.[19] Moreover, from the perspective of English lawyers, US law has in reality no model of floating charge for China to transplant, as a 'floating charge was never adopted in the United States'.[20] It is therefore submitted that the prevailing notion shared by the majority of Chinese scholars is not accurate. Taking all these factors into consideration, it is wise to undertake a detailed analysis of the specific rules to see in how far the Chinese version of the floating charge replicates the English version of the floating charge.

THE CREATION OF A FLOATING CHARGE

Eligible Chargor

The wording of article 396 of the Chinese Civil Code shows that those who have the capacity of creating a floating charge are threefold, namely, enterprises, industrial and commercial households, and agricultural manufacturers or traders. 'Enterprises' in Chinese law refers to for-profit legal persons and unincorporated organisations. For-profit legal persons are predominantly companies (i.e. those incorporated for the purpose of making profits and distributing profits to shareholders), with sub-categories of limited liability companies and companies limited by shares.[21] For-profit unincorporated organisations

---

Code [中华人民共和国民法典物权编理解与适用] (People's Court Press 2020) 1050.

[19] Long Jun, 'Research on Priority Rules regarding Charge over Movables [动产抵押对抗规则研究]' [2016] 3 The Jurist [法学家] 42, 46.

[20] Ewan McKendrick, *Goode and McKendrick on Commercial Law* (6th edn, Penguin 2020) para 25.33. This is conceptually correct, although one may argue that, functionally speaking, the US 'floating lien' provided in Uniform Commercial Code art 9 can be described as a functional equivalent to the English floating charge.

[21] Chinese Civil Code, art 76. Note that the limited liability companies/companies limited by shares contrast in Chinese company law is considerably different from the public/private company contrast in English company law. By English standards, all limited liability companies are private companies. However, for companies limited by shares, there are three sub-categories: listed companies whose shares are admitted to trading on senior stock exchanges (namely, the Shanghai Stock Exchange, the Shenzhen Stock Exchange and the Beijing Stock Exchange); companies whose shares are offered on junior stock exchanges (e.g. National Equities Exchange and Quotations); and companies whose shares cannot be offered to the public, which would not be public companies under English law. Moreover, China does not accept concepts like unlimited companies or companies limited by guarantee in which members' liabilities are not limited by shares.

refers to organisations which, though without the status of legal persons, are capable of holding rights and carrying out juridical acts in their own name, including sole proprietorships, partnership enterprises, and professional service organisations (such as law firms and accounting firms), all being registered entities.[22] 'Industrial and commercial households' and 'agricultural manufacturers or traders' are not legal persons, nor do they have the capacity to hold rights or carry out juridical acts, but they are essentially a commercial shell for individuals normally running a small business. 'Industrial and commercial household' is a technical legal term,[23] while 'agricultural manufacturer or trader' is not, but the latter is interpreted to be equivalent to 'rural contracted management household',[24] meaning 'member household of a rural collective economic organization which acquires the right to land contractual management in accordance with the law on conducting household contractual management'.[25] Technicalities aside, 'industrial and commercial households' essentially means those shopkeepers and craftsmen running a registered business (with or without a business name different from their own), while 'agricultural manufacturers or traders' essentially means those running an unregistered farming business, predominantly agrarian businesses.

Eligible Assets for a Floating Charge

Regarding the assets which can fall within the ambit of a floating charge, again, an ostensible answer can be found in the wording of article 396 of the Chinese Civil Code. A floating charge can be created over four types of things, namely, 'existing and future manufacturing equipment, raw materials, semi-finished products, and products'. This implies that immovables cannot be subject to a floating charge, nor can personal rights (e.g. book debts as often seen

---

[22] Chinese Civil Code, art 102.

[23] Chinese Civil Code, art 54.

[24] Huang Wei, *Interpretation of the Chinese Civil Code: Book on Property Rights [中华人民共和国民法典解读]* (China Legal Publishing House 2020) 483.

[25] Chinese Civil Code, art 55. 'Rural contracted management household' is a technical legal term quite particular to Chinese law, mainly owing to the Reform and Opening-up Policy in 1978, when this term was gradually developed for the purpose of modifying the rigid public land ownership regime. Basically, most of the rural lands are owned by the collective economic organisation (as a socialist collectivist concept). By having the concept of 'rural contracted management household', household members (farmers) can be granted by the collective economic organisation a right to exclusive possession over a plot of land for agrarian purposes for a renewable certain period of time ranging from 30 to 70 years each session.

in English case law[26]).[27] However, this by no means can be taken to indicate that if a product subject to a floating charge is sold for proceeds or receivables, such proceeds or receivables are not subject to that charge, as article 396 only governs eligible assets at the time of creation of the floating charge, but poses no limits to the pool of assets thereafter. Additionally, some scholars argue that the phrase 'existing and future manufacturing equipment, raw materials, semi-finished products, and products' in article 396 should be interpreted in an extensive way for the purpose of determining whether a class of assets can be used to create a floating charge covering all types of movables.[28]

There is a general provision that expressly limits the scope of assets that can be subject to a charge, which applies to both fixed and floating charges. A textual interpretation of article 399 of the Chinese Civil Code shows that (1) movables the ownership of which is 'equivocal or under dispute'[29] and (2) movables that are seized, detained, or under public investigation are incapable of being subject to a floating charge. However, there are disputes over what exactly these two scenarios mean. The legislator supports the view that a floating charge created over these two types of things is simply void.[30] The Supreme Court supports the view that in the case where a floating charge is created over movables that are seized, detained, or under public investigation, the floating charge is not void, but is merely inferior to the personal right for the realisation of which the movables in question are seized, detained, or under public investigation.[31] The Judicial Interpretation on the Guarantee System stated that where a floating charge is created over movables the ownership of which is equivocal or under dispute, and is later on determined to be an *ultra vires* disposition, the chargee may still be able to acquire the charge by

---

[26] Duncan Sheehan, The Principles of Personal Property Law (2nd edn, Hart Publishing 2017) 348–350.

[27] Enforcement of Civil Code Group of the Supreme People's Court (ed.), *Understanding and Applying the Book on Property Rights of the Chinese Civil Code [中华人民共和国民法典物权编理解与适用]* (People's Court Press 2020) 1047–1048.

[28] Xie Hongfei, 'Summary Description of Security Assets and Its Completeness [担保财产的概括描述及其充分性]' [2021] 11 The Jurist [法学] 99, 109.

[29] If it turns out that a chargor tries to create a charge over an asset (or a class of assets) for which the chargor has no power of disposition, then the juridical act of creating such a charge is void *ab initio*.

[30] Huang Wei, *Interpretation of the Chinese Civil Code: Book on Property Rights [中华人民共和国民法典解读]* (China Legal Publishing House 2020) 493.

[31] Enforcement of Civil Code Group of the Supreme People's Court (ed.), *Understanding and Applying the Book on Property Rights of the Chinese Civil Code [中华人民共和国民法典物权编理解与适用]* (People's Court Press 2020) 1061.

bona fide acquisition.[32] Where a floating charge is created over movables that have been seized or detained or are under public investigation, the charge cannot bind the execution creditor for whom the movables in question have been seized or detained or are under public investigation, but can bind others.[33] If the seizure, detention or public investigation order is revoked, the floating charge becomes binding in relation to the execution creditor as well.[34]

Manifestation of Intent

When it comes to the creation of a fixed charge or a floating charge, the outcome depends largely on the manifestation of the relevant intent. Similarly to English law, distinguishing a floating charge from a fixed charge under Chinese law primarily depends on the characteristic that a floating charge is a charge on a class of assets both 'present and future', not 'present' assets only. In contrast to English law, however, the second characteristic that a floating charge is a charge on a class of assets, the exact contents of which are expected to change in the normal course of business is no longer expressly stated in Chinese law specifically relating to floating charges.[35] This is because the Chinese Civil Code has modified Property Law 2007 in a way that, in the case where the subject-matter of a charge is a movable thing, even if the parties' manifestation of intent is that the subject-matter can change in the normal course of business, this does not negate the possibility that this is a fixed charge. This is because a fixed charge over movables no longer can bind bona fide purchasers for value without notice in the ordinary course of business either.[36] Consequently, the core test has to be reduced to the first one, i.e. whether the parties have a common manifestation of intent to have a charge over present and future assets (then floating charge), or present assets only (then fixed charge).

---

32 Chinese Civil Code, arts 311 and 313.

33 *Judicial Interpretation of the Supreme People's Court of the Application of the Relevant Guarantee System of the Chinese Civil Code* (Supreme Court Interpretation No 28, 2020) art 37. A judicial interpretation is a set of rules written by the Chinese Supreme Court in the name of explaining a particular statute in an abstract way (i.e. without mentioning any particular party in litigation). Given that the statutory provisions are often stated in a general way, sometimes with considerable ambiguity, a juridical interpretation is widely seen by lawyers as an extension of the corresponding statute.

34 *Jiangsu Golden Phoenix Investment Co Ltd v Jiangyin Urban Construction and Development Co Ltd* [2018] S0281MC No 15295 (Jiangyin City Court, 10 April 2019).

35 *Re Yorkshire Woolcombers Association Ltd* [1903] 2 ch 284.

36 Chinese Civil Code, art 404.

Formality

As stated above, the contract to create a floating charge shall take the form of writing.[37] This is especially relevant for determining the scope of the assets subject to the floating charge. The contract may stipulate for the charge to cover all present and future movables of the chargor (i.e. a general floating charge). Alternatively, it may be stipulated in such a way as to cover certain type(s) of the present and future movables of the chargor (i.e. a limited floating charge over a class or group of assets).[38] A general description suffices as long as the court can reasonably identify the scope of the floating charge in question.[39] Notably, Chinese law follows the specificity principle of property law, and there is no persuasive doctrinal justification raised by Chinese scholars for adopting the floating charge while upholding the specificity principle. The reason for such a legal transplant in 2007, as briefly stated in section 2 of this chapter, was based on policy, not principle. Specifically, the policy consideration was to facilitate the financing of small and medium enterprises and farmers in China, and there was no policy change in this regard during the codification era.[40]

CRYSTALLISATION EVENTS

Crystallisation is seen in Chinese law as a mechanism, the main consequence of which is that after crystallisation, the floating charge becomes fixed in relation to assets covered by the security, and consequently, the chargee can materialise the secured debt by enforcing the charge with priority over the chargor's unsecured creditors. Put differently, crystallisation is a prerequisite for the chargee to realise the security interest. Article 411 of the Chinese Civil Code expressly recognises four events of crystallisation. The first event is where 'the personal right is not yet satisfied when the debt becomes due', meaning that the secured debt in question becomes an unpaid due debt. The second event is where 'the chargor is declared insolvent or is dissolved'. By mentioning 'insolvency', the

---

[37] Chinese Civil Code, art 400.

[38] Gao Shengping, *Understanding and Applying Security Systems in the Chinese Civil Code and Accompanying Judicial Interpretations [民法典担保制度及其配套司法解释理解与适用] vol 1* (China Legal Publishing House 2021) 448.

[39] *Judicial Interpretation of the Supreme People's Court of the Application of the Relevant Guarantee System of the Chinese Civil Code* (Supreme Court Interpretation No 28, 2020) art 53.

[40] HU Kangsheng (ed), *Explaining the Property Law 2007 [中华人民共和国物权法释义]* (Law Press 2007) 398.

law mainly refers to corporate insolvency.[41] Insolvency liquidation can apply analogously to sole proprietorships[42] and partnership enterprises,[43] despite the member(s) being jointly and severally liable for the undischarged debts. Where the chargor is an individual (such as an industrial and commercial household, or an agricultural manufacturer or trader), Chinese law does not provide for a mechanism of insolvency, although there is a functionally similar mechanism called 'participation in distribution', which provides for collectiveness and pari passu distribution among unsecured creditors, but without the effect of discharging the debt, which is limited to monetary obligations that have become due.[44] The only exception is the city of Shenzhen, where there has been a local regulation recognising individual bankruptcy since March 2021.[45] By mentioning 'dissolution', article 411 refers to the general rule on the dissolution of legal persons.[46] The third event triggering crystallisation lies 'in other circumstances of enforcing the charge as agreed by the parties', referring to contractually stipulated events. Specified events such as that the 'chargor carries out any related-party transaction or transaction at an under value' or 'commodities in store fall below a certain amount' are often seen in commercial practice.[47] The fourth event is an open-ended one, namely 'other circumstances which severely affect the realisation of the personal right'. This especially encompasses the chargor company entering serious financial or economic distress or the chargor carrying out sham transactions.[48]

The second event in Chinese law (insolvency or dissolution) roughly corresponds to the de facto cessation of business in English law,[49] which may

---

41 Enterprise Bankruptcy Law 2006, art 2.

42 Sole Proprietorship Law 1999, arts 26–32.

43 Partnership Enterprise Law (2006 Revision), arts 85–92.

44 *Judicial Interpretation of the Supreme People's Court of Several Issues concerning the Enforcement Procedures* (Supreme Court Interpretation No 15, 1998) arts 88–96.

45 Regulation of Shenzhen Special Economic Zone on Individual Bankruptcy 2020, art 173. For an overview of this regulation, see Pingyao Xie, 'Chinese Personal Bankruptcy Regulation: the Shenzhen Experience' (2021) 30 International Insolvency Review 410.

46 Chinese Civil Code, art 69.

47 Enforcement of Civil Code Group of the Supreme People's Court (ed.), *Understanding and Applying the Book on Property Rights of the Chinese Civil Code [中华人民共和国民法典物权编理解与适用]* (People's Court Press 2020) 1114.

48 Sun Xianzhong and Zhu Guangxin (eds), *Commentaries of the Civil Code [民法典评注:物权编]* (China Legal Publishing House 2020) 206.

49 *National Westminster Bank plc v Jones* [2001] EWCA Civ 1541, [2002] 1 BCLC 55.

be voluntary[50] or in response to a winding-up petition.[51] The third event in Chinese law (contractual stipulation) largely corresponds to express crystallisation in English law, in that they both refer to consensually stipulated events expressly laid down in crystallisation clauses which effectively crystallise a floating charge despite no active step having been taken by the chargee.[52] The difference, in comparison with English law, lies in the first (debt having fallen due without satisfaction) and fourth (other circumstances) events, and implies a fundamentally different way of understanding crystallisation. Specifically, Chinese law treats crystallisation as an automatically triggered event, in the sense that it does not depend on any active step taken by the chargee. The chargee may choose not to enforce after crystallisation, but this has nothing to do with the legal position that the charge in question has crystallised. In contrast, the English position is that the chargee's application matters. For instance, the chargee's appointment of a receiver (whether an ordinary receiver[53] or administrative receiver[54]) counts as a crystallisation event. From the perspective of a Chinese lawyer, one may question, if the secured debt has become due and is still unpaid (i.e. the first event in Chinese law), why should English law bother to wait for the chargee to elect to crystallise the charge by appointing an ordinary receiver? If the chargor company has entered into such serious financial or economic distress that it is unable to pay its debts owing to cash-flow insolvency or balance-sheet insolvency (i.e. the fourth event in Chinese law), why should English law bother to wait for the chargee to elect to crystallise the charge by appointing an administrative receiver or administrator?

Another difference is that English law allows partial crystallisation while Chinese law does not. Under Chinese law, a debtor can use some of its movables to create a 'partial' floating charge at the outset (i.e. over a class or group of assets), yet once a charge is created, whether over some or all of the debtor's movables, it can only be 100% floating or 100% crystallised. In comparison, under English law, as long as partial crystallisation has been clearly stipulated (in the charge instrument) and its scope is identifiable, it is possible for the

50 *Re Woodroffe's Musical Instruments Ltd* [1985] 2 All ER 908, 913–914; *Edward Nelson & Co Ltd v Faber & Co* [1903] 2 KB 367.

51 *Re Victoria Steamboats Ltd* [1897] 1 ch 158.

52 *Re Home & Hellard* (1885) 29 ch D 736; *Davey & Co v Williamson and Sons* [1898] 2 QB 194.

53 *Evans v Rival Granite Quarries Ltd* [1910] 2 KB 979.

54 Insolvency Act 1986, ss 72A–H.

charge to crystallise and specifically attach to a particular set of assets, leaving the charge floating as to the remaining assets.[55]

EFFECTS AS BETWEEN CHARGOR AND CHARGEE

With regard to property law, crystallisation turns a floating charge into a fixed charge, so that rules for enforcement of the debt secured by a fixed charge apply.[56] Specifically, the chargee may enter into an agreement with the chargor to have the debt repaid by converting the charged asset(s) to its value,[57] or by the proceeds of an auction or sale by reference to the market price. If they cannot reach an agreement as to the method of executing the charge, the chargee is entitled to ask the court for a court-ordered auction or sale of the charged asset(s), also by reference to the market price.

Notably, unlike English law, Chinese law has no rule empowering the secured creditor to take possession, if that means by self-help without a court order and without entering the premises of the debtor.[58] As far as sale is concerned, unlike English law, Chinese law does not provide that if there is a surplus, it is held on trust for the chargor, and that the chargee shall account to the chargor for profits made from holding or using the surplus,[59] regardless of the fact that Chinese law also recognises trusts, and that the concept of fiduciary duty is well-known to judges and scholars. Instead, the Chinese position is that the chargor has a purely personal right rather than a right under a trust against the chargee for the restitution of the surplus.[60]

Where the chargor of a floating charge is a company and has become cash-flow or balance-sheet insolvent, the adequate responses for the chargee are not those in property law, but those in corporate insolvency law. Unlike the position under English law, there is no such thing as an administrative receiver for the chargee to appoint under Chinese law. The chargee cannot appoint

---

55 Ewan McKendrick, *Goode and McKendrick on Commercial Law* (6th edn, Penguin 2020) para 25.22.

56 Chinese Civil Code, art 410.

57 Chinese Civil Code, art. 401.

58 Criminal Law Act 1977, s 6(1).

59 *Charles v Jones* (1887) 35 ch D 544; Law of Property Act 1925, s 109; *Mathew v TM Sutton Ltd* [1994] 4 All ER 793. While these authorities involve pledge and fixed charge but not floating charge, it may be considered a generally applicable point of English security law that the surplus is held on trust. The authors would like to express their sincere gratitude to the co-editor Alisdair MacPherson for his kind help by adding more authorities on this point to an earlier draft of this chapter.

60 Chinese Civil Code, art 413.

an insolvency administrator or liquidator either; the office-holder is appointed by the court.[61] In fact, Chinese corporate insolvency law does not distinguish between an administrator and a liquidator; there is only one insolvency official called an administrator, whose exact role depends on which specific insolvency proceeding the case undergoes: reorganisation,[62] compromise,[63] or liquidation.[64]

As stated at the beginning of section IV of this chapter, the core consequence of crystallisation is that a floating charge becomes a fixed one, meaning that the main debt can now be said to be secured by specific assets of the chargor, and consequently, the right of a chargee as a secured creditor to receive preferential treatment (compared to unsecured creditors) is triggered. Chinese insolvency law provides that a person who has a security interest over any specific asset of the insolvent company (including the chargee after crystallisation) can have the secured debt repaid with priority from this specific asset.[65] If the amount of the secured debt exceeds the proceeds of sale of the charged asset(s), the outstanding amount remaining unpaid becomes an unsecured debt, for which the chargee has to join the queue of unsecured creditors for rateable distribution.[66] As long as the value of the encumbered assets is higher than the secured debt, the floating chargee can get fully repaid in priority to the office-holder's expenses, employees' claims, not to speak of unsecured creditors (including social security debts and tax debts), contractually subordinated creditors, and shareholders of the chargor company.[67] This is different from the position of English law where the floating charge holder does not have priority over a liquidator's expenses approved by the floating charge holder,[68] an administrator's expenses,[69] preferential creditors (mainly

[61] Enterprise Bankruptcy Law 2006, art 22.

[62] Enterprise Bankruptcy Law 2006, ch 8. This mechanism is to some extent akin to the UK restructuring plan (Companies Act 2006, Pt 26A), in the sense that the court has the power to sanction the proposed reorganisation plan to bind all creditors if the vote fails to reach the legally required threshold.

[63] Enterprise Bankruptcy Law 2006, ch 9. This mechanism is to some extent akin to the UK company voluntary arrangement (Insolvency Act 1986, Pt 1), in the sense that the court has no power to sanction the proposed compromise plan to bind all creditors if the vote fails to reach the legally required threshold.

[64] Enterprise Bankruptcy Law 2006, ch 10.

[65] Enterprise Bankruptcy Law 2006, art 109.

[66] Enterprise Bankruptcy Law 2006, art 110.

[67] Enterprise Bankruptcy Law 2006, art 113.

[68] Insolvency Act 1986, s 176ZA.

[69] Insolvency Act 1986, sch B1, para 99(3)(b).

referring to employees and the reintroduced Crown preference for certain unpaid taxes),[70] and the prescribed part.[71]

EFFECTS AS BETWEEN CHARGEE AND THIRD PARTIES

Dealings with Third-party Buyers in the Ordinary Course of Business

So far as the effects as between chargee and third parties are concerned, unlike English law, Chinese law does not separate the effects before and after crystallisation. This is due to art 404 of the Chinese Civil Code, according to which a charge over movables (whether floating or fixed) does not bind a third-party purchaser of these movables who has acquired them in the chargor's ordinary course of business for a reasonable price. Under English law, before crystallisation, the chargor has the power to transfer assets covered by a floating charge to a third-party buyer in the ordinary course of business, so that the buyer acquires them free from the charge.[72] After crystallisation, the chargor no longer has actual or implied authority to do the same thing, though a bona fide third-party buyer may still be able to acquire the asset(s) free from the charge thanks to the chargor's apparent authority, provided that the crystallisation event has a low degree of publicity.[73] In contrast, under Chinese law, a third-party buyer can always acquire ownership of the movables subject to a floating charge, whether the transaction is completed before or after crystallisation.

Notably, Chinese law does not generally have the same rules of agency as its English counterpart, and this is relevant in relation to the chargor's authority regarding disposition. Chinese scholars also explain that one of the effects of crystallisation is the end of the authority to dispose of the charged assets in the ordinary course of business.[74] It logically follows that Chinese law should have provided that, after crystallisation, whether the charge can bind a third-party purchaser in the ordinary course of business shall largely depend on whether the purchaser had notice (either actual or constructive) of crystallisation, although art 404 of the Chinese Civil Code does not take this logical step.

---

[70] Insolvency Act 1986, s 175(2)(b); Companies Act 2006, s 754(2).

[71] Insolvency Act 1986, s 176A.

[72] *Re Florence Land and Public Works Co* (1878) 10 ch D 530; *Wallace v Universal Automatic Centre Pty Ltd* [1984] 2 ch 547.

[73] Ewan McKendrick, *Goode and McKendrick on Commercial Law* (6th edn, Penguin 2020) para 25.30.

[74] Gao Shengping, *Understanding and Applying Security Systems in the Chinese Civil Code and Accompanying Judicial Interpretations [民法典担保制度及其配套司法解释理解与适用] vol 1* (China Legal Publishing House 2021) 709–710.

According to the Chinese Supreme Court, the reason was a policy-motivated one; the legislator decided to give extremely strong protection to third-party purchasers in the ordinary course of business by completely exonerating the purchaser from the burden of investigating whether the asset(s) sold is subject to a charge, as long as the purchase happens in the chargor's ordinary course of business.[75] Consequently, as long as the subject matter of a charge (whether floating or fixed) is a movable thing, any third-party purchaser can sit back and simply buy and acquire unencumbered ownership, as long as the sale takes place in the ordinary course of business.[76] This is because art 404 of the Chinese Civil Code is a joker card for such a purchaser in the ordinary course of business, just as art 311 is for a bona fide purchaser for value without notice (i.e. bona fide acquisition). Article 404 is even stronger than art 311 in that the former even protects mala fide purchasers for value in the ordinary course of business, whereas the latter expressly includes good faith as a constituent element of bona fide acquisition.[77] Put differently, in the spectrum between the security of transaction and the security of ownership,[78] art 404 chooses to radically stand for the former.

In order to allay the radical position of art 404, the Chinese Supreme Court later used a provision in the Judicial Interpretation on Guarantee System to restrict the scope of scenarios amounting to an 'ordinary course of business', which is in considerable contrast to the English position, tending to interpret this technical term in a loose way.[79] Specifically, under Chinese law, a sale is not in the ordinary course of business if (i) the number of goods sold is obviously higher than an ordinary purchaser would order, (ii) the goods sold are the chargor's equipment for producing goods, (iii) the purpose of the contract

---

75 Supreme People's Court, *Understanding and Applying the Judicial Interpretation of the Guarantee System of the Chinese Civil Code [最高人民法院民法典担保制度司法解释理解与适用]* (People's Court Press 2021) 486.

76 Cui Jianyuan, *Commentaries of the Chinese Civil Code: Book on Property Rights [中国民法典释评·物权编] vol 2* (Renmin University Press 2020) 375–376.

77 Gao Shengping, 'Interpreting the Rules of Registration Confrontation regarding Security Rights in the Chinese Civil Code [民法典动产担保权登记对抗规则的解释论]' [2020] 4 Peking University Law Journal [中外法学] 951, 970–971; LONG Jun, 'Security Interests System over Movables and Rights in the Chinese Civil Code [民法典中的动产和权利担保体系]' [2020] 6 Chinese Journal of Law [法学研究] 22.

78 William Swadling, 'Restitution and Bona Fide Purchase' in William Swadling (ed.), *The Limits of Restitutionary Claims: A Comparative Analysis* (UKNCCL 1997) 80.

79 *Countryside Banking Corpn Ltd v Dean* [1998] AC 338; *Ashborder BV v Green Gas Power Ltd* [2004] EWHC 1517, [2005] 1 BCLC 623 [227].

of sale in question is to secure the chargor's or a third-party's debt, or (iv) there is a direct or indirect controlling relationship between the purchaser and the chargor. Apart from these negative rules, this provision also positively explains the meaning of 'ordinary course of business', the constituent elements of which are (i) that the transaction in question falls within the chargor's registered scope of business shown in its business certificate and (ii) that the chargor has been continually selling the same type of goods.[80]

Other Types of Third-party Right-holders

The conflict between the chargee and a third-party purchaser for value in the ordinary course of business is not the end of the story. There are other scenarios of competing interests. A typical one is the chargee vs. a subsequent chargee over the same asset(s). In English law, the answer seems to be that before crystallisation, a subsequently created floating charge does not take priority over the pre-existing floating charge, even if the subsequent charge crystallises earlier,[81] whereas a subsequently created fixed charge takes priority over the pre-existing floating charge (subject to the potential effects of a negative pledge).[82] After crystallisation, a subsequently created fixed charge normally cannot take priority over the pre-existing charge (which is now a fixed one too), owing to the priority doctrine of 'first in time'. Given that the Chinese legislator has aimed to establish a uniform registration system for movables as stated in section II of this chapter, Chinese law relies on the priority doctrine of 'first in registration' while discarding the priority of 'first in time' for unregistered charges. Whether the rival charges are both fixed, both floating, or one floating vs. one fixed, and whether before or after crystallisation, the rule is: (i) that the charge that is registered first takes priority; (ii) that a registered charge takes priority over an unregistered charge; and (iii) that between two unregistered charges, the answer is not that the one created first in time takes priority, but that the two chargees receive a pro rata distribution of the proceeds of the sale (of the charged asset(s)) in proportion to their secured debts.[83] Notably, while it is possible for a creditor to hold and enforce an unregistered charge over movables against the chargor, such a charge does not bind third parties, with the consequence that the creditor secured by the

---

[80] *Judicial Interpretation of the Supreme People's Court of the Application of the Relevant Guarantee System of the Chinese Civil Code* (Supreme Court Interpretation No 28, 2020) art 56.

[81] *Re Benjamin Cope & Sons Ltd* [1914] 1 ch 800.

[82] *Wheatley v Silkstone and Haigh Moor Coal Co* (1885) 29 ch D 715.

[83] Chinese Civil Code, art 414.

unregistered charge cannot receive the proceeds of sale of the charged asset(s) in priority to the chargor's unsecured creditors.[84]

Another scenario of rival right-holders arises between a pre-existing floating charge and a subsequently created fixed charge to secure the purchaser's (i.e. the chargor's) full payment for the asset(s) that will be acquired and thus be covered by the floating charge – put differently, a purchase money security interest. Specifically, if another charge is created to secure the payment of the price of the assets falling under the floating charge, and if such a charge is registered within 10 days from the delivery date of the assets, then it takes priority over other pledges, floating and fixed charges over the assets even if they were created and registered earlier.[85] The Chinese Supreme Court has confirmed that such a timely registered purchase money security interest also takes priority over the creditors' rights in retention of title and finance lease arrangements.[86]

Finally, a pre-existing floating charge can enter into a conflict with a lien. The lien is a statutory unregistered possessory security interest,[87] which occurs where the debtor fails to perform a due debt, so that the creditor retains possession of the debtor's movable asset which has already lawfully entered the creditor's possession (e.g. for the purposes of undertaking repairs, warehousing, carriage and so on), and consequently the creditor becomes the lien holder.[88] Where a movable is subject to a lien while it is also subject to another security interest, no matter what the latter security interest is (including a floating charge and a purchase money security interest), no matter whether the rival security interest was registered before or after the lien arising, and no matter whether the lien holder has knowledge of the existence of any pre-existing

---

84 Chinese Civil Code, art 403.

85 Chinese Civil Code, art 416.

86 Supreme People's Court, *Understanding and Applying the Judicial Interpretation of the Guarantee System of the Chinese Civil Code [最高人民法院民法典担保制度司法解释理解与适用]* (People's Court Press 2021) 492, citing *Judicial Interpretation of the Supreme People's Court of the Application of the Relevant Guarantee System of the Chinese Civil Code* (Supreme Court Interpretation No 28, 2020) art 57.

87 English lawyers often describe a lien as a non-consensual form of security, as opposed to consensual forms of security such as fixed and floating charges: William Swadling, 'Property: General Principles' in Andrew Burrows (ed.), *English Private Law* (3rd edn, Oxford University Press 2013) para 4.137. One may say that this is in principle the position in Chinese law too, although Chinese law explicitly provides that the parties may *consensually* stipulate in an agreement in advance to preclude certain movables from being subject to a lien: Chinese Civil Code, art 449.

88 Chinese Civil Code, art 447.

security interest, the lien always prevails.[89] This is particularly meaningful in Chinese law compared with English law, as an English common law lien in principle only gives rise to a right to retain possession until the debt is paid, but not a power of sale.[90] In contrast, a lien holder under Chinese law has and can exercise the power of sale. Specifically, the lien holder and the debtor shall stipulate a time limit for satisfying the debt after the creation of a lien. Where such stipulation does not exist or there is ambiguity, the lien holder shall give the debtor at least 60 days to pay the debt, except where the subject matter of the lien is difficult to keep in good condition, such as fresh and perishable goods. When the debtor fails to perform within the time limit, the lien holder may enter into an agreement with the debtor for accord and satisfaction (代物清偿, *daiwu qingchang*), or straightforwardly satisfy the secured debt by the proceeds of an auction or sale.[91]

SUMMARY

Chinese law has expressly recognised a floating charge since 2007, introducing it in Property Law 2007, and carrying it over into the Chinese Civil Code of 2020. This type of security was introduced by the legislator in the context of reforming property law, not insolvency law reform. While the style of the entire Chinese property law is typically Civilian, the adoption of this type of property right is due to the influence of Common Law jurisdictions. The main policy consideration was the facilitation of trade, allowing small and medium enterprises and entrepreneurs to choose from more financing alternatives when entering into secured transactions, at the expense of the pre-existing doctrine based on Civil Law. Those who have the capacity of creating a floating charge are threefold, namely, enterprises, industrial and commercial households, and agricultural manufacturers or traders. One can create a floating charge over four types of things, namely, existing and future manufacturing equipment, raw materials, semi-finished products, and products. A liberal interpretation shows that this can be understood to cover all types of corporeal movables, while immovables and personal rights (e.g. book debts, receivables, negotiable instruments) cannot be used as collateral for a floating charge. To

[89] Chinese Civil Code, art 456; Huang Wei, *Interpretation of the Chinese Civil Code: Book on Property Rights [中华人民共和国民法典解读]* (China Legal Publishing House 2020) 623–624.

[90] There are exceptional scenarios: e.g. Tort (Interference with Goods) Act 1977, ss 12 (bailee's power of sale of uncollected goods); Innkeeper's Act 1878, s 1 (innkeeper's power of sale); Sale of Goods Act 1979, s 48 (unpaid seller's power of resale).

[91] Chinese Civil Code, art 453.

effectively create a floating charge, the underlying contract must be in writing. Registration is not a constitutive requirement, although it is necessary in order to give the floating charge any third-party binding effect and determine priority. Compared with the English counterpart, two notable characteristics of the Chinese version of the floating charge are that there is no difference before and after crystallisation as to the 'chargee vs. third-party right-holder' rivalry, and that it generally takes the priority doctrine of the first in registration rather than the first (created) in time. Moreover, crystallisation renders specific assets encumbered, the most prominent feature being that Chinese law treats crystallisation as automatically triggered by certain events, in the sense that it does not depend on any active step taken by the chargee. An encumbered asset can become unencumbered by the extinction of the charge (e.g. owing to the discharge of the secured debt). It can also become unencumbered by subsequent bona fide acquisition, or by subsequent purchase for value in the chargor's ordinary course of business. Where there is another charge that was registered earlier than the floating charge, accord and satisfaction, compulsory sale or auction also renders the asset unencumbered. Thus, if a prior-ranking chargee enforces the charge and consequently the ownership of the asset is transferred to the chargee or someone else, that asset is no longer encumbered by the floating charge. Like other charges, a floating charge is enforced by accord and satisfaction (consensually between the chargor and the chargee), or by compulsory sale or auction (either consensually or by court order). A floating charge in principle can bind other holders of security interests over the same asset as long as the floating charge was registered prior to those rival security interests. However, a floating charge cannot bind purchasers for value in the chargor's ordinary course of business, even if the floating charge was registered and has crystallised, and the purchaser has knowledge. A floating charge cannot bind holders of purchase money security interests which were registered within 10 days from the delivery date of the asset. A floating charge cannot bind the holder of a lien over the same asset.

8. The English floating charge and the conceptualisation of a French global security

Muriel Renaudin

INTRODUCTION

The essential feature of a security interest is to confer rights in the debtor's property assets to the secured creditor as security for the performance of an obligation such as the repayment of a debt. Personal property security law entitles secured creditors to a priority of repayment from the encumbered assets over unsecured creditors. In the event of default, the secured creditor will normally have a right of sale over the encumbered assets. Secured creditors therefore have greater leverage than unsecured creditors. Despite significant debates questioning the economic rationale for the institution of personal property security law,[1] it is submitted that access to credit and secured financing is of crucial importance for businesses to thrive and for modern economies to develop.[2] It is well established that an efficient personal property security law fosters economic development and that without it, it would be almost impossible for a national economy to develop.[3] A particularly significant type of security available to creditors is the floating charge which developed at Common law, more precisely, in equity in England in the 19th century.[4] It is a type of

---

[1] See for example, Thomas Jackson and others, 'Secured Financing and Priorities Among Creditors' (1979) 88 YaleLJ 1143; Alan Schwartz, 'The Continuing Puzzle of Secured Debt' (1984) 37 VandLRev 1051; and Vanessa Finch, 'Security, Insolvency and Risk: Who Pays the Price?' (1999) 62 MLR 633.

[2] Roy Goode and Louise Gullifer, *Goode and Gullifer on Legal Problems of Credit and Security* (6th edn 2017). See also Michael Bridge, 'The Quistclose Trust in a World of Secured Transactions' (1992) 12 OJLS 333, 341.

[3] Roy Goode, 'Security in Cross-Border Transactions' (1998) 33 TexIntlLJ 47.

[4] On this point, see Eilis Ferran, 'Floating Charges, the Nature of the Security' (1988) 47(2) CLJ 213 and John Armour, 'The Chequered History of the Floating

non-possessory security that can be created over all the debtor's assets, present and future, immoveable and moveable, corporeal and incorporeal.[5] The floating charge is said to 'hover' over the debtor's changing fund of assets until it crystallises,[6] at which point it becomes a fixed charge. The floating charge provides many advantages and great flexibility for lenders and borrowers. Notably, the debtor remains free to use the encumbered assets in the ordinary course of business until crystallisation, which is not possible with a fixed charge. Despite the attractiveness of this security device, it has been subject to many criticisms, mainly relating to the uncertain characterisation of the charge[7] and unfavourable priority rules within the insolvency context.[8] As a result, many academics in England and Wales are of the opinion that the floating charge should be axed.[9] Common law jurisdictions such as New Zealand and Australia have already abolished it[10] and adopted the functional

Charge' (2004) 13 GriffithLR 25.

[5] Ibid.

[6] Crystallisation generally occurs when the company ceases to do business, when the creditor intervenes, usually when a receiver or liquidator is appointed, or upon the occurrence of a particular event agreed upon in a clause (express crystallisation).

[7] Louise Gullifer and Jennifer Payne, *Corporate Finance Law* (Hart 2015) 308. See also *National Westminster Bank v Spectrum Plus* [2005] 2 AC 680 (HL).

[8] Kayode Akintola, 'The Treatment of Secured Creditors' in Kayode Akintola (ed.), *Creditor Treatment in Corporate Insolvency Law* (Edward Elgar Publishing 2020) 5.77.

[9] Roy Goode, 'The Case for the Abolition of the Floating Charge' in Joshua Getzler and Jennifer Payne (eds), *Company Charges; Spectrum and Beyond* (Oxford University Press 2006) and Riz Mokal, 'The Floating Charge: An Elegy' in Sarah Worthington (ed.), *Commercial Law and Commercial Practice* (Hart 2003) 502. On the proposals for reforms in England and Wales, see Richard Calnan, 'The Reform of the Law of Security' (2004) BJIBFL 88 and Hugh Beale, 'Reform of the Law of Security – Another View' (2004) BJIBFL 117.

[10] David Brown, 'The New Zealand Personal Property Securities Act 1999' and Simon Fisher, 'Personal Property Security Law Reform in Australia: History, Influences, Themes and the Future' (2009) in John De Lacy (ed.), *The Reform of UK Personal Property Security Law: Comparative Perspectives* (Routledge-Cavendish, 2009) 328.

approach[11] developed by Personal Property Security Acts (PPSA) legislations and art. 9 of the American Uniform Commercial Code (UCC).[12]

The aim of a modern and efficient personal property security law regime is to facilitate the granting of credit at low costs, thanks to clear, certain and easily accessible rules. It has been argued that an efficient secured credit law regime should allow the debtor to use all categories of assets to raise finance while remaining free to use them. In addition, it should enable simple and easy access to accurate information regarding the status of the property to be encumbered through effective publicity systems.[13] It should also provide a fast and cheap security enforcement mechanism to creditors.[14] Offering these features would enable lower transaction and monitoring costs and generate cheaper interest rates for debtors, thereby ensuring efficiency.[15] Despite the lack of a functional approach in England and Wales, the possibility for the debtor to use all categories of assets to raise finance is also a key feature of the floating charge. This type of security does not exist in the Civil law jurisdiction of France, but its features have aroused interest in academia.[16] French

---

[11] On the functional approach, see Iwan Davies, 'The Reform of English Personal Property Security Law: Functionalism and Article 9 of the Uniform Commercial Code' (2004) 24(3) LS 295 and Michael Bridge and others, 'Formalism, Functionalism, and Understanding the Law of Secured Transactions' (1999) 44 McGillLJ 567.

[12] Legislative text available at <https://www.law.cornell.edu/ucc/9> accessed 20 February 2024.

[13] See Louise Gullifer, 'Discussion Paper Series: Registration' (2017) Secured Transactions Law Reform Project available at <https://stlrp.files.wordpress.com/2017/01/gullifer-registration.pdf> accessed 20 February 2024.

[14] Louise Gullifer, 'Policy Paper' (2016) Secured Transactions Law Reform Project available at <https://securedtransactionslawreformproject.org/draft-policy-paper/> accessed 20 February 2024.

[15] Ibid. On the question of economic efficiency, see also, Thomas Jackson and Anthony Kronman, 'Secured Financing and Priorities Amongst Creditors' (1979) 88 Yale LJ 1143.

[16] Claude Witz, 'Les Sûretés Réelles Anglo-Américaines au Regard du Droit Français des Sûretés' (1992) RDBB 143, 143–147; Michael Elland-Goldsmith, 'Les Sûretés Réelles Mobilières en Droit Anglais' (1995) IBLJ 145; Jean François Riffard, *Le Security Interest ou l'Approche Fonctionnelle et Unitaire des Sûretés Réelles, Contribution à une Rationalisation du Droit Français* (LGDJ 1998); Jean François Riffard, 'L'Harmonisation Internationale des Droits des Sûretés Mobilières: Ne Ratons Pas le Train' (2016) RDBF dossier 11; Christophe Juillet, 'La Sûreté Hypothécaire Unique en Droit Français' (2016) RDBF étude 12; Jean François Riffard, 'Bis Repetita (Non) Placent. L'Ordonnance du 29 janvier 2016 sur le Gage des Stocks à l'Aune de la Nécessaire Unification des

law belongs to the Civil law tradition and does not recognise the concept of equity in its legal system. As a result, a true equivalent security mechanism to the English floating charge does not exist in French personal property security law. Yet this chapter provides evidence that several French personal property security law reforms[17] have adopted some of the features of the floating charge. Despite the fact that French law does not currently recognise the possibility to create a security over both movable and immovable property, the reforms suggest that French law is beginning to develop the conceptual foundations of a global security.

A global security would encompass different categories of assets such as movable and immovable, corporeal and incorporeal, and fungible or non-fungible assets. It would also be adapted to businesses by enabling debtors to freely continue using encumbered assets in the course of business. No doubt, the concept of a global security similar to the English floating charge or the American security interest has aroused interest from national legislators, including France, as part of the drive to enhance legal and economic competitiveness and thus boost economic growth.[18] It is contended that a global security would bring many advantages to debtors and creditors, including the possibility for the debtor to charge all of his assets, thereby increasing access to credit opportunities while remaining free to use the assets in the ordinary course of business.[19] Before 2006, traditional French personal property security law was characterised by a myriad of different types of securities with regimes that made the validity of a personal property security subject to the dispossession of the debtor and to inconsistent publicity requirements.[20] French personal property security law was therefore described as archaic and complex. The 2006 and subsequent French security law reforms[21] substan-

Sûretés Mobilières' (2016) RDBF étude 15; and Yannick Blandin, 'Sûretés et Bien Circulant: Contribution à la Réception d'une Sûreté Réelle Globale' (Thèse, Université Panthéon-Assas – Paris II 2014).

[17] The main legislative measures are Ordinance No 2006-346 of 23 March 2006 on Security Rights; Law No 2007-211 of 19 February 2007 on the *Fiducie;* Ordinance No 2009-15 of 8 January 2009 on financial instruments; and Ordinance No 2021-1192 of 15 September 2021 on the reform of security rights.

[18] See Nicolas Borga and Olivier Gout (eds), *L'Attractivité Du Droit Français Des Sûretés Réelles: 10 Ans Après la Réforme* (LGDJ 2016).

[19] Jean François Riffard, *Le Security Interest ou l'Approche Fonctionnelle et Unitaire des Sûretés Réelles, Contribution à une Rationalisation du Droit Français* (n 16).

[20] Christian Mouly, 'Procédures Collectives: Assainir le Régime des Sûretés' in Mélanges Roblot (ed.) *Aspects Actuels du Droit Commercial Français* (LGDJ 1984) 529.

[21] Ibid.

tially modernised the law, but the reforms fell short of adopting the concept of a global security. French law reforms have been piecemeal and failed to comprehensively rationalise the law.[22] Many argue that adopting the concept of a global security would contribute significantly to a more comprehensive rationalisation and modernisation of the law.[23] In particular, it would circumvent the excessive use of property-based security such as the retention of title clause and the *fiducie*,[24] and would also simplify the French security landscape by suppressing the specific regimes of securities which, for some, are still in force.

Many international initiatives have actively fostered the adoption of this kind of global security (in particular art. 9 UCC) by incorporating the concept into model laws (for example, those of the European Bank for Reconstruction and Development (EBRD)[25] or the United Nations Commission on International Trade Law (UNCITRAL)[26]). Many jurisdictions, including Civil law jurisdictions, have been influenced by these international initiatives and have reformed their secured credit laws accordingly. Quebec and Mexico are examples of Civil law jurisdictions that have embraced the idea of a global security inspired by art. 9 UCC and these international endeavours.[27] In a context of growing pressure on legislators to remain economically competitive, combined with the desire to remain attractive to business, France may also follow suit.[28] Comparative analysis of both Civil and Common law models of global securities can therefore make a useful contribution to any attempt to conceptualise a French global security.

---

[22] Olivier Gout, 'Quel Droit Commun Pour les Sûretés Réelles?' (2013) RTDC 255 and Christophe Juillet, 'Les Sûretés Réelles en Quête de Droit Commun' (2014) RDBF Dossier 33.

[23] Blandin (n 16); Anne Marijke Morgan de Rivery-Guillaud, *Le Droit Nord Américain des Sûretés Mobilières* (LGDJ 1998); Riffard, *Le Security Interest ou l'Approche Fonctionnelle et Unitaire des Sûretés Réelles, Contribution à une Rationalisation du Droit Français* (n 16); Michel Deschamps, 'Le Droit des Sûretés au Quebec', in Marie Elodie Ancel (ed.), *Repenser le Droit des Sûretés Mobilières* (LGDJ 2005) 73.

[24] The *fiducie* is a property-based security which was introduced by Law No 2007–211 of 19 February 2007.

[25] EBRD Model Law on Secured Transactions (2004) available at <https://www.ebrd.com/sites/Satellite?c=Content&cid=1395238855784&d=&pagename=EBRD%2FContent%2FDownloadDocument> accessed 20 February 2024.

[26] UNCITRAL Model Law on Secured Transactions (2019) available at <https://uncitral.un.org/sites/uncitral.un.org/files/media-documents/uncitral/en/19-08779_e_ebook.pdf> accessed 20 February 2024.

[27] See below, point IIA.

[28] Borga and Gout (n 18).

This chapter is organised in two parts. The second section contributes to a better understanding of the nature of the English floating charge by drawing out and analysing its key characteristics in order to identify possible functional equivalents in the French law of secured credit. Given the absence of a true equivalent to the floating charge in French law, the third section explores the experience of foreign Civil law jurisdictions such as Quebec and Mexico which have adopted the concept of a global security into their legal systems and which may contribute to the conceptualisation of a French global security for future legal reforms.

TOWARDS A RATIONALISED PERSONAL PROPERTY SECURITY LAW WHICH FALLS SHORT OF A GLOBAL SECURITY

Definition and Key Characteristics of the English Floating Charge: The Search for a French Functional Equivalent

The English floating charge did not develop by statute but was created in legal practice during the nineteenth century. Several definitions can be identified from judicial precedents, but the following two will be used to examine the nature of the floating charge. In *Government Stock and Other Securities Investment Co v Manila Railway Co*,[29] Lord Macnaghten explained that:

> A floating security is an equitable charge on the asset for the time being of a going concern. It attaches to the subject charged in the varying condition in which it happens to be from time to time. It is of the essence of such charge that it remains dormant until the undertaking charged ceases to be a going concern, or until the person in whose favour the charge is created intervenes.[30]

This first definition would suggest the floating charge to create a proprietary interest over all of the debtor's assets from time to time (i.e. on an ongoing basis) coupled with the freedom to use the assets in the ordinary course of business until crystallisation. In *Re Yorkshire Woolcombers Association*,[31] Lord Macnaghten further provided that:

> a floating charge [...] is ambulatory and shifting in its nature, hovering over and so to speak floating with the property which is intended to affect until some event

[29] *Government Stock and Other Securities Investment Co v Manila Railway Co* [1897] AC 8.

[30] Ibid para 86.

[31] *Re Yorkshire Woolcombers Association* [1903] 2 Ch 284.

> occurs or some act is done which causes it to settle and fasten on the subject of the charge within its reach and grasp.[32]

Despite the security already covering the assets, this second quote confirms the fundamental characteristic of the floating charge, which is the freedom of the debtor to deal with the assets in the ordinary course of business. The security is said to 'hover' over the debtor company's pool of assets until it crystallises, at which point the security will attach specifically to the debtor's assets.[33] Goods used by the debtor in the ordinary course of business are freed from the charge, and newly acquired assets become automatically charged. There is no transfer of property to the creditor. Rather, the charge entitles the creditor to an interest in property, analysed in English law as an equitable interest.[34] The lack of a doctrine of equity in France prevents the recognition of equitable interests in property and, *a fortiori*, of the floating charge.

The first hurdle in recognising an equivalent to the floating charge in France therefore resides in the conceptual nature of the proprietary interests conferred to the holder of a floating charge, which seems incompatible with the current French concept of *droit réel* (real right). Real right means a right in a *res* (or asset). The concept of ownership in France is indeed very different from that in Common law jurisdictions. French property law recognises the possibility for ownership to 'be dismembered' so that certain attributes of ownership can be conferred to third parties, such as the right to use, enjoy and destroy the property, but it cannot be separated out as legal or equitable interests in property.[35] Dismembered ownership provides for limited real rights for third parties and for a residual real right for the legal owner. In contrast, the Common law concepts of legal and equitable ownership constitute distinctive forms of ownership allowing for more flexibility and relativity in the notions of property and ownership. This would also suggest that Common law jurisdictions tend to place less emphasis on the concept of ownership and legal title than Civil law jurisdictions such as France. There is also no transfer of property under French security law (except under a retention of title clause or a *fiducie*) and the debtor remains the owner of the encumbered assets.

French law analyses the creditor's security as a 'secondary' real right on the charged assets, while the debtor has the primary real right of ownership. A feature of the creditor's security is that it is accessory to the debt and so will be subject to the same outcome as the debt itself. Should the debt become

---

32 Ibid paras 291–292.

33 Ferran (n 4) 214.

34 Ibid 214–217.

35 Yaëll Emerich, 'Regard Civiliste sur le Droit des Biens de la Common Law: pour une Conception Transsystémique de la Propriété' (2008) 38(2) RGD 339.

extinguished, the security would also disappear.[36] This qualification of the real right has important consequences for creditors under French law. First, the creditor is entitled to a *droit de préférence* (preferential right to repayment), entitling him to a priority of repayment over unsecured creditors upon the debtor's insolvency. Secondly, the creditor is entitled to a *droit de suite* (right to trace), which allows him to trace the encumbered asset in the hands of third parties. In contrast, there is no right to trace for the holder of a floating charge. An asset used by the debtor, such as through an outright sale, is automatically freed from any encumbrances.

The above analysis confirms that the conceptual analysis of the floating chargee's proprietary interest as an equitable interest prevents the identification of a true equivalent to the floating charge in French law. Nonetheless, a more detailed and functional analysis of the floating charge may contribute to the identification of common features with some French security devices. Such an analysis of the key characteristics and values of the floating charge has been developed through case law. The leading authority dealing with this particular issue is *Re Yorkshire Woolcombers Association Ltd.*,[37] where the key categorisation is that of Romer LJ, who stated that a security is a floating charge if:

> (1) If it is a charge on a class of assets of a company, present and future; (2) if that class is one which, in the ordinary course of business of the company, would be changing from time to time; and (3) if you find that by the charge it is contemplated that, until some future step is taken by or on behalf of those interested in the charge, the company may carry on its business in the ordinary way as far as concerns the particular class of assets.[38]

These elements will now be considered in relation to French law to determine the extent to which there is an equivalent.

'A non-possessory security created on a class of assets present and future'

Non-possessory security

The floating charge is a type of non-possessory security and shares this feature with some French security devices. The security in business components (*nantissement de fonds de commerce*) is an example of non-possessory security created on a class of assets, both present and future. Yet the recognition of this security device as a true equivalent to the English floating charge remains

---

[36] Laurent Aynès and others (eds), *Droit des Sûretés* (LGDJ 2021) 271.

[37] *Re Yorkshire Woolcombers Association Ltd.* [1903] 2 Ch 284.

[38] Ibid 295.

limited. Article 142-2 of the French Commercial Code restricts the category of chargeable assets to particular incorporeal movables (namely the trading sign and name, the right of lease and the clientele and goodwill). It further provides that the security can also encompass commercial furniture, equipment or tools used in the operation of the business and the intellectual property rights attached thereto (patents, licences, trademarks, industrial designs and models) only if it is expressly agreed by the parties.[39] The chargeable assets listed in art. 142-2 are exclusive and therefore exclude other assets such as immovable property, trade stocks and book debts. Given these limitations, the charged assets subject to the security in business components are less likely to 'circulate' than with the floating charge. In addition, art. 143-1 of the French Commercial Code imposes some limitations on the ability of the debtor to use charged assets in the course of business. It provides that if the debtor decides to modify the components of his business (e.g. sell all or parts of the business), he would need to seek prior authorisation from the creditor. As such, the similarities to the floating charge remain limited to this first characteristic, that the security in business components is a non-possessory security created on a class of (albeit limited) assets, both present and future.

On a more general scale, French law only recognised the possibility for the debtor to create a non-possessory security in 2006.[40] Traditional French personal property law subjected the validity of a security agreement to the debtor's dispossession. This position supporting publicity was justified by the need to protect creditors and third parties against the debtor's default. This principle was firmly established both in the Napoleonic Civil Code and in French jurisprudence.[41] However, the requirement of the debtor's dispossession was not practical in that it considerably reduced the pool of assets available to debtors for raising finance through security arrangements. The evolution towards the recognition of non-possessory securities first happened with the adoption of specific non-possessory securities such as the maritime hypothec,[42] the agricultural warrant,[43] the security on professional tools and

[39] There is no need to set up a detailed list of the corporeal movable assets forming part of the security because the security is conceptualised as a universality of assets which can depreciate or increase in value.

[40] Ordinance No 2006-346, 23 March 2006.

[41] See for example Cass. Crim., 20 April 1901, (1901) Dalloz 369 or Cass. Com., 7 July 1998, No 96-15-296, Bull. Civ. IV 182.

[42] Law 10 December 1874, reformed by Law No 67-5 of 3 January 1967.

[43] Law 18 July 1898.

equipment materials,[44] and the security on motor vehicles.[45] This list is non-exhaustive.[46] These specific regimes were abolished by the 2021 secured credit law reform,[47] but at the time of their adoption, these specific types of security laid the first stone on the path towards recognition of a general principle of a security without dispossession. Given the well-enshrined principle of protection of creditors and third parties, the possibility to create a security without dispossession was a significant innovation for French personal property law. The policy argument that it was necessary to protect interested parties was accommodated by a system of publicity through registration of non-possessory securities.[48] The 2021 secured credit law reform further modernised the French registration mechanism with the adoption of a new centralised online register.[49]

In addition to the recognition of the general principle of a security without dispossession, the 2006 law reform operated a partial rationalisation[50] of the law which now broadly distinguishes between two types of security, namely the *gage*[51] and the *nantissement*.[52] Both can be created by all parties, including individuals (except for the specific securities of the Commercial Code (e.g. security in business components) which can only be created by businesses). The *gage* allows the debtor to create a possessory or non-possessory security

---

44 Law No 51-59 of 18 January 1951. On the security on professional tools and equipment materials, see Georges Ripert, 'Le Nantissement de l'Outillage et du Matériel d'Équipement' (1951) Dalloz, Chronique, 41.

45 Law 29 December 1934 '*Loi Malingre*', replaced by Decree No 53-968 of 30 September 1953, incorporated into the Civil Code in arts 2351–2353.

46 On the different types of specific regimes of non-possessory securities, see Riffard, *Le Security Interest ou l'Approche Fonctionnelle et Unitaire des Sûretés Mobilières* (n 16) 59.

47 Ordinance No 2021-1192 of 15 September 2021.

48 Decree No 2021-1887 of 29 December 2021. See Frédéric Kieffer, 'Réforme des Sûretés: Registre Des Sûretés Mobilières et Autres Opérations Connexes' (2022) Dalloz Actualités <https://www.dalloz-actualite.fr/flash/reforme-des-suretes-registre-des-suretes-mobilieres-et-autres-operations-connexes> accessed 20 February 2024.

49 Ibid.

50 On this point, see, for example Philippe Simler, 'Avant-Propos' (2006) JCP G, supplement No 20, 3.

51 The *gage* is defined in arts 2333–2353 of the French Civil Code. It is a security created on corporeal movables property (present or future) which can be possessory or non-possessory.

52 The *nantissement* is defined in arts 2355–2366 of the French Civil Code. The *nantissement* is a security created on incorporeal movables property (present or future) which can be possessory or non-possessory.

over present and future corporeal movable property (art. 2333 French Civil Code), while the *nantissement* allows him to create a security over incorporeal present and future movable property (art. 2355 French Civil Code). Despite an overall simplification of the law, many academics argue that this reform was not entirely satisfactory given that the new legislation kept some of the specific regimes of securities created over particular classes of assets such as agricultural assets or motor vehicles.[53] The law reform even added a particular regime for a security created over stock-in-trade, which created a duplication with the existing general regime for the non-possessory security created over movable fungible property.[54] The more recent 2021 law has now repealed many of the specific regimes that were left untouched by the 2006 law reform including the security created over stock-in-trade.[55] Yet the French secured credit law reforms evidenced that a security created over movable property without dispossession can be valid and enforceable. This characteristic is shared with the English floating charge.

Security over present and future assets

The English floating charge enables borrowers to charge present and future assets. The House of Lords in *Holroyd v Marshall*[56] concluded clearly that a future asset owned by the debtor and which falls within the description of the charged assets automatically becomes charged in favour of the creditor. French law only recognised the possibility of creating a security over future assets in 2006. Traditionally, French law subjected the validity and enforceability of a security to the transfer of possession, which meant that the borrower could not create a security over future assets. The recognition of non-possessory securities provided more flexibility to the recognition of security over future assets. It is now possible for borrowers to charge present and future assets to secure present and future debts,[57] which confirms the willingness of the French legislator to adopt a more flexible approach to baseline personal property security law

---

[53] See for example, Reinhard Dammann, 'La Réforme des Sûretés Mobilières: Une Occasion Manquée' (2006) Dalloz 1298 and Pierre Crocq, 'La Réforme des Sûretés Mobilières' in Yves Picod and others (eds), *Le Droit des Sûretés à l'Epreuve des Réformes* (2006 Editions Juridique et Technique) No 34.

[54] On the security created over stock-in-trade (gage des stocks), see Patrice Bouteiller, 'Le Gage des Stocks de Biens ou de Marchandises' (2006) JCP E 808 and Dominique Legeais, 'Le Gage sur Stocks' (2006) RTDC 639.

[55] The security created over stock-in-trade (gage des stocks) was repealed by Ordinance No 2021-1192 of 15 September 2021.

[56] *Holroyd v Marshall* [1861–62] 10 HLC 191.

[57] Both arts 2333 and 2355 of the French Civil Code provide that the *gage* and *nantissement* can include future goods.

concepts such as the French law *principe de spécialité* (specificity principle).[58] Since 2006, the law no longer requires the security agreement to specifically identify the debts covered by the security[59] but requires that they must be at least determinable.[60] As such, future debts can now be affected by a *gage* or *nantissement* as long as they are determinable. The condition of 'determinability' is not precisely defined in the Civil code as the legislator left it to the courts to assess the conditions of determinability in each particular situation of facts, but elements such as the identity of the debtor, the amount due and, if applicable, the due date will be relevant.[61]

'A charge on a class of assets which would be changing from time to time in the ordinary course of business'

A reform which recognises the possibility of creating a security over fluctuating fungible assets

A significant innovation introduced by the French 2006 secured credit law reform was the introduction of art. 2342 of the French Civil Code, which permits the creation of a security over revolving fungible assets (*le gage sur choses fongibles*).[62] Article 587 of the French Civil Code defines fungible goods as those which are 'of the same quantity and quality' and art. 1892 as those 'of the same kind and quality'. According to the formula of Cornu, fungible things are 'strictly equivalent as instruments of payment or restitution'.[63] Accordingly, fungible goods are interchangeable and can be replaced with goods of the same kind, nature and quantity such as steel, machinery, vehicles

---

[58] The *principe de spécialité* or specificity principle requires the security agreement to specifically identify the debts affected to the security. On the '*principe de spécialité*', see Pierre Crocq, 'Le Principe de Spécialité des Sûretés Réelles Chronique d'un Déclin Annoncé' (2001) Droit et Patrimoine 63. See also Corine Dauchez, *Le Principe de Spécialité en Droit des Sûretés Réelles* (2013, Université Panthéon Assas) Thesis.

[59] Former art. 2074 French Civil Code.

[60] See art. 2336 French Civil Code (*gage*) and art. 2356 French Civil Code (*nantissement*).

[61] On the question of determinability, see Philippe Malaurie and others (eds), *Droit des Obligations* (2017 Lextenso) No 1410.

[62] On this point, see Stéphane Torck, 'Les Garanties Réelles Mobilières sur Biens Fongibles Après l'Ordonnance du 23 Mars 2006 Relative aux Sûretés' (2006) RDB 39.

[63] Gérard Cornu, 'Choses Fongibles' in Gérard Cornu (ed.), *Vocabulaire Juridique* (Dalloz 9th edn, 2011) 171 and François Terré and Philippe Simler, *Droit civil, Les Biens* (Précis Dalloz, 8th edn, 2010) 15.

or agricultural products. In order to ascertain fungible goods, it is generally necessary to perform an action of measurement or counting.

The security over revolving fungible assets represents a significant innovation for French law as it enables the borrower to use the charged assets (sell, encumber with further security, transform and destroy) as long as they are replaced by the same quantity of equivalent things (art. 2341 al. 2 French Civil Code). The legal innovation truly lies in the effects of such a security device because it effectively removes the right to trace of creditors. In other words, third-party purchasers are protected from any proprietary claims by secured creditors. Similar to the English floating charge, the security automatically attaches to newly acquired assets and frees the used assets from any encumbrance. Newly acquired assets will automatically be covered by the security via the mechanism of subrogation.[64] Accordingly, the pool of assets affected to the security fluctuates and shares this key characteristic with the floating charge. The difference lies in the obligation to replace used fungible goods under French law, which is not required with the English floating charge.[65]

A security device more restrictive in its scope than the floating charge

The French security over revolving fungible assets is, however, more restricted in its scope than the floating charge. First, this security device is effectively limited to the sole category of fungible goods, whereas the floating charge can extend to any type of assets. In addition, art. 2336 of the French Civil Code requires that the pool of fungible assets is determined or at least determinable (specificity principle); in other words, the fungible goods must be specified as to their kind and nature, quantity and quality. Furthermore, the fungible goods can be used by the debtor without seeking the creditor's consent, but must be replaced by the same quantity of equivalent goods so that the pool of assets can fluctuate without diminishing its value. Finally, it is to be reiterated that the proprietary right of the creditor under French law cannot be conceptualised

---

[64] There is no general regime for real subrogation (*subrogation réelle*). It is allowed when the existence of a right is threatened by the disappearance of the property to which it relates. The type of right in question is irrelevant. The right is automatically exercisable over the replacement property. On this concept, see Véronique Ranouil, *La Subrogation Réelle en Droit Civil Français* (LGDJ 1985) 218.

[65] Article 2342 of the French Civil Code provides that a debtor can use the encumbered fungible assets on the condition that he replaces them with the same quantity of equivalent goods. There is a statutory obligation to replace the used assets with goods of the same kind, nature and quantity. French law provides for contractual and statutory safeguards against non-compliance with the requirement of replacement (see below).

as an equitable interest. It has, however, been described by some academics as a real right subject to a suspensive condition,[66] the condition being the ascertainment of the goods forming the pool of assets available for repayment upon the debtor's default. Other academics use different terminology by analysing the real right of the creditor as being 'suspended' so that the real right of the creditor would only emerge upon the debtor's default and upon the ascertainment of the borrower's assets (or upon crystallisation to use the Common law terminology).[67] The creditor's suspension of his real right until crystallisation appears logical because of the implied right of the borrower to freely use the assets until realisation of the security.

The parties contemplated that the [debtor] can continue to deal with the assets in the ordinary course of business (control)

The freedom to use assets in the ordinary course of business

The English floating charge enables the debtor company to freely use all of its assets in the ordinary course of business until crystallisation. In other words, the debtor can sell some or all of its assets in the ordinary course of business without the creditor's consent, even if the assets sold amount to the entire business.[68] The debtor can also use its assets by way of security. It can mortgage or charge the encumbered assets, thereby granting a priority which will, however, overtake the rank of the floating charge (subject to the operation and effects of negative pledges).[69] As long as the transaction falls within the ordinary course of business and occurs before crystallisation, the debtor is free to use all of its assets without seeking prior authorisation from the creditor. Courts adopt a broad approach to the interpretation of 'transactions made in the ordinary course of business', considering that if the company has not stopped business, then almost all transactions will be deemed in the ordinary course of business.[70] The freedom to use assets in the ordinary course of business is therefore very wide under a floating charge. There is also no obligation to replace used assets as under French law. The freedom to deal with charged assets under the floating charge constitutes one of its great strengths and its key appeal for debtor companies.

---

66 See Michel Cabrillac and others, *Droit des Sûretés* (LGDJ 2015) 572.

67 Blandin (n 16) 141.

68 *Re Borax Company* [1901] 1 Ch 326.

69 *Re Hamilton's Windsor Ironworks Co, ex parte Pitman & Edwards* [1879] LR 12 Ch D 707.

70 *Cotton L.J. in Willmott v London Celluloid Company* [1886] LR 34 Ch D 147, 151.

The French security on revolving fungible assets also enables the debtor to use the fungible goods without seeking the creditor's consent. The most common example of fungible goods is stock-in-trade, the disposal of which would normally occur in the ordinary course of business, but omitting this restriction could arguably create a greater risk of asset diversion. Its inclusion could provide a useful limitation to propose in the conceptualisation of a French global security. French law, however, requires the debtor to replace the encumbered fungible assets with the same quantity of equivalent assets which cannot be the proceeds of resale. This requirement to replace assets is enabled via the subrogation mechanism, with replacement assets automatically forming part of the security's pool of assets without the need to create a new security. This requirement constitutes a significant difference from the English floating charge as replacement is not necessitated, but French law shares the characteristic with the floating charge that newly acquired assets automatically become charged while used fungible assets are automatically freed from the security. In this perspective, the French security on revolving fungible assets could, to a certain extent, be envisaged as a functional equivalent to the floating charge since it performs a similar function albeit via different mechanisms.

Safeguards against misbehaviour by debtors

Without an obligation of replacement, the freedom to use charged assets in the ordinary course of business under the English floating charge poses the risk of assets being diverted by misbehaving debtors. To avoid the risk of asset diversion, modern floating charges usually contractually limit the debtor's freedom to use the charged assets. The floating charge may contain express provisions preventing the company from using some of its assets in a certain way. For example, to avoid the situation where the debtor under a floating charge sells a substantial part of the business, the floating charge may restrict the freedom of the debtor to use assets in the 'course of business' to the use of assets in the 'course of trading' – in the anticipation that the concept of 'ordinary course of trading' is more restrictive than the concept of 'in the ordinary course of business'.[71] Furthermore, most floating charges contain restrictions preventing the debtor from using the company's assets by way of security without first obtaining the consent of the floating chargee. The most common express provision contained in the floating charge is the negative pledge clause. This clause prevents the debtor from creating fixed charges on assets subject to

[71] Lexis Nexis, Taking Security > Part B Types of Security > Chapter 5 Floating Charges > Part 3: The position before crystallisation, 5.52 available at <https://www.lexisnexis.com/uk/lexispsl/bankingandfinance/document/391290/55KX-XBB1-F185-S2XM-00000-00/Crystallisation_of_floating_charges> accessed 20 February 2024.

the floating charge which would effectively rank ahead of the floating charge holder's interest. However, these clauses are only enforceable if third parties are aware of them or have constructive knowledge.[72] The risk of asset diversion being important for holders of floating charges, the costs of monitoring the debtor's behaviour can constitute a deterrent to this type of security. In practice, secured creditors often opt for a combination of floating and fixed charges to protect them upon the debtor's insolvency.

French law also provides for contractual and statutory safeguards against the debtor's misbehaviour, specifically against non-compliance with the requirement of replacement. For example, legal sanctions are in place if the debtor fails to maintain the same kind and value within the pool of encumbered assets. Article 2342 of the French Civil Code provides that the debtor must maintain the material value of the charged assets. Article 2344, paragraph 2, allows the creditor to request an immediate repayment of the debt or to request additional encumbered assets if the debtor fails to maintain the same material value of the pool of charged assets. Obviously, the nature of commercial transactions means that replacement of fungible assets, usually stock, cannot be immediate; it may take a few days or even longer to replace assets. As such, parties can also contractually agree on terms to protect the creditor against the risk of asset diversion by including a *clause d'arrosage*[73] in the security agreement, which provides for a value threshold under which the debtor's pool of secured fungible assets cannot go. If it does, the creditor is entitled to request an immediate repayment of the debt in court.

Validity and Enforceability of the Floating Charge: Comparative Perspectives

The creation of the floating charge

Common contract law principles

The English floating charge and the French security over fungible revolving assets (which comes under the general regime of *gage)* are both subject to specific validity requirements. Both require the security agreement to comply with formalities contained in general contract law principles. Under French law, the *gage* must be created in writing (art. 2336, French Civil Code). English consensual security rights can be created by oral contract, but in practice, there will be a written contract to include all significant details. The key difference

---

72 *Re Castell & Brown* [1898] 1 Ch 315; *Re Standard Rotary Machine Company Ltd* [1906] 95 LT 829, and *Wilson v Kelland* [1910] 2 Ch 306.

73 Blandin (n 16), 145 and Dominique Legeais, *Sûretés et Garanties du Crédit* (LGDJ 2021) 364.

between the floating charge and the French gage relates to the eligible contractual parties. The floating charge can only be created by companies or Limited Liability Partnerships (LLPs). In contrast, the provisions of the general gage are contained in the Civil Code, which can apply to any contractual parties, including individuals.

A common publicity principle

Despite significant differences in their intrinsic nature, the English floating charge and the French non-possessory security over fungible revolving assets share similar economic aims and functions. Both security devices enable the creditor to mitigate credit risks thanks to a preferential ranking in the event of the debtor's insolvency and enable the debtor to continue using the charged assets for profit in the ordinary course of business. Both legal systems, to varying degrees, also share the same requirement for non-possessory security devices to be publicised as a core condition for their validity and enforceability. It has been argued that the publicity principle avoids the problem of the debtor's 'false wealth' and reduces information asymmetries.[74] It is further contended that publicity contributes to the efficiency of secured transactions, reduces costs for the parties, and enables the establishment of priority in the event of the debtor's insolvency, in addition to providing public notice of proprietary interests in movable assets to third parties.[75] Most prominent international and national secured credit legislation subjects the validity and enforceability of non-possessory securities to the requirement of publicity through a mechanism of registration.[76]

Part 25 of the Companies Act 2006 requires all charges created by UK companies and LLPs to be registered at Companies House within 21 days, apart from a few exceptions listed in s 859A(6). Since 2013, companies can electronically file the charge through simplified formalities. The charge so registered can be tracked on the database by third parties. French law also requires all

[74] According to the DTI 'Regulatory Impact Assessment on Proposals for the Registration of Companies' Security Interests' (London, DTI, July 2005) at para 2.7, 'The system of registration of company charges is needed to address the following risks: the concealment of secured credit with markets being misled by the apparent unencumbered ownership by companies of assets which in fact are encumbered in favour of prior creditors, uncertainty over the rights of secured parties in the event of the borrower's insolvency, uncertainty over the rights of those who buy assets that are subject to security interests.' See also Giuliano Castellano, 'Reforming Non-Possessory Secured Transactions Laws: A New Strategy?' (2015) 78(4) MLR 611, 618.

[75] Gullifer (n 13).

[76] Eva Micheler, *Property in Securities. A Comparative Study* (CUP 2007).

non-possessory securities to be registered, including the non-possessory security in revolving fungible assets. Non-possessory securities must be registered on a special registry held at the local commercial tribunal where the debtor's business is registered (art. 2337 French Civil Code) or where the debtor normally resides if the debtor is an individual. The registration is valid for five years and must be renewed to maintain validity. Since 2021, French law has significantly modernised the current registration system and created a centralised online system.[77] The Decree adopted on 29 December 2021 provides the details of the registration modalities of this new centralised register.[78] The new online register is accessible since 1 January 2023 through a unique online portal overseen by the National Council of Commercial Court Clerks.[79] This new registration mechanism aims to simplify the publicity process for non-possessory personal property securities. It also enables creditors to get immediate information on existing securities given by a particular debtor, thereby reducing the risk of information asymmetries. The modernisation of the French registration system for personal property securities is a significant reform that evidences an approximation of laws between French secured credit law and other prominent other personal property security law regimes.

The effects of the floating charge and of the French security over revolving fungible goods within the insolvency context

When the floating charge crystallises, it becomes a fixed charge which attaches to all of the debtor's assets at that point in time and which is covered by the security, including newly acquired assets since the creation of the security.[80] It is also upon crystallisation that the debtor's freedom to deal with the charged assets ceases and that the order of repayment of creditors can be determined.[81] Under the French security created over revolving fungible assets, the debtor also loses his freedom to deal with the encumbered assets upon default. This would be the equivalent of the moment of 'crystallisation' in the Common law terminology, but French law does not use this term. French academic writings

---

[77] Ordinance No 2021-1192 of 15 September 2021.

[78] Decree No 2021-1887 of 29 December 2021. See Yannick Blandin, 'Aperçu de la Réforme du Droit des Sûretés par l'Ordonnance No 2021-1192 du 15 September 2021' (2021) 37 GazPal, 14.

[79] See arts R. 521–529 à R. 521–530 French Commercial code. See also Conseil National des Greffiers des Tribunaux de Commerce. <https://www.cngtc.fr/fr/> accessed 20 February 2024. The new online portal can be accessed here: <https://suretesmobilieres.fr/rechercheParSiren> accessed 20 March 2024.

[80] *NW Robbie & Co v Witney Warehouse Co* [1963] 1 WLR 1324.

[81] Sarah Worthington, 'Floating Charge – An Alternative Theory' (1994) 53(1) CLJ 81, 89.

refer to the moment when the creditor can enforce his security,[82] that is when the debtor's company ceases to do business, when he defaults or when a liquidator is appointed. It is also at this moment that the fungible goods subject to the security are ascertained[83] and that the order of repayment can be determined under French law.

Despite these common features, significant differences can be highlighted in relation to preferential repayment mechanisms between the holder of a floating charge and the holder of a security over revolving fungible assets. Under English law, fixed charges created prior to crystallisation will generally prevail over the repayment of the floating charge holder, even if registered after the floating charge. As a result, the question of the characterisation of the charge as fixed or floating truly becomes relevant when looking at the insolvency context and at the effects of the charge. It is not the aim of this analysis to revisit the debate surrounding the characterisation of the floating charge,[84] but it is worth summarising why the distinction is important in the insolvency context. Primarily, the order of repayment in the case of the debtor's insolvency can make the floating charge vulnerable. Besides the rights of prior registered fixed charges taking priority, several preferential creditors also rank ahead of the floating charge holder. His Majesty's Revenue and Customs (HMRC) and the rights of preferential creditors such as claims made by employees rank in priority over the floating charge (but not over fixed charge holders).[85] Secondly, a prescribed part of the company's net property subject to floating charges will be set aside for unsecured creditors.[86] Thirdly, the administrator or liquidator can set aside the floating charge if created less than a year before the beginning of the insolvency process and if at the time of its creation the debtor was already insolvent.[87] Finally, the administrator or liquidator can pay their fees and expenses out of the realisation of the floating charge.[88] These

---

[82] Arts 2346, 2347 and 2458 French Civil Code provide that upon the debtor's default, the creditor can either get repayment through the sale of the encumbered assets or through the transfer of title in the charged property.

[83] Fungible goods which are subject to the security are ascertained at the moment when the debtor defaults.

[84] Louise Gullifer and Jennifer Payne, 'The Characterization of Fixed and Floating Charges' in Joshua Getzler and Jennifer Payne (eds), *Company Charges Spectrum and Beyond* (OUP 2006) 51.

[85] The Finance Act (FA) 2020 reinstituted the HMRC preferential status (s 98 FA). On preferential debts priority, see ss 175 and 176 Insolvency Act 1986.

[86] Enterprise Act 2002, s 252; Insolvency Act 1986, s 176. Fixed charges are not subject to the prescribed part.

[87] Insolvency Act 1986, s 245.

[88] Insolvency Act 1986, Sch B1, para 99(3)(b); Insolvency Act 1986, s 176ZA.

factors indubitably weaken the position of the floating charge holder within the insolvency context and have led to some academics arguing for the abolition of the floating charge.[89] However, these disadvantages belong to the insolvency context and should not overshadow the advantages of the floating charge for the creditor in the ability to charge all of the debtor's present and future assets and for the debtor in the ability to remain free to use the assets in the ordinary course of business.

The security created over revolving fungible assets arguably provides a better position for the creditor upon the debtor's insolvency. When the debtor defaults, the creditor is entitled to enforce the security through the sale or transfer of property of the charged assets. The major difference compared to the floating charge lies in the priority system and the preferential repayment ranking of secured and unsecured creditors. In contrast to the floating charge, the creditor of a security over revolving fungible assets takes priority according to the time of creation and not the time of 'crystallisation'. However, it should be pointed out that this is subject to the effects of negative pledge clauses, which can often apply in practice.

The order of repayment for secured creditors is determined according to the time of the creation of the relevant securities. However, and similarly to the floating charge, French law also provides for a portion of the debtor's assets to be distributed in priority to administrative expenses (legal fees, including judicial winding-up procedure expenses) and to employees, but that principle applies to all types of securities and not just the security over revolving fungible assets.

---

89 Kayode Akintola, 'What is Left of the Floating Charge?' (PhD University of Nottingham 2016) 38; Riz Mokal, 'The Floating Charge – An Elegy' in Sarah Worthington (ed.), *Commercial Law and Commercial Practice* (Hart 2003) 502; Roy Goode, 'The Case for the Abolition of the Floating Charge' in Joshua Getzler and Jennifer Payne (eds), *Company Charges; Spectrum and Beyond* (OUP 2006) Ch 2; and Sarah Paterson, 'The Insolvency Consequences of the Abolition of the Fixed/Floating Charge Distinction' Secured Transactions Law Reform Project 2016.

CONCEPTUALISING A FRENCH GLOBAL SECURITY: THE APPROXIMATION OF PERSONAL PROPERTY SECURITY LAW REGIMES

Learning from Foreign Experiences: The Cases of Quebec and Mexico

The global security model and its attraction

In a context of growing reforms in the field of secured credit law, the functional and pragmatic approach of PPSA legislations such as art. 9 UCC has aroused much interest from legal reformers on the other side of the Atlantic.[90] The unitary concept of the security interest, as enshrined in art. 9 UCC, offers comprehensive coverage and adopts a functional approach. The global nature of the security effectively means that it can cover all categories of personal property, tangible and intangible, future and present as a single class of assets.[91] Its scope is wide and delimited according to the function served, so that the parties are free to apply the structure best suited to their transactions.[92] This functional approach is defined by a single set of rules applicable to the security interest. Similar to the English floating charge, the debtor can freely use the encumbered assets in the ordinary course of business without seeking prior authorisation from the creditor. The security automatically extends to transformed goods and proceeds of resale without the need to register a new security. Article 9 UCC further introduces a notice-filing registration and a first-to-file priority rule system. One of the key differences from the English floating charge lies in the priority system. While the priority of the floating charge holder is settled at the point of crystallisation, the priority of the holder of a security interest under art. 9 UCC is determined according to the time of its registration. The American system would therefore seem closer to the French insolvency law principles on priority. Since 2001, art. 9 UCC has been applied uniformly in all fifty states of the USA and the District of Columbia.[93]

---

[90] Art. 9 UCC was introduced in the 1950s by two sponsoring organisations: The American Law Institute and the National Conference of Commissioners on Uniform State Law. It has since served as a model for reforms in many jurisdictions, including (but not limited to) Canada, South America, Australia and New Zealand.

[91] § 9-109 UCC. See Harry Sigman, 'The Security Interest in the United States: A Unitary Functional Solution' in Marie Elodie Ancel (ed.), *Repenser le Droit des Sûretés Mobilières* (LGDJ 2005) 59.

[92] *Ibid*, 60.

[93] In 2001, the revised art. 9 of the UCC was approved by the National Conference of Commissioners on Uniform State Laws. Revised art. 9 was applied effectively uniformly in all 50 states and the District of Columbia on 1 July 2001.

The significant positive economic impact derived from the simplicity, lower costs, transparency and reliability of this global security has been cited by other jurisdictions as reasons to reform their own laws on this model.[94] While the adoption of a global security modelled on art. 9 UCC has predominantly occurred in Common law jurisdictions, several Civil law jurisdictions have successfully imported the concept of a global security but without replicating the art. 9 UCC functionalist model and have instead adopted approaches in keeping with their traditions.

Examples of global security regimes in Civil law jurisdictions: Quebec and Mexico

Quebec is an interesting example of a Civil law jurisdiction that successfully implemented the concept of a global security into its personal property security law, without the Common law concept of the security interest, thereby preserving its property law baseline concepts such as the notion of real right.[95] A new Civil Code in 1994 significantly modernised its secured credit law regime[96] by introducing a unitary concept of security over movables and immovables called the hypothec. A centralised province-wide registration system, to a certain extent similar to PPSA registration systems, was also adopted.[97] The regime of the hypothec is governed by Book Six of the Civil Code of Quebec, entitled 'Prior claims and hypothecs' (art. 2665 Civil Code of Quebec). The hypothec enables the debtor to use all of the company's assets present and

---

[94] See for example, Henry Deeb Gabriel, 'The New Zealand Personal Property Securities Act: A Comparison with the North American Model for Personal Property Security' (2000) 34(4) IntLawyer 1123, and Anthony Duggan, 'UCC Influences on the Development of Australian Commercial Law' (1996) 29 LoyLALRev 992.

[95] On the criticism addressed against the presumption of hypothec in Quebec, see Roderick Macdonald, 'Faut-il s'Assurer qu'on Appelle un Chat un Chat? Observations sur la Méthodologie Législative à Travers l'Énumération Limitative des Sûretés, "La Présomption d'Hypothèque" et le Principe "de l'Essence de l'Opération"', in Ernest Caparros (ed.), *Mélanges Germain Brière* (Montréal, Wilson et Lafleur, Coll. Bleue 1993) 551–562.

[96] Civil Code of Quebec is available at <https://www.legisquebec.gouv.qc.ca/fr/document/lc/ccq-1991> accessed 24 February 2024. On the secured credit law reform in Quebec, see Roderick Macdonald, 'Change of Terminology? Change of Law? An Overall Assessment of the Provisions of the Civil Code of Quebec Relating to Prior Claims and Hypothecs' (1992) 23 RGD 537.

[97] For a comprehensive analysis of the difference between the law of secured credit in Quebec and PPSA jurisdictions, see Aline Grenon, 'Major Differences Between PPSA Legislation and Security Over Movables in Quebec Under the New Civil Code' (1995) 36 CBLJ 391.

future, corporeal and incorporeal, movable and immovable as security (art. 2684 Civil Code of Quebec). In line with the fundamental Civilian property law *summa divisio,* the law of Quebec distinguishes hypothecs created in movable assets and hypothecs created in immovable assets (art. 2665 Civil Code of Quebec). A hypothec created over movable property can encompass corporeal and incorporeal assets and can comprise an individual asset or a 'universality' of assets (arts 2666 and 2674 Civil Code of Quebec).

Quebec did not adopt the concept of interest in property, but conceptualised the global hypothec over movable assets as a secondary real right, thereby conferring on the creditor a right to trace and a preferential right of repayment upon the debtor's default (art. 2660 Civil Code of Quebec). One of the key features of the hypothec in Quebec, shared with the English floating charge and the American security interest, is the possibility for the debtor to freely use the assets in the ordinary course of business. This is a key economic incentive for the debtor. The Civil Code of Quebec, however, provides limitations to this freedom. For example, if the debtor uses the encumbered assets in the manufacturing process, the real right created by the security will follow into the newly created assets. If the hypothec is created over a universality of movable assets and the debtor uses some of the assets in the ordinary course of business, the hypothec will automatically attach to newly acquired assets of the same nature which replace the assets disposed of. If there is no replacement for the used assets, the hypothec can also subsist by attaching to the proceeds of resale if identifiable (art. 2674 Civil Code of Quebec). The hypothec of Quebec offers more flexibility in its legal regime and a broader scope than the current French security over fungible assets, notwithstanding its use of well-entrenched Civil property law concepts.

Mexico also underwent significant reforms of its personal property security law in 2000, 2003, 2009, 2010 and 2014. Unlike PPSA jurisdictions, Mexico did not adopt the functional approach with the unitary concept of the security interest. Instead, Mexican personal property law remains characterised by different types of security devices which have developed over time.[98] The successive reforms in Mexico have been rather slow and piecemeal over the last two decades. This is partly due to some opposition to the adoption of a PPSA-type legislation. Some academics argued that the Mexican legal system was incompatible with the concept of a security without dispossession and with

[98] Todd Nelson, 'Receivables Financing to Mexican Borrowers: Perfection of Article 9 Security Interests in Cross-Border Accounts' (1998) 29 Miami IALR 525, 550–551, and Harry Sigman, 'Security Over Movables in Mexico New Registro Único de Garantias Mobiliarias (RUG)' (2013) Universidad Nacional Autónoma de Mexico, Instituto de Investigaciones 389.

a notice-filing mechanism.[99] However, given the geo-economic position of Mexico,[100] law reforms were adopted to make Mexican law more aligned with the law of secured lending currently applicable in North American trade partners the United States and Canada. It was argued that the old law in Mexico did not provide North American lenders with sufficient security, predictability and transparency.[101] As a result, Mexican policymakers recognised the economic benefits of adopting a regime modelled on the security law of powerful economic partners.[102] In 2000 and 2003,[103] Mexico modernised its personal property security law but fell short of adopting the functional approach of art. 9 UCC.[104] Still, these reforms simplified the law by introducing a non-possessory pledge (*prenda sin transmisión de posesión*) and the guarantee trust

---

[99] Sigman, ibid.

[100] Mexico joined the North American Free Trade Agreement (NAFTA) in 1994, which created a tariff-free trading relationship with the United States of America and Canada. The United States–Mexico–Canada Agreement (USMCA) now replaces NAFTA since 1 July 2020.

[101] See Dale Beck Furnish, 'Mexico Emergent New Law of Secured Transactions' (2011) 38(1) ArizJIntl&CompL 143, 145 and Dale Beck Furnish, 'Mexican Law of Secured Transactions' in Leon Trakman and others (eds), *Doing Business in Mexico* (2004).

[102] Boris Kozolchyk, 'Secured Lending and its Poverty Reduction Effect' (2007) 42 TexIntlLJ 727.

[103] In 2000, the Mexican Congress adopted a Decree that amends, adds and repeals various provisions of the General Law of Credit Instruments and Operations, the Commercial Code and the Law of Credit Institution published on 23 May 2000 and a Decree that Amends, Adds and Repeals Various Provisions of the Civil Code for the Federal District in Common Matters and for the Whole Country in Federal Matters, the Federal Code of Civil Procedure, the Commercial Code and the Federal Consumer Protection Law, published on 29 May 2000. These law reforms introduced broad changes for Mexican commercial law, including a Commercial Registry. In 2003, the Congress adopted the Decree that Amends, Adds and Repeals Various Provisions of the General Law of Credit Instruments and Operations, the Commercial Code, the Law of Credit Institutions, the Securities Market Law, the General Law on Insurance Companies, the Federal Law on Bonding Institutions and the General Law of Organisations and Activities Ancillary to Credit, published on 13 June 2003. Regulations for the Public Registry of Commerce, as amended, were published on 24 October 2003. On the reforms introducing the public registry in Mexico, see Deck Beck Furnish, 'Accommodating Registry Systems for the OAS Model Law: Mexico's New Registry Regulations' (2005) 37(4) UCCLJ 3.

[104] Alejandro Lopez-Velarde and John Wilson 'A Practical Point by Point Comparison of Secured Transactions Law in the United States and Mexico' (2004) 36 UCCLJ 3, 12–16.

(*fideicomiso de garantía*). While the latter requires the transfer of property to a trustee similar to the French *fiducie*, the former implements the concept of a global security similar to the hypothec created over a universality of movable assets in Quebec. This Mexican non-possessory security enables businesses to create a floating security over present and future movable assets, whether they are identified individually, generically or by categories of assets (arts 353, 354 and 355 *Ley General de Títulos y Operaciones de Crédito* or Legislation on Secured Credit thereafter). This security can be created in different types of assets such as equipment, inventory, receivables, intellectual property rights and other revolving property (art. 355 Legislation on Secured Credit). In addition, the Mexican non-possessory pledge is subject to the principle of specificity as to the debt, rather than assets covered by the security. Article 348 of the Legislation on Secured Credit requires that present and future debts must at least be determinable. In line with traditional Civilian property law concepts, the security is constructed as a real right entitling the creditor to a right to trace and a preferential repayment right (art. 346 Legislation on Secured Credit). In addition, the debtor can freely use the pledged assets in the ordinary course of business, but this is subject to some restrictions. For example, the debtor can use the pledged goods in the manufacturing process as long as their value does not decrease (art. 356 Legislation on Secured Credit). The debtor can also sell the encumbered assets to third parties without affecting the creditor's real right, in particular its right to trace the assets in the hands of third parties. Article 340 of the Legislation on Secured Credit further provides that if the value of the encumbered assets falls by more than 20%, the creditor may request the judge to sell the encumbered assets (arts 340, 341 and 342 Legislation on Secured Credit). The creditor is further entitled to inspect the pool of encumbered assets to verify that the debtor is complying with its duty of care over the company's encumbered assets (art. 362 Legislation on Secured Credit). The parties can further agree to include a clause in the contract requesting the debtor to add assets to the security if the value of the encumbered assets decreases significantly. Debtors are precluded from using assets by way of security (if already encumbered), but they can use newly acquired assets for security purposes under a purchase money security interest mechanism (art. 358 Legislation on Secured Credit). The freedom to use assets in the ordinary course of business is therefore more restricted than under the hypothec of Quebec or the French non-possessory charge (*gage*), but does provide for a stronger protection of the creditor than under the English floating charge.

In terms of validity and enforceability requirements, the Mexican non-possessory pledge agreement must provide for a detailed description of the encumbered assets, which can be quite cumbersome in relation to certain types of assets, such as inventory (art. 357 Legislation on Secured Credit). Priority of repayment is determined according to the time of the registration of the security rights (art. 368 Legislation on Secured Credit). In that respect, further reforms were introduced in Mexico with several Acts enacted in 2009 and 2010.[105] The reforms introduced a unique notice-filing registration system for personal property security devices, the RUG (*Registro Único de Garantías Mobiliarias*).[106] The aim of the RUG is 'to promote the use of personal property as collateral for micro-, small- and medium-sized enterprises, to obtain financing under more favourable conditions, to stimulate investment, growth and competitiveness of the economy'.[107] This reform was substantial in terms of the modernisation of Mexican secured credit law but also in terms of its approximation with North American secured credit law legislations. The latest reform of 2014 further reformed Mexican personal property security law by modifying judicial and extra-judicial enforcement procedures and strengthening the position of creditors.[108]

An analysis of the hypothec over movables of Quebec and the Mexican non-possessory pledge evidences some substantial similarities, but above all demonstrates that the adoption of a global security over personal property is not incompatible with civil law property baseline concepts, and *a fortiori* with French personal property security law.

---

105 The Mexican Congress adopted a Decree that Amends and Adds Various Provisions to the Commercial Code, published on 27 August 2009, which introduced a unique register for personal property securities. The Congress adopted further legislation in 2010 which finalised the implementation of the new registry. The Congress adopted a Decree that Amends and Adds Various Provisions of the Regulations of the Public Commercial Registry, published on 23 September 2010; the Accord Establishing the Forms by Which to Carry Out Registrations and Annotations in the Public Commercial Registry and the Single Registry of Security Interests, published 12 October 2010; and the Clarification of the Accord Establishing the Forms by Which to Carry Out Registrations and Annotations in the Public Commercial Registry and the Single Registry of Security Interests, also published 12 October 2010. See Deck Bale Furnish, ´Mexico's Emergent New Law of Secured Transactions: Recent Developments 2000–2010' (2011) 28(1) ArizJIntl&CompL 143.

106 Available at <https://rug.economia.gob.mx/Rug/home/inicio.do> accessed 20 February 2024.

107 Original extract: 'Potenciar el uso de bienes muebles como garantías para que las micro, pequeñas y medianas empresas obtengan financiamiento en mejores condiciones, estimulando la inversión, el crecimiento y la competitividad de la Economía' available from <https://rug.economia.gob.mx/Rug/home/inicio.do> accessed 20 February 2024.

108 See Isis Isunza, 'The Impact of Secured Transactions Reforms in Mexico and Colombia' (2016) 33(1) AJICL 125, 126 and Sigman (n 98) 391.

A French Global Security: Convergence Towards International Standards and the Approximation of Law

The adoption of a global security has been widely embraced by national legislatures and extensively promoted by several international initiatives. Giving creditors the opportunity to take security over all of the debtor's assets would increase access to credit and reduce credit costs.[109] International instruments such as the EBRD Model Law on Secured Transactions[110] or the UNCITRAL Model Law on Secured Transactions[111] play a significant part in fostering the adoption of a global security modelled, to a certain extent, on the American art. 9 UCC.[112] Further international initiatives such as that of the Organization of American States (OAS)[113] and the Doing Business Reports of the World Bank further support the adoption of an art. 9 UCC type regime.[114] From 2004 until 2021, the Doing Business Reports have ranked the law of national jurisdictions: the criteria used are based on how far legislative frameworks promote the ease of doing business. One of the criteria relates to secured credit. The methodology used by the Doing Business Reports rewards jurisdictions with a high score if their secured credit law displays, amongst others,[115] the following features: (1) a unified legal regime for secured transactions that extends to the creation, publicity and enforcement of fiduciary transfers of title; financial leases; assignments or transfers of receivables, and sales with retention of title; (2) the possibility to create a non-possessory security right in a single category

---

[109] Gerard McCormack, *Secured Credit and the Harmonisation of the Law – The UNCITRAL Experience* (Edward Elgar Publishing 2011) 1.

[110] For the content of the Model Law, see <www.ebrd.com> accessed 24 February 2024. See also Jan Hendrick Röver, *Secured Lending in Eastern Europe: Comparative Law of Secured Transactions and the EBRD Model Law* (OUP 2007); Duncan Fairgrieve, 'Reforming Secured Transactions Laws in Central and Eastern Europe' (1998) EBLR 245 and Gerard McCormack and Frédérique Dahan, 'The EBRD Model Law on Secured Transactions: Comparisons and Convergence' (1989) CFILR 65.

[111] UNCITRAL Model Law on Secured Credit 2019.

[112] See Neil Cohen, 'The Private International Law of Secured Transactions: Rules in Search of Harmonization' (2018) 81 L&CP 203.

[113] <https://www.oas.org/en/default.asp> accessed 20 February 2024.

[114] Reports (since 2004) are available at <https://archive.doingbusiness.org/en/doingbusiness> accessed 20 February 2024.

[115] The latest 2020 Report identifies 12 different features used to measure and rank national secured credit legislation. Eight features relate to legal rights in personal property security law, and four relate to bankruptcy. A score of '1' is assigned for each of the features contained in the law of a particular jurisdiction. The greater the grade, the better the ranking a particular jurisdiction gets.

of movable assets without the need for a specific description of the collateral; (3) the possibility to create a non-possessory security right in all movable assets without the need for specific description of the collateral; (4) the possibility to create a security over future and after-acquired assets which automatically extend to products, proceeds and replacements of the original assets; (5) a security that can secure all types of debts and obligations without the need for specific description; (6) a unified registry to operate as regards security interests granted over movable property; (7) a notice filing system (that only provides notice of the security interest and not a review of the transaction); and (8) an online, modern and efficient registry. These features evidently promote a more functional approach to the regulation of secured credit and promote the adoption of a global security, to a certain extent modelled on art. 9 UCC.[116]

There is no doubt that such international initiatives can create significant political and economic pressures on national legislatures to remain legally competitive and to reform their laws according to the proposed models. However, it does not mean that one size can fit all legal systems and can suit the legal environment of a particular jurisdiction. As such, France has been quite cautious in its approach to adopting the concept of a global security. One of the aims emphasised within the latest 2021 law reform was to achieve a balance between the need for the protection of debtors and the need for economic efficiency within secured transactions.[117]

However, recent law reforms do point towards a willingness to move towards a more functional approach and *a fortiori* towards a more all-encompassing security. Some French academics are of the opinion that the adoption of a global security would complete the rationalisation of French secured credit law and would also contribute to the approximation of law in relation to other systems.[118] The successive personal property security law reforms that followed the 2006 reform considerably softened French conceptual principles underpinning personal property security and now provide an opportunity to develop the foundations of a global security.[119]

---

[116] The United States scored 95 on a scale of 0–100 in both 2019 and 2020 reports in respect of the 'getting credit' category. New Zealand scored 100 and Australia 95. Score tables are available at <https://subnational.doingbusiness.org/en/data/exploretopics/getting-credit/score> accessed 20 February 2024.

[117] Michel Grimaldi and others, 'Présentation d'un Avant-Projet de Réforme des Sûretés' (2017) Recueil Dalloz 1717.

[118] Juillet (n 16); Riffard, 'L'Harmonisation Internationale des Droits des Sûretés Mobilières: Ne Ratons pas le Train' (n 16); and Blandin (n 16).

[119] Ibid.

CONCLUDING REMARKS ON THE CONCEPTUALISATION OF A FRENCH GLOBAL SECURITY

An analysis of the nature of the floating charge and of other global security models has proved useful in this contribution to the conceptualisation of a French global security. It revealed that French law already shares many features with these models and that its traditional Civilian property law concepts can be further softened to accommodate the concept of a global security. Besides the question of its desirability,[120] the conceptualisation of a new global security under French secured credit law appears feasible and could borrow from the English floating charge, art. 9 UCC and Civil law models. It was not the aim of this study to provide a comprehensive analysis of what a French global security could or should be, but the following conclusions can contribute to such a discussion.

This chapter has evidenced that a French global security could theoretically encompass all types of assets, including present and future, movables, corporeal and incorporeal, while preserving the creditor's real right. Mexico and Quebec demonstrate this possibility, however, with the *proviso* that the classic *summa divisio* between movable and immovable assets could prevent the recognition of an all-encompassing security such as the floating charge. In order to overcome the potential conceptual hurdle raised by the *principe de spécialité* (specificity principle), Quebec uses the property law concept of the 'universality' of assets, which is useful but requires the debtor to maintain the kind and value of the charged assets within this universality. The concept of 'universality' of assets has also been put forward by some French academics as part of the proposal for a French global security, but proponents of the adoption of a PPSA model argue that the concept of 'universality' remains limited because it does not theoretically justify the replacement of assets used by the debtor in the course of business by different kinds of goods. Consequently, it is contended that the notion of the security being extended to the manufactured goods or proceeds of resale as under art. 9 UCC would offer a better justification.[121]

As to the effects of global security, the above analysis evidenced that all models recognise the need for the debtor to remain free to use the encumbered assets in the ordinary course of business. This is usually subject to limitations

[120] Riffard, *Le Security Interest ou l'Approche Fonctionnelle et Unitaire des Sûretés Réelles, Contribution à une Rationalisation du Droit Français* (n 16).

[121] Riffard, 'L'Harmonisation Internationale des Droits des Sûretés Mobilières: Ne Ratons pas le Train' (n 16).

aimed at protecting the creditor against the debtor's misbehaviour. For example, it is suggested that contractually limiting the freedom of the debtor to use the assets in the ordinary course of business (as with the English floating charge) can be useful. Such limits could also be adopted within the French legal regime for global security. However, given the more interventionist approach to French commercial legislation, it is likely that further statutory and conventional control measures, such as those adopted by the Mexican and Quebec models, will appeal to the French legislator.[122]

Finally, in relation to validity and enforceability requirements, the 2021 French secured credit law reform has adopted a unitary and centralised registration mechanism comparable with most prominent national and international standards.[123] A French global security would most certainly be subject to registration within this newly created centralised register. In terms of priority entitlements upon the debtor's default, this chapter has explained that priority of repayment in France is determined according to the time of registration and follows the principle of *prior tempore, potior jure* (or 'first in time, first in right'). These principles are also followed in art. 9 UCC and in Civil law jurisdictions such as Quebec and Mexico. It would theoretically be difficult for France to subject the global security to the principles applicable under English law whereby the floating charge holder effectively ranks behind fixed charge holders (even where fixed charges are registered after the floating charge). Modifying the extant French principles would arguably also undermine the French secured credit law rationalisation efforts and the attractiveness of the global security.[124]

It is anticipated that the traditional French contract law requirement that the validity of any consensual agreement requires a document in writing would apply. This is especially so given that the validity of current non-possessory securities created over present and future assets (and *a fortiori* any form of global security) is currently subject to the requirement of determinability. As for the eligible parties to the agreement, all foreign experiences limit the possibility to create a global security to businesses. Currently, France allows all

---

[122] On a comparative analysis of state interventionism in Civil law and Common law jurisdictions, see, for example Mariana Pargendler, 'The Role of the State in Contract Law: The Common–Civil Law Divide' (2018) 43 Yale J Int'l L 143.

[123] See for example, UNCITRAL Guide on the Implementation of a Security Rights Registry. <https://uncitral.un.org/sites/uncitral.un.org/files/media-documents/uncitral/en/security-rights-registry-guide-e.pdf> accessed 20 February 2024.

[124] See above on the disadvantages of the floating charge in the insolvency context.

kinds of parties to create non-possessory securities (except for the specific securities provided by the French Commercial Code). However, the fluctuating nature of the encumbered assets of a global security suggests that only businesses should be able to agree to such a security. It is in the very nature of businesses to continue using encumbered assets, and as such, it would make sense that the creation of a French global security should also be limited to professionals.[125]

A French global security, which encompasses all types of movable assets, present and future, and which provides the debtor with the freedom to use assets in the ordinary course of business, seems more plausible than ever, despite traditional civil law concepts of property. Although the position of the debtor may be weakened by allowing him to use all of his assets as security, the position of the creditor would continue to be strong thanks to control measures against asset diversion. Furthermore, debtors could benefit from additional protection through specific restrictive measures. For example, the legislator could decide to restrict access to the global security to businesses only (businesses are usually seen as better informed than consumers). The legislator could also decide to increase formal requirements for this type of security.

Economic imperatives have transformed traditional and rigid civilian property law concepts, allowing for more economically efficient security devices to emerge. As such, many French academics are of the view that France should continue its modernisation efforts and adopt a global security right.[126]

---

125 Blandin (n 16), 239–240.

126 Blandin (n 16); Riffard, *Le Security Interest ou l'Approche Fonctionnelle et Unitaire des Sûretés Mobilières* (n 16); Riffard, 'Bis Repetita (non) Placent. L'Ordonnance du 29 janvier 2016 sur le Gage des Stocks à l'Aune de la Nécessaire Unification des Sûretés Mobilières' (n 16); Jean François Riffard, 'The Still Uncompleted Evolution of the French Law on Secured Transactions Towards Modernity' in L Gullifer and O Akseli (eds), *Secured Transactions Law Reform Principles, Policies and Practice* (2019, Bloomsbury) Ch 17; Nathalie Martial-Braz, 'L'Existence de Modèles Alternatifs. L'Approche Unitaire des Sûretés Mobilières, Solution Pour le Droit Français?' in Nicolas Borga and Olivier Gout (eds), *L'Attractivité du Droit Français des Sûretés Réelles. 10 Ans Après la Réforme* (LGDJ 2016) 35; Nicolas Borga, 'Les Conditions de Validité de l'Hypothèque Unique' (2016) RDBF No 13; Nathalie Martial-Braz, 'L'Opposabilité de l'Hypothèque Unique' (2016) RDBF No 14; and Maxime Julienne, 'Les Attributs de l'Hypothèque Unique' (2016) RDBF No 15.

9. Floating security in Québec? Hypothecs on a universality of movable property

Catherine Walsh

INTRODUCTION

Canada's federal constitutional structure assigns law-making authority over matters relating to "property and civil rights" to the provinces.[1] While the private law in Canada's other provinces (and three federal territories) derives from the common law tradition, in Québec it is rooted in French civil law.[2]

The Québec law of security on property is today set out in the Civil Code of Québec/*Code civil du Québec* (CCQ).[3] In force since 1 January 1994, the CCQ emerged from a lengthy reform process aimed at modernizing and rationalizing the whole of Québec private law.[4] On coming into force, the CCQ repealed and replaced the Civil Code of Lower Canada/*Code civil du Bas-Canada* (CCLC).[5] The CCLC had come into effect in 1866 in anticipation of what is now the province of Québec joining the Canadian Confederation in 1867. Its purpose was to consolidate the mix of legal sources that had emerged after

[1] The Constitution Act, 1867, 30 & 31 Vict, c 3 (known before 1982 as the British North America Act), s 92(13).

[2] After what is now the province of Québec came under British colonial rule, the British Parliament passed the Québec Act of 1774, 14 George III, c. 83 (UK). Section VIII specified that French law applied to matters of property and civil rights and English common law to matters of criminal and public law. That division was later reflected in The Constitution Act, 1867.

[3] S.Q. 1991, c. 64.

[4] See generally John EC Brierley, "The Renewal of Québec's Distinct Legal Culture: The New Civil Code of Québec" (1992) 42:4 UTLJ 484.

[5] 29 Vict., ch. 41 (1865).

the Province of Québec was created in 1763 in a civil code modelled on the structure and legislative style of the French *Code Civil.*[6]

In line with the then traditional civilian view,[7] the pledge was the only security device recognized by the CCLC for movables.[8] The non-possessory hypothec was reserved for immovables[9] and the hypothecation of movables was expressly prohibited.[10]

The inability of the pledge to address the financing needs of enterprise debtors soon forced exceptions to be made. From the late nineteenth century onwards, federal banking legislation enabled federally regulated banks operating in Québec to obtain security over the circulating inventory of primary producers and commercial enterprises.[11] In 1914, the Québec legislator authorized corporations (and later limited partnerships) to grant a form of non-possessory trust deed security on their present and future assets.[12] The trust deed, which had to be executed in notarial form and publicized by registration, typically provided for a fixed security on capital assets and a floating security on circulating assets such as inventory. The floating security allowed the debtor to sell the assets subject to it in the ordinary course of its business free of the security and attached only to those assets still owned by the debtor on default.

---

6 On the history and sources of the CCLC, see JEC Brierley, "Quebec's Civil Code Codification: Viewed and Reviewed" (1968) 14 McGill LJ 521.

7 Paul-A Crépeau, "Civil Code Revision in Quebec' (1974) 34 La L Rev 921, 944–945.

8 CCLC arts 1966–1979; arts 1971 and 1979 also recognized the pledge of documents of title representing corporeal movables.

9 CCLC art. 2016. While CCLC art. 1967 recognized the possessory pledge of immovables (*antichrese*), this was considered anachronistic even at that time.

10 CCLC art. 2022.

11 For details, see John EC Brierley and Roderick Macdonald (eds), *Quebec Civil Law: An Introduction to Quebec Private Law* (Emond Montgomery 1993). For the current version of this security, see the Bank Act, S.C. 1991, c. 46, s 427.

12 Special Corporate Powers Act, R.S.Q. 1977, c. P-16, ss 27–31 (first introduced in 1914 by An Act to Amend the Revised Statutes, 1909, S.Q. 1913–1914, c. 51). In 1983, CCLC art. 1883.1 extended this form of security to limited partnerships: S.Q. 1983, c. 28. For details, see: Brierley & Macdonald (eds) *ibid*, para 719; Jacques Auger, Les sûretés mobilières sans dépossession sur des biens en stock en vertu de la Loi sur les banques et du droit québécois (1983–1984) 14 RDUS 221, 260–263; Martin Boodman, "The Nature and Diversity of Personal Property Security Systems in Canada" (1992) 23 RGD 23, at 132; Y Renaud, "Loi des pouvoirs spéciaux des corporations: deux régimes de sûretés?" (1971) 73 R du N 383. On the distinctly civilian character of the floating aspect of this security, see Louis Payette, "La charge flottante" in [1976] Meredith Memorial Lectures (Richard De Boo 1978).

As against other creditors, the security ranked behind the privileges assigned by the CCLC to specific classes of unsecured creditors. Moreover, the debtor company could, even after registration, grant prior-ranking security to other creditors including the agricultural pledge (extended to forestry operations in 1974) and the commercial pledge introduced by amendments to the CCLC in 1940 and 1962[13] (despite the term pledge, these were non-possessory security devices). In 1951, the Québec legislator amended the CCLC to allow commercial enterprises to assign present and future book debts (receivables) as security,[14] and in 1984, it introduced an inventory security mechanism inspired by the federal banking legislation—transfer of "property in stock"—but available to all creditors.[15] Parallel to these statutory developments, the Québec courts came to endorse the use of a transfer or reservation of ownership of corporeal movables to secure loan and sale credit (including such variants as the double sale, sale-leaseback, lease with an option to purchase and finance lease), albeit these functionalist substitutes were increasingly made subject to consumer protection legislation when engaged in with consumers.[16]

This ad hoc evolution of the law of security on property, especially movable property, produced a fragmented and confusing hodgepodge, and the CCQ revision project early on recognized the need for a wholesale rationalization and modernization.[17] At a policy level, the drafters sought to preserve Québec's distinct civil law tradition while modernizing the law of security, and especially movable security on enterprise assets, to achieve similar functionalist outcomes to UCC Article 9 in the United States and the Personal Property Security Acts in Canada's common law jurisdictions.[18]

---

[13] CCLC arts 1979a–1979d (agricultural and forestry pledge), arts 1979e–1979e (commercial pledge). For details, see Brierley & Macdonald, *supra* para 709.

[14] CCLC art. 1571d. For details, see Brierley & Macdonald *supra*, para 719. Boodman, *supra* at 132. The CCLC was amended in 1968 to rank competing assignees by the time of registration of the assignment rather than the time of publication of the newspaper notice of enforcement: Brierley & Macdonald *supra*, para 721, Boodman, *supra* at 128.

[15] An Act respecting the transfer of property in stock, amending the Bills of Lading Act, S.Q. 1982, c. 55. For details and critiques, see RA Macdonald, "Inventory Financing in Quebec After Bill 97'" (1984) 9 CBLJ 153; Auger, supra.

[16] For details, see: Brierley & Macdonald, *supra* paras 715, 716, 722; Boodman, *supra* at 125–126; G LeDain, "Security Upon Moveable Property in the Province of Quebec" (1956–1957) McGill LJ 77, 78–89.

[17] Civil Code Revision Office, *Report on the Civil Code* (1977), volume I, p. xxxiv, and volume II, tome I, pp. 346–372.

[18] Roderick A Macdonald, "Change of Terminology? Change of Law?" (1992) 23 RGD 357, 358–359.

The security regime that emerged is organized primarily around the hypothec, conceived as "a real right on a movable or immovable property made liable for the performance of an obligation".[19] A hypothec may be conventional—constituted by agreement of the parties—or legal—constituted by operation of law.[20] Subject to limitations to protect non-enterprise debtors, a debtor's corporeal or incorporeal property, present or future, may be the object of a conventional hypothec. Moreover, it may be granted on "specific corporeal or incorporeal property, whether individual or multiple, or *on all the property comprised in a universality*" (emphasis supplied).[21] As elaborated later, a universality is understood to include all property within a generic class or category including a universality comprising all the grantor's present and future property. The idea is that it is the universality that is the real object of the hypothec, although it also charges each specific item within the universality.

While a hypothec on a universality is the closest functional equivalent in the CCQ to the floating charge of English law, as we shall see, it generally ranks as a "fixed" security right once the specified creation and publicity rules are observed. This is true, however, only for movable hypothecs.[22] Although hypothecary agreements may purport to charge a universality of present and future immovables, an immovable hypothec is effective against third persons only when registered against each immovable in the land register and ranks only from the time of registration.[23]

The analysis that follows therefore focusses on the CCQ movable security regime, and specifically on hypothecs on a universality of movables.

The next three sections respectively address the CCQ rules on the creation and publicity, ranking and enforcement of movable hypothecs. This includes, at particular points, consideration of the intersection between the ranking and enforcement rules for hypothecs and the CCQ's continued recognition of contracts for the transfer and retention of ownership for security purposes. Secured transactions law is deeply interconnected with bankruptcy and insolvency law over which the federal Parliament has constitutional authority. Consequently, this is followed by a consideration of the effects of federal insolvency law on the ranking and enforcement of pre-existing security rights. The final substantive section addresses the special rules for movable hypothecs on investment

---

[19] CCQ art. 2660.

[20] CCQ art. 2664(2).

[21] CCQ art. 2666.

[22] Movable property is defined broadly by the CCQ as a residual category, comprising not just "things which can be moved" but "all other property, not otherwise characterized by law", including claims and incorporeal rights generally: CCQ arts 905, 907.

[23] CCQ arts 2949, 2945(1), 2663.

securities and security entitlements and on monetary claims (the latter concept includes claims to the credit balance of a deposit account with a financial institution). These deviate in complex ways from the general rules addressed in the preceding parts and so require separate analysis. The last section summarizes and offers concluding observations.

Length restrictions mean that many issues are addressed only superficially in the analysis that follows or have had to be omitted altogether. Important exclusions include the CCQ conflict of law rules on the law applicable to the validity, publicity and priority of movable security rights.[24] The chapter also does not address the interaction between the CCQ regime and federal legislation on matters other than insolvency (specifically its effects on ranking and enforcement) over which Parliament also has exclusive authority, such as maritime law, banking, intellectual property rights and negotiable instruments. Also omitted is the impact of Canada's ratification of the Cape Town Convention and Aircraft Protocol on security over commercial aircraft assets and the subsequent adoption of implementing legislation by all jurisdictions, including Québec.[25]

CREATION AND PUBLICITY

Conventional Movable Hypothecs: General Rules

The CCQ rules for creating a valid conventional movable hypothec differ depending on whether it is a hypothec with or without delivery.[26] A "movable hypothec with delivery" (traditional pledge) requires "physical" delivery of the hypothecated property to the creditor.[27] The agreement constituting a "movable hypothec without delivery" need only be in writing to avoid absolute nullity.[28] And while the agreement must provide "a sufficient description of the

24 CCQ arts 3102–3108.8.

25 For Québec, see an Act to implement the Convention on International Interests in Mobile Equipment and the Protocol to the Convention on International Interests in Mobile Equipment on Matters Specific to Aircraft Equipment, CQLR c M-35.1.2.1.

26 CCQ art. 2665.

27 CCQ arts 2702, 2709.

28 CCQ art. 2696. No special form of writing is required unless the hypothec is in favour of a "hypothecary representative" of multiple present or future creditors (as in a syndicated loan arrangement) where the hypothec must be granted "by notarial act *en minute*": art. 2692(4). In contrast, an immovable hypothec must be granted "by notarial act *en minute*" (art. 2693) and "is valid only so far as the constituting act describes in a precise manner the hypothecated property" (art. 2694).

hypothecated property", for a movable hypothec on a universality "an indication of the nature of that universality" suffices.[29] The Minister's comments indicate this was a deliberate change from pre-CCQ law, aimed at forestalling arguments that a generic description might make the security invalid.[30]

The doctrine and case law affirm that a specific description of the movables within a universality is unnecessary if the description enables a determination of whether a specific movable falls within its scope.[31] Thus generic descriptions like "all present and future claims" or "all present and future inventory" or indeed all "present and future movables" suffice.

A conventional hypothec is effective between the parties on creation,[32] but must be "published" to take effect against third persons,[33] even if they knew of its existence.[34] For a movable hypothec with delivery, physical delivery of the hypothecated movable to the creditor constitutes publication for as long as the creditor has possession.[35] However, a movable hypothec without delivery must be published by registration in the register of personal and movable real rights/*registre des droits personnels et réels mobiliers* (RDPRM or movable registry).[36]

The movable registry is centralized, publicly accessible, and digitalized, facilitating the online submission of registration data by creditors and search requests by interested third persons.[37] Registration is notice-based, meaning that a registration application need only set out the basic details: names and addresses of the parties, date of birth if the grantor is a natural person, sum for which the hypothec is granted,[38] date and place of signature of the

---

29 CCQ art. 2697.

30 Ministère de la Justice, *Commentaires du ministre de la Justice: Le Code civil du Québec, Tome* II, Québec, Publication du Québec, 1993, CCQ art. 2697. And see Yaëll Emerich, "L'hypothèque Mobilière Universelle: Entre Impératifs Économiques et Protection du Débiteur" (2009) 111:3 Revue du notariat 463, note 56.

31 Emerich, *ibid* at 480, citing among other sources: *Duchesneau c. Graton*, EYB 2003–45105 (C.S.), paras 33–34; *Caisse Desjardins de Salaberry-de-Valleyfield c. General Motors Acceptance Corporation of Canada Ltd.*, 2007 QCCA 1342, para 18.

32 CCQ art. 2941(2).

33 CCQ arts 2663, 2941(1).

34 CCQ art. 2963.

35 CCQ art. 2703. A movable hypothec with delivery is extinguished on termination of the creditor's possession: CCQ art. 2798(2). For immovable hypothecs, the sole mode of publication is registration in the land register: CCQ art. 2934.

36 CCQ art. 2934.

37 https://www.rdprm.gouv.qc.ca/fr/Pages/Accueil.html.

38 On this requirement, see below.

hypothecary agreement,[39] and duration of the registration up to 10 years but renewable before expiration.[40] While the application must also describe the charged property, the description of a hypothec on a universality need only indicate the nature of the universality.[41]

When determining if errors in submitted information invalidate a registration, the key is whether the error affects the registry's publicity function. Since the grantor's name is the principal search criterion,[42] an error in the grantor's name that prevents retrieval on a search using the correct name voids the hypothec's published status.[43]

Limitations on Who Can Hypothecate a Universality of Present and Future Movables

While allowing grantors to hypothecate present and future movables facilitates access to credit for enterprises, there is less need or demand – and greater potential for abuse – in the consumer secured credit market.[44] Reflecting these competing tensions, the CCQ initially allowed only legal and natural persons, partnerships and trustees operating enterprises to grant a hypothec on a universality of present and future corporeal or incorporeal property.[45] The negative impact of an *absolute* prohibition on access to personal credit proved difficult to sustain and the CCQ was later amended to allow non-enterprise debtors to hypothecate a universality of their present and future investment securities

---

39 One can therefore infer that it is not possible to register in advance of the agreement constituting the hypothec.

40 CCQ arts 2798(1).

41 CCQ art. 2950.

42 Although the grantor's name is the main search criterion, if the hypothec is on a specific road vehicle, its identification number (VIN) must be entered in a separate field in the registration application. VIN searching ensures disclosure of hypothecs granted by prior owners. VINs are not needed for hypothecs on a universality of vehicles held by the grantor as inventory, as these are released on each vehicle's sale in the grantor's ordinary course of business; see below.

43 See, for example, *Québec inc. (Syndic de),* (C.A), 2003 CanLII 8040.

44 Emerich, *supra* at 472, citing *Caisse Desjardins de Salaberry-de-Valleyfield, supra*, para 11.

45 CCQ art. 2684. Art. 1525(3) defines the operation of an enterprise in broad terms as the "carrying on by one or more persons of an organized economic activity, whether or not it is commercial in nature, consisting of producing, administering or alienating property, or providing a service". *An Act respecting the special powers of legal persons*, CQLR c P-16, also allows certain legal entities not carrying on an enterprise to grant a hypothec on a universality if empowered by their charter or the law governing them: arts 27, 34.

or security entitlements and monetary claims including bank account credit balances.[46]

Limitations on the Grant of Hypothecs Without Delivery on Current Movables

The CCQ restricts the current movables on which natural persons not operating enterprises can grant a hypothec without delivery to road vehicles and other movable property specified by regulation.[47] The regulation has been amended since the CCQ was initially adopted to allow individuals who do not operate enterprises to grant hypothecs without delivery on their current incorporeal property and claims generally, excepting only claims to registered tax savings and education funds.[48] The limitation has also been relaxed for corporeal movables. Initially permitted only for road vehicles, caravans, mobile homes, boats, personal watercraft and aircraft,[49] non-enterprise debtors can now hypothecate assets like art, jewellery and rare collectibles without having to give up possession.[50]

The continued exclusion of other potentially high-value corporeal assets[51] is difficult to explain other than as an atavistic remnant of the general pre-CCQ prohibition on the hypothecation of movables. After all, no such limitation applies where non-possessory security on corporeal property is instead achieved under the CCQ via a transfer or reservation of ownership.[52] Consumers engaging in these functional alternatives to the hypothec are instead protected, as they increasingly were under pre-CCQ law, by consumer protection legislation.[53]

---

[46] CCQ art. 2684.1. On these two categories of movables, see below.

[47] CCQ art. 2683.

[48] *Regulation respecting the Register of personal and movable real rights*, CQLR c CCQ, r 8, art. 15.02(3).

[49] *Ibid*, art. 15.02(1).

[50] *Ibid*, art. 15.02(2).

[51] See e.g. *9263–8766 Quebec inc. c Développement du faubourg Fortier inc.*, 2021 QCCS 4429 (hypothec on a Vermeer trencher granted by a natural person who did not operate an enterprise declared invalid as this was not a category of movable property excepted by regulation from the limitation).

[52] On the extent to which the CCQ continues to recognize these functional alternatives to hypothecs, see below.

[53] *Consumer Protection Act*, CQLR c P-40.1, arts 66–181. And note CCQ art. 1749(1).

What Obligations Can be Secured?

The CCQ incorporates the classic principle that a hypothec is an accessory right and exists only as long as the secured obligation exists.[54] However, to facilitate credit practices in both the consumer and enterprise markets, it allows a conventional hypothec to secure any obligation,[55] including lines of credit and future and indeterminate obligations,[56] until positively cancelled.[57]

Overcollateralization

Allowing a hypothec to secure all present and future movables can lead to overcollateralization, where the value of the hypothecated property far exceeds the obligations secured by it, thereby limiting the debtor's ability to obtain new secured financing from another creditor on the residual value. To address this concern, the CCQ requires the sum/*somme* for which a hypothec is granted to be stated in the hypothecary agreement[58] and registration application.[59] However, this sum need not match the actual financing,[60] and creditors often specify a sum equal to the value of the hypothecated property to maintain ranking priority for future financing even if not contemplated at the time of the transaction. This undermines the policy goal unless the grantor can negotiate a sum that realistically corresponds to the anticipated financing.

---

54 CCQ art. 2661.

55 CCQ art. 2687.

56 CCQ, art. 2688. And see *St-Jacques c. Charbonneau* [1999] R.D.I. 200 (C.A.); *HSBC Bank Canada c. 9082–3659 Québec Inc.*, 2005 CanLII 6442 (QC CS). While allowed, all present and future obligations clauses in contracts with unsophisticated borrowers will be construed strictly: *Royal Bank of Canada c. Lavoie*, 2022 QCCS 4876.

57 CCQ arts 2797, 2691.

58 CCQ art. 2689.

59 For movable hypothecs, see Registre des droits personnels et réels mobiliers, *Informations générales pour remplir les formulaires* (June 2022) at 7, available at https://www.rdprm.gouv.qc.ca/fr/Documents/Publications/Information_generale_remplir_formulaires.pdf.

60 *Francoeur c. Hypothèques CIBC inc.*, 2012 QCCS 1639, paras 15–19.

RANKING

General Rule

The CCQ sets out the classic civil law principle that debtors' assets are the "common pledge" of their creditors.[61] Creditors seeking seizure and sale of a debtor's assets are thus presumed to share the proceeds equally, proportionately to their claims.[62] This is subject, however, to the preferential right of hypothecary creditors to be paid first out of the proceeds of enforcement against the hypothecated asset.[63]

Generally, movable hypothecs rank from the time of publication, whether published by registration or physical delivery of the movable,[64] and whether they charge a specific movable or a universality of present and future movables.[65] Of course, a hypothec only charges a future movable when the grantor acquires rights to it[66] but ranking is determined by the anterior time of publication.[67]

The principal exceptions and qualifications are detailed below, while the special ranking rules for hypothecs on investment securities and security entitlements and monetary claims are addressed in a later section.

Hypothecs on Circulating Assets (Inventory and Claims)

The English common law floating charge aims to reconcile the concept of security as a real right with an enterprise grantor's practical need to deal with circulating assets—inventory and receivables and cash proceeds—in the ordinary course of business without having to obtain a release from the creditor on each dealing. How does the CCQ address that challenge?

Hypothecary creditors generally have the right to follow the hypothecated property[68] and exercise their enforcement rights against subsequent acquirers.[69] The CCQ creates an exception aimed at ensuring buyers obtain clear title to hypothecated property sold by an enterprise in the ordinary course of

---

61 CCQ art. 2644.
62 CCQ art. 2646.
63 CCQ art. 2647.
64 CCQ arts 2941(1), 2945.
65 CCQ art. 2950.
66 CCQ art. 2670.
67 CCQ arts 2950, 2941(1).
68 CCQ art. 2660.
69 CCQ art. 2751.

its business while also facilitating automatic roll-over inventory financing.[70] Thus, a hypothec on a universality that includes property destined for sale by the grantor is released on each item on its sale in the ordinary course of the grantor's business.[71] However, the hypothec still subsists and instead charges property that replaces property of the same nature as the property sold.[72]

The hypothec also charges monetary proceeds received from the sale of items alienated by the grantor in the ordinary course of business.[73] Although inspired by the proceeds provisions of the Personal Property Security Acts (PPSAs) in the common law provinces,[74] the CCQ rule is narrower. First, it lacks the equitable rules for tracing funds into a bank account incorporated into the PPSAs. Consequently, monetary proceeds become unidentifiable once deposited into the grantor's general account and mixed with other funds.[75] To address this limitation, the creditor can require proceeds to be deposited into a dedicated account or otherwise closely monitor the grantor's dealings with them. Second, the hypothec only charges monetary proceeds and then only if no other property replaces the property sold.[76] To address this limitation, the hypothec can explicitly charge a universality comprised of all potential categories of present and future proceeds (claims, receivables, trade-ins, etc.).

As for hypothecs on a universality of claims, the CCQ offers an interesting solution to the frequent practical need for grantors to continue collecting their receivables and using the proceeds in the operation of the enterprise. By default, the creditor has the *immediate* right to collect the claims and apply the proceeds to the obligation secured *even if it is not due*.[77] However, the hypothecary agreement may instead authorize grantors to continue collecting their claims.[78] While the effect of authorization is to release the creditor's hypothec, the creditor may withdraw its authorization at any time by notifying the grantor and the debtors on the claims and registering notice of the withdrawal in

---

[70] CCQ art. 2674(1). The wording is obscure, but see, e.g. *Federated Insurance Co. of Canada c. Galp Inc.*, 2004 CanLII 1214 (QC CA), paras 83–85.

[71] *Ibid.*

[72] *Ibid.*

[73] CCQ art. 2674(3).

[74] For a detailed analysis of the PPSA proceeds provisions, see Ronald CC Cuming, Catherine Walsh and Roderick J Wood, *Personal Property Security Law* (3rd edn, Irwin 2022) 613–641.

[75] See, e.g. *Bombardier Capital Ltée c. Caisse populaire St-Charles Garnier*, 2004 CanLII 20018 (QC CS).

[76] CCQ art. 2674(3).

[77] CCQ art. 2743.

[78] CCQ art. 2744.

the movable registry.[79] The creditor's default collection right is not conceived as a hypothecary enforcement right; thus, the authorization may be withdrawn even if the grantor is not in default and the creditor need not give the grantor advance notice of its intention.[80] Amounts collected by the creditor that exceed the obligation owed must of course be remitted to the grantor.[81]

It may happen that a grantor hypothecates its claims to two different creditors, and both have authorized the grantor to continue collecting them. What happens if the lower-ranking creditor withdraws its authorization and registers notice of the withdrawal before the first-ranking creditor does so? The jurisprudence confirms that the lower-ranking creditor can collect *and retain* the proceeds of collection until the prior-ranking creditor completes the formalities for withdrawal of its authorization.[82] But once that occurs, the general order of publication ranking rule applies, and the lower ranking creditor loses its right to direct collection.[83]

Floating Hypothec/*Hypothèque Ouverte*

The CCQ provides for a sub-species of hypothec called a floating hypothec/*hypothèque ouverte* capable of charging the property of a legal or natural person or other entity operating an enterprise.[84] The floating security concept was carried over from the form of corporate trust deed security introduced by special legislation in pre-CCQ law in 1914 and suffers from the same weak ranking.[85] Unlike an ordinary hypothec/*hypothèque ordinaire* on a universality of an enterprise's property, a floating hypothec has effect only if published beforehand[86] and its effects are suspended until the creditor serves the grantor with a notice of default and crystallization.[87] Only at that point

---

[79] CCQ art. 2745.

[80] See, e.g. *Syndic of 9324–3533 Québec inc.*, 2023 QCCS 125, at paras 28–33, citing Louis Payette, *Les sûretés réelles dans le Code civil du Québec* (6th edn, Yvon Blais 2022) at paras 1137 and 1138, 1142 and 1143.

[81] CCQ art. 2747.

[82] *Caisse populaire St-Albert-le-Grand c. Royal Bank of Canada*, 2000 CanLII 11388 (QC CA); *9264-1414 Québec inc. c. 4210310 Canada inc.*, 2015 QCCS 3049.

[83] *Caisse populaire St-Albert-le-Grand*, *ibid* at para 29. This is a change from pre-CCQ law, under which the date of notification also conferred rank.

[84] CCQ art. 2686.

[85] *Supra*, note 12.

[86] CCQ art. 2716(1). If immovables are charged, it has effect only when published by registration in the land register against each immovable.

[87] CCQ art. 2715(1).

does it have the effect of an ordinary hypothec on the charged property.[88] Moreover, it is effective against third persons only on registration of the notice of crystallization,[89] and ranks only from then.[90]

Its weak ranking means that the floating hypothec is simply not used in practice. The floating character of a hypothec must be expressly stipulated in the hypothecary agreement,[91] eliminating any risk that an ordinary hypothec on a universality of inventory or claims might be presumed floating owing to some similarities in its effects.[92]

Seller's Hypothec

The CCQ gives special priority to a movable hypothec granted by a buyer to a seller on the object of a credit sale in their sale agreement. If registered within 15 days, it ranks ahead of a prior registered hypothec on a universality of present and future movables of the same kind.[93] This ensures debtor access to sale credit but requires the prior hypothecary creditor to monitor the registry before making new advances on the security of new assets. Unlike the PPSAs[94] (and UCC Article 9), the CCQ does not give a similar super-priority to secured lenders financing the grantor's acquisition of new assets from third-party sellers.

Ownership as Security (*Sûretés-Propriétés*)

Although the hypothec is the only nominate security device, the CCQ recognizes that certain contracts for the transfer or reservation of ownership of property can continue to be deployed for security purposes (*sûretés-propriétés*):

- a trust established by contract to secure an obligation owed by the settlor to the beneficiary;[95]

---

[88] CCQ art. 2719.
[89] CCQ art. 2716(2).
[90] CCQ art. 2955.
[91] CCQ art. 2715(2).
[92] *Groupe TVA inc. c. 2420-7441 Québec inc.*, 2001 CanLII 24674 (QC CS), para 23.
[93] CCQ art. 2954.
[94] Cuming et al, *supra*, at 488–492.
[95] CCQ art. 1263(1). Unlike the common law trust, the CCQ trust does not rely on divided ownership but results from the transfer of property by the settlor to an autonomous patrimony administered by a trustee and appropriated for a particular purpose: art. 1260.

- a sale of property to secure an obligation owed to the buyer/lender subject to the seller/borrower's right to redeem ownership;[96]
- a term sale subject to a reservation of ownership by the seller to secure payment of the price;[97]
- a finance lease (*crédit-bail*);[98]
- depending on the terms, a long-term (for more than one year) ordinary lease (*louage*).[99]

With limited exceptions,[100] these functionalist alternatives to the hypothec must also be published by registration to take effect against third persons.[101] Registration of a transfer of ownership under a trust or sale with a right of redemption for security purposes does not confer any ranking advantage over a hypothec.[102] However, the situation is different when a seller's reservation of ownership, or a lessor's continued ownership rights, are used to secure the buyer's or lessee's payment obligations. If published in due time, their continued ownership means that their rights will effectively rank ahead of prior published hypothecs granted by the buyer or lessee on a universality of present and future movables of the same kind. Conversely, absence of publication or late publication means that the buyer or lessee implicitly had the power to convey real rights in the sold or leased movables, even though vis-à-vis the seller or lessor, they have not (yet) acquired ownership.[103]

It is common practice to have master sales and lease agreements extending a seller's reservation of ownership or a lessor's continued ownership rights to a universality of movables to be sold or leased from time to time to an enterprise.

---

96 CCQ art. 1756.

97 CCQ art. 1745. Publication of a lease for a term or more than one year is required whether or not it functions in substance to secure payment of the acquisition price of the leased object.

98 CCQ art. 1842.

99 CCQ art. 1851.

100 Sales with a right of redemption, sales subject to a reservation of ownership, and ordinary leases for a term of more than one year require publication only if the movable is used in an enterprise or is a type of movable on which a hypothec without delivery may be granted by a non-enterprise natural person (see above): CCQ arts 1750(2), 1745, 1852.

101 CCQ arts 1263(1), 1750(2), 1745(2), 1847, 1852(2). Note that except for security trusts, the creditor's ownership can be set up against third parties from the date of the transaction if published within seven days: *ibid.*

102 CCQ art. 2941(1).

103 *Maschinenfabrik Rieter, a.g. v. Canadian Fidelity Mills Ltd.*, 2005 QCCA 1033, at para 62.

While publication is still required for third-party effectiveness,[104] a one-time registration in the movable registry is effective for renewable periods of up to 10 years.[105] Registration preserves the seller's or lessor's rights on all future movables of the same kind supplied to the enterprise[106] except as against third persons who acquire movables from the enterprise in the ordinary course of its business.[107] The seller's or lessor's continuing ownership has the effect of giving it super-priority over a prior-published hypothec on a universality of movable property of the enterprise of the same kind.

Unlike the PPSAs (and UCC Article 9), the CCQ does not give a similar super-priority to secured lenders financing the grantor's acquisition of movables from third-party sellers.[108] Nor, unlike these regimes, is a seller who finances the debtor's ongoing acquisition of inventory required to give notice to prior registered creditors for its registration to have super-priority effect.[109] To address the priority risk, the prior hypothecary creditor instead must monitor the registry before advancing new credit against new movables, including new inventory, acquired by the enterprise.

Intercreditor Agreements

The holder of a prior ranking conventional hypothec can cede its ranking to another creditor.[110] While the wording of the CCQ provision suggests that a cession of priority between hypothecary creditors must be published, jurisprudence confirms that a subordination is effective between the parties without publication.[111]

---

104 For judicial confirmation, see *Mière Enterprises Inc. (Syndic de)*, 2012 QCCA.

105 CCQ art. 2961.1.

106 *Ibid.* It is questionable whether their rights extend to the monetary proceeds: *GE Financement commercial aux détaillants Canada c. Banque Nationale du Canada*, 2009 QCCS 5843 at paras 104–107. It was unnecessary to decide the issue on the facts and the Court of Appeal declined to do so on the appeal: 2011 QCCA 961.

107 *Ibid.*

108 *Cuming et al, supra,* at 490–493.

109 *Ibid*, at 496–499.

110 CCQ art. 2956.

111 See, e.g. *Lévesque c. 9161-0832 Québec inc.*, 2009 QCCS 5609 at para 165.

Legal Hypothecs and Prior Claims

The CCQ recognizes legal hypothecs (hypothecs established by law) to secure the unpaid claims of five categories of creditors:

1. Suppliers of services or materials used to construct or renovate immovable property.
2. Condominium syndicates for co-owners' contributions to common expenses.
3. The Québec government and legal persons established in the public interest for claims under fiscal laws and for other claims provided for in specific statutes.
4. Judgment creditors.[112]

Only the legal hypothecs of the Québec government and public bodies and of judgment creditors can charge the debtor's movable property, taking effect on registration in the movable registry.[113] Neither benefits from any special ranking rule and so ranks like conventional hypothecs from the time of registration.[114]

In contrast, prior claims (*priorités*) entitle the holder to preferential satisfaction from the proceeds of enforcement against a debtor's property over other creditors, *including even hypothecary creditors*,[115] without publication[116] or regard to date.[117]

The CCQ recognises five categories of prior claimants:[118]

1. Enforcing creditors for legal costs and expenses incurred in the common interest—executable against both movable and immovable property.[119]

---

[112] CCQ art. 2724.

[113] CCQ arts 2725, 2730. The registered notice must be served on the debtor and describe the charged property. *Ibid.* In *Plasticon Canada Inc.* v. *Corbec Inc.* 2019 QCCS 2110, the court concluded that notice of a legal hypothec resulting from a judgment can describe the property as a universality of all present and future movables.

[114] CCQ, art. 2945(1).

[115] CCQ art. 2650.

[116] CCQ art. 2655.

[117] CCQ art. 2657.

[118] CCQ art. 2651.

[119] CCQ art. 2652.

2. Unpaid vendors for the price of a movable sold to a non-enterprise natural person.[120]
3. Persons with the right to retain movable property until paid for services or materials provided in relation to the property.[121]
4. The Québec government for amounts due under fiscal laws, executable against movable property only.[122]
5. Municipalities and school boards for property taxes on immovables and other taxes on immovables and movables in respect of which the taxes are due.

Although they rank ahead of hypothecs,[123] prior claims differ from hypothecs in important respects. First, the creditor generally does not benefit from any special enforcement rights, but must employ ordinary execution procedures after obtaining a judgment against the debtor or claim a preference to payment from the proceeds of enforcement by a hypothecary or other creditor.[124] Second, except for the tax claims of municipalities and school boards,[125] a prior claim is not a real right and so the creditor cannot follow the debtor's property into the hands of subsequent acquirers.[126]

Effects of Federal Bankruptcy and Insolvency Law on Ranking

The principal federal insolvency statutes are the Bankruptcy and Insolvency Act (BIA)[127] and the Companies' Creditors Arrangement Act (CCAA).[128]

---

[120] CCQ art. 1741.

[121] Of the dozen or so rights of retention recognized by the CCQ, the most relevant here are those in favour of: (1) warehouse keepers (art. 2283); (2) carriers (art. 2058); (3) charterers (art. 2003); (4) persons in possession of property with the owner's consent if the claim relates to the property (art. 1592); (5) persons whose labour or materials have contributed to the production of new assets (art. 974).

[122] CCQ art. 2653. Registration by the Québec government of a legal hypothec does not prevent it from enforcing its prior claim: art. 2725(3).

[123] CCQ art. 2650. Prior claims rank between themselves according to the order listed in the text: arts 2651, 2567(1). If multiple prior claims of the same rank attach to the same property, the creditors share the proceeds proportionately: art. 2657(2).

[124] CCQ art. 2656. For details and qualifications, see Code of Civil Procedure, CQLR c C-25.01, arts 517, 700, 766, 776.

[125] CCQ art. 2654(1).

[126] CCQ art. 2655.

[127] RSC 1985, c B-3.

[128] RSC 1985, c C-36.

While both apply to liquidation and reorganization proceedings,[129] the CCAA does not apply to individuals and is restricted to corporate debtors owing at least $5M to creditors.

The BIA generally preserves the priority of pre-existing security rights over unsecured creditor claims in liquidation proceedings.[130] However, certain statutorily prescribed super-priority rights rank ahead of the claims of secured creditors in bankruptcy or receivership proceedings. The main ones are listed below in the order in which they rank against each other.

1. Unpaid claims of suppliers of goods: the BIA gives unpaid suppliers a super-priority right to repossess goods from a buyer who becomes bankrupt or is placed in receivership within 30 days after delivery.[131] The aim is to discourage debtors on the verge of insolvency from enlarging their inventory asset base to benefit secured creditors (referred to as "juicing the trades").[132] However, the rigid conditions imposed on the exercise of this right render it largely ineffective in practice.
2. Unpaid claims of suppliers of certain perishable products: with the same policy aim, the BIA creates a deemed super-priority charge on the debtor's inventory to secure the unpaid claims of farmers, fishers, and aquaculturists for perishable products supplied within 15 days preceding bankruptcy or receivership.[133] The stringent conditions that must be met to qualify also render this protection largely ineffective in practice.
3. Unremitted source deductions: ranking next in super-priority are governmental claims for unremitted "source deductions"—amounts required to be deducted by employers from employees' wages and remitted to the relevant level of government to pay their income tax obligations, employment

[129] The CCAA was originally intended to be solely a reorganization vehicle. However, "liquidating CCAAs" are increasingly common, as now reflected in CCAA s 36. On this trend, see *9354-9186 Québec inc. v. Callidus Capital Corp.*, 2020 SCC 10, paras 40–44.

[130] BIA s 136(1). Despite the advent of "liquidating CCAAs" (*ibid*), there is still no scheme of distribution in the CCAA. In principle, "absent a contradiction between the CCAA and the BIA, the BIA scheme of distribution should apply in a liquidating CCAA": *Arrangement relatif à Bloom Lake*, 2017 QCCS 4057, para 208.

[131] BIA s 81.1.

[132] Tamara Buckwold and Roderick J Wood, "Priorities" in Stephanie Ben-Ishai and Anthony Duggan (eds), *Canadian Bankruptcy and Insolvency Law: Bill C-55, Statute c. 47 and Beyond* (LexisNexis Canada Inc 2007) 121.

[133] BIA s 81.2.

insurance premiums and governmental pension plan contributions.[134] The BIA expressly preserves the super-priority deemed trusts on the debtor's assets created by federal and provincial legislation to secure these claims.[135]

4. Unpaid employee wage claims: next in ranking is the super-priority deemed charge on a debtor's current assets (essentially inventory and receivables) created by the BIA to secure employee claims for unpaid wages earned within six months preceding the debtor's bankruptcy or receivership (to a maximum of C$2,000 per employee) and salespersons' claims for reimbursement of expenses in the same period (to a maximum of C$1000).[136] Employees enjoy more immediate and more generous protection under the *Wage Earner Protection Program Act*[137] (WEPA) under which the federal government compensates employees directly for amounts up to seven times the maximum weekly insurable earnings under the *Employment Insurance Act* (C$8,507.66 for 2024). The government is then subrogated to the rights of the unpaid employee and has a priority claim against the current assets of the debtor company but only up to the BIA maximum.
5. Unpaid pension contributions: the BIA establishes a deemed charge on the assets of a bankrupt employer or an employer in receivership to secure unremitted pension contributions deducted from employees' wages and unpaid employer contributions to a prescribed pension plan.[138] The 2023 *Pension Protection Act*[139] extends super priority treatment to all employer obligations under defined pension plans, including unpaid special payments and amounts to liquidate an unfunded liability or solvency deficiency. These protections will take effect only in April 2027, allowing employers and their financiers time to assess the impact on the availability and cost of credit, leading to concerns that the Act will accelerate the shift to defined-contribution plans.

In reorganization proceedings under the BIA and CCA, equivalent super-priority status for unremitted source deductions,[140] unpaid wages,[141] and unpaid

134 BIA s 86(3).

135 *Ibid.* For the Québec deemed trust provisions, see Tax Administration Act, CQLR c A-6.002, s 20; Supplemental Pension Plans Act, CQLR c R-15.1, art. 49.

136 BIA ss 81.3, 81.4.

137 SC 2005, c 47.

138 BIA ss 81.5, 81.6.

139 S.C. 2023, c. 6.

140 BIA ss 60(1.1)–(1.2); CCAA, ss 6(3)–(4).

141 BIA, s 60(1.3); CCAA, s 6(5).

pension plan contributions[142] is achieved by provisions that prevent court approval of a BIA proposal or CCAA arrangement or liquidating sale unless it is satisfied that these claims will be paid. Courts can also order super-priority charges on the debtor's assets in favour of creditors whose involvement is considered necessary to achieving a successful restructuring or an orderly liquidation. These so-called priming charges rank ahead of the claims of pre-filing secured creditors and will survive a bankruptcy if the reorganisation fails. Typical examples include a debtor-in-possession (DIP) charge in favour of creditors who finance the continued operation of the debtor company while it attempts to return to solvency or liquidate in an orderly fashion[143] and an administration charge to secure payment of the fees and costs of the CCAA monitor or BIA trustee and the legal, financial and other experts engaged by the debtor to assist it in the proceeding.[144]

On the other hand, the BIA provides that bankruptcy proceedings take precedence over provincial judgment enforcement measures.[145] This has been interpreted to render the legal hypothecs of judgment creditors ineffective once the debtor's property vests in the debtor's trustee on behalf of the insolvency estate.[146] In practice, the beneficiary of this demotion is not the general body of creditors but the holder of a conventional hypothec that would have ranked behind the legal hypothec but for the debtor's bankruptcy. Recognizing that the legal hypothec's ineffectiveness mainly benefits conventional hypothecary creditors, the Québec Court of Appeal has insisted on a strict interpretation of the BIA provision.[147]

---

142 BIA, s 60(1.5); CCAA, s 6(6).

143 CCAA s 11.2; BIA s 50.6.

144 CCAA s 11.52; BIA s 64.2. On the broad discretion of courts in CCAA proceedings, and increasingly in BIA proceedings, to order priming charges in favour of other key creditors and to otherwise disrupt ranking, see: Miranda Spence, Karen Kimel and Anastasia Jones, More Flexible Than You Think: An Exploration of Creative Uses of the BIA Proposal Regime for Corporate Restructuring, 2022 20 *Annual Review of Insolvency Law*, 2022 CanLIIDocs 4305 <https://canlii.ca/t/7n173>; Eamonn Watson, Gray Monczka and Jordan Schultz, Anything You Can Do, I Can Do Better: Does the CCAA Provide Broader Discretionary Relief than the BIA?, 2022 20 *Annual Review of Insolvency Law*, 2022 CanLIIDocs 4309 https://canlii.ca/t/7n177>.

145 BIA, s 70(1).

146 *Larue v. Royal Bank of Canada*, 1926 CanLII 49 (SCC), aff'd *Quebec (Attorney General) v. Larue*, 1928 CanLII 514 (UK JCPC) *Guévremont c. Radmore*, (1974) CA 194.

147 In *3095-7252 Quebec inc. c. Mickeck Jacyno*, 2010 QCCA 940, the Court, reversing a prior jurisprudential trend it had set itself, ruled that to benefit from the termination of the legal hypothecs of judgment creditors under the BIA, the

Conventional secured creditors also benefit from the general demotion of federal and provincial governmental claims to unsecured status in BIA and CCAA proceedings.[148] The most important exception is governmental claims for unremitted "source deductions" noted above.[149] Other governmental security rights and preferences are preserved only if they are of a kind that can be obtained by creditors generally or are registered in a general security rights registry.[150] While the legal hypothecs of Québec governmental creditors fall within the latter exception, they are only effective under the BIA to secure amounts owed at the time of registration, necessitating successive registrations as new arrears arise.[151]

ENFORCEMENT

Enforcement Rights of Hypothecary Creditors Under the CCQ

The CCQ stipulates that hypothecary creditors may exercise *only* the following real rights on the debtor's default: take possession of the charged property to administer it, take it in payment, sell it under court supervision or sell it themselves.[152] The creditor must provide advance notice to the debtor and publish it in the appropriate registry.[153] Enforcement cannot begin until the notice period expires: 20 days for movables, 60 days for immovables (10 days if the creditor plans to take possession) and 30 days for movables charged by a hypothec accessory to a consumer contract.[154] The purpose of requiring advance notice is to give the debtor and interested third persons enough time to terminate enforcement by paying what is owed and rectifying any other defaults.[155] While advance notice is mandatory, the creditor can seek a court

holder of a conventional hypothec must not have exercised its right under the CCQ to take ownership of the property in satisfaction of the secured claim before the grantor's bankruptcy.

[148] BIA s 86(1); CCAA s 38(1).

[149] BIA s 86(3), CCAA s 38(3). For the Québec deemed trust provisions, see Tax Administration Act, CQLR c A-6.002, s 20; Supplemental Pension Plans Act, CQLR c R-15.1, art. 49.

[150] BIA s 86(2), CCAA s 38(2).

[151] BIA s 87, CCAA s 39.

[152] CCQ art. 2748. As noted earlier, a creditor's right to collect hypothecated claims directly is not conceived by the CCQ as a hypothecary enforcement right.

[153] CCQ art. 2757. The registrar is required to notify third persons who have registered a right in the encumbered assets covered by the notice: CCQ art. 3017.

[154] CCQ art. 2758.

[155] CCQ art. 2761(1).

order for immediate surrender if recovery of the claim is otherwise jeopardized or the property is at risk of rapid deterioration.[156] In the latter scenario, the creditor can enforce immediately.

Extension of the Hypothecary Enforcement Regime to *Sûretés-Propriétés*[157]

While formally distinguishing hypothecs from ownership-based security, creditors who deploy a trust or a sale subject to a right of redemption to secure an obligation must adhere to the rules governing the enforcement of hypothecs on the debtor's default.[158] The same applies to sellers who reserve ownership under a term sale to secure payment of the purchase price,[159] although stricter rules of consumer protection legislation apply if the buyer is a consumer.[160] Freedom of contract generally prevails on the default of a lessee, even if in economic substance the lease performs a purchase money financing function. However, finance leases can be entered into only for enterprise purposes[161] and the lessor's enforcement rights under a long-term lease with a consumer lessee are strictly regulated by consumer protection legislation.[162]

Appointment of a Receiver Under the BIA

The focus of this chapter is on conventional hypothecs on a universality comprised of the present and future movables of an enterprise. In this scenario, selling the assets on a going concern basis will often yield higher value than selling them piecemeal. In Canada's common law jurisdictions, secured creditors can appoint a receiver, by agreement or court application, to manage the debtor's business before selling it as a going concern or conducting a liquidation sale.[163] Receivership is a common law institution and the CCQ hypothecary enforcement regime lacks an equivalent.[164] However, hypothecary creditors

---

156 CCQ art. 2767.

157 On these functional alternatives to hypothecs, see above.

158 CCQ arts 1263(2), 1750(2).

159 CCQ art. 1749(1).

160 Consumer Protection Act, CQLR c P-40.1, arts 132–149.

161 CCQ art. 1842(3).

162 Consumer Protection Act, CQLR c P-40.1, arts 150.1–150.32.

163 Cuming *et al*, *supra*, at 727–733.

164 The CCQ hypothecary recourses include the creditor's right to appoint an administrator of the property of another: arts 2773–2777. However, the administration is temporary, and the administrator's powers do not allow for the sale of the hypothecated property.

can seek a court-appointed receivership under the BIA[165] if the debtor is insolvent, the security interest covers substantially all the assets used by the debtor in relation to a business and the creditor gives 10 days' advance notice.[166] The court may order additional actions, typically authorizing the receiver to solicit bids and then seek court approval of a going-concern or liquidation sale to the successful bidder free of any claims.

In the absence of a comparable CCQ recourse, a BIA receivership is commonly used by hypothecary creditors if the BIA criteria are met. The 2015 Supreme Court of Canada decision in *Saskatchewan (Attorney General) v. Lemare Lake Logging Ltd.*[167] raised doubts about the availability of this alternative. In *Lemare*, the Court had to determine whether a secured creditor seeking to enforce a mortgage on Saskatchewan farmland via a BIA receivership had to adhere only to the BIA's 10-day advance notice period or also respect the 150-day advance notice requirement of the Saskatchewan *Farm Security Act* (SFSA). In a six-to-three ruling, the majority held that the provincial SFSA did not "frustrate" the "purpose" of the BIA receivership mechanism, which it considered to be to facilitate the appointment of a "national" receiver where the debtor had assets in multiple provinces. Therefore, as a constitutional matter, the BIA did not exclude the concurrent application of the longer Saskatchewan notice period, and the mortgagee had to wait for that period to elapse before seeking a BIA receivership order.

After *Lemare*, some Québec judges concluded that hypothecary creditors were restricted to their CCQ enforcement recourses unless the appointment of a "national" receiver under the BIA was necessary. The controversy was resolved by the Québec Court of Appeal in 2020 in *Séquestre de Media Corporation*.[168] The Court unanimously decided that federal constitutional authority over bankruptcy and insolvency law included providing additional enforcement options to secured creditors against insolvent debtors[169] and that appointing a receiver under the BIA was not limited to cases where the debtor holds property in more than one province. On the contrary, in *Lemare* the debtor only owned assets in Saskatchewan, as is typical in most BIA receivership applications.[170] Rather, the key lesson from *Lemare* was that, along with satisfying the BIA prerequisites, hypothecary creditors had to adhere to the

---

165 RSC 1985, c B-3.

166 BIA ss 243–244.

167 2015 SCC 53.

168 2020 QCCA 943, leave to appeal to Supreme Court of Canada dismissed, 2021 CanLII 24824 (CSC).

169 *Ibid*, paras 71–72.

170 *Ibid*, paras 75–78.

CCQ substantive and procedural prerequisites to enforcement,[171] including waiting for the relevant CCQ advance notice period to expire except where the CCQ itself permitted a court order for immediate enforcement.[172]

In reaching its decision, the Court recognized that judicial discretion to appoint a receiver under the BIA to facilitate a sale of the debtor's business as a going concern had become an essential aspect of Canadian and Québec insolvency practice.[173] However, it also emphasized that the receivership recourse was a significant departure from the Québec civil law tradition, and that the court's exercise of discretion should consider the particularities of Québec civil law rather than relying solely on criteria developed by courts in the common law provinces.[174] Thus, the court should ensure that the creditor acts in good faith as required by both the BIA and CCQ and more generally that the receiver's powers align with the policy objectives of federal bankruptcy and insolvency legislation.[175]

Effect of Federal Insolvency Law on Enforcement of Security

Subject to certain provisos, secured creditors may proceed to enforce their security despite the grantor's bankruptcy.[176] The situation is different in reorganization proceedings to allow time to explore the possibility of a successful reorganization. Thus, a non-consumer debtor's filing of a notice of intention to propose a reorganization under the BIA triggers an automatic stay of enforcement by both secured and unsecured creditors.[177] While a stay is not automatic in CCAA reorganization proceedings, the court will usually exercise its discretion to order a similarly comprehensive stay. Under both Acts, the stay is subject to exceptions for security on aircraft objects and financial collateral.[178]

---

171 *Ibid*, paras 87–88.

172 *Ibid*, para 97. As for the advance notice periods, see above.

173 *Ibid*, paras 73–75.

174 *Ibid*, paras 90–92.

175 *Ibid*, paras 93–96, 98.

176 This follows from the combined effect of BIA ss 136, 70(1) and 71.

177 BIA ss 69(1), 69.4.

178 If the charged asset is an aircraft object covered by the Cape Town Convention/Aircraft Protocol, the stay is limited to 60 days: BIA ss 2, 69(2)(d), CCAA ss 2, 11.07. The stay also does not affect enforcement by secured creditors on eligible financial collateral (e.g. securities, securities entitlements, futures contracts, derivatives): BIA ss 2, 84.2(8), CCAA ss 2, 34(8).

HYPOTHECS ON INVESTMENT SECURITIES AND MONETARY CLAIMS

Investment Securities

In 2009, the Québec legislator adopted legislation (STA)[179] on the private law aspects of the acquisition and transfer of investment securities accompanied by complementary reforms to the CCQ hypothecary regime.[180] Although the rules reflect the civilian drafting style and concepts, the reform was part of a pan-Canadian initiative aimed at aligning the law in all provinces and territories[181] with UCC Articles 8 and 9 in the US.[182]

The reform addressed two key developments: the shift from paper certificates to uncertificated securities represented by digital entries to evidence an investor's rights against an issuer and the emergence of an intermediated system for publicly issued securities in which the ultimate investor no longer has a direct relationship with the issuer.[183] In the intermediated system (as it operates in Canada and the US), a top-tier intermediary—usually a clearing corporation like the Canadian Depository for Securities (CDS) or the US Depository Trust Company (DTC)—is registered as the holder in the issuer's records. Trading then occurs through a chain of intermediaries. The top-tier intermediary maintains accounts for participants—banks, brokers and trust companies—to which securities are credited. These participants then hold the securities credited to their accounts for their own customers, forming a second tier, and so on down the chain until one reaches the securities account of the ultimate investor.

---

179 An act respecting the transfer of securities and the establishment of security entitlements, RSQ c T-11.002 (STA).

180 CCQ arts 2701.1, 2714.1–2714.7. New conflict of laws rules for this type of collateral were added to the CCQ at the same time: arts 3108.1– 3108.8.

181 STA, s 1: "The purpose of this Act is to establish a legal framework for certain private law aspects of the transfer of securities and the establishment of security entitlements to financial assets, as part of an effort by the Canadian provinces and territories to harmonize their laws on the matter".

182 See Eric T Spink, "The Securities Transfer Act—Fitting New Concepts in Canadian Law" (2007) 45 Can Bus LJ 167; James S Rogers, "The Revision of Canadian Law on Securities Holding through Intermediaries: Who, What, When, Where, How and Why" (2007) 45 Can Bus LJ 49.

183 The reform was led by the Canadian Securities Administrators, who considered that the interconnectedness of the US and Canadian investment markets required alignment between Canadian and US law even for private law transactions: Spink and Rogers, *ibid.*

The first development is reflected in the recognition that traditional directly held securities/*valeurs mobilières* may be certificated or uncertificated. The second development is reflected in the characterization of an account holder's right in the intermediated system as a new type of movable property—security entitlements/*titres intermédiés*—distinct from the securities to which the entry in the securities account relates.[184]

The rules are intimidatingly complex. Even a summary is beyond the scope of this chapter. The important point is that they significantly diverge from the general CCQ rules for movable hypothecs. At the core of this divergence is the concept of control. A movable hypothec with delivery on securities and security entitlements can be constituted and set up against third parties by the creditor obtaining control of them.[185]

For certificated securities, control entails physically delivering the certificate to the creditor.[186] This method aligns with the general rule requiring *physical* delivery to the creditor for a hypothec with delivery to be constituted and set up against third parties.[187] However, for uncertificated securities, control can be obtained by the creditor becoming the registered holder on the issuer's register or concluding a so-called control agreement under which the issuer agrees to comply with the creditor's orders without needing further consent from the grantor.[188] For security entitlements, the creditor can obtain control either by entering into a control agreement with the grantor's intermediary or by itself becoming the entitlement holder.[189] The latter method necessitates debiting the securities to which the security entitlement relates from the grantor's securities account and crediting them to the securities account of the creditor or its representative.[190]

Obtaining control via a control agreement clearly deviates from the usual requirement for physical delivery for a movable hypothec with delivery to be

---

184 For an analysis of the new framework for intermediated securities, albeit referencing Ontario sources, see Robert M Scavone, "Stronger than Fictions: Canada Rethinks the Law of Securities Transfers in the Indirect Holding System" (2007) 45 Can Bus LJ 67.

185 CCQ art. 2714.1.

186 For certificated securities in bearer form, physical delivery of the certificate to the creditor gives it control; if the certificate is in registered form, the creditor obtains control if the certificate is delivered to the creditor, *and* the certificate is *either* endorsed to the creditor or in blank, *or* the security is registered in the name of the creditor on the issuer's securities register: STA arts 55, 50.

187 CCQ arts 2702, 2703.

188 STA arts 56. 51.

189 STA art. 113.

190 STA art. 103.

set up against third persons. The creditor's control is not publicized[191] nor need it be exclusive: the creditor has control even if the grantor retains the right under the control agreement to deal with and dispose of its uncertificated securities or securities entitlements.[192] In this latter respect, the hypothec might be considered to have floating characteristics since it will only attach to whatever assets remain on default and enforcement.

The hypothec of a creditor who obtains control of securities or security entitlements ranks ahead of any other hypothec – prior or subsequent – published by other means.[193] Consequently, it can be argued that there is no value in requiring formal publicity since prior creditors and other interested third parties should be taken to know that their rights will rank behind a hypothecary creditor (or outright transferee) who later obtains control.

On the other hand, the availability of alternative control methods means multiple persons can have control of the same securities or security entitlements, complicating the ranking assessment.[194] Moreover, the ranking rules heavily favour financial intermediaries and their hypothecary creditors. If a hypothec on security entitlements is granted in favour of the grantor's own intermediary, the intermediary automatically has control and its hypothec ranks ahead of all other hypothecs.[195] More troubling, if an intermediary—through negligence or fraud—does not hold enough financial assets in its securities account to satisfy the claims of both its account holders and its hypothecary creditor, its creditor has priority if it obtains control.[196]

Monetary Claims

The CCQ was amended effective January 2016 to introduce a special regime for hypothecs with delivery on "monetary claims". A monetary claim refers to any claim requiring the debtor on the claim to "reimburse, return or restore an amount of money or make any other payment in respect of an amount

[191] The issuer or intermediary is not required to disclose the existence of the control agreement to third persons unless the grantor consents: STA arts 57, 114.

[192] STA arts 56, 113.

[193] CCQ art. 2714.2(1). The creditor is also protected from other adverse claims except in very limited circumstances: STA, arts 53, 111, 112.

[194] CCQ art. 2714.2(2)–(3). Note that under art. 2714.3, a movable hypothec with delivery on security entitlements in favour of the grantor's securities intermediary ranks ahead of any other hypothec.

[195] CCQ art. 2714.3.

[196] STA, art. 129. If the intermediary is a clearing agency, its hypothecary creditor has priority without needing to obtain control: art. 130.

of money".[197] The new regime was largely inspired by the rules governing deposit accounts in UCC Article 9 in the US.[198] Monetary claims thus include grantors' claims to the credit balance of their accounts with financial institutions.[199] However, the CCQ concept is broader, also including, for example, claims to the return of money transferred to a landlord or utility company to secure the grantor's payment obligations to it.[200]

Under the new regime, the requirement for the property to be delivered to the creditor for a movable hypothec with delivery on a monetary claim to be constituted and set up against third persons may be met by the creditor obtaining control of the claim,[201] whether the claim is against the creditor or against a third person.[202]

A detailed exposition of the methods of obtaining control and the complex ranking rules is beyond the scope of this chapter. It is sufficient here to emphasize two points. First, the creditor has control even if the grantor retains the right to give instructions regarding the hypothecated claim to the debtor on the claim until default (for example, to the bank with whom the grantor holds its bank account).[203] In this respect, the hypothec might be considered to have floating characteristics. Second, the rules are highly favourable where a monetary claim that the grantor has against the creditor secures an obligation the grantor owes to the creditor. In this scenario, the creditor acquires control simply by obtaining the grantor's consent that the monetary claim secures payment of the grantor's obligation to it.[204] Consent need not even be given in writing (although invariably it will be in practice). Thus, financial institutions that loan money to their customers can obtain control of their customers' claims to the credit balance of their deposit accounts simply by obtaining their consent that their claims secure the loan. Moreover, the institution's hypothec ranks ahead of all other hypothecs, including those previously published by registration[205] or held by creditors who previously obtained control by entering into a control agreement with the institution.[206] The only exception is where

---

[197] CCQ art. 2713.1(2).

[198] UCC § 9-104, § 9-203, § 9-327.

[199] CCQ art. 2713.5.

[200] Michel Deschamps, "Les sûretés sur dépôts bancaires et autres créances pécuniaires" (2016) R du B 433.

[201] CCQ art. 2713.1 (2).

[202] CCQ art. 2713.2.

[203] CCQ art. 2713.7.

[204] CCQ art. 2713.3.

[205] CCQ art. 2713.8(1).

[206] CCQ, art. 2713.8(3).

the other creditor obtained control by becoming the account holder,[207] but this is a mode of control to which the institution needs to consent as a practical matter.

SUMMARY AND CONCLUSIONS

Summary

The CCQ aimed to rationalize and modernize the law of security and specifically to facilitate access to credit by enterprises on the security of their present and future movables and claims. It has largely succeeded in that ambition.

Creation and publicity modalities are simplified and unified. Hypothecs can secure any obligation, present or future, determinate or indeterminate. Although the traditional pledge survives (hypothec with delivery), a non-possessory hypothec (hypothec without delivery) is created simply by the written agreement of the parties. Any legal or natural person or entity operating an enterprise can grant a hypothec on a universality of present and future corporeal and incorporeal property. The hypothecary agreement need only indicate the nature of the universality without further specificity and gives the creditor rights in future movables, once acquired, as if owned by the grantor from the outset. While publicity is required for third-party effect, registration substitutes for possession. The movable registry is centralized, digitalized, publicly accessible online and based on notice-filing, minimizing transaction costs for both creditors and third-party searchers.

The CCQ aimed to balance easy access to hypothecary credit for enterprises on the security of their present and future movables with strict limitations on the grant of non-possessory movable security by consumer debtors. In the face of market demand, that policy has been relaxed over time. Consumers can now grant a hypothec on a universality of present and future securities or security entitlements and monetary claims including the credit balances of bank accounts. And while initially they could only grant a hypothec without delivery on a limited range of their current movables, this limitation too has been relaxed to the point that the exceptions (almost) swallow the rule. The CCQ also sought to address the potential negative impact of overcollateralization on a grantor's access to new hypothecary credit from other sources. While that policy aim is a sympathetic one, the solution in practice often fails to achieve its objective.

Ranking in general is determined by the time of publication—whether by possession or registration—and whether the hypothec charges a specific

[207] CCQ art. 2713.8(3).

movable or a universality of present and future movables. The fixed/floating distinction is rejected. This might not be obvious to the uninformed reader considering the atavistic retention of a version of the form of floating security recognized by pre-CCQ law. However, the floating hypothec is not used in practice since an ordinary hypothec on a universality of present and future movables benefits from the general ranking rule. That said, a hypothec on circulating inventory is automatically released on the sale of each specific item of inventory in the ordinary course of the enterprise's business while attaching to new replacement inventory. The creditor may likewise authorize the enterprise to directly collect hypothecated receivables while preserving the right to withdraw that authorization at any time and claim the benefit of the general ranking rule. In these respects, the fixed movable hypothec on a universality can be said to have floating characteristics. Otherwise, as between competing hypothecary creditors, the general ranking rule is subject only to the super priority given to a hypothec granted by a buyer to a seller in their sale agreement to secure payment of the purchase price.

However, the CCQ hypothecary concept is formal, not functional, meaning that contracts for the transfer or reservation of ownership can still be deployed for security purposes. These functional alternatives to the hypothec are limited to five prototypes and most must be registered to have third-party effect. They disrupt the general ranking rule in the case of a reservation of ownership by sellers in a term credit sale or the continuing ownership rights of lessors in finance and long-term leases. Conceptually, a prior-published hypothec on future assets of the same kind cannot attach until the buyer or lessee acquires ownership. Even more than the seller's hypothec, the resultant super priority facilitates access to new purchase money credit from sellers and lessors since ownership can secure an enterprise's acquisition of present and future inventory under a master agreement. On the other hand, it also means that holders of prior-published hypothecs on assets of the same kind must monitor the registry before advancing credit against new assets acquired by the grantor, including incoming inventory.

Allowing enterprises to grant fixed security on a universality of their present and future movables means that if the enterprise becomes insolvent, there are likely to be few unencumbered assets left to pay their claims. Should insolvency law at least afford preferential treatment to involuntary creditors or creditors who cannot adjust to the insolvency risk by negotiating a security interest or a higher interest rate?

In Canada, this is a matter ultimately determined by federal bankruptcy and insolvency law, which provides very limited protection. The legal hypothecs of judgment creditors are rendered ineffective in bankruptcy proceedings, and most governmental claims are reduced to unsecured status in insolvency proceedings generally. However, rather than increasing the assets available for distribution to ordinary creditors, in practice, the usual beneficiaries of these priority inversions are conventional secured creditors.

Federal law does create super-priority rights in favour of certain specified creditors that rank ahead of the claims of secured creditors. However, while these include unpaid suppliers of goods to the debtor on the eve of bankruptcy or receivership, they are rarely able to satisfy the rigid conditions necessary to qualify to benefit in practice. Employees also benefit from super-priority for unpaid wages and unremitted employer pension plan contributions in both liquidation and reorganization proceedings. However, the wage protection is too modest to provide much practical benefit. And while the federal government has established a more generous statutory wage protection plan, the additional coverage is paid out of general revenue, so secured creditors are not further affected.

The CCQ establishes a unified enforcement regime for hypothecs on both movable and immovable property and further advances functional equivalence by mandating the application of the same rules to creditors, excepting lessors, secured by a transfer or reservation of ownership. The enforcement rights of secured creditors under the CCQ are generally not affected by the commencement of liquidation proceedings under federal bankruptcy and insolvency law but are typically subject to an initial stay on the institution of reorganization proceedings to allow time to explore the feasibility of a successful reorganization.

The CCQ failed to address the practical need for an enforcement recourse that would allow a creditor with a hypothec on substantially all the movable assets of an enterprise to facilitate its sale as a going concern. In practice, creditors have relied on the receivership recourse created by federal bankruptcy law to fill the gap. However, the courts have ruled that the CCQ advance notice and other requirements for a judicial sale of hypothecated assets concurrently apply. Despite receivership not having played much of a role in the Québec civil law tradition, a more efficient made-in-Québec dedicated recourse would have been preferable.

Québec's reform of the law of movable security was undoubtedly influenced by the practical demand for its secured credit market to give Québec enterprises access to credit opportunities analogous to those available under the UCC Article 9-influenced PPSAs in the rest of Canada. That influence has continued, as evidenced by the special CCQ regime for hypothecs on securities and security entitlements subsequently adopted as part of a pan-Canadian initiative aimed at harmonizing the law in all provinces and territories with UCC Articles 8 and 9 in the US. While the new regime clearly deviates from the general CCQ rules, the same is true for the PPSA jurisdictions and reflects the rapid evolution of international commercial transactions and financial markets, and the demand to prioritize easy access to credit for financial intermediaries. Indeed, Québec has most recently gone even further than the PPSA jurisdictions in introducing a similar special regime for hypothecs on monetary claims. In great part inspired by the UCC Article 9 rules for security interests on bank deposits, this new regime is highly favourable to financial institutions taking security on their customers' credit balances. Importantly, the grant of a hypothec under both regimes is effective even if the grantor retains the right to deal with its security entitlements or the credit balance in its bank account until default and enforcement. In this respect, the hypothec might be considered to have floating characteristics.

Concluding Observations

Overall, the Québec reform experience demonstrates that the practical demand for a form of fixed non-possessory security over an enterprise's present and future circulating assets is achievable within a private law framework that remains faithful to the civil law tradition.

Is the Québec experience transplantable to other civil law and mixed jurisdictions? Only arguably yes, and subject to qualifications.

First, the willingness of the Québec legislator to embrace fundamental change was heavily influenced by the close trade and economic relations between Québec and the rest of Canada and the US. This nudged them to embrace reforms that would give Québec enterprises competitive access to secured credit. Importantly, it also meant that the Québec legal and business communities were already sufficiently familiar with the liberal movable security statutory regimes in these common law jurisdictions to appreciate how they could be adapted to the Québec civil law tradition.

Second, path dependence means that even the most ambitious legal reform will end up preserving some arguably atavistic pre-reform concepts and practices. How this plays out will differ for each jurisdiction, depending on its own pre-reform history and the timing of reform.

Third, the ranking and enforcement of security rights, especially security on enterprise assets, are increasingly determined by insolvency law, which is undergoing its own rapid evolution. In Canada, for better or worse, the allocation of constitutional authority over insolvency law to the federal Parliament means it increasingly has the final say on how to address the policy concerns for ordinary creditors raised by allowing fixed security over substantially all the assets of an enterprise.

10. Drifting in the currents: floating charges under Romanian law

Radu Rizoiu

This chapter will focus on the specific challenges the floating charge has encountered under Romanian law. Since its formal introduction in 1999, this institution was seen with reluctance by the local players, being pushed mostly by international financing practices. We will delve into the history of the concept and its tumultuous history in the transition period Romanian law underwent from a centralized economy to a market-based one. As a result of these challenges, Romanian law was forced to change at an accelerated pace, moving from a nineteenth-century static structure directly into twenty-first-century dynamic security techniques. A new system was put in place at the turn of the century which created some adaptation issues to the local practices. However, the main traits of a modern floating charge device were regulated by the new system in a coherent manner. The giant leap intended to transform Romania directly into a (post)modern neoliberal market economy caused certain tremors in practice while the case law hesitated in giving the new device the whole power encapsulated in the legal texts. In these troubled waters, the floating charge survived and is looking for the sunny calm waters of an established practice to sail on into the future.

BACKGROUND AND CONTEXT

The year 1996 was an eventful year for Romania and its market. The general elections held at the end of that year showed a clear will towards (Western) European values and marked the beginning of building a real market economy. While the Constitution enacted at the end of 1991 proclaimed that the Romanian economy follows the model of a market economy (even if article 1 para. 3 maintained that Romania is a 'social state'[1]), the governments that

---

[1] On the dynamics between the two constitutional concepts, see E.S. Tănăsescu, 'Human Dignity and the Circumstantial Protection of Social Rights',

were in power in the first half of the 1990s tried to ensure a 'long transition' from a state-controlled economy towards a 'new model' (i.e. a third path, to avoid 'real' capitalism[2]).

This social and political turmoil eclipsed another important event (as it would later prove itself): in the autumn of 1996, the first two GSM (2G) licenses were awarded by the Romanian Government to two newly created joint ventures (Connex and Dialog). By the end of that electoral cycle (in 2000), they had risen to a staggering number of over 2 million users (i.e. 10% of the country's population). However, back in 1996, the future was not sounding so great.[3] Each company was supposed to pay about US$75 million for 15 years of operation, out of which about US$ 30 million was to be paid upfront. In addition, they assumed covenants to cover most of the national territory within 10 years. They needed a lot of cash, and quickly. And they got it. Connex raised US$190 million from a consortium of banks led by the European Bank for Reconstruction and Development (EBRD) in September 1997,[4] followed by Dialog raising US$210 million the same year from a consortium of banks

in M. Zubik (ed.), *Human Rights in Contemporary World – Essays in Honour of Professor Leszeck Garlicki*, Wydawnictwo Sejmowe, Warsaw, 2017, 306–316.

2 In what was later called 'the lost decade' (for some economic charts using this designation owing to stagnation in development during that decade, see Razvan Diaconu, 'Puțină istorie foarte recentă în 6 grafice: economia comparativă a României înainte de, precum și de la căderea comunismului încoace' (*Curs de Guvernare*, 31 January 2021) <https://cursdeguvernare.ro/putina-istorie-in-6-grafice-economia-comparativa-a-romaniei-inainte-de-precum-si-de-la-caderea-comunismului-incoace.html> accessed 12 November 2022; Romania struggled during the 1990s to avoid implementing a 'shock therapy' with large-scale privatization as suggested by the World Bank for the former communist states in Eastern Europe. The main proponent of this 'long transition' was the former president Ion Iliescu (President of Romania during 1990–1996 and 2001–2004), who asked the Government to follow the 'Swedish model'. By that, he wanted to keep in place a socialist model that he knew (he was a second-tier communist leader before 1989), but with a facelift, or a capitalist interface. The outcome of this 'experiment' was that Romania was the only Eastern European country with negative GDP development during that decade.

3 The advertising phrase of one of the mobile operators was for many years 'The future sounds great'.

4 See the company press release available at <http://www.cosconor.fr/GSM/Divers/Publicitate%20si%20altele/CONNEX/Site%20rip/Noutati/Arhive/1997%20-%201998/1997/Imprumut%20BERD.pdf> accessed 12 November 2022.

led by the International Financial Corporation (IFC).[5] These were the largest private financings in Romania by far at that time.

The secret behind securing this massive financial influx for an (extremely) risky business with no or minimal (tangible) assets was the floating security right or, as it was known at that time in Romania, the 'enterprise mortgage' (*gaj asupra fondului de comert*, in Romanian). Indeed, back then, Romania still held on to an old mix of the nineteenth-century legacy of security rules[6] based on the Napoleonic Civil Code-style personal property pledge (joined by a similarly coined real estate mortgage benefitting from mid-nineteenth-century Belgian improvements) seasoned with a few improvements in the commercial area where a 'pledge without dispossession' was allowed by a regulation inspired by the Italian Commercial Code at the end of the nineteenth century.

At the beginning of the twentieth century, Romanian legal literature,[7] inspired by its French counterparts discussing the '*gage du fonds de commerce*', explored the possibility of creating a pledge over the enterprise as a whole ('*fond de comert*' in Romanian). While Romanian law lacked special regulation[8] (comparable with the 1886 and 1909 French laws on the subject), the case-law soon followed the idea and validated such operations based on the theory that the collateral consists of an asset (which was qualified as a movable asset) comprising all the goodwill of a certain business. As the devil is in the detail, fierce debates focused on whether the merchandise was included in the enterprise or whether its debts were also included. The latter issue was resolved easily since debts could not be transferred, while the former did not reach a final conclusion. The whole debate was 'frozen' during the communist period owing to a lack of interest (as there were no more private businesses).

---

5 See IFC press release available at <https://pressroom.ifc.org/all/pages/PressDetail.aspx?ID=20324> accessed 12 November 2022.

6 For details, see R. Rizoiu, *20 ans après: L'unification du droit des sûretés réelles en Roumanie*, in C.-L. Popescu (ed.), *Colloque Franco-Roumain: '20 ans et le temps du droit'. Actes du colloque*, Hamangiu, Bucharest, 2019, 144–157.

7 See M.A. Dumitrescu, *Manual de drept comercial*, vol. IV, Alcalay, Bucharest, 1926, 769; I.N. Fințescu, *Curs de drept comercial*, vol. I, Doicescu, Bucharest, 1929, 175–176; I.L. Georgescu, *Drept comercial român*, vol. I, Socec, Bucharest, 1946, 527–530; D. Gălășescu, *Drept comercial*, TUB, Bucharest, 1948, 361–364; St.D. Cărpenaru, *Drept comercial român* , All, Bucharest, 1995, 111–112; I. Turcu, *Tratat teoretic și practic de drept comercial*, vol. I, C.H. Beck, Bucharest, 2008, 335–336.

8 For the discussion on the lack of positive law in this area, see the comment of the Legislative Council on art. 118 of the Draft Commercial Code of 1939 (which was passed but never entered into force owing to the war), in M.A. Demetrescu, I.L. Georgescu, *Codul comercial Carol al II-lea. Comentariu*, Cartea Românească, București, 1939, 89.

In 1990, after the fall of communism, a new law allowed for private companies to be established and organized a public ledger for companies (i.e. the 'Companies Registry'). The Law no. 26/1990 organizing this Companies Registry included a text mentioning that the Registry would also record operations dealing with the enterprise, including the pledging thereof. For a decade, this was the only mention of such an operation in Romanian law, but it was sufficient to start a practice. Keeping in mind that the system of security devices available at that time was scarce and almost all devices dealing with movable collateral required physical dispossession of the debtor (pledgor), the pledge over the enterprise was a tempting alternative.

This tiny legal reference was the key to opening the path for the large GSM financings of 1997. Indeed, for a company with basically no (tangible) assets, there was no possibility for (standard) pledges or mortgages. Actually, the loans were needed exactly for financing the acquisition of the equipment required for building the network, in a context where the law did not provide anything for the purchase money security interest schemes. The gamble paid off. In 1999–2000, when many businesses in the region were collapsing because of the 1998–1999 crisis wave sweeping from the 'Asian tigers' (i.e. the developed East Asian economies of Hong Kong, Singapore, South Korea and Taiwan) throughout Russia into Eastern Europe, the two Romanian GSM operators increased their exposure to US$295 million[9] and US$245 million[10] respectively.

And the success story is more remarkable if we compare it with the tragic experience of local banks in the same period. Indeed, using the 'traditional' banking security devices such as pledges over (fleets of) trucks, local banks faced fierce legal battles where the insolvent debtors claimed such security to be invalid because the trucks were left in possession of the debtor itself, hence breaching the dispossession requirement of the law. It was only by the bold move of the Romanian High Court, which issued a landmark decision in 1998, that this kind of security was 'saved' by adapting it to the realities of the twentieth-century global economy.[11]

---

[9] See Connex company press release available at <http://www.cosconor.fr/GSM/Divers/Publicitate%20si%20altele/CONNEX/Site%20rip/Date%20de%20refrinta.pdf> accessed 12 November 2022.

[10] See IFC press release available at <https://pressroom.ifc.org/all/pages/PressDetail.aspx?ID=25161> accessed 12 November 2022.

[11] See R. Rizoiu, *Sailing in a Stormy Sea: Recent Romanian High Court Decisions Affecting Secured Transactions*, 'Zeitschrift für Europäisches Privatrecht' no. 3/2019, 554–570.

At the turn of the millennium, in April 1999, Romania enacted a specialized law dealing with security interests in personal property (the '1999 Act').[12] This piece of legislation was drafted based on the template of Article 9 of the Uniform Commercial Code. The sponsors of the new draft law were none other than the EBRD and IFC.[13] This law specifically regulated the 'security interests in *universitas facti*'. Later on, in 2011, the Romanian Civil Code (since it is much younger than its 1864 forefather, it is still called the 'New Civil Code' or 'NCC') was enacted, taking over the concept but 'rebranding' it as 'universal hypothec'.[14]

A SHORT OVERVIEW OF THE ROMANIAN SECURITY INTEREST SYSTEM

Under Romanian law, an obligation can be secured by taking a proprietary security interest (i.e. an *in rem* device), by having another person guarantee personally for the debtor's obligation or by employing various legal techniques that were designed originally for other purposes (e.g. a reservation of title). The core regulation of this system is contained in the New Civil Code. The NCC is seconded by a law for applying the Code (the 'LPA'[15]), which contains many useful guiding rules. Under the NCC, the proprietary security is divided based on the possession requirement into possessory devices and non-possessory devices. The first category contains the pledge (which is limited to tangible movable assets), while the second category is represented by a generic device called the 'hypothec'. As such, under Romanian law, hypothec is the brand

[12] The security device for immovable assets remained unchanged at the time, as the old-school hypothec under the 1864 Civil Code. There were only minor 'backdoors', such as considering that certain immovable assets are in fact movables (e.g. fixtures).

[13] On the history of the regulation, see R. Rizoiu, *Garantii civile (Textbook on civil guarantees and secured transactions)*, Hamangiu, Bucharest, 2022, 159–173. *Adde* Fr. Dahan, J. Simpson, *The European Bank for Reconstruction and Development's Secured Transactions Project: A Model Law and Ten Core Principles for a Modern Secured Transactions Law in Countries of Central and Eastern Europe (and Elsewhere!)*, in E.-M. Kieninger (ed.), *Security Rights in Movable Property in European Private Law*, Cambridge University Press, Cambridge, 2004, 98–104; N. de la Peña, H.W. Fleisig, 'Romania: Law on Security Interests in Personal Property and Commentaries', Review of Central and East European Law, vol. 29, no. 2/2004, 133–217.

[14] This time, the reform went all the way and also encompassed also security interests in immovable property.

[15] In Romanian, *Legea de punere in aplicare a Codului civil*, hence the usual abbreviation – LPA.

name of any non-possessory security device,[16] irrespective of the nature of the collateral (tangible or intangible, movable or immovable). While replacing the security interest defined by the 1999 act with the (movable) hypothec, the NCC, however, retained much of the initial design of a functional approach (and only extended most of it to the immovable hypothec as well).

With respect to the general layout of the legal regime of assets, the NCC is also trying to bring a unitary approach. As a matter of law, any 'thing' that forms the object of a 'right' will be considered an 'asset'.[17] Moreover, art. 535 NCC[18] expressly provides that the term 'thing' is not limited to tangible reality, but it also includes intangible values. In addition, art. 542 NCC[19] mentions that 'rights' are not 'things', but when they are themselves able to create 'superstructure' models where a right is created in another right,[20] their legal treatment will be that of an asset. In doing so, the law declares rights to be 'assimilated assets'.[21]

In this landscape, art. 541 NCC[22] defines the concept of *universitas facti* ('*universalitate de fapt*' in Romanian) as a collection of assets that are viewed (and treated) as a whole by their owner.[23] Nonetheless, the text adds that such a

---

16 While this terminology goes back to the Roman law tradition, it was lost in the struggles of the *Ancien Regime* in sixteenth-century France ('*meubles n'ont point de suite par hypothèque*') and, therefore, Romanian law considered that the hypothec is reserved for immovable assets only.

17 For a more detailed presentation, see R. Rizoiu, 'How "Real" is a Security Interest? Security Interests as Derivative Proprietary Interests', in O. Remien and L. Zidaru (eds), *Gemeineuropäisches Privatrecht in Rumänien. Neue Kodifikationen zwischen französischen, deutschen oder österreichischen und europäisch internationalen Einflüssen*, Duncker & Humblot, Berlin, 2023, 129–146.

18 Article 535 NCC: 'Assets are the goods, tangible or intangible, that are subject to a patrimonial right'.

19 Article 542 NCC: '(1) Unless otherwise stated, the rights *in rem* over the movable assets are subject to the rules regarding the movable assets. (2) The other patrimonial rights are, within the limits provided by the law, subject to the rules regarding the movable assets'.

20 For example, the law refers to the usufruct over a claim right (art. 737–744 NCC) or the hypothec over a receivable (art. 2398 NCC).

21 See R. Rizoiu, *Curs de garantii civile (Textbook on civil guarantees and secured transactions)*, Hamangiu, Bucharest, 2020, 90–91.

22 Article 541 NCC: '(1) A *universitas facti* is comprised of assets belonging to the same person and that have a common destination set by her will or by law. (2) The assets comprising the *universitas facti* can together or individually be subjected to distinct legal relations'.

23 See Constanta Appellate Court, decision no. 17/2022, stating that there are three cumulative conditions to have a *universitas facti*: (i) a collection of more than

private statement shall not affect the special legal rules applicable to each item within the collection. For example, if the *universitas facti* contains a piece of real estate together with certain movable assets, the owner cannot transfer the collection without observing the specific rules applying to the transfer of real estate (for that particular item). While it is not apparent from the text, the *universitas facti* is not considered, therefore, an asset in itself, but only a modality the parties could use to define a collection of assets ensuring its dynamics over time.[24] In other words, the content of *universitas facti* will change in time without affecting its identity (subject only to fraudulent practices). The *universitas facti* can hold both real estate and personal property, and both tangible assets and choses in action.[25] For example, a portfolio of receivables is considered a species of *universitas facti* [art. 174 LPA].[26]

The consequence of this structure with regard to security interests is that anything that has a (monetary) value can be used as collateral. As such, a hypothec (*ipoteca* in Romanian) could cover all sorts of assets (both real estate and personal property) irrespective of their nature (either tangible or intangible[27]) and it could also cover assimilated assets such as receivables and choses

one asset; (ii) the assets belonging to the same owner; and (iii) all assets have a common destination. As such, if an assignment refers to only one receivable, this is not a *universitas facti*. Also, if there are several receivables but they do not have a *nexum* consisting of a common destination, there is no *universitas facti* (Craiova Appellate Court, decision no. 436/2016).

[24] In the early years, the courts had difficulties in understanding that a *universitas facti* is different from the entire wealth of the debtor (consisting of rights and debts). See, for example, Brasov Appellate Court, decision no. 749/2013, where the court considered that a tax lien failing to describe the collateral should be treated as a hypothec over all assets (present and future) of the debtor. Later on, once the law prohibited any description of collateral that was so broad to cover 'all assets', the courts were able to disqualify such general security interests altogether. See Cluj Specialized Tribunal, decision no. 588/2017, where the court considered a security agreement as null and void because the description of collateral included therein was 'all movable assets of the debtor, present and future, tangible and intangible, meaning all assets including all receivables against third parties'.

[25] By 'choses in action' we mean a large category that includes items such as claim rights (receivables, rights of use that are not rights *in rem* under the Continental legal system, etc.) and certain intangible assets (intellectual property rights, clientele rights, goodwill, etc.).

[26] Article 174 LPA: 'The portfolio of receivables is a *universitas facti* of receivables within the meaning of art. 2398 of the Civil Code'.

[27] For the special case of intellectual property as collateral, see R. Rizoiu, R. Dinca, *Security Rights in Intellectual Property in Romania*, in E.-M. Kieninger (ed.), *Security Rights in Intellectual Property*, Springer, 2020, 555–595.

in action (art. 2350 NCC[28]). Among the valuables that could constitute collateral under a hypothec, the law expressly lists the *universitas facti*.

Indeed, once the 1999 Act reshaped the security interests in personal property by eliminating the requirement of dispossession, it also expressly mentioned the possibility of creating a security interest in a *universitas facti*. Again, the legal literature unanimously recognized[29] that an enterprise is a species of *universitas facti*, and the legal practice flourished with many security interest agreements concluded over the enterprise. Under the 1999 Act, the *universitas facti* was perceived as an asset in its own right, but it mentioned that the security interest attached to every item in the collection once it entered therein and continued to follow that asset after it left the collection.[30] In this respect, this device functioned more like a traditional fixed security than like a floating charge.[31]

While the initial practice continued to focus on the old concept of enterprise, new structures started to be explored. For example, when the major Romanian '4-play operator'[32] RCS&RDS sought financing from ING Bank in 2001, it secured it by creating a security interest in the *universitas facti* comprising all assets in its network (which was expanding at a tremendous pace at the time). Also, by the middle of the decade, consumer finance skyrocketed and the 2007 EU accession gave a boost to the market of consumer electronics. As such, a lot of stock-in-trade financing was developing in the decade, and one of the main

---

28 Article 2350 NCC: '(1) The collateral may be movable or immovable, tangible or intangible. (2) It may be determined or determinable assets or *universitas facti*'.

29 See St.D. Cărpenaru, *Tratat de drept comercial*, Universul Juridic, Bucharest, 2009, 130–150; S. Angheni, *Drept comercial. Tratat*, C.H. Beck, Bucharest, 2019, 89–100; Gh. Piperea, *Drept comercial român. Teoria generală, întreprinderea și insolvența*, C.H. Beck, Bucharest, 2020, 75–80.

30 In other words, the description of collateral in the security agreement as being a *universitas facti* was meant only to determine a class of assets that are subject to the security interest. Once an asset meeting such a description was acquired by the securing party, it automatically entered under the security. If later on that asset was transferred to a third party, the security (which was already attached to it) would follow the asset.

31 See R. Rizoiu, *Garanția reală mobiliară asupra universalităților de bunuri (Security interests in universitas facti)*, in 'Pandectele române', no. 2/2005, 137–170.

32 In the entertainment industry, a '4-play operator' is a company that provides integrated services for TV, landline telephony, cellular network and internet.

security devices used in this area was the security interest over stock-in-trade seen as a *universitas facti*.[33]

Building on the experience of the decade since the enactment of the 1999 Act, the New Civil Code integrated the security interest in *universitas facti* as part of the larger project of unifying the security devices within a more inclusive concept of 'hypothec'. Under current Romanian law, the hypothec is a security device created over virtually any type of collateral for securing the performance of any type of (monetary) obligation.[34] The main trait of the hypothec is that it is a flexible security interest devoid of the need for the creditor to take possession of the collateral. Hence, the debtor continues to have (almost[35]) full control over the collateral. As such, under art. 2373 NCC: 'The securing debtor is free to use, administrate and dispose of the collateral without prejudice to the secured creditor's rights'. This means that the debtor can freely use the assets within the *universitas facti*, including by transferring or consuming them, hence depleting the content of the universality.[36] All other security devices (i.e. liens, pledge, security-like operations – conditional sales, reservation of title, assignment of receivables for security purposes – and the

---

33 See Cluj Appellate Court, decision no. 304/2016, stating that a stock of merchandise represents a *universitas facti* and as such could be considered collateral for a hypothec. In the same line, see Timisoara Appellate Court, decision no 1092/2015, stating that the medicine stock of a pharmacy represents a *universitas facti* subject to a valid hypothec.

34 Article 2323 NCC: 'This section regulates the liens, as well as the security interests meant to ensure the performance of an obligation that has a value appraisable in money'.

35 However, the debtor should refrain from causing an abnormal decrease in the value of the collateral. See art. 2374 NCC: 'The securing debtor cannot destroy or damage the collateral and cannot diminish its value unless it occurs during a normal usage of the collateral or during a state of emergency'.

36 See Cluj Appellate Court, decision no. 450/2021, stating that a hypothec over *universitas facti* has no value when the content of the universality was fully depleted at the time the receiver finalized the inventory report. In the same line, see Bacau Appellate Court, decision no. 238/2021. Both courts analyzed the status of a wholesaler who had a hypothec over the stock of building materials sold to certain construction firms. At the time the receiver made the inventory of the assets of those firms, there were no materials left in stock (because they were incorporated in the works rendered to clients). For a detailed analysis of the loss of a hypothec once the materials are incorporated in the construction, see Cluj Appellate Court, decision no. 106/2021, stating that once incorporated the materials do not form part of the stock of the contractor anymore.

like) received a legal status similar to the hypothec in terms of having a unified priorities system and similar enforcement treatment.[37]

THE ROMANIAN FUNCTIONAL EQUIVALENT TO THE FLOATING CHARGE

The French system was the blueprint of the modern Romanian legal system since 1864 (when Romania enacted a Civil Code based on the Napoleonic template). It still maintains its legacy on the overall legal system nowadays. The transition to a market economy showed increased US influence, with the Canadian system used as a middle ground between the common law and civil law traditions. The NCC is greatly inspired by the 1994 Quebec Civil Code, but the chapter regulating the hypothec is closer to Article 9 UCC and the Canadian Personal Property Security Acts.[38] English law had an indirect influence through its floating charge mechanism. This *common law*-inspired lineage resulted in Romanian security interests functioning similarly to their English-language security devices. For example, in the case of the Romanian equivalent of the floating charge (i.e. the hypothec over *universitas facti*), art. 2357 NCC[39] together with art. 160 LPA[40] explains the mechanics in terms of generic attachment followed by crystallization.

The floating charge is generally created by a business owner (either a company or a private entrepreneur), since the hypothec should be created by the owner of the collateral.[41] Nonetheless, this person could be different from the

---

[37] Therefore, all these encumbrances could be placed in the same list and ordered using the *prior tempore potior iure* rule. Also, in case of enforcement, all secured creditors have the same rights (ordered only based on their ranking) over the collateral.

[38] In Canada, all provinces apart from Quebec have adopted a uniform model of regulation for security interests in personal property, based on a model similar to that of the United States of America.

[39] Article 2357 NCC: 'The hypothec over a collateral consisting in a pool of assets attaches to every asset thereof. (2) The hypothec survives over the pool of assets even when such assets have perished, if the securing debtor replaces them in a reasonable amount of time, taking into consideration the quantity and nature of the assets.'

[40] Article 160 LPA: '(1) In the case of a hypothec over a collateral consisting in a pool of assets, if an asset is transferred, it will be made clear of the security. (2) The provisions of art. 1562–1565 of the Civil Code [dealing with *actio pauliana*] remain applicable.'

[41] Article 2365 NCC: 'The security agreement can be concluded only by the holder of the rights in the collateral and who can dispose of it'.

debtor of the secured obligation.[42] Also, it is not mandatory that the creator is the (full) owner of the *universitas facti*. For example, they could have a limited right in that *universitas facti*, such as a usufruct, or even a lease.[43] In these cases, of course, the hypothec will cover only the limited rights the securing party has in the collateral.

Romanian law has an equivalent of the floating charge. It is called a hypothec over a *universitas facti* (or, simplified, a 'general hypothec'[44]). Article 2368 NCC[45] expressly mentions the possibility of creating a hypothec over a *universitas facti* (that could comprise movable as well as immovable assets), provided that such a *universitas facti* comprises assets used by a (corporate or individual) business. Therefore, nowadays the hypothec over a *universitas facti* is limited to the business sector, similar to the limitation included in the Quebec Civil Code.

Moreover, art. 2398 NCC,[46] which mentions that claims can also be used as collateral, expressly states that a portfolio of receivables (i.e. a *universitas facti* comprising claims) can also be used as collateral. However, if immovable property is included in the *universitas facti*, specific formalities for creating the mortgage are required (i.e. notarial deed and registration in the Land Registry), limiting the usefulness of the flexibility ensured by a floating charge.

Based on these texts, it can be stated that Romanian law allows an equivalent of a floating charge to be created over all types of assets, i.e. movable and immovable, tangible and intangible, provided that such assets are used by a business. The main trait of this security device is that it allows for the free flow of assets within the *universitas facti* and only captures under the security those items that are found inside at the time that enforcement starts.

---

42 Article 2366 NCC: 'The security agreement can be concluded by the debtor of the secured obligation or by a third party'.

43 The construction here creates some problems, since these rights have the *universitas facti* itself as their object; they are not parts of it. For example, a business owns a certain enterprise but decides to lease the operations thereof to another company. The latter will only have a lease right over the enterprise. Nonetheless, the lessee of the enterprise could create a security interest over such a lease.

44 Article 2424 NCC (Priorities between general hypothecs and special hypothecs): 'Between a hypothec over a collateral consisting of a pool of movable assets and a hypothec over a collateral consisting of individual movable assets shall prevail the hypothec which was registered or perfected first'.

45 Article 2368 NCC: 'The conventional hypothec over a collateral consisting in a pool of movable or immovable, present or future, tangible or intangible assets can only be concluded regarding the assets used by an enterprise'.

46 Article 2398 NCC: 'The hypothec [on receivables] can have as its object either one or several receivables, or a *universitas facti* of receivables'.

The creation of the hypothec over a *universitas facti* is done by executing a security agreement.[47] This agreement should be executed in written format and be signed by both parties (i.e. the securing party – usually, the debtor – and the secured party – the creditor). The attachment occurs once the secured obligation is effective and the security provider (i.e. the debtor) acquires rights over the collateral (i.e. the *universitas facti*)[48] (art. 2387 NCC).

In order to perfect such a security, a notice should be filed with the National Register of Publicity in Movables ('RNPM'). This is an electronic database that can be searched freely by anyone anytime via a web interface. The agreement itself is not published, but only relevant data (identification of the parties and description of the collateral), based on a notice filed by any of the parties. The description of the collateral can be as general as the parties want as long as it can reasonably[49] describe the *universitas facti*.[50] As a general guideline,

[47] Article 2388 NCC: 'The security agreement shall be drafted and acknowledged by a Civil Law Notary or concluded as a document under private signature, under the pain of contract's absolute nullity'.

[48] Article 2387 NCC: 'A movable hypothec is created by the conclusion of the security agreement, but it takes effect as of the date on which the secured obligation comes into existence and the grantor acquires rights in the collateral'.

[49] The law does not offer a definition of reasonability, and this is the reason it employs the term in the first place. It remains to the judge to decide on a case-by-case basis what was reasonable for the (third) parties to consider a proper description. For example, where the security agreement was created over the crops of the debtor and the description of collateral indicated the land surface without identifying the plots of land, the court decided that the hypothec is valid, but it only covers one-third of the lands of the debtor (*pro rata* with the indicated surface). See Craiova Appellate Court, decision no. 722/2021. In another case, the court decided that the description of collateral stating that it contains all assets that the creditor sold to the debtor under a certain sales contract is a valid description (Cluj Appellate Court, decision no. 450/2021). On the contrary, another court stated that the general description of the assets being sold was not sufficient, especially when it was about building materials that were afterward incorporated into a building (Ploiești Appellate Court, decision no. 882/2016). More generally, one court stated that 'the description of the collateral should be, at the end of the day, able to allow the identification of the asset in case of enforcement of the security' (Cluj Appellate Court, decision no. 441/2014). Even a very broad description covering all inventory, stocks of pharmaceuticals and receivables against the National Health Insurance Administration is a reasonable description of the enterprise (Bucharest Appellate Court, decision no. 339/2016).

[50] Article 2391 NCC: 'The security agreement shall comprise a reasonable description of the collateral. (2) The description is reasonable, even if the collateral is not individualized, as long as it can be reasonably identified. (3) The description can be made by compiling a list of the collaterals, by determining the

the description should indicate 'the nature and the content'[51] of the collection. This means that the risk of an unclear description lies with the creditor because the security agreement could be found null and void for lack of collateral[52] or the enforcement shall be limited only to those assets that are clearly identifiable.

Once filed, the hypothec is perfected, and notice is considered to be given to any third party[53] (art. 2409 NCC). No other formality is required. Filing an otherwise invalid hypothec will not cure the defects of the security agreement (art. 2414 NCC).

In case the *universitas facti* also includes immovable property, the agreement should be passed in authentic (i.e. notarized) form (art. 2378 NCC) and should identify the real estate by its cadastral number. Moreover, as a general

---

category to which they belong, by indicating the quantity, by establishing a determination formula and by any other means of reasonable identification of the collateral. (4) When the hypothec bears upon a pool of assets, the security agreement shall describe the nature and content of the pool of assets. (5) It is not considered a reasonable description within the meaning of paragraph (1) the stipulation according to which the hypothec bears upon all assets of the debtor or upon all present and future assets of the debtor. (6) If the hypothec bears upon a bank account, it shall be distinctly individualized in the security agreement.'

[51] See Timisoara Appellate Court, decision no. 1092/2015, drawing this conclusion from article 2391 para (4) NCC. For a more detailed analysis, see Bucharest Appellate Court, decision no. 399/2016, stating that a collateral description including the universality of inventory placed in certain locations operated by the debtor, plus the stock of pharmaceutical drugs located thereunder, plus the portfolio of receivables the debtor had against the National Health Insurance House are sufficiently clear. Also, if the description of the *universitas facti*, however broadly used, is meant to cover the entire enterprise (*fond du commerce*) of the debtor, this is sufficient since it has a functional link. See Cluj Appellate Court, decision no. 956/2016, stating that the inclusion of all assets, inventory, merchandise and receivables related to the business of the debtor is a fair description of collateral. However, if the description is too broad and tries to tie in all the assets of the debtor's wealth, the hypothec shall not attach. See Cluj Appellate Court, decision no. 441/2014, stating that a description stating only 'the universality of debtor's assets' is not sufficiently clear.

[52] Article 2372 para (2) NCC: 'On pain of nullity, the hypothec contract must (…) give a sufficiently precise description of the collateral'.

[53] Article 2409 NCC: '(1) The hypothec is perfected when it is effective according to the provisions of art. 2387 and the publicity formalities required by law are met. (2) The publicity of movable hypothecs is ensured by registration in the [RNPM], unless otherwise provided by law. (3) The perfected hypothec is opposable to the other creditors of the securing debtor, to those who acquire rights over the collateral and as well as to every other third party.'

rule, such a hypothec will not be validly created unless recorded in the Land Registry.[54] However, this rule does not apply yet to all of Romania but only to those areas of the country where the general cadaster has been finalized (i.e. less than 10%[55]). For the rest of the country, recordation only ensures perfection.[56] While the texts do not transform the floating security into a fixed one *per se*, they surely create problems of interpretation. Owing to these formal constraints, in practice immovable assets are not included within such *universitas facti*. Therefore, the parties prefer to include only the movable assets within the definition of the *universitas facti* and to create (separate) fixed hypothecs over various plots of real estate.

Article 2357 NCC mentions that the hypothec covers all assets within the *universitas facti* at any time and from time to time. This means that attachment occurs automatically once a specific asset enters the collection (by meeting the criteria set for its belonging there after being acquired by the owner of the collection). Article 160 LPA provides that once a specific asset exits the *universitas facti*, it is no longer encumbered. This means that assets can move freely in and out of the collection, while the hypothec encumbers only those assets presently covered by it. In practical terms, this mechanism functions like the crystallization of a floating charge, which covers only those elements that are in the collateral class at the time of enforcement. Indeed, if at the time of the creation of the security interest the *universitas facti* contained 10 items and then four of them were transferred to other persons, when the secured creditor starts the enforcement of the security it will only have access to the remaining six elements within the *universitas facti*. On the contrary, in the case of a fixed security over the 10 items, the security would have remained

[54] Article 2377 para (2) NCC: 'The hypothec over a universality does not attach to the immovable property contained therein until the hypothec is registered in the land register in respect of each of the immovable properties'. Moreover, art. 888 NCC: 'Entries in the land register shall be made on the basis of an authentic notarial document, an enforceable court judgment, a certificate of succession or another document issued by the administrative authorities, where the law so provides'.

[55] See the latest report of the National Agency for Cadaster and Land Registration (ANCPI), dated December 2023, available at <https://www.ancpi.ro/wp-content/uploads/2024/01/NOTA-privind-activitatea-ANCPI-la-data-de-31.12.2023.pdf> accessed March 1, 2024.

[56] Romanian legal system still bears the legacy of the French legal system in this area as well. As such, interests in real estate are freely created/transferred by the simple agreement passed between the parties. Such agreements are valid and legally binding as between the parties thereto. However, they are not opposable to third parties until they are recorded in the land registry. Therefore, registration is just a condition for their effectiveness against third parties.

in place over each of them irrespective of any transfer. The law also observes that the rules against fraudulent transfers remain applicable to prevent fraud in dealing with assets within a hypothecated *universitas facti*.[57]

A difficult issue is encountered in relation to the legal treatment of the proceeds generated by the sale of (parts of) a *universitas facti*. For example, if the debtor sells items in that universality for cash, is the money received in return covered by the hypothec? Under art. 2393 NCC,[58] if the sale is made in the ordinary course of business,[59] the seller (i.e. the debtor) should deposit the proceeds in a dedicated bank account subject to the hypothec. Moreover, if the sale refers to the entire *universitas facti* as a whole,[60] the money is considered proceeds of the collateral and therefore covered by the hypothec.[61] No special formality is needed in case the cash proceeds can be traced.[62] If the cash is

---

57 See G. Boroi, A. Ilie, *Comentariile Codului civil. Garanțiile personale. Privilegiile și garanțiile reale (Civil code commentary. Personal guarantees. Liens and security interests)*, Hamangiu, Bucharest, 2012, 136.

58 Article 2393 NCC: '(1) The asset acquired in the ordinary course of business of an enterprise alienating assets of the same kind no longer acts as a collateral for the securing debtor even if the hypothec is perfected and the acquirer had knowledge of it. (2) In this case, the hypothec transfers to the proceeds of the sale.'

59 However, sometimes the bulk sale of the entire content of the *universitas facti* could indicate that a fraudulent transfer took place. See Cluj Appellate Court, decision no. 711/2019, stating that the sale of a livestock of chickens to cover an unsecured debt is fraudulent when the same livestock was used as collateral for securing another loan.

60 See Arges Tribunal, decision no. 3079/2015, stating that the sale of a livestock of pigs shall transfer the hypothec over all the bank accounts the price was cashed in (within the limits of the sale price). Where the *universitas facti* contains also immovable assets, the process will be further complicated by the fact that the procedure of real estate judicial sale is cumbersome.

61 Article 2392 NCC: '(1) The hypothec extends over the fruits and products of the collateral, as well as over every asset acquired by the securing debtor as a result of an administrative or disposal act regarding the collateral. (2) It is considered to be a proceed of the movable collateral any asset that replaces it or acquires its value.'

62 Article 2412 NCC: '(1) In case the initial filing was not sufficiently descriptive as to encompass the proceeds, the hypothec maintains its rank over the proceeds only if the secured creditor files an additional statement describing the resulted proceeds within 15 days since their occurrence. (2) When the proceeds are traceable amounts of money, the hypothec maintains its rank over them without filing an additional statement.' For special difficulties in tracing under Romanian law, see R. Rizoiu, *Unele aspecte particulare ale garanțiilor reale mobiliare constituite asupra conturilor curente deschise la instituții bancare (Some specific issues on security interests in personal property created over current accounts*

used to acquire assets of the type included in the original *universitas facti*, no special problems arise, since the new assets automatically enter the collection (and form part of the collateral). The status of the non-cash proceeds (including receivables) is different. In order to be able to trace such items (assuming they do not fall under the definition the parties set for the *universitas facti*), additional steps need to be undertaken by the secured creditor, including the filing of an amended notice with RNPM describing the new collateral (i.e. the proceeds) within 15 days from their occurrence.

While there is no specific crystallization procedure under Romanian law, a similar mechanism is implied by the way the hypothec over a *universitas facti* works. Indeed, enforcement of a hypothec over a *universitas facti* is started by the creditor deciding to act (when the debtor is in default[63] or the value of the collateral is endangered[64]). To this end, the creditor has to go to a bailiff (‘*executor judecatoresc*’ in Romanian) and ask for assistance. The bailiff can either carry out the whole enforcement process or, according to the creditor's choice, can only serve the debtor an enforcement notice.

In cases where the bailiff is in charge of the whole process, she should ask a court to confirm the enforcement.[65] This is done by a summary proceeding, where the court only checks the existence of the security agreement and its perfection. The debtor is not subpoenaed, since the law declares the security agreement as a writ of execution. Once the enforcement is confirmed, the bailiff will seize the content of the *universitas facti* that she can find at that moment and decide to sell it in any way (in block or separately) in order to repay the secured debt from the proceeds. Dismembering the collection (for a piece-by-piece sale), could mean the loss of value resulting from the initial

---

opened with banking institutions), in ‘Revista română de drept privat’, no. 2/2007, 198–222.

63 Article 2429 NCC: ‘If the securing debtor does not willingly perform his obligations, the secured creditor can enforce the hypothec, according to the provisions of this Chapter’.

64 Article 2396 para (1) NCC: ‘The secured creditor may accelerate his secured claim and enforce the hypothec when he finds the lack of a proper maintenance of the collateral or other events attributable to the securing debtor affecting the prospects of enforcement, as they were determined by the security agreement’.

65 Article 2445, para. (1) NCC: ‘The secured creditor may ask the court the permission to enforce the hypothec over movable assets by selling the collateral. It shall file the application together with the documents attesting the existence of the secured claim and of the hypothec, together with the evidence of the hypothec being perfected. The court shall analyze the existence of the claim and of the validly perfected hypothec and shall allow the sale.’

aggregation of assets into a functional enterprise, but this is not a concern for the secured creditor since he is not required to obtain the best value.[66]

In case the creditor chooses to go with private enforcement, once the bailiff has served the notice of enforcement to the debtor, the creditor can use any reasonable means (as provided for in the security agreement[67]) to cash in on the collateral. In doing so, the creditor is precluded from breaching the peace,[68] meaning that it cannot act in a threatening or violent manner.[69] However, the creditor is not limited to selling the assets found in the *universitas facti*, but it can also manage them (as a whole enterprise) and collect the revenues to use them in order to reduce the secured claim.[70] In case the debtor and any other

---

[66] Article 2446 NCC: '(1) The sale of collateral is commercially reasonable if it takes place: (a) in the manner in which goods of the same kind are normally disposed of on an organized market; (b) at the price established on an organized market and valid at the time of sale; (c) in accordance with reasonable commercial practices followed by those who ordinarily sell property of the same kind; (d) in accordance with the rules laid down in the security agreement, where there is no organized market for the hypothecated property or where there are no standard commercial practices. (2) In the circumstances referred to in paragraph (1), the mere fact that a higher price could have been obtained if the sale had taken place at a different time or by a different method from that chosen by the creditor shall not render the sale commercially unreasonable.'

[67] In case the agreement is silent on this matter, the law allows the secured creditor to sell the collateral (as a whole or piece by piece) in an auction sale or in a private sale (art. 2445 NCC), as well as to operate the collateral as a business (without owning it, but only as a manager) and apply the profits of such management against the secured claim (art. 2468 NCC). Article 2445 paras (2)–(5) NCC: '(2) The secured creditor may sell the collateral in the condition in which they are found or after taking commercially reasonable steps for their realization. (3) The creditor may sell the collateral at public auction or by direct negotiation, by one or more contracts, at once or separately, at any time or place, on reasonable commercial terms. (4) The parties may agree, by means of the hypothec contract, on the manner of realization of the collateral. (5) In all cases, the sale must be conducted in a commercially reasonable manner as to method, time, place, conditions and all other aspects of the sale.'

[68] Article 2440 para (2) NCC: 'The secured creditor [exercising the self-help remedy] cannot breach the peace and it cannot resort directly or indirectly to constraint even if the action shall not qualify as a misdemeanor'.

[69] For more details, see R. Rizoiu, *Scurte considerații istorico-teleologice asupra modalității de executare a garanțiilor reale mobiliare*, in 'Pandectele române', Supplement no 1/2006, 308–349.

[70] Article 2468 NCC: '(1) If the collateral belongs to an enterprise, the secured creditor can take it over for management purposes if he notifies the persons referred to in art. 2450 and he files an enforcement notice according to the provisions of

person claiming rights in the collateral agree, the creditor can also take full ownership of the collateral against the full discharge of the secured debt.[71] Article 2433 NCC[72] prohibits the inclusion of a *lex commissoria* in the security agreement.[73] The creditor cannot take ownership of the collateral without observing the enforcement procedures mentioned above. Any surplus obtained from the enforcement has to be returned to the debtor. Conversely, any deficiency resulting from the enforcement proceeds not covering the secured debt in full can be collected from the debtor by way of a personal (unsecured) claim.[74]

DOES THE ROMANIAN 'FLOATING CHARGE' REALLY WORK?

When the Financial Crisis hit Romania in 2009, the shock wave swept over the economy. The first businesses to be affected were those relying on consumer credit. Once the lending criteria changed abruptly and the influx of customers disappeared overnight, many retailers faced insolvency. As a matter of fact, several large electronics retailers collapsed, some never to recover. These large-scale insolvency procedures tested the endurance of the security interests in *universitas facti*. For example, when the financing banks discovered that the warehouses of K Tech Ultra Pro were nearly empty a few days before filing for bankruptcy, the surprise was a harsh one, and the security interest they held in the stock of electronics proved inadequate.[75] Nonetheless, the banks later

---

arts 2449–2451. (2) The takeover of the collateral is temporary, at most until the performance of his secured claim.'

71 Article 2460 para (1) NCC: 'The secured creditor may take over the collateral in exchange for the secured claim, if the law does not preclude him from doing so, the owner of collateral agrees and the [interested] persons do not oppose'.

72 Article 2433 NCC: 'Any clause according to which the collateral is automatically transferred to the secured creditor or he can dispose of it without meeting the formalities provided by law, in order to secure his claim, is considered unwritten'.

73 While there are some debates on the possibility of the parties agreeing on a certain manner of enforcement after the default, the procedure regulated under art. 2460 NCC sqq suggests that the parties alone cannot agree on the enforcement unless the other interested parties are not also involved.

74 Article 2432 NCC: 'The provisions of this Chapter do not affect the possibility of the secured creditor to enforce his claim by way of a personal action or to take any measures deemed necessary for the enforcement of the hypothec, according to the Civil Procedure Code'.

75 See Otilia Haraga, 'K Tech Ultra Pro goes bankrupt with debts of EUR 28 million' (BR Business Review 14 June 2010) <https://business-review.eu/

proved that some of these transfers had been fraudulent (i.e. the debtor had transferred large stocks of merchandise to some of its subsidiaries just before filing for bankruptcy[76]) and the assets were seized after all. Also in 2009, ING Bank found itself engulfed in a similar scenario after discovering that large quantities of stock had disappeared from its debtor, Flanco. However, after a few years of restructuring the debt, the financing banks had enough leverage (mainly through their security interest in the existing and future stock-in-trade) to obtain a recovery plan meant to repay their loans.[77] These events seemed to confirm the bleak analysis considering working capital facilities secured with stock-in-trade as risky business.[78]

The cases described above raised the awareness of the creditors of the pitfalls of security over *universitas facti*. One major drawback that emerged was the composite structure of the *universitas facti*. Given the broad definition of 'asset' under the NCC, the hypothec over a *universitas facti* has an equally broad scope. In fact, the *universitas facti* is not even an asset *per se*, but a collection of multiple assets contained therein. This means that this *mixtum compositum* is difficult to place in a single asset category. It is rather a receptacle of various assets, each of which has a specific legal status. Since the legal treatment of any element in the *universitas facti* remains the one linked with the category the asset belongs to, the rules of the general law of property (or even obligations, in case the collateral consists of a portfolio of claims) apply to each such category. For immovable assets, this refers to the notarial form of the agreement, identification of the real estate and recording in the Land Registry, which makes the floating charge very difficult to handle in practice, as shown above. For movable assets, there can be particular rules for certain assets. For example, in the case of securities, the rules of the relevant stock

---

news/k-tech-ultra-pro-goes-bankrupt-with-debts-of-euIr-28-million-9390-7875> accessed November 12, 2022.

[76] See Catalin Lupateanu, 'Fostul patron al firmei care gestiona magazinele Ultra Pro Computers, audiat la DIICOT' (Medifax 17 September 2014) <https://www.mediafax.ro/social/fostul-patron-al-firmei-care-gestiona-magazinele-ultra-pro-computers-audiat-la-diicot-13284196> accessed November 12, 2022.

[77] See <https://newskeeper.ro/articol?id=C95624554EE3BD3D46374AC4A774C617&data=2010-08-25> accessed November 12, 2022.

[78] See A. Staicu, *Garanția reală mobiliară fără deposedare, între legalitate și eficiență (Security interest without dispossession – between legality and efficiency)*, in 'Revista de drept bancar și financiar' no. 1/2008, 14–17, criticizing the 1999 Act for allowing the debtor to dispose of the stock used as collateral and thus proving the security interest in stock-in-trade (totally) inefficient.

exchange apply.[79] In the case of claims, the law declares them as freely tradable as a rule; exceptions are only those claims that are closely connected to the person (*intuitu personae*).

The general rule of competing security rights over the same asset is *prior tempore potior jure*, meaning that the first creditor to make her security interest public shall have preferred rank. The same rule applies in the case one of the concurrent security rights is a hypothec over a *universitas facti*. This means that for each asset in the *universitas facti* at the time of enforcement, the time of the publication (of a security notice[80]) of the hypothec will be compared with that of the competing security right, and the prior one will take precedence. This means that the hypothec over a *universitas facti* does not have a singular ranking, but it depends on the security it enters into competition with. For example, if a *universitas facti* contains three assets (a1, a2, a3) and it is registered at the moment T1 while another security interest over a1 (as an individual asset) was already registered (since T0), this fixed security will take precedence over the floating charge, but only with respect to a1. If another lien is created over a2 (as an individual asset) later on (at T2), then the floating charge is second ranking to the fixed charge over a1, but first ranking as against the fixed charge over a2.

Now, all these rules are put to the test in practice by the occurrence of an insolvency event. As it is often said, an interest is 'real' only inasmuch as it resists in insolvency. In other words, insolvency is the litmus test of property interests: if it ignores them, they are simple claims; if it gives them priority, they are interests *in rem*. A great debate involves the treatment a hypothec over *universitas facti* should receive in insolvency.[81] The possibility to save the business activity of the debtor is at stake. If the trustee in bankruptcy were

---

79 In practice, there is some uncertainty in the case of securities included in a *universitas facti*. See R. Rizoiu, *Garanțiile reale și piața de capital: între nevoia de celeritate și obsesia supravegherii totale (Security interests and capital markets: Between the need for speed and the obsession of total control)*, in 'Curierul judiciar', no. 5/2013, 258–270.

80 In case of personal property, the registration is performed quite instantly since the security notice is processed by the RNPM operator within minutes of its submission. The priority is given by the moment of the actual uploading of the notice into the electronic database by the RNPM operator. In the case of real estate, the registration with the land registry takes several days, but the priority is provided by the date of the application, not the date of actual registration. Anyhow, as a rule, in case of real estate, once an application is filed, no one else can file other encumbrances until the first application is resolved.

81 See F.I. Motu, *Atypical guarantees during insolvency procedures. Guarantees created before the start of the procedure*, in 'Phoenix' no. 68 (2019), 17–29.

to give full effect to such a hypothec, then the secured creditor might pull the plug and bring the business to an end. Indeed, enforcing a hypothec over the entire enterprise (as a business concern) makes any effort to restructure the company impossible owing to the lack of resources. On the other hand, ignoring the hypothec altogether means trying to recover the company at the expense of one, often important (secured), creditor. As the percentage of successful reorganizations is about 1% in Romania,[82] this question is a harsh one for secured creditors who complain that the law gives preference to inefficient solutions only in order to try to save insolvent businesses.

As a general rule, insolvency imposes a general stay on all claims, including the ability of a secured creditor to have access to the collateral. Under Romanian law, this stay is indefinite, and in practice it takes 3–5 years between the start of an insolvency procedure and the distribution of proceeds to the creditors. This is particularly inconvenient in cases of security over *universitas facti* because the content thereof is intrinsically dynamic and changes over time. Moreover, in times of distress, it tends to deplete dramatically. While the secured creditors can ask for an exemption from the stay, this only works for cases when collateral is not to be used in the attempted reorganization. In cases where the collateral is the enterprise as a business concern, this exception shall be inapplicable.

In legal terms, a problem arises when a hypothec over a *universitas facti* can be considered to crystallize in an insolvency. There are several moments that could be considered. The obvious candidate is the moment of declaring the insolvency,[83] when all claims against the debtor are stayed. One should 'freeze' the content of the *universitas facti* in that instant and consider all assets within the universality to be covered by the hypothec. However, in practice, this proves more difficult than it seems. This is because the appointed receiver needs some time to create a complete inventory list (generally, this takes more than one year). In the meantime, the *universitas facti* cannot be 'frozen' because stock-in-trade should continue to be able to circulate[84] in order not to stop all activity of the debtor and, as such, generate immediate bankruptcy. Another possible moment is the content at the time of liquidation of the assets

[82] See *OECD Economic Surveys: Romania, 2022*, 88, available at <https://www.gov.ro/fisiere/stiri_fisiere/Romania_Survey_2022_VRD.pdf> accessed November 12, 2022. Also, the recovery rate in insolvency is around 35% (*idem*).

[83] The debtor or any relevant creditor could file for insolvency, but the insolvency is to be declared by the court after analyzing the application. Therefore, the moment the insolvency is declared is the moment the court ruling is issued.

[84] While a hypothec covering 'all assets' of the debtor is not allowed (art. 2391 para. 5 NCC), there are cases when the description of the enterprise covers most of the assets of the debtor's business.

of the debtor. However, that moment (which could be 3–5 years in the future) is hard to assess and the danger of depleting the assets rises exponentially. Some courts decided on an interim moment, i.e. the date the inventory list is ready.[85] However, this implies that the debtor should continue business as usual and try to keep the content of the *universitas facti* as close as possible to that which would result in normal circumstances. As one can imagine, this ideal concept is hard to achieve if not impossible. Nonetheless, this seems to be the reasonable approach, since the main purpose of the initial stage of an insolvency procedure is to stabilize the business of the debtor by providing a 'breathing aid' in the form of the automatic stay. If the debtor's stock continues to diminish despite this aid, then it is not fair for the secured creditors to have to look on passively while the debtor is being kept alive only by using the value of their collateral (like being connected to an artificial lung). A possible solution would be to assess the feasibility of the reorganization plan by comparing the prospective evolution of the value of collateral in the various scenarios laid down in the plan. In case the plan says (as it often does) that the assets in the *universitas facti* are to be depleted (used, transferred, consumed) without providing for suitable alternative security for the affected secured creditor, maybe the latter should have the right to trigger the crystallization event. This solution is already implemented in the Romanian Insolvency Law no. 85/2014 (the 'RIL') in case of the security over bank accounts.[86]

Of course, the parties could take precautions themselves and include a crystallization mechanism or event in the security agreement.[87] This is a safe option, but it continues to create difficulties in practice. For example, the RIL provides that contractual clauses attempting to define the declaration of insolvency as an event of default or as triggering effects similar to default are to be considered null and void (art. 123 para. 1 RIL). Since crystallization is a

[85] See Cluj Appellate Court, decision no. 304/2016. The solution is proposed as a 'rule of thumb' by the judge issuing the opinion in F.I. Motu, *The legal regime of the secured creditors in the insolvency proceedings*, doctoral thesis defended on March 31, 2022, at the West University in Timisoara.

[86] Under art. 75 para (7) RIL, the secured creditor having a hypothec over the bank accounts of the debtor has the option to collect the amounts in those bank accounts in the first 3 months after the insolvency was declared by the court. The trustee in bankruptcy has, under para (9) of the same text, the right to refuse such collection provided it secures the consent of the secured creditor or by providing an 'equivalent' security over liquid unencumbered assets of the debtor.

[87] For example, the parties could agree that once the content of the *universitas facti* decreases below a certain threshold, the secured creditor may declare default and 'freeze' the content thereof.

preliminary step generally linked to the enforcement of the security interest, such clauses could be invalidated by the courts.[88]

For all these reasons, the effectiveness of the floating charge is still under debate. This is especially true when it comes to the insolvency of the debtor. The case-law still struggles with the realization that most of the time the *universitas facti* is already depleted once the default occurs. As such, the courts often reject claims from the secured creditors on the argument that there are no assets within the *universitas facti* at the time the insolvency was declared. While the law would allow more inquiry from the courts into the causes of such depletion,[89] the courts were not reported to address such cases.

Especially in the insolvency context, crystallization is fiercely opposed by the receivers who fear that it will put a swift end to any attempt to achieve a reorganization of the debtor's activity. As a matter of policy, reorganization is the desired result in any insolvency, but it should also be backed by solid economic assumptions. When successful workout procedures amount to 1% of all insolvencies, one could wonder if sacrificing the floating charge on the workout shrine is worthwhile. Maybe it is a learning curve here, and the legal system needs some time to build up the know-how of successful workouts. If this is the case, then the sacrifice could pay off. Maybe a better understanding by secured creditors of their role in supporting feasible workouts would help increase the success rate.

CONCLUSION: A CANDLE IN THE RAIN

Romanian law has most of the ingredients for a floating charge-like device. All the building blocks are in place, and the mortar provided by the general legislation is also flexible enough to accommodate this legal instrument.

By regulating the general and all-encompassing concept of 'hypothec' as the local denominator for the security interest without dispossession (regardless of the nature of the collateral), the law specifically provides the possibility of having a *universitas facti* as collateral (when the grantor is a business). Once the security interest covers a *universitas facti*, it is the collection itself and not its individual components that are seized by the hypothec. This means that the items could flow freely in and out of the recipient during the normal course of

---

[88] While there is no reported case law to this effect, the reason is merely due merely to the fact that, in practice, the trustee in bankruptcy takes the initiative of restructuring the activity of the insolvent debtor before asking the creditors about it.

[89] The provisions of art. 160 para. (2) LPA allow the secured creditor to invalidate the transfer of (some) assets from the *universitas facti* when they are proved to be fraudulent.

business of the debtor. Only when there is a default and the secured creditor starts enforcing the hypothec will the actual content of the *universitas facti* be scrutinized and only those items currently in the collection at the time of enforcement is started shall be part of the foreclosure proceedings. This means that the hypothec over *universitas facti* functions like a floating security interest for the normal duration of its existence, but it crystallizes once an enforcement event (i.e. default) occurs.

However, for more than 20 years the case-law has still been hesitant in unleashing the full potential of this security device. Sometimes, the courts failed to notice the effectiveness of the creation of the hypothec over *universitas facti* by considering that the security interest does not attach unless the items within the collection are described in detail, despite the law providing for a broad spectrum of valid descriptions of collateral. Other courts have had difficulties in determining the clear limits of the description offered by the parties in their security agreement when confronted with generic descriptions mentioned in the security notice filed with the relevant public registry. Yet most of all, the main issue keeping this device in the shadows is the way the bankruptcy courts alter the crystallization event. In particular, the syndic judge will continue to stress that the automatic stay triggered by the insolvency effectively precludes the secured creditor from declaring default and obtaining a snapshot of the content of collateral, and so the usefulness of the hypothec over *universitas facti* will remain limited. Hopefully, the legal literature (including that produced by some judges) suggests that this simplistic approach is about to change by allowing the parties to the security agreement to provide a more detailed crystallization process in case of insolvency as well as putting some options on the table for the secured creditor: either to limit its enforcement to the items at the time of the insolvency event or to allow it to have a dynamic approach if it leaves the enterprise to continue its business as usual during the reorganization period.

Like a candle in the rain, it needs a lot of energy to keep it lit. I am confident that the domestic courts will have this degree of energy in store to be able to give the hypothec over *universitas facti* a significant boost in the near future.

11. The short history of the Hungarian floating security

Tibor Tajti

INTRODUCTION

Prologue

The Hungarian floating security, metaphrased as the 'property encumbering charge,' was introduced with the reforms assisted by the European Bank for Reconstruction and Development (EBRD) in 1996, through the amendment of the Civil Code, which had been enacted during the communist period in 1959.[1] Notwithstanding its quickly acquired popularity, the drafters of the new Civil Code passed in 2013 discarded the device based on hardly substantiated grounds. What one can ascertain from the laconic Hungarian semi-official comments[2] are no more than scant hints at the possible reasons. Hungarian-language scholarship has remained silent as well. Since no English-language study has seen daylight on this topic either, this writing is the first holistic account of these, so far systematically not analyzed and largely untold, developments in either language.

The unhappy fate and the scholarly vacuum notwithstanding, the study of the Hungarian floating charge provides a valuable contribution to comparative law and the understanding of not only blanket securities as the most complex types of proprietary security devices but also secured transactions law more broadly. This is so as the Hungarian approach, not followed by other similarly situated countries of Central and Eastern Europe, might figure as

---

[1] Polgári Törvénykönyv (Hungarian Civil Code), abbreviated as Ptk. The first was introduced by Act No. IV of the year 1959 and the second with Act No. V of the year 2013 on the Civil Code (in Hungarian: A Polgári Törvénykönyvről szóló 2013. évi V. törvény).

[2] I Gárdos, 'Comments on Title VII of the Civil Code on Liens' in L Vékás, *A Polgári Törvénykönyv magyarázatokkal* (Complex 2013) 430.

such a peculiar reform path that countries planning to modernize their secured transactions systems could learn a lot from it. Its analysis is, in other words, a valuable addendum to legal reform studies as well. Time will tell whether the Hungarian path can be considered an example of inevitable refinement or instead a backpedaled reform, if not legal engineering gone wrong.

The Systemic Features of the Hungarian Legal System

It is useful to start by positioning Hungary among the legal traditions of the world as a legal system belonging to the Civil Law legal tradition. It has been primarily influenced historically first by Austrian law during the existence of the Austro-Hungarian Empire, a prestigious place thereafter gradually taken over by German law, although traces of the influences of Franco-Latin law,[3] and more recently, of Anglo-American laws, can be found, too. The Hungarian system of notaries, for example, belongs to the so-called Latin Public Notarial system,[4] and the secured transactions reforms (to be focused upon here) were significantly influenced by Common Law systems.[5]

Another relevant feature of the Hungarian legal system is that it is a monist regime in the sense that both the old and the new Civil Codes are the repositories of both private and commercial law. In other words, the law of proprietary securities to be discussed below applies to both consumer and business finance. If needed, distinct provisions ensure the protection of consumer-debtors,

---

[3] On the impact of Italian law and legal scholarship on Hungary and Hungarian scholars, see T Tajti, 'Italian Law in Hungary' in Mauro Bussani (ed.), *Il diritto italiano in Europa (1861–2014) – Scienza, giurisprudenza, legislazione*, vol V (Edizioni Scientifiche Italiana 2014). The Italian language version of the paper was published in Rodolfo Sacco (ed.), *Diritto italiano in Ungheria 1861–2018* (UTET Giuridica, Wolters Kluwer Italia 2018) 183–203.

[4] See, e.g. T Molnár, 'The Assertion of Fundamental Principles Relating to Civil Law Notaries in the 21st Century with Special Focus on Hungary' (2019) 4 ProFuturo 25, 26. See also the English language pages of the Notarial Office of István Mándoky in Kecskemét at <http://www.notaryoffice.hu/english.html> accessed 18 August 2023.

[5] See T Tajti, 'Comparative Secured Transactions Law' (Akadémiai kiadó 2002) 293–316; T Tajti, 'Central and Eastern European Systems – Hungary, Poland and Lithuania' in G McCormack and R Bork (eds), *Security Rights and the European Insolvency Regulation* (Intersentia 2017) 571–693; T Tajti, 'Secured Transactions and Financial Contracts in Hungary on the Eve of Joining the European Union' (2002) 9 J of East Eur L 259–299.

typically by stricter preconditions or additional duties imposed on the strategically stronger party: the secured creditor.[6]

SYNOPSIS OF THE HISTORY AND KEY FEATURES OF THE HUNGARIAN FLOATING SECURITY

Why Cast a Word on the Pre-reforms Era?

Understanding the secured transactions reforms starting in the 1990s necessitates casting a word on the preceding two radically different eras: the pre-WWII capitalist period and the post-WWII credit-hostile communist regime. The first is the period in Hungarian history during which the increased need for credit and the concomitant utilization of movables and intangibles as collateral surfaced forcefully, along with the appearance of the 'security idea.' The first limited version of a floating security right also appeared in this period.

The latter, the era of communism, deserves attention as a negative example of a failed regime characterized by extreme hostility toward credit and credit securities. Comprehending its implications also helps to understand the post-1990s developments, including the reasons behind the incomprehension and occasional hostility as well as the mistakes made in shaping the contours of the new market economy-based Hungarian secured transactions laws.

The Pre-WWII Beginnings

Although Hungarian legal solutions were at some periods of the Middle Ages on par with those of leading Western European countries, that radically changed for the worse after the occupation of a large portion of the country by Ottoman Turks after 1526, the Battle of Mohács. The ensuing versions of feudalism were hardly conducive to credit, especially owing to the institution of 'entail'[7] (*'ősiség'*) making mortgaging of land, in which wealth was primarily

---

[6] See, for example, § 5:91 of the 2013 Civil Code on security agreements concluded with consumers.

[7] In Latin, the official language of Hungary in the Middle Ages, it was known as 'aviticitas'. The *Oxford Dictionary of the Middle Ages*, edited by Robert E Bjork (OUP 2010), defined it as 'Entail in medieval Hungary. The inalienable status of noble property, based on a tribal tradition that the descensus estate should descend to brothers, collateral relatives, and kinsmen. It was extended to donations by King St. Stephen, and though King Andrew II's 1222 "Golden Bull" introduced free alienation, was reestablished by King Louis the Great in 1351.' The Dictionary refers to the monograph of Antal Murarik, *Az ősiség alapintézményének eredete* [*The Origins of the Basic Institution of Entail*], published in Budapest in

locked, impossible. Consequently, it suffices to start with two notes on the nineteenth century and the pre-WWI period, the decades of gradual introduction of capitalist concepts and discarding of feudal ones.[8]

The first is that the peak of Hungarian industrial development is linked to the period between the Austro-Hungarian Compromise of 1867[9] and the beginning of WWI in 1914. This period was characterized by laying down the modern foundations of the banking and financial system, and the linked legal system. Modernization ensued, however, not only via the legislature: Hungary was back then unique also for its semi-precedential system[10] under which high court decisions served as primary sources of law essentially until the arrival of communism after WWII.

There is, however, another point of crucial importance to the evolution of credit and its role in the economy, or the 'credit idea,'[11] as the *sine qua non* of

---

1938. The entail was first abolished by the revolutionary Hungarian government in 1848. However, as the revolution was foiled by Austria (with tzarist Russia's assistance) and the law lost its effectiveness, the entail had to be abolished (again) by the decree of the Austrian Kaiser in 1852 (1852. évi ősiségi nyílt pátens). For further detail on the history of Hungarian entails, see György Képes, 'Az ősiség intézményének felszámolása és a modern magánjog létrejötte Magyarországon' in *350 éves az Eötvös Loránd Tudományegyetem Állam- és Jogtudományi Kara* (vol. 2, ELTE Eötvös Kiadó 2018) 1018–1028. In English, see Martyn Rady, *Nobility, Land and Service in Medieval Hungary* (Palgrave Macmillan 2000) 97ff.

[8] See also E Steiner, 'A vagyont terhelő zálogjog és története' (2001) 10 Közjegyzők Közlönye [Bulletin of Public Notaries] 3–9. It is commonly subscribed to that feudal elements remained part of Hungarian law until the regime change after WWII.

[9] Albeit the Kingdom of Hungary remained part of the Monarchy, the Compromise partially reestablished the Kingdom's sovereignty with many of the concomitant powers lost as a result of the break of the 1848 Revolution and the ensuing Austrian absolutist rule.

[10] D Márkus (ed.), *Magyar jogi lexikon* [*Hungarian Legal Lexicon*] (Vol. III, Pallas Irodalmi és Nyomdai Rt 1900), 84.

[11] By the phrase 'credit idea,' what is meant is the pivotal (*sine qua non*) role that credit (both loan- and sale-credit) and credit securities play in market economies, or as the French writer M Gustave du Puynode put it back in 1834: 'However fruitful have been the mines of Mexico and Peru, in which for a long time after Columbus, seemed buried the fortune of the world, there is yet a discovery more precious for humanity, and which has already produced more wealth than that of America: that is the discovery of Credit, a world altogether imaginary, but vast as space, as inexhaustible as the resources of the mind.' M Gustave du Puynode, *De la Monnaie du Credit et de l'Impot* (1834) 110, cited in H D Macleod, *The Principles of Economical Philosophy* (2nd edn, Longmans, Green, Reader, and Dyer 1872) 2.

capitalist credit economies, albeit little known outside Hungary: the pivotal role Count *István Széchenyi* played. Apart from financing the founding of the Hungarian Academy of Sciences, the construction of the world-famous Chain Bridge in Budapest, the regulation of the river Tisza and making the lower parts of the Danube navigable, he also published a highly influential book titled 'Credit' ('*Hitel*') in 1830. As the outcome of his visit to England, which in those days was at the helm of the industrial revolution, the quintessence of this work could be expressed in his oft-cited saying according to which 'the lack of credit stymies almost all [economic] activities';[12] a realization that not only echoes the similarly often-quoted excerpt from the speech of Daniel Webster in the Senate of the United States,[13] but also played a crucial role in the country's transition from feudalism to capitalism, especially as the Count also forcefully worked on the dissemination of the credit idea.

It might be little known outside the country that, in those days, the publication record of Hungarian scholars was quite remarkable throughout the pre-WWII period. This undoubtedly influenced the advancements occurring in the legal arena, including financing and credit securities, in those years. Although a number of internationally renowned legal scholars also appeared during communism, the pre-WWII period publications understandably devoted more attention to credit and the linked legal institutions, in particular, to the role that various security devices play.[14]

The drastic shortage of affordable credit in the early 1920s, to a great extent owing to the war that had lasted for four years and had brought the war-torn country to its knees, was the catalyst for change. The equipment of industrial enterprises was obsolete and depreciated. The latter half of the 1920s consequently was filled with quite intense legislative activity aimed at ameliorating these financing problems. The draft statute (bill) No. 1185 from 1926 on Chattel Mortgages, unfortunately, did not become law, although it would have

---

12 Hungarian original text: '*A hitel híja szinte minden mozgást elakaszt.*'

13 As Webster put it in 1834: 'Credit is the vital air of the system of modern commerce. It has done more, a thousand times, to enrich nations, than all the mines of all the world. It has excited labour, stimulated manufactures, pushed commerce over every sea, and brought every nation, every kingdom, and every small tribe among the races of men to be known to all the rest.' Quoted by H D Macleod, *The Principles of Economical Philosophy* (2nd edn, Longmans, Green, Reader, and Dyer 1872) 2.

14 See, e.g. P Ágoston, *A magyar zálogjog története* [*The History of Hungarian Charges*] (Politzer 1905); Endre Nizsalovszky, *A zálogjogok és a telki teher néhány főkérdése* [*Main Issues Related to Charges and Estate Encumbrances*] (Budapest 1928); E Nizsalovszky, 'Dologi jog' ['Property Rights'] in Károly Szladits (ed.), *Magyar Magánjog* [*Hungarian Private Law*] (Budapest 1930).

been the first generally applicable piece of legislation providing that security interests over movables could be perfected by registration in a proposed public register.

Some other acts of narrower reach were nonetheless enacted. An early version of floating security[15] was, indeed, introduced into the Hungarian legal system. The volte face is attributable to Law No. 35 of the year 1927 on Mortgages,[16] and the Law No. 21 of the year 1928 on Industrial Debentures.[17] The latter one is of primary importance because it could be taken as the law that introduced a version of floating security for the very first time in Hungary. The innominate proprietary security device did resemble the English floating charge. In particular, it extended to all types of assets an enterprise may possess, from machinery and equipment to raw materials needed for manufacturing, semi-finalized products and inventory (i.e. finalized products) and intellectual property rights, as well as receivables, rights and claims.[18] The law also gave unfettered dominion to the debtor-enterprise, entitling it to dispose

[15] None of the Hungarian floating securities was an exact replica of either the English floating charge or the US concept of 'floating lien', notwithstanding the undeniable impact of the former, as will be clear based on the ensuing more detailed description, especially of the version introduced in the 1990s. The same could be said also about the first floating security variant in the period between the two World Wars, notwithstanding the dearth of literature about it. They shared two crucial features of the English and US contemporary variants: first, they could be established on all, or a substantial part of, the property of an enterprise. This is why the exact designation of the new floating security was – metaphrased – a property encumbering charge, property meaning not a single movable asset. Initially, in practice, for example, there were numerous cases with all assets of a restaurant business being encumbered. Second, the security was floating (hovering) over the collateral in the sense that assets could come in and leave the debtor's encumbered estate during its existence. As far as the ranking position is concerned, the priority position was defined unfortunately vaguely; see the related discussion below.

[16] The Hungarian title was: *A jelzálogról szóló 1927. évi XXXV. törvénycikk*. This act was meant to be used in the agricultural sector, which was the reason it relied on the already existing developed system of land registers. See in National Collection of Law (Országos Törvénytár), Általános és részletes indokolás (General and Detailed Commentary), 584–639 (No. 4, 1927). Note that the title of this act could also be translated also as the Act on Charges.

[17] The Hungarian title was: *Az ipari záloglevelekről szóló 1928. évi XXI. törvénycikk* (the 1928 Industrial Debentures Act). The Hungarian text is available at <https://net.jogtar.hu/getpdf?docid=92800021.TV&targetdate=&printTitle=1928.+%C3%A9vi+XXI.+t%C3%B6rv%C3%A9nycikk&referer=1000ev> accessed 25 July 2023.

[18] §3 of the 1928 Industrial Debentures Act.

of the property in the ordinary course of business.[19] Enforcement was possible only on the enterprise as a whole, encompassing all the property owned by it as a juridical person.[20] The main function of the act, however, was not the introduction of a novel comprehensive security but rather the simplification of securitization[21] of long-term credits, secured by a mortgage on immovables as well as movables, rights and claims of the debtor.

If we take either the year 1862 and the case of *Holroyd v Marshall*,[22] or the 1870 *Re Panama* case,[23] as the cradle of the English floating charge, then 60-some years were needed for the emergence of its Hungarian kin, about the use of which little is known. However, the 12 years of near-normalcy allotted to the new device to prove its utility between its introduction and the outbreak of WWII, harmed also by the spillover effects of the Great Depression originating in the US, were hardly sufficient to make a genuine success story out of it.

The Impact of the Communist Decades

The communist regime imposed after WWII, named 'socialism' within the Eastern Bloc, had devastating effects on the financial system during the four and a half decades of its existence in the region. One could say that, contrary to the institutions of the capital market (e.g. the stock exchange, company shares[24]), at least credit and credit securities were not completely eradicated

---

19 §5 of the 1928 Industrial Debentures Act.

20 §4 of the 1928 Industrial Debentures Act.

21 Securitization in the sense known in the twenty-first century was obviously not known in 1920s Hungary, yet one should not forget that the German *Pfandbriefe* (often referred to as 'covered bonds') system resembling modern securitization was known in Central Europe since 1769. Whether this system was a source of inspiration for Hungarians with or without the English floating charge is unknown, though. See, e.g. Hal S Scott, *International Finance – Transactions, Policy, and Regulation* (17th edn, Foundation Press 2010) 646ff.

22 *Holroyd v Marshall* [1862] 10 HLC 191, 11 ER 999.

23 *Re Panama* [1870] 5 Ch App 318.

24 The Budapest Stock Exchange, which began its trading on 18 January 1864, was, for example, closed down as part of the nationalization of the industry on 25 May 1948. It was reopened after the fall of the socialist regime on 21 June 1990. The non-existence of a stock exchange between 1948 and 1990 meant also that there was no need for shares (stocks) either; nor was there a need to devote much attention (if anything at all) to shares as paradigm securities of capital markets.

from the legal system in this period. However, their prestige, as well as their use in practice, did subside drastically.[25]

Notwithstanding such hostility, the first-ever Hungarian Civil Code, enacted in 1959, did devote some attention to *in rem* securities, although essentially limiting the available security devices to the tandem of real property (immovables) mortgages ('*ingatlan jelzálogjog*') and possessory pledges over movables ('*kézizálogjog*'). The only peculiarity was a *sui generis* proprietary security device specifically designed to secure loans extended by banks being in exclusive state ownership, which basically persisted until the fall of the Berlin Wall in 1989. According to Harmathy, these were not fully-fledged proprietary securities[26] but rather some local limited-use idiosyncratic products of those times.

This state of affairs was the product of a handful of communist policies that aimed at finding new functional substitutes for such capitalist legal categories as 'credit' and 'security.' For example, housing issues were predominantly solved on a non-commercial basis, with evictions for defaulting on the repayment of loans essentially being unknown. The few surviving *in rem* securities were rarely used (although in the case of possessory pledges, this claim can only be an estimate based on anecdotal evidence). Indirectly, this may be concluded from a report on the activities of courts from 1965, which listed only one case involving *in rem* securities.[27] No major changes seem to have occurred in this respect until the mid-1990s.

Moreover, as an overwhelming number of enterprises were state-owned, basically no insolvency system was in place. Instead, enterprises facing the abyss were bailed out by the government, often based on political rather than economic grounds. Most importantly, however, non-possessory securities over movables, intangibles and rights were unknown creatures of law. Although in this respect Hungary was ahead of most other members of the Eastern Bloc thanks to its westernmost geographic position and its comparably strong legal tradition inherited from the past, its legal system nonetheless remained credit-hostile, having also eradicated all the progressive developments

---

[25] For example, the comparative law treatise authored by Gyula Eörsi, the leading internationally renowned comparatist, failed to tackle the topic of proprietary securities. See Gy Eörsi, *Összehasonlító Polgári Jog* [*Comparative Civil Law*] (Akadémiai Kiadó 1975).

[26] See in general A Harmathy, 'A hitelbiztosítékok jogának változásáról' ['On the Changing of Credit Security Law'] in *Kemenes-Emlékkönyv* (József Attila University, Szeged-Hungary, 1993).

[27] See B Bodzási, 'A keretbiztosítéki jelzálogjog szabályozása a magyar jogban' (2010) 3 Állam és Jogtudomány, 259, 282, referring to K Benedek and M Világhy, *A Polgári Törvénykönyv a Gyakorlatban* [*The Civil Code in Practice*] (Közgazdasági és Jogi Könyvkiadó 1965) 255.

from the pre-WWII era mentioned (see the section entitled 'The Pre-WWII Beginnings'). The English floating charge was a foreign peculiarity known perhaps by no more than a handful of comparatists. This should be borne in mind in order to understand the hardships and errors corollary to the reform path starting with the amendment of the Civil Code in 1996.

The Reform Era of the 1990s and Subsequent Developments

The socio-economic circumstances and impetus for the reform of Hungarian secured transactions laws

A version of floating security was introduced in Hungary with the 1996 secured transactions law reforms, as part of which a separate statute was passed: the 26th Act of the year 1996 on the Amendment of Certain Provisions of the Hungarian Republic's Civil Code[28] (hereinafter, the First Reform Act).[29] This device was an exact replica of neither the English floating charge nor the US floating lien, for which reason it is more appropriate to refer to it with the metaphrased expression 'property encumbering charge.'[30]

---

[28] The text of the old Civil Code in Hungarian is available at <https://njt.hu/jogszabaly/1959-4-00-00> accessed 18 August 2023. An English language version is downloadable from <https://gss.unicreditgroup.eu/sites/default/files/markets/documents/Civil_Code_effective_on_24_July_2012_.pdf> accessed 18 August 2023.

[29] See on the Hungarian reforms up until the year 2002, the chapter on Hungary in Tibor Tajti, *Comparative Secured Transactions Law* (Akadémiai kiadó 2002) 293–315. For further developments, see Tibor Tajti, 'Security Rights and Insolvency Law in the Central and Eastern European Systems' in Gerard McCormack and Reinhard Bork (eds), *Security Rights and the European Insolvency Regulation* (Intersentia 2017) 571–692. The property encumbering charge was defined in section 254(1) of the First Reform Act (*első zálogjogi novella*) [note the numbering of sections changed subsequently].

[30] The Hungarian designation '*vagyont terhelő zálogjog*' was exactly 'property encumbering charge,' although it would be correct to translate it as 'property encumbering consensual lien' or 'property encumbering security interest.' I opted for 'charge' because among the three English expressions, this one seems to be the most widely known and used among Hungarian lawyers, bankers and other finance experts dealing with the device. See section 266 of the old Civil Code from 1959 (as amended). The term 'charge' is not, however, being used in the technical sense of English law of equity. Note also that unlike English legal terminology, the Hungarian designation of the floating security (as well as pledge and mortgage) includes the term 'right,' and it is not expressing the name of a distinct security device. This required adaptations in some of the translated quotations in the text to make them fit English legal terminology.

This reform effort ensued at the initiative of the EBRD (European Bank for Reconstruction and Development) after its meeting held in Budapest in 1992, discussing the financing needs of the region, the obstacles to affordable financing and the deficiencies of the connected laws.[31] As even the titles of some commentators' publications prove, the reception of Common Law-originated legal institutions was, however, not necessarily wholeheartedly welcomed by all.[32] The final commonly subscribed-to verdict nonetheless is that the reform was a success as it significantly boosted credit and lending.

The most important reason for the reform of the secured transactions law was, however, related to the hardships prevailing in agriculture at the beginning of the 1990s. This sector was in desperate need of modern technologies, and although banks were, in principle, ready to lend to the sector, the secured transactions law inherited from communism was completely ill-suited for the task. In particular, there were no non-possessory security devices that would have facilitated the taking of agricultural machines and equipment, crops and other agricultural products as collateral.

Title finance or acquisition finance transactions were missing because these make use of the newly acquired equipment to generate income from which the credit installments could (also) be paid. Consequently, a strong competitor for the newly introduced 'registered pledges' appeared on the market parallel with the centrally orchestrated reforms to solve not only the problems of agriculture, but also those of the acquisition of motor vehicles, in the form of a distinct largely non-statutory law of 'fiduciary securities' (*'fiduciárius hitelbiztosítékok'*). These were actually various contracts relying on retained title (ownership), from versions of 'leasing' contracts to 'simple' sales contracts containing a retention of title clause. Essentially, until their eradication from the legal system by the 2013 new Civil Code,[33] or the subjection of some of them to registration in the new register of non-possessory securities over movables, they were used to bypass the rules and registration requirements introduced by the reforms. Owing to the limbo caused by the coexistence of the two parallel and competing legal regimes, the positions of courts were also diverging,[34] similarly to the authors of related publications. Some courts and

---

31 See A Harmathy, 'The EBRD Model Law and the Hungarian Law' in JJ Norton and M Andenas, *Emerging Financial Markets and Secured Transactions* (Kluwer 1998), 197–209.

32 See, e.g. T Anka, 'Halva született' ['Born Dead'] (1998) 2 Közjegyzők közlönye [Bulletin of Public Notaries] 7.

33 §6:99 of the new Civil Code.

34 Gárdos (n 2), 458 and 574 para 5. The fiduciary securities, however, were not abolished only because of their latent nature but rather because they, as claimed, provide the creditor with more rights to the detriment of the debtor than what is

authors vouched for the legitimacy of the non-registrable fiduciary securities, and yet others were of the contrary opinion.

As the reform was both initiated and supported by the EBRD, it was primarily influenced by the 1994 EBRD Model Law[35] and its basic principles, which in turn were drafted following English law – including the floating charge.

As far as the impact of English and American law is concerned, it makes sense to distinguish two phases in the life of the new secured transactions law. With the introduction of the new system in 1996, this impact was, at first, indirect through the related documents of the EBRD. In this initial phase, resorting to the above-mentioned pre-WWII device was also noticeable, more as some kind of historic justification for the reforms rather than to satisfy practical needs; this seems to have subsided later. The second phase was characterized by rather more courageous reliance on the laws of the United States, first and foremost on Article 9 of the Uniform Commercial Code as the number one international model. Consequently, the 2013 Civil Code provisions already display features resembling concepts borrowed from the other side of the Atlantic; the best example being the import of the American concept of 'commercially reasonable disposition.'[36]

The key features of the property encumbering charge

The basic rules on the creation (attachment and perfection in the nomenclature of Uniform Commercial Code Article 9) – or making the property encumbering charge valid against the entire world (*erga omnes* effect) – were, in general, similar to those applicable to the English floating charge or the US floating lien. The security agreement had to be concluded in written form, the type of the security device had to be declared (in the title of the agreement), and it had to be registered as such in the newly established electronic database operated by the National Association of Public Notaries ('MOKK') in operation from

legally necessary and just, as well as for their conflict with the prohibition of *lex commissoria,* or prohibition of 'strict foreclosure' known by common law systems.

35 Text available at <https://www.ebrd.com/news/publications/guides/model-law-on-secured-transactions.html> accessed 18 August 2023. See also LA Mistelis, 'The EBRD Model Law on Secured Transactions and Its Impact on Collateral Law Reform in Central and Eastern Europe and the Former Soviet Union' (1998) 5 Parker Sch JE Eur L 455. For critical comments see JA Spagnole, 'A Functional Analysis of the EBRD Model Law on Secured Transactions' (1997) 3-SPG NAFTA: L & Bus Rev Am 82.

36 Gárdos (n 2), 470. This was, though, an indirect borrowing from US law through the intermediation of the European Union Directive 2002/47/EC on financial collateral arrangements (6 June 2002). In UCC Article 9, see section 9-610(b).

1997.[37] Although traditionally following German law – which remains characterized by latent[38] (i.e. non-publicized) security interests as far as movables, rights and claims are concerned (save for some specific asset types such as ships and aircraft), Hungary had thereby joined the predominant pattern of leading common law systems, which place greater reliance on registration, at least to make the security fully effective. As the register was not established solely for the registration of the property encumbering charge but also for the registration of security interests, *inter alia,* on movables, machines and equipment, and receivables, it has been functioning ever since.

This database was distinct not only from the real property (immovables) register but also from those for motor vehicles, ships and aircraft, and some intellectual property rights, as well as some types of securities issued by companies.[39] For these, registration in physically separate registries (called: '*lajstrom*') was, and remains, necessary. In respect of the requirements of registration of these specific types of assets, Hungary is no exception.[40]

---

[37] See the related clarification on the two registers in Hungarian on the website of the Hungarian National Association of Public Notaries (in Hungarian: Magyar Országos Közjegyzői Kamara, abbreviated as MOKK) at <https://www.mokk.hu/ugyfeleknek/ZONY.php> accessed 28 July 2023. While the first was named 'Charge Registry' ('*Zálogjogi Nyilvántartás*'), translatable also as 'Registry of Security Interests,' the new one introduced in March 2014 is called 'the Registry of Credit Securities' ('*Hitelbiztosítékok Nyilvántartása*'). Their widely used acronyms are 'ZONY' for the first and 'HBNY' for the latter.

[38] By latent security interests, what is meant are interests for which no publicity is provided regarding their existence. Put simply, they are not registered in a publicly accessible register or otherwise publicized. The main reason for there being no perceived need for such a public register in Germany (applicable also to Austria), as formulated by Ulrich Drobnig, the doyen of German commercial law, is that '[m]erchants are expected to know that nowadays most items of major equipment are bought on credit and that the purchased items serve as security. [...] In short, publicity by registration is replaced by a presumption of constructive knowledge of the security right.' He admitted though that 'it is true to say that the rate of litigation in cases of the buyers' bankruptcies is very high and as a result at least some of the initial saving of cost and time due to non-registration is later lost in litigating with the insolvency administrator.' Quoted from U Drobnig, 'Basic issues of European rules on security in movables' in John de Lacy (ed.), *The Reform of UK Personal Property Security Law – Comparative Perspectives* (Routledge 2010) 448.

[39] For details of these separate registries, see Gárdos (n 2), 430.

[40] See, e.g. §5:93 of the 2013 Civil Code on the constitutive effects of registration in these distinct registers. For the regime applicable to the recording of security interests over motor vehicles, see T Tajti, 'Security Rights and Insolvency Law in the Central and Eastern European Systems' in Gerard McCormack and Reinhard

The 2013 Civil Code changes also included the introduction of a new electronic register for the registration of security interests ('registered pledges') introduced with the 1996 reforms, the operation of which was also entrusted to the National Association of Public Notaries but under a different designation.[41] Hence, researchers can find references to property encumbering charges only in the pre-2013 Civil Code, as amended, after 15 March 2014, the starting date of the implementation of the new Civil Code.

It is also interesting to add that until 2013, the registration of security interests in the new register largely operated analogously to the rules applicable to real property registers. This meant, in particular, that the security agreement creating the property encumbering charge had to be drafted, explained and counter-signed by a public notary before entry into the register. The fee payable to notaries was based on the value of the collateral, a pattern that was radically reduced to a fixed amount by the 2013 Civil Code and the implementing acts.

Similarly to English law,[42] provisions introducing a statutory prescribed part (carve-out) for non-secured creditors were also added by the Fourth Amendment of the Insolvency Act in 2006.[43] As Juhász, a leading Hungarian insolvency expert, emphasized, this specifically involved having foreign examples in sight.[44] According to this rule, the secured creditor holding a property encumbering charge was entitled to get 50% of the price received for the sold collateral in insolvency proceedings immediately upon the receipt of these moneys.[45] For the remaining 50%, the secured creditor had to stand in line and compete with a number of other unsecured and statutory claimants.[46]

Bork, *Security Rights and the European Insolvency Regulation* (Intersentia 2017) para 1.5., 652–653.

[41] The implementing laws and regulations were the '2013. évi CCXXI. törvény a hitelbiztosítéki nyilvántartásról, 18/2014 (III 13)' and the 'KIM rendelet a hitelbiztosítéki nyilvántartás részletes szabályainak megállapításáról.'

[42] UK Insolvency Act 1986 s 176A. See also L Gullifer and J Payne, *Corporate Finance Law: Principles and Policy* (3rd edn, Hart Publishing 2020), para 3.3.1.2.3. at 103.

[43] Law No. VI of the year 2006 on the Amendment of the Act on Reorganizations, Liquidations and of the Act No. XLIX of the year 1991 on Dissolution [of Companies] ['*2006. évi VI. törvény a csődeljárásról, a felszámolási eljárásról és a végelszámolásról szóló 1991. évi XLIX. törvény módosításáról*'].

[44] L Juhász, *A magyar fizetésképtelenségi jog kézikönyve* [*The Handbook of Hungarian Insolvency Law*] (Vol. II, Novotni Publisher 2014) 758.

[45] See §49/D of the Insolvency Act in the version then in force. Juhász (n 44) vol. II 758–59.

[46] §57(1) of the Insolvency Act in the version back then in force.

Another similarity with English law was that the Hungarian floating security was available only to businesses, but to both those with and without juridical entity status, on the entirety of their assets or on their independently operating economic units (*'önálló gazdasági egységként működtethető részén'*).[47] It could extend to immovables (real property) as well.

One more point ought to be added to make the picture clearer. Namely, the drafting technique of the 1996 reforms was a bit inconsistent, especially as far as the naming of the newly introduced proprietary securities was concerned. Most, including the property encumbering charge, were made part of the system under a specific designation,[48] which was then consistently used not only in the statutory text but also in business life.

In addition to that, there was a device that appeared in the provisions of the Civil Code in a descriptive format. More precisely, the descriptive provision ended with a specific designation added in brackets.[49] Its metaphrased translation to English would be 'fixed-limit mortgage' or 'fixed-limit property encumbering charge' (*'keretbiztosítéki jelzálog'*) as its main feature was that besides identifying which debts are secured by it, the upper monetary limit up to which the secured creditor could enforce its security interest also had to be fixed. Eventually, this arrangement evolved into a distinct kind of *in rem* security, though strictly speaking, it was merely a sub-type of other nominated types of security devices. Statistics nonetheless listed it as a separate item, for example, in the form of a 'fixed-limit property encumbering charge.' In English translations, this may cause misunderstandings as occasionally it was translated as a blanket (floating) security. The fixed-limit charge, contrary to the property encumbering charge, was not abolished by the 2013 Civil Code.[50]

As these details may suggest, the not necessarily consistent nomination of security devices must have created some unease, if not practical hardships, during the implementation of the new law, given that the proprietary securities-related chapter's section titles of the new Civil Code are no longer based on the names of the recognized (nominated) security devices but rather they

47 §266(1) of the old Civil Code.

48 The nominated securities in the 1996 reform act amending the old Civil Code were: (1) the newly introduced chattel mortgage (*'jelzálogjog'* in §261), (2) the possessory pledge (*'kézizálogjog'* in §265), (3) the novel property encumbering charge (*'vagyont terhelő zálogjog'* in §266), (4) charges on rights and claims (*'zálogjog jogon és követelésen'* in §267), (5) the independent charge – also newly introduced (*'önálló zálogjog'* in § 269), and (6) the special possessory security inherited from the past which we will refer to as 'security-bailment' (*'óvadék'* in §270).

49 See §263(1) of the old Civil Code.

50 §5:98(3) of the 2013 Civil Code.

follow the phases of the existence of *in rem* security rights, from their constitution to enforcement and deletion from the register.[51] This applies also to the fixed-limit charge, the designation of which nonetheless has seemingly remained a useful aid in business activities.

Remedying the inconsistencies: the amendments of the Civil Code of 2000

Unfortunately, the language of the provision[52] on the ranking position of the property encumbering charge[53] in the first version of the amendment from 1996 was incomplete and thus misleading. It was not specified whether the priority of the property encumbering charge was the date of its registration or, rather, the date of its 'concretization', the latter being similar to the crystallization of a floating charge in English law based on default. This was a serious deficiency, suggesting that more prescriptive drafting would have been needed.

Put differently, the dilemma was whether the new Hungarian property-encumbering charge was modeled on the English floating charge, or rather it resembled the US concept of a floating (blanket) lien.[54] In English law, the floating charge gets a priority position not upon registration with the Companies Register, but only later, upon crystallization.[55] As opposed to

---

51 Gárdos (n 2) 417.

52 Section 250 of the 1996 amendments of the Civil Code. Note that the numbering subsequently changed. The second amendment of the secured transactions-related part of the Civil Code already expressly provided clear rules on the ranking of the property-encumbering charge in section 266(3). See the Hungarian text of the old Civil Code, and the secured transactions law-related amendments, at <https://jogkodex.hu/jsz/ptk_1959_4_torveny_5861514?ts=2006-08-24#ss1608> accessed 4 August 2023.

53 I Mándoki, 'A vagyont terhelő zálogjog ranghelye' (2006) 7–8 Közjegyzők Közlönye 14–17. It is noteworthy that the author of this short article was the acting public notary in the case that reached the Supreme Court. His position was identical with that of the subsequent interpretation of the Court. As the case involved great monetary value, his office was consequently exposed to considerable risk in the form of possible monetary damages not covered by the mandatory liability insurance of public notaries in case of an unfavorable interpretation.

54 In the United States, both phrases are in use. Grant Gilmore, the chief editor of the team drafting Article 9 of the Uniform Commercial Code (UCC), used primarily the term 'floating lien.' See G Gilmore, *Security Interests in Personal Property* (Little, Brown and Company 1965) §11.7, 359.

55 However, in English law, this is subject to rules regarding negative pledges, which can cause a floating charge to rank from its creation against (certain) competing interests. This concretely means that '[a] party taking a subsequent fixed charge with notice of the negative pledge clause will cede priority to the

that, the US floating lien gets its priority immediately upon filing (registration), unless explicitly postponed by the parties (which in practice is normally not the case). That this admittedly imprecise analogy has legitimacy could be deduced also from the fact that the term 'crystallization' in its Hungarian version (*kristályosítás*') was also used occasionally.[56] Otherwise, 'concretization' or 'crystallization' was in effect a written declaration of the secured creditor in which it was specified with regard to which assets he wanted to enforce the charge.[57]

As the stakes were high, the drafting flaw generated an unusually heated debate involving not only scholars but also judges, public notaries and scholars. As a commentator aptly put it, as 'the drafters had failed to pay due attention to the ranking of security rights that come into being by transformation, they had created a cause for a serious debate.'[58]

The opinions were diametrically opposite, some rejecting the property encumbering charge being equal to other types of proprietary security rights and others pronouncing their equality. As one of the deniers put it: 'this legal institution originating in Anglo-Saxon law is so foreign to Hungarian law that it cannot be considered as equal to other types of proprietary security rights, especially in its "floating" shape because in this phase it is only in a "preparatory form" that cannot serve as an object of enforcement.'[59] One author was even of the opinion that the property encumbering charge was not a proprietary security right but rather merely an option to obtain such a right.[60]

---

floating charge, but if the fixed chargee does not have notice, it will take free of, and in priority to, the floating charge.' L Gullifer and J Payne, *Corporate Finance Law: Principles and Policy* (3rd edn, Hart 2020) para 7.4.4. at 335 citing *English and Scottish Mercantile Investment Co v Brunton* [1892] 2 QB 700, and *Welch v Bowmaker (Ireland) Ltd* [1980] IR 251 (Sup Ct Ireland). See also Ewan McKendrick, *Goode and McKendrick on Commercial Law* (6th edn, Penguin 2020) paras 22.45, 22.46, and 24.47.

[56] E.g. L Leszkoven, 'Néhány zálogjogi gondolat' ['A Few Thoughts on Security Law'] (2000) 5 Magyar Jog 277.

[57] Section 266(2) of the old Civil Code.

[58] L Kovács, 'A vagyont terhelő zálogjog' ['The Property Encumbering Charge'] (2002) 12 Közjegyzők közlönye 33, cited by Mándoki (n 53) 15 [translation by the author].

[59] T Zámbó, *A zálogszerződés* [*The Security Contract*] (Közgazdasági és Jogi Könyvkiadó 1999) 118, cited by Mándoki (n 53) 15. Zámbó has, however, changed his opinion since the Supreme Court decision.

[60] B Bodzási, 'Néhány szó a keretbiztosítéki vagyont terhelő jelzálogjogról' ['Few Words about the Frame-Security Property Encumbering Charge'] (2004) Themis, the ELTE Law School Doctoral School Journal 17, cited by Mándoki (n 53).

In addition to some other refinements and filling of gaps, the function of the amendments of the respective provisions of the Civil Code by the Second Reform Act in the year 2000[61] was to clarify this pivotal issue. In fact, more cases reached the Supreme Court asking for the resolution of this question.[62] As some of the cases had been launched before the 2000 amendments and were concluded after them, a further dilemma came up: whether the ranking of the pre-2000 and post-2000 property encumbering charges ought to be the same. The Supreme Court cut the Gordian Knot by the following holding:

> In deciding the disputed legal question we need to proceed from the fact that the Civil Code defines the property encumbering charge as one type of security right. The security right, being the subject matter of this case, comes into being by constitution according to § 260(2) of the Civil Code, its registration in the register maintained by the public notaries, and it has the same absolute effects, *and has the same ranking [...] as other types of security right.* [...]. The secured creditor's declaration unifies and concretizes it, but with this act no new security right is being created; only the type of security right is changing. [Emphasis added]

Put simply, and as *ex post* declared by the 2000 amendments,[63] the date of registration determined the priority position of the property encumbering charge.

Some quantitative and empirical data from the heyday of the Hungarian floating security

The quantitative data available on the property encumbering charge was primarily published by the National Association of Public Notaries. According to their sources, in the period between 5 May 1997, the start of the work of the charge register, and 31 December 2006, 12,217 property-encumbering charges were registered in total. This is a figure to which one could also add the two hybrid types of floating securities: the 98 independent and the 13,918 fixed-limit property encumbering charges. The total number of these securities was topped only by the 51,837 chattel mortgages established on single, identifiable movable assets. The total number of in rem security devices registered with

61 The 137th Act of the year 2000 on the Amendment of the Law Regulating Charges (Official Gazette No. 2000/129, at 8645).

62 Gfv. IX. 30. 247.

63 See Old Civil Code §266(3) and the Governmental Decree No. 7-1997 (of January 22) on the Registry of Chattel Mortgages and Property Encumbering Charges ['*7/1997 (I 22) Korm. rendelet az ingó dolgokat terhelő jelzálogjog és a vagyont terhelő zálogjog nyilvántartásáról*'].

the charge register operated by the National Association of Public Notaries was 94,135, a considerable figure given the size of the Hungarian economy.[64]

What the data reveals is that the Hungarian floating security became rather popular within a short period of time, notwithstanding the teething problems. For this reason, its abolition came as a surprise for banks and public notaries. Anka, one of the most prolific practicing public notaries who regularly comments on security laws, noted:

> The resolute law-maker was not deterred from carrying out the abolition of the property encumbering charge notwithstanding that no such request was made by those applying the law. [Moreover,] those financial institutions that made most use of it were decidedly for keeping it.[65]

In the agricultural sector, however, it was not the property-encumbering charge that became the 'workhorse' of the system but rather a few warehousing companies (initially four, later three) operating nationwide based on a technique called 'artificial warehousing' ('*művi raktározás*'). The label stemmed from the fact that it was not the farmer or the agricultural enterprise that had to carry their crop used as collateral to a public warehouse in cities and towns, but rather the warehousing companies went out to the field to erect an artificial facility on the premises of the debtors. This was very similar, if not identical, to what used to be known in the United States as 'field warehousing', which Gilmore spoke of as one of the 'independent security devices' that were then integrated into UCC Article 9.[66]

In the early days, though, these hardly worked perfectly. Indeed, investigative journalists reported how debtors abused the gaps in the system by pledging their crop to a bank and then secretly selling it, or pledging it to another creditor in return for more credit. Today, however, most of these problems are solved efficiently by the application of such new technologies as GPS (Global Positioning System) or telemetry, as combined with such new services on the market as collateral management or collateral certification.[67]

The reason why artificial warehousing deserves mention here is that, according to Roy Goode, the doyen of English commercial law, field warehousing has not appeared in the United Kingdom exactly because of the availability of the

---

64 S Póka, 'Statisztika' ['Statistics'] (2007) 3 Közjegyzők Közlönye [Bulletin of Public Notaries] 9.

65 T Anka, 'A zálogjog az új Polgári Törvénykönyvben' ['The Charge in the New Civil Code'] (2014) 1 Közjegyzők Közlönye 28, 33.

66 G Gilmore, *Security Interests in Personal Property* (1965) ch 6.

67 For a detailed study on this topic, see T Tajti, 'The Resurrection of Field Warehousing' (2014) 55/3 Acta Juridica Hungarica 185–235.

floating charge in England and the US courts' intolerance of the floating device lasting until the arrival of the UCC with almost a century-long delay.[68] Even if his claim may have merits in Britain, it obviously has not been confirmed by Hungarian developments. What the Hungarian experiences suggest is that the introduction of the floating security did not make artificial warehousing superfluous. Rather, they co-existed, the critical advantage of the 'artificial' and the earlier American 'field' warehousing as to the floating charge being that in the case of warehousing, the collateral is in the safekeeping of a professional company, preventing it from being misappropriated by the debtor. In other words, the critical formula is hidden in the difference between the *possessory* artificial warehousing versus the floating security as a *non-possessory* security device and the critically reduced opportunities for abuse by the debtor in the case of warehousing.

The 2013 new Civil Code: abandonment of the floating security device

As already noted, notwithstanding the successful introduction of the device, and contrary to the views of the Hungarian Chamber of Public Notaries, the device was unexpectedly abolished with the adoption of the new Civil Code ('*Polgári törvénykönyv*') of Hungary in 2013.[69] More precisely, although the device as such was discarded, some of its features remain available in a limited format, namely, the possibility of identification of the collateral by description instead of by specification,[70] and giving the debtor unfettered dominion to deal with the collateral in the ordinary course of business.[71] However, these are now possibilities only with respect to specific individualized assets and not to the entire property, present and future, of the debtor.

The drafters of the Code justified the abolition using two interlinked reasons. The first was related to the impossibility of enforcing the property encumbering charge by selling the debtor's enterprise as an economic unit ('*vagyon egységének fentartása mellett*') outside insolvency proceedings.[72] According to commentators, this simply did not work in practice, which is why it was assumed that the enforcement of the floating security could occur only

---

[68] Ewan McKendrick, *Goode and McKendrick on Commercial Law* (6th edn, Penguin 2020) para 29.10 at 784.

[69] The 5th Law of Year 2013 on the Civil Code [hereinafter the 2013 or new Civil Code].

[70] Namely, as per §5:89(3), the basic rule is that the collateral must be specified. As a supplementary rule, as per §5:89(4), the collateral may be specified, however, also by type, quantity, or other appropriate method of description of the asset used as collateral. See also §5:102 of the 2013 Civil Code.

[71] §5:108 of the 2013 Civil Code.

[72] Gárdos (n 2), 417.

within insolvency proceedings.[73] Although they also referred to some out-of-court enforcement problems, it is not fully clear what they meant, as self-help and extra-judicial enforcement have always been limited to some very exceptional situations under Hungarian law but have not been applicable to floating security.

The most probable explanation is that little attention, if any, was given to the role receivers, administrative receivers, and more recently administrators[74] have played in enforcing floating charges in England or Scotland (or other relevant systems) and more precisely, the fact that especially before the adoption of the Enterprise Act 2002, weakening the position of floating chargees, floating charges were typically enforced 'outside any insolvency proceedings by appointing an administrative receiver',[75] third party experts whose mandate was to 'utilize the charged assets to the best advantage of the appointing creditor',[76] the holder of a floating charge. The administrative receiver was not a liquidator but rather a 'receiver and manager',[77] as its original designation suggests. Such professionals who could perform managerial tasks, potentially continue running the debtor company as a going concern or if needed sell the debtor company's assets, have not existed in Hungary, nor was training of such experts planned parallel with the introduction of the local version of the floating security.

The second reason, also originating in the idea of disposal of the debtor's property as a unit, was that such a sale of the collateral could be undertaken only in insolvency proceedings,[78] or as the semi-official comments stated: 'Enforcement of the property encumbering charge by keeping the unity of its

---

[73] Gárdos (n 2), 417.

[74] The English 'receiver' later came to be named 'administrative receiver,' and they could have been appointed by floating chargees over all the assets of a company out of court. This power has been abolished, except in some limited cases (e.g. project finance), and now the floating chargee can appoint an administrator out of court. The administrator, contrary to the receiver, '*owes a duty to act in the interests of all the company's creditors, unless he has decided that he cannot either rescue the company or achieve a better result for the company's creditors as a whole than if it were wound up.*' Gullifer & Payne (n 42) para 7.5.1.4. at 342–343.

[75] Gullifer & Payne (n 42) para 7.5. at 337.

[76] Ewan McKendrick, *Goode and McKendrick on Commercial Law* (6th edn, Penguin 2020) para 23.40.

[77] Ibid., note 101 at 743, referring to *Lightman and Moss on the Law of Administrators and Receivers of Companies*, note 99.

[78] Gárdos (n 2), 417.

assets [could] not be effectuated within the confines of civil law; such enforcement would inevitably transgress into the domain of insolvency law.'[79]

Unfortunately, the sparing words of the semi-official commentary are limited to this statement and do not specify why enforcement in insolvency proceedings would also be difficult in more concrete terms. The reasons, though, might have been quite mundane and self-explanatory, although a little disheartening too: the insolvency system was new and consequently it had suffered from numerous imperfections ever since the enactment of Hungary's first modern insolvency act in 1991.[80] This included problems with the training and incentivization as well as the control of insolvency practitioners, who received only minimal training to enforce property-encumbering charges by selling the debtor's company as a whole, let alone perform tasks of company managers. This claim is corroborated by the succinct qualification of Andrea Csőke from 2011, another of the very few experts on Hungarian insolvency law. As she put it: 'In Hungary, everybody has known for years that the insolvency system does not work. The system is very expensive and ineffective, but nobody is prepared to do anything about it, to think about changes, or to decide even basic issues.'[81]

Even bigger obstacles were created by the lack of stiff contempt of court rules or equivalent rules, which meant that the directors and officers of bankrupt companies, especially the smaller ones in which the owners also performed the functions of managers, could not be properly disciplined and forced to fulfill their statutory duties in time. Not much has changed in this respect ever since, notwithstanding that since 1 September 2009 (NB: introduced only about 18 years after the passage of the Insolvency Act in 1991) the Chief Executive Officer (CEO) can be fined for not cooperating with the insolvency practitioners.[82] These questions are part of a more general problem: how to make bankruptcy courts more respected.

---

79 Gárdos (n 2), 417. The Hungarian original reads: 'A vagyont terhelő zálogjog vagyonegység fenntartása melletti érvényesítése ... nem oldható meg a polgári jog keretei között, az szükségképpen átcsúszik a fizetésképtelenségi jog területére.'

80 Act No. 49 of Year 1991 on Restructuring and Liquidation Proceedings ['*1991. évi XLIX. törvény a csődeljárásról és a felszámolási eljárásról*']. Note that owing to some unknown reasons the first chapter of the Act – content-wise covering the restructuring or reorganization proceedings in many respects similarly to Chapter 11 of the US Bankruptcy Code – was named 'bankruptcy proceedings' if we metaphrase the title of this chapter ('*Csődeljárás*').

81 A Csőke, 'Preservation Measures in Hungarian Insolvency Proceedings' in Heinz Vallender (ed.), *Regulations and Measures of Protection in National Legislations within the European Union* (INSOL Europe 2011) 89.

82 Juhász (n 44) vol. I 224.

Although empirical evidence on how insolvency proceedings are conducted in the country is generally scarce, László Juhász, the author of a two-volume *Insolvency Law Handbook*, has found it important to stress, for example, that insolvency practitioners often face '[hardships in finding] the avoidable contracts of the bankrupt debtor because its officers had [by that time] cautiously hid them.'[83] This is the consequence of an unfortunately quite widespread practice according to which by the time liquidation proceedings are started and the insolvency practitioner is appointed, the CEO's mandate has been terminated by resignation, removal, or otherwise (e.g. death), as a result of which there is nobody to hand over financial documents to the insolvency administrator and fulfilll other statutory duties.[84]

These are just a few of the defects of the insolvency system that persist today. Thus, although not spelled out by the drafters of the 2013 Civil Code, one can presume that they have been, indeed, decisive when discarding the most complex security device imaginable: the property encumbering charge or the Hungarian variant of the floating security.

On top of that, reorganization has remained unpopular throughout the post-1991 period largely owing to fear about the intense stigma of bankruptcy and its negative consequences.[85] As evidence, it is sufficient to point to the extremely large number of abandoned companies, the volume of which remains very high.[86] These are clearly living proof not only of the excessive uncooperativeness of company officers of insolvent businesses but also of the obstacles such behavior created for the enforcement of property-encumbering charges.

---

[83] Juhász (n 44) vol. II 551.

[84] Juhász (n 44) vol. I 448.

[85] Juhász (n 44) vol. I 145. According to the official statistics for the year 2019 only 123 reorganizations (csődeljárás) were initiated. As compared with that, even fewer, 77 were initiated in 2015. As opposed to that, the number of liquidations was 11,689 in 2019. Based on a document 'Ügyforgalmi Elemzés – 2019. Év' ['Analysis of the Activities of Courts for Year 2019'] available at <https://birosag.hu/sites/default/files/2020-05/reszletes_elemzes_a_2019._evi_birosagi_ugyforgalomrol.pdf> accessed 28 July 2023.

[86] These are subject to special proceedings called 'forced deletions' – deletions from the Company Register – regulated outside the Insolvency Act, in Act No. V of Year 2006 on Company Publicity, Court Company Registration, and on Final Accounting ('*2006. évi V. törvény a cégnyilvánosságról, a bírósági eljárásról és a végelszámolásról*'). The number of such forced deletions, similarly to liquidations, is also counted in thousands from year to year up until today. See also T Tajti, 'Unprotected Consumers in the Digital Age: The Consumer-Creditors of Bankrupt, Abandoned, Defunct and of Zombie Companies' (2019) 24(1) Tilburg L Rev 3–26, 23–24.

Yet, to get a closer insight into the atmosphere in which the drafters were working, the confused treatment of another device introduced in 1996, the so-called 'independent charge,' should be looked at. This German law-inspired device[87] was abolished simultaneously with the property encumbering charge but, contrary to the latter, was reintroduced in 2016.[88] While the main reason for the independent charge's abolition officially was its abusive use to the detriment of consumer-debtors, given that owing to its non-accessory nature it could have been easily disposed of by banks even into the hands of less regulated, or unregulated, buyers, incomprehension undoubtedly contributed too.

The reintroduction was explained by the need to fit the Civil Code's related rules with the expectations of the 2010 Third Basel Accord[89] enshrined in EU *Regulation 575/2013 on prudential requirements for credit institutions and investment firms and Amending Regulation 648/2012*,[90] which sees the independent charge as a risk-exposure reducing device.[91] Consequently, its availability is crucial for banks, which are expected under Basel III to keep the required leverage ratio and to maintain certain levels of reserve capital.

87 The model for the Hungarian independent charge was the German *Grundschuld,* commonly translated into English as 'land charge,' as opposed to *Hypothek,* or mortgage. While the latter is accessory, the land charge is not, and this is the reason why it became 'the common security right in German legal practice having replaced the "Hypothek" entirely. It can secure different claims without the need to repeat its registration in the Land Register every time.' See Reinhard Bork, 'Security Rights and Insolvency Law in the Germanic Legal System' in Gerard McCormack and Reinhard Bork (eds), *Security Rights and the European Insolvency Regulation* (Intersentia 2017) para 21 at 180.

88 The independent charge was reintroduced by the 77th Act of Year 2016 on the Amendment of the Law of Year 2013 on the Civil Code ['*2016. évi LXXVII törvény a Polgári Törvénykönyvről szóló 2013. évi V. törvény módosításáról*'].

89 Basel III was passed as a reaction to the global financial crisis of 2007–2008 caused by the US Credit Crunch. Initially, it was foreseen to be implemented in the period of 2013–2015, yet the deadline was extended first to 2019 and then to 1 January 2023.

90 OJ L 176, 27.6.20131–337.

91 Official Comments on the 2016 77th Act on the Amendment of the Law No. LXXVII of the year 2013 on the Civil Code [*2016. évi LXXVII. törvény indokolása a Polgári Törvénykönyvről szóló 2013. évi V. törvény módosításáról*].

NEGLECTED BUT CRUCIAL QUESTIONS

The Impact of Invisible Presumptions

In hindsight, and with the lack of a more detailed explanation of the reasons that led to discarding the property encumbering charge, it ought to be added that a few hardly palpable, subtle presumptions have most probably impacted the fate of the device from the outset. No word seems to have been cast on these. As a result, it is hard to prove both their existence and the intensity of their impact. Still, it can be quite firmly claimed that they have been widely and uncritically shared by Hungarian lawyers, especially as they were inferences drawn based on widely known legal concepts. Two ought to be mentioned.

The first was the presumption that the property encumbering charge, similarly to all the other proprietary security devices, was to operate overwhelmingly outside the context of insolvency law. The logic of this rests on the reasons already mentioned: the extremely intense bankruptcy stigma, including the ignorance and fear of insolvency laws, the myriad defects of the insolvency system and the generally shared opinion that the insolvency regime is dysfunctional. That these claims are meritorious can be seen also in the above-quoted one-paragraph-long reasons of the drafters of the new 2013 Civil Code, discarding the device exactly by referring to the enforcement problems transgressing the confines of private law.[92] This presumption, implying that the value of in rem security devices can and should be assessed principally outside the context of insolvency proceedings, equally applied to the other known *in rem* security devices. In other words, the number one presumption commonly subscribed to in leading common law systems, according to which security interests primarily exist as protections against the insolvency of their debtors, has not been the dominant one in Hungary (and presumably in much of the region).[93]

The second presumption seems to have been that the property encumbering charge in the overwhelming number of cases ensures full recovery for the secured creditor. When thinking about the reasons, recall that upon the arrival of the transitory phase in the 1990s, only two *in rem* security devices were

[92] See Gárdos (n 2).

[93] Interestingly, this idea was most succinctly put forward by the doyen of German commercial law, Ulrich Drobnig, who, irrespective of coming from a country still struggling with making its insolvency law work properly, rightly underlined that, indeed, '*The acid test of security is, of course, its status and effectiveness in the event of the debtor's insolvency*.' U Drobnig, 'Basic Issues of European Rules on Security in Movables' in J de Lacy, *The Reform of UK Personal Property Security Law* (Cavendish 2010) 449.

known by the system: the possessory pledge and the mortgage of immovables. The common characteristic of these was that the asset used as collateral had a firm physical existence and normally could not vanish out of sight of the secured creditor. As opposed to that, the Hungarian floating security was established on shifting assets, which was a novelty of such magnitude that its myriad consequences hardly could have been 'digested' within the few years of the device's existence. In particular, as opposed to a piece of land or an apartment, the existence of which does not need to be checked on a weekly or monthly basis to ensure their existence, the fluctuating assets of a company should be monitored (in the vocabulary of UCC Article 9: 'policed') to guarantee the same end. Yet policing, no matter how named, was not only something new but also not necessarily stressed even by foreign advisors as a *sine qua non* corollary of floating securities.[94]

Although impossible to prove, presumably the dominant vision that Hungary's lawyers had regarding the English floating charge was also that it ensures full, or nearly full, recoveries in most cases. This is a mistaken perception of the device as the available empirical data from the UK[95] and the commentaries of UK scholars[96] prove. Given that English law, through the

[94] For a comparative account of the topic of policing in the context of secured transactions, see T Tajti, 'The Overlooked Building Blocks of Secured Transactions Law Reforms: Policing and the Role of Organized Industries' (2022) 27 Uniform Law Review 320–343.

[95] See in particular the recent dataset from Scotland compiled by J Hardman and A MacPherson, 'Scottish Companies Who Have Filed Certain Insolvency Forms Between 1 October 2019 and 30 September 2020' 2019–2020 [dataset]. University of Edinburgh School of Law at <https://doi.org/10.7488/ds/3040> accessed 28 July 2023; and see J Hardman and ADJ MacPherson, 'Small and State Funded: An Empirical Study of Liquidations in Scotland' (2023) 32 International Insolvency Review 420 for analysis of the data. This dataset, containing data on 505 Scottish company insolvency cases (specifically liquidations) yet not focused only on floating charges, indicates that full recoveries by holders of floating charges are far from being the rule. The floating charge seems to have become a weak security device held more for strategic reasons. Note that although the Scottish floating charge works in practice similarly to its English and Welsh kin, the underlying law contains significant discrepancies. See in general ADJ MacPherson, *The Floating Charge* (Edinburgh Legal Education Trust 2020).

[96] That the recoveries of holders of floating charges are low could be primarily linked to the fact that the insolvency proceedings are financed from the assets encumbered by the floating charge, as well as the mandatory prescribed part to be set aside for unsecured creditors, preferred claims and fixed charges. In extreme cases, the expenses of either administration or liquidation might consume a large part of the floating charge collateral, as it includes the fees of administrators and

intermediation of EBRD, had undeniably played a noticeable role during the reform years, the incomplete picture formed about the English floating charge in Hungary might have played a role in shaping the contours of the Hungarian floating security as well.

The perception that the floating charge is an exclusively 'priority-based'[97] security device seems to have been problematic as well, although in the UK this has been a hotly debated issue for the last few decades (at least). While Mokal propounded already in 2005 that '[the floating charge] is in fact not a priority-based device at all,'[98] Akintola, relying on more recent data, disagreed with this contention.[99] The point made is that the Hungarians should have recognized that the English floating charge is also a control device, or a 'residual management displacement device which can work optimally only when it is part of a package of security interests covering the whole or substantially the whole of the debtor's property, and generally, only when this package includes fixed security over assets strategically important to the debtor's business.'[100]

This should have been of crucial relevance from the very beginning of the Hungarian reform process because it would have made the reformers realize that the successful functioning of the new Hungarian floating security, in particular its enforcement within and outside the context of insolvency law, would have required professionals trained to step into the shoes of the management of the debtor company.

The other presumption was that the Hungarian floating security should survive unscathed until insolvency or, similarly to possessory pledges or real property mortgages, be subject to the effects of negative movements on the relevant market and depreciation at worst. Express provisions supporting such a conclusion could be found in the 2013 Civil Code Comments, in particular the ones providing the secured creditor with protection aimed to ensure 'that his security right, possibly without diminished value, survives until enforcement.'[101] Express Civil Code provisions thus equip the secured creditor with the right to police (monitor) the collateral and to protect it against harms

---

liquidators, and also the debts from contracts entered into by them. See Gullifer & Payne (n 42) para 7.3.3.3.4(a) at 315.

[97] MacPherson, *The Floating Charge* (n 95) para 3–12.

[98] RJ Mokal, *Corporate Insolvency Law: Theory and Application* (OUP 2005) 191.

[99] K Akintola, 'What is Left of the Floating Charge? An Empirical Outlook' (2015) Butterworths JIBFL 404.

[100] Mokal (n 98) 194.

[101] §5:109 of the 2013 Civil Code. See also Gárdos (n 2), 449.

that would decrease the value of the assets exploited as collateral.[102] This is, however, a different set of questions from the reasons that explain the relatively low recovery rates of floating charge holders in the UK,[103] an issue of utmost relevance yet on which no quantitative data seems to have ever been collected in Hungary.

Floating Securities and the Role of Receivers

Pondering the reasons behind the abolition of the Hungarian property encumbering charge inevitably requires casting a word on the role receivers (and equivalents) have played in the life of floating securities, especially in the UK and, to a lesser extent, in the US. The central related question is whether floating securities can efficiently work without receivers, administrative receivers or their present-time legal successors, the administrators?[104] Namely, these – all referred to herein as 'receivers' – have all been *sui generis* classes of professionals capable of performing the tasks of both liquidators and managers.[105]

---

102 While §5:109(1) empowers secured creditors to police (control) the collateral, §5:109(2) directs them to resort to the Code's general provisions on the prevention or elimination of harm. Moreover, as per §5:109(3), if the debtor fails to take steps to remedy the situation upon the secured creditor's request to do so (e.g. by providing additional collateral or new collateral), the secured creditor may sell the collateral.

103 UK sources primarily refer to Mokal (n 98) and the sources referred to by him, among others, the 9th Survey of Business Recovery in the United Kingdom (22 Nov 2001) of the Association of Business Recovery Professionals (ABRP), according to which the recoveries in 2001 were: 35% for preferential creditors, 53% for secured creditors, and 7% for unsecured (trade) creditors (Mokal, 2005), 191 note 92. MacPherson's data, obtained via a Freedom of Information request to the Insolvency Service, end in 2015, but relate to 165 administrations from 2012 to 2013. These are more specific and thus more expressive regarding floating charges. According to these data, the recoveries were as follows: while preferential creditors got back 26% of their debt, secured creditors excluding floating chargees got back 50% and unsecured creditors merely 0.3%. The recoveries of floating charge holders were only 13% (ADJ MacPherson, *The Floating Charge* (Edinburgh Legal Education Trust 2020) paras 3–14, note 43).

104 On the history and the meaning of pertinent designations, see Kayode Akintola and David Milman, 'The Rise, Fall and Potential for a Rebirth of Receivership in UK Corporate Law' (2020) 20(1) Journal of Corporate Law Studies 99–119.

105 Indeed, as the old case law proves, '[w]here a receiver is required for the purposes not only of receiving rents and profits, or of getting in outstanding property, but also of carrying on or superintending a trade, business or undertaking, they

Similarly to other civil law systems, Hungary has always possessed only one class of professionals primarily trained to perform the tasks of liquidators, whose key duty is selling the bankrupt debtor's assets and hardly stepping into the shoes of company officers. Although it seems that some isolated voices raised this issue during the 1990s,[106] the topic has never become a thoroughly discussed mainstream issue in Hungary.

From this perspective, it would have been illuminating for Hungarians to also take a look at the pertinent Scottish developments, besides English law dominating mainstream international legal scholarship. Scotland, being a mixed legal system, was faced with the same problem as Hungary just a few decades earlier. In both countries, floating security was introduced statutorily; in Scotland, this was by the Companies (Floating Charges) (Scotland) Act 1961.[107] Notwithstanding academic and judicial criticism, the device became popular even without borrowing receivership from English law as well. Receivership was, however, introduced by the Companies (Floating Charges and Receivers) (Scotland) Act 1972, although to a great extent led also by the consideration of 'reviv[ing] the fortunes of a company and preven[ting] unnecessary liquidation.'[108]

Still, the main reason behind the introduction of receivership in Scotland was that '[t]he 1961 Act did not provide the holder of a floating charge with

---

are called a manager, or more usually a receiver and manager' – Thomas Robinson and Peter Walton (eds), *Kerr and Hunter on Receivers and Administrations* (21st edn, Sweet & Maxwell – Thomson Reuters 2020) introduction to Chapter 11 titled 'Managers'.

[106] I Mándoki mentioned in his above-cited paper (Mándoki (n 53), note 39 that during the initial phase of the reforms in the early 1990s, András Hanák, a Hungarian attorney, pointed to the possible usefulness of the introduction of receivership as part of the secured transactions law reforms; an idea that was allegedly not supported by the Scottish experience as described by Professor George L Gretton (see e.g. GL Gretton, 'Should Floating Charges and Receivership Be Abolished?' 1986 Scots Law Times (News) 325; and, later, GL Gretton, 'Reception Without Integration? Floating Charges and Mixed Systems' (2003) 78 Tulane LR 307 at 325).

[107] For details, see ADJ MacPherson, *The Floating Charge* (Edinburgh Legal Education Trust 2020) para 1-01 at 1. See also ADJ MacPherson, 'The Genesis of the Scottish Floating Charge' in J Hardman and ADJ MacPherson (eds), *Floating Charges in Scotland: New Perspectives and Current Issues* (Edinburgh University Press 2022).

[108] Scottish Law Commission, *Report on the Companies (Floating Charges) (Scotland) Act 1961* (Scot Law Com No. 14, 1970) para 37. See also ADJ MacPherson, *The Floating Charge* (Edinburgh Legal Education Trust 2020) para 3-03 at 29.

an effective remedy to realise his security.'[109] The January 1970 Scottish Law Commission Report, therefore, determined that 'the charge-holder required a method of directly intervening in the affairs of the company to realise his security, which would not necessarily entail the full consequences of liquidation.'[110] That the introduction of receivership was needed could also be concluded based on the 1986 Memorandum of the Commission noting that 'receivership had become [since 1972] the dominant procedure for the conduct of the affairs of insolvent companies.'[111]

The role of receivers has, however, changed owing to UK-wide reforms of the insolvency system. These also included restrictions on the appointment of administrative receivers by the UK Enterprise Act 2002.[112] Save for a limited number of cases, consequently, the floating chargee may only appoint an administrator now which, contrary to the receiver, 'owes a duty to act in the interests of all the company's creditors.'[113] In theory, therefore, the administrator is the champion of all creditors, not advancing the interests only of the floating chargee. Its position and duties, in other words, are supposed to be similar to those of the Hungarian insolvency practitioner or the US bankruptcy trustee.

In practice, however, contrary to the legislative rhetoric, floating chargees still control the process notwithstanding that in most cases formally the administrators are appointed by the company or its directors.[114] This is primarily

---

[109] Sandra Frisby, Malcolm Davis-White, Michael Jones and David Bennett (eds), *Kerr and Hunter on Receivers and Administrations* (19th edn, Sweet & Maxwell – Thomson Reuters 2010) para 27-4.

[110] Ibid., Frisby et al., referring to the Scottish Law Commission, *Report on the Companies (Floating Charges) (Scotland) Act 1961* (Scot Law Com No. 14, 1970).

[111] Scottish Law Commission, *Floating Charges and Receivers* (Consultative Memorandum No. 72, 1986) para 1.3.

[112] Sandra Frisby, Malcolm Davis-White, Michael Jones and David Bennett (eds), *Kerr and Hunter on Receivers and Administrations* (19th edn, Sweet & Maxwell – Thomson Reuters 2010) para 27-7. Insolvency Act 1986, s 72A, inserted by Enterprise Act 2002 c. 40, s 250(1).

[113] Gullifer & Payne (n 42) para 7.5.1.4. at 343. Insolvency Act 1986, Sch B1 para 3(2).

[114] According to the empirical study of Akintola involving 2129 randomly chosen administration and creditors' voluntary liquidation cases in the period between 2006 and 2011, out of which administrators were appointed in 1087 cases, administrators were appointed in 852 cases appointed by the company or its directors, in 210 cases by the floating charge holder and in 25 by the court. However, the secured creditors have played a crucial role also where formally the company or its directors made the appointment. In fact, fearing the reputation risk, floating

possible because the costs and expenditures of administration are covered by the principal lender, which is the floating chargee, although strengthened with fixed charges on key assets of the company-debtor.[115] This enables the floating chargee to also choose the identity of the administrator, who 'has an incentive to comply with the lender's wishes to ensure future business.'[116] Such a strong strategic position of the floating charge holder eventually allows it to 'broker a decision to sell the business with little or no consultation with the other creditors.'[117]

This discrepancy between theory and practice should, however, not have disheartened Hungarian law reformers, because out-of-court enforcement of security interests has never played such a crucial role in modern times as it does in England. Similarly, neither insolvency practitioners nor other legal professionals capable of stepping into the shoes of company managers were available in the 1990s, and for years thereafter. Mindset shift, and mission-specific training, obviously both time-consuming, would have been the real challenges.

It is instructive in this context to cast a word on receivers in the United States, where after the federal centralization of the bankruptcy system in 1978 and the passage of the Bankruptcy Code, the importance and the role played by receivers have drastically decreased. Consequently, receivership is now less conspicuous in US law compared with earlier historic times because the receiver – named in the Bankruptcy Code as 'custodian' – has become an officer ancillary to the bankruptcy trustee. As Tabb put it, 'the bankruptcy case generally supersedes the nonbankruptcy custodianship.'[118] The Code does, however, permit the appointment of a custodian also to 'enforce a lien or to administer the property for the benefit of creditors.'[119] Otherwise, the receivers are regulated at the State level, and besides the centralization of the bankruptcy system at the federal level in 1978, the frequency of their appointments has subsided to a great extent also because they are deemed to be expensive.[120]

---

chargees did not want to appear as the ones making the appointments, yet were in the position to ensure that 'the company would have appointed an insolvency practitioner the creditor approved of' – K Akintola, 'What is Left of the Floating Charge? An Empirical Outlook' (2015) Butterworths JIBFL 406.

115 Gullifer & Payne (n 42) para 7.3.3.4. at 319–320.

116 Ibid 320.

117 Ibid.

118 C J Tabb, *Law of Bankruptcy* (5th edn, West Academic 2020) para §5.12 at 438.

119 Ibid with reference to §543 of the US Bankruptcy Code.

120 See, e.g. PA Davidson, 'Wise Receivers' (2008) 31 LA Lawyer 24, 26, referring to receivers as 'legal luxuries'.

If these thoughts on the role of receivers might seem misplaced or impractical tasks for civilian lawyers, a reminder of the ever-stronger emphasis placed on restructuring by the European Union should be added. Namely, as already hinted at above, it ought to be realized that restructuring inevitably presumes managerial capabilities from insolvency practitioners as well, unless the system relies exclusively on the incumbent management, a concept known as 'debtor-in-possession' (DIP). Thus, it is not far-fetched to claim that developing an efficient restructuring regime in Hungary would require steps similar to those that the promulgation of receivers, administrative receivers and eventually administrators in Scotland presupposed as well. The conclusion that lends itself to be formulated based on these thoughts is that the existence of better-trained insolvency practitioners in Hungary during the observed period might have made the property encumbering charge work and might have made its abolition unnecessary.

EPILOGUE

The value of the above discussion, at the center of which is a security device that no longer exists, could be dismissed by strict positivists. However, for those with a broader horizon, and to law reformers, the unhappy and short life-story of the Hungarian floating security can be instructive because the wise learn not only from the successes but perhaps even more from the failures of others. Moreover, the quest for the reasons leading to the abolition of the device has brought to the surface a number of topics, the exploration of which would be desirable generally and not only in the context of Hungarian law. These range from broader theoretical issues like the pitfalls of contemporary comparative law's obsession with 'major' jurisdictions only, to the more practical ones best exemplified by the myriad dilemmas surrounding the security–insolvency law interface or the role receivers play.

Although the introduction of the floating security, just like the entire secured transactions project in Hungary, was driven by meta-legal reasons of making affordable financing possible and boosting the credit economy, nothing has been said about these aspects of the topic above. The reason is simple: the extreme scarcity of related quantitative data. This also unfortunately prevents formulating a proper answer to the paramount question of what the economic effects of the concept's discarding were. The tentative response cannot be but inconclusive for the time being, although it is a fact that credit has not ground to a halt because of the disappearance of floating security from the system. Moreover, unfortunately, one could hardly expect in-depth studies in Hungary on any of the related economic issues or on the utility of floating security in light of pre- and post-abandonment data. This contribution, consequently, was inevitably doomed to be law-focused, although it points toward further value that could be found anchored in economics and finance, which seem to have unfortunately escaped attention in Hungary.

The life story of an outcast legal institution, having disappeared from the Hungarian legal system (whether forever or until its future return), should be judged with all of these considerations in sight.

12. Floating charges in the Nordic countries

Bjørn Løtveit, Astrid Millung-Christoffersen, Patrik Lindskoug and Teemu Juutilainen

INTRODUCTION

This chapter analyses floating charges in the Nordic countries. 'Nordic' is a collective term for a group of countries and autonomous areas located in the northern part of Europe.[1] For the purposes of this text, we include Denmark, Norway, Sweden and Finland.[2] The Nordic countries do not constitute a unified legal system, and membership in the group has few substantial legal implications.[3] While the Nordic countries have strong historical, cultural and linguistic connections, they are sovereign states with their own parliaments, governments and courts.[4]

The Nordic countries are known for their distinctive functional approach to property law. A frequently cited example concerns the concept of ownership in property law. Whereas many other jurisdictions approach property law problems by asking who owns an object, the Nordic approach commonly asks who

1 While the terms 'Nordic' and 'Scandinavian' are often understood as interchangeable in English usage, 'Scandinavian' also has a narrower meaning in which it refers to Denmark, Norway and Sweden. See e.g. Astrid Millung-Christoffersen, 'The Scandinavian "functional" approach to movable property from a Danish view – including the question of "tradition"' [2019] EPLJ 8(1) 4, n. 2.

2 The law of the fifth Nordic country, Iceland, will not be discussed owing to limitations of space and the authors' expertise.

3 See Patrik Lindskoug, 'Property and its limits' in Pia Letto-Vanamo, Ditlev Tamm and Bent Ole Gram Mortensen (eds), *Nordic Law in European Context* (Springer 2019) 135–151, 135–137.

4 See Mads Bryde Andersen, 'Nordens betydning i nordisk formueret' in Hans Henrik Edlund, Torsten Iversen, Susanne Karstoft and Birgit Liin (eds), *Festskrift til Palle Bo Madsen* (Djøf Forlag 2021) 15–33, 17–21.

has a better right to the object.[5] This can be viewed as a case-specific approach, where ownership of an asset does not necessarily include every 'function' of a property right, and where questions concerning transfer of ownership must be answered independently for each 'function'.[6] Since property law rules in the Nordic countries are more fragmentary than in countries with more comprehensive and codified models, Nordic law deconstructs concepts like ownership to consider all relevant aspects in the situation at hand and to create space for legal argumentation.

Nordic security rights law, however, is more codified than property law in general. Consequently, the functional approach has not had the same impact on the rules on floating charges as it has had on other aspects of property law. When it comes to security rights, the Nordic countries are just as concerned with questions of priority and ranking as other jurisdictions. Since questions of priority are not that different from questions of who has the better right, the Nordic functional approach does not render Nordic security rights law fundamentally different from what applies in other jurisdictions when it comes to priority between competing rights.

The four Nordic countries discussed in this chapter all have rules on the granting of floating charges. While the term 'floating charge' might have strong connotations with an English-style security right, it is nevertheless used in certain public translations of Nordic security rights law without referring to the English model. In these translations, the term 'floating charge' simply refers to non-possessory security rights where the grantor is permitted to sell or otherwise dispose of encumbered assets without the consent of the secured creditor.[7] Similarly, when the term 'mortgage' is used in public translations of Nordic security rights law, it generally does not refer to the English transfer of title model but to a mere security right where the grantor retains ownership and title.

The rules on floating charges were introduced in the Nordic countries mainly to facilitate a more effective use of movables as security. Before the introduction of floating charges, possessory pledges were essentially the only

---

5 See Patrik Lindskoug, 'Property and its limits' in Pia Letto-Vanamo, Ditlev Tamm and Bent Ole Gram Mortensen (eds), *Nordic Law in European Context* (Springer 2019) 135–151, 135–137.

6 See Sverre Magnus Bergslid Salvesen, *Kreditorvern* (Cappelen 2021) 35–36; Hilde Hauge, *Løsøreerververs kreditorvern* (Fagbokforlaget 2016) 58–60; and Patrik Lindskoug, 'Property and its limits' in Pia Letto-Vanamo, Ditlev Tamm and Bent Ole Gram Mortensen (eds), *Nordic Law in European Context* (Springer 2019) 135–151, 135–137.

7 UNCITRAL, *Legislative Guide on Secured Transactions* (New York 2010) 47.

available option for creating security rights over movables. This solution was impractical for grantors, as they were deprived of the opportunity to use encumbered assets during the security period. Rules on floating charges were therefore developed.

While the Nordic countries are sovereign and thus legally independent, there has been extensive legislative collaboration between them. Firstly, many Nordic legislative acts in the field of private law are products of common drafting and have resulted in regional harmonisation.[8] In addition, the Nordic legal community has traditionally encouraged the sharing of legal research findings, thus fostering the direct and indirect transfer of legal principles and concepts between the Nordic countries.[9] Secondly, EU and EEA legislation has contributed extensively to the European harmonisation of many areas of law.

Floating charges in the Nordic countries were not developed through Nordic, or even international, collaboration, and formal collaboration has generally had a very limited impact on Nordic security rights law. Nevertheless, it is clear that some informal exchange of ideas has occurred. This is apparent from, for example, the similarities between the floating charge regime adopted in Norway in 1980 and the Danish rules. The preparatory works to the Norwegian Mortgage Act (*panteloven*) of 1980 briefly discuss security rights law in a wide range of foreign jurisdictions, including Denmark.[10] Although these findings did not make any explicit normative contributions to Norwegian law, nevertheless, Norwegian law ended up including rules similar to Danish floating charge rules in force at that time – presumably the result of an informal exchange of ideas rather than a direct adoption of the Danish rules. Since then, the rules have been further developed in both countries.

---

[8] In 1934, Denmark, Norway, Sweden and Finland collaborated on preparing a common Act on Promissory Notes, and in 1964, the same countries collaborated on drafting patent legislation. See also Severin Blomstrand, 'Nordic Co-operation on Legislation in the Field of Private Law' in Peter Wahlgren (ed.), *Scandinavian Studies in Law*, vol. 39 (Stockholm Institute for Scandinavian Law 2000).

[9] See Thomas Wilhelmsson, *Critical Studies in Private Law* (Kluwer 1992) 17 and Mads Bryde Andersen, 'Nordens betydning i nordisk formueret' in Hans Henrik Edlund, Torsten Iversen, Susanne Karstoft and Birgit Liin (eds), *Festskrift til Palle Bo Madsen* (Djøf Forlag 2021) 15–33, 21–29.

[10] See NUT 1970:2, 178–225, which explains security rights law in Denmark, Finland, Iceland, Sweden, England, France, the Netherlands, Switzerland, Germany and the United States. Similarly, the Finnish Committee Report 1981:56, which resulted in the Government Proposal for the current Enterprise Mortgage Act, contains an annex with a review of the corresponding legislation in Sweden, Norway and Denmark. The Act, in turn, has notable similarities with Swedish law.

Historically, the rules on floating charges in the Nordic countries were developed to safeguard the interests of domestic businesses. The purpose of introducing floating charges was not to harmonise Nordic security rights legislation, but rather to increase national business competitiveness by improving access to low-cost credit and thus improve businesses' financing options. The motivation for adopting rules on floating charges was thus the same in each country, but was linked to domestic, rather than international, interests.

The following sections discuss the rules on floating charges applicable in four Nordic countries. While there are some similarities between the countries, the national regimes have largely developed independently, and the rules differ considerably. Denmark and Norway have the most similar rules and are therefore considered first. As Danish law appears to have inspired Norwegian law, the Danish rules form the starting point for the discussion. The Norwegian rules are examined next. The Finnish and Swedish rules also share some characteristics, and Finnish law appears to have adopted several Swedish solutions. The discussion therefore continues with the Swedish rules before concluding with the Finnish provisions. Finally, some comparative conclusions are presented based on observations from each country.

FLOATING CHARGES IN DENMARK

Floating Charges in General

In Denmark, floating charges are regulated by the Registration of Property Act (*tinglysningsloven*).[11] Contracts creating floating charges are limited by mandatory rules, of which the following three are of particular importance:[12] (1) the rule against *general charges* (according to which a charge may not encompass everything the grantor owns or will acquire in the future);[13] (2) the rule against *mortgaging negotiable instruments, simple debt instruments and other receivables*;[14] and (3) the rule against *mortgaging a collection of chattels*[15]

[11] Additionally, floating charges over crops are regulated by *Lov nr. 271 af 22. maj 1986 med senere ændringer om høstpant.*

[12] See Bent Iversen, Lars Hedegaard Kristensen and Lars Henrik Gam Madsen, *Panteret*, 5th edn (Karnov Group 2015) 103 *et seq.*, Astrid Millung-Christoffersen, *Virksomhedspant* (Karnov Group 2016) 27 *et seq.*, Lars Henrik Gam Madsen, *Virksomhedspant, fordringspant og pantsætningsforbud* (Karnov Group 2020) 129 *et seq.*

[13] See section 47a of the Registration of Property Act.

[14] See section 47(10) of the Registration of Property Act.

[15] See section 47b(1) of the Registration of Property Act.

(according to which a charge may not encompass collections of things that are described in general terms only, such as changeable stock).[16]

In general, this means that Danish law traditionally offers very limited scope for establishing a floating charge, owing especially to the rule prohibiting general charges. However, there are some exceptions to the mandatory rules, including the rule against mortgaging collections of chattels. Such exceptions are provided in sections 37 and 47b(2) of the Registration of Property Act, which permit the mortgaging of working plant and operating equipment (e.g. machinery) belonging to a business that is operated from real property owned by the proprietor, see section 37 (*tilbehørspant*), or leased from a third party, see section 47b(2).[17] Charges of this kind are commonly created to protect separate rights in connection with the acquisition of business equipment. However, section 37 and section 47b(2) do not prevent a separate financing arrangement based on chattel security rights, as they must respect separate movable property rights, e.g. in a machine.[18] The question is when the charges must respect the separate right. The separate right must exist at the time the asset is included in the category of working plant. If unencumbered movable property is included in the category of working plant, separate financing is thus excluded unless the mortgagee in the property waives the mortgage.[19]

With the (limited) exception of these provisions, the general rule prior to the introduction of floating business charges was that floating charges could not be established, or at least not with the scope now permitted for a floating business charge. Since 1 January 2006, it has been possible to create a *floating business charge* (*virksomhedspant*) or a *floating charge on receivables* (*fordringspant*).[20] Such charges are now used by many businesses and are of great practical relevance. The provisions governing these charges deviate

---

16 Rules against general charges and mortgaging a collection of chattels were introduced as early as in the Bankruptcy Act 1872, but in 1977 the rules were transferred to the Registration of Property Act. See Vagn Carstensen and Thomas Rørdam, *Pant*, 7th edn (Jurist- og Økonomforbundets Forlag 2002) 56 and 319.

17 Bent Iversen, Lars Hedegaard Kristensen and Lars Henrik Gam Madsen, *Panteret*, 5th edn (Karnov Group 2015) 238 *et seq.*, and 392 *et seq.*

18 Hans Willumsen, *Tinglysningsloven med kommentarer* (Jurist- og Økonomforbundets Forlag 1997) 300, Astrid Millung-Christoffersen, *Virksomhedspant – særligt ud fra et tingsretligt perspektiv* (Karnov Group 2015) 76.

19 Anders Ørgaard, *Sikkerhed i løsøre*, 10th edn (Karnov Group 2020) 100.

20 See *lov nr. 560/2005 om ændring af tinglysningsloven, konkursloven og andre love.* Betænkning nr. 560/2005 om virksomhedspant (white paper on floating business charge). The preparatory works relating to the floating business charge in Denmark were inspired by other jurisdictions; see Betænkning nr. 1459/2005, chapter 5.

somewhat from the previously mentioned mandatory rules. Floating business charges are regulated by section 47c of the Registration of Property Act and make a broader type of floating charge available under Danish law compared to the provisions mentioned above, which are less comprehensive.

Floating Business Charge

The scope of the floating business charge

Floating business charges may be created by any business owner (grantor) – whether an individual or a company.[21] When the grantor charges all assets in certain asset groups that the business *owns or may acquire in the future*, this is known as a floating charge (*flydende pant*).[22]

The assets that may be covered by a floating business charge are specified in section 47c(3) of the Registration of Property Act, and include (1) receivables deriving from the sale of goods and services, (2) inventories of raw materials, semi-manufactured products and finished goods, (3) vehicles which have not previously been registered in Denmark (or in similar foreign registers), (4) working plant and operating equipment, (5) fuel and other ancillary materials, (6) livestock, (7) intellectual property rights and (8) vehicles that are or have previously been registered in Denmark (or in similar foreign registers), provided that the grantor manages an enterprise involving the sale and purchase of vehicles.

A floating business charge may not encompass assets other than those falling into the eight categories listed above. Accordingly, assets such as shares, real property, bank accounts, vessels and aircraft may not be included in the floating business charge. Security rights over such assets must therefore be created separately.

Section 47c(4) of the Registration of Property Act contains rules that either exempt certain assets from the floating business charge – for example, vehicles that are exempted from registration in the Danish Vehicle Registration Act (*lov om registrering af køretøjer*)[23] – or regulate the position of the floating

---

[21] Floating business charges are not available to private individuals other than in their capacity as a business owner. Foreign companies can grant a floating business charge if they are registered according to the Danish rules, e.g. assigned a CVR number if necessary.

[22] See section 47c(1) of the Registration of Property Act.

[23] A vehicle can, among other things, be exempted from registration if it is predominantly used outside public roads, e.g. in the area of a company.

business charge vis-à-vis other mortgaging arrangements and floating charges pursuant to section 37 of the Registration of Property Act.[24]

Section 47d of the Registration of Property Act also contains rules on floating charges that relate only to receivables stemming from the sale of goods and services, *i.e. floating charge on receivables* (*fordringspant*). Such floating charges include both present and future receivables. It is not permitted to have both a floating business charge and a floating charge on receivables simultaneously.[25] A business must therefore choose which one of the two charges it wants to use. If the business wants to encompass other assets than receivables, it should therefore choose the floating business charge.

A floating business charge is based on an agreement between the grantor and the secured creditor. It can be linked to different types of mortgage instruments, namely an all-moneys instrument (*skadesløsbreve*) or an owner's charge instrument (*ejerpantebreve*).[26] Whether a floating business charge can be transferred or reused depends on the mortgage instruments and the underlying rules regulating these situations, since there are differences depending on whether an all-moneys instrument or an owner's charge instrument has been used.[27]

A floating business charge is registered in the Danish Chattel Mortgage Registry (*personbogen*), which the Land Registration Court maintains centrally for the whole country.[28] Registration is undertaken digitally.[29] If the formal registration requirements are not met, the document is rejected.[30] However, if the requirements are met, the document is registered immediately.[31] The

---

24 Regarding the ranking of floating business charges and floating charges under section 47b(2), it is regulated in section 47e(3) of the Registration of Property Act, pursuant to which registration of the charges is decisive.

25 See section 47e(2) of the Danish Registration of Property Act.

26 The Danish rules regulating the use of all-money instruments and owner's charge instruments – not least when these are combined with a floating business charge – are extensive and will not be addressed further. See Bent Iversen, Lars Hedegaard Kristensen and Lars Henrik Gam Madsen, *Panteret*, 5th edn (Karnov Group 2015) 170 *et seq.*

27 See Lars Henrik Gam Madsen, *Virksomhedspant, fordringspant og pantsætningsforbud* (Karnov Group 2020) 157 *et seq.*

28 <https://domstol.dk/tinglysningsretten/> accessed 18 February 2025.

29 <https://www.tinglysning.dk/tinglysning/landingpage/landingpage.xhtml> accessed 18 February 2025.

30 For instance, the secured obligation (the secured amount) has to be specified in the registration form.

31 The Land Registration Court does not check the existence of the object described in the mortgage. If the object does not exist, the risk that the secured creditor's right is a 'fiction' is borne by the creditor.

registration rules are set out in the Danish Registration of Property Act and are supplemented by a number of executive orders.

Floating business charge *in rem*

An act of perfection must be observed for each individual asset covered by a security as this is a condition for the security to be protected *in rem* against the grantor's transferees and other creditors who take legal action. Third-party effectiveness of a *floating business charge* requires registration.[32] Registration (or perfection) of the floating business charge only has to be completed once to cover both present and future assets in the stipulated asset categories. In a number of respects, a floating business charge has the effect as if all the assets involved had been individually mortgaged in accordance with section 47 of the Registration of Property Act (*individuelt underpant*). In other respects, however, the special conditions applicable to floating business charges mean that such charges differ significantly from security relating to individual objects.

Owing to the special conditions applicable to floating business charges, the position *in rem* of such a charge raises issues such as when the floating business charge attaches to a specific asset, when the act of perfection takes effect, the extinctive effect of the floating business charge[33] and the ranking of the floating business charge with respect to future assets.[34]

A floating business charge becomes applicable to a newly acquired asset when the asset becomes part of the grantor's business.[35] There is no requirement for the asset to be connected to the grantor's business physically. If an asset group is included in the general description of the floating business charge, the charge automatically covers newly acquired assets of that type. Except for receivables, the grantor may dispose of assets encumbered by a floating business charge. However, if a disposal does not form part of regular business operations, the secured creditor can enforce the charge.[36]

---

[32] See section 47c(2) of the Registration of Property Act.

[33] Contrary to the floating business charge, charges under sections 37 and 47b(2) of the Registration of Property Act do not have extinctive effect.

[34] See Astrid Millung-Christoffersen, *Virksomhedspant – særligt ud fra et tingsretligt perspektiv* (Karnov Group 2015) 255 *et seq.*, Lars Henrik Gam Madsen, *Virksomhedspant, fordringspant og pantsætningsforbud* (Karnov Group 2020) 339 *et seq.*

[35] Further, regarding when the asset becomes part of the grantor's business, see Astrid Millung-Christoffersen, 'The Scandinavian "functional" approach to movable property from a Danish view – including the question of "tradition"' [2019] EPLJ 8(1) 4.

[36] Lars Henrik Gam Madsen, *Virksomhedspant, fordringspant og pantsætningsforbud* (Karnov Group 2020) 427.

The extinctive effect of a floating business charge entails that the charge extinguishes rights that are unperfected at the time the floating business charge is created and registered.[37] The extinctive effect also means that subsequent rights that are unperfected at the time an asset becomes subject to the floating business charge are extinguished by the floating business charge.[38] However, pursuant to section 47c(6) and (7) of the Registration of Property Act, a secured creditor holding a floating business charge must respect subsequent mortgages over movable property and vehicles which have been agreed and registered no later than at the time of delivery of the asset to the business.[39] In other words, this means that the subsequent mortgage which fulfils the requirements has a better right over the movable property than the floating business charge. In other instances, the floating business charge takes priority over any subsequent mortgage.[40]

As regards trade receivables subject to a floating business charge, the secured creditor's priority is not regulated by legislation,[41] as illustrated by priority conflicts concerning movable property. The conflicts that may arise between a *factoring agreement* and a *floating business charge* (resting on a different legal basis) with respect to future trade receivables are much discussed in theory.[42] Factoring arrangements are particularly challenged by the extinctive effect of the floating business charge. This was also the question in a case where the High Court[43] was faced with determining the respective legal positions of a factoring arrangement and a subsequent floating business charge. However, the specific problem was solved according to bona fide, since the grantors of the floating business charges were in bad faith.

In theory, it has been proposed that the floating business charge in general should be changed into a *residual charge* without extinctive effect, in order to

---

[37] To fulfil the requirements for extinction, the grantor also needs to be in good faith at the time of the registration of the floating business charge.

[38] Astrid Millung-Christoffersen, *Virksomhedspant – særligt ud fra et tingsretligt perspektiv* (Karnov Group 2015) 71 *et seq.*, Lars Henrik Gam Madsen, *Virksomhedspant, fordringspant og pantsætningsforbud* (Karnov Group 2020) 312 *et seq.*

[39] This also applies to the retention of title to movable property and vehicles.

[40] Peter Mortensen, *Virksomhedspant og fordringspant* (Pejus 2014) 39.

[41] In other words, the legislation is silent.

[42] For example, Astrid Millung-Christoffersen, 'Virkningstidspunktet for sikringsakter – særligt med henblik på forholdet mellem factoring og virksomhedspant i fordringer' [2017] UfR 2017B.51, Lars Henrik Gam Madsen, *Virksomhedspant, fordringspant og pantsætningsforbud* (Karnov Group 2020) 348 *et seq.*, Ulrik Rammeskow Bang-Pedersen, 'Konflikter mellem virksomhedspant og factoring' [2016] UfR 2016B.388.

[43] ØLD dated 4 December 2009 (utr. Sag nr. B-1712–09).

preserve the purpose of the rules while avoiding uncertainty for businesses and their security interest.[44]

Negative pledge and enforcement

In general, a negative pledge (*pantsætningsforbud*) is a private declaration where the grantor undertakes not to pledge (willingly) to a third party unless the pledgee's consent is given.[45]

Section 43(2) of the Registration of Property Act regulates a specific rule on negative pledge. The rule prohibits certain types of pledges, including floating business charges. A negative pledge regarding a floating business charge can be limited to one or more of the provisions in section 47c(3) of the Registration of Property Act (i.e. asset groups such as livestock). On the other hand, it is not possible to exclude one specific object from the floating business charge, e.g. a particular machine among the grantor's operating equipment. A negative pledge in section 43(2) of the Registration of Property Act cannot prevent prosecution.

A secured creditor who holds a floating business charge must respect a subsequent execution lien (*udlæg*) over the encumbered assets if the holder of the lien has announced it to the debtor no later than three days after its creation.[46] If these conditions are met, the secured creditor must respect the higher priority of the execution lien.

If insolvency proceedings are commenced with respect to the grantor, the floating business charge 'freezes', i.e. the charge will not encompass assets acquired by the grantor after the time of the bankruptcy notice.[47] Freezing of the charge also means that the grantor may no longer alienate (transfer) assets subject to the floating business charge in regards to fulfilment of the secured creditor. This is in accordance with the principle of equality under insolvency law, which dictates that assets acquired by a grantor in the course of insolvency proceedings as the main rule must benefit all creditors.[48]

---

[44] Lars Henrik Gam Madsen, *Virksomhedspant, fordringspant og pantsætningsforbud* (Karnov Group 2020) 77 and 312.

[45] Lars Henrik Gam Madsen, *Virksomhedspant, fordringspant og pantsætningsforbud* (Karnov Group 2020) 599.

[46] See section 47c(5) of the Registration of Property Act.

[47] See section 47f of the Registration of Property Act.

[48] Further, regarding the principle of equality in relation to floating business charges, see Lasse Søholm Lindekilde, *Virksomhedspant i en insolvensretlig belysning* (Djøf Forlag 2022) chapter 5.

FLOATING CHARGES IN NORWAY

Six Different Floating Charges

Six different, and independent, floating charges are available under Norwegian law: (1) one relating to operating assets; (2) one relating to inventory (goods intended for sale); (3) one relating to motor vehicles; (4) one relating to trade receivables (factoring); (5) one relating to agriculture; and (6) one relating to fishing equipment. Two or more of these charges may be combined to secure the same obligation(s), and this is commonly done in the case of operating assets, inventory and trade receivables. However, even in combination, the floating charges may not encumber all assets of the grantor. In addition, real property, registered ships and aircraft may never be included in a floating charge. This is because there are separate registries for these assets where security rights are to be registered. To register a security right in one of these special registries, the security right must be connected to a specific asset and not to an abstract category of assets. Consequently, real property, ships and aircraft must be charged individually and not as part of a floating charge.

The Norwegian Mortgage Act (*panteloven*) of 1980 introduced the floating charges available today. Although floating charges were not an entirely new concept in Norway at the time, the 1980 Act reformed the existing rules.[49] One significant change was to generalise floating charges, making most of them available to all businesses and allowing them to be used to secure loans from any lender. Prior to 1980, the law governing floating charges had become inconsistent, disorganised and uneven, with complex special rules applying dependent on the type of enterprise and type of lender.[50] The Mortgage Act of 1980 cleaned up this area of law.[51]

The floating charge over *operating assets* includes machines, tools and other equipment, making it a comprehensive charge.[52] It only encompasses assets that are intended for use in the grantor's business, but it is not limited to equipment intended for industrial purposes; it may also include items like office furniture. A wide range of intellectual property is also included – not only intellectual property which is wholly owned by the grantor, but also co-owned intellectual property and licences to intellectual property owned

---

49 The older floating charges are described in Francis Hagerup, *Den norske panteret*, 4th edn (Aschehoug 1925) 110–111; Sjur Brækhus, *Omsetning og kreditt 2*, 3rd edn (Universitetsforlaget 2005) 77; and Carl Jacob Arnholm, *Panteretten*, 3rd edn (Tanum 1962) 108–109, 129.

50 NUT 1970:2, 20 (preparatory works to the Mortgage Act).

51 Ot.prp. nr. 39 (1977–1978), 9–10 (preparatory works to the Mortgage Act).

52 The Mortgage Act, section 3–4 (2).

by third parties, provided that such licences are transferrable.[53] Further, the charge covers permissions to search for mineral resources.

The floating charge over *inventory* encompasses raw materials and trade goods, both finished and unfinished.[54] It also includes fuel and other goods consumed in business activities, as well as product packaging. *Motor vehicles, construction machinery and railroad materials* are excluded from general floating charges over operating assets or inventory. Instead, these assets have to be secured by an independent floating charge, primarily based on the same structure as the floating charge over operating assets.[55] However, a floating charge over motor vehicles may be restricted to certain vehicles, rather than all vehicles owned by the grantor.

The floating charge over *trade receivables* includes present and future trade receivables linked to payment for goods or services delivered by the grantor's business.[56] There is no requirement to list the claims or to name the debtors of these claims. By default, both present and future claims are included, but the charge may be restricted to only present or only future trade receivables.

A separate category of floating charge is available for *agriculture*, applicable to both operating assets and inventory.[57] The reason for this separate charge type is that the distinction between operating assets and inventory is less clear-cut in agriculture businesses, since animals, for example, could function as operating assets one day and as inventory the next.

Finally, a distinct type of floating charge exists for *fishing equipment*. Businesses that use movable objects in connection with fishing vessels can create a floating charge over such movables, provided that the assets are not considered accessories to the vessels themselves.[58] Assets that can be encumbered with a motor vehicle floating charge, an agricultural floating charge or a fishing equipment floating charge may not also be encumbered with a general floating charge over operating assets or inventory.[59]

---

53 See Bjørn Løtveit, *Pantsettelse av immaterialrettigheter* (Universitetsforlaget 2021) 190–233.

54 The Mortgage Act, section 3-11 (2).

55 The Mortgage Act, section 3-8.

56 The Mortgage Act, section 4-10 (1).

57 The Mortgage Act, section 3-9.

58 The Mortgage Act, section 3-10.

59 The Mortgage Act, sections 3-4 (4) and 3-11 (4).

General Conditions for Granting Floating Charges

According to the Mortgage Act, a valid and enforceable security right can only be created if statutory law explicitly provides for it.[60] The list of floating charges in the sections above is therefore exhaustive. Further, floating charges may only be granted by undertakings registered in the Register of Business Enterprises (*Foretaksregisteret*) and institutions like hospitals, nursing homes, schools and universities.[61] Foreign undertakings that are carrying out business operations in Norway are obliged to register in the Register of Business Enterprises,[62] and consequently such undertakings can, once registered, grant floating charges over their Norwegian assets. Norwegian sole proprietorships are not obliged to register but can choose to do so.[63] If they choose to register, they can grant floating charges.

Each type of floating charge has pre-defined content. The included assets are specified in the relevant provision of the Mortgage Act and, as a general rule, the scope of a floating charge may not be customised by the security agreement creating the charge.[64] This has also been the view of the Supreme Court of Norway.[65] Further, for an asset to be covered by a floating charge, the grantor must be entitled to transfer the asset, typically by selling it.[66] In addition, an asset can only be included in a floating charge if it is intended for use in the grantor's business, not private use.[67]

Acquiring New Assets and Disposing of Encumbered Assets

If the grantor acquires new assets during the security period and those assets fall within the general description of an existing floating charge, the general rule is that the charge automatically covers the newly acquired assets.[68]

---

[60] The Mortgage Act, section 1-2 (2).

[61] The Mortgage Act, section 3-5, see also sections 3-4 (1), 3-8 (1), 3-9 (1), 3-10 (1), 3-11 (1) and 4-10 (1). See also Jens Edvin A. Skoghøy, *Panterett*, 5th edn (Universitetsforlaget 2021) 56–59.

[62] The Business Enterprises Register Act (*foretaksregisterloven*), section 2-1 (2).

[63] The Business Enterprises Register Act (*foretaksregisterloven*), section 2-2.

[64] The Mortgage Act, section 1-3 (1), thus prohibits the use of general floating charges over all assets of a grantor.

[65] See Rt. 1992 p. 1629 (18 December 1992).

[66] The Mortgage Act, section 1-3 (2).

[67] The Mortgage Act, sections 3-4 (1), 3-8 (1), 3-9 (1), 3-10 (1), 3-11 (1) and 4-10 (1).

[68] The Mortgage Act, sections 3-4 (5), 3-9 (5), 3-10 (3) and 3-11 (3).

However, if a newly acquired asset is subject to a sale lien (the Norwegian equivalent of retention of title), the sale lien will always have priority over the floating charge.[69] This applies regardless of whether the sale lien has obtained third-party effectiveness or not, which has been confirmed by the Supreme Court of Norway.[70]

Except for claims encumbered by a floating charge over trade receivables, the grantor may dispose of assets covered by a floating charge as long as such disposal is consistent with sound business operations and does not significantly impair the secured creditor's security interest.[71] In the event of such a disposal, the floating charge will cease to encumber the disposed assets. The grantor's power to dispose of encumbered assets is even more comprehensive in the case of a floating charge over inventory, where the grantor may dispose of any asset included in the charge on the condition that disposal occurs in the ordinary course of business.[72] Consequently, within the grantor's ordinary course of business, disposal of encumbered inventory can be carried out regardless of whether it impairs the secured creditor's security interest.

Third-party Effectiveness

The effectiveness of a floating charge between the involved parties (*inter partes*) is conditional on the existence of a valid security agreement between the grantor and the secured creditor, and on statutory law recognising the granting of such a floating charge. Third-party effectiveness, however, requires that the floating charge is registered in the Norwegian Register of Mortgaged Movable Property (*Løsøreregisteret*).[73] The registration application must be made on a form prescribed by the registration authority.[74] All standard application forms, except the form for a floating charge over trade receivables, include an acknowledgement of debt, and the registered document thus constitutes a transferable promissory note (*pantobligasjon*), unless the parties choose a different application form than the standard version.

Up until the Supreme Court of Norway's ruling in HR-2020-837-A it was commonly assumed that a floating charge over trade receivables could also obtain third-party effectiveness by giving the debtors of the receivables notice

---

69 The Mortgage Act, sections 3-4 (3), 3-8 (5), 3-9 (5), 3-10 (3) and 3-11 (5).

70 See Rt. 2000 p. 1360 (31 August 2000).

71 The Mortgage Act, sections 3-7 (1), 3-8 (5), 3-9 (5) and 3-10 (3).

72 The Mortgage Act, section 3-13 (1).

73 The Mortgage Act, sections 3-6, 3-8 (2), 3-9 (3), 3-10 (2), 3-12 (1) and 4-10 (2).

74 Available online: <https://www.brreg.no/tinglysing/skjema-for-tinglysing/> accessed 16 March 2024.

of the charge.[75] However, the Supreme Court of Norway held that notification can only provide third-party effectiveness if the security agreement lists the names of the debtors of these claims and for future claims the basis for the claims must also be specified. The extent to which the viewpoints of the Supreme Court are applicable to both current and future trade receivables remains ambiguous, prompting criticism of the decision.[76] However, to eliminate any risk of non-perfection, a general floating charge over trade receivables (i.e. a charge where the security agreement does not list the debtors or claims) should always be registered in the Register of Mortgaged Movable Property to obtain third-party effectiveness.

For registration to secure third-party effectiveness of any Norwegian floating charge, the application must specify the maximum amount of money the floating charge may cover.[77] This registered maximum does not have to correspond to the actual secured obligations, and is often set higher. Despite the general rule that the charge cannot cover claims exceeding the registered amount, certain claims – such as for interest accumulated in the two years preceding enforcement and for necessary collection costs – may be added to the registered amount.[78]

Registration secures effectiveness in the event of insolvency proceedings against the grantor, provided that the charge was registered no later than the day before the proceedings commenced.[79] In addition, registration establishes priority over subsequent execution liens over the assets encumbered by the charge, as well as priority over subsequent conflicting charges.[80] However, if registration applications are filed for two or more conflicting encumbrances at the same time, the charges will share priority. Although a floating charge is well protected once registered, registration does not mean that the charge will continue to encumber individual assets that have been the subject of subsequent transactions (alienation).[81] If an asset is wrongfully sold by the grantor

---

[75] See e.g. Jens Edvin A. Skoghøy, *Factoringpant* (Universitetsforlaget 1990) 320.

[76] See Jens Edvin A. Skoghøy, '*Rettsvern for factoring og factoringpant – hva gjelder etter HR-2020-837-A Bergen Bunkers?*', Jussens Venner 2021, 299–314.

[77] The Mortgage Act, section 1-4 (1).

[78] The Mortgage Act, section 1-5 (1).

[79] Act of 7 June 1935 No. 2, the Land Registration Act (*tinglysingsloven*), sections 34(3) and 23.

[80] The Land Registration Act, sections 34 (3) and 20.

[81] The Mortgage Act, sections 1-2 (4) and 4-10 (2).

to a third party in good faith, the third party acquires the asset unencumbered by the floating charge, even if the charge is registered.[82]

Moreover, even if a registered floating charge has the best priority, this priority may be compromised by rules on statutory security rights. Specifically, secured creditors should be aware of statutory security rights in favour of the grantor's bankruptcy estate. In the event of bankruptcy, the estate will be granted a statutory security right over any asset owned by the grantor that is encumbered by a security right in favour of a third party.[83] Such a statutory security will automatically rank above all other encumbrances. However, statutory security is limited to 5 per cent of the total value of the asset in question (capped at 700 times the standard court fee), and statutory security may only be used to secure coverage of necessary expenses incurred in administering the estate.[84]

If a floating charge is to be reused or transferred to a new secured creditor, it is necessary either to re-establish the charge for the benefit of a new creditor or, if retaining priority is an issue, that the first creditor transfers the charge to the new creditor.[85] In the event of re-establishment, the first creditor's charge is deleted and a new independent charge is created for the benefit of the new creditor, which must be registered to secure third-party effectiveness. Consequently, a charge can only be re-established with the grantor's consent and involvement. However, a charge can be transferred without involving the grantor, if the secured obligations are transferrable.[86] In the

---

[82] It is unclear whether the same rules apply to intellectual property encumbered with a floating charge over operating assets. It has been argued that the same rules should apply: Bjørn Løtveit, *Pantsettelse av immaterialrettigheter* (Universitetsforlaget 2021) 359–362.

[83] The Mortgage Act, section 6-4.

[84] Similar statutory security rights are also granted to creditors whose claims relate to funding the grantor's reconstruction proceedings according to the Reconstruction Act (*rekonstruksjonsloven*), see the Mortgage Act, section 6-5. Furthermore, with the approval of the reconstruction administrator, such claims can also be secured by the grantor creating new floating charges in favour of the creditors funding the reconstruction proceedings. Such new floating charges will automatically rank above any pre-existing encumbrances, see the Reconstruction Act, section 19. However, the Reconstruction Act is at this point only temporary and will be repealed on 1 July 2023.

[85] Re-establishing a charge does not always compromise the priority of the charge. Priority can be kept after a re-establishment if the secured obligations are the same and the maximum secured amount is not increased.

[86] The Mortgage Act, section 1-10. The main rule in Norwegian law is that monetary claims are freely transferable, see the Supreme Court of Norway's ruling in Rt. 2008 p. 385 (section 61).

event of transfer, effectiveness against the grantor's successors (creditors or transferees) is already ensured by the first creditor's registration of the charge. However, when the charge is transferred to a new creditor, additional perfection requirements need to be fulfilled for the transfer to obtain effectiveness against the first creditor's successors. It is unclear whether, in such cases, third-party effectiveness is obtained by registering the transfer in the Register of Mortgaged Movable Property (*Løsøreregisteret*) or by following the procedures for transferring claims, i.e. by transferring a connected debt instrument or, if the secured obligations are not connected to a debt instrument, by notifying the debtor of the transfer.[87] While this question has been discussed by legal scholars, no clear answer has yet been found.[88] The preparatory works to the Mortgage Act appear to imply that, in such cases, third-party effectiveness is secured through the procedures for the transfer of claims.[89]

Enforcement

In the event of the grantor's bankruptcy, the bankruptcy estate liquidates the encumbered assets. When a default occurs outside the bankruptcy context and a floating charge is in place, this can be enforced by the secured creditor. Generally speaking, enforcement is undertaken by public enforcement officers in accordance with procedures laid down in the Norwegian Enforcement Act (*tvangsfullbyrdelsesloven*).[90] The parties to a security agreement may not agree to customised enforcement arrangements prior to default but can make such arrangements after default has occurred.[91] However, in the case of a floating charge over trade receivables, the parties may agree in advance not to involve public enforcement officers in the enforcement process. In such cases, enforcement is normally effected by the secured creditor notifying the debtors that the trade receivables have been assigned to the secured creditor and that the grantor is no longer entitled to collect them. Once the debtors have been notified that payment is to be made to the secured creditor and not to the

[87] See the Land Registration Act, sections 34 (3), 20 and 23, see also section 22, which pursuant to section 34 (3) does not apply to the Register of Mortgaged Movable Property.

[88] See Hans Fredrik Marthinussen, *Forholdet mellom panteretten og det sikrede kravet* (Cappelen 2010) 445–466.

[89] See Ot. prp. nr. 39 (1977–1978), 26 and 94, and Jens Edvin A. Skoghøy, *Panterett*, 5th edn (Universitetsforlaget 2021) 260.

[90] Act of 26 June 1992 No. 86 (the Enforcement Act).

[91] The Enforcement Act, section 1-3 (2).

grantor, they are obliged to make payment to the secured creditor and will no longer be discharged of their obligations if payment is made to the grantor.[92]

A registered floating charge can constitute sufficient title for enforcement purposes.[93] In such cases, no additional court judgment, verdict or decision is required.

FLOATING CHARGES IN SWEDEN

Background

In Sweden, a primary issue discussed with regard to security rights over movable property in general is third-party effectiveness, particularly vis-à-vis other creditors of the grantor. Traditionally, the most commonly used mechanisms in Sweden have been retention of title and pledging of property. The basic rules on pledging can be traced to a provision dated 1734,[94] and are quite strict. For example, the possession of the object must be transferred to the secured creditor and it must remain in the creditor's possession until the debt is settled. Further, the grantor – owing to retaining ownership of the object – must be denied all autonomous access to the pledged object. Legitimate credit security in the form of a pledge can only be created over individualised property remaining in the grantor's possession when the matter involves pledging of a) real property, b) ships or c) aircrafts, and the pledge is registered.[95] These strict rules can constitute hurdles for enterprises that do not own real property and/or are unable to transfer possession of goods required for conducting business. For a long time, therefore, enterprises have had the option of securing credit on non-individualised property forming part of their business.[96] The applicable legislation, which is closely related to the method for granting security over real property, has been amended several times over the years, most recently in 2008 by the Limited Floating Charges Act (*lag om företagshypotek*).[97] According to Chapter 1, Section 1, a limited floating charge is to be understood as 'a security interest pursuant to the provisions of this Act'. As set out below,

---

[92] The Act on Promissory Notes (*gjeldsbrevloven*), section 27.

[93] The Enforcement Act, section 8-2 (1) (a).

[94] Handelsbalken 10:1.

[95] An alternative, where the object may otherwise be left in the transferor's or grantor's possession, is to register the transaction as an acquisition of goods in accordance with the Bills of Sales Act (*lösöreköplagen*). For various reasons, as a bureaucratic and rigid procedure, this alternative appeals to few.

[96] The first act focused on floating security dates to 1883; see *lagen (1883:16 s. 1) angående förlagsinteckning.*

[97] Limited Floating Charges Act (SFS 2008:990).

it involves no transfer of title to the secured creditor and, in contrast to the traditional pledge, the limited floating charge is thus a special type of security interest – registration-based, non-possessory and floating. Today, any company owner (trader) – whether an individual or the company itself – can establish a floating credit security right over certain types of business asset.

Creation

To grant credit security under the Limited Floating Charges Act (*företagshypotek*), a trader or the company must first apply to the Swedish Companies Registration Office (*Bolagsverket*) for a business mortgage for a specific sum of money.[98] This business mortgage is created through registration and confirmed by a mortgage certificate (*företagsinteckningsbrev*). Thereafter, the trader must deliver the mortgage certificate to the creditor as security for the claim. This procedure complies with the strict requirements applicable to transfers of pledged chattels.

The application to register the business mortgage certificate must be made in writing using a specific form, including a specification of the grantor's name and social security number or company registration number, and must state the amount secured by the business mortgage certificate. If the currency involved is not Swedish krona (SEK), this must also be noted. The sum of money secured by the certificate correlates with the maximum amount of credit security granted over the movable property. Additionally, if the trader wants to issue two or more certificates, the application must indicate the relative ranking of these, i.e. whether or not the mortgages shall have equal priority. If there are previously issued business mortgages, the older instruments will automatically rank above more recent ones. The trader can choose to have the business mortgage certificate issued in either electronic or printed form. However, there is no difference between these two forms regarding the effect of the certificate.

To establish actual security over the movable property covered by the business mortgage, the certificate must be transferred to the creditor. If the certificate is not in the creditor's direct or indirect custody, the granted security will be invalid. If, as is usually the case nowadays, the mortgage is issued electronically, the traditional transfer of the business mortgage certificate is replaced by registration with the Companies Registration Office. Such registration can already be arranged when applying for a business mortgage.

98 Available online: <https://bolagsverket.se/en/sjalvservice/blanketterochmallar/ovrigablanketterochmallar/foretagsinteckning.1757.html> accessed 16 March 2024.

To summarise, the mortgage certificate can be said to represent a proportion of the value of movable property. Credit security is granted by transferring the certificate, which must subsequently be returned to the trader once the debt secured by the certificate has been settled. The trader is then free to reuse the certificate as security for new credit. If a printed mortgage certificate is lost and more than 10 years have passed since it was last used, it can be cancelled by application to the Companies Registration Office. Such cancellation does not cancel the actual registration. Accordingly, the trader can apply for a new mortgage certificate based on the mortgage registration that facilitated the issuing of the first (now cancelled) certificate. For obvious reasons, an electronic mortgage certificate cannot be cancelled.

Encumbered and Exempted Assets

The assets covered by the mortgage certificate are regulated in section 2:1 of the Limited Floating Charges Act. The principal rule is that all movable property, including intangibles, belonging to the grantor is included. This means that only assets owned by the grantor falls within the scope of the mortgage. Leased and hired assets are excluded, even if they happen to be in the grantor's possession. In theory, the grantor's lease and hire rights might be included, but the possibility for a third party to exercise this right is entirely dependent on the grantor's contract with the lessor, and such a right can, in any case be expected to have a very limited financial scope.

Section 2:1 states that the following assets are exempted: (1) cash and funds in a bank; (2) shares and other financial instruments intended for general trading; (3) assets which can be the subject of a pledge owing to a mortgage or registration (for example, certain land rights, waterfall rights, rights in ships or shipbuilding, aircraft and mortgageable spare parts for aircraft); or (4) assets which can neither be subject to a levy of execution nor included in a bankruptcy/insolvency liquidation.

It is clear that the business mortgage is an uncertain form of security in several respects. A secured creditor can never be sure of the total value of the security. Further, the assets included in a business mortgage is defined by law, and the parties cannot validly agree on different content. The security right over each asset expires when the asset is sold.[99] Accordingly, since movable assets may be used in regular business transactions, creditors may find that their security has eroded to the point where the remaining assets are of little,

[99] This rule covers all sales. Should there, however, be any irregularities, the property in question may be subject to recovery in bankruptcy, but – if so – the bankruptcy estate will then benefit and not the creditor with a business mortgage.

or no, value. On the other hand, future assets are also included in the security, which in any case means a strengthening of it.

If a business subject to a business mortgage is transferred and the transfer includes encumbered assets, the mortgage remains valid against the assets as held by the transferee.[100] In such cases, the security right no longer attaches to a category of assets but only to the specific objects which were encumbered by the original mortgage and which remain in the transferee's possession. If the transferee has resold, damaged, lost or used up the assets through letting or by other means that give the transferee a claim for compensation, the mortgage may also apply to this claim. However, the secured creditor loses his right to enforce the mortgage against the transferee if he does not, within six months after the transferor or transferee notifies him of the transfer and at the latest 18 months from the date on which the business was relinquished, commence an action against the transferee for payment from the assets and provide notice thereof to the registration authority.

Effect and Priority

Section 2:5 of the Limited Floating Charges Act sets out the consequences of a creditor having a floating charge (*företagshypotek*) as security for a claim. The provision states that, in the event of enforcement or bankruptcy proceedings, the holders of a business mortgage may exercise their right to secure payment from the assets covered by the mortgage. In the first instance, an amount corresponding to the principal sum specified in the mortgage certificate can be reserved.[101] In addition, a supplement can be demanded if necessary. Such supplements consist of two parts: a maximum of 15 per cent of the principal sum and an annual interest rate specified by law. The purpose of the supplement is not to stress a sale of the goods remaining in the business. In case of foreclosure or insolvency, some creditors demand a quick sale and distribution of the payment from the assets to prevent further losses. The supplement prevents these kinds of actions.

Section 2:8 of the Limited Floating Charges Act states that a creditor has the right to apply for payment from assets subject to a business mortgage even if the claim has not fallen due for payment. However, this right may only be exercised in one of the following three cases: (1) if the mortgaged business, or a substantial part thereof, is transferred, terminated or assigned to a third party through assignment of the assets of a trading company or through division of

---

[100] See the Limited Floating Charges Act, Chapter 2, section 3.

[101] The creditor's right to payment from the property is always limited by the actual claim (plus interest, if any), and also by the fact that the secured claim may have become smaller, e.g., by partial repayment.

assets for any reason other than the death of the trader; (2) if the assets – as a result of neglect or a natural event, or for any other comparable reason – is impaired or reduced such that the value of the security decreases significantly; or (3) in the event of enforcement (by another creditor) of a business mortgage over assets. In these cases, the mortgage creditor is entitled to payment from the assets in accordance with the Enforcement Code (*utsökningsbalken*) even if the claim has not yet fallen due for payment.

As regards priority between different mortgages, an earlier mortgage certificate has priority over a subsequent one (see above). Where applications are made on the same date, the resulting mortgage certificates share the same priority ranking unless otherwise specified in the applications. The system thus permits reuse of a mortgage certificate that has been returned to a trader after repayment of a loan as credit security with unchanged priority. Before accepting a business mortgage as security, creditors normally request information about the total mortgage burden, priority order and other information recorded in the business mortgage register. Such information may be given to third parties, usually in the form of a 'certificate of search' (*gravationsbevis*) issued by the Companies Registration Office on application.

Enforcement

As indicated above, a creditor is only entitled to payment before a claim has fallen due for payment in three exceptional instances. In all other cases, the creditor requires a basis for enforcement (e.g. a court judgment, verdict or decision) in accordance with Chapter 3 of the Enforcement Code in order to engage the enforcement authority. In the event of the grantor's bankruptcy, encumbered assets will not be separated out and protected against other creditors, and secured creditors are not entitled to realise such assets autonomously. The *ius separationis* granted to ordinary pledgees does not encompass business mortgages. Instead, the bankruptcy estate must realise assets connected to such mortgages.[102]

As regards restructuring, the situation is somewhat complicated. A secured creditor is exposed to the risk that receivables, stock-in-trade and other assets may be sold or otherwise realised prior to an imminent bankruptcy. To protect business mortgage creditors, a so-called administration account is often opened to receive significant payments stemming from the sale of business

[102] The provisions regulating the order in which the grantor's property must be used to cover claims in a bankruptcy situation or in enforcement proceedings can be found in the Preferential Rights Act (*förmånsrättslagen*).

mortgage assets.[103] In the event of a subsequent bankruptcy, the account is handed over to the bankruptcy estate.

FLOATING CHARGES IN FINLAND

Enterprise Mortgages as the Finnish Equivalent of Floating Charges

The sources of Finnish law on security over movables are fragmentary and of varying ages.[104] They could hardly be regarded as a system if not for the systematisation efforts of legal scholars. These efforts include the articulation of principles that condense the normative content of the law. A key principle of the law governing security over movables (and property law more generally) is the principle of specificity. It requires that the content and the object of a security right must be sufficiently specified for the security right to be effective and enforceable between the parties and against third parties.[105]

Enterprise mortgages (*yrityskiinnitys*; *företagsinteckning*) can be regarded as a deviation from the principle of specificity, or perhaps as an example of a more relaxed attitude towards it.[106] Subject to certain exceptions, enterprise mortgages allow enterprises (i.e. traders registered in the Finnish Trade Register) to use all their movable assets – including both tangibles and intangibles – as the object of a floating security in accordance with the Enterprise Mortgage Act (*yrityskiinnityslaki*; *företagsinteckningslag*; 634/1984). On the other hand, enterprise mortgages do not necessarily have to be viewed as a systemic deviation, since their reduced specificity comes at a price: weaker

---

[103] It must be noted that a new act regarding restructuring entered into force in 2022 (*Lag (2022:964) om företagsrekonstruktion*) and it is not certain to what extent the old solutions will continue to be carried out in these matters. Most of those involved in restructuring seem to continue to use such accounts. To what extent, only the future can tell.

[104] For example, some provisions on pledging originate in the Trade Code of the Swedish Law of the Realm of 1734. See chapter 10 of the Trade Code (*kauppakaari*; *handelsbalk*; 3/1734).

[105] Eva Tammi-Salminen, *Esinevakuusoikeuden perusteet* (Alma Talent 2015) 111–118.

[106] 'Enterprise mortgage' may be a misleading translation if it leads one to think of the characteristics of mortgages in other legal systems. In the Finnish context, it refers to a type of security which is registration-based, non-possessory and floating, but involves no transfer of title to the secured creditor. The Finnish Patent and Registration Office uses this translation, noting that the type of security is 'also called business mortgage or floating charge'. Patent and Registration Office website: <https://www.prh.fi/en/yrityskiinnitykset.html> accessed 13 March 2024.

control for the secured creditor over the encumbered assets and lower priority in relation to other creditors, as compared with other types of security.[107] These and other main characteristics of enterprise mortgages are discussed in the sections below.

The Enterprise Mortgage Act was enacted in 1984 and entered into force in 1986. Its main purpose was to support the financing of enterprises – especially small and medium-sized businesses – by facilitating the use of movable assets as security for credit without sacrificing the possibility of productive use of those assets. A further objective was to reduce the need for enterprises to resort to security provided by third parties.[108] The advantages of enterprise mortgages are clearest with respect to tangible (corporeal) movables. As a rule, tangible movable assets can otherwise only be used as security by means of a possessory pledge (or a functionally equivalent security right, with the same conditions for effectiveness), meaning that the assets cannot simultaneously be used productively in the grantor's business.[109]

To make use of enterprise mortgages, the grantor must be registered in the Finnish Trade Register (*kaupparekisteri*; *handelsregistret*) in accordance with the Trade Register Act (*kaupparekisterilaki*; *handelsregisterlag*; 564/2023).[110] The obligation to register (to file a start-up notification) is not limited to Finnish traders, but extends to, for example, branches of foreign traders.[111] As a result,

---

107 Tammi-Salminen, *Esinevakuusoikeuden perusteet*, cit., 118–119, 389.

108 Government Proposal 190/1983, 1–2.

109 However, certain means of transport are separately mortgageable under special acts and can be used both as security and in the grantor's business at the same time. See section 'Encumbered Assets' below. It should also be noted that certain combinations of security and contractual arrangements may have floating charge-type characteristics. See e.g. Jarno Tepora, 'Irtaimen vakuusluovutuksesta ja panttioikeuden oikeudellisesta määräysvallasta erilaisissa toimintaympäristöissä' in Esa Kolehmainen (ed.), *Business Law Forum 2005* (Edita Publishing 2005). Tepora discusses, among other things, the use of securities portfolios as security.

110 Enterprise Mortgage Act, section 1. See Jarmo Tuomisto, *Yrityskiinnitys* (Alma Talent 2007) 30. According to Tuomisto, 'trader' (*elinkeinonharjoittaja*; *näringsidkare*), as meant in section 1 of the Enterprise Mortgage Act, includes everyone who is obliged to register in the Trade Register or can register in it voluntarily. The majority of registered traders are limited liability companies and private traders. See the Patent and Registration Office website: <https://www.prh.fi/en/kaupparekisteri.html> accessed 13 March 2024.

111 Trade Register Act, section 3(1). The Patent and Registration Office defines a branch of a foreign trader as 'a part of a foreign organisation or foundation that professionally runs business activities in Finland, from this country, in the name of or on behalf of the foreign business or foundation' and notes that while branches 'must operate in the same line of business as the foreign trader', branches

the movable assets of a foreign trader's registered Finnish branch can be used as the object of a floating security by enterprise mortgage.[112]

The Enterprise Mortgage Act is not the first instance of floating security in Finnish law. It was preceded by the Chattel Mortgage Act of 1923 (*laki irtaimistokiinnityksestä*; *lagen om lösöreinteckning*; 55/1923), which had a significantly narrower personal and asset scope than the Enterprise Mortgage Act. Initially, the Chattel Mortgage Act only applied to 'mechanical or industrial plants' and certain artisanal and agricultural enterprises, but its scope was expanded in 1979. Even more limited forms of mortgage over movables existed before the Chattel Mortgage Act, dating back to the eighteenth century (when Finland was part of the Kingdom of Sweden). Under the mercantilist legislation of the time, such mortgages were initially only available for mining enterprises and certain industrial and artisanal enterprises.[113]

Creation and Third-party Effectiveness

As a first step in securing a creditor's claim by enterprise mortgage, the grantor must apply for mortgage registration with the Finnish Patent and Registration Office (*Patentti- ja rekisterihallitus*; *Patent- och registerstyrelsen*).[114] The application must enclose a negotiable promissory note for use as the mortgage instrument. Both the application and the promissory note must use forms issued by the Patent and Registration Office.[115] The promissory note specifies the maximum amount of money the registered mortgage will cover (i.e. a monetary cap on the claims it secures), but does not set out any actual debt owed by the applicant. Moreover, it does not relate to any specific debt relationship.

Next, the Patent and Registration Office records the mortgage in the Register of Enterprise Mortgages (*yrityskiinnitysrekisteri*; *företagsinteckningsregistret*)

---

with a narrower line of business have been approved for registration. Patent and Registration Office website: <https://www.prh.fi/en/kaupparekisteri/yrityksen_perustaminen/sivuliikkeen_perustaminen.html> accessed 13 March 2024.

112 Tuomisto, *Yrityskiinnitys*, cit., 108.

113 Committee Report 1981:56 (to the Ministry of Justice), 14–21. See Ilmari Caselius, *Laki irtaimistokiinnityksestä, annettu helmikuun 17 päivänä 1923, siihen liittyvine asetuksineen ja selityksineen* (Werner Söderström Osakeyhtiö 1924) 6–8.

114 The mortgage registration procedure is set out in chapter 3 of the Enterprise Mortgage Act. Under section 17, the applicant may also be a creditor. See the Patent and Registration Office webpages on enterprise mortgages: <https://www.prh.fi/en/yrityskiinnitykset.html> accessed 13 March 2024.

115 The latter form has the English title 'Promissory note secured by a pledge' (*Panttivelkakirja*; *Pantskuldebrev*) and is specified to be a 'bearer bond'.

and, importantly, adds a mortgage certificate to the promissory note, which is then returned to the applicant. To create a security right effective against third parties, and thus secure a creditor's claim, the grantor must additionally enter into a security agreement with the creditor, and the creditor must take possession of the promissory note containing the mortgage certificate.[116]

Once a secured claim is repaid, the promissory note containing the mortgage certificate is returned to the grantor. The grantor may then reuse the promissory note to secure other claims, whether belonging to the same or to a different creditor, with the same priority in relation to the other enterprise mortgages that the grantor may have registered.[117] Reuse is possible because the promissory note is not related to any specific debt relationship between the grantor and a creditor,[118] because the priority between several enterprise mortgages (and promissory notes) is fixed at the time of mortgage registration by the date of application, so that earlier ones take priority over later ones,[119] and because a mortgage registration (and a promissory note) remains valid until it is cancelled, upon application.[120]

---

116 Enterprise Mortgage Act, section 7; Government Proposal 190/1983, 9. See Tuomisto, *Yrityskiinnitys*, cit., 9–13. Section 7 of the Enterprise Mortgage Act does not distinguish between the creation of a security right and achieving third-party effectiveness, but suggests that both occur at the same time. In the Act's terminology, the security right is a 'right of pledge' (*panttioikeus*; *panträtt*). The term 'enterprise mortgage' can refer either to the type of security in a general sense or to the act of mortgage registration or a registered mortgage (regardless of whether a security right has been created). It should also be possible to create a secondary security right. For third-party effectiveness, this requires notification to the secured creditor in possession of the promissory note containing the mortgage certificate.

117 Indeed, the grantor may have applied for several mortgage registrations and may thus have obtained several promissory notes with a mortgage certificate. A registered mortgage and the existence of a promissory note with a mortgage certificate do not as such mean the existence of a security right, but can rather be regarded as a precondition or a preparatory step for creating a security right. The grantor may use the promissory notes to create security rights for one and the same or different creditors.

118 Enterprise Mortgage Act, section 7.

119 Enterprise Mortgage Act, section 8.

120 Enterprise Mortgage Act, sections 22 and 23. See section 27 on situations in which a mortgage registration will be removed.

Encumbered Assets

The assets that are included in an enterprise mortgage – insofar as they form part of the business activities of the enterprise – are listed in the Enterprise Mortgage Act. These 'mortgageable assets' are the following: (1) buildings, structures, machines, equipment, and comparable fixed assets; (2) trademarks, trade names, industrial designs, patents, other intellectual property rights, lease rights, rights of use, rights of extraction (e.g. relating to land or mineral resources), other 'special rights' (a category of rights in the Real Estate Code (*maakaari*; *jordabalk*; 540/1995)), and other fixed assets; (3) materials, supplies, finished products, goods, and other current assets; and (4) cash, receivables, securities, book entries, and other financial assets.[121]

Despite the reference to buildings in the list above, an enterprise mortgage only covers movable assets. As a rule, all assets that are deemed to belong to real estate (land), as its component or accessory, are excluded from mortgageable assets under the Enterprise Mortgage Act.[122] Depending on the circumstances, buildings may be regarded as movable assets, and thus mortgageable under the Enterprise Mortgage Act, or as part of real estate, and thus mortgageable under the Real Estate Code, but not under the Enterprise Mortgage Act.[123] Generally, buildings are regarded as movable assets if they are owned by someone other than the person who owns the real estate on which they are located, and conversely, as part of real estate if they are owned by the same person who owns the real estate.[124]

Tax refunds are explicitly excluded from the list of mortgageable assets. Further exclusions include assets mortgageable under other legislation, notably the Real Estate Code,[125] the Vessel Mortgage Act (*aluskiinnityslaki*; *lag*

---

121 Enterprise Mortgage Act, section 3(1).

122 Government Proposal 190/1983, 6–7. See the Real Estate Code, chapter 14, section 5, on delimitation of components and accessories by registration.

123 It is also possible that a building is not regarded as part of real estate, but as part of a lease or other fixed-term usufruct on real estate owned by another person. Such rights may be mortgageable under chapter 19 of the Real Estate Code. If so, the right and the building are not mortgageable under the Enterprise Mortgage Act. See section 4(1).

124 Section 4(2) of the Enterprise Mortgage Act deals with changes in such circumstances, e.g. when the owner of a building acquires the real estate on which the building is located, and the building becomes part of the real estate.

125 The reference here is to leases and other fixed-term usufructs on real estate owned by another person, which under certain circumstances are mortgageable in accordance with chapter 19 of the Real Estate Code. See Tuomisto, *Yrityskiinnitys*, cit., 112–121.

om inteckning i fartyg; 211/1927) and the Aircraft Mortgage Act (*laki kiinnityksistä ilma-aluksiin*; *lag om inteckning i luftfartyg*; 211/1928). The only exception to this is assets mortgageable under the Vehicle Mortgage Act (*autokiinnityslaki*; *lag om inteckning i bil*; 810/1972), which are subject to an enterprise mortgage. However, a previously registered vehicle mortgage takes priority over a subsequently registered enterprise mortgage upon the sale of the mortgaged vehicle.[126]

Generally speaking, an enterprise mortgage covers all assets that are mortgageable under the Enterprise Mortgage Act and belong to the enterprise at the time of mortgage registration, as well as all such subsequently acquired assets.[127] The enterprise is permitted to use and alienate assets subject to an enterprise mortgage in the ordinary course of business, including the regular exchange of goods and necessary asset renewal. When alienated in this way, assets become unencumbered. This also applies even if the alienation does not occur in the ordinary course of business, provided that the acquirer acts in good faith. Rules exist to protect secured creditors, for example, in situations where the mortgaged assets have been alienated wholly or for the most part.[128]

Priority

An enterprise can register several enterprise mortgages. The priority between these is determined by the application date: mortgage registrations applied for earlier take priority over mortgage registrations applied for later.[129]

Further rules exist on priority between an enterprise mortgage and a competing pledge (or charge) of a specific object. An earlier pledge takes priority

---

[126] Enterprise Mortgage Act, sections 3(2) and 4(1). Perhaps counterintuitively, ordinary cars (automobiles) and vans are not mortgageable under the Vehicle Mortgage Act. On interpretation of the priority rule, see Tuomisto, *Yrityskiinnitys*, cit., 126–129.

[127] Enterprise Mortgage Act, section 5. Exceptions are caused by subsequently acquired assets that are subject to a retention of title (or a functionally equivalent) clause, provided that the clause fulfils the conditions of third-party effectiveness. See Tuomisto, *Yrityskiinnitys*, cit., 159–163. In addition, section 5(2) permits restriction of mortgage registration to a certain part of the enterprise's business activity, or on certain geographical grounds. Other than that, an enterprise mortgage cannot be limited to certain groups or classes of assets.

[128] Enterprise Mortgage Act, sections 9 and 15. See Government Proposal 139/1990, 5. For an example of the related case law, see Finnish Supreme Court decision KKO 1999:49.

[129] Enterprise Mortgage Act, section 8. Mortgage registrations applied for on the same date share the same priority, unless otherwise decided based on the application.

over a later mortgage, while a later pledge is ineffective against ('does not bind') the holder of an earlier mortgage.[130] The wording of this rule and its preparatory works are unclear, but legal literature suggests that priority should be determined based on the time of the relevant publicity measures (e.g. taking possession of a pledged object versus taking possession of the promissory note containing the mortgage certificate).[131] An exception exists for securities, book entries and receivables, which may be pledged (or charged) regardless of – and with better priority than – an enterprise mortgage.[132]

In the event of the grantor's bankruptcy (collective liquidation) proceedings or debt enforcement proceedings, the priority of claims secured by an enterprise mortgage is subject to limitations.[133] First, certain other claims take precedence, including claims secured by a right of pledge or a right of retention, claims which have arisen in connection with enterprise restructuring (collective rehabilitation) proceedings, and child maintenance claims. Second, in bankruptcy proceedings (but not in debt enforcement proceedings), claims secured by an enterprise mortgage take priority over other claims only with respect to 50 per cent of the value of the mortgaged assets.[134] Owing to these

---

[130] Enterprise Mortgage Act, section 4(3).

[131] Tuomisto, *Yrityskiinnitys*, cit., 143–151. Here, 'publicity measure' refers to the step required in addition to a security agreement for achieving third-party effectiveness. Put simply, the main options under Finnish law on security over movables are possession, notification and registration.

[132] Enterprise Mortgage Act, section 4(3); Government Proposal 190/1983, 7. This exception permits, e.g., a separate factoring arrangement.

[133] In debt enforcement proceedings initiated by another creditor, a secured creditor (holder of an enterprise mortgage) is not entitled to payment from the proceeds of realisation of the mortgaged assets if the remaining mortgaged assets suffice as full security. See Enterprise Mortgage Act, section 14(3); Enforcement Code (*ulosottokaari*; *utsökningsbalk*; 705/2007), chapter 5, section 29.

[134] Enterprise Mortgage Act, section 14; Act on the Ranking of Claims (*laki velkojien maksunsaantijärjestyksestä*; *lag om den ordning i vilken borgenärer skall få betalning*; 1578/1992), section 5. The '50 per cent rule' was introduced as part of a general reform of priority rules in 1993, with the explicit aim of promoting creditor equality by reserving assets for unsecured creditors. This reform saw the abolition of most statutory privileges, including those for tax and wage claims. The intention behind the '50 per cent rule' was to maintain the priority position enterprise mortgages had enjoyed while the statutory privileges still existed. See Government Proposal 181/1992, 17–19; Teemu Juutilainen, *Secured Credit in Europe: From Conflicts to Compatibility* (Hart Publishing 2018) 146–147.

limitations and the fact that secured creditors have little control over mortgaged assets, enterprise mortgages are typically used as supplementary security.[135]

Enforcement

An enterprise mortgage does not entitle the secured creditor to effect independent realisation of mortgaged assets in the event of non-payment by the grantor. Instead, the secured creditor has to obtain a court judgment and seek enforcement by the Enforcement Authority (*Ulosottolaitos*; *Utsökningsverket*).[136] In the event of the grantor's bankruptcy, the secured creditor has no separate position in relation to the bankruptcy estate based on the existence of an enterprise mortgage. Accordingly, the bankruptcy estate (or, in some cases, the Enforcement Authority) undertakes realisation of the mortgaged assets.[137] If a grantor becomes subject to enterprise restructuring, claims secured by an enterprise mortgage may count wholly or partly as 'secured debt' which is protected against certain alterations of debt relationships otherwise available in restructuring proceedings.[138]

COMPARATIVE CONCLUSIONS

As can be identified from the previous sections, there are several similarities between the floating charge regimes applicable in the Nordic countries. Floating charges are mainly focused on encumbering movables, but each country also has arrangements that allow trade receivables and certain intellectual property rights to be included in a floating charge. A further similarity is the restriction of floating charges to a maximum secured amount specified in the mortgage instrument, mirroring tendencies outside the Nordic region.[139] An additional similarity is that, while there are a few exceptions, the Nordic rules on floating charges generally do not allow secured creditors to self-enforce their security rights. Further, Nordic floating charges are subject to the same inherent risks as floating charges in general. In other words, a secured creditor can never be

---

135 See Jarno Tepora, *Rahoitusmuodot ja vakuudet* (2nd edn, Kauppakamari 2022) 29.

136 See Tammi-Salminen, *Esinevakuusoikeuden perusteet*, cit., 418–422.

137 Bankruptcy Act (*konkurssilaki*; *konkurslag*; 120/2004), chapter 17, section 17. See also section 11.

138 Restructuring of Enterprise Act (*laki yrityksen saneerauksesta*; *lag om företagssanering*; 47/1993), sections 3(1) and 45. See Jarno Tepora, Janne Kaisto and Esa Hakkola, *Esinevakuudet* (2nd edn, Kauppakamari 2016) 317–320.

139 See UNCITRAL, *Legislative Guide on Secured Transactions* (New York 2010) 71 and 75–76.

certain about which assets are presently encumbered, cannot control the grantor's disposal of encumbered assets, and cannot be sure that the value of the encumbered assets is equal to, or higher than, the secured obligations.

Examination of the main 'structural' similarities and differences between Nordic laws on floating charges shows relatively clearly that the four jurisdictions discussed above can be grouped into two pairs, in that Denmark and Norway are closer to each other than to Sweden and Finland, and vice versa. The clearest indication in this regard is that Danish and Norwegian law provide for several types of floating charges, while Swedish and Finnish law only offer one type each. Moreover, Sweden and Finland have adopted very similar mortgage certificate concepts, whereas floating charges in Denmark and Norway can be linked to different kinds of debt instrument. Although the Swedish and Finnish rules differ significantly at the level of detail, they are broadly similar in many other respects, including the role of registration, mortgage instruments, creation, and third-party effectiveness.

All of the Nordic countries presuppose some connection between the floating charge and a debt instrument, but there are differences in how strong this connection must be. Finnish law requires a registration application to enclose a negotiable promissory note, which can be physically transferred to a secured creditor.[140] Similarly, Swedish law requires the grantor to obtain an official mortgage certificate for physical transfer to the secured creditor, although an electronic mortgage certificate is also available.[141] In Denmark, a floating business charge can be transferred, but the third-party effect depends on the type of mortgage instrument and the applicable rules.[142] Similarly, Norwegian law contains no legal requirement to connect a floating charge to a transferable debt instrument, but the registration application forms contain fields for information which, if provided, turn the application into a negotiable promissory note.

Further, in Finland and Sweden, a grantor may reuse a registered floating charge once the secured obligations have been repaid in full, and the connected debt instrument has been returned to the grantor. In such cases, the grantor reuses the floating charge simply by transferring the physical debt instrument to a new secured creditor. In Denmark, the scope for reusing a floating business charge depends on the mortgage instrument in question, as the rules differ significantly. In Norway, however, the registration of a floating charge always

140 See Patrik Lindskoug, 'Property and its limits' in Pia Letto-Vanamo, Ditlev Tamm and Bent Ole Gram Mortensen (eds), *Nordic Law in European Context* (Springer 2019) 135–151, 149–150.

141 *Ibid.*

142 See Lars Henrik Gam Madsen, *Virksomhedspant, fordringspant og pantsætningsforbud* (Karnov Group 2020) 157 *et seq.*

specifies the secured creditor. If a floating charge is to be reused, it is necessary either to re-register it to the new secured creditor or for the previous creditor to transfer the charge to the new creditor. As the rules on third-party effectiveness of transfers of floating charges are somewhat unclear in Norway, as described above, the formal connection between a floating charge and a debt instrument is also less clear under Norwegian law than in the other Nordic countries.

The differences between the rules on floating charges may entail increased transaction costs for international businesses. When dealing with different sets of rules, it will often be necessary to seek legal counsel in multiple jurisdictions. Since a grantor usually covers both its own and the secured creditor's legal costs in secured transactions, the credit arrangement gets increasingly expensive for the grantor as the number of jurisdictions increases. More harmonised rules on floating charges may enable lawyers to advise on matters relating to foreign jurisdictions as well, thus decreasing transaction costs. Harmonisation could thus be beneficial to inter-Nordic trade and commerce, and larger-scale harmonisation might aid European, or even global, cross-border transactions. However, for the time being, the Nordic countries' solutions in the area of credit security law continue to differ considerably.

ACKNOWLEDGEMENTS

While this chapter is the result of a collaborative effort, primary authorship of the parts on individual jurisdictions is as follows: Norway, B.L.; Denmark, A.M.-C.; Sweden, P.L.; Finland, T.J. The Introduction and Comparative Conclusions were drafted by B.L.

13. The encumbrance of intermediated securities in Switzerland

Alexandra Dal Molin-Kränzlin

INTRODUCTION

Unlike many Common Law countries, the Swiss legal system, which evolved from the Civil Law tradition, does not have a history of non-possessory security rights such as floating charges.[1] However, there is one notable recent exception. In 2010, intermediated securities – a new type of asset – were introduced into the Swiss legal system. This type of asset may be encumbered with security rights which to some extent resemble floating charges and serve similar purposes.

The focus of this contribution lies in considering encumbrances of intermediated securities as one special case relating to floating security rights under Swiss law. The contribution is structured as follows: I begin with a brief discussion of Swiss security law and its governing concepts, followed by a discussion on whether there is any room for floating security rights in Swiss law. Thereafter, a detailed analysis of intermediated securities in general and their encumbrance in particular will follow. In the next section I will compare and contrast the encumbrances of Swiss law-based intermediated securities with floating charges under English law. The contribution then finishes with concluding remarks.

1 'Floating charges' for the purpose of this paper are understood as security instruments which enable companies to mortgage their assets present and future in whole or at least to a large extent by recording such charges in a special register while the company's power of disposal of its assets is not impaired. As a consequence, the amount of assets covered by such floating charges may change. The power of disposal ends once the company is wound up or a receiver over the charged assets of the company is appointed. At this point in time, the charge stops floating and becomes a fixed charge (so-called 'crystallisation'). Cf. Manfred Wenckstern, 'Die englische Floating Charge im deutschen Internationalen Privatrecht' (1992) 56 RabelsZ 624, 692 et seq.

SWISS SECURITY RIGHTS LAW

This chapter starts with an overview of traditional legal concepts governing Swiss security rights law and gives a brief description of the ongoing evolution of securities (financial instruments, not to be confused with security rights) as physical deeds towards becoming dematerialised equivalents. In the second part of this section, I will provide an initial classification of (dematerialised) intermediated securities, which were introduced to Swiss law relatively recently, and which can be encumbered by security rights that bear certain similarities to floating charges. I will also point out possible discrepancies with traditional legal concepts.

General Concepts

Swiss security rights law is governed by several property law-based principles which have been developed by jurisprudence and doctrine over the years.[2] In the present context, the following principles are of particular interest:

- *Principle of speciality* (in German '*Spezialitätsprinzip*'): according to the principle of speciality, rights *in rem* (encompassing also security rights) can only comprise single, individualised and specific objects or rights. In particular, rights *in rem* cannot relate to a totality of objects (such as e.g. all items in a warehouse or assets belonging to a company).[3]
- *Principle of publicity* (in German '*Publizitätsprinzip*'): owing to the *erga omnes* effect of rights *in rem*, a certain level of publicity is required with regard to such rights encompassing objects. The means of publication for rights in movable property is in general the concept of possession, while

---

[2] Cf. Dieter Zobl and Dieter Gericke, 'Systematischer Teil FISA nos 78–108' in Dieter Zobl, Martin Hess and Ansgar Schott (eds), *Kommentar zum Bucheffektengesetz (BEG)* (Schulthess Juristische Medien AG 2013). Regarding liens, which are of particular interest for this contribution: Reto Arpagaus, 'Teil 3: Kreditgeschäft' in Reto Arpagaus, Ralph Stadler and Thomas Werlen (eds), *Das Schweizerische Bankgeschäft* (8th edn, Schulthess Juristische Medien AG 2021) paras 1405–1415.

[3] Arpagaus (n 2) para 1408; Christina Schmid-Tschirren, 'Perspektiven des sachenrechtlichen Spezialitätsprinzips: insbesondere zur Bedeutung dieses Prinzips bei Pfandrechten' (2016) 97 ZBGR 1, 2; Jörg Schmid and Bettina Hürlimann-Kaup, *Sachenrecht* (5th edn, Schulthess Juristische Medien AG 2017) para 70; Zobl and Gericke (n 2) no 87.

the means of publication for rights in immovable property is an entry into a register.[4]

- *Pledge principle* (in German '*Faustpfandprinzip*'): according to the pledge principle, a security right cannot be created as long as the person granting the security right has sole power of disposal over the encumbered object.[5]
- *Principle of age priority* (in German '*Prinzip der Alterspriorität*'): according to the principle of age priority, the order of priority among limited rights *in rem* is determined by the date of their creation. The right created earlier takes precedence over the right created later (*prior tempore, potior iure*).[6]

These principles work well when applied to security rights over securities that follow the traditional concept of securities being physical pieces of paper embodying membership rights and other rights comprising three functions:[7]

- *Transport function* (in German '*Transportfunktion*'): physical securities are intended to facilitate the transferability of rights.
- *Legitimacy function* (in German '*Legitimationsfunktion*'): physical securities also have a legitimacy function insofar as possession and presentation of securities legitimise creditors to demand performance of relevant debts.
- *Market protection function* (in German '*Verkehrsschutzfunktion*'): through the protection of bona fide acquisitions from the possessor of the security, a physical security also ensures legal certainty and protects market transactions.

The link between rights and securities is a central element of the Swiss concept of securities. In the past, this concept, together with the corresponding legal principles, was the foundation stone for enabling the mobilisation of claims and other rights. With the resulting mass distribution of securities, however,

---

4 Arpagaus (n 2) para 1409; Schmid and Hürlimann-Kaup (n 3) paras 63–69; Zobl and Gericke (n 2) no 92.

5 Arpagaus (n 2) para 1410. The pledge principle is stated in art 884 para 3 of the Swiss Civil Code (CC): 'The general lien is not established as long as the pledgor retains exclusive possession of the chattel'. However, according to art 884 para 1 CC, the law may state exceptions to this general principle.

6 Schmid and Hürlimann-Kaup (n 3) paras 77 et seq; Zobl and Gericke (n 2) no 103.

7 Botschaft zum Bucheffektengesetz sowie zum Haager Wertpapierübereinkommen, BBl 2006 9315, 9321 (Dispatch Intermediated Securities); Martin Hess and Alain Friedrich, 'Das neue Bucheffektengesetz (BEG): Hinweise auf Grundlagen und praktische Auswirkungen' (2008) 2 GesKR 98, 99.

obstacles in legal transactions soon arose. The greater the number of traded securities, the more difficult and cumbersome it became to safely store and trade them. The administration and trading of securities had to be streamlined. As a result, and to solve these problems, a process of dematerialising securities started, and the Swiss legislator introduced so-called uncertificated securities (in German '*Wertrechte*') (i.e. non-physical securities with the same functions as traditional physical securities). This process is still ongoing, and a relatively recent development has been the introduction of intermediated securities (in German '*Bucheffekten*'), enabling the mediatised custody of uncertificated securities (i.e. custody of securities with financial intermediaries).[8] In the following sub-section, I will discuss some of the legal challenges that have emerged alongside this dematerialisation evolution with the example of intermediated securities.

Floating Securities? No, but ...

Bearing the above-mentioned traditional property law principles in mind, the concept of floating security rights poses various challenges to the Swiss legal system. In legal systems that acknowledge the concept of floating charges, a company can sometimes charge all its present and future property with a floating charge.[9] This seems to undermine the principle of speciality, which requires the encumbered object to be previously specified. Depending on their legal structure, floating security rights may also pose challenges to the principle of publicity and the pledge principle, especially if such a collateral transaction is not visible to a third party.

Despite the previously outlined conceptual challenges, in 2010 the Swiss legislator introduced so-called intermediated securities (in German '*Bucheffekten*') with the newly created Federal Act on Intermediated Securities (FISA). Its major aim was to keep up with the international trend of dematerialisation of securities and to facilitate the custody of intermediated securities (in German '*mediatisierte Wertpapierverwahrung*'). Part of this new legal act was also the introduction of a special form of security right according to art 25 FISA, which – as I will elaborate in this contribution – has similarities to the concept of the floating charge. The predominant reason for this new form of security right provided by art 25 para 2 lit b and c FISA seems to have been a practical one: the Federal Council explains in the legislative materials that,

8 Dispatch Intermediated Securities, 9321 et seq; Hess and Friedrich (n 7) 98 et seq. For more information regarding the introduction of intermediated securities, see the following chapter.

9 Manfred Wenckstern (n 1) 630. See also the other chapters in this book, and the sources cited therein.

in practice, creditors are in most cases interested in having a certain percentage of the intermediated securities count as encumbered assets and not one or more particular intermediated securities as such. In addition to that, the Federal Council mentions that it would be very cumbersome to strictly follow the principle of speciality in such cases (for example, each and every intermediated security would need to be described with its identification number).[10] The legal scholars add to this that this new form of security right in intermediated securities could also be especially helpful for securing monetary claims of the custodian towards the account holder from current accounts, the amount of which constantly varies.[11]

INTERMEDIATED SECURITIES

This section will commence with an overview of the general characteristics of intermediated securities. Thereafter, I will elaborate in detail on how intermediated securities can be encumbered with security rights and how and when such security rights can be enforced.

General Characteristics

With intermediated securities, the FISA introduced a new legal object *sui generis* to the Swiss legal system: these securities have the characteristics of both a contractual claim and a property object. Although they do not have a corporeal dimension according to the traditional property law understanding, they nevertheless have all the functional characteristics of securities.[12]

According to art 1 para 1 FISA, the 'Act applies to intermediated securities that are credited to a securities account by a custodian'. Custodians can be banks, securities dealers, fund management companies, central securities depositories, the Swiss National Bank and the Swiss Post.[13] Intermediated securities, within the meaning of art 3 FISA 'are personal or corporate rights of a fungible nature against an issuer which are credited to a securities account, and may be disposed of by the account holder in accordance with

---

[10] Dispatch Intermediated Securities, 9321–9338, 9370 et seq.

[11] Arpagaus (n 2) para 1557.

[12] Dispatch Intermediated Securities, 9339. Regarding the functional characteristics of a security cf. art 965 of the Federal Act on the Amendment of the Swiss Civil Code (Part Five: The Code of Obligations) (CO) (emphasis added by the author): 'A negotiable security is any *instrument* to which a *right attaches* in such a manner that it may *not be exercised or transferred to another without the instrument*.'

[13] See art 4 FISA.

the provisions of this Act'. Intermediated securities are created in a twofold process: firstly, a deposit of certificated securities[14] or global certificates[15] with a custodian or a registration of uncertificated securities[16] in the main register of a custodian is required. Secondly, the respective rights need to be credited to one or more securities accounts of the account holder.[17] Similarly, intermediated securities will cease to exist once they are decredited from the holder's account and the underlying certificated securities or global certificate are delivered to the beneficiary or the uncertificated securities are deregistered from the main register.[18]

In contrast to traditional securities and their concepts of physicality and transfer via possession, intermediated securities are characterised by the concepts of immateriality, collective deposit and electronic transfer via credit assignment or control agreement.[19]

---

[14] For a definition of certificated securities/negotiable securities cf. art 965 CO.

[15] For a definition of global certificates, cf. art 973b CO:

> (1) The obligor may issue global certificates or replace two or more fungible negotiable securities entrusted to a single bailee with a global certificate, provided the conditions for issue or the articles of association of the company provide therefor or the bailors have consented thereto.
> (2) The global certificate is a negotiable security in the same form as the individual rights that it represents. It is jointly owned by the participant bailors, in proportion to their shares. [...]

[16] For a definition of uncertificated securities, cf. art 973c CO:

> (1) The obligor may issue uncertificated securities or replace fungible negotiable securities or global certificates that have been entrusted to a single bailee with uncertificated securities, provided the conditions for issue or the articles of association provide therefor or the bailors have consented thereto.
> (2) The obligor shall keep a book on the uncertificated securities that he has issued, in which details of the number and denomination of the uncertificated securities issued and of the creditors are recorded. The book is not open for public inspection.
> (3) The uncertificated securities are created on entry in the book and continue to exist only in accordance with such entry.
> (4) The transfer of uncertificated securities requires a written declaration of assignment. Their pledging is governed by the provisions on the pledging of claims.

[17] Article 6 FISA; Dispatch Intermediated Securities, 9339.

[18] Article 8 FISA; Dispatch Intermediated Securities, 9339.

[19] See arts 24 and 25 FISA and the following chapter.

Encumbrance of Intermediated Securities

In this sub-section I will first elaborate on the possibilities of creating security rights over intermediated securities. Thereafter, I will examine an existing security right over intermediated securities with an emphasis on analysing the power of the parties to dispose of the encumbered security, the scope of the security right and its enforcement.

Creation

There are two possibilities for creating security rights over intermediated securities:

- Firstly, a security right over intermediated securities may be created based on a contract of security and the actual act of disposition of the affected intermediated securities from the collateral provider to the acquirer's securities account in accordance with art 24 FISA. According to the mentioned article, the act of disposition encompasses two elements: both an instruction from the account holder to its custodian to transfer the intermediated securities and a credit of the intermediated securities to the acquirer's account are required. Once these two elements are fulfilled, the collateral provider ceases to be in control of the affected intermediated securities, and the beneficiary receives – at least in relation to third parties – a right *in rem* in the intermediated security.[20] This method is primarily useful for security rights which are based on title transfers such as the transfer of securities (in German '*Sicherungsübereignung*') or irregular pledging (*pignus irregulare*).[21]
- Secondly, a security interest over intermediated securities may also be created via a control agreement according to art 25 para 1 FISA:

> An act of disposal for intermediated securities may also be created, and becomes effective against third parties, when the account holder and the custodian agree irrevocably that the custodian must carry out instructions from

[20] Dispatch Intermediated Securities, 9367–9369; Hess and Friedrich (n 7) 116.

[21] In the mentioned use cases, the person granting security ceases to be 'in possession' or 'in control' of the intermediated security. With regards to physical items, we would use the terminology ownership/property. See Hess and Friedrich (n 7) 116; Ansgar Schott, 'art 24 FISA no 14' in Dieter Zobl, Martin Hess and Ansgar Schott (eds), *Kommentar zum Bucheffektengesetz (BEG)* (Schulthess Juristische Medien AG 2013).

the acquirer without any further consent or cooperation on the part of the account holder.

This method of creating a security right over intermediated securities is also based on a twofold process: firstly, a contract of security between the person granting security and the secured party must be concluded. Secondly, a control agreement, which is mentioned in the title of art 25 FISA, must be concluded between the person granting security and the custodian (and potentially also the secured party being the beneficiary), which constitutes the actual act of disposition. The security interest is perfected and valid also vis-à-vis third parties once the control agreement is concluded. No further act of publicity is either necessary or possible. According to this method, no transfer of intermediated securities from the person granting security to the secured party takes place.[22] This means that the traditional principle of publicity (including the supporting means of possession with movable objects or entry into a register with immovable objects) and the pledge principle have been replaced with the concept of control (in German '*Kontrollprinzip*').[23] In order to protect third-party acquirers, art 29 FISA provides for a protection of the *bona fide* purchaser.

In this scenario, the person granting the security right remains the right *in rem* holder. However, in relation to the beneficiary of the security right and depending on the wording of the contractual agreement between the security provider and the security beneficiary, this right *in rem* may be reduced to nothing but *nuda proprietas*.[24]

Only the second method of creating a security right over intermediated securities is functionally similar to the concept of floating charges. The following parts of this contribution will, therefore, focus on this method.

Existence of the security interest

In the first part of this sub-section, I will elaborate on the scope of the parties' disposal power once an intermediated security has been encumbered with a security right. In particular, I will distinguish between the two concepts of positive and negative control. In the second part of this sub-section, we will

[22] Hans Kuhn, 'art 25 FISA nos 1–4' in Vito Roberto and Hans Rudolf Trüeb (eds), *CHK – Handkommentar zum Schweizerischen Privatrecht* (3rd edn, Schulthess Juristische Medien AG 2016).

[23] Arpagaus (n 2) para 1549 (regarding pledge principle); Rashid Bahar and Martin Peyer, 'art 25 FISA nos 11–13 (regarding principle of publicity)' in Heinrich Honsell, Nedim Peter Vogt and Rolf Watter (eds), *Basler Kommentar: Wertpapierrecht* (Helbing Lichtenhahn Verlag 2012).

[24] Luca Dalla Torre et al., 'Sicherheiten nach Bucheffektengesetz – theoretische und praktische Aspekte' (2010) recht 16, 21 with further references.

have a closer look at the scope of a security right that has been created over intermediated securities.

Scope of power of disposal

As long as a security right in the encumbered intermediated securities exists, the beneficiary may, without any further consent or cooperation on the part of the account holder, dispose of the encumbered intermediated securities upon the occurrence of the enforcement event.[25] This power of disposal is referred to as *positive control* by Swiss doctrine.[26]

There is a debate amongst Swiss scholars about whether, in addition to the positive control of the beneficiary, the person granting security – who is still the formal holder of the encumbered intermediated securities – is legally excluded from disposing of the asset without the consent of the beneficiary of the security right with regard to the encumbered intermediated securities (so-called *negative control*).[27] The majority of legal scholars are of the opinion that, subject to an agreement between the parties stating the contrary or contractually limiting the security provider's power of disposal, no such negative control is necessary, and thus affirm the ongoing parallel existence of an independent and unrestricted right of disposal of the person granting security.[28] A minority of scholars, however, consider that negative control is required.[29] In the present author's opinion, the arguments of the majority of the legal scholars are stronger and more convincing. Firstly, the wording of art 25 FISA only mentions positive control by the beneficiary of the security and is silent regarding negative control. Such a requirement also cannot be inferred from

---

[25] Article 25 para 1 FISA; Dispatch Intermediated Securities, 9369 et seq.

[26] Kuhn (n 22) art 25 FISA no 5. Cf. also Official Commentary on the UNIDROIT Convention on Substantive Rules for Intermediated Securities, 'art 1 no 54' in Hideki Kanda et al. (eds) (Oxford University Press 2012) (UCC).

[27] UCC, art 1 no 54.

[28] See Frédérique Bensahel, Sébastien Micotti and Marco Villa, 'L'objet et le rang des sûretés selon la loi sur les titres intermédiés (LTI) – Questions choisies' (2009) SJ 321, 332; Bahar and Peyer (n 23) art 25 FISA no 15; Bénédict Foëx, 'Les sûretés sur les titres détenus auprès d'une banque en Suisse selon la loi sur les titres intermédiés' in Luc Thévenoz and Christian Bovet (eds), *Journée 2008 de droit bancaire et financier* (Schulthess Juristische Medien AG 2009) 134 et seq; Marion Hanten, *Das Bucheffektengesetz: Eine rechtliche Analyse der schweizerischen Lösung für die sogenannte mediatisierte Wertpapierverwahrung* (Helbing Lichtenhahn Verlag 2012), 133; Kuhn (n 22) art 25 FISA no 5; Schott (n 21) art 25 FISA nos 57 et seq.

[29] Harald Bärtschi, 'Die rechtliche Umsetzung des Bucheffektengesetzes' (2009) 9 AJP 1071, 1080. Similar also the Federal Council in the Dispatch Intermediated Securities, 9370; Hess and Friedrich (n 7) 116 n 163.

automatically applying general property law principles governing pledges of corporeal movables (chattels)[30] because the FISA as *lex specialis* in some areas follows its own concepts and must be interpreted on its own.[31] Secondly, the FISA being a (relatively) new law in Switzerland, it should be interpreted in line with similar international legislation. As an example, the UNIDROIT Convention on Substantive Rules for Intermediated Securities does not require exclusive negative control by the beneficiary of the security.[32]

Scope of security right

In order to determine the scope of the security right, art 25 para 2 FISA is relevant. It reads as follows:

> The act of disposal may relate to:
>
> a. specific intermediated securities;
> b. all intermediated securities credited to a securities account; or
> c. a proportion of the intermediated securities credited to a securities account up to a specified value.

According to lit a) of the provision, a security right may relate to specific intermediated securities. This means that the parties determine which individual intermediated security will be encumbered by the security right (e.g. by referencing a security or ISIN number).[33] From a property law perspective this first possibility does not bring any particular challenges to the traditional principles. In particular, the principle of speciality is complied with.

Let us have a closer look at the two other options mentioned in the provision: according to lit (b), all intermediated securities credited to a securities account – including intermediated securities which come into existence in the

30 In particular, art 884 para 1 CC as a *lex generalis* stating the pledge principle *(Faustpfandprinzip)* is not automatically applicable to intermediated securities.

31 Hess and Friedrich (n 7) 113.

32 The Dispatch Intermediated Securities, 9335, explicitly mentions that the FISA and the UNIDROIT Convention on Substantive Rules for Intermediated Securities are largely compatible with one another. Cf. art 12 no 1 in connection with art 1 lit k of the Unidroit Convention and UCC, art 1 no 54. The Directive 2002/47/EC of the European Parliament and of the Council of 6 June 2002 on financial collateral arrangements, however, seems to be a bit more restrictive. Cf. art 2 para 2 of the EU Directive and Foëx (n 28) 135 n 100 with further references. Cf. also Dalla Torre et al (n 24) 21 with further references.

33 Bahar and Peyer (n 23) art 25 FISA no 72; Schott (n 21) art 25 FISA nos 68–70.

future[34] – may be encumbered. Furthermore, lit (c) allows for an encumbrance of only a proportion of the intermediated securities credited to a securities account up to a specified value, without any requirement of individualising the encumbered intermediated securities. In the event of realisation of the security right, the beneficiary in this option may choose which intermediated securities they wish to liquidate.[35]

It is obvious that the degree of individualisation of the encumbered objects is decreased in comparison to lit (a). The majority of the legal scholars in Switzerland qualify this peculiarity as a deviation from the principle of speciality.[36] A minority of legal scholars are of the opinion that the principle of speciality is nevertheless adhered to.[37] This question, which is of a rather dogmatic nature, may, however, be left open for the present analysis. Rather, what is of interest here is that art 25 FISA – being a *lex specialis* compared with the property law statutory provisions as *leges generales* and thus prevailing over them – in its lit (b) and (c) explicitly allows for a continuous 'change of stock' within the encumbered substrate of intermediated securities, which is also one of the main characteristics of floating charges. This type of encumbrance is therefore sometimes also in Swiss literature referred to as a floating charge.[38] As will be discussed in a later section, there certainly are similarities between these two types of security interests. However, there are also a few important differences.[39]

Enforcement of the security right

In this sub-section I will first explain the general prerequisites of realising a security right in intermediated securities. Secondly, I will analyse the

---

[34] Kuhn (n 22) art 25 FISA no 9; Schott (n 21) art 25 FISA no 71.

[35] Schott (n 21) art 25 FISA no 73.

[36] Arpagaus (n 2) para 1549; Bahar and Peyer (n 23) art 25 FISA nos 74 and 75; Peter Jung, 'art 622 CO no 147' in Lukas Handschin (ed), *Zürcher Kommentar* (2nd edn, Schulthess Juristische Medien AG 2016) (concerning art 25 para 2 lit c FISA); Foëx (n 28) 139; Hanten (n 28) 133; Kuhn (n 22) art 25 FISA no 7; Schmid-Tschirren (n 3) 17 (concerning art 25 para 2 lit c FISA); Schott (n 21) art 25 FISA no 66 (concerning art 25 para 2 lit c FISA). Cf. also Dispatch Intermediated Securities, 9370 et seq.

[37] Mirjam Eggen, 'Sicherheiten an Wertrechten – eine Untersuchung der Rechtslage ab Inkrafttreten des Bucheffektengesetzes' (2009) SZW 116, 123; Florian Louis Steiner, 'Zur Revision des Bucheffektengesetzes' (2016) GesKR 335, 343.

[38] Arpagaus (n 2) para 1557. Concerning art 25 para 2 lit c FISA: Bärtschi (n 29) 1081; Hess and Friedrich (n 7) 116; Jung (n 36) art 622 CO no 147; Schmid-Tschirren (n 3) 17.

[39] Cf. the final substantive section below.

particular scenario when, upon realisation of such a security right, the relevant intermediated security is encumbered by two or more competing rights, and I will elaborate on the ranking of competing rights.

Realisation of collateral

With the introduction of the FISA, the legislator wanted to provide a fast and easy procedure for realising collateral in intermediated securities. It has thus codified in art 31 FISA private realisation (in German '*Privatverwertung*') as the standard, while a governmental enforcement proceeding (in German '*Zwangsvollstreckungsverfahren*'), which usually takes much longer than a private realisation, is also possible.[40] Article 31 FISA reads as follows:

> (1) The secured party may realise intermediated securities in which a security interest has been created according to the terms and conditions stipulated in the security agreement by:
> a. selling the intermediated securities and offsetting the proceeds against the secured debt; or
> b. appropriating the intermediated securities whose value can be determined objectively and offsetting their value against the secured debt.
> (2) This power is not affected by the commencement of debt enforcement, reorganisation or protective proceedings in respect of the provider of the security interest.
> (3) The custodian is not bound or entitled to verify whether the conditions for realisation of the intermediated securities are fulfilled.
> (4) The foregoing is without prejudice to the liability of the beneficiary of a security interest who realises intermediated securities where the conditions for realisation are not fulfilled.

Article 32 FISA adds a notice and accounting obligation to this:

> (1) The secured party shall give notice to the provider of the security interest before realisation. A provider of a security interest who is a custodian or a qualified investor may waive the notice requirement.
> (2) The secured party shall account to the provider of the security interest and remit to the latter any excess proceeds of the realisation.

Although it is not explicitly mentioned in the FISA, the beneficiary can, as a general rule, only realise a security right if the secured claim is not settled

[40] Dispatch Intermediated Securities, 9380; Dalla Torre et al. (n 24) 25; Benedikt Maurenbrecher and Christoph Bauer, 'art 31 FISA no 4' in Dieter Zobl, Martin Hess and Ansgar Schott (eds), *Kommentar zum Bucheffektengesetz (BEG)* (Schulthess Juristische Medien AG 2013); Zobl and Gericke (n 2) Systematischer Teil FISA nos 116–123.

although it is due. However, the parties may contractually agree on provisions deviating therefrom (so-called 'enforcement events').[41]

Ranking

Like other assets, intermediated securities may be encumbered by two or more competing rights (e.g. by multiple security rights). For these situations, an order of priority of such competing rights is determined by art 30 para 1 FISA, which states as a general principle that where intermediated securities or rights in intermediated securities are disposed of pursuant to the FISA, the disposition first in time shall prevail over further dispositions. This rule is in line with the traditional principle of age priority (*prior tempore, potior iure*).[42] In relation to third parties and their legal position, this rule is mandatory law. *Inter partes*, the rule is not binding law, and the priorities of rights may be modified.[43]

The relevant point in time to determine the creation of a right in intermediated securities is the conclusion of the control agreement.[44] In this regard it is irrelevant whether specific intermediated securities, all intermediated securities credited to a securities account, or a proportion of the intermediated

41 Arpagaus (n 2) para 1559; Bahar and Peyer (n 23) art 31 FISA nos 8–9; Dalla Torre et al (n 24) 25.

42 Dispatch Intermediated Securities, 9379; Arpagaus (n 2) para 1556; Bahar and Peyer (n 23) art 30 FISA nos 1–2; Daniel Daeniker and Benjamin Leisinger, 'art 30 FISA no 13' in Dieter Zobl, Martin Hess and Ansgar Schott (eds), *Kommentar zum Bucheffektengesetz (BEG)* (Schulthess Juristische Medien AG 2013); Kuhn (n 22) art 30 FISA no 3. Cf. also art 19 Unidroit Convention on Substantive Rules for Intermediated Securities and UCC, art 19 no 11, which is also based on the same principle, which is referred to as 'first-in-time priority rule'.

43 Art 30 para 4 FISA; Dispatch Intermediated Securities, 9380; Bahar and Peyer (n 23) art 30 FISA no 5; Daeniker and Leisinger (n 42) art 30 FISA nos 39–43; Kuhn (n 22) art 30 FISA no 10. Article 30 FISA is not applicable, however, if a conflict of priorities *per se* is excluded. In other words, art 30 FISA presupposes that the competing rights in relation to intermediated securities can exist simultaneously. Such a situation of competing existence is typically excluded in the case of 'full rights' (i.e. ownership), since at any given time only one person can be entitled to ownership. In such cases, the validity of the disposition in accordance with art 24 FISA and the rules regarding the protection of *bona fide* purchasers according to art 29 FISA must be taken into account. See Bahar and Peyer (n 23) art 30 FISA no 7.

44 Dispatch Intermediated Securities, 9379; Daeniker and Leisinger (n 42) art 30 FISA no 14.

securities credited to a securities account up to a specific value is encumbered with the particular right in question.[45]

FLOATING CHARGES VERSUS ENCUMBRANCE OF INTERMEDIATED SECURITIES

In this section I will analyse the similarities and differences between security rights over intermediated securities under Swiss law and floating charges under English law.

Similarities

Comparing the two security interests – floating charges under English law and encumbrances of intermediated securities in Swiss law – we can detect several similarities:

Firstly, both floating charges and encumbrances of intermediated securities, according to art 25 para 2 lit (b) and (c) FISA, allow for the collateralisation of assets which, during the term of the existence of the security right, may vary in their value and composition.[46]

Secondly, the person granting security usually keeps – to a larger or smaller extent, as shown in this contribution – the power of disposal over the security objects.[47] This trait is a significant advantage of these security instruments, as it enables the person granting security, who for example encumbers assets of their company, to maintain their economic existence. It is obvious that the maintenance of an ongoing business is also in the interest of both the secured beneficiary and the other creditors.

Thirdly, both security instruments allow for a private or state realisation of collateral.[48]

---

45 Bahar and Peyer (n 23) art 30 FISA no 11.

46 Bahar and Peyer (n 23) art 25 FISA no 78; Barbara Graham-Siegenthaler, *Kreditsicherungsrechte im internationalen Rechtsverkehr: Eine rechtsvergleichende und international-privatrechtliche Untersuchung* (Stämpfli Verlag Bern AG 2005) 418 et seq (regarding floating charges). For more details regarding the English floating charge and relevant sources, see the chapter on English law in this volume.

47 Bärtschi (n 29) 1081.

48 Graham-Siegenthaler (n 46), 422 (regarding floating charges); Wenckstern (n 1) 629.

Differences

Despite these similarities, there are also a number of differences between floating charges under English law and security rights in intermediated securities which vary in stock under Swiss law.

- Scope of potential debtors:
  - *Floating charge:* floating charges are limited, at least in practice, to incorporated companies (and other incorporated entities) as debtors.[49]
  - *Security right in intermediated securities*: in contrast, there is no such limitation with regards to security rights in intermediated securities. Such security rights may thus be created by both natural and legal persons in favour of creditors.
- Legal status of the involved persons:
  - *Floating charge:* prior to crystallisation, the person granting security can, '*in the ordinary course of carrying on [its] business*' freely dispose of the security property,[50] without regard to the good faith of an acquirer.[51] Assets which are newly acquired are automatically covered by the floating charge. The right to realise the security right of a floating charge is suspended until the occurrence of the condition mentioned in the security agreement (so-called 'crystallisation').[52] Up to that point in time and unless otherwise agreed, the person granting security may also charge the property encumbered by a floating charge with fixed charges, which will be prior in ranking in case of the realisation of the security right, subject to the existence of a negative pledge accompanying the floating charge and requirements of notice.[53] Upon crystallisation, the charge ceases floating and turns into a fixed charge.[54] Only now does the beneficiary of the charge receive an equitable proprietary interest in specific items of the charged property.[55]
  - *Security right in intermediated securities* (art 25 para 2 lit (b) and (c) FISA): in contrast to floating charges, the ranking of competing rights to intermediated securities is determined (as mentioned above) at an

---

[49] Graham-Siegenthaler (n 46) 416.

[50] *Re Panama, New Zealand and Australian Royal Mail Co.* (1870), LR 5 ChApp 318 (322).

[51] Graham-Siegenthaler (n 46) 419 et seq.

[52] Graham-Siegenthaler (n 46) 415; Wenckstern (n 1) 692 et seq.

[53] Graham-Siegenthaler (n 46) 420; Ewan McKendrick, *Goode on Commercial Law* (5th edn, Penguin Books 2016) para 25.25.

[54] McKendrick (n 55) para 25.08.

[55] Graham-Siegenthaler (n 46) 417; Wenckstern (n 1) 639.

earlier stage with the conclusion of the control agreement.[56] In other words, the beneficiary's right *in rem* is not suspended until realisation of the security right. In this regard, security rights in intermediated securities – also those variations which cover collateral varying in composition – are from the very beginning 'fixed' and not 'floating', even though they may be considered floating in other respects.

- Creation and third-party effectiveness:
  - *Floating charge:* in order to obtain third-party effectiveness, a floating charge must be registered in the companies charges register.[57] From a Swiss law perspective this would be compatible with the property law principle of publicity.
  - *Security right in intermediated securities* (art 25 para 2 lit (b) and (c) FISA): in contrast, and as already mentioned above, security rights in intermediated securities cannot and must not be registered in a special register. The principle of publicity does not apply and is replaced by the control principle, which is a significant deviation compared with other security rights under Swiss law. Third-party effectiveness is determined by the rules regarding good faith acquisition (cf. art 29 FISA).
- Realisation:
  - *Floating charge:* upon crystallisation, the beneficiary of a floating charge can either introduce judicial liquidation proceedings (or equivalent) or initiate extrajudicial enforcement. However, the latter is only possible if the parties have agreed on this in the security agreement. In both cases, the realisation of the security right is led by an independent receiver, administrator or liquidator and not the beneficiary of the security right him- or herself.[58]
  - *Security right in intermediated securities* (art 25 para 2 lit (b) and (c) FISA): security rights in intermediated securities may also – depending on the parties' agreement – be enforced through either a judicial or an extrajudicial process. In contrast to the extrajudicial realisation of floating charges, security rights in intermediated securities may in this case be realised by the beneficiaries themselves.[59]

CONCLUDING REMARKS

This contribution has shown that, in general the Swiss legal system, owing to its long-standing property law principles (in particular, the principles of

[56] Bahar and Peyer (n 23) art 25 FISA no 78; Kuhn (n 22) art 25 FISA no 11.

[57] Graham-Siegenthaler (n 46) 416; Wenckstern (n 1) 633 et seq.

[58] Graham-Siegenthaler (n 46) 421 et seq; Wenckstern (n 1) 637 et seq.

[59] Bahar and Peyer (n 23) art 25 FISA no 10 et seq.

speciality and publicity), is not familiar with non-possessory, floating security rights. However, there is one notable recent exception: intermediated securities may be encumbered with security rights which are, at least in some regards, similar to floating charges. In particular, it is possible to encumber accounts of intermediated securities as a whole or parts of them, which vary in stock and where the security right's substrate is not determined from the beginning. Moreover, similar to floating charges, the person granting security generally retains some power of disposal and thus can maintain economic independence.

The reasons for introducing this 'legal transplant' into the Swiss legal system while softening traditional legal concepts are practical ones: the secured parties are usually interested in having a certain percentage of the intermediated securities account as collateral and not one or more particular intermediated securities as such. In these cases, it would be very cumbersome to strictly follow the principle of speciality. Also, this form of security is especially helpful for securing claims of the custodian towards the account holder from current accounts, the amount of which constantly varies.

So far, this new form of security has caused neither positive nor negative headlines in Switzerland. The future will show whether this security right proves its worth and whether other similar security rights might be introduced into Swiss law.

Index